THE

ENGLISH CHURCH

IN THE

EIGHTEENTH CENTURY

BY

CHARLES J. ABBEY

RECTOR OF CHECKENDON, OXON : LATE FELLOW OF UNIVERSITY COLLEGE, OXFORD

and

JOHN H. OVERTON

VICAR OF LEGBOURNE, LINCOLNSHIRE : LATE SCHOLAR OF LINCOLN COLLEGE, OXFORD

IN TWO VOLUMES

VOL. I.

LONDON

LONGMANS, GREEN, AND CO.

1878

All rights reserved.

This scarce antiquarian book is included in our special *Legacy Reprint Series*. In the interest of creating a more extensive selection of rare historical book reprints, we have chosen to reproduce this title even though it may possibly have occasional imperfections such as missing and blurred pages, missing text, poor pictures, markings, dark backgrounds and other reproduction issues beyond our control. Because this work is culturally important, we have made it available as a part of our commitment to protecting, preserving and promoting the world's literature.

PREFACE.

SOME YEARS have elapsed since the authors of this work first entertained the idea of writing upon certain aspects of religious life and thought in the Eighteenth Century. If the ground is no longer so unoccupied as it was then, it appears to them that there is still abundant room for the book which they now lay before the public. Their main subject is expressly the English Church, and they write as English Churchmen, taking, however, no narrower basis than that of the National Church itself.

They desire to be responsible each for his own opinions only, and therefore the initials of the writer are attached to each chapter he has written.

CONTENTS

OF

THE FIRST VOLUME.

——◦◦◦——

CHAPTER I.

INTRODUCTORY.

(C. J. Abbey.)

CHAPTER II.

THE CHURCH AND THE JACOBITES.

(*J. H. Overton.*)

CHAPTER III.

ROBERT NELSON : HIS FRIENDS, AND CHURCH PRINCIPLES.

(C. J. Abbey.)

CHAPTER IV.

THE DEISTS.

(*J. H. Overton.*)

CHAPTER VII.

THE ESSAYISTS.

(*J. H. Overton.*)

CHAPTER VIII.

THE TRINITARIAN CONTROVERSY.

(*J. H. Overton.*)

CHAPTER IX.

' ENTHUSIASM.'

(C. J. Abbey.)

Errata

Page 7, line 11 from bottom, *for* nineteenth *read* eighteenth

,, 9, ,, 9 from top (and in two or three other places), 1689 should be, more correctly, 1688

., 15, ,, 14 from top, *for* 'until the accession of George III.' *read* ' in the early part of the century '

,, 55, ,, 11 from bottom, *for* where *read* were

,, 64, Note 3 (and in some other places), *for* Nichol's *read* Nichols'

,, 82, line 5 from bottom, *for* Stewarts *read* Stuarts

,, 85, Note 1, *for* Tartufe *read* Tartuffe

,, 125, line 14 from bottom, *for* St. Asaphs *read* St. Asaph

,, 130, Note 5, *for* Clark *read* Clarke

,, 132, line 12 from top, *for* Kennett *read* Kennet

· ,, 163, ,, 10 from bottom, *for* limitation *read* limitations

,, 167, First sentence of fresh paragraph, *for* 'chapter, as they' *read* ' chapter. As they '

,, 199, Note 1 (and in some other places), *for* Farrer *read* Farrar

,, 311, line 11 from bottom, *for* Giotto *read* Orgagna

.. 325, Note 2, *for* trying *read* crying

,, 335, ,, 1, should be only 'so also does Atterbury '

,, 357, line 7 from top, *for* more *read* mere

,, 383, ,, 9 from top, the sentence beginning 'Archbishop Grindal' should be omitted. There was only *one* such case ; and even then (as a Reviewer in the 'Church Times' has shown) the license was granted, not by Grindal himself, who was then suspended, but by his Vicar-General

., 491, ,, 5 from bottom, *for* which *read* whom

,, 526, ,, 15 from top, *for* our Lord *read* one Lord

.. 530, ,, 11 from bottom, after Church history *insert* of the period

,, 574, ,, 15 ,, *for* Elijah's *read* Elisha's

.. 577, Note 1, *for* F. S. Maurice *read* F. D. Maurice

vacuum which was not yet supplied. As for loyalty, the half-hearted feeling of necessity or expedience, which for more than half the century was the main support of the German dynasty, was something different not in degree only, but in kind, from that which had upheld the throne in time past. Jacobitism, on the other hand, was not strong enough to be more than a faction; and the Republican party, who had once been equal to the Royalists in fervour of enthusiasm, and superior to them in intensity of purpose, were now wholly extinct. The country increased rapidly in strength and in material prosperity; its growth was uninterrupted; its resources continued to develop; its political constitution gained in power and consolidation. But there was a deficiency of disinterested principle. There was an open field for the operation of such sordid motives and debasing tactics as those which disgraced Walpole's lengthened administration.

In the following chapters there will be only too frequent occasion to refer to a somewhat corresponding state of things in the religious life of the country. For two full centuries the land had laboured under the throes of the Reformation. Even when William III. died, it could scarcely be said that England had decisively settled the form which her National Church should take. The 'Church in danger' cries of Queen Anne's reign, and the bitter war of pamphlets, were outward indications that suspense was not yet completely over, and that both friends and enemies felt they had still occasion to calculate the chances alike of Presbyterianism and of the Papacy. But when George I. ascended the throne in peace, it was at last generally realized that the 'Settlement' of which so much had been spoken was now effectually attained. Church and State were so far secured from change, that their defenders might rest from anxiety. It was not a wholesome rest that followed. Long-standing disputes and the old familiar controversies were almost lulled to silence, but in their place a sluggish calm rapidly spread over the Church, not only over the established National Church, but over it and also over every community of Nonconformists. It is remarkable how closely the beginning of the season of spiritual lassitude corresponds with the accession of the first George. The country had never altogether recovered from the reaction of lax indifference into which it had fallen after the Restoration. Nevertheless, a good deal had occurred since that time to keep the minds of Churchmen, as well as of politicians, awake and active ; and a good deal had been done to stem the tide of immorality which had then broken over the kingdom. The Church of England was certainly not asleep either in the time of the Seven Bishops, when James II. was King, or under its Whig rulers at the end of the century. And in Queen Anne's time, amid all the virulence of hostile Church parties, there was a healthy stream of life which made itself very visible in the numerous religious associations which sprang up everywhere in the great towns. It might seem as if there were a certain heaviness in the English mind, which requires some outward stimulus to keep alive its zeal. For so soon as the press of danger ceased, and party strifes abated, with the accession of the House of Brunswick, Christianity began forthwith to slumber. The trumpet of Wesley and of Whitefield was needed before that unseemly slumber could again be broken.

It will not, however, be forgotten that twice in successive generations the Church of England had been deprived, through misfortune or through folly, of some of her best men. She had suffered on either hand. By the ejection of 1662, through a too stringent enforcement of the new Act of Uniformity, she had lost the services of some of the most devoted of her Puritan sons, men whose views were in many cases no way distinguishable from those which had been held without rebuke by some of the most honoured bishops of Elizabeth's time. By the ejection of 1689, through what was surely a needless strain upon their allegiance, many high-minded men of a different order of thought were driven, if not from her communion, at all events from her ministrations. It was a juncture when the Church could ill afford to be weakened by the defection of some of the most earnest and disinterested upholders of the Primitive and Catholic, as contrasted with the more directly Protestant elements of her Constitution. This twofold drain upon her strength could scarcely have failed to impair the robust vitality which was soon to be so greatly needed to combat the early beginnings of the dead-resistance of spiritual lethargy.

But this listlessness in most branches of practical religion must partly be attributed to a cause which gives the history of religious thought in the eighteenth century its principal importance. In proportion as the Church Constitution approached its final settlement, and as the controversies, which from the beginning of the Reformation had been unceasingly under dispute, gradually wore themselves out, new questions came forward, far more profound and fundamental, and far more important in their speculative and practical bearings, than those which had attracted so much notice and stirred so much excitement during the two preceding centuries. The existence of God was scarcely called into question by the boldest doubters; or such doubts, if they found place at all, were expressed only under the most covert implications. But, short of this, all the mysteries of religion were scrutinized; all the deep and hidden things of faith were brought in question, and submitted to the test of reason. Is there such a thing as a revelation from God to men of Himself and of His will? If so, what is its nature, its purposes, its limits? What are the attributes of God? What is the meaning of life? What is man's hereafter? Does a divine spirit work in man? and if it does, what are its operations, and how are they distinguishable? What is spirit? and what is matter? What does faith rest upon? What is to be said of inspiration, and authority, and the essential attributes of a church? These, and other questions of the most essential religious importance, as the nature and signification of the doctrines of the Trinity, of the Incarnation of Christ, of Redemption, of Atonement, discussions as to the relations between faith and morals, and on the old, inevitable enigmas of necessity and liberty, all more or less entered into that mixed whirl of earnest inquiry and flippant scepticism which is summed up under the general name of the Deistic Controversy. For it is not hard to see how intimately the secondary controversies of the time were connected with that main and central one, which not only engrossed so much attention on the part of theologians and students, but became a subject of too general conversation in every coffee-house and place of public resort.

In mental, as well as in physical science, it seems to be a

law that force cannot be expended in one direction without some corresponding relaxation of it in another. And thus the disproportionate energies which were diverted to the intellectual side of religion were exercised at some cost to its practical part. Bishops were writing in their libraries, when otherwise they might have been travelling round their dioceses. Men were pondering over abstract questions of faith and morality, who else might have been engaged in planning or carrying out plans for the more active propagation of the faith, or a more general improvement in popular morals. The defenders of Christianity were searching out evidences, and battling with deistical objections, while they slackened in their fight against the more palpable assaults of the world and the flesh. Pulpits sounded with theological arguments where admonitions were more urgently needed. Above all, reason was called to decide upon questions before which man's reason stands impotent ; and imagination and emotion, those great auxiliaries to all deep religious feeling, were bid to stand rebuked in her presence, as hinderers of the rational faculty, and upstart pretenders to rights which were not theirs. 'Enthusiasm ' was frowned down, and no small part of the light and fire of religion fell with it.

Yet an age in which great questions were handled by great men could not be either an unfruitful or an uninteresting one. It might be unfruitful, in the sense of reaping no great harvest of results ; and it might be uninteresting, in respect of not having much to show upon the surface, and exhibiting no great variety of active life. But much good fruit for the future was being developed and matured ; and no one, who cares to see how the present grows out of the past, will readily allow that the religious thought and the religious action of the eighteenth century are deficient in interest to our times. Our debt is greater than many are inclined to acknowledge. People see clearly that the Church of that age was, in many respects, in an undoubtedly unsatisfactory condition, sleepy and full of abuses, and are sometimes apt to think that the Evangelical revival (the expression being used in its widest sense) was the one redeeming feature of it. And as in theological and ecclesiastical thought, in philosophy, in art, in poetry, the general tendency has been reactionary, the students and writers of the eighteenth century have in many respects scarcely received their due share of appreciation. Moreover, negative results make little display. There is not much to show for the earnest toil that has very likely been spent in arriving at them ; and a great deal of the intellectual labour of the last century was of this kind. Reason had been more completely emancipated at the Reformation than it was at first at all aware of. Men who were engaged in battling against certain definite abuses, and certain specified errors, scarcely discovered at first, nor indeed for long afterwards, that they were in reality contending also for principles which would affect for the future the whole groundwork of religious conviction. They were not yet in a position to see that henceforward authority could take only a secondary place, and that they were installing in its room either reason or a more subtle spiritual faculty superior even to reason in the perception of spiritual things. It was not until near the end of the seventeenth century that the mind began to awaken to a full perception of the freedom it had won—a freedom far more complete in principle than was as yet allowed in prac- tice. In the eighteenth century this fundamental postulate of the Reformation became for the first time a prominent, and, to many minds, an absorbing subject of inquiry. For the first time, it was no longer disguised from sight by the incidental interest of its side issues. The assertors of the supremacy of reason were at first arrogantly, or even inso- lently, self-confident, as those who were secure of carrying all before them. Gradually, the wiser of them began to feel that their ambition must be largely moderated, and that they must be content with far more negative results than they had at first imagined. The question came to be, what is reason unable to do? What are its limits? and how is it to be supplemented? An immensity of learning, and of arguments good and bad, was lavished on either side in the controversy between the deists and the orthodox. In the end, it may perhaps be said that two axioms were established, which may sound in our own day like commonplaces, but which were certainly very insufficiently realised when the controversy began. It was seen on the one hand that reason was free, and that on the other it was encompassed by limitations against which it strives in vain. The Deists lost the day. Their objections to revelation fell through ; and Christianity rose again, strengthened rather than weakened by their attack. Yet they had not laboured in vain, if success may be measured, not by the gaining of an immediate purpose, but by solid good effected, however contrary in kind to the object proposed. So far as a man works with a single-hearted desire to win truth, he should rejoice if his very errors are made, in the hands of an overruling Providence, instrumental in establishing truth. Christianity in England had arrived in the eighteenth century at one of those periods of revision when it has become absolutely necessary to examine the foundations of its teaching, at any risk. of temporary disturbance to the faith of individuals. The advantage ultimately gained was twofold. It was not only that the vital doctrines of Christian faith had been scrutinised both by friends and enemies, and were felt to have stood the proof. But also defenders of received doctrine learnt, almost insensibly, very much from its opponents. They became aware—or if not they, at all events their successors became aware—that orthodoxy must, in some respects, modify the stringency of its conclusions ; that there was need, in other instances, of disentangling Christian verities from the scholastic refinements which had gradually grown up around them ; and that there were many questions which might safely be left open to debate without in any way impairing the real defences of Christianity. A sixteenth or seventeenth-century theologian regarded most religious questions from a standing point widely different in general character from that of his equal in piety and learning in the nineteenth century. The circumstances and tone of thought which gave rise to the Deistic and its attendant controversies mark with tolerable definiteness the chief period of transition.

The Evangelical revival, both that which is chiefly connected with the name of the Wesleys and of Whitefield, and that which was carried on more exclusively within the Church of England, closely corresponded in many of its details to what had often occurred before in the history of the Christian Church. But it had also a special connection with the controversies which preceded it. When minds had become

tranquillised through the subsidence of discussions which had
threatened to overthrow their faith, they were the more
prepared to listen with attention and respect to the stirring
calls of the Evangelical preacher. The very sense of weari-
ness, now that long controversy had at last come to its termination, tended to give a more entirely practical form to the
new religious movement. And although many of its leaders
were men who had not come to their prime till the Deistical
controversy was almost over, and who would probably have
viewed the strife, if it had still been raging, with scarcely any
other feeling than one of alarmed concern, this was at all
events not the case with John Wesley. There are tolerably
clear signs that it had materially modified the character of
his opinions. The train of thought which produced the
younger Dodwell's 'Christianity not Founded upon Argument'
—a book of which people scarcely knew, when it appeared,
whether it were a serious blow to the Deist cause, or a
formidable assistance to it—considerably influenced Wesley's
mind, as it also did that of William Law and his followers.
He entirely repudiated the mysticism which at one time had
begun to attract him ; but, like the German pietists, who were
in some sense the religious complement of Rationalism, he
never ceased to be comparatively indifferent to orthodoxy,
so long as a man had the witness of the Spirit proving itself
in works of faith. In whatever age of the Church Wesley
had lived, he would have been no doubt an active agent in
the holy work of evangelisation. But opposed as he was to
prevailing influences, he was yet a man of his time. We can
hardly fancy the John Wesley whom we know, living in any
other century than his own. Spending the most plastic,
perhaps also the most reflective period of his life in a chief
centre of theological activity, he was not unimpressed by the
storm of argument which was at that time going on around
him. It was uncongenial to his temper, but it did not fail to
leave upon him its lasting mark.

The Deistical and other theological controversies of the
earlier half of the century, and the Wesleyan and Evangelical
revival in its latter half, are quite sufficient in themselves to
make the Church history of the period exceedingly important.
They are beyond doubt its principal and leading events. But

there was much more besides in the religious life of the country that is well worthy of note. The Revolution which had so lately preceded the opening of the century, and the far more pregnant and eventful Revolution which convulsed Europe at its close, had both of them many bearings, though of course in very different ways, upon the development of religious and ecclesiastical thought in this country. One of the first and principal effects of the change of dynasty in 1689 had been to give an immense impetus to Protestant feeling. This was something altogether different in kind from the Puritanism which had entered so largely into all the earlier history of that century. It was hardly a theological movement; neither was it one that bore primarily and directly upon personal religion. It was, so to say, a strategical movement of self-defence. The aggression of James II. upon the Constitution had not excited half the anger and alarm which had been caused by his attempts to reintroduce Popery. And now that the exiled King had found a refuge in the court of the monarch who was not only regarded as the hereditary enemy of England, but was recognised throughout Europe as the great champion of the Roman Catholic cause, religion, pride, interest, and fear combined to make all parties in England stand by their common Protestantism. There had never before been such unanimity, and even cordiality, between the highest of High Churchmen and thorough-paced Dissenters, as during the interval between the despotic proclamation of King James and his final abdication. This harmony was speedily interrupted by the doubts and difficulties which attended William's accession to the throne. Many who had even joyfully hailed his arrival as a temporary defender of their liberties, looked with very different eyes upon a sovereignty which they could not regard in any other light than as an unlawful usurpation. They might acknowledge, under the emergency, an interregnum, a vicegerent, or a protector; but James was still their king *de jure*, he was still the Lord's anointed. Nevertheless, although there was no longer the comparative unanimity that had prevailed before, and although, even in the great majority of the supporters of the new dynasty, their advocacy of it was marked by a cold and calculating spirit singularly at variance with the en-

thusiasm which a great cause demanded, the strength of that
Protestant feeling which had been aroused was not much
abated.   In fact, it was hardly possible that it should abate
so long as the fortune of the conflict with Louis XIV.
hung still in the balance.   Not only was England prime
leader in the struggle against Papal dominion ; but Churchmen of all views, the great bulk of the Nonconformists, and
all the reformed Churches abroad, agreed in thinking of the
English Church as the chief bulwark of the Protestant interest.

One of the most interesting, as it might have been one of
the most important, incidents of this outburst of Protestant
feeling had been the attempt made to increase the comprehensiveness of the English Church.   It was a difficult undertaking, and the principles on which it should have been carried
out were not at that time sufficiently understood.   Its promoters thought with reason that if it could be successfully
achieved, the Protestant cause, which was so sorely threatened,
and which they had so much at heart, would be materially
and permanently strengthened.   But the very strength of
their feeling cramped and narrowed a movement which
needed to be based on larger principles.   There was too much
policy in it, and a too exclusive regard for that particular
element in the English Church which was then thought to be
endangered.   Nothing could be gained by making the National
Church a mere amalgam of Protestant sects ; or if this
danger were avoided, it would have been a great wrong to an
ancient and honoured section of the Church, and one that
numbered among its ranks some of her greatest ornaments,
if room were to be made for others only at their expense.
There would be small gain in conciliating, or attempting to
conciliate, Presbyterians at the certain cost of alienating
Anglicans.   This was no imaginary hazard.   Many of the
reforms or alterations suggested by the commissioners were
in themselves reasonable enough, and such as Churchmen
might have willingly conceded, if they thought them likely
to add strength to the Church, and to promote a general
unity.   But there was a spirit abroad, which those who loved
the teaching of the English Church had good cause to be
afraid of.   They might well hesitate to admit of any change
in the old formularies at a time when, both in Church and

State, party feeling ran high, and when it was obvious that there were many who would gladly seize any opportunity of assimilating the Church of England, as far as might be, to that of Scotland or of Holland. There had been an interval during which circumstances had been singularly favourable for a wisely conceived measure of comprehension. It had passed by, so soon as William and Mary had been actually crowned.

These projects had ended in failure before the eighteenth century opened. But they were still fresh in memory, and men who had taken great interest in them were still living, and holding places of honour. For years to come there were many who greatly regretted that the scheme of comprehension had not been carried out, and whose minds constantly recurred to the possibility of another opportunity coming about in their time. Such ideas, though they scarcely took any practical form, cannot be left out of account in the Church history of the period. In the midst of all that strife of parties which characterised Queen Anne's reign, a longing desire for Church unity was by no means absent. Only these aspirations had taken by this time a somewhat altered form. The history of the English Constitution has ever been marked by altera-tions, in which Conservatism and attachment to established authority have sometimes been altogether predominant, at other times a resolute, even passionate contention for the security and increase of liberty. In Queen Anne's reign a reaction of the former kind set in, not indeed by any means universal, but sufficient to contrast very strongly with the period which had preceded it. One of the symptoms of it was a very decided current of popular feeling in favour of the Church. People began to think it possible, or even pro-bable, that with the existing generation of Dissenters English Nonconformity would so nearly end, as to be no longer a power that would have to be taken into any practical account. Con-cession, therefore, to the scruples of ‘weak brethren’ seemed to be no longer needful ; and if alterations were not really called for, evidently they would be only useless and unsettling. In this reign, therefore, aspirations after unity chiefly took the form of friendly overtures between Church dignitaries in England and the Lutheran and other reformed communities abroad, as also with such leaders of the Gallican party as were inclined, if possible, to throw off the Papal supremacy and to effect at the same time certain religious and ecclesiastical reforms. Throughout the middle of the century there was not so much any craving for unity as what bore some outward resemblance to it, an indolent love of mere tranquillity. The correspondence, however, that passed between Doddridge and some of the bishops, and the interest excited by the ' Free and Candid Disquisitions,' showed that ideas of Church comprehension were not yet forgotten. About this date, another cause, in addition to the *quieta non movere* principle, interfered to the hindrance of any such proposals. Persons who entertained Arian and other heterodox opinions upon the doctrine of the Trinity were an active and increasing party ; and there was fear lest any attempt to enlarge the borders of the Church should only, or chiefly, result in their procuring some modifications of the Liturgy in their favour. Later in the century, the general question revived in immediate interest under a new form. It was no longer asked, how shall we win to our national communion those who have hitherto declined to recognise its authority ? The great ecclesiastical question of the day—if only it could have been taken in hand with sufficient earnestness—was rather this : how shall we keep among us in true Church fellowship this great body of religiously minded men and women who, by the mouth of their principal leader, profess real attachment to the Church of England and yet want a liberty and freedom from rule which we know not how to give ? No doubt it was a difficulty —more difficult than may at first appear—to incorporate the activities of Methodism into the general system of the National Church. Only it is very certain that obstacles which might have been overcome were not generally grappled with in the spirit, or with the seriousness of purpose, which the crisis deserved. Meanwhile, at the close of the period when this question had scarcely been finally decided, the Revolution broke out in France. In the terror of that convulsion, whe Christianity itself was for the first time deposed in France, and none knew how widely the outbreak would extend, or what would be the bound of such insurrection against laws human and divine, the unity of a common Christianity could not fail to be felt more strongly than any lesser causes of disunion.

There was a kindness and sympathy of feeling manifested towards the banished French clergy, which was something almost new in the history of Protestantism. The same cause contributed to promote the good understanding which at this time subsisted between a considerable section of Churchmen and Dissenters. Possibly some practical efforts might have been set on foot towards healing religious divisions, if the open war waged against Christianity had long been in suspense. As it was, other feelings came in, which tended rather to widen than to diminish the breach between men of strong and earnest opinions on different sides. In some men of warm religious feeling the Revolution excited a fervent spirit of Radicalism. However much they deplored the excesses and horrors which had taken place in France, they did not cease to contemplate with passionate hope the tumultuous upheaval of all old institutions, trusting that out of the ruins of the past a new and better future would derive its birth. The great majority of Englishmen, on the other hand, startled and terrified with what they saw, became fixed in a resolute determination that they would endure no sort of tampering with the English Constitution in Church or State. Whatever changes might be made for better or for worse, they would in any case have no change now. Conservatism became in their eyes a sort of religious principle, from which they could not deviate without peril of treason to their faith. This was an exceedingly common feeling ; among none more so than with that general bulk of steady sober-minded people of the middle classes, without whose consent changes, in which they would feel strongly interested, could never be carried out. The extreme end of the last century was not a time when Church legislation, for however excellent an object, was likely to be carried out, or even thought of.

To return to the beginning of the period under review. ' Divine right,' ' Passive obedience,' ' Non-resistance,' are phrases which long ago have lost life, and which sound over the gulf of time like faint and shadowy echoes of controversies which belong to an already distant past. Even in the middle of the century it must have been difficult to realise the vehemence with which the semi-religious, semi-political, doctrines contained in those terms had been disputed and maintained in the genera-

tion preceding. Yet round those doctrines, in defence or in
opposition, some of the best and most honourable principles
of human nature used to be gathered—a high-minded love of
liberty on the one hand, a no less lofty spirit of self-sacrifice
and loyalty on the other. However untenable their opinion
might prove to be, there can be no question that many of the
High Churchmen of King William's and Queen Anne's time,
who held the doctrine of passive obedience, did indeed regard
it not only as 'a special glory of the Church of England,' not
only as 'a truly Catholic doctrine,' but as verily, in a special
sense, 'a doctrine of the Cross.' It had not only brought
upon many of them suffering and loss of possessions for conscience' sake, but it was, in their estimation, pre-eminently
an act of obedience to the Christian law of patience and forbearance. Apart from considerations thus nearly connected
with religion, it had been the traditional tenet, courageously
adhered to through many trials, of men whose opinions on
many subjects may have been narrow or mistaken, but who
had been endowed with much nobility of character and disinterestedness of purpose. Statesmen and divines in the
Georgian age might take pleasure in thinking that their
views on these and on many other matters were in some points
more national, more enlightened, more liberal-minded ; but
they could not afford to speak with scorn of men whose general
type of character had been often higher than their own. The
eighteenth century saw the last in England of a dogma
which had ennobled loyalty by infusing it so largely with
religion, even while it dishonoured religion by investing with
something of its sanctity even the most arbitrary acts of royal
power. Faction and intrigue sullied, in its later years, the
expiring cause ; yet it cannot be dismissed from the history
of the English Church during the period under review without
a genuine tribute of respect.

Hostility to the reigning monarch was almost a new thing
in the history of the Church of England. Often in past days
the clergy had been in warm contention with the King in
defence of what they deemed their rights ; and there had
been times when they had taken an honourable place in
maintaining the general liberties of the subject against royal
usurpation. During the wars of the Roses, the right of suc-

cession was never in any way a Church question. Perhaps a majority of the clergy were Lancastrian rather than Yorkist in their sympathies. But they were divided, as other citizens were, sometimes by a judicial preference of one or the other claim, oftener by local, personal, and social considerations. They did not feel that any special principle was involved, and, as a body, they readily acknowledged the prince who at the time was in possession of the throne. During all the centuries that had passed between the reign of the second and the third William, neither the English Church nor any considerable section of it had ever been really disaffected towards the person and family of the King.

The open or half-concealed Jacobitism which, until the accession of George III., prevailed in perhaps the majority of eighteenth-century parsonages could scarcely fail of influencing the English Church at large, both in its general action, and in its relation to the State. This influence was in many respects a very mischievous one. In country parishes, and still more so in the universities, it fostered an unquiet political spirit which was prejudicial both to steady pastoral work and to the advancement of sound learning. It also greatly disturbed the internal unity of the Church, and that in a manner peculiarly prejudicial to its well-being. Strong doctrinal and ecclesiastical differences within a Church may do much more good in stirring a wholesome spirit of emulation, and in keeping thought alive and preventing a Church from narrowing into a sect, than they do harm by creating a spirit of division. But the semi-political element which infused its bitterness into Church parties during the first half of the eighteenth century, had no such merit. It did nothing to promote either practical activity or theological inquiry. Under its influence High and Broad Church were too often not so much rival schools of religious thought, and representatives of different tones of religious feeling, as rival factions. King William's bishops—a set of men who, on the whole, did very high honour to his selection—were regarded by a number of the clergy with suspicion and aversion, as his pledged supporters, both in political and ecclesiastical matters, no less ready to upset the established order of the Church than they had been to change the ancient succession of the throne.

These, in their turn, scarcely cared to conceal, if not their scorn, at all events their supreme mistrust, for men who seemed in their eyes like bigoted disturbers of a Constitution in which the country had every reason to rejoice.

More than this, Jacobitism brought the National Church into peril of downright schism. There was already a nucleus for it. If the Nonjuring separation had been nothing more than the secession of a number of High Churchmen—some of them conspicuous for their piety and learning, and almost all worthy of respect as disinterested men who had strong convictions and stood by them—the loss of such men would, even so, have been a serious matter. But the evil did not end there. Although the Nonjurors, especially after the return of Nelson and others into the lay communion of the Established Church, were often spoken of with contempt as an insignificant body, an important Jacobite success might at any time have vastly swelled their number. A great many clergymen and leading country families had simply acquiesced in the rule of William as king *de facto*, and would have transferred their allegiance without a scruple if there had seemed a strong likelihood that James or the Pretender would win the crown back again. In this case the Nonjuring communion, which always proudly insisted that it alone was the true old Church of England, might have received an immense accession of adherents. It would not by any means have based its distinctive character upon mere Jacobite principles. It would have claimed to be peculiarly representative of the Catholic claims of the English Church, while Whigs and Low Churchmen would have been more than ever convertible terms. As it was, High Churchism among country squires took a different turn. But if the Stuart cause had become once more a promising one, and had associated itself, in its relations towards the Church, with the opinions and ritual to which the Nonjurors were no less attached than Laud and his followers were in Charles I.'s day, it is easy to guess that such distinctive usages might soon be welcomed with enthusiasm by Jacobites, if for no other reason, yet as hallowed symbols of a party. At the beginning of the eighteenth century, Church parties had been already strained and most unhappily embittered by political dissensions; under the circumstances supposed, division might readily have been aggravated into hopeless schism. But Jacobitism declined; and a less, but still a serious evil to the Church ensued. Jacobitism and the Papacy had become in most people's minds closely connected ideas. Hence the opinions upon Church matters prevalent among Nonjurors and their ecclesiastical sympathisers in the Established Church became also unpopular, and tainted with an unmerited suspicion of leaning towards Rome. This was no gain to the Church of the Georgian era. Quite independently of any bias which a person may feel towards this or that shade of opinion upon debated questions, it may be asserted with perfect confidence that the Church of that period would decidedly have gained by an increase of life and earnestness in any one section of its members. A colourless indifferentism was the pest of the age. Some movement in the too still waters was sorely needed. A few Ritualists, as they would now be called, in the metropolitan churches, zealous and active men, would have stimulated within the Church a certain interest and excitement which, whether it were friendly or hostile, would have been almost certainly beneficial. But, in the middle of the century, High Churchmen of this type would scarcely be found, except in Nonjuror 'conventicles,' and among the oppressed Episcopalians of Scotland.

The public relations of civil society towards religion attracted in the eighteenth century—especially in the earlier part of it—very universal attention. Of the various questions that come under this head, there was none of such practical and immediate importance as that which was concerned with the toleration of religious differences. The Toleration Act had been carried amid general approval. There had been little enthusiasm about it, but also very little opposition. Though it fell far short of what would now be understood by tolerance, it was fully up to the level of the times. It fairly expressed what was thoroughly the case; that the spirit of intolerance had very much decreased, and that a feeling in favour of religious liberty was decidedly gaining ground. Meanwhile, in King William's reign, and still more so in that of his successor, there was a very strongly marked contention and perplexity of feeling as to what was really meant by toleration, and where its limits were to be fixed. Everybody professed to be in favour of it, so long as it was interpreted according to his own rule. The principle was granted, but there were few who had any clear ideas as to the grounds upon which they granted it, and still fewer who did not think it was a principle to be carefully fenced round with limitations. The Act of Toleration had been itself based in great measure upon mere temporary considerations, there being a very strong wish to consolidate the Protestant interest against Papal aggression. Its benefits were strictly confined to the orthodox Protestant dissenters ; and even they were left under many oppressive disabilities. A great principle had been conceded, and a great injustice materially abated. Henceforth English Dissenters, whose teachers had duly attested their allegiance, and duly subscribed to the thirty-six doctrinal articles of the Church of England, might attend their certified place of worship without molestation from vexatious penal laws. It was bare toleration, accorded to certain favoured bodies ; and there for a long time it ended. Two wide-reaching limitations of the principle of tolerance intervened to close the gate against other Nonconformists than these. Open heresy could not be permitted, nor any worship that was adjudged to be distinctly prejudicial to the interests of the State. No word could yet be spoken, without risk of heavy penalty, against the received doctrine of the Trinity. Nonjurors and Scotch Episcopalians could only meet by stealth in private houses. As for Romanists, so far from their condition being in any way mitigated, their yoke was made the harder, and they might complain, with Rehoboam's subjects, that they were no longer chastised with whips, but with scorpions. William's reign was marked by a long list of new penal laws directed against them. There were many who quoted with great approval the advice (published in 1690, and republished in 1716) of 'a good patriot, guided by a prophetic spirit.' His 'short and easy method' was, to 'expel the whole sect from the British dominions,' and, laying aside 'the feminine weakness' of an unchristian toleration, 'once for all, to clear the land of these monsters, and force them to transplant themselves.' Much in the same way there were many good people who would have very much liked to adopt violent physical measures against 'freethinkers' and 'atheists.' Steele in the 'Tatler,' Budgell in the 'Spectator,' and Bishop Berkeley in the 'Guardian,' all express a curious mixture of satisfaction and regret that such opinions could not be summarily punished, if not by the severest penalties of the law, at the very least by the cudgel and the horsepond. Whiston seems to have thought it possible that heterodox opinions upon the mystery of the Trinity might even yet, under certain contingencies, bring a man into peril of his life. In a noticeable passage of his memoirs, written perhaps in a moment of depression, he speaks of learning the prayer of Polycarp, 'if it should be my lot to die a martyr.' The early part of the eighteenth century abounds in indications that amid a great deal of superficial talk about the excellence of toleration the older spirit of persecution was quite alive, ready, if circumstances favoured it, to burst forth again, not perhaps with firebrand and sword, but with the no less familiar weapons of confiscations and imprisonment. Toleration was not only very imperfectly understood, even by those who most lauded it, but it was often loudly vaunted by men whose lives and opinions were very far from recommending it. In an age notorious for laxity and profaneness, it was only too obvious that great professions of toleration were in very many cases only the fair-sounding disguise of flippant scepticism or shallow indifference. The number of such instances made some excuse for those who so misunderstood the Christian liberalism of such men as Locke and Lord Somers, as to charge it with irreligion or even atheism.

Nevertheless the growth of toleration was one of the most conspicuous marks of the eighteenth century. If one were to judge only from the slowness of legislation in this respect, and the grudging reluctance with which it conceded to Nonconformists the first scanty instalments of complete civil freedom, or from the words and conduct of a considerable number of the clergy, or from certain fierce outbursts of mob riot against Roman Catholics, Methodists, and Jews, it might be argued that if toleration did indeed advance, it was but at tortoise speed. In reality, the advance was very great. Mosheim, writing before the middle of the century, spoke of the 'unbounded liberty' of religious thought which existed in England. Perhaps the expression was somewhat exaggerated. But in what previous age could it have been used at all without evident absurdity? Dark as was the general view which Doddridge, in his sermon on the Lisbon Earthquake, took of the sins and corruption of the age, freedom from religious oppression he considered to be the one most redeeming feature of it. The stern intolerant spirit, which for ages past had prompted multitudes, even of the kindest and most humane of men, to regard religious error as more mischievous than crime, was not to be altogether rooted out in the course of a generation or two. But all the most influential and characteristic thought of the eighteenth century set full against it. In this one respect, the virtues and vices of the day made, it might almost be said, common cause. It might be hard to say whether its carelessness and indifference had most to do with the general growth of toleration, or its practical common sense, its professed veneration for sound reason, its love of sincerity. It is more remarkable that there was so much toleration in the last century, than that there was also so much intolerance.

Closely connected with these questions came another which also attracted a great deal of attention during the whole of the period, What is the nature of the connection that subsists between a State and the National Church? and what are their respective duties toward one another? Until near the end of the preceding century, however great might be the practical difficulties which from time to time arose, the general theory had been simple enough. The State was bound to provide for the spiritual and moral, as well as for the material needs of the people. Therefore it established and supported the Church. Reformed or unreformed, it was *the* Church, and all others were assumed to be in error. The King, as head and father of the people, was also the supreme temporal ruler of the National Church; and, since the Reformation, the English people, loving in their hearts an embodied, personal ruler, had invested their sovereign with many attributes of a Pope. But subsequently to the restoration of Charles II. this theory, which had scarcely suffered from the strain put upon it by the events of the Commonwealth, had received a shock which required it to be re-stated in somewhat altered terms. The

Toleration Act had given a legal standing to persons who neither acknowledged the authority of the National Church nor attended its services. The Revolution of 1689 had materially changed the character of the royal supremacy. The final decline of belief in a certain divine right inherent in royalty, the secession of the Nonjurors, the rise of a new school of philosophical thought under Locke, the establishment under an English king of a differently constituted church in Scotland— all these circumstances contributed among others to bring forward into greater prominence the relation of Church and State.

The personal supremacy of the sovereign had very much disguised the true character of a National Church. Ultimately the will of the nation was of course supreme in all matters connected with the ecclesiastical, as with the civil constitution of the realm. But even before the Reformation the authority of the King had been very great. Since that time, notwithstanding the assertion of Queen Elizabeth that she claimed no supremacy but such as had been attached to the Crown from time immemorial, the Roman Catholics had only too much reason in their taunts upon the ecclesiastical powers conferred by the English upon their sovereign. Parker, Grindal, Whitgift, and many others, had struggled hard against the ecclesiastical despotism of the Tudors. But Cranmer, than whom scarce any other man had left a deeper mark upon the constitution of the English Church, had entertained the most exalted views of the authority with which the King was invested as the spiritual as well as the temporal ruler of the nation. Latimer had spoken of the young King Edward as ' God's high Vicar upon earth ; ' and the people in general loved to have it so. The axiom, ' Rex Angliæ est persona mixta cum sacerdote,' pleased them well ; they liked to think of their monarch as being in a manner their high priest as well as their king. For his supremacy was the plain visible token of their independence of the Pope ; the idea of a national will, unrepresented by a living person, was as yet too abstract an idea to convey much meaning to them. It appeared to be a doctrine suited to the times, and, as such, may have been productive of more good than evil. The growth, however, of the Constitution had been forced into hastier development by the Revolution which placed William upon the throne. Year by year it became more evident that the King held all his authority not as an intrinsic personal right, but as derived from the nation and representative of it, and that his will had little power so far as it was not expressive of the national will. Henceforth Court influence in the Church became in most respects an unmixed evil. A sort of solemnity and responsibility had hitherto attached itself to the exercise of the royal prerogative in Church matters, saving it not so much from the essential evils of the system as from a baser spirit of sordidness and intrigue. There had been no servility in the deferential homage rendered to their King by those who regarded him as the Lord's anointed. It would have been well for the Church, if, when this sentiment had passed away, the principle had been clearly recognised that the King, as temporal head of the Church, acted only under the advice of a Ministry responsible to the people. But he still retained the appearance of his old authority, and some of its reality. Shortly before the Revolution Tillotson, speaking of this influence, had quoted the words :—

> Non sic inflectere sensus
> Humanos edicta valent ut vita Regentis.

Some time had yet to elapse before these words, as used in reference to the King's supremacy, could be held to represent a state of feeling that had quite passed away. William and Mary both exercised a very considerable personal influence in the administration of the Church. So also did Queen Anne ; the more so because her Stuart birth gave her a title which William had not, and because her attachment to the Church of England was the one point on which the general feebleness of her character was not apparent. Queen Caroline's influence in Church matters was great ; but it was too different in kind to be even compared with that of a Tudor or even a Stuart sovereign. It was simply a commanding Court influence, exercised by a clever woman who was keenly interested in theological controversies. George III.'s ecclesiastical authority was of a social rather than of a constitutional character—just that which would naturally attach itself to the chief personage in the realm, if his opinions, though somewhat narrow, were known to be conscientious and worthy of much

respect. Before the eighteenth century had run through half
its course, the King's supremacy, so far as it represented his
individual will, had chiefly come to this, that he had a principal
voice in the dispensing of Church dignities. 'Church and
King' had once contained the full meaning of 'Church and
Nation.' But in proportion to the dignity of the ideas which
this phrase had formerly suggested, and still suggested to the
minds of many who used it, so much greater was the ignominy,
wherever it might rather be interpreted as 'Church and
Court,' and became chiefly connected with the self-seeking
and coarse worldly motives which are nowhere more painfully
visible than among the constant seekers after place and
patronage.

Bishops, both as fathers of the Church and as holding
high places, and living therefore in presence of the public,
cannot, without grave injury not to themselves only, but to
the body over which they preside, suffer their names to be in
any way mixed up with the cabals of self-interest and faction.
At the beginning of the eighteenth century, the Episcopal
bench numbered among its occupants many men, both of
High and Low Church views, who were distinctly eminent
for piety, activity, and learning. And throughout the century
there were always some bishops who were thoroughly worthy
of their high post. But towards the middle of it, and on to
its very close, there was an undoubted lowering in the general
tone of the Episcopal order. Average men, who had succeeded
in making themselves agreeable at Court, or who had shown
that they could be of political service to the administration of
the time, too often received a mitre for their reward. Amid
the general relaxation of principle which by the universal
confession of all contemporary writers had pervaded society,
even worthy and good men seem to have condescended at
times to a discreditable fulsomeness of manner, and to an
immoderate thirst for preferments. There were many scan-
dals in the Church which greatly needed reform, but none
which were so keenly watched, or which did so much to lower
its reputation, as unworthy acts of subserviency on the part of
certain bishops. The evil belonged to the individuals and to
the period, not by any means to the system of a National
Church. Yet those who disapproved of that system found no

illustration more practically effective to illustrate their argument.

Apart from all such grounds of reproach, and from questions suggested by the altered character of the King's supremacy, other causes, already slightly alluded to, compelled attention to the relations of the Church towards the civil power. Some of the most distinguished of the Nonjurors, ejected from their spheres of pastoral labour, and unable to join any longer in the public prayers, but still firmly convinced that they, more truly than any others, represented the genuine historical Church of England, charged the body they had left with sacrificing its independence, and sinking into Erastian compliance with mere secular authority. Others, unaccustomed to draw distinctions between the essentials of Christianity, and secondary points of discipline and government, were thoroughly perplexed at their sovereign being the supreme temporal head of an Episcopalian Church in England, of a Presbyterian one in Scotland. Was there not, they asked, something profane, and even monstrous, in the notion of two religions established under one chief governor? two bodies combined under one head? For a similar reason, people who had grown up under a vague but fixed impression that it was the special office of the State, in matters of religion, to uphold and protect the truest creed, and to put down or discourage heresies, were puzzled how to reconcile the existence of a National Church with the duty—which they were no less ready to acknowledge—of freely tolerating differences in religious opinion. On the other hand, there were some who repudiated the paternal theory of government, and declared the Commonwealth to be a mere compact for the promotion of civil interests, yet could not shut their eyes to the immense importance of religious motive, even in matters relating only to the temporal welfare of mankind. These also were in want of a satisfactory exposition of the duties of government in securing provision for religious needs of evident public concern. Yet again, there was a numerous band of Deists and Sceptics, who would have been willing enough that the State should undertake responsibility for inculcating among the people the primary truths of natural religion, but disliked its giving countenance and public authority to any particular doctrines, and to a prescribed form of worship. Lastly, there were Dissenters—very few, if any, at the beginning of the century, but an increasing number as years went on—who asserted that toleration was not complete until all privilege was finally removed.

A crowd of writers, therefore, of every variety of opinion, had something to write or say on the subject of Church establishments. But until the time of Priestley few ever disputed the advantages derivable from a National Church. Many would have warmly agreed with Hoadly that 'an establishment which did not allow of toleration would be a blight and a lethargy.' So long as this was conceded, scarcely any one wished that the ancient union of Church and State should be dissolved. With rare exceptions, even Nonconformists did not wish it. However much fault they might find with the existing constitution of the Church, however much they might inveigh against what they considered to be its errors, however much they might point to the abuses which deformed it, and to the uncharitable spirit of some of its clergy, they by no means desired its downfall. Probably, it is not too much to say that to some extent they were even proud of it, as the chief bulwark in Europe of the reformed faith. The Presbyterians at the beginning of the century, a declining, but still a strong body, were almost Churchmen in their support of the national communion. Doddridge, towards the middle of the century, was a hearty advocate of religious establishments. Even Watts, a more decided Dissenter than he, in a poem written in the earlier part of Queen Anne's reign, spoke as if he would be thoroughly content to see a National Church working side by side with voluntary bodies, each labouring in the way most fitted to its spirit in the common cause of religion. Mrs. Barbauld, towards the end of the century, expressed the same thought ; and a great number of the more intelligent and moderate Dissenters would have agreed in it. On the general question, we are told that about the time of the Revolution of 1689 there was scarcely one Dissenter in a hundred who did not think the State was bound to use its authority in the interests of the religion of the people. Half the last century had passed before any considerable number of them had begun to think

differently. John Wesley is sometimes quoted as unfavourable
to the connection of Church and State. Doubtless he did not
greatly value it, and perhaps he may have used some expressions which, taken by themselves, might seem in some degree
to warrant the inference just mentioned. But the love and
loyalty which, all his life through, he bore towards the English
Church was certainly connected not only with a high estimation of its doctrines and modes of worship, but with respect
for it as the acknowledged Church of the realm. It should be
added that, in his answer to Toogood's 'Dissent Justified,' he
distinctly asserted the rights of the civil power in things
indifferent, and insisted that allegiance to the National Church
in no way affected the allegiance due to Christ. The
Evangelical party in the Church were, without exception,
thorough Church and State men. John Newton's 'Apologia'
was, in particular, a very vigorous defence of Church establishments. During the earlier stages of the French Revolution—
a period when unaccustomed thoughts of radical changes in
society became very attractive to some ardent minds in every
class—the party among the Dissenters who would have
welcomed disestablishment received the accession of a few
cultivated Churchmen. But Samuel Coleridge, Southey, and
Wordsworth found reason afterwards wholly to change their
views in this, as in many other respects. Furthermore, the
increased radicalism of the few was more than counterbalanced by the intensified conservatism of the many. The
glowing sentences in which Edmund Burke dwelt upon religion as the basis of civil society, and proclaimed the purpose
of Englishmen, that, instead of quarrelling 'with establishments as some do, who have made a philosophy and a religion
of their hostility to such institutions, they would cleave
closely to them,' found an echo in the minds of the vast
majority of his countrymen. This had been the general
feeling throughout the century. With all its faults—and in
many respects its condition was by no means satisfactory—
the Church of England had never ceased to be popular.
Sometimes it met with contumely, often with neglect, and
occasionally its alleged faults and shortcomings were sharply
criticised, and people never ceased to relish a jest at the
expense of its ministers. But they were not the least inclined

to subvert an institution which had not only rooted itself into the national habits, but was felt to be the mainstay throughout the country of religion and morals. Although too often deficient in the power of evoking and sustaining the more fervent emotions of piety, it was representative to the great bulk of society of most of their aspirations towards a higher life, most of their realisations of spiritual things. It was sleepy, but it was not corrupt ; it was genuine in its kind, so that the good it did was received without distrust. Nor could anyone deny that throughout the country it did an immense deal of quiet but not unrecognised good. There were few places where the general level would not have been lower without it. It had fought a good battle against Rome, and against the Deists ; and the hold which, since the middle of the century, had been gained in it by the Evangelical revival proved it not incapable of kindling with a zeal which some had begun to think was foreign to its nature. The Church, therefore, as a great national institution, was perfectly safe. Circumstances had no doubt forced a good deal of attention to its relation with the State. But these discussions had few direct practical bearings. Hence the theoretical and abstract character which they wear in the writings of Warburton and others.

In casting a general glance over the history of the English Church in the eighteenth century, it will be at once seen that there is a greater variety of incident in its earlier years than in any subsequent portion of the period. There were controversies with Rome, with Dissenters, with Nonjurors, with Arians, and above all, with Deists. There was correspondence and negotiation with the French and Swiss Reformed Churches, with German Lutherans, with French Gallicans. Schemes of comprehension, though no longer likely to be carried out, were discussed with strong feeling on either side. There was much to be said about occasional conformity, about toleration, about the relation between Church and State. There was the exciting subject of 'danger to the Church' from Rome, or from Presbyterianism, or from treason within. For there was vehement party feeling and hot discussion in ecclesiastical matters. Some looked upon the Low or Broad Church bishops as the most distinguished ornaments of the English Church ; others thought that if they had their

way, they would break down all the barriers of the Church,
and speedily bring it to ruin. With some, High Churchmen
were the only orthodox representatives of the English Church;
in the eyes of others they were firebrands, Jacobites, if not
Jesuits, in disguise, a greater danger to the ecclesiastical
establishment than any peril from without. No doubt party
feeling ran mischievously high. There was much bigotry,
and much virulence. Such times, however, were more favourable to religious activity than the dull and heavy stormless
days that followed. In the earlier part of the eighteenth
century there were very many men worthy to be spoken of
with the utmost honour, both in the High and Low Church
parties. A great deal of active Christian work was set on
foot about this time. Thus the Society for Promoting Christian Knowledge was founded, and gathered round the table
of its committee room men of very different opinions, but all
filled with the same earnest desire to promote God's glory,
and to make an earnest effort to stem the irreligion of the
times. From its infancy, this society did a vast deal to
promote the object for which it had been established. The
sister Society for the Propagation of the Gospel in Foreign
Parts attested the rise of missionary activity. Societies for
the suppression of vice, and for the reformation of public
manners, sprang up in most of the large towns, and displayed
a great, some thought an excessive, zeal in bringing to the
bar of justice offenders against morality. Numerous associations were formed—on much the same model as that adopted
in later years by the founders of the Methodist movement—
of men who banded to further their mutual edification, and a
more devotional life, through a constant religious observance
of the ordinances and services of the Church. In many cases
they made arrangements to provide public daily prayers where
before there had been none, or to keep them up when otherwise they would have fallen through. Parochial libraries were
organised in many parts of the kingdom, sometimes to provide
religious and sound moral literature for general public use,
more often to give the poorer clergy increased facilities for
theological study. A most beneficent work was set on foot
in the foundation of Charity Schools. During the five years
which elapsed between the forming of the Christian Know-

ledge Society in 1699, and the first assemblage of the Metropolitan Charity School children in 1704, fifty-four schools had started in and about London alone ; and their good work went on increasing. The fifty churches built in London and Westminster by public grant were another proof of the desire to administer to spiritual needs. Nor should mention be omitted of the provision made by Queen Anne's Bounty for the augmentation of poor livings, many of which had become miserably depauperised. By this liberal act the Queen gave up to Church uses the first fruits and tenths, which before the Reformation had been levied on the 'English clergy by the Pope, but from Henry VIII.'s time had swelled the income of the Crown.

The Sacheverell 'phrensy,' and the circumstances which led to the prorogation of Convocation, are less satisfactory incidents in the Church history of Queen Anne's reign. In either case we find ourselves in the very midst of that semi-ecclesiastical, semi-political strife, which is so especially jarring upon the mind, when brought into connection with the true interests of religion. In either case there is an uncomfortable feeling of being in a mob. There is little greater edification in the crowd of excited clergymen who collected in the Jerusalem Chamber, than in the medley throng which huzzaed round Westminster Hall and behind the wheels of Sacheverell's chariot. The Lower House of Convocation evidently contained a great many men who had been returned as proctors for the clergy, not so much for the higher qualifications of learning, piety, and prudence, as for the active part they took in Church politics. There were some excellent men in it, and plenty of a kind of zeal ; but the general temper of the House was prejudiced, intemperate, and inquisitorial. The Whig bishops, on the other hand, in the Upper House were impatient of opposition, and often inconsiderate and ungracious to the lower clergy. Such, for example, were just the conditions which brought out the worse and disguised the more excellent traits of Burnet's character. It is not much to be wondered at, that many people who were very well affected to the Church thought it no great evil, but perhaps rather a good thing, that Convocation should be permanently suspended. Reason and common sense demand that a great Church should have some sort of deliberative assembly. If it were no longer what it ought to be, and the reason for this were not merely temporary, a remedy should have been found in reform, not in compelled silence. But even in the midst of the factions which disturbed its peace and hindered its usefulness, Convocation had by no means wholly neglected to deliberate on practical matters of direct religious concern. And unless its condition had been indeed degenerate, there can be little doubt that it would have materially assisted to keep up that healthy current of thought which the stagnation of Church spirit in the Georgian age so sorely needed. The history, therefore, of Convocation in Queen Anne's reign, turbulent as it was, had considerable interest of its own. So also the Sacheverell riots (for they deserve no more honourable name) have much historical value as an index of feeling. Ignorance and party faction, and a variety of such other unworthy components, entered largely into them. Yet after every abatement has been made, they showed a strength of popular attachment to the Church which is very noteworthy. The undisputed hold it had gained upon the masses ought to have been a great power for good, and it has been shown that there was about this time a good deal of genuine activity stirring in the English Church. Unhappily, those signs of activity in it decreased, instead of being enlarged and deepened. In whatever other respects during the years that followed it fulfilled some portion of its mission, it certainly lost, through its own want of energy, a great part of the influence it had enjoyed at this earlier date.

The first twenty years of the period include also a principal part of the history of the nonjurors. Later in the century, they had entirely drifted away from any direct association with the Church of England. Their numbers had dwindled ; and as there seemed to be no longer any tangible reason for their continued schism, sympathy with them had also faded away. There are some interesting incidents in their later history, but these are more nearly related to the annals of the Episcopal Church of Scotland than to our own. Step by step in the earlier years of the century the ties which linked them with the English Church were broken. First came the death of the venerable bishops, Ken and Frampton ;

then the return to the established communion of Nelson and Dodwell, and other moderate Nonjurors ; then the wilful perpetuation of the schism by the consecration of bishops ; then the division into two parties of those who adopted the Communion Book of Edward VI., with its distinctive usages, and those who were opposed to any change. All this took place before 1718. By that time the schism was complete.

One more characteristic feature of the early part of the century must be mentioned. The essayists belong not only to the social history of the period, but also to that of the Church. Few preachers were so effective from their pulpits as were Addison and his fellow-contributors in the pages of the 'Spectator' and other kindred serials. It was not only in those Saturday papers which were specially devoted to graver musings that they served the cause of religion and morality. They were true sons of the Church ; and if they did not go far below the surface, nor profess to do more as a rule than satirise follies and censure venial forms of vice, their tone was ever that of Christian moralists. They did no scanty service as mediators, so to say, between religion and the world. This phase of literature lived on later into the century, but it became duller and less popular. It never again was what it had been in Addison's time, and never regained more than a small fraction of the social power which it had then commanded.

After Queen Anne's reign, the main interest of English Church history rests for a time on the religious thought of the age rather than on its practice. The controversy with the Deists (which lasted for several years longer with unabated force), and that in which Waterland and Clarke were the principal figures, are discussed separately in this work. But our readers are spared the once famous Bangorian controversy. Its tedious complications are almost a by-word to those who are at all acquainted with the Church history of the period. Some of the subjects with which it dealt have ceased to be disputed questions, or no longer attract much interest. Above all, its course was clouded and confused by verbal misunderstandings, arising in part perhaps from the occasional prolixity of Hoadly's style, but chiefly from the distorting influence of strong prejudices. Gibbon has spoken

of Hoadly as 'the object of Whig idolatry and Tory abhorrence.' The expression is scarcely an exaggerated one.
Not even Sacheverell received such extravagant encomiums,
nor, on the other hand, such furious abuse. There ought
to be no great difficulty in forming a dispassionate judgment. But justice is scarcely done to his memory even by
those who would most fall in with his opinions. No one
in our day is disposed to say much for a bishop who could
leave his diocese wholly unvisited for six years. Such gross
negligence is justly held unpardonable, and makes it impossible to estimate as highly as they deserve other points of
his character. In the last century such absenteeism was by
no means so generally regarded as a distinct blot upon his
fame. Unhappily, it was not so exceptional a thing as to
appear a crying scandal. The odious system of pluralities
had made non-residence so common, that if a man were seen
to be laudably active in some of the duties that devolved upon
him, they were inclined to look very leniently on neglect of
those that lay in an altogether different sphere of labour.
Besides, when Hoadly was appointed to Bangor, it was
becoming common enough to think that the chief function
of a bishop was to be a theologian rather than a chief pastor
of the Church. If Hoadly's great theological talents had
been exercised on subjects less apt to give offence, his fame
as a writer would quite have eclipsed his inactivity in other
respects ; the more so as it was well known that infirmities,
which amounted almost to deformity, made physical exertion
very difficult to him. In fact, the fault was more in the
system than in the man. It was a time when every thinking
man saw clearly that Christianity had good need to put forth
all its intellectual strength. But the proper place for Hoadly
would have been a deanery or a professor's chair rather than
the episcopate.

As a writer, Hoadly had some very great merits. He
loved truth, liberty, and reason with all his heart, and cared
not what obloquy he met while he was engaged in what he
thought to be the furtherance of any of these objects. He
was called by some 'a political bishop.' In the age, however, in which he lived, it is difficult to see how a man of
earnest patriotism and strong convictions could do otherwise

than take a deep interest in politics. Politically and ecclesiastically he was a very embodiment of the Whiggism of the
period. Cassan, in the 'Lives of the Bishops of Winchester,'
has called him 'the greatest Dissenter that ever held preferment in the Church.' His own contemporary, Calamy,
remarked that his views on the nature of the Church and
Church authority were thought to be more those of a moderate
Dissenter, than of the Church of England. Hearne, the
Jacobite, called him, naturally enough, 'a vile republican.'
Hoadly was neither this nor anything approaching to it. He
was warmly attached to the Crown, as it had been settled by
the Revolution of 1689 ; and he was thoroughly loyal, from a
Low Churchman's point of view, to the National Church. But
Tories in politics, and High Churchmen in religious and
ecclesiastical questions, had much reason to dislike and dread
him. With great argumentative power, and with a command
of temper which was by no means common in his age, and
which irritated them the more, he opposed them on all the
varied questions over which the controversy ranged. Whether
the debated subject related to Church authority, or to the
rights of private judgment and man's responsibility or irre-
sponsibility. for conscientious error, or to the limits which
should bound all State interference in matters of conscience,
or to the foundations of royal power, or to the grounds upon
which the Episcopate rests, or to the nature of the Sacraments, or to questions about taxes, and toleration, and subscription, and oaths, Hoadly was always ready with a more
or less able treatise, pamphlet, or sermon on the Whig and
Low Church side. He was often misrepresented or misunderstood, both by Nonconformists, who would gladly have
claimed his authority for opinions in accordance with their own,
and by High Churchmen, who would have rejoiced to show
that his position in the Church of England was an untenable
one. This was especially the case in regard of that leading
subject which brought him into direct collision with Convocation—the authority of human legislation in matters
pertaining to the interests of Christ's kingdom. It may
be that he used, in the first instance, some rather unguarded
expressions. But few unprejudiced persons could carefully
read his 'Answer to the Representation of the Committee of

Convocation' without acknowledging that his statements were grossly misinterpreted, and that inferences which his words by no means justified were presumed to follow from them.

Whatever opinion may be formed of Hoadly's reasonings, it is at least clear that he was thoroughly in earnest, and firmly convinced that the questions agitated were of great importance. ' I have used,' he said, ' my best endeavours to serve a cause upon which the Gospel, the Reformation, and the Church of England, as well as the common rights of mankind, entirely depend. . . . It is a cause in which I could more willingly spend the rest of my life, and a cause in which I could with more certain and well-grounded satisfaction suffer all that this world can bring upon me, than in any with which I have ever been acquainted. I have done, and resolve to do, everything in my power for its support. And I now offer up the whole of what I have done, and can do, to the glory of God, the honour of Christianity, the interest of the Reformation, and the good of human society.'

It is unquestionable that Hoadly's influence upon his generation was great. Some, looking upon the defects of the period that followed, have thought of that influence as distinctly injurious. They have considered that it strongly conduced to a negligent belief and indifference to the specific doctrines of Christian faith, making men careless of truth, so long as they thought themselves to be sincere; also that it loosened the hold of the Church on the people by impairing respect for authority, and by tending to reduce all varieties of Christian faith to one equal level. It is a charge which has some foundation. The religious characteristics of the age, whatever they were, were independent in the main of anything the Whig bishop did or wrote. Still, he was one of those representative men who give form and substance to a great deal of floating thought. He caught the ear of the public, and engrossed an attention which was certainly very remarkable. In this character as a leader of religious thought he was deficient in some very essential points. He was too much of a controversialist, and his tone was too political. There was more light than heat in what he wrote. So long as it was principally a question of right reason, of sincerity, or of justice, he deserved much praise, and did much good. In all the qualities which give fire, energy, enthusiasm, he was wanting. The form in which his religion was cast might suit some natures, but was too cold and dispassionate for general use. It fell in only too well with the prevailing tendencies of the times. It might promote, under favouring circumstances, a kind of piety which could be genuine, reflective, and deeply impressed by many of the divine attributes, but which, in most cases, would need to be largely reinforced by other properties not so easily to be found in Hoadly's writings—tenderness, imagination, sympathy, practical activity, spiritual intensity.

The rise and advance of Methodism, and its relationship with the English Church, is a subject of very great interest, and one that has occupied the attention of many writers. In these papers it has been chiefly discussed as one of the two principal branches of the general Evangelical movement.

Treatises on the evidences of Christianity constitute a principal part of the theological literature of the eighteenth century. No systematic record of the religious history of that period could omit a careful survey of what was said and thought on a topic which absorbed so great an amount of interest. But if the subject is not entered into at length, a writer upon it can do little more than repeat what has already been concisely and comprehensively told in Mr. Pattison's well-known essay. The authors, therefore, of this work have felt that they might be dispensed from devoting to it a separate chapter. Many incidental remarks, however, which have a direct bearing upon the search into evidences will be found scattered here and there in the course of this work. The controversy with the Deists necessitated a perpetual reference to the grounds upon which belief is based both in the Christian revelation, and in those fundamental truths of natural religion upon which arguers on either side were agreed. A great deal also which in the eighteenth century was proscribed under the name of 'enthusiasm' was nothing else in reality than an appeal of the soul of man to the evidence of God's spirit within him to facts which cannot be grasped by any mere intellectual power. By the greater part of the writers of that period all reference to an inward light of spiritual discernment was regarded with utter distrust as an illusion and a snare. From the beginning to the end of the century, theological thought was mainly concentrated on the effort to make use of reason—God's plain and universal gift to man— as the one divinely appointed instrument for the discovery or investigation of all truth. The examination of evidences, although closely connected with the Deistical controversy, was nevertheless independent of it. Horror of fanaticism, distrust of authority, an increasing neglect of the earlier history of Christianity, the comparative cessation of minor disputes, and the greater emancipation of reason through the recent Act of Toleration, all combined to encourage it. Besides this, physical science was making great strides. The revolution of ideas effected by Newton's great discovery made a strangely wide gap between seventeenth and eighteenth century modes of thinking and speaking on many points connected with the material universe. It was felt more or less clearly by most thinking men that the relations of theology to the things of outward sense needed readjustment. Newton himself, like his contemporaries, Boyle, Flamsteed, and Halley, was a thoroughly religious man, and his general faith as a Christian was confirmed rather than weakened by his perception of the vast laws which had become disclosed to him. On many others the first effect was different. Either they were impressed with exorbitant ideas of the majesty of that faculty of reasoning which could thus transcend the bounds of all earthly space, or else the sense of a higher spiritual life was overpowered by the revelation of uniform physical laws operating through a seeming infinite expanse of material existence. The one cause tended to create a notion that unassisted reason was sufficient for all human needs; the other developed a frequent bias to materialism. Both alike rendered it imperative to earnest minds that felt competent to the task to inquire what reason had to say about the nature of our spiritual life, and the principles and religious motives which chiefly govern it. Difficulties arising out of man's position as a part of universal nature had scarcely been felt before. Nor even in the last century did they assume the proportions they have since attained. But they deserve to be largely taken into account in any review of the evidence writers of that period. Not to speak of Derham's ' Physico-Theology ' and other works of that class, neither Berkeley, Butler, nor Paley—three great names—can be properly understood without reference to the greatly increased attention which was being given to the physical sciences. Berkeley's suggestive philosophy was distinctly based upon an earnest wish to release the essence of all theology from an embarrassing dependence upon the outward world of sense. Butler's 'Analogy'—by far the greatest theological work of the century—aims throughout at creating a strong sense of the unity and harmony which subsists between the operations of God's providence in the material world of nature, and in that inner spiritual world which finds its chiefmost exposition in Revelation. Paley's ' Natural Theology,' though not the most valuable, is by no means the least interesting of his works, and was intended by him to stand in the same relation to natural, as his ' Evidences ' to revealed religion.

The evidence writers did a great work, not lightly to be disparaged. The results of their labours were not of a kind to be very perceptible on the surface, and are therefore particularly liable to be under-estimated. There was neither show nor excitement in the gradual process by which Christianity regained throughout the country the confidence which for a time had been most evidently shaken. Proofs and evidences had been often dinned into careless ears without much visible effect, and often before weary listeners, to whom the great bulk of what they heard was unintelligible and profitless. Very often in the hands of well-intentioned, but uninstructed and narrow-minded men, fallacious or thoroughly inconclusive arguments had been confidently used, to the detriment rather than to the advantage of the cause they had at heart. But at the very least, a certain acquiescence in the ' reasonableness of Christianity,' and a respect for its teaching, had been secured which could hardly be said to have been generally the case about the time when Bishop Butler began to write. Meanwhile the revived ardour of religion which had sprung up among Methodists and Evangelicals, and which at the end of the century was stirring, in different forms but with the same spirit, in the hearts of some of the most cultivated and intellectual of our countrymen, was a greater practical witness to the living power of Christianity than all other evidences.

In quite the early part of the period with which these chapters deal there was, as we have seen, a considerable amount of active and hopeful work in the Church of England. The same may be said of its closing years. The Evangelical movement had done good even in quarters where it had been looked upon with disfavour. A better care for the religious education of the masses, an increased attention to Church missions, the foundation of new religious societies, greater parochial activity, improvement in the style of sermons, a disposition on the part of Parliament to reform some glaring Church abuses — all showed that a stir and movement had begun, which might be slow to make any great advance, but which was at all events promising for the future. Agitation against slavery had been in great part a result of quickened Christian feeling, and, in a still greater degree, a promoting cause of it. And when the French Revolution broke out, it quickly appeared how resolutely bent the vast majority of the people were to hold all the more firmly to their Christianity and their Church. Some of the influences which in the early part of the century had done so much to counteract the religious promise of the time, were no longer, or no longer in the same degree, actively at work. There was cause, therefore, for confident hope that the good work which had begun might go on increasing. How far this was the case, and what agencies contributed to hinder or to advance religious life in the Church of England and elsewhere, belongs to the history of a time yet nearer to our own.

Throughout the whole of the eighteenth century, almost all writers who had occasion to speak of the general condition of society joined in one wail of lament over the irreligion and immorality that they saw around them. This complaint was far too universal to mean little more than a general, and somewhat conventional tirade upon the widespread corruption of human nature. The only doubt is whether it might in some measure have arisen out of a keener perception, on the part of the more cultivated and thoughtful portion of society, of brutal habits which in coarser ages had been passed over with far less comment. Perhaps also greater liberty of thought and speech caused irreligion to take a more avowed and visible form. Yet even if the severe judgment passed by contemporary writers upon the spiritual and moral condition of their age may be fairly qualified by some such considerations, it must certainly be allowed that religion and morality were, generally speaking, at a lower ebb than they have been at many other periods. For this the National Church must take a full share, but not more than a full share, of responsibility. The causes which elevate or depress the general tone of society have a corresponding influence, in kind if not in degree, upon the whole body of the clergy. Church history, throughout its whole course, shows very clearly that although the average level of their spiritual and moral life has always been, except, possibly, in certain very exceptional times, higher in some degree than that of the people over which they are set as pastors, yet that this level ordinarily rises or sinks with the general condition of Christianity in the Church and country at large. If, for instance, a corrupt state of politics have lowered the standard of public virtue, and have widely introduced into society the unblushing avowal of self-seeking motives, which in better times would be everywhere reprobated, the edge of principle is likely to become somewhat blunted even where it might be least expected. In the last century unworthy acts were sometimes done by men who were universally held in high honour and esteem, which would most certainly not have been thought of by those same persons if they had lived in our own day. The national clergy, taken as they are from the general mass of educated society, are sure to share very largely both in the merits and defects of the class from which they come. Except under some strong impulse, they are not likely, as a body, to assume a very much higher tone, or a very much greater degree of spiritual activity, than that which they had been accustomed to in all their earlier years. It was so with the clergy of the eighteenth century. Their general morality and propriety was never impeached, and their lives were for the most part formed on a higher standard than that of most of the people among whom

they dwelt. But they were (speaking again generally) not
nearly active enough ; the spiritual inertness which clung
over the face of the country prevailed also among them
Although, therefore, the Church retained the respect and to a
certain extent the affection of the people, it fell evidently short
in the Divine work entrusted to it.

C. J. A.

CHAPTER II.

THE CHURCH AND THE JACOBITES.

THE Revolution of 1688 created at least as great a stir in the Church as it did in the State. Its influence upon the former, though not so permanent nor so really important as upon the latter, was for the time being quite as conspicuous; and its principles were even more fiercely canvassed by Churchmen than by statesmen.[1] In fact, had it not been for the religious question, it is highly probable that the Revolution would never have taken place at all. For men's minds were far more sensitive on the subject of religious than on that of civil liberty. King James's one unpardonable sin was, that he was a Papist and more than suspected of designing to destroy the National Church and to establish Popery upon its ruins. King William's great merit was that he was the champion of Protestantism. He was the nation's ' Deliverer,' not so much from civil bondage as from the iron yoke of Rome, which his infatuated father-in-law was endeavouring to rivet upon his country's neck, through the instrumentality of the Most Christian King.

For many years after the Revolution the dynastic question occupied a greater share of the attention of Churchmen as well as statesmen than any other. It was in many ways most unfortunate for the true interests of the Church that this was so. It gave an unwholesome prominence to the political element in ecclesiastical affairs. It diverted the attention of the Church from her own proper work, to questions in which she should have been only remotely concerned. It for some time alienated the vast majority of the clergy, who took one

---

[1] 'The Revolution is justly entitled to honour as the era of religious in a far greater degree than of civil liberty.'—Hallam's *Constitutional History*, vol. iii. ch. xv. p. 168.

side, from the vast majority of the laity, who took the other side in the dispute ; and the result of the struggle, issuing as it did in the total defeat of Jacobitism, paralysed for many years the energies of a most important party which has always found a home within the pale of the National Church ; while, from a kindred, though not altogether identical cause, it eliminated from religion much of its poetical, its ideal, its venerable character, and gave a hard, dry, prosaic, modern tone to the Church of the period.

In fact it is impossible to look back upon this vexed question of Jacobitism, in which our forefathers were so intensely interested, without mixed feelings. Reason leads us to sympathize with one side, sentiment with the other. While we may thankfully own that the Church was delivered from an imminent danger, we must also admit that the victory was not won without a grievous loss. There was much that was noble, much that was lovely, much that harmonized with a very high type of Christian character in the unselfish devotion which was conspicuous in the adherents to the ancient line of sovereigns. The cold, calculating spirit of interest, the highest feeling with which the advocates of the new *régime* regarded the foreigners who were eventually brought over from Germany to reign over us, was but a poor substitute for the generous, enthusiastic loyalty which was a redeeming feature in some even of the worst of the supporters of the Stuarts. This will abundantly appear in the sequel, when we have examined the details of the relationship between the Church and the Jacobites.

In order to understand the very embarrassing position which the Church of England held in reference to the change of dynasty which took place at the Revolution, it is necessary to glance back at the controversies which raged during the preceding centuries.

When our National Church broke off in the sixteenth century her connection with the Church of Rome, the great principle upon which she took her stand was this ; that the King within his own dominions has no earthly superior. This has been well termed the turning-point of the English Reformation.[1] From that time forward, the royal supremacy formed one of

---

[1] Massingberd's *English Reformation*, pp. 275, 276.

the essential distinctions between the Anglican and the Romanist, the former professing an undivided loyalty to the sovereign ; the latter (so at least said his opponents) being, if he acted consistently, divided in his loyalty between the King and the Pope.

Again, in the convulsions which distracted our country during the seventeenth century, while the various Protestant sects all more or less identified themselves with the anti-monarchical principle, the Church unswervingly attached herself to the monarchical.

In fact, loyalty to her lawful sovereign had for a long time been the distinguishing characteristic of the English Church.[1] She had felt so keenly the evils which had resulted from the interference of a foreign potentate on the one side, and from anarchy and military despotism on the other, that she had been tempted to proclaim her loyalty in wild and extravagant terms, and to use arguments which, if pushed to their logical conclusion, would lead to absolute slavery. When this kind of language was first used after the Restoration, such a case as that which actually occurred in 1688 had probably not been taken into account. Hence, when it did occur, the position of the Church, committed as she was to the principle of loyalty in its extremest form, was a very difficult one. Many of the clergy were suddenly called upon either to eat their own words, or else to resign their preferments and their spheres of usefulness, and to live in a state of disaffection to that government which the nation had all but unanimously chosen. Their case seemed all the more hard because the dispute which raised the difficulty was mainly a dispute between Popery and Protestantism : and so far were they from siding with Popery that they could point with honest pride to the fact that their order had made the boldest, ablest, and most effectual stand against both the doctrines and the practical encroachments of Rome during the reign of the late King.

The points at issue between the Jacobites and the William-ites were argued at great length, and, it must be added, with great ability on both sides.

---

[1] 'Like Hippocrates' twins, the Church and the King rejoiced and wept together.'—Stillingfleet, quoted by Dr. Hunt, *Religious Thought in England*, ii. 2.

The Jacobites asked, was it consistent with common honesty and common justice, and above all with the unbounded loyalty which the Church of England had profusely expressed, for men who had sworn an oath of fealty to one sovereign to transfer their allegiance on any pretence whatever to another ? If a solemn oath might be tampered with and explained away in this fashion, the distinctions between right and wrong would become utterly confused. The Church of England had been for many years preaching up the doctrines of the divine, hereditary, indefeasible right of anointed sovereigns, and the duty of non-resistance and passive obedience, (that is, 'a submissive and patient suffering of the punishment due to the obstinate refusal of actively obeying the commands and injunctions of superiors that are either inconsistent with or opposite to the laws of the divine Creator ')[1] without qualification and without reserve.[2] Were these doctrines suddenly to be scattered to the winds ? were the men who had been preaching them so long to act in direct opposition to them on the very first occasion which arose to test whether they really believed them or not ? And, if they set at naught the teaching of their Church, were they also to set at naught the teaching of their Bibles ? Had not God expressly declared in His Word, 'By Me kings reign and princes decree judgment' (Prov. viii. 15) ? had He not said, 'Who can stretch forth his hand against the Lord's anointed and be guiltless' (1 Sam. xxvi. 9) ? what could be more positively evinced than monarchy *jure divino* from such texts as these ? or, if the Old Testament were disregarded, did not the New Testament teach precisely the same lesson ? Were not such passages as Romans xii. and xiii. so diametrically opposite to the doctrines then fashionable, that it was impossible to find a more cogent argument or positive command for absolute, unlimited obedience than these were ? was not the oath of allegiance 'so express and positive, so firm and binding an obligation that

---

[1] See 'A Dialogue between a Jacobite and a Williamite' in the collection of State tracts published on the occasion of the late Revolution in 1688, and during the reign of King William III. published in London, 1705.

[2] Both Tillotson and Burnet, who may be regarded as the ruling spirits of the anti-Jacobite party, had 'pressed Lord Russell on the unlawfulness of resistance,' and had been severely censured for so doing.—See Birch's *Life of Tillotson*, p. 115.

nothing could be a firmer tie to secure obedience to King James, viz. not to take up arms against the King on any pretence whatever?' And to give this oath of fidelity to another, was not this, not only a contradiction in itself, but a downright violation of that former sacred obligation? Did not the Homily against Rebellion expressly forbid to carry arms against the King on any pretence whatever? were not the sermons and theological writings of many who took the oaths, in direct contradiction to their present practice? ' I have been scandalized,' wrote Ken to Burnet, 'at many persons of our own coat who for several years together preached up passive obedience to a much greater height than ever I did, it being a subject with which I very rarely meddled, and on a sudden, without acknowledgment of past error, preached and acted quite contrary.' [1] When some of the complying clergy complained that they were libelled by the Jacobites, Charles Leslie replied with crushing force : ' These gentlemen had need talk of libels when they have taken such extraordinary pains to libel themselves. Dr. Patrick's paraphrases are a notorious libel against him ; and Dr. Stillingfleet's Preface to the Jesuits' Loyalty, is a terrible libel against him ; and Dr. Sherlock's Case of Resistance,[2] and all his books and sermons before the oath are venomous and inveterate libels against him, and against all that he hath preached and written since. These are libels, and perpetual libels, and will remain

[1] Bowles's *Life of Ken*, p. 170.

[2] Dr. Sherlock's desertion of the Nonjurors raised a violent outcry against him on all sides. He attributed his change of opinion to reading Dr. Overall's Convocation book ; but his enemies said his conversion was 'due to the Devil and Mrs. Sherlock.' A wit seeing him handing Mrs. Sherlock into a coach, said, ' There goes the Doctor with his reasons for complying at his fingers' ends.' He was called the 'trimming Court divine.' Hickes accounted for his change by saying ' a providential King in possession hath bishoprics and deaneries at his disposal, but the legal King out of possession hath nothing to bestow.' ' I have heard,' writes Locke (*Works*, ix. 401) ' of a Master of the Temple, who, during the siege of Limerick, writ over hither to be sure to let him know by the first opportunity, whenever it came to be surrendered, which was done accordingly ; and immediately the good doctor's eyes were opened, and he plainly saw the oaths were not only expedient, but lawful and our duty.' ' Where,' wrote Defoe, ' is the famous Dr. Sherlock, who, having stood out long in his doctrines and confirmed the faith of his suffering brethren by strong and wonderful arguments, at last, at the powerful instigation of a wife and a good salary, has sold all his loyalty for a mess of pottage, fathering his conversion upon honest Dr. Overall ?'—*New Test of the Church of England's Loyalty*, p. 17.

everlasting monuments of their infamy, except they can persuade the people to burn all their books, and forget all their sermons.' It was said that the evils of the King's administration rendered the Revolution necessary; but 'no evils in the King's administration can be of such hurtful consequences to the people as those of anarchy. Placing power in the people and a coercive power over the Crown is anarchy. In case of a personal incapacity in the Prince to administer government, as infancy, lunacy, or madness, the next in blood that is capable ought to administer, but in the name of the Prince and by his authority.'[1] This was what the Jacobite clergy meant when they invited the Prince of Orange to come over. He was to be a Regent at most, not King.

On the other side, it was urged[2] with considerable force that the reciprocal duties in civil societies are protection and allegiance; and wheresoever the one fails wholly, the other falls with it. The end and design of the oaths of supremacy and allegiance was to secure us against the danger of Popery, as any one may see in the Acts by which they were imposed. And though all these oaths are still to the King, yet that is to a prince who subsists upon law, and rules by law; and therefore if the King ceases to *be* King, by subverting our constitution first, and deserting us next, then all our oaths fall to the ground; the next heir becomes the only lawful and rightful King; and if the next heir is a *femme covert*, then by

---

[1] *The Rehearsals: A View of the Times, their Principles and Practices*, by *Philalethes* [Charles Leslie]. London: W. Bowen, 1750, vol. i. p. 150.

[2] The arguments in favour of anti-Jacobitism have been culled mainly from the State tracts published on the occasion of the late Revolution in 1688 and during the reign of King William III. In many cases the quotations have been made verbatim, which will account for some quaint phraseology and peculiar orthography in the text. The names of the principal of these tracts are as follows:—

1. 'An Enquiry into the Present State of Affairs, December 1688, published by authority.'
2. 'Dialogue between a Jacobite and a Williamite.'
3. 'An Examination of Scruples about the Oath of Allegiance.'
4. 'Case of Allegiance considered.'
5. 'A Resolution of certain Queries concerning Submission to Government.'
6. 'Historical Account of the English Government.'
7. 'Unreasonableness of a New Separation,' and
8. 'Vindication of the Above.'
9. 'Letter from a Clergyman to his Neighbour on Allegiance.'—See also the *Somers' Tracts*, passim.

the law of nations her rights are communicated to her husband. A Protestant kingdom is incompatible with a Popish king, which many thought before the King came to the throne ; and he has so managed the matter since, that he has convinced the whole nation of it. Least of all can it be imagined that the great and learned body which has so triumphed over Popery in their late contests with it should now let themselves be so misled with the narrow notions of an unbounded loyalty as to oppose or even dislike such a complete settlement. All the laws forbid the acknowledgment of the Pope for the head of the Church. They make the King of England head of the English Church, and it is high treason to say otherwise. King James made a shift to thrust himself into the throne in spite of all these obstacles. But the English Government is not in the hands of one person. The Parliament partakes of legislative authority with the King ; the people have their privileges, which the King and Parliament cannot take from them. The conscientious objection to transferring sworn allegiance from one sovereign to another is ' very plausible and of great importance.' But ' oaths are only obligatory in the sense of those persons who invent and impose them, if their intention may clearly and rationally appear from the words as expressed in the oath. Did the great council of the nation assembled in Parliament, who composed this oath of fidelity and enjoined it to be given to the Prince, design it only for the preservation and safety of the King, especially when he placed his personal interest and safety in opposition to that of the public weal ? In ordinary circumstances, the Prince is so nearly allied to the public, and so much a part of it, that the safety and happiness of the latter is in a very high measure involved in the prosperity and welfare of the former. But kings were made for the people, not the people for kings.[1] ' Rei illicitæ nulla obligatio.' The oath is ' res illicita,' from its opposition to piety and destructiveness to religion. His Majesty, to whom you have given this oath of fidelity, is by profession a Roman Catholic, and ' quâ talis ' he is obliged, not only by the principles of his religion, but ' sub pœnâ ' of excommunication,

---

[1] It is hardly necessary to add that this doctrine was vehemently repudiated by the Jacobites.

deposition, yea damnation, to extirpate the Protestant religion to the utmost of his power, and to propagate superstition and idolatry. The oath only obliges us to protect and defend the interest of the supreme magistrate when his interest is subservient to the welfare of the whole society. In the baptismal vow men oblige themselves to works of piety, justice, and charity. An after obligation can never bind such to opposite duties. ' Obligatio prior præjudicat posteriori.' The oath of allegiance (in the Jacobite sense) becomes void because it finds men formerly engaged to contrary duties. ' When the English reformers have writ that the people cannot break the oath of allegiance sworn to the King, it was only to beat down the unjust power the Pope pretends to, of absolving subjects from their oaths of allegiance upon their being deposed or excommunicated by him. Reciprocal oaths are dissolved and made void by the non-performance of one of the parties. The oath supposeth the King ought to keep the coronation oath ; which oath he having violated, it follows that this oath can no longer oblige those who have taken it. James deserted the kingdom, made no provision for the administration in his absence, took away the public seals and cancelled writs of Parliament, put himself into the hands of the French King, the greatest enemy of our religion and country, without whom he cannot return to us, and with whom he cannot return without apparent ruin to this kingdom. He doth thereby cease *de facto* to be our King, and we are discharged from our allegiance. The pretended Prince of Wales, lying under a general and vehement suspicion of being an impostor, and being at present under the conduct and disposal of the King of France, hath no right. As to the " distinguishing characteristic of the Church of England," [1] if it had been foreseen that a king should arise that would exercise arbitrary power, subject the kingdom to the Pope, and destroy the religion and properties of his subjects, (a case so odious and improbable that it could not well be supposed), the doctrines of non-resistance and passive obe-

[1] On the argument of the ' distinguishing doctrine,' &c., Hoadly writes: ' When they speak of the peculiar doctrine of the Church of England, answer, It is a scandal to the Church of England to suppose it has peculiar doctrine apart from the Gospel.'—' Preservative against Nonjurors.—To the Christian laity.'—Hoadly, *Works*, vol. i.

dience would not have been pressed to those ends (which were intended to the contrary), viz. to make way for Popery, tyranny, and confusion. But as a matter of fact, what have the clergy acted contrary to those doctrines? While the King continued in the government, they continued to their obedience, even when their liberties and properties were actually taken away and their lives were at stake.' 'As to the oath of non-resistance,' wrote a complying clergyman to his wavering neighbour, 'your submission to King William implies no violation of it, nor departure from it. I have not heard that you took arms against James, nor intend to do; and I am persuaded King William will not press it on you. Clergymen are dispensed with as to the point of carrying arms, and therefore, if you have not broken this oath already, there's no danger that you have any temptation to it, and therefore it can no way hinder your submitting to King William, whatsoever it bound you to suffer with patience at the hands of King James. Scripture, when rightly understood, is in no way opposed to the revolution principles. Those passages which seem to evidence the divine right of the kings of *Israel* prove nothing for the kings of *England.* The Evangelical precepts confine us to no particular platform of civil government. Those places in the New Testament that enjoin obedience, enjoin obedience to all *lawful* commands, and prohibit resistance under the greatest punishment when legally imposed; and our late transactions were only acted to preserve our pure and apostolical religion and secure our fundamental *laws* and ancient government.' One more passage is worth quoting, because it brings out more distinctly than those quoted above the constitutional view of the question. 'If,' argues the writer, 'this be the difference between an absolute and political king, or king of England, that the will of the first is his law, but the law is the rule of the will of the second, that a king ruling arbitrarily, and fundamentally overturning the laws, is no such king as our Constitution owns or ever did admit of, and therefore that no allegiance can be due to him by law, whom the law knows not, nor ever did suppose, but always did exclude, he must be none of the kings to whom we swore allegiance, and by refusing to be a political king, the only king our laws will own, he must have absolved his subjects from that allegiance which is due only to such a king. If "rebus sic stantibus" be, as Bishop Sanderson says, a condition of all oaths, if the matter of the oaths must be then judged to cease when things so change, that if a change could have been foreseen the oath would not have been taken, then much more the obligation must cease when so great a change is made as from a political to an absolute king—from a king ruling by law and protecting the Church, to a king ruling against law, and subverting the Church against both his oath and law.'[1]

Another question closely connected with the foregoing arose soon after the Revolution. Had the civil power a right to deprive the nonjuring bishops of their sees, and to appoint fresh bishops in their room? This question, too, was argued on both sides at great length, but the main points are capable of being stated very briefly.

The Jacobites urged that 'to erect another altar against the hitherto acknowledged altar of the deprived fathers was schism. If their places be not vacant, the new consecrations must be null, invalid, and schismatical. 'Tis not agreeable to the mind of God that the Church should so concorporate with the State as that bishops should be deprivable at the pleasure of the civil magistrates. The civil power cannot, but in a synodical way, deprive bishops. The intruders are " secundi," and therefore " nulli ; " they cannot be defended as valid bishops, but by principles destructive of the Church, as a society distinct from the State. *They* are the schismatics,

---

[1] The opinion of Archbishop Sharp is worth quoting, not only for its intrinsic good sense, but on account of the character of the man. Dr. Sharp was universally respected ; no one would have accused him of temporising. He was distinctly a High Churchman of the older and better type, and he respected the scruples of the Nonjurors, though he did not share them. In answer to one who asked him how a person who had sworn allegiance to James could do the same to William, he replied, ' The laws of the land are the only rule of our conscience in this matter, and we are no further bound to pay obedience to governors than the laws enjoin. If William be king in the eye of the law, we must in conscience pay him obedience as such. As the law makes a king, so the same law extends or limits, or transfers our allegiance ; only with this proviso, that it be not contradictory to the laws of God. In that case we must obey passively, though we cannot actively ; and with this tacit condition, I do suppose all oaths of fidelity in the world are given and taken.'—*Life of Archbishop Sharp*, by his Son. Edit. G. T. Newcome, 1825, p. 264.

not *we.* They divide from us, not we from them. A lay authority cannot take away what it never gave.'[1]

To this it was replied, 'The secular powers depose a bishop not by way of deprivation, but of exclusion. They exclude him, not from his orders, as if he had them not, but from the gift, that he may not exercise it. And not from that neither absolutely, but after a sort; that he should not exercise his office as to their subjects nor in their dominions; a power which the holiest princes in the best and primitive times have often exercised. A prince cannot give, and so cannot take away the *intrinsic* power of the Word and Sacraments proceeding from the keys of ordination; but the *extrinsical* power and licence of exercising the ministerial office, received by ordination, he can in his dominions confer and again take away, if the case so requires. A *State* deprivation does not concern the character. Such a man may be a bishop of the Catholic Church still, if he do not fall under Church censures for heresy or other crimes; but it only concerns the exercise of his episcopal authority in any diocese within the dominions of that State, or enjoying any ecclesiastical benefice in it. This power the bishops had from the nomination of the King, as they themselves swore. The lay power does not concern itself with capacities within, but only that it be not exercised to the hazard of the public. It *may* take away what it never gave, as, for instance, life and property. Every government has a right of self-preservation; to deprive bishops for this end, therefore, is not to go beyond the limits of the civil powers.'[2]

For convenience' sake, the case has been stated as it stood between the Jurors and the Nonjurors. It must not, however, be supposed that 'Nonjuror' and 'Jacobite' were synonymous terms. There were Nonjurors who were in no active sense of the term Jacobites, men who would have been content to live quietly under the new government, and were only prevented by tenderness of conscience from taking the oaths;

---

[1] See Henry Dodwell's *Works,* passim; Lathbury's *History of the Nonjurors;* Kettlewell's, Ken's, Hickes' and Leslie's *Works,* passim.

[2] See Hoadly's *Works,* vol. i. 'Preservative against the Nonjurors. To the Christian Laity;' also State tracts referred to above, especially, 'The Vindication of their Majesty's Authority to fill the Sees of deprived Bishops.'

and there were Jurors who were still Jacobites at heart, and
were ready to embrace the first opportunity, if they were not
actually scheming to find an opportunity of restoring the
Stuart dynasty. The eight bishops, four hundred clergy, and
small sprinkling of laity who formed the original nonjuring
schism, by no means represented the full strength of Jacobitism.
In fact, it is very difficult to estimate what the real strength
of the Jacobite party was during the period immediately
subsequent to the Revolution. From the nature of the case,
there must have been many who could not acquiesce at once
in the new order of things. One of our most thoughtful
historians, who was certainly no friend of the Jacobites, admits
that 'the encroachments of James II. were rather felt in
prospect than much actual injury.'[1] Few had personally
experienced suffering or even inconvenience from the mal-
administration of the King, though they would probably
soon have done so. Under these circumstances, was it likely
that all those who had been accustomed to throw up their
caps for King James would be ready at a moment's notice to
throw up their caps for King William? Men cannot change
their principles as easily as they change their coats, especially
when they have suffered personally no harm from those
principles.

Hence it was very necessary to blow the trumpet of alarm
to rouse the apathetic against the dangers of Jacobitism.
If men did not make themselves ready for the battle, it
certainly was not because that trumpet gave an uncertain
sound. Its blasts were loud and frequent, and the loudest
and most frequent of all was that which warned men of the
danger to their National Church from Popery—another proof
of what was asserted at the beginning of this paper, viz., that
the religious element was by far the most important element
in the Revolution. 'You shall trot about in wooden shoes,
à la mode de France,' writes an alarmist in 1690. 'Monsieur
will make your souls suffer as well as your bodies. These are
the means he will make use of to pervert Protestants to the
idolatrous Popish religion. He will send his infallible apostolic
dragoons amongst you.' (Then follows a graphic description
of the horrible tortures which had been inflicted upon Protes-

---

[1] Hallam's *Constitutional History*, vol. iii. ch. xv. p 109.

tants elsewhere). 'If you fall into French hands, your bodies
will be condemned to irretrievable slavery, and your souls (as
far as it lies in their power) shall be consigned to the Devil.
If you regard neither body nor soul, I have done with you;
and so, farewell!'[1] Another writer, who styles himself 'a
person of quality,' warns his countrymen against Jacobitism
by sketching 'the character of a Jacobite by what name or
title soever dignified, 1690.' Here, too, the danger to religion
is brought far more prominently forward than any other.
'The Jacobites,' he writes, 'are a sort of animals sprung from
the corruptions of King James's evil government, and carry
two shapes in one body like a centaur, or the Irish virgin with
a fish in her tail, half Protestant half Papist. If they are of
the temporal nobility, they believe the glitter of their honour
to be only the reflection of King James's favour, and that the
rays of their grandeur cannot shine with that lustre as they
ought, unless, like glow-worms' tails, they may be permitted to
glisten in the dark of Popery and tyranny. Some lay claim
to conscience, and upon that score pretend whole ounces of
loyalty and fidelity to King James. . . . They are the most
believing persons in the world. They believe that sympathy
and antipathy, the Mass and the Common Prayer, will kiss
each other upon his coming back in two chapels under the
same roof; that his Italian wife will forgive 'em, his priests
will pardon 'em, and himself exonerate 'em for assisting to
lift him out of his kingdom; that young Perkin was truly
begot; that the French King will not sue by fire and sword
for the vast sums lent upon mortgage of the British dominions,'
and so forth. It is, however, upon the Jacobite clergy that
this writer chiefly pours the vials of his wrath. 'The Jacobite
clergy are a generation of vipers, envenomed with the poi-
sonous pamphlets of the "Observator."[2] They are a numerous
gang, and haunt S——'s coffee house in shoals, where they
sit croaking like frogs in March against the government.
They cannot study for hearkening after news; and in Parliament time the Court of Requests is so crowded with 'em, as
if the Pope's consistory sate in the Painted Chamber. If
they can get to be a lord's chaplain, they presently whip on a

---

[1] 'Jacobites' Hopes Frustrated' (from the Harleian Miscellany).
[2] That is, of course, Tutchin's 'Observator' not L'Estrange's.

long scarf, and then Lucifer was not prouder when he exalted himself upon the mount of the congregation in Isaiah. They are a sort of divinity meteors that run whisking up and down to misguide the wandering people. You cannot perceive 'em to be mere cripples, and yet there is not one of 'em but halts most conspicuously between God and Baal. They pretend to be Protestants with an extraordinary inclination to Popery, that they may have two strings to their bow, and be ready on the return of their idol to fall down and worship his will and pleasure.

'They idolize King James as the heathens did their false gods—first make their idol, and then worship it. They pretend to be true sons of the Church, but use her no better than a stepmother, to offer the price of her preservation for the redemption of her professed enemy. Nothing is more frequent among 'em than envy, passion, repining, and supplanting of each other. Their sermons are a sort of lampoons upon Scripture.[1] They pray for King James, spend all their most fervent ejaculations in their cups and over their coffee for King James, as if they thought God were a favourer of Popery, tyranny, and slavery. They set up King James like the Brazen Serpent, thinking to be safe by looking upon him when stung by the fiery serpents of Rome. They are afraid of heaven (that is, happiness under King William), and place their hopes on the Devil's future civility. They are for a king *de jure* that has forfeited his right by breach of faith, breach of oaths, breach of all things by which a sovereign claims his sovereignty, a vain terror of their own erecting. Heaven pulled him down, and they would heave him up again.'

'The other sort of Levitical Jacobites, as they are more highly dignified and farther stricken in years, carry themselves

---

[1] There certainly were some grounds for this remark. It is said that one clergyman took for his text on the occasion of the funeral of Queen Mary, 'Go see to this cursed woman and bury her, for she is a king's daughter;' another in allusion to the House of Hanover, whose crest was a white horse, preached from the text, 'And I looked and behold a pale horse; and his name that sat on him was Death, and Hell followed with him.' But the other side was equally open to the charge. One preacher is said to have explained the reason why Jacob's name was changed to Israel, 'because God would not have his chosen people called Jacobites.'

with more reservedness ; and as they have gained a greater reputation, so they are more dangerous to government ; yet they walk upon the same grounds and move upon the same principles as the inferior crew, who received their instructions from them. These are a moody, sullen sort of Jacobites that would make all the world believe there are but so many knowing, pious men in the nation, and by an affected ostentation of conscience would riggle themselves into the honour of having all the nation dance after their pipes. . . . . How near to reconciliation these Jacobites and the Romanists are ! They are linked together against William, like the wicked against King David. Some great Jacobites conform on purpose to do mischief ; for they can then give bad counsel unsuspected. These Levitical champions for King James draw after 'em some numbers of the commonalty and the gentry :— Bullies, Beaux, Hectors, Bravoes, St. Nicholas' Clerks, Alsatians, &c.—all these are of the society of Jacobites,—the dregs and *caput mortuum* of human society.'

The above are really not unfair specimens of the sort of language that was used, and the opinions that were held respecting the Jacobites at the close of the seventeenth century. They were hated and proscribed, and at the same time feared. The very mystery that hung about them and the uncertainty as to their real strength intensified these feelings of indefinite alarm and dislike.

As the Jacobites could not join in the services of the National Church on account of what they called ' the immoral prayers,' that is, those in which King William and Queen Mary were prayed for by name, they held secret meetings of their own, which where in all probability partly of a devotional and partly of a political character. A doggrel poem written in 1692 gives an amusing description of ' a Jacobite conventicle.' It is, of course, impossible to say whether the writer described what he actually saw and heard, or whether he drew upon his imagination ; but there is every reason to believe that, after making due allowances for the prejudices of an enemy, it may be taken as a substantially correct account of what often took place, and it is therefore worth quoting.

After having described how he dogged the steps of a

'moody Jacobite' to the place of rendezvous, the writer proceeds :—

> But hold—Before to Fetter Lane I go
> 'Tis requisite the entrance word I know ;
> Last Sunday 'twas commandèment the fifth,
> And now St. Germains is the Shibboleth.
> 'Tis so,—and now with eager steps I fly
> To the true Church of England's ministry,
> To hear a sort of men who ever knew
> Still to be faithful, loyal, firm, and true,
> Who for their souls detest the swearing vice,
> Either to get or keep a benefice.
>
> I sate me down upon a hassock,
> Expecting clergyman in cassock ;
> That Holy Smith who blows the coals
> Of discontent, and saves their souls
> By telling them that no salvation
> Can be to men of abdication,
> And that, a Hell is still appointed
> For those resist the Lord's anointed;
> But he, it seems, was not come yet,
> But staid behind to take a whet
> Of white wine in a brimming taster
> In mem'ry of his absent master.

Before the clergyman comes, all talk politics. The room is crowded with both men and women, all of whom are sullen and discontented. At last the clergyman arrives, and then :—

> His surplice on, they then prepare
> To joyn with him in Common Prayer ;
> Nor Psalms nor prayers did he omit any,
> Till coming to that place i' th' Litany,
> Wherein obliged by name to pray
> For those who bear the Sovereign sway,
> He did in 's prayers no name put in,
> But those of gracious King and Queen ;
> Which prayer, no sooner did it reach the
> Ears of them all, but 'we beseech Thee'
> Echoed more loud by persons there
> Than the response to any prayer
> Which in the Liturgy we read
> From the Lord's Prayer to Nicene Creed.

The clergyman then gives out his text, Romans xiii. 1, 2, and proceeds thus :—

> The text (quoth he), belovèd, plainly
> Holds forth that every one should mainly
> Strive who should most enrichèd be
> With that dear jewel, Loyalty.
> I do not mean the counterfeit
> Which every one that swears may get
> To save their purses having a mind ;
> Theirs is a Bristol stone, no diamond.

Then he exhorts parents how to instruct their children :—

> Tell 'em the dignity of crown'd heads,
> And make 'em learn to hate the Roundheads.
> Tell 'em there nothing is in nature
> So monstrous as a Whiggish creature ;
> Tell 'em,—nay, tell 'em anything
> T' advance the glory of a king.

Then he comments on the words ' Let every soul *be subject,*' &c. :—

> That is, let every soul be ready
> With a fixt mind resolved and steddy
> To part with life, estate, and all,
> Whene'er it is his Prince's call.
> But never let him hum and haw
> And question if 'tis done by law ;
> His Prince's will to him should be
> The rule of law and equity.

Then he apostrophizes his adversaries thus :—

> What mighty havock have ye done,
> Ye wicked men of Forty One !
> Nay, I might farther here rejoyn,
> Ye Belial's sons of Eighty Nine !

The meeting is here interrupted by a constable and party of musketeers, who drag them all before the magistrates. The oath is tendered and refused, and every one has to pay a fine of forty shillings.

At the beginning of the eighteenth century, Jacobitism in

many respects assumed a new form.   In the first place, lapse
of time had considerably widened the breach between those
who ostensibly acquiesced in the Revolution settlement and
those who refused to take the oaths.   At the outset of the
dispute, many instances of good feeling had been displayed
on both sides.   Sancroft, the most obstinate of Nonjurors,
still kept his chaplains who had taken the oaths, and trusted
'that though the swearers and they (the Nonjurors) went by
different ways, Heaven's gates would be wide enough to
receive both.'[1]   Ken expressed a kindly feeling towards
the actual holders of power, though his conscience prevented
him from swearing allegiance to them, and said to Hooper,
' I am satisfied that you take the oaths with as clear and well-
resolved conscience as I refused them !'[2]   Many of the Nonjurors continued to attend their parish churches, though
they could not say 'Amen' to the prayers for the reigning
sovereigns.

On the other side, the complying clergy had shown a
generous unwillingness to occupy the sees vacant by deprivation.   Some, as Sharp and Beveridge, absolutely refused to
accept such bishoprics, and those who did accept them were
with difficulty persuaded to do so.   To render the oath less
objectionable, the words 'rightful and lawful' sovereign were
omitted.   King William himself offered to excuse the oath
altogether, if Dissenters might be excused the sacramental
test.   A large body of the complying clergy interceded in
behalf of their non-complying brethren in the most earnest
and generous language.[3]

Unhappily, these friendly relations were of short duration.
The Nonjurors became more and more convinced that the
primitive and Catholic doctrines of the Church of England
were being undermined by latitudinarian and Erastian notions, emanating from high places and gradually leavening·
the mass.[4]

---

[1] *Life of Kettlewell*, iii. 159.
[2] Bowles's *Life of Ken*, ii. 255.
[3] See the address in full in Lathbury's *History of the Nonjurors*.
[4] 'The clergy continued to be much divided ; all moderate divines were
looked upon by some hot men with an ill eye, as persons who were cold and
indifferent in the matters of the Church. That which flowed from a gentleness of
temper and principle was represented as an inclination to favour Dissenters,

The Jurors complained more and more that the Nonjurors were factious and narrow; that by their politics they were playing into the hands of France, by their religion into the hands of Rome.

Several circumstances contributed to bring about these unhappy results. In the interval which elapsed between the suspension and deprivation of the nonjuring bishops, one of their number (Turner of Ely) was suspected of having been concerned in Lord Preston's conspiracy. In some intercepted letters supposed to have been written by the bishop to James, these ominous expressions occurred : ' Sir, I speak in the plural number, because I write my elder brothers' sentiments as well as my own, and the rest of our family.' This cast a shade of suspicion upon all the Nonjurors, although they vehemently protested their innocence of any share whatever in the plot.

The violent and unchristian tone in which some of the Nonjurors spoke and wrote of the newly appointed dignitaries exasperated their enemies and grieved the hearts of their more moderate friends.[1] The death of Queen Mary in 1694 naturally tended to alienate disaffected Churchmen still further from the sovereign power. The Queen had been a Church-woman by conviction, and had won the esteem of Church people of almost every shade. Her husband had left the management of ecclesiastical affairs to a great extent in her hands, and she had exercised her influence wisely and well according to her light. As to King William himself, he was quite incapacitated by his early training for appreciating one very important side of the Church's teaching. He could

which passed among many for a more heinous thing than leaning to Popery itself. Those men, who began now to be called the High Church party, had all along expressed a coldness if not an opposition to the present settlement. . . . . They were now soured with a leaven that had gone too deep to be rooted out,' &c. Burnet's *History of His own Times*, vol. iii. book vi. p. 318. See also page 446 of the same volume.

[1] Tillotson was a special object of abuse. ' His politics,' it was said, ' are Leviathan and his religion Latitudinarian, which is none. He is owned by the atheistical wits of all England as their true Primate and Apostle. He leads them not only the length of Socinianism (they are but slender Beaux have got no farther than that), but to call in question all revelation. His principles are diabolical, and by them he has deeply poisoned the nation.' ' He came into the Church a thief and a robber, and has continued so.' R. Nelson was deeply annoyed at the treatment of his friend by the Nonjurors. Burnet was equally abused.

sympathize with its negative character, so far as it protested against the corruptions and innovations of mediæval Rome. But its position as the guardian of primitive and Catholic truth, as the consistent maintainer of Apostolical order combined with Evangelical doctrine, as the skilful pilot steering clear of the Scylla of mediæval superstitions on the one side, and the Charybdis of modern disorders on the other, could not be realised, much less appreciated, by one who had never shaken off his predilection for Dutch Presbyterianism. Moreover, among the many turbulent elements of his troubled reign, none were more disturbing than those which arose from ecclesiastical affairs. His relationship with the great body of the clergy had never been cordial, and after the Queen's death it was less cordial than ever.[1] Thus various circumstances concurred to convert passive Nonjurors into active Jacobites, as well as to incense the friends of Revolution principles against all who would not cordially co-operate with them.

The very first year of the new century witnessed a marked change in the aspect of affairs. The death of the Duke of Gloucester, sole surviving child of the Princess of Denmark, and, after his mother, heir to the crown, greatly revived the hopes of the Jacobites.[2] Providence, they thought, itself seemed to open a way for the restoration of the ancient line. The Act of Settlement (1701), which gave the reversion of the crown to a Lutheran and a foreigner, far removed from the direct order of succession, afforded them another handle for appealing both to the Catholic sympathies and the *jure divino* doctrines of the High Churchmen. They were also freed from

---

[1] 'The King seemed to grow weary of us and of our affairs ; and partly by the fret from the opposition he had of late met with, partly from his ill-health, he was falling, as it were, into a lethargy of mind.'—Burnet's *History of His own Times*, vol. iii. bk. vi. p. 315. An anonymous writer of a ' Letter to King William, first printed in 1696,' on ' The Foundation of the English Monarchy,' writes : ' It cannot be expected that the clergy should upon the Revolution be contented to cry " peccavi " by a hearty, active conformity to your government ; therefore you have received so little respect from the body of the clergy, though we have received all that we enjoy from you,' &c.

[2] ' His death,' writes Burnet (*History of His own Times*, vol. iii. bk. vi. p. 315), 'gave a great alarm to the whole nation ; the Jacobites grew insolent upon it, and said now the chief difficulty was removed out of the way of the Prince of Wales's succession.'

a serious embarrassment by the opportune death of their very impracticable King over the water. Even before his death, the thoughts of the Jacobites had begun to be turned from James II. to James III. It was felt to be an utterly hopeless task to attempt to restore the aged father. But sympathy with a young prince who had had no share in that father's errors might surely be awakened. Why should the sins of the guilty father. (supposing he *was* guilty) be visited upon the innocent son? *He* had not violated the much-talked-of pact between the nation and its lawful sovereign. Why should he be deprived of his rightful inheritance? And once more, the Abjuration oath, placing as it did a stumbling-block in the way of many who might otherwise have given at least a tacit allegiance to the government, tended to strengthen the Jacobite cause.[1]

Under these circumstances it may seem strange that upon the death of King William, which took place immediately after the Abjuration oath had been imposed, no attempt should have been made to seat the Pretender upon the vacant throne. But the Jacobites judged rightly in postponing their efforts. The pear was not yet ripe. There were several insuperable objections to their candidate, which for the present at least rendered his chances of success hopeless. He was a mere boy; his interests were inseparably bound up with those of France, England's sworn foe; his legitimacy was questioned; and, above all, he was a Romanist. As this work is concerned only with the religious aspect of Jacobitism, the last objection alone need be dwelt upon. And it was in itself quite sufficient to disqualify him. In vain did his partisans represent that the evil effects of early training might easily be eradicated from one so young, if he were once detached from the scheming priests and bigoted mother under whose influence he was at St. Germains. In vain did they hold out hopes of a general toleration under his rule. 'It's as easy,' wrote an anonymous pamphleteer some years before, 'for the Arctick and

---

[1] The admirable letter of Bishop Wilson on the Abjuration oath, which was so highly valued by Lord Chancellor King that it was printed at his desire, is well worth reading not only for its intrinsic excellence, but as illustrating the sentiments of a conscientious High Churchman who was not a Jacobite, on a subject which was once a great stumbling-block to many good men. It is published *in extenso* in Stowell's *Life of Wilson*, pp. 206-212.

Antarctick Poles to meet together, or for the East and West to be in conjunction, as to reconcile infallibility of one religion with a toleration of all ; the necessity of extirpating all Heretics with a connivance at all Heresies.'[1]   And this was still the general sentiment of the nation.   Its horror of Popery was unbounded.   Within the last two years it had passed a most cruel law against the growth of Popery.[2]   England had once for all shaken off the yoke of Rome, and had thoroughly determined not to run the slightest risk of having to submit to that yoke again.

Moreover, the High Churchmen, upon whose dissatisfaction at the Latitudinarianism and Erastianism into which the Church was thought to be drifting the Jacobites counted as favourable to their cause, had more reason to be satisfied with the new Queen than with the late King.   Anne had no leaning towards Dutch Calvinism, or Presbyterianism, or Latitudinarianism.   She was a staunch and conscientious, if not a very enlightened, member of the Church of England, not from policy but from conviction, and she made no secret of her intention to extend the influence and increase the resources of the Church in every way.[3]

Thus Jacobitism for some years lay in abeyance.   With the single exception of the feeble and abortive attempt of 1708, no active steps appear to have been taken for eight years in favour of the Chevalier.   But though no overt act was done in his behalf, secret schemes were constantly going on.   Nor was this scheming confined to the much maligned party of the Nonjurors.   Men of all parties and all principles were implicated in it—Whigs as well as Tories, Low Churchmen as well as High Churchmen.   Marlborough himself, the hero of the Protestant cause, was strongly suspected of holding communications with the exiled Court.   So was Godolphin, so was Harley, so was Sunderland, so was Bolingbroke.   'Jacobitism' was still at times a useful political cry.   For instance,

---

[1] 'Advantages of the Present Settlement and Danger of Relapse.'   One of the 'State tracts' on the Revolution.   See *supra.*

[2] Act against the growth of Popery, passed in 1700.

[3] See Queen Anne's speech at the close of her first Parliament in 1702.   'My own principles must always keep me entirely firm to the interests and religion of the Church of England, and will incline me to countenance those who have the truest zeal to support it.'

when an attempt was made to pass the bill against occasional conformity by the somewhat sharp practice of 'tacking' it to a grant of money, its opponents found Jacobitism a convenient charge to bring against the tackers. 'A tacker,' writes a pamphleteer in 1705, 'is the motley spawn of the nonjuring clergy, and with a pious supererogation damns himself with oaths which he takes to destroy. A tacker is one whose zeal for the Church shakes hands with the Devil ; and for fear of Geneva, joins the Jesuit and Turk to oppose it. A tacker is one that maintains that we had better unite with a Church we differ from in fundamentals than one we dissent from only in circumstantials. A tacker is one that holds Popery, which is condemned by our laws, is more eligible than Presbytery, which our law allows. A tacker is a Jacobite in disguise, who, having refused the oaths all the late reign, took them only in this to destroy it. A tacker is one that is fool enough to believe (if absurdities are properly the objects of faith) that the supposed son of King James has a divine right to be King of England, and is knave enough to take a solemn oath to a contrary government and in the presence of God to abjure this divine right, that he may get into the legislature and embroil our affairs to establish it. A tacker is one that, while he would have all mankind but kings beasts of burthen, is so himself *ex confesso*, and therefore, as he owns himself to be a beast, ought to be used like one by all true Englishmen, and justly excluded from that religion and property which he declares we have no right to. A tacker, in fine, is one who, denying that we ought to live by law, ought by his own rule to be hanged without law. And so, there is an end of the tacker.' [1]

An anti-tacker, on the other hand, 'is one who hates Popery and Church Papists as he would so many toads. His heart is truly English, and he knows no enemies but the Devil, the Pope, the French King, and their adherents.'

Indeed it was the constant policy of the Whigs to represent the Tories in general, and the Tory clergy especially, as being all Jacobites at heart. But this the Tories indignantly denied. 'There are not ten clergymen (except Nonjurors),'

[1] 'Character of a Tacker' and 'Character of an Anti-Tacker.' *Somers' Tracts*, vol. xii.

wrote Swift, 'who do not abhor the thoughts of the Pretender reigning over us.'[1] 'Dodwell, Hickes, and Lesley are quoted to prove that the Tories design to bring in the Pretender ; and if I should quote them to prove that the same thing is intended by the Whigs, it would be full as reasonable ; since I am sure they have as much to do with Nonjurors as we.'[2] 'I charge him (the Observator),' writes Leslie, 'with keeping up the name of him whom he means by Perkin. There has not been a word of him from his own party, if any such are left in England. They have all been hush since her Majesty's accession to the throne, as if they were well pleased. At least they are modest. And the name of Perkin might have been dead among us by this time, but for the Observator and some hypochondriac sinners who dream of him all night, and rave upon him all day.'[3]

But, however true it may be that during the first decade of the eighteenth century, there was no serious danger from Jacobitism, the same cannot be said of the last four years of Queen Anne's reign. The period from 1710 to 1714 was perhaps the only period when Jacobite projects really seemed to have a fair chance of being crowned with success. Jacobitism was then no mere panic cry raised by a party in the State to create political capital for themselves. Everyone who could read the signs of the times felt that the restoration of the exiled Stuarts after the Queen's death was highly probable. The political circumstances which helped to bring

---

[1] 'Public Spirit of the Whigs.' 'This,' adds the Dean with more vigour than elegance, 'is the spittle of the Bishop of Sarum, which our author [Steele, in 'The Crisis '] licks up and swallows and then coughs out again with an addition of his own phlegm.'

[2] *Examiner*, No. xxxiii. In the absurd affair of Partridge and Squire Bickerstaff, Swift, in allusion to the unreasonable charges of Jacobitism brought against the Tories, makes Partridge say, 'I shall demonstrate to the judicious that France and Rome are at the bottom of this horrid conspiracy [to prove that he was dead, according to Bickerstaff's prophecy] against me ; and that the culprit aforesaid is a Popish emissary, has paid his visits to St. Germain's, and is now in measure with Louis XIV. That thro' my sides a wound is given to all Protestant Almanack makers.'

[3] *The Rehearsals*, vol. i. 'John Wesley says of those who called his father a Jacobite, 'Most that gave him the title of Jacobite did not distinguish between Jacobite and Tory, whereby I mean one that believes God, not the people, to be the origin of all civil power,' quoted in Nichol's *Literary Anecdotes*, v. 244.

about this change in the posture of affairs do not fall within the compass of this work. But ecclesiastical, or rather politico-ecclesiastical events had far more to do with the crisis than secular politics had. The storm which at last burst forth on the impeachment of Dr. Sacheverel had long been brewing. The High Churchmen, that is, the vast majority of the clergy,[1] had for some time been dissatisfied with the conduct of affairs. The Queen herself had not realised the fair promise which she had given, both before and immediately after her accession to the throne. Instead of being a true nursing-mother to the Church, she had been too much like a step-mother, or a dry-nurse.

> When she was the church's daughter
> She acted as her mother taught her ;
> But now she's mother of the church,
> She's left her daughter in the lurch.

This had been a favourite distich with High Churchmen for some years. Not but what they admitted that the Queen was still sound at heart ; only she had been too much in-fluenced by evil counsellors, and it was high time to remove them. The Sacheverel impeachment was simply the last straw which broke the camel's back. There is little doubt that this 'roasting of the parson,' as it was called, was chief among the proximate causes which brought about the change of Ministry in 1710, and there is hardly less doubt that the new Ministry were all more or less implicated in the Jacobite cause ; and least of all can it be doubted that the clergy of the Church of England were, whether rightly or wrongly, regarded as the main *fons et origo mali.*

Certainly, if the most violent assertions of the doctrines of divine hereditary right, non-resistance, passive obedience, and the rest of the old High Church programme, were, as they were assumed to be, the best methods of paving the way for the return of the exiles, there can be no doubt that a vast number of the clergy of the period were, in fact, fuglemen of the Jacobites. Sacheverel's famous sermon was pronounced rank Jacobitism. ' Had he,' wrote Dr. Burges, 'made use of

---

[1] 'Those they call the High Church,—by which they mean the far greatest part of the English clergy.'—'Wolf stript of the Shepherd's Clothing.' Leslie's *Theological Works,* vol. iii. p. 396.

those wild notions in a Jacobite conventicle, or before his royal master the Pretender, at St. Germains, few on this side of the water would have troubled their heads about it.'[1] 'Could this fanatical doctor,' writes another, 'strike the fifth commandment out of the Decalogue, the Pretender's interest would thrive with a witness. The city and country would abandon their true mothers, the Queen and the Church, and betake them to a Jackish conventicle and French Restoration; for which some of our wolves in sheep's clothing, our Lesleyan and Sa——n false brethren, most heartily wish and pray. The Jacobites spare no pains to poison her Majesty's subjects with pamphlets and sermons that insinuate the danger of the Church, by which they mean the Jacobite synagogues; the ruin of the monarchy, by which they mean the exclusion of the Pretender. How well would it be for Church and State if these ecclesiastical knaves would throw off the mask, quit the Church of which they are no true members, and shake hands with the Jacobites, whose creatures and tools they really are, and not eat her bread and lie in wait for her ruin.'[2]

The Tory addresses to the Queen which poured in after the Sacheverel trial, were mostly drawn up at the instigation of the High Church clergy, and were vehemently condemned on the ground that they simply played into the hands of the Jacobites. The Jacobites themselves, it was said, looked upon them in this light. 'Leslie, a professed Jacobite,' writes Hoadly, 'calls these addresses *loyal*. Nothing can be loyal to him but what promotes James III.'s interest. Addresses which condemn all resistance, he knows, condemn the Revolution and the throwing off King James. Addresses which cry up hereditary right, condemn excluding the Popish line; therefore he calls them loyal addresses. If the word Parliamentary be a word not fit to be mentioned by a true Briton, he knows what condition they are in who have only a late Parliamentary title to plead. The addresses are the fruits of Jacobite principles.'[3]

---

[1] A tract entitled 'Dr. Burges' Answer to Dr. Sacheverel.'

[2] 'The Cherubim with a flaming sword that appeared last November 5, in St. Paul's, to the Lord Mayor.'—'Remarks to the Lord Mayor on Dr. S.'s Sermon,' 1709.

[3] 'The Jacobites' Hopes revived by our late Tumults and Addresses,' or 'Remarks on Lesley's good old Cause.'—Hoadly's *Works*, vol. i.

Among the 'Somers Tracts,' there is an amusing parody entitled 'A True Genuine Tory Address of 1710,' which points to the same conclusion. 'As we have cultivated peace and quiet,' wrote the supposed addressers, 'by encouraging and conniving at the most outrageous tumults, and mutual love and affection by the most endearing provocations and abuses ; as we have manifested our unfeigned resolution to maintain the Protestant succession by our zeal for that hereditary right which cannot belong to it, and our concern for the common good by doing everything agreeable to the wishes of the common enemy ; so your Majesty may certainly depend upon it that we will ever give the like convincing proofs of our sincere affection to your person and government. We will ever continue faithfully to support the Constitution and Church by reviling the Revolution and railing at the toleration. We will to the last defend your Majesty's title to the crown as far only as it is hereditary, and we will effectually keep out the Pretender and all the Popish line by constantly adhering to the principles of unalienable right and unlimited non-resistance, by which they were at first excluded ; principles which, as we have shewed in the face of the whole world, sweeten the tempers and quiet the passions of those who profess them, and are peculiarly adapted to reconcile the affections of men to our perfect establishment' (an allusion to the Sacheverel riots). 'By all, therefore, that is worthy of consideration, we most earnestly entreat your Majesty's favour ; by the meekness of our tumults and the good temper of our addresses ; by our tender regard to consciences truly scrupulous ; by our uncommon zeal for the hereditary right of the illustrious House of Hanover ; by the moving cry of the Church's danger, so agreeable a sound in your royal ears ; by our sincere promise to suppress all disorderly tumults, now they are over, and our unfeigned resolution to be very peaceable and submissive when we are uppermost ; by the entire conformity of our practices to our professions ; by the passiveness of our principles and the activeness of our natures ; by the wishes of the common adversary abroad, who boasts of what we are now doing, and by the entreaties of all the Papists and Nonjurors at home, who are acting the same part with us, &c. &c.; by everything dear and sacred to us, we beseech your Majesty to be guided by our infallible wisdom,' &c.

The sermons of the period, especially those preached on Jan. 30, adopt the same sort of language as the addresses, but in a still more violent strain.[1] 'Blood, royal blood,' said one, 'cries aloud to God for vengeance ; and never, never must we expect to be free from the guilt and punishment of it as long as there are so many left among us who are daily murdering our Blessed Martyr over again ; nay some (good God, is it credible?) who are this day [Jan. 30] feasting to hinder the good effects of our fasting.   Let us shew that we can never enough admire in *his undoubted heir and successor* those many excellent graces and virtues, which we knew not how to value in our Blessed Martyr.'[2]   Another speaks of 'the supreme authority with which he [Charles I.] was invested as a King, which rendered his person sacred and inviolable and himself *unaccountable to any human tribunal,* had he been what they endeavoured to represent him.   'We Christian ministers have a strict charge to put people in mind to be subject unto powers, but *not one to arm against them.'*[3]   'So fatal,' exclaimed another, 'is the tendency and so natural the progress of those mischiefs which arise from what our *forefathers* called the doctrines of *Rebellion,* but what others in *our* days have not scrupled to enjoin as *the duty of resistance.*   The duty of resistance ! a sound not heard before by English ears or in a Christian country.   A language this from which the most barbarous of subjects had hitherto abstained under the smart of oppression and in the heat of their resentments.   God heard all the while the babblings of their teachers and the blasphemies of the multitude and saw that it was time more openly to declare himself ; and therefore, to let them see that He had not forsaken His anointed, He caused his grace to shine out in the sufferings of his servant and His glory to appear in the confusion of his enemies.   When many even of those whom the misfortunes of his life had tempted to desert

---

[1] It should, however, be stated that the sermons of the seventeenth century on these topics were still more violent.   For some curious specimens of them, see Mr. Lecky's most interesting *History of England in the Eighteenth Century,* vol. i. ch. i. p. 64, 65, &c.

[2] Sermon on January 30, 1710, by the Bishop of Chester.

[3] Sermon on January 30, 1710, by the Rev. — Higden.

or disposed to censure him, were by the wonders of his death prevailed upon to acknowledge that surely this was a righteous person ; and as soon as they beheld the ruins of the temple and the shakings of the government and the darkness at noon-day, which so surprisingly attended it, they laid their hands upon their breast, &c. &c. Who, then, shall lay anything to the charge of God's anointed? Now know we that the Lord hath favoured His anointed, that He hath heard his prayers, and fulfilled his prophecies, by restoring with his posterity the laws and religion we had wantonly departed from, and by his still vouchsafing to continue and preserve them under the government of a Queen, in whom the Crown and the virtues of the Martyr are *hereditary*. These things happened to us for examples, to the intent that we should not lust after change of government as they also lusted ; neither murmur against our Sovereign as some of them also murmured, and were destroyed of the destroyer.'[1]

The sermons from which the above quotations are made were addressed to the laity. But the clergy too were exhorted to be faithful to the doctrines of non-resistance and hereditary right. 'The malignant influence,' said a preacher before the Lower House of Convocation on Jan 30, 1710, 'of those rebellious and seditious principles, which are propagated among us with so much industry, which make the people the fountain of honour and power, directly strike at her Majesty's hereditary right to the crown and weaken the Protestant succession. . . . Upon such an occasion as this, to speak carelessly and disrespectfully of the royal cause and the loyal adherents to it, to flirt at that primitive doctrine of passive obedience, and to start intricate and perplexed cases which may, upon any pretence whatever, suppose the necessity of resisting the supreme power ; what is it but to erect a scaffold every year for the righteous martyr, and without a vizard continue to repeat the mournful stroak of the executioner? Assure men of the certain judgment of eternal damnation which hangs over the heads of those who resist the ordinance of God.'[2] Another preacher put the

[1] Sermon on January 30, 17¼¼, by the Rev. Pawlett St. John, Rector of Yelden.

[2] Sermon by Archer before the Lower House of Convocation, January 30, 1710.

matter still more plainly. 'If,' he said, 'the King should by his royal command execute the greatest violence upon either our person or estate, our duty is to submit by prayers and tears to God Almighty to turn the wrath of his viceregent. But to lift up the hand against the Lord's anointed, or resist the evil of punishment he thinks fit to inflict, this was a crime unpardonable either before God or man, and a crime which, we bless God, the principles of our ever loyal mother, the Church of England, abhors and detests.'[1]

It is certainly not easy to reconcile such language as all this, either with a cordial approval of what took place at the Revolution or with a true zeal for the Hanoverian succession, the hereditary right of which it would be somewhat difficult to prove. Still, neither the addresses nor the sermons went, except perhaps by implication, the full length of Jacobitism. It was of course convenient for the Whigs to represent them as doing so. 'The Whigs,' wrote a Tory pamphleteer in 1711, who professed at least to be in favour of the Protestant line, 'would not lose him (the Pretender) for the world, considering how useful he is to them by furnishing them with matter of lies and scandal upon those who, they know, abhor his interest much more than themselves.'[2] But from a purely anti-Jacobite point of view it was not, perhaps, wise thus to drive possible friends into a corner, and force them either to renounce their most cherished principles or to apply them in a way which some of them at least never intended. Moreover, those who asserted that the sentiments of the addresses and sermons were downright Jacobitism laid themselves open

[1] Sermon of Dr. B——ge, quoted by Defoe in his 'New Test of the Church of England's Loyalty.' See Wilson's *Memoirs of Daniel Defoe*, ii. 23.

Among the *Somers' Tracts*, vol. xii., is one entitled 'The History of Resistance, or Mr. Agate's Sermon at Exeter on January 30,' by J. Withers, 1710. 'Agate,' he writes, 'undertakes to prove that resistance to the higher powers on any pretence whatever is absolutely unlawful. But suppose the Prince should endeavour to overthrow the Constitution and bring in Popery, may he not be resisted in such a case? Oh no, God forbid! for he that resisteth, resisteth the ordinance of God, and shall receive to himself damnation. If any who have been baptized into our Church are for the doctrine of resistance, I pronounce t'em to be enemies both to our Church and Constitution. None but Atheists and Deists, Papists and Dissenters, ever thought it lawful to resist the higher power upon any pretence whatsoever!'

[2] A Tract entitled, 'The character and principles of the present set of Whigs,' 1711.

to a very easy retort. If the inculcation of the doctrine of divine hereditary right necessarily led to the succession of King James's son, what became of the favourite argument that the Pretender was *not* his son? For if he was illegitimate, he had of course no hereditary right to the throne. And again, if the inculcation of the doctrine of non-resistance necessarily involved a condemnation of the Revolution settlement, what became of the favourite argument that the Revolution took place because the throne was vacant by the voluntary desertion of its occupant? An accomplished controversialist like Charles Leslie was naturally not slow to detect and point out these inconsistencies. 'They have of late,' he writes in 1710, 'begun to deny the Queen's hereditary right. All the last reign they gave the Pretender no other name than Perkin and Impostor. Now they plead for his birth and own it. *Abdication* is now run down and the Revolution must be all resistance. These arguments are ranged against the Church. Having made the Revolution resistance and given up the birth of the Pretender, if the Church should preach any more her old doctrine of non-resistance she must be against the Revolution, and if she owns heredity, she must be for the Pretender.'[1] The Low Churchman, who in those days of political churchmanship was almost identical with the Whig, constantly represented the High Churchman or Tory as necessarily a Jacobite if he acted consistently with his principles. The last question in a clever brochure entitled, 'A New Catechism, with Dr. Hickes' Thirty-nine Articles,' is, 'How could the High Church clergy on their principles withdraw their allegiance from King James, declare King William to be rightful and lawful King, abjure the Pretender, and swear to the present Government and the Protestant suc-

---

[1] 'The Good Old Cause further discussed' in a letter to the author of 'The Jacobites' Hopes revived,' 1710. The writer goes on, 'This has been long bellowed against her by "Observators," "Reviewers," &c. For now they think they have got full proof in the "Good Old Cause." For having made that author a professed Jacobite and a High Churchman, is it not plain that all High Churchmen are Jacobites? But if this be very ridiculous, then it can be no more laid against them what a Jacobite says, than what a Whig or a Dissenter says. For these, too, agree with High Churchmen in some things. Must they, therefore, agree when they differ? A non-resistance man would be glad to see his *principle* prevail, on what side soever it had been. . . . Everybody sees that this [Jacobitism] is a groundless handle taken against the Church at this juncture.'

cession?' And the answer is, 'Egad, Sir, I shall tell you plainly, that I am not at leisure, nor shall not be at leisure, nor want to be at leisure, to say one word to you about this matter.'[1]   But as a matter of fact, the Hanoverian Tories, as the High Churchmen who were not Jacobites were called, *did* find leisure to say a good many words about the matter. Dean Swift, writing of the very time of which we are now speaking, declares that 'the whole nation, almost to a man, excepting a few professed Nonjurors, had conceived the utmost abhorrence of a Popish successor ; the scruple of conscience upon the point of loyalty was wholly confined to a few antiquated Nonjurors, who lay starving in obscurity.'[2]

But if the Dean really meant what he wrote, he must have been strangely ignorant of the true state of affairs.   Whether or not the 'high-fliers' were intentionally paving the way for the Pretender may be doubtful ; but there is not the slightest doubt that there was the most serious cause for alarm to all who really had the Protestant succession at heart.   The fate of both Church and State in England was trembling in the balance.   And the crisis was all the more alarming because men knew not who were their friends and who were their foes. What, for example, were the real sentiments of the Queen ? Almost every speech from the throne declared emphatically and in the most unequivocal language that she had the Hanoverian succession very near at heart.[3]   But it is known now, and was suspected then, that the men who put such language into her mouth were actually at the time in negotiation with St. Germains.   It has never indeed been positively proved that the Queen was in the secret of those plots which were being hatched for the succession of her brother.[4]   But it can

---

[1] *Somers Tracts*, vol. xii.

[2] 'Inquiry into the Behaviour of the Queen's Last Ministry.'

[3] Of the Queen's speech to Parliament in 1713, Burnet remarks, 'It was observed, that there was not, in all her speech, one word of the Pretender or of the Protestant succession.'—Burnet's *History of His own Times*,' vol. iv. 390.   But this was an exception which proved the rule.

[4] Sir A. Alison, in his *Life of Marlborough*, ii. 255, says, 'The Queen was silently taking measures for the succession of her brother,' but he gives no proof of his assertion.   Burnet, indeed (*History of His own Times*, vol. iv. p. 290, &c.) describes a lecture which he read the Queen on her supposed partiality to the Pretender's cause, but he gives no positive proof of her active co-operation in Jacobite plots.   See Hallam's *Constitutional History*, ii. 577, Lathbury's *History*

hardly be conceived that she was really anxious for the succession of a foreigner, against whom she notoriously had a strong personal repugnance. Was it not natural that a childless, lonely woman, who was endowed with an affectionate disposition but not a very strong mind, should yearn after the only near relation she had in the world ? The Chevalier himself afterwards declared that he was well assured of his sister's intentions in his favour.[1] And this was a very general impression. 'When I see,' writes Lord Chesterfield, 'how far things had already gone in favour of the Pretender and of Popery, and that we were within an inch of slavery, I consider the death of this woman (Queen Anne) as the greatest happiness that has ever befallen England ; for if she had lived three months longer, she would have established her religion and tyranny ; and would have left us after her death a bastard king as foolish as herself, and who, like her, would have been led by the nose by a band of rascals.'[2] There are two assertions in this passage, which were utterly groundless slanders, and as they were commonly reported at the time it may be well to notice them. The insinuation that High Churchmen generally, and the Queen in particular, were in favour of Popery, is grossly untrue ; they were far more consistent members, and would have been far more staunch and unflinching supporters of the Reformed Church of England than men like Lord Chesterfield. This point will be noticed presently, and therefore need not be further dwelt upon in this place.[3] 'The bastard King,' as Lord Chesterfield

of the Nonjurors, p. 240, Palin's *History of the Church of England* (1688-1717), ch. xv. 320, &c.

[1] In his manifesto, dated August 29, 1714, he wrote : 'Contrary to our expectation, on the death of our sister (of whose good intentions to us we could not for some time past doubt, therefore we sat still expecting the good effects thereof, which were prevented by death) the people proclaimed a foreign prince.' There was some little doubt about the genuineness of this manifesto ; but the Duke of Lorraine declared it to be genuine, and said the Prince himself had given him one of them.—See Continuation of *Rapin's History* by Tindal, 3rd ed. 1763, vol. xviii. p. 338.

[2] See Mrs. Oliphant's *Historical Sketches of the Reign of George II.* Sketch iii. 'The Man of the World.' To the same effect the writer of a pamphlet in 1714, 'Her death delivered us all from the Pretender, Popery, and slavery. She was a Stuart born, and a chip of the old block.'

[3] 'There appeared,' writes Burnet, 'at this time [1712] an inclination, in many of the clergy, to a nearer approach towards the Church of Rome ;' and he

contemptuously calls the Pretender, was no bastard ; the fable
of his supposititious birth is utterly exploded, and was, in all
probability, not seriously believed at the time when it was
industriously propagated.[1]   But whether he was legitimate
or illegitimate, the apprehensions of his succession to the
throne were both unfeigned and well-grounded.   The evidences
of this are so numerous that the only difficulty consists in
selecting the most striking.   In the preface to Bishop Fleetwood's ' Works,' published in 1737, the writer speaks of ' that
spirit of rage and madness which broke out in 1710, and
which continued to the end of the Queen's reign, when party
rage ran higher and the spirit of Jacobitism was more insolent
and barefaced than in any former time since the Revolution.'[2]
Bishop Fleetwood himself remarks in a Fast-day sermon
preached on January 16, 171½ : ' When I consider how the
sorceries of France prevail and with what contempt the Protestant interest and religion abroad are treated by many
among us, and with what tenderness and ill-concealed content
many speak of *one* who, if ever he comes, will bring a sure
destruction to this Church and State along with him,' &c.
And again in that brave preface to his four sermons, published
the same year, which was ordered to be burnt by the House
of Commons, ' I have lived to see our deliverance from arbitrary power and Popery vilified by some who thought it their
greatest glory to have had a little share in bringing it about. . . .
After seven years of glory, God for our sins permitted a
spirit of discord to go forth, and by troubling camp, city, and
country (and oh that it had altogether spared the places
sacred to His worship !) to spoil for a time this beautiful and
pleasing prospect, and give us in its stead I know not what,

instances ' Hicks, an ill-tempered man, who was now at the head of the Jacobite
party,' and ' one Brett ; ' but the proofs which he gives are only the preaching of
those doctrines, which had always been held by the High Church party in the
Church of England.—*History of His own Times*, vol. iv. bk. vii. 353.

[1] One is sorry to find a man of the reputation and ability of Bishop Hoadly
helping to propagate the fable.   In the preface to his *Preservative against
Nonjurors*, he alludes to ' the *Person*, who pretends to be the son of King James,'
and doubts whether the King ever had a son, or if so, whether this be he,' &c.
See Hoadly's *Works*, 3 vols, folio, vol. i.

[2] Bishop Fleetwood's *Works* (1 vol. folio), Preface, p. iv.   ' The clergy,' adds
the writer, ' differed almost to a man from him [Fleetwood, when he was Bishop
of St. Asaph] in principle,' i.e. were more or less inclined to Jacobitism.

our enemies will tell the rest with pleasure.'[1] Daniel Defoe in the same year asks, 'Why is it that England's neighbours expect every hour to hear that she is going back to Egypt and, having given up her liberty, submit to the stripes of task-masters?' He complains that 'the enemies of England persuade the common people that the Ministry, by giving up the war with France, are for the Pretender, and suggest that the common people are more in his favour.' This, he thinks, is 'a cheat ; whatever the Jacobite party may promise themselves from the Ministry, the Ministry do not act avowedly for the Pretender.' Nevertheless he is fully alive to the danger. ' Swarms of Popish priests from abroad and Jacobite emissaries at home in disguise run up and down mingling with all companies and in coffee-houses and private conversations pave the way for the Pretender. They say that he is Protestant at heart and will abjure the errors of Popery. If he is a Protestant, why do the Papists seek his favour? He must be a Frenchman by honour and obligation, a Papist by inclination, and a tyrant by education.'[2] In the next year the same writer complains that 'the strife is got into our kitchens. ' There is a feud of cook-maids, who is for the Protestant succession, who for the Pretender. The scullions cry, " High Church, no Dutch Kings, no Hanover," or " no French peace, no Pretender, no Popery!" It is the same in the shops, the same among the ladies.'[3] And in the same year he published two stirring pamphlets, whose titles tell their own tales, 'What if the Pretender should come?' and 'What if the Queen should die?'[4] in the latter of which he speaks without any qualification of the professed Jacobitism of the nation. In fact, the whole tone of the anti-Jacobite pamphlets which at this period poured forth in luxuriant abundance

[1] Bishop Fleetwood's *Works.*

[2] Defoe's ' Seasonable Warning and Caution againt the Insinuations of Papists and Jacobites in favour of the Pretender'—(Letter from an Englishman at the Court of Hanover, 1712).

[3] ' Reasons against the Succession of the House of Hanover,' 1713.

[4] So utterly were these pamphlets misunderstood that a *Whig* commenced a prosecution against Defoe for desiring to favour the Jacobite succession. The judges told him that they contained matter for which he might be hanged, drawn, and quartered. He was thrown into Newgate and would have been pilloried, had not Harley interceded for him with the Queen. See *Historical and Biographical Essays,* by John Forster, vol. ii.—' Daniel Defoe.'

indicates the most serious alarm. 'Jacobitism,' writes one, ' has so much spread within these three last years among all sorts of people that a stranger would be apt to think that the Elector of Hanover was (as the Jacobites impudently call him) the Pretender, whom the nation was obliged to abjure, especially had he seen in how many Churches the doctrines of hereditary right and non-resistance (on which the Pretender wholly builds his claim) were preached up, at least with as much zeal as in the conventicles of the Jacobites ; and that the people chuse rather to fill their addresses with contradictions than to omit those doctrines so powerfully recommended from the pulpit.' [1] In another pamphlet he complains that 'the Jacobites who, like the devil, are indefatigable in mischief, apply to the passions of the clergy against Dissenters.' [2] No stone was left unturned to warn the people of their danger.[3] Now an appeal is made to the honour of the nation, which had taken the abjuration oath. With some ingenuity this oath is shown to be of much greater force than the oath of allegiance which the Jacobites accused their adversaries of breaking. ' Was ever poor deluded nation so religiously mocked as this? What do these people think of oaths? Alas! an abjuration is a quite different thing from an oath of allegiance. There you promise peaceable behaviour, &c. ; but here you call God to witness that you never will submit to him and that he has no right to demand it. When you swear *to* a Prince, the oath

---

[1] 'Dissuasive from Jacobitism,' 1713.

[2] Second Part of ' Dissuasive from Jacobitism,' 1713.

[3] The *Flying Post* of March 7th, 171⅜, publishes a list of sufferers for the Protestant religion in France, ' to convince Jacobite Protestants what treatment they are to expect if ever the Pretender should come to the throne, since he must necessarily act according to the bloody House of B——, without whose assistance he can never be able to keep possession, if he should happen to get it.' The *Examiner* wrote a paper to confute ' the grand epidemical lye, that the Tories in power are about to bring in Popery.' 'But,' adds the Whig Boyer (*Quadriennium Annæ postremum*, v. 120), 'the author of the *Examiner* is generally accounted to be the same person that wrote the *Tale of a Tub*; and what can be expected from an apostate priest who has derided and ridiculed all religion in so flagrant a manner, but that he should be profligately abandoned to all honour, truth, and modesty ?'

On March 14, 171⅜, 'the *Examiner* wrote against mentioning the Hanover succession in our addresses, on the pretence that her Majesty ought not to have her winding-sheet continually laid before her.'—*Quadriennium Annæ postremum*, vol. v.

is of no force when that Prince can no longer possess sovereignty. The other can never be dispensed with. It is not a
common oath of allegiance that ends with any national revolution. It is a solemn renouncing of your allegiance for ever ;
not the cunningest sophister under heaven can bring you
out of it. Thus *National Perjury* is the first thing that must
attend bringing in the Pretender, and the second is *National
Apostacy*. Pretender and Popery are the same. They say
he has turned Protestant. Then why are all the Papists in
England for bringing him in ? Would they side with an
apostate ? They would as soon take part with a Jew. But
they know what his conversion means.' [1]

Now he appeals to the temporal interests of the clergy,
telling them that ' if they would once again infuse into the
people (over whom Providence seems to have given them so
great influence for this end), the same apprehension of a
Popish succession as at the Revolution, we should be saved.
The Pretender, he reminds them, is under obligation to
foreign priests, and must repay them with English benefices.
He will have scarce any left even to reward the Nonjuring
priests who have been so long confessors for his sake. The
clergy have so great a power over the nation (much greater
than they themselves, till of late, imagined), that there is nothing they need despair of under a Protestant government,
which must court and caress them as long as they keep such
an interest with the people.' [2]

On the other side, the Jacobites were evidently lifting up

[1] *The History of the Jacobite Clubs*, 1712.—The iniquity of breaking the
abjuration oath is thus described in a doggerel poem entitled 'The Tories' Address
to King G——e,' published in 1716:—

> ' Then throwing off the mask, declare
> At once for the pretended Heir ;
> Whom we've ofttimes abjur'd before,
> And you our rightful monarch swore.
> This proves us Papists in disguise,
> Who can dispense with perjuries,
> And the most heinous crimes remit,
> When Holy Church is served by it.
> A charge so just, we must of course
> Acknowledge, or confess a worse ;
> For perjury's allow'd to no man
> By any kind of faith but Roman.'

[2] ' Dissuasive from Jacobitism,' and second part of the same.

their heads.[1] They spoke of 'a glorious revolution now going
on to perfection,' ostensibly referring simply to the change of
Ministry, but obviously with an eye to another change which
should bring their King back to the throne of his ancestors.
The Jacobite Clubs flourished.   Here is a description of one
in 1712, written by an enemy and therefore of course to be
taken *cum grano*.   A festival was to be held in honour of the
Peace.   No one was to be admitted that had not the attestation
of two or more persons belonging to the Society of his being
tooth and nail for indefeasible and hereditary right, that is,
for the exclusion of the Hanover line.   These were the regulations for the toasts—1. The Queen's health may be drunk,
because it is equivocal (there being one at St. Germains), but
not without the Church being put before her out of respect
to his Holiness, whom we are to believe to be Head of it.
2. The Protestant succession, because it is given out both in
France and England that our young master has renounced
Popery and is instructed by a divine of the Church of
England. 3. The great officers of State, because our young
master on the other side of the water has doubtless provided
himself with them,—and so on.[2]

In the Jacobite pamphlets of the day, the principles of
Jacobitism are not veiled as of yore, but avowed without any
disguise.   One out of the many is worth quoting for the
ingenious way in which it contrives not only to twist Scripture
to Jacobite purposes, but also to use the very language of the
English Revolution to describe events held out to us as warnings in the Bible.[3]   'All the Patriarchs, both ante- and post-
diluvians were very silly fellows, because they had a parcel of
tyrannical notions inconsistent with the liberties of the people.

---

[1] Great complaints were made that the Society for promoting Christian
Knowledge encouraged Jacobitism in connexion with the Charity Schools. 'While
the Protestant succession was doubtful,' writes Bishop Gibson, 'some persons,
otherwise virtuous and good men, endeavoured to get the management of Charity
Schools into their hands, and to make them instrumental in rousing and
spreading an aversion to the Protestant Settlement.'—'Instructions to Masters
and Mistresses of Charity Schools,' 1724, 'Charges,' &c., 145.   Archbishop
Wake complained of the attempt in 1716. See Skeat's *History of the Free Churches*,
p. 272.

[2] *History of the Jacobite Clubs*, 1712.

[3] A tract entitled 'Some Whig Principles demonstrated to be good Sense and
sound Divinity from their natural Consequences,' 1713.

This discovery I happened lately to make by stumbling upon an old, musty, worm-eaten book, written in a strange language. I found it amongst the archives of a Right Reverend Prelate, who had never worn sleeves if he had read it, no, not for 2,000*l*. a year. Now, I say, these old Patriarchs were very tyrants in their nature, for they thought that every one of them, forsooth, had a right to govern his own family. But they were egregiously mistaken, because undoubtedly their families, their children, nay even their servants, both collectively and representatively, had a right to depose them and to exercise the faculties and powers of these Lords Patriarchs with which they were invested by the original instrument of government, the pre-Adamitical *contract*. So that the people in those days shewed very great *moderation* when they allowed themselves to be governed and ruled by these same Patriarchs, when indeed the Patriarchs did owe the peaceable possession and exercise of that power which they vainly and tyranically imagined they were invested with, wholly to the good nature and good will of their families, who had a well-founded, original, natural and pre-Adamitical right to kick them out of doors whenever they thought fit to do so. Why? Because they were the people, and naturally free. And can anybody be so stupid as to imagine that a silly Patriarch, a single person, was to be preferred to all his children, servants, and family? Or that these old Patriarchs were born for any other end, but to beget children and to hire servants, to depose or govern themselves, whichever they, the majority, should think fit? Besides it was very impudent in these old fellows and very tyrannical to pretend a right from God over their families. This alone was reason enough for their children and servants to have made them glad to *abdicate* had they not exceeded in *moderation*.' Then we pass on to a later stage in Bible history. 'The children of Israel elected God to be their King once upon a time when they were in a good humour; but they took care to settle the *Pacta conventa* previously to their election, by which they articled to change him, to depose him, to renounce him, whenever they thought fit.[1] But these children of Israel had but just settled their

---

[1] Here the writer adds, 'My voucher is a doctor of a fine college in a famous University, which has a statute binding its fellows down to the hard task of being

government in the hands of their newly made King, the Lord of Hosts, when they soon repented that they had not foreseen and capitulated for farther limitations. And therefore, that they, as good patriots, might not be found fault with by their posterity, for giving up their liberties upon such conditions, they very soon endeavoured to put the *deposing doctrine* in practice. And having in a general *convention* met upon that *extraordinary occasion*, for the *Preservation* of their *religion, liberties*, and *property*, they found that Moses, who was the vice-gerent of their newly-elected King, had *abdicated*; and therefore they *declared* the *throne vacant*. And because, as they were then posted and situated, it was of dangerous consequence to keep the throne vacant long; they, therefore, immediately took care to fill it with a dumb idol calf,[1] the most inoffensive and best sort of King in the world, because he never could dwindle into a tyrant. And it was remarkable enough that they never danced so heartily nor so nimbly while they were a people as they did before this royal calf. Why? That dumb royal calf was the *choice of the people*, exerting themselves in defence of religion, laws, and liberties; religion, I say, for some of the priests were consenting, who had their religion, no doubt, very much at heart. . . . 'Tis true, they happened to miscarry; for there were *Nonjurors* both amongst the priests and also among the people, who could not be brought to worship nor do homage to this, their new king, the calf. And they had well nigh lost themselves, but that their *King de jure*, their *true King*, was very merciful unto them and gave them an indemnity.' Then we pass on to another scene in the history. ' They came off at a loss when they tried to exert their *original power* against their King himself, and after several unsuccessful attempts, and a great many growlings and grumblings and mobs, they at last resolved to try their skill by destroying the High Priest, a

---

"mediocriter docti." He was a Papist twenty-six years ago, and has never renounced it, and he wrote a book with the help of a great many friends, called the *Rights of a Christian Church*, by which he plainly shews that no Christian Church has any right at all !' The 'fine college' was of course ' All Souls;' the doctor, Matthew Tindal.

[1] Query—in allusion to the silence and reserve of King William, or to the limitations which were placed on the monarchy, making (the Jacobites might think) the king no better than a dummy? or to both?

chief minister among them. This they did by a *Presbyterian Plot.* They were true blue, staunch Presbyterians (and, by the way, this shows the antiquity of the sect, this being the first account I have met with of their foundation, tho' their establishment was above three thousand years after) ; [1] but unluckily this contrivance was spoiled ; for, by a *fortuitous concourse of atoms,* [2] the earth happened to open just in that critical nick of time and just in the spot where the three ringleaders of the *Popular Faction* happened to stand ; and, by another surprising concourse of fiery atoms, the accomplices were devoured ; and, by a third concourse of plaguy atoms, a multitude were struck dead.' Passing on to the times of the Kings, he proceeds, ' My old musty book says that God chose David and made him His Vicegerent without asking any of the People, Peers or Commons, any advice at all about it. And he entailed the Kingdom (according to my old book) upon King David's family hereditarily, without allowing the people any vote in that affair at all. But who doubts the People had power to depose King David by virtue and right of their original contract ? They set up King David's son against him—I mean Absalom—and Achitophel was his principal Secretary of State or first minister, and he who had been an eminent Privy Counsellor to the Father helped to contrive the revolution for the son.[3] 'Tis true they happened to be very unlucky in this undertaking also ; for their *Revolution King, created* by the *people,* against the express constitution of the Kingdom, happened to have too tall a Beast on which he rode, which proved the death of him.[4] And then, after some time, God's King was restored, and the restoration publickly solemnised, and he was very merciful, &c. And then there was an end of Revolution Principles for a good many years.' [5] He

---

[1] An allusion, of course, to the abolition of Episcopacy and establishment of Presbyterianism in Scotland.

[2] To appreciate the point of this allusion, it must be remembered that the High Churchmen accused the Low Churchmen of encouraging Deists and Freethinkers, like Tindal, already alluded to, who explained away the miracles, especially of the Old Testament, by natural causes.

[3] Churchill ? or Clarendon ? or Danby ?

[4] An allusion to the horse which caused the death of King William. ' Sorrel's health ' was a favourite toast with the Jacobites.

A neat compliment to Queen Anne, whose hereditary right was at this time much insisted on by the Jacobites.

then proceeds to describe Jeroboam's rebellion after the same fashion. ' Their King was their own deputy, and the calves were their gods they chose to preserve their liberties, lest the people, by going to worship the true God at Jerusalem, had returned to their allegiance, and so had confounded the usurper and their revolution principles at once.[1] They were unfortunate in this exercise of their original right, for they never had the good fortune to have so much as one good or tolerable Revolution King for ever hereafter ; tho' they changed and altered the *succession* about eight times, and new settled in so many different families, and with a great deal of judgment too ; for they all worshipped the two calves.[2]   And after all their sense and wit and conduct, their zeal for their religion, their calves, and their jealousy of everything that could attempt upon their liberties, they never made choice of one for their King who was so good as the worst of those God had chosen for them.'   At last they were dispersed, and the nation was ruined.   ' Yet still they were a free people, for all this, so long as God's Vicegerent in the Family of David did not reign over them.   For any slavery is supportable and tolerable except that which God Almighty enjoins.   But to yield to that is to be a slave indeed, and shows a mean spirit which has no regard for natural freedom, which every fine gentleman and pretty fellow ought to have.'   The dullest of anti-Jacobites could scarcely fail to read the moral ; there was scarcely need of the italics to remind him, ' *Mutato nomine de te, Fabula narratur.*'

There is no need to give further proof of what must be patent to every student of history.   An able writer of the present day does not state the case too strongly when he says, ' If the Stewarts had come back in 1714, it is highly improbable they would have been turned out again for long years.   It was difficult as it was to get up sufficient public feeling to prevent their restoration.   When we think of this crisis in our fate, it is impossible not to look back almost with bated

---

[1] An allusion to the encouragement of Dissenters, insinuating that if the people had been encouraged to attend to the true teaching of the Church of England they would have been Jacobites.

[2] I.e. they were all Dissenters.   King William was a Presbyterian Calvinist, George I. was a Lutheran.

breath on the desperate party struggles which eddied round the throne of Anne.'[1] 'Nothing,' wrote Bishop Talbot in 1714, 'but a direct interposition of Providence can save us.'[2] How the crisis was averted is a question rather for the civil than for the ecclesiastical historian. Suffice it to say that the Queen died somewhat unexpectedly, before the Jacobites, open or concealed, had matured their plans.[3] The friends of the House of Hanover were better prepared for the emergency. A regency had been settled upon, which on the death of the Queen at once took the government into its own hands, and a Secretary of State went off post haste to Hanover to bring over the new monarch. The aged Electress had died only a few weeks before. Her son was therefore proclaimed under the title of George I., and, owing to the prompt measures of his friends, ascended what he called 'the throne of his ancestors' as peaceably as if the succession had come to him in the direct line from father to son. And, on the whole, the Church had as much reason as the State to be thankful that the struggle ended as it did; for though her prospects were not very bright under the new King, who, so far as he had any religion at all, was a Lutheran, and had no real sympathy with the peculiar position of that great national institution of which he was now the temporal head, they were not so dark as they would have been under the priest-ridden, woman-ridden bigot, who would probably have been a mere puppet in the hands of France and Rome. If, so far as the interests of the Church were concerned, George was a King Log, James in such hands would have been a King Stork, and of the two evils the former was undoubtedly the least.[4]

---

[1] T. E. Kebbel on 'Lord Stanhope's Reign of Queen Anne,' in the *Fortnightly Review* for May 1870.

[2] Letter from the Bishop of Oxford to Mrs. Clayton, written in July 1714. See *Memoirs of Lady Sundon* and the *Court and Times of George II.*, by Mrs. Thomson, i. 64.

[3] Macpherson's *Original Papers*, vol. ii. *passim*.

[4] There is little doubt that the Queen's supposed Jacobitism rendered her very unpopular at the close of her life. In a tract entitled *The True Character of her Late Majesty*, written in 1714, it is said, 'A poor old woman upon Tower Hill, seeing a crowd of people rejoicing that the Queen was dead, burst into tears, saying, "I can't but cry and lament, not that the Queen is dead (for she was the best friend the Pretender ever had), but that her Majesty, after twelve years' reign, should so lose the affection of all her subjects as not one tear has been shed for her."'

Before entering upon the new state of affairs which the accession of the House of Hanover brought about, it is necessary to add a few words on the part which the English clergy took in the events which preceded and followed that change in which their interests were so largely involved. During the reign of Queen Anne the Nonjurors had fallen off both in numbers and influence.[1] The comparatively few who remained were divided among themselves, some arguing that the separation from the Established Church should cease when the cause which had originated it had been removed ; others desiring to perpetuate the schism by the consecration of fresh bishops. The former party, represented by such men as Ken among the clergy, and Dodwell and Nelson among the laity, contended that when by death or resignation the sees of the deprived bishops were lawfully vacant, the then holders might be lawfully recognised as their spiritual fathers, and that even their lax and heterodox views constituted no valid reason for a continuance of the separation. The latter, of whom Hickes and Wagstaffe were leading representatives, would admit of no compromise. The Nonjuring Church was the sole lawful remnant of the true Church of England, and, as such, ought to continue its separation from faithless brethren. How far either of these parties as a body was implicated in the schemes for promoting the interests of the exiled Stuarts is not very clear. That individual Nonjurors were engaged in most of the Jacobite plots is unquestionable. But the Nonjurors were not the most formidable enemies, even among the clergy, whom the House of Hanover had to fear. It was convenient to make them the scapegoats ; hence every vituperative epithet which language could supply was lavished upon them. They were 'that most wicked and abominable crew ;' they were a 'stupid, illiterate, stubborn, positive, noisy and impudent generation,' and 'ought not only to be kept under and discouraged, but also ridiculed and made contemptible, both in print and conversation.' In fact, in the excited writings of the period they were loaded with every villanous imputa-

---

[1] 'The poor Nonjurants,' wrote Leslie, 'are not worth the stroke of such a hero. Alas ! let them die in their hopes ; they are trod underfoot and crushed to nothing ; they trouble nobody now.'—'Wolf Stript,' Leslie's *Theological Works*, vol. vi. p. 384.

tion.[1] But beyond vague, general charges it is not easy to find evidence that there was any organisation among them as a body for the purpose of restoring the Stuarts.[2] Indeed, the religion of the Chevalier would have been as disastrous to them as to the rest of the clergy; for though they were constantly charged with favouring Popery, they were, in fact, as sincerely attached to the doctrines of the Church of England as any of their complying brethren, and would probably have been found far less yielding to a Popish sovereign than many whose theological views were modified by their temporal interests. Even those Nonjurors who were actively engaged in the interests of the Pretender fondly clung to the notion that he would change his religion. One of the ablest of their number[3] was sent over to Lorraine for the express purpose of bringing the Prince into the fold of the English Church.

That the clergy generally, however, were, especially during the last four years of Queen Anne's reign and the early part of George I.'s, more or less in favour of restoring the legitimate line is very probable. The evidence of this from all sides is too strong to be resisted. Hickes 'thanked God that the main body of the clergy were in their hearts Jacobites.' The archbishops and bishops in and near London, in their loyal address to King George in 1715, admit that 'the chief hopes of our enemies seem to arise from discontents artificially raised among us' (the clergy). Many of the clergy had of course received their training at Oxford; and Oxford, ever since the days when her martyred King had held his Court

---

[1] See, *inter alia*, Monk's *Life of Bentley*. The writer says, 'The Nonjurors were not numerous, and appear to have shown no disposition to disturb the Government which they declined to acknowledge. They were peaceable in their demeanour.' But he adds, 'The writings then in fashion [1716] were full of abuse to them.' Colley Cibber's adaptation of Molière's *Tartufe* under the title of *The Nonjuror*, in which the author played the part of Dr. Wolf, a Nonjuror and concealed Papist, and was rewarded by a present of 200*l*. from the King in 1717, is another instance.

[2] A contemporary historian writes of the Nonjurors, 'This schism is nothing but a political faction arising out of a deadly feud, an abhorrence of the Revolution, and the Protestant succession, and King George. They are a spiritual army for the Pretender, to take up carnal weapons when they can.'—*Quadriennium Annæ postremum*, or *The Political State of Great Britain*, by G. Boyer, 2nd ed. 1718, vol. xii. p. 427.

[3] Charles Leslie.

and Parliament within her walls, had always been enthusiastically devoted to the Stuart cause.[1] A clergyman—not a Nonjuror—was the only man of high rank who, on the death of Queen Anne, proposed a rising in favour of her brother.[2]

When the new King became known to his subjects, the knowledge was not conducive to his popularity with that Church of which he was officially the head, but of which he could hardly be reckoned as personally even a member. 'Howsoever religious the King is,' wrote Atterbury, 'it cannot be imagined that he hath any extraordinary veneration for a religion which he came into but the other day, and to which he was an absolute stranger before. The Lutheran, wherein he was educated, and which he professed to the very hour of his landing, is entirely different, both in doctrine and discipline, from ours. So that since his Majesty, to qualify himself for the Crown, was pleased to depart from his own to embrace a religion so different, it is no remote thought to apprehend he may consent to the alteration of ours, for a valuable consideration to himself.'[3] The reaction against the 'reign of the Saints' had by no means yet died out; and though there was certainly not very much of the saint about George I., still Lutheranism and Puritanism were not very clearly discriminated by the English mind. The new King's personal character was singularly unattractive: his immorality was notorious;[4] he understood little of our English

---

[1] 'Oxford,' writes Philopoliticus about the time of the rebellion of 1715, 'is debauched with Jacobitism. They call the Parliament "the Rump," and riots in the streets, with cries of "Down with the Rump!" are of daily occurrence.' Even fellows and heads of colleges were disposed to Jacobite opinions; and the Jacobites expected that the city would be the Chevalier's head-quarters, as it had been of Charles I. See *Memoirs of the Jacobites of* 1715 *and* 1745, by Mrs. Thomson.

[2] Atterbury, Bishop of Rochester, who proposed to Bolingbroke to proclaim King James at Charing Cross, and offered to lead the procession in his lawn sleeves. Bolingbroke shrank from the enterprise, and Atterbury cried in a passion, 'Then is the best cause in Europe lost for want of spirit.'

[3] See *Somers' Tracts*, vol. xiii., 'English Advice to the Freeholders of England,' by Bishop Atterbury, 1714.

[4] George le Ier de cette race insignifiante était un Stuart allemand; il était passionné à sa manière, cruel même et abominable sous des apparences de bourgeoisie sans façon. Le peuple anglais, qui s'était trop avancé pour reculer, qui voulait le protestantisme, et demandait à grands cris la ruine de la monarchie de Louis XIV., se contenta de lui. Un monstre lui eut convenu, pourvu qu'il fût pro-

language and nothing of our English ways. His name was connected with none of the traditions which Englishmen cherish. It was simply impossible for an English Churchman to transfer that enthusiastic loyalty which had become almost a part of his creed to such a man. There was a sort of glamour of romantic interest about the King over the water; he might—at least so long as he was at a distance—be made the object of that kind of semi-religious attachment to the monarch which was still a tradition of English Churchmanship; but any such sentiment towards the very uninteresting person now in possession of the throne was out of the question. It is by no means denied that King George had merits in which his rival was deficient; only they were not the kind of merits to satisfy that sentimentalism with which the Church had, before the Revolution and during a short period of Queen Anne's time, regarded the reigning sovereign.[1]

Taking all this into account, we need not wonder that the calm which attended the accession of King George was of short duration, and still less need we wonder that many of the clergy saw with secret satisfaction the outbreak of the storm, and that some took an active part in raising it. It broke out on the general election which immediately followed the King's accession, and reached its climax in the rebellion of the ensuing year. At the election 'The Church' was the watchword on both sides. Whigs and Tories appealed each to a point on which the English nation was peculiarly sensitive. The Whigs tried to inflame the passions of the electors against Popery, the Tories against Puritanism. 'If,' said the former, 'you would lose your Protestant King, your religion, and your liberties, if you would have the Pretender, the Mass, and the wooden shoes, send his good friends the Tories to represent you. Can you imagine that one bred up by the

testant et ennemi de la France. George Ier réunissait ces qualités ; c'était un misérable et un protestant.'—*Le* 18me *Siècle en Angleterre.* Philarète Chasles, vol. i. 185.

[1] Bishop Fleetwood, in his charge to the clergy of the diocese of Ely in 1716, complains bitterly of the unpopularity of George I., which he seems to attribute greatly to the influence of the Church. 'There is an evil, lying spirit gone forth among us, filling every corner of the country with defamation and scandal, inventing things impossible, surmising things improbable, &c., to alienate the hearts of people from the King's person and family.' He goes on to speak of the ' silence and inactivity of ecclesiastics on the one side,' and, ' on the other side, the numbers, strength, and influence' of Jacobite clergy.

most bigoted and tyrannical even of all Popish Courts, and altogether a most bitter enemy to our religion and nation, would not, were it in his power, establish Popery, not out of conscience, but out of revenge for the treatment he has met with from the Protestant Church of England? Besides, Toryism and Popery in many things differ only as that which is absurd differs from that which is more absurd. If ever the Tories should gain their end, and the Pretender come, there would soon be an end of the purest Church in the world. It is objected that King George is a foreigner. But what is their Pretender but a foreigner? Is he ever the better an Englishman for having been rocked four or five months in an English cradle, and been bred for twenty-seven years in a French Court?[1] Or do you want a return of arbitrary power? Will you listen to the slavish doctrines of those clergy who preach the people into damnation if the stingy wretches should refuse even to send their heads in a bandbox, were it their sovereign's will and pleasure to ask for them?'[2]

On the other side, the populace was roused by the dread of a return to Puritanism. Riots took place in several places. 'Down with the Roundheads!' 'No Hanover!' 'High Church and Dr. Sacheverell!' 'High Church and the Duke of Ormond for ever!' were the popular cries; and if the elections had been in the hands of the mob, it is highly probable that the so-called Church party would have gained a victory; but the electors returned a large majority of Whigs, and the hopes of the Jacobites were for a time baffled.

The Church was unhappily mixed up far too much with these disputes. Two clergymen of high standing were the ablest and most energetic supporters of either side; Atterbury, Bishop of Rochester, employed his great powers in behalf of the Tories, and Hoadly, who was very soon after the election made Bishop of Bangor—perhaps in reward for his services—was an able advocate of the Whig cause. These election disturbances naturally exasperated the friends of the Government. The new Ministry was urged to take very

[1] 'English Advice to Freeholders' (Whig), 1714. See *Somers' Tracts*, vol. xiii.

[2] *The Conventicle; or, A Narrative of the Dissenters' New Plot*, 1714.

decisive measures for 'the entire rooting out of Jacobitism in Great Britain.' The author of this ' Bold Advice,' as he calls it, admits that ' it is not indeed in the power of the Ministry to remove the foundation of this mischief. The Pretender is, and will, and must be in being, as long as Heaven permits the despicable creature to breathe in His air. But,' he adds, ' Jacobitism is an evil harboured in the bosom of the nation, which, like a running sore, exhausts the vitals, and will in time, if not healed, taint the blood and turn to an incurable plague.' Then he proposes his remedy. ' Blessed be God, this Jacobitism is now laid on its back, knock'd down, stunn'd, and bruised in a happy manner by the coming of King George so seasonably, quietly, and with general consent to the Crown. Since Jacobitism is low and underfoot, let the present Ministry take occasion to crush it. Hitherto we have trifled with the Jacobites, and treated them with leniency and clemency. What hardships have they suffered ? Paying double taxes is all they have yet felt. Not a man should be suffered to live in the nation who refused abjuration of the Pretender, and the oath should be immediately tendered to every adult in the nation.' ' The pulpit,' he continues, ' is now become a trumpet of sedition, and clergymen, under the protection and in pretence of preaching the Gospel spread abroad sedition and preach treason and rebellion at pleasure.'

There was, no doubt, some ground for this complaint. In the rebellion of 1715 it is probable that a large proportion of the clergy were unfavourable to the Hanoverian cause. Incendiary sermons and speeches had become so common that a Bill had to be passed forbidding the clergy to mix themselves up with State affairs ; but such laws are easily evaded, and, in spite of this prohibition, it is clear that the bulk of the clergy exercised the great influence which they possessed against the Government. But they must have been sadly embarrassed by the conduct of the Chevalier. As a rule, even the highest of High Churchmen were as Protestant as the Low Churchmen themselves. What could they do to help a man who, conscious as he must have been of the almost morbid dread of Romanism which those whom he desired to rule felt, strengthened his relation with Rome in every way? To render his chances the more hopeless, he married a bigoted Romanist; and when his claims were no longer allowed by France, he retired—of all places in the world—to the Papal States, where he lived under the special favour of the Pope. Even when he wanted the help of the Protestants in 1716 he would promise nothing to the Church of England but security and protection in the enjoyment of its property. What would he have done when his throne was secure?[1]

Indeed this question, 'How could the Church of England be preserved when the Temporal Head of that Church was not only of a different religion himself, but actually of a religion which rendered it his bounden duty to extirpate heretics, of whom English Churchmen were the chief?' was always the most difficult question which the Protestant Jacobites had to answer; and it was pressed home with an almost wearisome iteration by their adversaries. Thus the writer of the 'Dissuasive from Jacobitism' in 1713 argues, 'The Romish Church in the Council of Constance determined that faith is not to be kept with a heretic. Popish kings are under a prior obligation to destroy heretics. Always to fear death is a most dismal thing. This is no more than Protestants may expect under Popish princes, for they make no scruple to have recourse to massacres. No Popish prince will think himself safe amid the crowd of Protestants in London.' He then proceeds to depict in glowing colours the treatment which the Protestants had met with from the French kings, and declares that there would be a danger of the Inquisition being set up in England.[2] 'A Popish outlaw,' exclaimed an indignant preacher on January 30, 171⅔, 'seated on the throne of Protestant kingdoms to be the defender of their faith! Though these perjured hypocrites (who had taken the oath of abjuration of the Pretender and were yet scheming for his return), under fulsome and treacherous pretences of great zeal and honour for the Church, had the skill for a time to abuse the easy nature and too credulous simplicity of many honest and well-meaning people, yet, now the mask is off, all must see that the *real* danger of the Church was from those

---

[1] See Cook's *Memoirs of Lord Bolingbroke*, ii. 7.
[2] *Dissuasive from Jacobitism*, 1713.

false pretenders to it who, at the same time they were doing the mean and abject drudgery of Popish cruelty and malice under the false colours of the Church of England, were only paving the way for her overthrow.' Among the articles of a Tory's creed Addison gives the following :—(1) 'That the Church of England will always be in danger till it has a Popish king for its defender. (2) That, for the safety of the Church, no subject should be tolerated in any religion different from the established, but that the head of the Church may be of that religion which is most repugnant to it. (3) That the Protestant interest could not but flourish under the protection of one who thinks himself obliged, on pain of damnation, to do all that lies in his power for the extirpation of it.' And after enumerating two or three articles which do not directly bear upon our subject—(7) 'That a man has no opportunities of learning how to govern England in any foreign country so well as in France.'[1] 'We have only the *vices* of a Protestant to fear,' he writes in another place, 'and may be made happy by his virtues ; but in a Popish prince we have no chance for our prosperity ; his very piety obliges him to our destruction ; and in proportion as he is more religious he becomes more insupportable.'[2]

The difficulty was ably dealt with by Charles Leslie in his ' Case of the Regale and Pontificate.' Instead of dwelling upon the hope that the Prince might be induced to change his religion or to grant a general toleration, as some others did, he boldly cut the Gordian knot by asserting that if the relations of Church and State were rightly adjusted, the King's personal opinions were of no consequence. The point is an interesting one, because, unlike most of the points connected with the Jacobite question, it is not merely part of a defunct controversy, but has a distinct bearing upon the controversies of the present day. The object of the treatise is to show that the regal and ecclesiastical authorities are entirely distinct. 'The sacred and civil powers are like two parallel lines which can never meet or interfere with each other. The same criminal may be absolved by the Church and condemned by the State, and *vice versa*.' Therefore there would be no *imperium in imperio*. The regale should be supreme over all

---

[1] *Freeholder*, No. 14.   [2] *Ibid.* No. 36.

persons in all causes, ecclesiastical as well as civil, but in its proper sphere—that is, in their civil relations. The distinction between Christian and non-Christian, orthodox and heterodox princes would thus make no difference to their civil power. The pontificate has no more right to interfere with the regale than the regale with the pontificate. He shows with convincing force that this theory is totally opposed to the claims of Rome, and that those who accused the High Churchmen of being Romanists in disguise completely misunderstood their true position. But he also contends that the carrying out of his principles would free the Church from a danger on the other side. 'How can he be head of any Church who is not so much as a member of it? He may be the *civil* head, and exercise the power of the civil sword in all causes over all persons, as well ecclesiastical as civil, but to be ecclesiastical head, to have any sort of ecclesiastical power, is totally inconsistent.' 'We can have no security for our religion, at least none equal in all human appearance to the settling of the Church upon her own primitive bottom, whereon Christ did place her, independent, as to her whole spiritual authority, upon any earthly power. Then we need be in less pain for the religion of our prince, except for the good of his own soul; for he could then hurt our religion no otherwise than by open persecution, which, in England, could not be in his power, and it is not likely that he would ever attempt it. But he could no longer betray and undermine it; he could not then put in bishops that would be his tools and give up the rights of the Church to purchase his favour; nor would they hire under-workmen to employ their parts and learning to disarm their mother of all, even legal, defence against her ravisher, in hopes that they too in their turns may come to share his good graces.'[1]

This was a line of argument which was almost unintelligible to the political Churchmen of the day. They said that 'the new High Church was turned old Presbyterian, since they maintained the same doctrine of independency that they so bitterly exclaimed against in the Presbyterians. They would not submit to episcopal jurisdiction. Presbyters in the Lower

---

[1] 'Case of Regale and Pontificate,' i. 606, C. Leslie's *Theological Works*, in 2 vols. folio.

House of Convocation claimed a co-ordinate power with bishops.'[1]

It is not to the present purpose to enter further into the vast and complicated question suggested by Leslie's argument, involving as it does the whole relation between Church and State, a subject of even more pressing importance at the present day than in the early part of the eighteenth century. Suffice it to say that whether or not Leslie's theory was sound or his scheme practicable, he showed most conclusively that he and the Protestant Jacobites who agreed with him had a very clear and intelligible standpoint against the Romish system, though they were friends of the Romish claimant to the throne. Absurd as the accusation was, it was not one whit more absurd to accuse them of being Presbyterians than of being Papists.

The accusation of Popery was not the only unjust charge that was brought against the Jacobites in the early part of George I.'s reign. After the suppression of the 'unnatural' rebellion of 1715, it was the fashion to vilify that movement as if it had been merely the work of desperate adventurers without religion and without morality. Among others Addison's graceful pen was employed to represent the rebels in this light, and he executed the task in a manner worthy of the 'Spectator.' An extract from his amusing 'Memoirs of a Preston Rebel' will illustrate this view of the case. 'We laid our heads together,' writes the supposed rebel, 'over a bowl of punch to consider what grievances the nation had suffered under the reign of George. After having spent some hours upon this subject, without being able to discover any, we unanimously agreed to rebel first and to find out reasons for it afterwards. It was indeed easy to guess at some grievances of a private nature. One of us had spent his fortune ; another was a younger brother ; a third had the incumbrance of a father upon his estate.' Then of course follows the inevitable allusion to the religious question, which was always mixed up with Jacobite disputes. 'Being at length thoroughly inflamed with zeal and punch, we resolved to take horse next morning, being joined by many Roman Catholics whom we could rely on, knowing them to be the best Tories in the

[1] See a tract entitled *New High Church turned Old Presbyterian*, published in 1709

nation and avowed enemies to Presbyterianism.   On Sunday
we heard a most excellent sermon.   Our chaplain insisted
principally upon two heads.   (1) He proved to us that the
breach of public oaths is no perjury.   (2) He expounded the
nature of non-resistance, which might be interpreted from the
Hebrew to signify either loyalty or rebellion, according as the
sovereign bestowed his favours and preferments.   He concluded with exhorting us in a most pathetic manner to purge
the land by wholesome severities, and to propagate sound
principles by fire and sword.   Meeting with a refreshment of
October, all the officers assembled over it, among whom
were several Popish lords and gentlemen, who toasted many
loyal healths and confusions, and wept very plentifully for the
danger of the Church.' [1]

All this is very smart writing ; so also is the description of
the Jacobite fox-hunter and the Jacobite landlord of the inn.
' My fellow-traveller the fox-hunter observed there had been
no good weather since the Revolution, nor one good law since
William's accession to the throne, except the Act for preserving
game. . . . He told me he did not know what travelling was
good for, but to teach a man to ride the great horse, to jabber
French, and to talk against passive obedience ; he scarce ever
knew a traveller who had not forsook his principles and lost his
hunting seat. . . . The landlord of the inn was, he said, a jolly,
lusty fellow that lives well, at least three yards in the girth,
and the best Church of England man upon the road.   The
landlord had swelled his body to a prodigious size, and worked
up his complexion to a standing crimson, by his zeal for the
prosperity of the Church.   He had not time to go to church
himself, but had headed a mob at the pulling down two or
three meeting-houses. While supper was preparing he enlarged
on the happiness of the neighbouring shire, "for there is
scarce a Presbyterian in the whole county except the bishop."
I found he had learned a great deal of politics, but not one
word of religion, from the parson of his parish, and had scarce
any other notion of religion but that it consisted in hating
Presbyterians.' [2]   In a later number the fox-hunter reappears in
town, though 'he has a natural aversion to London, and
would never have come up had he not been subpœnaed to

---

[1] *Freeholder*, No. 3.   [2] *Ibid.* No. 22.

give his testimony for one of the rebels whom he knew to be a very fair sportsman.'[1]

There was, no doubt, a certain amount of truth in these witty sketches. An obstinate, unreasoning conservatism may have characterised a certain type of Jacobites, and the sacred name of the Church may have been dragged through the mire by men who had no real sense of religion and would have been a disgrace to any Christian community. But the elegant Whig essayist gave, to say the least of it, a very one-sided view of the character of the rebellion. Looking at it from a different point of view, a writer of our own day justly observes, 'It is remarkable that the adventurers in the unfortunate cause of the Chevalier St. George were, with rare exceptions, men of considerable credit, who had vast stakes in the country and had lost none of their due consideration in the eyes of others by extravagance or profligacy. This marks the insurrection of 1715 from others raised and supported by men of desperate fortunes.'[2] These are somewhat conflicting representations, but it certainly would be as easy to substantiate the latter as the former. The fact seems to have been that Jacobitism found its adherents principally among the higher and the lower classes; the great middle class was the chief support of the Government; and as this class was stronger than the other two put together, Jacobitism could make no head against it.[3] To adopt the whimsical but very expressive phraseology of a modern writer, it was in the Barbarian and Helot portion of the population that Jacobitism found its strength—among the old county families, whether noble or otherwise, and among the poor, who were still practically *ascripti glebæ*, and would naturally adopt the politics of the masters of the soil. The 'dregs of Romulus' also would, as a matter of course, side against the established order; and vagabonds generally would have a fellow-feeling with men who were in such a very unsettled condition as the Pretenders were. Add to these the whole of the Romanist interest, and we have the strength of

---

[1] *Freeholder*, No. 44.

[2] *Memoirs of the Jacobites of* 1715 *and* 1745, by Mrs. Thomson.

[3] 'The dynasty,' writes Sir A. Alison (*Life of Marlborough*, i. 80, &c.), 'brought in by the Revolution stood on the support of the moneyed power and the citizens of towns. They could not be expected to have the unbought loyalty which was felt by the rural population.'

Jacobitism. On the other hand, it was among the Philistines—
the *par excellence* respectable classes, as opposed to the noble
on the one side, and their retainers, supported by a strong
phalanx of Adullamites and Romanists, on the other—that
the anti-Jacobites found their strength.

And, on the whole, English Churchmen may be thankful
that the struggle ended as it did ; for, whatever may be thought
of Leslie's theory *as* a theory, there can be little doubt that in
the existing state of the English nation the religion of its king
would have been more than a personal matter ; and the Chevalier could never have been trusted not to play into the hands of
Rome and France. At the same time this thankfulness can be
by no means unalloyed. The triumphs of the Philistines introduced a vast amount of Philistinism into the Church. It was
painfully conspicuous in her outward fabrics. The taste
which 'crowned the edifice' of a conspicuous London church
with a full-sized statue of King George, which pushed the
bad old pew system to its most offensive height, glorifying
the well-to-do and practically excluding the poor from that
place where 'the rich and the poor' should 'meet together, for
the Lord is Maker of all,' which lined the walls of our churches
with hideous tablets filled with fulsome and mendacious
panegyrics—was sadly wanting in 'sweetness and light.' And
the outward was only too faithful a type of the internal condition of the Church in the eighteenth century. It would
of course be absurd to attribute these defects to the mere fact
that King George, not King James, was seated on the throne.
But they may be attributed, in a great degree, to the spread
of Philistinism, which was partly the cause, partly the effect,
of the decay of Jacobitism. Even the extravagant expressions
of loyalty which almost formed part of the religion of the
Stuart party were at any rate in less execrable taste than the
language which was often employed by the anti-Jacobites
when they wrote or spoke of their sovereign. There was
something grand, after all, in the sort of homage which was
paid by the adherents of the Stuarts to the 'divinity that doth
hedge a king ;' it was paid to the office rather than to the
man, and it was paid in most cases without any regard to
self-interest. But there was nothing grand in the clumsy
flattery which was paid both by preachers and writers to the

monarchs in the eighteenth century. If the outcries against monarchy *jure divino*, passive obedience, and non-resistance had led to a sturdy independence and self-respect which scorned to flatter any mortal man, we might have respected them ; but, as a rule, they did nothing of the sort. The glorification of King William, Queen Anne, and the first two Georges was quite as outrageous and more gross than that which extolled the Stuarts. Daniel Defoe, in the very same work in which he ridicules the opinion that 'kings came down from heaven with crowns upon their heads, and the people were all born with saddles upon their backs,' and that 'if a king wanted to walk across a dirty highway, his majesty might command twenty or thirty of the heads of his followers to be cut off to make steppings for him, that he might not dirty his sacred shoes,' could yet write thus of King William :—

> If any ask thee what high place remains,
> And what bright orb thy *William's* star contains,
>
> .   .   .   .
>
> There *he's a god indeed*, for th' heavenly face
> Gives high similitude to the immortal race ;
> There he possesses infinite, compleat,
> Whom here he cou'd no more than imitâte.
> A guard of glorious lights form'd his ascent,
> And wond'ring stars ador'd him as he went;
> The planetary gods eclips'd and fled,
> Resign'd their light, and veil'd their guilty head ;
> Superior glory lightn'd all the way,
> With beams shot out from everlasting day ;
> Harmonious musick, form'd in choirs of love,
> From the immortal symphony above,
> In charming measures all his *actions* sung
> And with seraphic *anthems* mov'd along.
> Thus *William* went. I saw the saint ascend,
> And sympathetick joy did optick powers extend :
> I saw th' exalted heroe at the gate :
> My soul went up with him ; 'tis hardly come back yet.
> Wonder no more new raptures fire my pen,
> When WILLIAM's name I chance to write, and when
> I search the lustre of his memory,
> The best of monarchs and of men to me.[1]

[1] *Jure Divino*, a satire in twelve books, by the author of the *True-born Englishman*, printed in the year 1706.

After the glowing description of William's Assumption (one can hardly use a milder term), there is rather a bathos in the last line. But to Defoe's credit it should be stated that his enthusiasm was kindled simply by gratitude for favours received, and not by the expectation of favours to come ; for the poem was written after his hero's death, and when the praise of his patron would be no passport to Court favour. Still the language is rather strong from a man who wrote immediately afterwards—

> For governments from heaven might first appear,
> But governours came from *the Lord knows where.*

If we do not know where governors come from, we at least know where one has gone to.

This is the way in which the Whig bishop Fleetwood—a good man and no sycophant—spoke from the pulpit of Queen Anne in her very presence :—' Did ever fair example shine at Court with so small influence ? where everybody praises what they will not imitate, as if they were so dazzled with its lustre that they rather lost their way than were directed by it. . . . The nation is almost an idoliser of its Queen.' [1]

This is the way in which Toland, the sworn foe of the *jure divino* doctrine, writes of George I. :—' Never before did Britain possess a king endued with so many glorious qualities ; as true piety, fortitude, temperance, prudence, justice, knowledge, industry, frugality, and every other virtue. . . . The Whigs admire King George almost to adoration.' [2]   This is the way in which a pious clergyman, like Dr. Young, writes of the same monarch :—' All Britain bends in humble thankfulness for such a blessing.' [3]   And this is the way in which a Dissenter (and therefore, of course, a Whig and anti-Jacobite) describes the same king's character :—' King George was born a heroe. His mind is vast and comprehensive, his imagination fruitful and sprightly. He is the choice both of God and the people, and the very darling of Heaven. He had a title to the crown (like William), even in nature and superior

---

[1] Fleetwood's *Sermon before the Queen at St. Paul's*, August 19, 1708, thanksgiving for victory.

[2] Toland's *Memorial to a Minister of State on the Accession of King George I.*

[3] Doran's *Queens of England of the House of Hanover*, vol. i. p. 171, Sophia Dorothea.

merit, before he wore it. He is religious without superstition, &c. &c. In a word, King George (who is hastening to us with all the affection of a tender father) carries on the noble designs of Heaven in raising up oppressed virtue, in securing the Protestant religion, and in procuring rest and happiness to the world.'[1] If a 'not' were inserted in some of these sentences they would be nearer the truth.

And this is the way in which Smollett (a Jacobite, by the way, and therefore, perhaps, ready to make the worst of the matter) tells us that George II. was spoken of :—'On the King's death he was extolled as above Alexander in courage, Augustus in liberality, Titus in clemency, Antoninus in piety and benevolence, Solomon in wisdom, and St. Edward in devotion. The two universities vied in lamenting his death, mingled with condolence and congratulation to his successor.'[2]

In extenuation of all this mendacious flattery it is only fair to remember that it was the fashion of the day to speak of great people in this sort of language, which did not therefore imply the same degree of servility as it would at the

---

[1] A tract entitled *The True Character of her Late Majesty*, published in 1714.

See also Tindal's continuation of Rapin, xix. p. 598, where George I. is thus described :—'As to his private virtues, the serenity and benignity of his mind discovered themselves in his countenance and captivated the love and veneration of all who approached him.' One Goode, a layman, in the dedication of a letter to Bishop Hoadly, calls George I. 'one of the best, the wisest, and bravest men the world ever produced.'—Hoadly's *Works*, in 3 vols. folio, vol. i. *ad initium.*

[2] Smollett's continuation of Hume, vol. v. p. 372.

See also Bishop Newton's *Sermon on the Death of Frederick, Prince of Wales.* 'Religion hath lost a defender ; liberty hath lost a guardian. We might have rested under his shadow, whenever God for our sins should have deprived us of his Majesty's mild and gracious government,' &c. &c. In a funeral sermon on Queen Anne we read, 'If we ascend yet higher, from her private to her more public character, such a scene of wonders will thence be opened to our memories as will deserve an historian equal to one of her noble ancestors [Earl of Clarendon], and yet will hardly find credit from posterity when so related.' 'A theme too big to be contracted within the narrow compass of a few cursory lines, and too magnificent for a pen which has not room nor ability to do it justice. . . . Let us rather, in this place, consider her clothed, as she always was, with the robes of righteousness,' &c. &c.—*The Royal Pattern*, preached July 8 and 15, 1714, by Nat. Marshall, Rector of Finchley and Lecturer of St. Mary, Aldermanbury.

George III. objected to such flattery. In the first year of his reign one of his chaplains 'having ventured to eulogise him in the pulpit while he was present in the Chapel Royal, the King at once took steps to prevent the recurrence of such mistimed flatteries. He desired his chaplains might be informed that he went to church to hear the praises of God, and not his own.'—Jesse's *Memoirs of the Life and Reign of George III.*, vol. i. pp. 51-2.

present day. But then, in common justice, the same allowance should be made for the Jacobites' extravagant expressions of loyalty.

The history of Jacobitism in its relation to the Church after the rising of 1715 may be quickly told. The rebellion was easily stamped out, but the seeds of disaffection which had been sown were not so easily eradicated. The Jacobites in England watched with an eager eye every unpopular step of the Government, and kept the Pretender informed of every occurrence which seemed calculated to advance his interests. In 1717 his hopes were raised by the discontent of the clergy at the indefinite prorogation of Convocation, and at the instigation of Leslie he renewed his assurances of 'maintaining inviolably to the Church of England all her just rights and privileges, of confirming those rights in our first Parliament, and of giving what further reasonable security on that head shall then seem good to our people.' This 'excellent letter,' we are told,[1] 'was received with great pleasure and entire satisfaction in England,' but nothing further resulted from it. In 1720 he is informed that disaffection and uneasiness will continue everywhere, and probably increase, and the bulk of the nation will be still in the true interest and on the side of justice ; but, owing to a reconciliation which had taken place between the King (George) and the Prince of Wales, all action must be postponed. In the following year he is informed that 'the time is now come when, with a very little assistance from your friends abroad, your way to your friends at home is become safe and easy. Your friends are in good earnest exerting themselves, under a full expectation that an opportunity may some time this summer be given them to show their zeal for your service. They will always think this the most promising juncture that has ever yet offered itself.'[2] In consequence of such information as this, the Pretender put forth his audacious declaration, which roused England from her apathy and caused her to rally round her king, who, whatever his faults might be—and they were many, and made his government very unpopular—was yet the sole hope of Protestantism.

[1] By Charles Leslie. *Stuart Papers*, vol. i. vi.
[2] The *Stuart Papers*, vol. i. No. xii. Letter from Atterbury to the Chevalier de St. George, dated April 21, 1721.

One memorable name will always be connected with this revival of the alarm of Jacobitism. Atterbury, Bishop of Rochester, was committed to the Tower on a grave suspicion of being concerned in the conspiracy for bringing back the Stuarts. Refusing to be tried by the Commons, he was brought before the bar of his peers in May 1723, and was accused of ' holding treasonable correspondence with the Pretender and of fomenting a conspiracy to invade this kingdom.' The evidence against him was not unimpeachable. His speech in his own defence was one of the most eloquent and masterly orations ever made within the walls of Parliament.[1] There was a strong feeling in his favour out of doors, especially among the clergy, who complained loudly that the whole sacred order was insulted and their rights violated by the committal of a bishop to the Tower; but the vote of his peers went against him, and among those who spoke and voted with the majority were several bishops. There were conflicting opinions as to his guilt not only in his own day, but for many years afterwards, and it is only within the present generation that the question has been for ever set at rest by the publication of the Stuart Papers, which prove his guilt beyond the shadow of a doubt.[2]

There can be but one opinion about the conduct of this able prelate. He had taken the oaths of allegiance and abjuration. He held office under the existing Government. He solemnly protested his innocence of all share in the plot, calling God to witness his protestation and imprecating upon himself the most awful curses if he did not speak the truth, while, in point of fact, he had been far more deeply implicated in the conspiracy than even his enemies were aware. Some Nonjuring clergymen were involved in his fall, but their conduct appears in a very different light from his : they were bound by no solemn obligations ; they were reaping no

---

[1] Hallam, however (an authority from whom one may well shrink from differing), thinks that ' Atterbury's own speech is certainly below his fame, especially the peroration ' (*Constitutional History*, vol. iii. p. 250, note). The opinion of the speech in the text was written before the writer, though he had read and re-read Hallam, happened to have observed this note. However, the speech is still extant, and the reader must be left to judge for himself of its merits.

[2] Bishop Hoadly always spoke and wrote most confidently of Atterbury's Jacobitism. See his *Works*, vol. iii. *passim.*

benefits from the Government against which they conspired ; they were open enemies, and could be guarded against as such. In his exile Atterbury openly entered into the Pretender's service, and during the remainder of his life was an indefatigable agent of the Jacobites abroad and a constant correspondent with Jacobites at home.[1]

But the cause of Jacobitism was doomed. The Jacobite element in the Church had almost died out. The old generation of Nonjurors had passed away, and their successors, whose reasons for scrupling the oaths rested on a different foundation, commanded little of the respect which had been felt even by enemies for their predecessors. They produced little or no appreciable effect upon the Church at large, which from the time of Atterbury's banishment seems to have abandoned its Jacobite proclivities.[2]

Nothing proves this more clearly than the contrast between the attitude of the clergy towards the rebellion of 1745 and that of 1715. Personally the young Pretender was far more calculated to attract the sympathies of the clergy than his father had been. The fatal barrier of a different religion was in his case far less strong. He had received part of his education from a Protestant tutor.[3] It was rumoured that he was not disinclined to become a Protestant himself. It was certain that he was not so hopelessly enslaved to Rome as his father and grandfather had been. There were many points in his character which were adapted to encourage that

[1] A full account of the correspondence between Atterbury and the Pretender will be found in the *Stuart Papers*, published in 1847. The estimation in which Atterbury was held by the Jacobites is shown by the language in which one of them—Mr. Salkeld—describes him after his death in 1732. 'Our great and illustrious prelate the Bishop of Rochester, that anchor of our hopes, that pillar of our cause, and that ornament of our Church and nation, is no more.'

[2] 'The Jacobite party,' writes Lord Hervey (*Memoirs of Reign of George II.*, i. 5), had fallen low [in 1727], and consisted only of a few veterans, and some who, educated in that calling, made it a point of honour not to quit the name, but their attachment to the person of the Pretender was quite worn out.'

The Jacobites, however, still nourished hopes of success. The Duke of Wharton wrote to Atterbury in 1725 (August 8), 'The disaffection of the common people daily increases in England, and I can with pleasure assure you that 'many considerable men in England are still sincerely attached to the King and his cause, and labour with more interest than ever in promoting of his Majesty's interest.'— *Stuart Papers*, vol. i. letter lv. See also the same work *passim* for evidence on this point.   [3] Murray.

old semi-religious spirit of loyalty which had formerly kindled
the hearts of English Churchmen. That spirit could scarcely
be roused in favour of so feeble a character as that of the
Chevalier de St. George ; it certainly had not found an object
to which it might attach itself in either of the foreign occupants of the English throne. But might it not be awakened in
behalf of the young adventurer who came unsupported by
foreign aid simply to throw himself upon the sympathies of
his countrymen and to recall his father's misguided subjects to
their duty ?[1] There was a romantic chivalry in the whole
enterprise, which harmonised well with the spirit of the loyal
Churchmen of ancient times. Might not the homage paid to
the memory of the royal martyr be transferred to his living
representative? The issue proved that it could not. The
clergy evidently used none of the great influence they possessed over their flocks to awaken a feeling in behalf of the
descendant of the martyr. Charles Edward and his High-
landers marched on to the very centre of England without
kindling one spark of enthusiasm in their favour. Hardly a
single recruit voluntarily joined their standard ; they were received everywhere with a sullen and mortifying silence.[2] 'We
will not have this man to reign over us' was the general feeling
of both clergy and laity.

There is abundant evidence of efforts made by the clergy

[1] The Prince himself seems to have been disappointed at the apathy and opposition of the clergy. In an interesting letter to his father, dated September 21,
1745, he writes, 'I have seen two or three gazettes filled with addresses and
mandates from the bishops to the clergy. The addresses are such as I expected,
and can impose on none but the weak and credulous. The mandates are of the
same sort, but more artfully drawn up. They order the clergy to make the
people sensible of the great blessings they enjoy under the present family that
governs them—of the great security of their religion, &c. . . . But they care
not to mention the dreadful growth of atheism and infidelity ; I hear many fashionable men are ashamed to own themselves Christians, and many of the lower sort
act as if they were none. Those who are louder in the cry of Popery and the
danger of the Protestant religion are not really Protestants, but profligate men of
good parts, &c. . . . Dr. Wagstaffe told me that I must not judge of the English clergy by the bishops, who were not promoted for piety and learning, but for
writing pamphlets, being active at elections, and voting as the Ministry directed
them. After another victory they will write for me.' See Ewald's *Life of Prince
Charles Stuart*, vol. i. p. 217, &c.

[2] At Manchester a few of the clergy and some of the populace showed a little
enthusiasm, but this was an exception which proves the rule.

in favour of the existing Government. Several eminent divines preached sensible sermons on the duty of supporting the powers that be;[1] the Archbishop of York composed a prayer for the success of the King's troops, which is a more beautiful one than could have been expected in that prosaic age;[2] and, what was the unkindest cut of all, even the diocese of Oxford, which had once been the hot-bed of Jacobitism, earned the congratulation of its bishop for the 'unanimous zeal it had expressed against the unnatural rebellion' and 'the proofs of loyalty and affection to Government in which it had abounded.'[3]

The last blow was inflicted upon the Stuart cause when a king ascended the English throne who gloried in the name of Briton. The outcry against foreign princes could no longer be raised. The most loyal of Churchmen found an object for their loyalty without looking across the seas to find it. 'They changed their idol, but preserved their idolatry.'[4] A faint echo of the cry which nearly a hundred years before had driven the Stuarts from the throne was heard in the Gordon riots of 1780, when it was absurdly hinted that the Pretender was coming to restore Popery through the supposed Scotch influence behind the throne. The rumour would be hardly worth mentioning did it not show how to the very last the religious question was connected with the Stuarts.

So ended this memorable struggle, which was a long and sometimes a doubtful one. As loyal Churchmen we may rejoice that it terminated as it did; but our joy cannot be altogether unmingled with regret. England was freed from superstition and tyranny, but it was at the cost of many a noble life and the loss of many a noble sentiment. The

---

[1] Among others, Secker, Sherlock, and Warburton.

[2] 'May the great God of battles stretch out His all-powerful hand to defend us; inspire an union of hearts and hands among all ranks of people, a clear wisdom into the councils of his Majesty, and a steady courage and resolution into the hearts of his generals,' &c.

[3] See Bishop Secker's *Third Charge to the Diocese of Oxford in* 1747. There was still, however, a strong element of Jacobitism in the university. Thus Pitt spoke of the Oxford Jacobites:—'The body was learned and respectable, and so much the more dangerous.' H. Walpole's *Memoirs of George II. in the Year* 1754. See also Fielding's *The True Patriot*, No. 24, April 1746, 'A Letter from a Nonjuror to his Son at Oxford.'

[4] Edmund Burke. See *Life of Gibbon*, ch. v. p. 148.

success of the Georges delivered the English Church from all danger from the side of Rome, a danger which, humanly speaking, could not have been averted if the Stuart line had been restored. It is scarcely too much to say that she owed her life as a reformed, established Church to their success ; but, looking at her career during the reigns of these two monarchs, one is almost tempted to add that her misfortune was *propter vitam vivendi perdere causas*. The low tone, the worldliness, the spiritual drowsiness, the want of elasticity, which characterised the Church of the Hanoverian period may be traced in no slight degree to her peculiar position under those foreign potentates. Instead of rising to the high level of the grand old Church of their adoption, they seem to have dragged her down to their own low level. While, then, we should be ungrateful if we refused to acknowledge our obligations to those who delivered us from the iron yoke of Rome, we may at least 'pay the passing tribute of a sigh' to a ruined cause whose downfall carried with it much that was noble along with much that was base and dangerous.

J. H. O.

CHAPTER III.

ROBERT NELSON, HIS FRIENDS, AND CHURCH PRINCIPLES.

HIGH CHURCHMANSHIP, as it was commonly understood in Queen Anne's reign, did not possess many attractive features. Its nobler and more spiritual elements were sadly obscured amid the angry strife of party warfare,[1] and all that was hard, or worldly, or intolerant in it was thrust into exaggerated prominence. Indeed, the very terms 'High' and 'Low' Church must have become odious in the ears of good men who heard them bandied to and fro like the merest watchwords of political faction.[2] It is a relief to turn from the noise and virulence with which so-called Church principles were contested in Parliament and Convocation, in lampoons and pamphlets, in taverns and coffee-houses, from Harley and Bolingbroke, from Swift, Atterbury, and Sacheverell, to a set of High Churchmen, belonging rather to the former than to the existing generation, whose names were not mixed up with these contentions, and whose pure and primitive piety did honour to the Church which had nurtured such faithful and worthy sons. If, at the opening of the eighteenth century, the English Church derived its chief lustre from the eminent qualities of some of the Broad Church bishops, it must not be forgotten that it was also adorned with the virtues of men of a very different order of thought, as represented by Ken and Nelson, Bull and Beveridge. Some of them, it is true,

[1] See a vigorous passage by Swift, beginning, ' How has the spirit of faction mingled itself with the mass of the people ! '—*Sentiments of a Church of England Man.* Works viii. 279. A choice selection from the vocabulary of abuse employed by Tories and High Churchmen is culled by Lord Somers, in his *Judgment of whole Kingdoms and Nations*, &c. § 190. It might be matched with the greatest ease on the other side. A writer in the *Qu. Rev.* (101, 415), on the political satires of that date, refers to an argument of the *Examiner* (No. 8), that a man of ' no party ' was in ' an infamous neutrality.'

[2] ' Our state parties . . . the more to inflame their passions, have mixed religious and civil animosities together ; borrowing all their appe'lations from the Church, with the addition of " High " and " Low," how little soever the disputes relate to these terms.' Swift's *Works*, viii. 226.

had been unable to take the oaths to the recently established Government, and were therefore, as by a kind of accident, excluded, if not from the services, at all events from the ministry of the National Church. But none as yet ventured to deny that, saving the question of political allegiance, they were thoroughly loyal alike to its doctrine and its order.

It is proposed in this chapter to make Robert Nelson the central figure, and to group around him some of the most distinguished of his Juror and Nonjuror friends. A special charm lingers around the memory of Bishop Ken, but his name can scarcely be made prominent in any sketch which deals only with the eighteenth century. He lived indeed through its first decade, but his active life was over before it began. Nelson, on the other hand, though he survived him by only four years, took an active part throughout Queen Anne's reign in every scheme of Church enterprise. He was a link, too, between those who accepted and those who declined the oaths. Even as a member of the Nonjuring communion he was intimately associated with many leading Churchmen of the Establishment; and when, to his great gratification, he felt that he could again with an easy conscience attend the services of his parish church, the ever-widening gap that had begun to open was in his case no hindrance to familiar intercourse with his old Nonjuring friends.

Greatly as Robert Nelson was respected and admired by his contemporaries, no complete record of his life was published until the present century. His friend Dr. Francis Lee, author of the 'Life of Kettlewell,' had taken the work on hand, but was prevented by death from carrying it out. There are now, however, three or four biographies of him, especially the full and interesting memoir published in 1860 by Mr. Secretan. It is needless, therefore, to go over ground which has already been completely traversed; a few notes only of the chief dates and incidents of his life may be sufficient to introduce the subject.

Robert Nelson was born in 1656. In his early boyhood he was at St. Paul's School, but the greater part of his education was received under the guidance of Mr. Bull, afterwards Bishop of St. Davids, by whose life and teaching he was profoundly influenced. The biography of his distinguished tutor occupied the labour of his last years, and was no doubt a grateful offering to the memory of a man to whom he owed many of his best impressions.   About 1679 he went to London, where he became intimate with Tillotson, then Dean of Canterbury.   In later years this intimacy was somewhat interrupted by great divergence of views on theological and ecclesiastical subjects ; but a strong feeling of mutual respect remained, and, in his last illness, Tillotson was nursed by his friend with the most affectionate love, and died in his arms.   In 1680 Nelson went to France with Halley, his old schoolfellow and fellow member of the Royal Society, and during their journey watched with his friend the celebrated comet which bears Halley's name.   While in Paris he received the offer of a place in Charles II.'s Court, but took the advice of Tillotson, who said he should be glad 'if England were so happy as that the Court might be a fit place for him to live in.'[1]   He therefore declined the offer, and travelled on to Rome, where he made the acquaintance of Lady Theophila Lucy and married her the next year.   It was no light trouble to him that on their return to London she avowed herself a Romanist. Cardinal Howard at Rome, and Bossuet at Paris, had gained her over to their faith, and with the ardour of a proselyte she even entered, on the Roman side, into the great controversy of the day.   Robert Nelson himself was entirely unaffected by the current which just at this time seemed to have set in in favour of Rome.   He maintained, indeed, a cordial friend-ship with Bossuet, but was not shaken by his arguments, and in 1688 published, as his first work, a treatise against tran-substantiation.   Though controversy was little to his taste, these were times when men of earnest conviction could scarcely avoid engaging in it.[2]   Nelson valued the name of Protestant next only to that of Catholic, and was therefore drawn almost necessarily into taking some part in the last great dispute with Rome.[3]   But polemics would be deprived of their gall of bitterness if combatants joined in the strife with as much charity and generosity of feeling as he did.[4]

From the first Nelson felt himself unable to transfer his

[1] Birch's *Life of Tillotson*, lxi.
[2] Ken and a few others are conspicuous as exceptions.
[3] W. H. Teale, *Life of Nelson*, 221.
[4] Dr. S. Clarke called him a model controversialist.   Teale, 330.

allegiance to the new Government. The only question in his mind was whether he could consistently join in Church services in which public prayers were offered in behalf of a prince whose claims he utterly repudiated. He consulted Archbishop Tillotson on the point; and his old friend answered with all candour that if his opinions were so decided that he was verily persuaded such a prayer was sinful, there could be no doubt as to what he should do. Upon this he at once joined the Nonjuring communion. He remained in it for nearly twenty years, on terms of cordial intimacy with most of its chief leaders. When, however, in 1709, Lloyd, the deprived Bishop of Norwich, died, Nelson wrote to Ken, now the sole survivor of the Nonjuring bishops, and asked whether he claimed his allegiance to him as his rightful spiritual father. As regards the State prayers, time had modified his views. He retained his Jacobite principles, but considered that non-concurrence in certain petitions in the service did not necessitate a prolonged breach of Church unity. Ken, who had welcomed the accession of his friend Hooper to the see of Bath and Wells, and who no longer subscribed himself under his old episcopal title, gave a glad consent, for he also longed to see the schism healed. Nelson accordingly, with Dodwell and other moderate Nonjurors, rejoined the communion of the National Church.

It is much to Robert Nelson's honour that in an age of strong party animosities he never suffered his political predilections to stand in the way of union for any benevolent purpose. He had taken an active interest in the religious associations of young men which sprung up in London and other towns and villages about 1678, a time when the zeal of many attached members of the Church of England was quickened by the dangers which were besetting it. A few years later, when 'Societies for the Reformation of Manners' were formed, to check the immorality and profaneness which was gaining alarming ground, he gave his hearty co-operation both to Churchmen and Dissenters in a movement which he held essential to the welfare of the country. Although a Jacobite and Nonjuror, he was enrolled, with not a few of the most distinguished Churchmen of the day, among the earliest members of the Society for Promoting Christian Knowledge, at its formation in 1699; and long before his re-entering into

the Established communion we find him not only a constant
attendant, but sometimes chairman at its weekly meetings.
He took a leading part in the organisation of the Society for
the Propagation of the Gospel in Foreign Parts, in 1701, and
sat at its board in friendly conference with Burnet and many
another whose very names were odious to his Nonjuring
friends.   And great as his disappointment must have been at
the frustration of Jacobite hopes in the quiet accession of
George I., the interest and honourable pride which he felt
in the London charity schools so far triumphed over his political
prejudices that he found pleasure in marshalling four thousand
of the children to witness the new sovereign's entry, and to
greet him with the psalm which bids the King rejoice in the
strength of the Lord and be exceeding glad in His salvation.

In such works as these—to which must be added his
labours as a commissioner in 1710 for the erection of new
churches in London, his efforts for the promotion of parochial
and circulating clerical libraries throughout the kingdom, for
advancing Christian teaching in grammar schools, for improving prisons, for giving help to French Protestants in
London and Eastern Christians in Armenia—Robert Nelson
found abundant scope for the beneficent energies of his public
life.   The undertakings he carried out were but a few of the
projects which engaged his thoughts.   If we cast our eyes
over the proposed institutions which he commended to the
notice of the influential and the rich, it is surprising to see in
how many directions he anticipated the philanthropical ideas
of the age in which we live.   Ophthalmic and consumptive
hospitals, and hospitals for the incurable ; ragged schools ;
penitentiaries ; homes for destitute infants ; associations of
gentlewomen for charitable and religious purposes ; theological,
training, and missionary colleges; houses for temporary
religious retirement and retreat—such were some of the designs
which, had he lived a few years longer, he would certainly
have attempted to carry into execution.[1]

He was no less active with his pen in efforts aimed at
infusing an earnest spirit of practical piety, and bringing
home to men's thoughts an appreciative feeling of the value of

---

[1] See his *Address to Persons of Quality,* and *Representation of the several Ways
of doing Good.*   Secretan, 149.   Teale, 338.

Church ordinances. He published his 'Practice of True Devotion' in 1698, an excellent work, which attracted little attention when it first came out, but reached at least its twenty-second edition before the next century was completed. His treatise on the 'Christian Sacrifice' appeared in 1706, his 'Life of Bishop Bull' in 1713; but it is by his 'Festivals and Fasts' that his name has been made familiar to every succeeding generation of Churchmen. Its catechetical form, and the somewhat formal composure of its style, did not strike past readers as defects. It certainly was in high favour among English Churchmen generally. Dr. Johnson said of it in 1776 that he understood it to have the greatest sale of any book ever printed in England except the Bible.[1] In the first four years and a half after its issue from the press more than 10,000 copies were printed.[2]

Robert Nelson died in the January of 1715, a man so universally esteemed that it would be probably impossible to find his name connected in any writer with a single word of disparagement. It would be folly to speak of one thus distinguished by singular personal qualities as if he were, to any great extent, representative of a class. If the Church of England had been adorned during Queen Anne's reign by many such men, it could never have been said of it that it failed to take advantage of the signal opportunities then placed within its reach. Yet his views on all Church questions, and many of the characteristic features of his character, were shared by many of his friends both in the Established Church and among the Nonjurors. He survived almost all of them, so that with him the type seemed nearly to pass away for a length of time, as if the spiritual atmosphere of the eighteenth century were uncongenial to it. His younger acquaintances in the Nonjuring body, however sincere and generous in temperament, were men of a different order. It was but natural that, as the schism became more pronounced and Jacobite hopes more desperate, the Church views of a dwindling minority should become continually narrower, and lose more and more of those larger sympathies which can scarcely be altogether absent in any section of a great national Church.

[1] *Life*, by Boswell, ii. 457.
[2] G. G. Perry, *History of the Church of England*, iii. 140.

First in order among Nelson's friends —not in intimacy, but in the affectionate honour with which he always remembered him—must be mentioned Bishop Ken. He was living in retirement at Longleat ; but Nelson must have frequently met him at the house of their common friend Mr. Cherry of Shottisbrooke,[1] and they occasionally corresponded. Nelson may have been the more practical, Ken the more meditative. The one was still in the full vigour of his benevolent activity while the other was waiting for rest, and soothing with sacred song the pains which told of coming dissolution. In his own words, to ' contemplate, hymn, love, joy, obey,' was the tranquil task which chiefly remained for him on earth. But they were congenial in their whole tone of thought. Their views on the disputed questions of the day very nearly coincided. Nelson, as might be expected of a layman who throughout his life had seen much of good men of all opinions, was the more tolerant ; but both were kindly and charitable towards those from whom they most differed, and both were attached with such deep loyalty of love to the Church in whose bosom they had been nurtured that they desired nothing more than to see what they believed to be its genuine principles fully carried out, and could neither sympathise with nor understand religious feelings which looked elsewhere for satisfaction. Both were unaffectedly devout, without the least tinge of moroseness or gloom. Nelson specially delighted in Ken's morning, evening, and midnight hymns. He entreated his readers to charge their memory with them. ' The daily repeating of them will make you perfect in them, and the good fruit of them will abide with you all your days.' [2] He subjoined them to his ' Practice of True Devotion ; ' and Samuel Wesley tells us that he personally knew how much he delighted in them. It was with these that—

> He oft, when night with holy hymns was worn,
> Prevented prime and wak'd the rising morn.[3]

He has also made use of many of Ken's prayers, together with some from Taylor, Kettlewell, and Hickes, in his ' Companion

[1] Secretan, 50, 71.
[2] *Practice of True Devotion,* 28.
[3] S. Wesley's poem on R. Nelson, prefixed to some editions of the *Practice, &c.* He adds in a note that this was a personal reminiscence of his friend.

for the Festivals and Fasts.' There is an intensity and effusion of spirit in them, in which his own more studied compositions are somewhat wanting.

Among the other nonjuring bishops Nelson was acquainted with, but not very intimately, were Sancroft and Frampton. The former he loved and admired; and spoke very highly of his learning and wisdom, his prudent zeal for the honour of God, his piety and self-denying integrity.[1] The little weaknesses and gentle intolerances of the good old man were not such as he would censure, nor would he be altogether out of sympathy with them. Bishop Frampton was in a manner an hereditary friend. He had gone out to Aleppo as a young man, half a century before, in capacity of chaplain of the Levant Company, at the urgent recommendation of John Nelson, father of Robert,[2] who had the highest opinion of his merits. From his cottage at Standish in Gloucestershire, where he had retired after his deprivation, he occasionally wrote to Robert Nelson, and must have often heard of him from John Kettlewell, the intimate and very valued friend of both. He was a man who could not fail to be esteemed[3] and loved by all who had the privilege of his acquaintance. He had been a preacher of great fame, whom people crowded to hear. Pepys said of him that 'he preached most like an apostle that he ever heard man;[4] and Evelyn, noting in his diary that he had been to hear him, calls him 'a pious and holy man, excellent in the pulpit for moving the affections.' His letters, of which several remain, written to Ken, Lloyd, and Sancroft, about the end of the seventeenth and the beginning of the eighteenth centuries, give the idea of a man of unaffected humility and simple piety, of a happy, kindly disposition, and full of spirit and innocent mirth. Though he could not take the oaths, he regularly communicated at the parish church.[5] Controversy he abhorred; it seemed to him, he

---

[1] Nelson's *Life of Bull*, 303. [2] Secretan, 2.

[3] 'A man,' says his biographer, 'of singular earnestness, honesty, and practical ability, who was never wanting in times of danger, and never hesitated to discharge his duty at the cost of worldly advantage.'—*Life of Frampton*, by T. S. Evans. Preface, x.

[4] Quoted in *Life of Ken*, by a Layman, 753.

[5] And even, by the permission of the Bishop of London assisted in the service. *Evans' Life*, 208.

said to Kettlewell, as if the one thing needful were scarcely heard, amidst the din and clashings of *pros* and *cons*, and he wished the men of war, the disputants, would follow his friend's example, and beat their swords and spears into ploughshares and pruning hooks.[1]

John Kettlewell died in 1695, to Nelson's great loss, for he was indeed a bosom friend. Nelson had unreservedly entrusted him with his schemes for doing good, his literary projects, his spiritual perplexities, and 'the nicest and most difficult emergencies of his life ; such an opinion had he of his wisdom, as well of his integrity.'[2] More than once, observes Dr. Lee, he said how much gratitude he owed to Kettlewell for his good influence, sometimes in animating him to stand out boldly in the cause of religion, sometimes in concerting with him schemes of benevolence, sometimes in suggesting what he could best write in the service of the Church. They planned out together the ' Companion for the Festivals and Fasts ;' they encouraged one another in that gentler mode of conducting controversy which must have seemed like mere weakness to many of the inflamed partisans of the period. Nelson proposed to preserve the memory of his friend in a biography. He carefully collected materials for the purpose, and though he had not leisure to carry out his design, was of great assistance to Francis Lee in the life which was eventually written.[3]

Bishop Ken used to speak of Kettlewell in terms of the highest reverence and esteem. In a letter to Nelson, acknowledging the receipt of some of Kettlewell's sermons, which his correspondent had lately edited, he calls their author ' as saintlike a man as ever I knew ;'[4] and when, in 1696, he was summoned before the Privy Council to give account for a pastoral letter drawn up by the nonjuring bishops on behalf of the deprived clergy, he spoke of it as having been first proposed by ' Mr. Kettlewell, that holy man who is now with God.'[5] There can be no doubt he well merited the admiration of his friends. Perhaps the most beautiful element in his character was his perfect guilelessness and transparent

---

[1] Frampton to Kettlewell. *Life of Kettlewell,* App. No. 18.
[2] *Life of Kettlewell,* p. 169.   [3] Id. 162. Secretan, 61.
[4] *Life of Kettlewell,* App. No. 25.   [5] *Life of Ken,* by a Layman, 676.

truth. Almost his last words, addressed to his nephew, were
'not to tell a lie, no, not to save a world, not to save your
King nor yourself.'[1] He had lived fully up to the spirit of
this rule. Anything like show and pretence, political shifts
and evasions, dissimulations for the sake of safety or under
an idea of doing good—'acting,' as he expressed it, 'deceit-
fully for God, and breaking religion to preserve religion,'
were things he would never in the smallest degree condescend
to. In no case would he allow that a jocose or conventional
departure from accuracy was justifiable, and even if a nonjuring
friend, under the displeasure, as might often be, of Government, assumed a disguise, he was uneasy and annoyed, and
declined to call him by his fictitious name.[2] Happily,
perhaps, for his peace of mind, his steady purpose 'to follow
truth wherever he might find it,'[3] without respect of persons
or fear of consequences, though it led to a sacrifice, con-
tentedly, and even joyfully borne, of worldly means, led him
no tittle astray from the ancient paths of orthodoxy. Like
most High Churchmen of his day, he held most exaggerated
views as to the duty of passive obedience, a doctrine which
he held to be vitally connected with the whole spirit of
Christian religion. He sorely lamented 'the great and
grievous breach' caused by the nonjuring separation,[4] and
earnestly trusted that a time of healing and reunion might
speedily arrive ; and though he adhered staunchly to the communion of the deprived bishops, whom he held to be the only
rightful fathers of the Church, and believed that there alone
he could find 'orthodox and holy ministrations,'[5] he never for
an instant supposed that he separated himself thereby from
the Church of England, in which, he said in his dying declaration, 'as he had lived and ministered, so he still continued
firm in its faith, worship, and communion.'[6] Such was
Kettlewell, a thorough type of the very best of the Nonjurors,
a man so kindly and large-hearted in many ways, and so
open to conviction, that the term bigoted would be harshly
applied to him, but whose ideas ran strongly and deeply in a

---

[1] *Life of Kettlewell*, 176.   [2] Id. pp. 95, 182.
[3] Id. 14.   [4] Id. 172.
[5] Id. 134.   [6] Id. 172.

narrow channel. He lived a life unspotted from the world ;
nor was there any purer and more fervent spirit in the list of
those whose active services were lost to the Church of England
by the new oath of allegiance.

Henry Dodwell was another of Robert Nelson's most
esteemed friends. After the loss of his Camdenian Professorship of History, he lived among his nonjuring acquaintances
at Shottisbrooke, immersed in abstruse studies. His profound
learning—for he was acknowledged to be one of the most
learned men in Europe[1]—especially his thorough familiarity
with all precedents drawn from patristic antiquity, made him
a great authority in the perplexities which from time to time
divided the Nonjurors. It was mainly to him that Nelson
owed his return to the established Communion. Dodwell
had been very ardent against the oaths ; when he conceived
the possibility of Ken's accepting them, he had written him a
long letter of anxious remonstrance ; he had written another
letter of indignant concern to Sherlock, on news of his
intended compliance.[2] But his special standing point was
based upon the argument that it was schism of the worst
order to side with bishops who had been intruded by mere
lay authority into sees which had other rightful occupiers.
When, therefore, this hindrance no longer existed, he was of
opinion that political differences, however great, should be no
bar to Church Communion, and that the State prayers were
no insurmountable difficulty. Nelson gladly agreed, and the
bells of Shottisbrooke rang merrily when he and Dodwell,
and the other Nonjurors resident in that place, returned to the
parish church.[3]

Dodwell is a well-known example of the extravagances
of opinion into which a student may be led, who, in perfect
seclusion from the world, follows up his views unguided by
practical considerations. Greatly as his friends respected his
judgment on all points of precedent and authority, they
readily allowed he had more of the innocency of the dove

---

[1] Schlosser, F. C., *History of the Eighteenth and Nineteenth Centuries*, chap.
i. § 2, p. 40.—Hearne said of him, 'I take him to be the greatest scholar in
Europe, when he died ; but what exceeds that, his piety and sanctity were beyond
compare.'—June 15, 1711, p. 228.

[2] *Life of Ken*, by a Layman, 540

[3] *Reliq. Hearniana*, 1710, March 4, p. 188.

than the wisdom of the serpent.[1] His faculties were in fact over-burdened with the weight of his learning, and his published works, which followed one another in quick succession, contained eccentricities, strange to the verge of madness. A layman himself, he held views as to the dignities and power of the priesthood, of which the 'Tatler'[2] might well say that Rome herself had never forged such chains for the consciences of the laity as he would have imposed. Starting upon an assumption, common to him with many whose general theological opinions he was most averse to, that the Divine counsels were wholly beyond the sphere of human faculties, and unimpeded therefore by any consideration of reason in his inferences from Scripture and primitive antiquity, he advanced a variety of startling theories, which created some dismay among his friends, and gave endless opportunity to his opponents. Much that he has written sounds far more like a grave caricature of high sacerdotalism, after the manner of De Foe's satires on intolerance, than the sober conviction of an earnest man.[3] It is needless to dwell upon crotchets for which, as Dr. Hunt properly observes, nobody was responsible but himself.[4] Ken, who had great respect for him—'the excellent' Mr. Dodwell, as he calls him—remarked of his strange ideas on the immortality of the soul, that he built high on feeble foundations, and would not have many proselytes to his hypotheses.[5] The same might be said of much else that he wrote on theological subjects. As for nonjuring principles, he was so wedded to them that he could see nothing but deadly schism outside the fold over which 'our late invalidly deprived fathers' presided. It only, as orthodox and unschismatic, 'was entitled to have its communions and excommunications ratified in heaven.'[6] No wonder he longed to see union restored, that so he might die in peace.[7]

---

[1] Brokesby's *Life of Dodwell*, 534.
[2] No. 187.
[3] Brokesby's *Life of Dodwell*, chap. x. 73.
[4] Hunt, J. *Religious Thought in England*, ii. 85.
[5] *Life of Ken*, by a Layman, 705.
[6] Dodwell's *Append. to Case in View, now in Fact*, and his *On Occasional Communion, Life*, pp. 474 and 419.
[7] *Life of Kettlewell*, 128.

With the ever understood proviso that they could not
fall in with many of his views, Nelson and most of his friends
loved Mr. Dodwell and were proud of him.   They admired his
great learning, his fervent and ascetic piety, his deep attachment to the doctrine and usages of the English Church, and
many attractive features in personal character.   'He was a
faithful and sincere friend,' says Hearne, 'very charitable to
the poor (notwithstanding the narrowness of his fortune), free
and open in his discourse and conversation (which he always
managed without the least personal reflection), courteous and
affable to all people, facetious upon all proper occasions, and
ever ready to give his counsel and advice, and extremely
communicative of his great knowledge.'[1]   Although a man
of retiring habits and much personal humility, he was bold
as a lion when occasion demanded, and never hesitated to
sacrifice interest of any kind to his sincere, but often strangely
contracted ideas of truth and duty.   It was his lot to suffer
loss of goods under either king, James II. and William.
Under the former he not only lost the rent of his Irish
estates,[2] but had his name[3] on the murderous act of attainder
to which James, to his great disgrace, attached his signature
in 1689.   Under the latter he was deprived of his preferment
in Oxford, and under a harsher rule might have incurred yet
graver penalties.   'He has set his heart,' said William of
him, 'on being a martyr, and I have set mine on disappointing him.'[4]   He died at Shottisbrooke in 1711.

After Kettlewell's death, no one was so intimate with
Robert Nelson as Dr. George Hickes.   They lived near
together[5] in Ormond Street, and for the last eleven years of
Nelson's life met almost daily.   In forming any estimate of
Hickes's character, the warm-hearted esteem with which Nelson
regarded him[6] should not be lost sight of.   Whatever were his
faults, he must have possessed many high qualities, to have
thus completely won the heart of so good a man.   The feeling
was fully reciprocated ; and those who knew with what
intensity of blind zeal Hickes attached himself to the interests

---

[1] Quoted in Brokesby's *Life of Dodwell*, 546.   [2] Id. 541.
[3] Macaulay's *History of England*, chap. 12.   [4] Id.
[5] Secretan, 63.
[6] Nelson's *Life of Bull*, 439.

of his party, must have been surprised that this intimacy was not interrupted even by his sore disappointment at Nelson's defection from the nonjuring communion. In Hickes there was nothing of the calm and tempered judgment which ruled in Nelson's mind. From the day that he vacated his deanery, and fixed up his indignant protest in Worcester Cathedral,[1] he threw his heart and soul into the nonjuring cause. Unity might be a blessing, and schism a disaster; but it is doubtful whether he would have made the smallest concession in order to attain the one, or avoid the other. Even Bishop Ken said of him that he showed zeal to make the schism incurable.[2] A good man, and a scholar of rare erudition, he possessed nevertheless the true temper of a bigot. In middle life he had been brought into close acquaintance with the fanatic extravagances of Scotch Covenanters, his aversion to which might seem to have taught him, not the excellence of a more temperate spirit, but the desirability of rushing toward similar extremes in an opposite direction. He delighted in controversy in proportion to its heat, and too often his pen was dipped in gall, when he directed the acuteness and learning which none denied to him against any who swerved, this way or that, from the narrow path of dogma and discipline which had been marked with his own approval. Tillotson was 'an atheist,'[3] freethinkers were 'the first-born sons of Satan,' the Established Church was 'fallen into mortal schism,'[4] Ken, for thinking of reunion, was 'a half-hearted wheedler,'[5] Roman Catholics were 'as gross idolaters as Egyptian worshippers of leeks,'[6] Nonconformists were 'fanatics,' Quakers were 'blasphemers.'[7] From the peaceful researches, on which he built a lasting name, in Anglo-Saxon and Scandinavian antiquities, he returned each time with renewed zest to polemical disputes, and found relaxation in the strife of words. It was no promising omen for the future of the nonjuring party, that the Court of St. Germains should have appointed him and Wagstaffe first bishops of that Communion. The consecration was kept for several years a close secret, and Robert

---

[1] *Life of Kettlewell*, App. No. 3.   [2] *Life of Ken*, &c., 718.
[3] Hunt, ii. 375.   [4] Letter to Nelson. *Life of Bull*, 441.
[5] *Life of Ken*, &c., 719.   [6] Hunt, ii. 76.
[7] Hickes, 9, *Enthusiasm Exorcised*, 64.

Nelson himself may probably have been ignorant [1] of the high dignity to which ' my neighbour the Dean ' had attained.

One other of Nelson's nonjuring friends must be mentioned. Francis Lee, a physician, had been a Fellow of St. John's, Oxford, but was deprived for declining the oaths. At the end of the seventeenth century, after travelling abroad, he joined [2] one of those societies of mystics which at that time abounded throughout Europe. A long correspondence with Dodwell ensued, and convinced at last that he had been in error, he not only left the brotherhood and its presiding ' prophetess ' (it appears to have been a society of a somewhat fanatical order), but published in 1709, under the title of ' A History of Montanism, by a Lay Gentleman,' a work directed against fanaticism in general. He writes it in the tone of one who has lately recovered from a sort of mental fever which may break out in anyone, and sometimes becomes epidemic, inflaming and throwing into disorder certain obscure impulses which are common to all human nature. [3] He became intimate with Nelson, and subscribes one of his letters to him, ' To the best of friends, from the most affectionate of friends.' [4] He helped him in his devotional publications ; took in hand, at his instigation, and from materials which Nelson and Hickes had collected, the life of Kettlewell ; and took an active part in furthering the benevolent schemes in which his friend was so deeply interested. It was he who suggested [5] to him the founding of charity schools after the model of the far-famed orphanage and other educational institutions lately established by Francke and Spener at Halle, the centre of German pietism. In other ways we see favourable traces of his earlier mystical associations. He had been cured of fanaticism ; but the higher element, the exalted vein of spiritual feeling, remained, and perceptibly communicated itself to Nelson, whose last work—a preface to Lee's edition of Thomas a Kempis—is far more in harmony with the general tone of mystical thought than any of his

---

[1] Lathbury's *History of the Nonjurors*, 216. Seward speaks of him as ' this learned prelate.'—*Anecdotes of Distinguished Persons*, 250.

[2] Secretan, 70. He was much fascinated by the writings of Madame Bourignon.— Hearne to Rawlinson, quoted in Wilson's *History of Merchant Taylors*, 957.

[3] *History of Montanism*, &c., 344.   [4] Secretan, 273.   [5] Id. 70.

former writings. During the last few months of Nelson's life, they were much together. One of the very last incidents in his life was a drive with Lee in the park, when they watched the sun 'burst from behind a cloud, and accepted it for an emblem of the eternal brightness that should shortly break upon him.'[1]

Nelson was more or less intimate with several other Non-jurors; such as were Francis Cherry, of Shottisbrooke, a generous and popular country gentleman, whose house was always a hospitable refuge for Nonjurors and Jacobites;[2] Brokesby, Mr. Cherry's chaplain, author of the 'Life of Dod-well,' and of a history of the Primitive Church, to whom Nelson owed much valuable help in his 'Festivals and Fasts;' Jeremy Collier, whom Macaulay ranks first among the Non-jurors in ability; Nathanael Spinckes,[3] afterwards raised to the shadowy honours and duties of the nonjuring episcopate, Nelson's trustee for the money bequeathed by him to assist the deprived clergy; and lastly, Charles Leslie, an ardent and accomplished controversialist, whom Dr. Johnson excepted from his dictum that no Nonjuror could reason.[4] It may be added here, that when Pepys, author of the well-known 'Diary,' cast about in 1703, the last year of his life, for a spiritual adviser among the nonjuring clergy, Robert Nelson was the one among his acquaintances to whom he naturally turned for information.

The decision of many a conscientious man hung wavering for a long time on the balance as he debated whether or not he could accept the new oath of allegiance. Friends, whose opinions on public matters and on Church questions were almost identical, might on this point very easily arrive at different determinations. But the resolve once made, those

---

[1] Secretan, 171. Wilson quotes from the Rawlinson MSS. a very beautiful prayer composed by Lee soon before his death, for 'all Christians, however divided or distinguished . . . . throughout the whole militant Church upon earth.'—*History of Merchant Taylors*, 956.

[2] Hearne dwells enthusiastically on his high qualities, his religious conscientiousness, his learning, modesty, sweet temper, his charity in prosperity, his resignation in adverse fortune.—*Reliquiæ*, i. 287.

[3] Secretan, 50, 69, 284. He was a learned man, a student of many languages.—*Nichols*, i. 124.

[4] Boswell's *Life of Johnson*, iv. 256.

who took different courses often became widely separated.
Many acquaintances, many friendships were broken off by
the divergence. Some of the more rigid Nonjurors, headed
by Sancroft himself, went so far as to refuse all Church communion with those among their late brethren who had incurred the sin of compliance ; and it was plainly impossible
to be on any terms of intimacy with one who could be welcomed back into the company of the faithful only as 'a true
penitent for the sin of schism.'[1]   There were some, on the
other hand, who were fully aware of the difficulties that beset
the question, and had not a word or thought of condemnation for those who did not share in the scruples they themselves felt. They could not take the oath, but neither did
they make it any cause of severance, or discontinue their
attendance at the public prayers. But for the most part even
those Nonjurors who held no extreme views fell gradually
into a set of their own, with its own ideas, hopes, prejudices,
and sympathies. They could scarcely help making a great
principle of right or wrong of that for which most of them had
sacrificed so much. It was intolerable, after loss of home and
property in the cause, as they believed, of truth and duty, to
be called factious separatists, authors of needless schism.
Hence, in very self-defence, they were driven to attach all
possible weight to the reasons which had placed them, loyal
Churchmen as they were, in a Nonconformist position, to
rally round their own standard, and to strive to the utmost of
their power to show that it was they, and not their opponents,
not the Jurors but the Nonjurors, who were the truest and most
faithful sons of the Anglican Church. Under such circumstances, the gap grew ever wider which had sprung up between
themselves and those who had not scrupled at the oath. Even
between such friends as Ken and Bull, Nelson and Tillotson,
a temporary estrangement was occasioned. But Robert
Nelson was not of a nature to allow minor differences, however much exaggerated in importance, to stand long in the
way of friendship or works of Christian usefulness. He lived
chiefly in a nonjuring circle ; but even during the years when

---

[1] A regular form of admission 'into the true and Catholic remnant of the
Britannick Churches,' was drawn up for this purpose.--*Life of Kettlewell*, App.
xvii.

he wholly absented himself from parochial worship, he was on friendly and even intimate terms with many leading members of the establishment, and their active co-operator in every scheme for extending its beneficial influences.

First in honour stood Bishop Bull, his old tutor and warm friend, to whom he always acknowledged a deep debt of gratitude. Three years after his death Nelson published his life and works, shortening, it is said, his own days by the too assiduous labour which he bestowed upon the task. But it was a work of love which he was exceedingly anxious to accomplish. In the preface, after recording his high admiration of his late friend's merits, he solemnly ends with the words, 'beseeching God to enable me to finish what I begin in His name, and dedicate it to His honour and glory.'[1]

Both in his lifetime and afterwards, Bull has always been held in deserved repute as one of the most illustrious names in the roll of English bishops. Nelson called him 'a consummate divine,' and by no means stood alone in his opinion. Those who attach a high value to original and comprehensive thought will scarcely consider him entitled to such an epithet. He was a man of great piety, sound judgment, and extensive learning, but not of the grasp and power which signally influences a generation, and leaves a mark in the history of religious progress. He loved the Church of England with that earnestness of affection which in the seventeenth century specially characterised those who remembered its prostration, and had shared its depressed fortunes. Dr. Skinner, ejected Bishop of Oxford, had admitted him into orders at the early age of twenty-one. The Canon, he said, could not be strictly observed in such times of difficulty and distress. They were not days when the Church could afford to wait for the services of so zealous and able an advocate. He proved an effective champion against all its real and presumed adversaries — Puritans and Nonconformists, Roman Catholics, Latitudinarians and Socinians. An acute controversialist, skilled in the critical knowledge of Scripture, thoroughly versed in the annals of primitive antiquity, he was an opponent not lightly to be challenged. A devoted adherent of the English Church,

[1] Nelson's *Life of Bull*, 4.

scrupulously observant of all its rites and usages, and convinced as of 'a certain and evident truth that the Church of England is in her doctrine, discipline, and worship, most agreeable to the primitive and apostolical institution,'[1] his only idea of improvement and reform in Church matters was to remove distinct abuses, and to restore ancient discipline. Yet he was not so completely the High Churchman as to be unable to appreciate and enter to some extent into the minds of those who within his own Church had adopted opposite views. He used to speak, for example, with the greatest respect of Dr. Conant, a distinguished Churchman of Puritan views, who had been his rector at Exeter College, and whose instructions and advice had made, he said, very deep impression on him.[2] So, on the other hand, although a strenuous opponent of Rome, he did not fail to discriminate and do justice to what was Catholic and true in her system. And it tells favourably for his candour, that while he defended Trinitarian doctrine with unequalled force and learning, he should have had to defend himself against a charge of Arian tendencies[3] simply because he did not withhold authorities which showed that the primitive fathers did not always express very defined views upon the subject. His most notable and unique distinction consisted in the thanks he received, through Bossuet, from the whole Gallican Church, for his defence of the Nicene faith ; his most practical service to religion was the energetic protest of his ' Harmonia Apostolica ' in favour of a healthy and fruitful faith in opposition to the Antinomian doctrines of arbitrary grace which, at the time when he published his ' Apostolic Harmony,' had become most widely prevalent in England.

Bull had been ordained at twenty-one ; he was consecrated, in 1705, Bishop of St. Davids, at the almost equally exceptional age of seventy. He succeeded a bad man who had been expelled from his see for glaring simony ; and it was felt, not without justice, that the cause of religion and the

---

[1] Speech before the House of Lords, 1705.—Nelson's *Life of Bull*, 355.

[2] Nelson's *Life of Bull*, 11. Archdeacon Conant stood very high in Tillotson's estimation, as a man ' whose learning, piety, and thorough knowledge of the true principles of Christianity would have adorned the highest station.'—Birch's *Life of Tillotson, Works*, i. ccxii.

[3] Nelson's *Life of Bull*, 243-9. Dorner, ii. 83.

honour of the Episcopate would gain more by the elevation of a man of the high repute in which Bull was universally held, than it would lose by the growing infirmities of his old age. He accepted the dignity with hesitation, in hopes that his son, the Archdeacon of Llandaff, who however died before him, would be able greatly to assist him in the discharge of his duties. But as he was determined that if he could not be as active as he would wish, he would at all events reside strictly in his diocese, he saw little or no more of his friend Nelson, of whom he had said that 'he scarce knew any one in the world for whom he had greater respect and love.'[1] During the first four years of the century there had been a frequent correspondence between them on the subject of his controversy with Bossuet, with whom Nelson had long been in the habit of interchanging friendly courtesies. The Bishop of Meaux had written, in 1700, to Nelson, expressing admiration of Bull's work on the Trinity, and wonder as to what he meant by the term 'Catholic,' and why it was that, having such respect for primitive antiquity, he remained nevertheless separated from the unity of Rome. Bull wrote in answer his 'Corruptions of the Church of Rome,' and sent the manuscript of it to Nelson in 1704. It did not, however, reach Bossuet, who died that year. Bishop Bull followed him in 1709.

Nelson was well acquainted, though scarcely intimate, with Bishop Beveridge, Bull's contemporary at St. Asaphs. The two prelates were men of much the same stamp. Both were divines of great theological learning; but while Bull's great talents were chiefly conspicuous in his controversial and argumentative works, Beveridge was chiefly eminent as a student and devotional writer. His 'Private Thoughts on Religion and Christian Life,' and his papers on 'Public Prayer' and 'Frequent Communions,' have always maintained a high reputation. Like Bull, he was profoundly read in the history of the primitive Church, but possessed an accomplishment which his brother bishop had not, in his understanding of several oriental languages. Like him, he had been an active and experienced parish clergyman, and, like him, he was attached almost to excess to a strict and rigid observance of

---

[1] Secretan, 255.

the appointed order of the English Church. It was to him that Dean Tillotson addressed the often quoted words, ' Doctor, Doctor, Charity is above rubrics.'[1] Yet it must not be inferred therefore, that he was stiffly set against all change. In a sermon preached before Convocation at their very important meeting of 1689, he had remarked of ecclesiastical laws other than those which are fundamental and eternal, ' that they ought not indeed to be altered without grave reasons ; but that such reasons were not at that moment wanting. To unite a scattered flock in one fold under one shepherd, to remove stumbling-blocks from the path of the weak, to reconcile hearts long estranged, to restore spiritual discipline to its primitive vigour, to place the best and purest of Christian societies on a base broad enough to stand against all the attacks of earth and hell—these were objects which might well justify some modification, not of Catholic institutions, but of national and provincial usages.'[2]

Beveridge was one of the bishops for whom the moderate Nonjurors had much regard. In most respects he was of their school of thought ; and although, like Wilson of Sodor and Man, and Hooper of Bath and Wells, he had no scruple, for his own part, to take the oath of allegiance to William and Mary, he fully understood the reasonings of those who had. He greatly doubted the legality and right of appointing new bishops to sees not canonically vacant, so that when he was nominated in the place of Ken, he after some deliberation declined the office. He and Nelson saw a good deal of each other. They were both constant attendants at the weekly meetings of the Society for Promoting Christian Knowledge, an association which Beveridge zealously promoted,[3] and to which he left the greater part of his property. The minutes of the society refer to private consultations between him and Nelson for arranging about a popular edition in Welsh of the Prayer-book, and to the bishop distributing largely in his diocese a translation of Nelson's tract on Confirmation. They also frequently met at the committees of the Society for the Propagation of the Gospel. In his ' Life of Bull ' Nelson

---

[1] Birch's *Life of Tillotson*, lxxxviii.
[2] ' Concio ad Synodum,' quoted by Macaulay, *History of England*, chap. xiv.
[3] Secretan, 135.

speaks in terms of much admiration for Beveridge, whom he calls 'a pattern of true primitive piety.' He praises his plain and affecting sermons, and says that ' he had a way of gaining people's hearts and touching their consciences which bore some resemblance to the apostolical age,' and that he could mention many 'who owed the change of their lives, under God, to his instructions.'[1] Like Bull and Ken, the latter of whom was born in the same year with him, his life belongs chiefly to the history of the preceding century, for he died in 1707 ; his short episcopal career however lay, as was the case with Bull, only in the first decade of the eighteenth.

Sharp, Archbishop of York, must by no means be omitted from the list of Robert Nelson's friends, the more so as he was mainly instrumental in overcoming the scruples which for many years had deterred Nelson from the communion of the national Church. ' It was impossible,' writes the Archbishop's son, ' that such religious men, who were so intimate with each other, and spent many hours together in private conversation, should not frequently discuss the reasons that divided them in Church communion.'[2] Sharp's diary shows that early in 1710 they had many interviews on the subject. His arguments prevailed ; and he records with satisfaction that on Easter Day that year his friend, for the first time since the Revolution, received the Communion at his hands. The Archbishop was well fitted to act this part of a conciliator. In the first place, Nelson held him in high esteem as a man of learning, piety, and discernment, 'who fills one of the archiepiscopal thrones with that universal applause which is due to his distinguishing merit.'[3] This general satisfaction which had attended his promotion qualified him the more for a peacemaker in the Church. At a time when party spirit was more than usually vehement, it was his rare lot to possess in a high degree the respect and confidence of men of all opinions. From his earliest youth he had learnt to appreciate high Christian worth under varied forms. His father had been a fervent Puritan, his mother a strenuous Royalist ; and he speaks with equal gratitude of the deep impressions left upon his mind by the grave piety of the

[1] *Life of Bull,* 64.   [2] Sharp's *Life,* by his Son, ii. 32.   Secretan, 78-9.
[3] *Life of Bull,* 238.

one, and of the admiration instilled into him by the other of the proscribed Liturgy of the English Church. He went up to Cambridge a Calvinist ; he learnt a larger, a happier, and no less spiritual theology under the teaching of More and Cudworth. His studies then took a wide range. He delighted in imaginative literature, especially in Greek poetry, became very fairly versed in Hebrew and the interpretation of the Old Testament, took much pleasure in botany and chemistry, and was at once fascinated with the Newtonian philosophy. He was also an accomplished antiquarian. At a later period, as rector of St. Giles in the Fields, and Friday lecturer at St. Lawrence Jewry, he gained much fame as one of the most persuasive and affecting preachers of his age. Tillotson and Clagett were his most intimate friends ; and among his acquaintances were Stillingfleet, Patrick, Beveridge, Cradock, Whichcot, Calamy, Scot, Sherlock, Wake, and Cave, including all that eminent circle of London clergy who were at that time the distinguishing ornament of the English Church, and who constantly met at one another's houses to confer on the religious and ecclesiastical questions of the day. There was perhaps no one eminent divine, at the end of the seventeenth and beginning of the eighteenth century, who had so much in sympathy with men of either section of the English Church. He was claimed by the Tories and High Churchmen ; and no doubt, on the majority of subjects his views agreed with theirs, particularly in the latter part of his life. But his opinions were very frequently modified by a more liberal training and by more generous and considerate ideas than were common among them. He voted with them against occasional Conformity, protested against any enfeebling of the Test Acts, and took, it must be acknowledged, a far from tolerant line generally in the debates of 1704-9 relating to the liberties of Dissenters. On the other hand, he indignantly resented the unworthy attempt of the more extreme Tories to force the occasional Conformity Act through the House of Lords by ' tacking ' it to a money bill. He expressed the utmost displeasure against anything like bitterness and invective ; he had been warmly in favour of a moderate comprehension of Dissenters, had voted that Tillotson should be prolocutor when the scheme was submitted to Convocation, and had himself taken part of the responsibility of revision. As in 1675 he had somewhat unadvisedly accepted, in the discussion with Nonconformists, the co-operation of Dodwell, so, in 1707, he bestowed much praise on Hickes' answer to Tindal (sent to him by Nelson) on behalf of the rights of the Christian priesthood. But Dodwell's Book of Schism maintained much more exclusive sentiments than Sharp's sermon on Conscience, of which it was professedly a defence ; nor could the Archbishop by any means coincide in the more immoderate opinions of the hot-tempered nonjuring Dean. And so far from agreeing with Hickes and Dodwell, who would acknowledge none other than Episcopal Churches, he said that if he were abroad he should communicate with the foreign Reformed Churches wherever he happened to be.[1] On many points of doctrine he was a High Churchman : he entirely agreed, for example, with Nelson and the Nonjurors in general, in regretting the omission in King Edward's second Prayer-book of the prayer of oblation.[2] He bestowed much pains in maintaining the dignity and efficiency of his cathedral ;[3] but, with a curious intermixture of Puritan feeling, told one of his Nonconformist correspondents that he did not much approve of musical services, and would be glad if the law would permit an alteration.[4] In regard of the questions specially at issue with the Nonjurors, he heartily assented for his own part to the principles of the Revolution, maintaining 'for a certain truth that as the law makes the king, so the same law extends or limits or transfers our obedience and allegiance.'[5] This being the case, it may at first appear unintelligible that an ardent nonjuring champion of passive obedience and non-resistance should assert that 'by none are these truly Catholic doctrines more openly avowed than by the present excellent metropolitan of York.'[6] But Dodwell was correct. Archbishop Sharp, with perfect consistency, combined with Whig politics the favourite High Church tenet of the Jacobean era. He strenuously maintained the duty of

---

[1] *Life*, by his Son, ii. 28.   [2] Secretan, 178.
[3] 'None,' said Willis in his *Survey of Cathedrals*, 'were so well served as that of York, under Sharp.'—*Life of Sharp*, i. 120.
[4] *Thoresby's Correspondence.* i. 274.   [5] *Life*, i. 264.
[6] Dodwell's 'Case in View,' quoted in Lathbury's *History of the Nonjurors*, 197.

passive obedience, not however to the sovereign monarch, but
to the sovereign law.[1] At the same time, he felt much sympathy with the Nonjurors, and was sometimes accused of Jacobitism because he would not drop his acquaintance with them,
nor disguise his pity for the sacrifices in which their principles
involved them.   When a choice was given him of two or
three of the sees vacated by the deprivation of the nonjuring
bishops, he declined the offer.   He would not allow that
there had been any real unlawfulness or irregularity in their
dispossession, but as a matter of personal feeling he disliked
the idea of accepting promotion under such circumstances.
Although therefore, in many ways, he differed much in opinion
from the Nonjurors, he possessed in a great degree their
attachment and respect.   Robert Nelson was neither the
only one of them with whom he was on terms of cordial
friendship, nor was he by any means the only one whom he
persuaded to return to the Established Communion.

Bishop Smalridge of Bristol should be referred to, however briefly, in connection with the truly worthy man who is
the main subject of this paper.   He was constantly associated
with Nelson in his various works of charity, especially in for-
warding missionary undertakings, in assisting Dr. Bray's
projects of parochial lending libraries, and as a royal commissioner with him for the increase of church accommodation.
Nelson bequeathed to him his Madonna by Correggio 'as a
small testimony of that great value and respect I bear to
his lordship ; '[2] and to his accomplished pen is owing the very
beautiful Latin epitaph placed to his friend's memory in St.
George's Chapel.[3] Under the name of ' Favonius,' he is spoken
of in the ' Tatler ' in the warmest language of admiring respect,
as a very humane and good man, of well-tempered zeal and
touching eloquence, and ' abounding with that sort of virtue
and knowledge which makes religion beautiful.'[4] Bishop
Newton has also spoken very highly of him, and adds that he
was a man of much gravity and dignity and of great complacency and sweetness of manner.[5] In reference to this last

---

[1] *Life*, i. 264.   [2] Secretan, 285.
[3] Nichol's Lit. An. i. 190.   [4] Nos. 72 and 114.
[5] Bishop Newton's *Life and Works*, i. 7.   Whiston spoke of him as ' one of the
most learned and excellent persons in the nation.'—*Life of Clark*, 30. A mention
occurs of him in Lady Cowper's Diary (1714-20) which gives a fair sample of the

feature of his character, it was said of him, when he succeeded Atterbury as Dean of Carlisle, that he carried the bucket to extinguish the fires which the other had kindled. His political sympathies, however, accorded with those of Atterbury, and brought him into close relation with the Nonjurors. Although he had submitted to the new Constitution, he was a thorough Jacobite in feeling. His Thirtieth of January sermons were sometimes marked with an extravagance of expression [1] foreign to his usual manner; and he and Atterbury, with whom he had recently edited Lord Clarendon's History, were the only bishops who refused to sign the declaration of abhorrence of the Rebellion of 1715.[2]

Smalridge and Nelson had a mutual friend,[3] whom they both highly valued, in Dr. Ernest Grabe, a Prussian of remarkable character and great erudition, who had settled in England under the especial favour of King William. Dissatisfied as to the validity of Lutheran orders, he had at first turned his thoughts to Rome, not unaware that he should find in that Church many departures from the simplicity of the early faith, but feeling that it possessed at all events that primitive constitution which he had learnt to consider essential. He was just about to take this step, when he met with Spener, the eminent leader of the German Pietists, to whom he communicated his difficulties, and who pointed out to him the Church of England as a communion likely to meet his wants. He came to this country,[4] at the end of the seventeenth century, received a royal pension, took priest's orders, and continued with indefatigable labour his patristic studies. It

theological and ecclesiastical gossip in Queen Caroline's court. Some had been extolling Smalridge to the Princess as 'the greatest saint upon earth.' Some one on the other side informs her, which 'till this morning she had never known, that he was one of Dr. Sacheverell's speechmakers.' Mrs. Clayton redresses the balance by observing that 'Dr. Smalridge had said to her that every private Christian was not obliged to believe every part of the Athanasian Creed.'—*Diary of Mary Countess Cowper*, 1864. Hearne records as a promising sign of the amelioration of the stage, that the bishop had been to the play to see Addison's 'Cato' acted.—*Reliquiæ*, ii. 163. Smalridge was one of the most distinguished adherents to Bishop Berkeley's philosophy.—Berkeley's *Life and Works*, iv. 62.

[1] 'Animadversions on the two last January 30 sermons,' 1702. The same might be said of his 'Sermon before the Court of Aldermen,' January 30, 1704.

[2] Lord Mahon's *History of England*, chap. 12.   [3] Secretan, 223.

[4] The parallel with an interesting portion of I. Casaubon's life is singularly close. See Pattison's *Isaac Casaubon*, chap. 5.

became the great project of his life to maintain a close communication between the English and Lutheran Churches,[1] to
bring about in Prussia a restoration of episcopacy, and to introduce there a liturgy composed upon the English model. It
cannot be said that the general course of theological thought
in England was at this time very congenial to his aspirations;
but his great learning and the earnest sincerity of his ideas
were widely appreciated, and within a somewhat confined
circle of High Churchmen and Nonjurors he was cordially
welcomed, and his services highly valued. He pushed his
conformity to what he considered the usages of the Primitive
Church to the verge of eccentricity. But 'indeed,' says Kennett
without any sympathy in his practices, but with a kindly
smile, 'his piety and our charity may cover all this.'[2]

Dr. Thomas Bray may stand as a fit representative of
another class of Nelson's friends and associates. So far from
agreeing with Nelson in his Nonjuring sentiments, the prospect of the constitutional change had kindled in him enthusiastic expectations 'Good Dr. Bray,' remarks Whiston, 'had
said how happy and religious the nation would become when
the House of Hanover came, and was very indignant when
Mr. Mason said that matters would not be mended.'[3] He
accepted a living which had been vacated by a Nonjuring
clergyman, but spent alike his clerical and private means in
the benevolent and Christian hearted schemes to which the
greater part of his life was dedicated.[4] It is not the purpose
of this chapter to discuss the missionary and other philanthropical activities which at the close of the seventeenth and the
opening of the eighteenth centuries resulted in the formation of
the Society for Promoting Christian Knowledge, the Society for
the Propagation of the Gospel in Foreign Parts, and other
kindred associations. It may be sufficient here to repeat the
warm-hearted encomium of his fellow labourer in this noble
work: 'I am sure he has been one of the greatest instruments for propagating Christian knowledge this age has pro-

---

[1] In conjunction with Archbishop Sharp, Smalridge, and Jablouski, &c. See
Chapter on 'Comprehension, &c.'

[2] Secretan, 221, note. Nelson gives a full account of Dr. Grabe in his *Life of
Bull*, 343-6.

[3] Memoirs, 154.   [4] *Life of Ken*, by a Layman, 619-20.

duced. The libraries abroad, our society (the S.P.C.K.), and the Corporation (the S.P.G.) are owing to his unwearied solicitations.'[1] In organising the American Church, in plans for civilising and christianising the Indians, in establishing libraries for the use of missionaries and the poorer clergy in the colonies, on shipboard, in seaport towns, and in the secluded parishes of England and Wales, in translations of the Liturgy and other devotional books, in the reformation of prisons, in measures taken for the better suppression of crime and profligacy,—Bray and Nelson, with General Oglethorpe and other active coadjutors, helped one another with all their heart. They met in the board-room of the two great societies, in one another's houses, and sometimes they may have talked over their projects with Bishop Ken at the seat of their generous supporter, Lord Weymouth.[2]

The names of many other men, more or less eminent in their day for piety or learning, might be added to the list of those who possessed and valued Robert Nelson's friendship ; among them may be mentioned—Dr. John Mapletoft, with whom he maintained a close correspondence for no less than forty years : a man who had travelled much and learnt many languages, a celebrated physician, and afterwards, when he took orders, an accomplished London preacher ; Francis Gastrell, Bishop of Chester, Mapletoft's son-in-law ;[3] Sir Richard Blackmore, another physician of note, and, like Mapletoft, most zealous in all plans for doing good, but whose unlucky taste for writing dull verses brought down upon him the unmerciful castigation of the wits ; John Johnson of Cranbrook, with whose writings on the Eucharistic Sacrifice Nelson most warmly sympathised ; Edmund Halley, the mathematician, his school playmate and life-long friend; Ralph Thoresby, an antiquarian of high repute, a moderate Dissenter in earlier life, a thoughtful and earnest Churchman in late years, but who throughout life maintained warm and intimate relations with many leading members of either communion ;

[1] Secretan, 142.

[2] Oglethorpe and Nelson sometimes met there. Secretan, 211.

[3] He was one of the many writers against the Deists. It was to his credit, that although he had been strongly opposed to Atterbury in controversy, he earnestly supported him in what he thought an oppressive prosecution.—Williams' *Memoirs of Atterbury*, i. 417.

Dr. Charlett, Master of University College, Oxford; Dr. Cave, the well-known writer of early Church History, to whose literary help he was frequently indebted; John Evelyn; Samuel, father of John and Charles Wesley, whose verses, written on the fly-leaf of his copy of the 'Festivals and Fasts,' commemorative of his attachment to Nelson and of his reverence for his virtues, used to be prefixed to some editions of his friend's works; nor should the list be closed without the addition of the name of the eminent Gallican bishop Bossuet, with whom he had become acquainted in France, and had kept up the interesting correspondence already noticed in connection with Bishop Bull.

The group composed of Nelson and his friends, of whom he had many, and never lost one, would be pleasant to contemplate, if for no other reason, yet as the picture of a set of earnest men, united in common attachment to one central figure, varying much on some points of opinion, but each endeavouring to live worthily of the Christian faith. From one point of view the features of dissimilarity among his friends are more interesting than those of resemblance. A Churchman, with whom Jurors and Nonjurors met on terms of equal cordiality, who was intimate alike with Tillotson and Hickes—whose love for Ken was nowise incompatible with much esteem for Kidder, the 'uncanonical usurper' of his see—and who consulted for the advancement of Christian knowledge as readily with Burnet, Patrick, and Fowler, as with Bull, Beveridge, and Sharp—represents a sort of character which every national Church ought to produce in abundance, but which stands out in grateful relief from the contentions which embittered the first years of the century and the spiritual dulness which set in soon afterwards.

Yet, though Robert Nelson had too warm a heart to sacrifice the friendship of a good man to any difference of opinion, and too hearty a zeal in good works to let his personal predilections stand in the way of them, he belonged very distinctively to the High Church party. Some of his best and most prominent characteristics did not connect him with one more than with another section of the Church. The philanthropical activity, which did so much to preserve him from narrowness and intolerance, was, as Tillotson has observed, one of the most redeeming features of the period in which he lived ;[1] the genial serenity of his religion is like the spirit that breathed in Addison. But all his deeper sympathies were with the High Churchmen and Nonjurors—men who had been brought up in that spirit of profound attachment to Anglo-Catholic theology and feeling which was prominent among Church of England divines in the age that succeeded the Commonwealth.

The Church party of which, at the beginning of the eighteenth century, Nelson and his friends were worthy representatives, was rapidly losing strength. Soon after his death it had almost ceased to exist as a visible and united power. The general tone of feeling in Church matters became so unfavourable to its continued vigour, that it gradually dwindled away. Not that there was no longer a High Church, and even a strong High Church party. There has been no period in the history of the Reformed English Church in which the three leading varieties of opinion, so familiar to us at the present day, may not be distinctly traced. The eighteenth century is certainly no exception ; from its first to its last year so-called High Churchmen were abundant everywhere, especially among the clergy. But they would scarcely have been recognised as such by Nelson, or by those with whom he chiefly sympathised. The type became altered, and not for the better. A change had already set in before the seventeenth century closed. When in quick succession Bull and Beveridge, Ken and Nelson, passed away, there were no new men who could exactly supply their places. The High Churchmen who belonged more distinctly to Queen Anne's reign, and those of the succeeding

---

[1] S. xx. *Works*, ii. 252. Similar observations frequently occur, e.g. *Guardian* (1713) No. 79 ; De Foe's *Tour through Great Britain* (1737) ii. 133 ; Worthington's *Essay on Redemption* (c. 1740) 136 ; Bishop Law's *Theory of Religion* (1745), 281 ; Fielding's *Covent Garden Journal* (1752), No. 44 ; Malcolm's *Manners of London* (1760–70) i. 17 ; Jortin's *Tracts on different subjects* (1755) ii. 530 ; Hannah More's *Religion of the Fashionable World* (1790) chap. ii. *Works*, xi. 87–9. But the *Guardian* added that such benevolence was mainly limited to those of the middle sort (see also W. Harte's *Poems, Eulogius*, ad finem) : and Hannah More bids those who regarded too complacently 'The Age of Benevolence' remember, that there was no longer so much of that private but widespread and thoughtful beneficence which was practised when 'great people staid at home.'

Georgian era, lacked some of the higher qualities of the preceding generations. They numbered many worthy, excellent men, but there was no longer the same depth of feeling, the same fervour, the same spirit of willing self-denial, the same constant reference to a supposed higher standard of primitive usage. Their High Churchmanship took rather the form of an ecclesiastical toryism, persuaded more than ever of the unique excellence of the English Church, its divinely constituted government, and its high, if not exclusive title to purity and orthodoxy of doctrine. The whole party shared, in fact, to a very great extent in the spiritual dulness which fell like a blight upon the religious life of the country at large. A secondary, but still an important difference, consisted in the change effected by the Revolution in the relation between the Church and the Crown. The harsh revulsion of sentiment, however beneficial in its ultimate consequences, could not fail to detract for the time from that peculiar tone of semi-religious loyalty which in previous generations had been at once the weakness and the glory of the English Church.

The nonjuring separation was a serious and long-lasting loss to the Church of England ; a loss corresponding in kind, if not in degree, to what it might have endured, if by a different turn of political and ecclesiastical circumstances, the most zealous members of the section headed by Tillotson and Burnet had been ejected from its fold. It is the distinguishing merit of the English Church that, to a greater extent probably than any other religious body, it is at once Catholic and Protestant, and that without any formal assumption of reconciling the respective claims of authority and private judgment, it admits a wide field for the latter, without ceasing to attach veneration and deference to primitive antiquity and to long established order. It is most true that 'the Church herself is greater, wider, older than any of the parties within her ;'[1] but it is no less certain that when a leading party becomes enfeebled in character and influence, as it was by the defection to the Nonjurors of so many learned and self-sacrificing High Churchmen, the diminution of vital energy in the whole body is likely to be far more than pro-

[1] Bishop Magee, Charge at Northampton, October 1872.

portionate to the number of the seceders, or even to their individual weight.

Judged by modern feeling, there might seem no very apparent reason why the Nonjurors should have belonged nearly, if not quite exclusively, to the same general school of theological thought. In our own days, the nature of a man's Churchmanship is no key whatever to his opinions upon matters which trench on politics. High sacramental theories, or profound reverence for Church tradition and ancient usage, or decided views as to the exclusive rights of an episcopally ordained ministry, are almost as likely to be combined with liberal, or even with democratic politics, as with the most staunch conservative opinions. No one imagines that any possible change of constitutional government would greatly affect the general bias, whatever it might be, of ecclesiastical thought. But the Nonjurors were all High Churchmen, and that in a much better sense of that word than when, in Queen's Anne's time, Tory and High Church were in popular language convertible terms. And though they were not by any means the sole representatives of the older High Church spirit—for some who were deeply imbued with it took the oath of allegiance with perfect conscientiousness, and without the least demur—yet in them it was chiefly embodied. Professor Blunt remarks with much truth, that to a great extent they carried away with them that regard for primitive times, which with them was destined by degrees almost to expire.[1] If the Nonjurors were nearly allied with the Jacobites on the one side, they were also the main supporters of religious opinions which were in no way related with one dynasty of sovereigns rather than with another, but which have always formed a very important element of English Church history, and could not pass for the time into comparative oblivion without a corresponding loss.

The doctrines of non-resistance and passive obedience, in defence of which so much was once written, and so many sacrifices endured, are now no longer heard of. Theories based upon the divine right of kings are regarded only as fictions, lingering here and there amongst the traditions of continental statecraft. Even before the close of the eighteenth

---

[1] J. J. Blunt, *Early Fathers*, 19 ; also Archbishop Manning's *Essays*, Series 2, 4.

century, Bishop Horsley, in a 30th of January sermon,[1] directed against republican opinions, called it 'an exploded notion' to believe that monarchs rule by any title more indefeasible than belongs to all duly constituted government. It is difficult now to realise with what passionate fervour of conviction these obsolete theories were once maintained by many Englishmen as a vital portion, not only of their political, but of their religious creed. Lord Chancellor Somers, whose able treatise upon the Rights of Kings brought to bear against the Nonjurors a vast array of arguments from Reason, Scripture, History, and Law, remarked in it that there were some divines of the Church of England who instilled notions of absolute power, passive obedience, and non-resistance, as essential points of religion, doctrines necessary to salvation.[2] Put in this extreme form, the belief might have been repudiated ; but undoubtedly passages may be quoted in great abundance from nonjuring and other writers which, literally understood, bear no other construction. At all events, sentiments scarcely less uncompromising were continually held, not by mere sycophants and courtiers, but by many whose opinions were adorned by noble Christian lives, willing self-sacrifice, and undaunted resolution. Good Bishop Lake of Chichester said on his deathbed that 'he looked upon the great doctrine of passive obedience as the distinguishing character of the Church of England,'[3] and that it was a doctrine for which he hoped he could lay down his life. Bishop Thomas of Worcester, who died the same year, expressed the same belief and the same hope. Robert Nelson spoke of it as the good and wholesome doctrine of the Church of England, 'wherein she has gloried as her special characteristic. . . . Papists and Presbyterians have both been tardy on these points, and I wish the practice of some in the Church of England had been more blameless,'[4] but he was sure that it had been the doctrine of the primitive Christians, and that it was very plainly avowed both by the Church and State of

---

[1] Horsley's Sermon before the House of Lords, January 30, 1793. In Wordsworth's *Christian Institutes*, iii. 34.

[2] Lord Somers' 'Judgment of whole Kingdoms. . . . As to Rights of Kings,' 1710, § 117.

[3] *Life of Kettlewell*, App. No. 13. Kettlewell uses the same words, Id. p. 87.

[4] Letter to his Nephew, Nichol's *Lit. An.* iv. 219.

England. Sancroft vehemently reproved ' the apostacy of the National Church' [1] in departing from this point of faith. Even Tillotson and Burnet [2] were at one time no less decided about it. The former urged it upon Lord Russell as 'the declared doctrine of all Protestant Churches,' and that the contrary was ' a very great and dangerous mistake,' and that if not a sin of ignorance, 'it will appear of a much more heinous nature, as in truth it is, and calls for a very particular and deep repentance.' [3] Just about the time when the new oath of allegiance was imposed, the doctrine of non resistance received the very aid it most needed, in the invention of a new term admirably adapted to inspire a warmer feeling of religious enthusiasm in those who were preparing to suffer in its cause. The expression appears to have originated with Kettlewell, who had strongly felt the force of an objection which had been raised to Bishop Lake's declaration. It had been said that to call this or that doctrine the distinguishing characteristic of a particular Church was so far forth to separate it from the Church Catholic. Kettlewell saw at once that this argument wounded High Churchmen in the very point where they were most sensitive, and for the future preferred to speak of non-resistance as characteristically ' a Doctrine of the Cross.' [4] The epithet was quickly adopted, and no doubt was frequently a source of consolation to Nonjurors. At other times it might have conveyed a painful sense of disproportion in its application to what, from another point of view, was a mere political revolution. But with them passive obedience and divine right had been raised to the level of a great religious principle for which they were well content to be confessors. It must have added much to the moral strength of the nonjuring separation. Argument or ridicule would not make much impression upon men who had always this to fall back upon, that ' non-resistance is after all too much a doctrine of the Cross, not to meet with great opposition from the prejudices and passions of men. Flesh and blood and corrupt reason will set up the great law of self-

---

[1] Lathbury, 94.
[2] A letter from Burnet to Compton, quoted from the Rawl. MSS. in *Life of Ken*, 527.
[3] Birch's *Tillotson*, lxxv.
[4] *Life of Kettlewell*, 87.

preservation against it, and find a thousand absurdities and contradictions in it.'[1]   How thoroughly Kettlewell's term was adopted, and how deeply the feeling which it represented was cherished by the saintliest of the High Churchmen of that age, is nowhere more remarkably instanced than in some very famous words of Bishop Ken.   In that often quoted passage of his will where he professed the faith in which he died, the closing words refer to the Church of England 'as it stands distinguished from all Papal and Puritan innovations, and as it adheres to the doctrine of the Cross.'   The special interpretation to be placed upon the final clause somewhat jars upon the ear, although not without interest in illustrating the strong religious principle which forbade the transfer of his political allegiance.   Dr. Lee, who had excellent opportunities of knowing, says, 'there cannot remain any manner of doubt'[2] that Ken used the expression with particular reference to the sense in which his friend Kettlewell had used it.

When once the Hanoverian succession was established, the doctrine of a divine right of kings, with the theories consequent upon it, passed gradually away; and many writers, forgetting that it was once a generally received dogma in Parliament as in Convocation, in the laws as much as in the homilies, have sought to attach to the Church of England the odium of servility and obsequiousness for its old adherence to it.   But as the tenet died not without honour, dignified in many instances by high Christian feeling, and noble sacrifice of worldly interest, so also it had gained much of its early strength in one of the most important principles of the Reformation.   When England rejected the Papacy, the Church, as in the old English days before the Conquest, gathered round its sovereign as the emblem and as the centre of its national independence.   Only the tie was a personal one; much in the same way as the Pope had been far more than an embodied symbol of Church authority.   The sovereign represented the people, but no one then spoke of 'sovereignty residing in the whole body of the people,'[3] or dreamt of as-

---

[1] Whaley, N., Sermon before the University of Oxford, January 30, 1710. 16.
[2] Lee's *Life of Kettlewell*, 167.
[3] Warburton's ' Alliance,' iv. 173.

serting that the supremacy of the King was a fiction, meaning only the supremacy of the three estates.[1] So it long continued, especially in the Church. Ecclesiastical is ever wont to lag somewhat in the rear of political improvement. In the State, the personal supremacy of the sovereign, though a very strong reality in the hands of the Tudors, had been tutored into a moderately close conformity with the wishes of the popular representatives. In the Church, the same process was going on, but it was a far more gradual one; and the spirit of loyal deference which long remained unaltered in the one, gained increasing strength in the other. Upon the reaction which succeeded after the Commonwealth, the Church, as it had been ever faithful to the royal fortunes in their time of reverse, shared to the full in the effusion with which the nation in general greeted the return of monarchy, and was more than ever dazzled by the 'divinity which hedges round a King.' But under James II., the Church had cause to feel the perils of arbitrary power as keenly, or even more keenly than the nation in its civil capacity. By a remarkable leading of events, the foremost of the High Church bishops found themselves, amid the acclamations of the multitude, in the very van of a resistance which was indeed in a sense passive, but which plainly paved the way to active resistance on the part of others, and which, as they must themselves have felt, strained to the utmost that doctrine of passive obedience which was still dear to them as ever. Some even of the most earnest champions of the divine right of kings were at last compelled to imagine circumstances under which the tenet would cease to be tenable. What if James should propose to hand over Ireland to France as the price of help against his own people? Ken, it is said, acknowledged that under such a contingency he should feel wholly released from his allegiance.

The revolution of 1688 dissipated the halo which had shed a fictitious light round the throne. Queen Anne may

---

[1] 'The supremacy of the Queen is, in the sense used by the noble lord, no better than a fiction. There might have been such a supremacy down to the times of James II., but now there is no supremacy but that of the three estates of the realm and the supremacy of the law. The Queen is the Chief of the Established Church.'—On the 'Ecclesiastical Titles Bill,' May 12, 1851. J. Bright's *Speeches,* ii. 475.

have flattered herself that it was already reviving. George I.
in his first speech to parliament laid claim to the ancient
prestige of it.[1] The old theories lingered long in manor-houses
and parsonages, and among all whose hearts were with the
banished Stuarts. But they could not permanently survive
under such altered auspices; and a sentiment which had once
been of real service both to Church and State, but which had
become injurious to both, was disrooted from the constitution·
and disentangled from the religion of the country. The
ultimate gain was great ; yet it must be acknowledged that
at the time a great price was paid for it. In the State, there
was a notable loss of the old loyalty, a blunting in public
matters of some of the finer feelings, an increase among State
officers of selfish and interested motives, a spirit of murmuring
and disaffection, a lowering of tone, an impaired national
unity. In the Church, as the revulsion was greater, and in
some respects the benefit greater, so also the temporary loss
was both greater and more permanent. The beginning of
the eighteenth century saw almost the last of the old-fashioned
Anglicans, who dated from the time of Henry VIII.—men
whose ardent love of what they considered primitive and
Catholic usage had no tinge of Popery, and whose devoted
attachment to the throne was wholly free from all unmanly
servility. The High Church party was deprived of some of the
best of its leaders, and was altogether divided, disorganised,
and above all, lowered in tone ; and the whole Church suffered in the deterioration of one of its principal sections.

Without here taking into account that widely diffused
Jacobite sentiment which consisted in various degrees of
affection for the late dynasty, and dislike of the house of
Hanover, there were many high-minded men of High Church
views whose principles of obedience and divine right were
amply sufficient, apart from all other considerations, to make
a transfer of their loyalty impossible. Dislike, too, of the religious principles prevalent in the Dutch republic, and a
number of other causes, combined to make Nonjurors.

But the oath of allegiance introduced among the difficulties of the time a new set of perplexing elements, directly
connected with great principles of religious and moral obliga-

---

[1] Campbell's *Lives of the Chancellors,* iv. 351.

tion. Until a comparatively recent period, the national conscience has been subjected to a demoralising strain by the imposition of needless oaths, exacted on a great variety of occasions, and frequently where, from carelessness, ignorance, or the very conditions of human nature, they were exceedingly liable to be broken. A hundred and eighty years ago, when oaths or subscriptions were required on numberless occasions as an all but invariable condition of office, there was certain to be a corresponding laxity with regard to the obligations contained in them. Whiston remarked severely upon it. He did not know, he said, which were most to be condemned— they who imposed so many doubtful oaths, or they who took them with doubtful and dissatisfied minds. It seemed to him that the 'custom-house oaths,' which had become a proverb, were not much more insincere than similar asseverations elsewhere. He quoted the words of Jeremiah, that 'because of swearing the land mourneth,' and was evidently of opinion that many had taken the new oaths carelessly, many dubiously, and not a few against their better consciences.[1] At the same time, it was generally understood that the oath of allegiance stands upon a peculiar footing of its own, and it was very natural that conscientious men should often have been much perplexed as to the interpretation which should be put upon it. There were probably no Whigs whose conscience compelled them to be Nonjurors, as being bound by the oaths they had taken under King James. Even the most scrupulous among them were unanimous in supposing that the oath rested upon an implied contract between sovereign and people, and that they had been absolved from its obligations by the King's pronounced violation of it. The question had been thoroughly discussed at the Revolution, and their opinion had been amply justified both by reason and precedent. All future doubts on the point were obviated by the clearer language of the statutes of William III.; but even from the most ancient times the idea of a compact had been always implied and sometimes expressed in the oath of allegiance, and distinguished jurists had declared in unmistakable terms for the subjection of the King to the supremacy of law. Many High Churchmen and Tories agreed in these views, and took the

[1] *Memoirs*, 32-3, 412.

oath,[1] when other considerations admitted of it, if not willingly; at all events without scruple as to its lawfulness ; some allowed the general principle, but disputed the application of it ; some, on the other hand, altogether denied that they could be dispensed from their previous obligation. There was in fact the greatest variety of opinion on the subject ; [2] and what Kettlewell chiefly found fault with in many of the clergy was not that they adopted one opinion rather than another, but that they should treat with so much indifference a matter where the morality of an oath was at stake. 'A true Christian,' he said, 'ought to be ready to suffer for any point of morality and justice as well as for any point of orthodoxy in faith or purity in divine worship.'[3] Amid so many perplexities and doubts, we can well understand how the final decision should in some cases form a spiritual crisis in a man's life. Thus, it is said of William Law that his refusal to take the oath was the first step taken towards a more perfect and entire devotion.[4]

The abrupt change in the State prayers was a point which, quite independently of political views, must have been a great jar to feelings of religion, truthfulness, and consistency. In 1687 and 1688 they had been called to pray for King James that 'his seed might endure for ever,' and 'be set up after him, and his house and kingdom be established,' that their 'gracious King might be prospered in all his undertakings,'[5] and that 'the princely infant might excel in all virtues becoming to the royal dignity to which God had ordained him.'[6] A few months after, public prayers were being offered that their late monarch as one of the enemies of the new King, might he 'vanquished and overcome,' and that not James, but William, might be 'protected in person and his hands strengthened.'[7] All this was no doubt unavoidable, and the inconsistency more apparent than real. When the country had decreed that James had broken the compact in virtue of

---

[1] Bishop Wilson's advice to a person who was uneasy about the oath of allegiance was concise and epigrammatic. 'It is safer to obey authority with a doubting conscience, than with a doubting conscience to disobey.'—Cruttwell's *Life of Wilson*, 129.

[2] *Life of Kettlewell*, 92. Whiston's *Memoirs*, 30.

[3] Id. 175.   [4] Tighe's *Life of W. Law*, 30.

[5] Id. 119.   [6] Id. App. xi. xvi.   [7] Id.

which he reigned, the prayers which had been offered for him as lawful sovereign must evidently cease. But to many, to the clergy especially, and to those of Jacobite sentiments most of all, the change was naturally productive of much uneasiness.

Even the Nonjurors did not altogether escape the difficulty. In relation both to them and to persons who, as a duty or a necessity, had accepted the new constitution, but were more or less Jacobite in their sympathies, a question arose of far more than temporary interest. It is one which frequently recurs, and is of much practical importance, namely, how far unity of worship implies, or ought to imply, a close unity of belief ; and secondly, how far a clergyman is justified in continuing his ministrations if, agreeing in all essentials, he strongly dissents to some particular petitions or expressions in the services of which he is constituted the mouthpiece. The point immediately at issue was whether those who dissented from the State prayers could join with propriety in the public services. This was very variously decided. There were some who denied that this was possible to persons who had any strict regard to consistency and truth.[1] How, said they, could they assist by their presence at public prayers which were utterly contradictory to their private ones ? Many Nonjurors therefore, and many who had taken the oath on the understanding that it only bound them to submission, absented themselves entirely from public worship, or attended none other than nonjuring services. There was a considerable party, headed unfortunately by Sancroft himself, whose regret at the separation thus caused was greatly tempered by a kind of exultation at being, as they maintained, the ' orthodox and Catholic remnant ' from which the main body of the English Church had apostatised.[2] Far different were the feelings of those whose opinions on the subject were less strangely exaggerated. If they joined the nonjuring communion, and forsook the familiar parish church, they did so sadly and reluctantly, and looked forward in hope to some change of circumstances which might remove their scruples and end the schism. It was thoroughly dis-

---

[1] Lathbury, 129. *Life of Kettlewell,* 139.
[2] Lathbury, 94.

tasteful to men like Ken, Nelson, and Dodwell, to break away
from a communion to which they were deeply attached, and
which they were quite persuaded was the purest and best in
Christendom.   When the new Government was fairly established, when the heat of feeling was somewhat cooled by
time, when the High Church sympathies of Anne had begun
to reconcile them to the new succession, and when the last of
the ejected bishops had withdrawn all claim on their obedience,
many moderate Nonjurors were once more seen in church.
They agreed that the offence of the State prayers should be
no longer an insuperable bar.[1]   They could at all events
sufficiently signify their objection to the obnoxious words by
declining to say Amen, or by rising from their knees, or by
various other more or less demonstrative signs of disapproba-
tion.   Some indeed of the Nonjurors, among whom Bishop
Frampton was prominent, and a great number of Jacobites,
had never from the first lent any countenance to the schism,
and attended the Church services as heretofore.   The oath of
allegiance being required before a clergyman could take
office, it is of course impossible to tell whether any nonjuring
clergyman would have consented to read, as well as to listen
to, the State prayers.   But there was undoubtedly a large
body of Jacobite clergymen who in various ways reconciled
this to their conscience.   Their argument, founded on the
sort of provisional loyalty due to a *de facto* sovereignty, was
a tolerably valid one in its kind ; a far more important one,
in the extent and gravity of its bearings, was that which met
the difficulty in the face.   It was that which rests on the answer
to the question whether a clergyman is guilty of insincerity,
either in reality or in semblance, in continuing to read a
service to part of which he strongly objects, though he is
completely in accord with the general tone and spirit of the
whole.   The answer must evidently be a qualified one.
Nothing could be worse for the interests of religion, than that
its ministers should be suspected of saying what they do not
mean ; on the other hand, unless a Church concedes to its
clergy a sufficiently ample latitude in their mode of interpreting its formularies, it will greatly suffer by losing the

---

[1] Dodwell's *Further Prospect of the Case in View*, 1707, 19, 111, quoted in
Lathbury, 201, 203.

services of men of independent thought or strongly marked religious convictions. Among clergymen who submitted to the reigning powers, though their hopes and sympathies were centred at St. Germains, the alternative of either reading the State prayers or relinquishing office in the English Church must have been singularly embarrassing. To offer up a prayer in which the heart wholly belies the lip is infinitely more repugnant to religious and moral feeling than to put a legitimate, though it may not be the most usual, interpretation on words which contain a disputed point of doctrine or discipline. Yet, from another point of view, it was quite certain that as little weight as possible ought to be attached to a quasi-political difference of opinion which in itself was no sort of interruption to that confidence and sympathy in religious matters which should subsist between pastor and people. It was a great strait for a conscientious man to be placed in, and a difficulty which might fairly be left to the individual conscience to solve.

As for those Nonjurors and Jacobites who joined as laymen in the public services, undeterred by prayers which they objected to, it is just that question of dissent within, instead of without the Church, which has gained increased attention in our own days. When Robert Nelson was in doubt upon the subject, and asked Tillotson for his advice, the Archbishop made reply, 'As to the case you put, I wonder men should be divided in opinion about it. I think it plain, that no man can join in prayers in which there is any petition which he is verily persuaded is sinful. I cannot endure a trick anywhere, much less in religion.'[1] This honest and outspoken answer was however extremely superficial, and, coming from a man of so much eminence, must have had an unfortunate effect in extending the nonjuring schism. Although his opinion was perfectly sound under the precise terms in which it is stated, the whole force of it rests on the word 'sinful.' If any word is used which falls the least short of this, Tillotson's remark becomes altogether questionable. Of course no one can be justified in countenancing what 'he is verily persuaded is sinful.' From this point of view, there were some Nonjurors to whom separation from the National

[1] Birch's *Life of Tillotson*, clxxxiii.

L 2

Church was a moral necessity. Those among them, for
instance, who drew up, or cordially approved, the 'Form for
admitting penitents,' in which the sorrow-stricken wanderer
in ways of conformity returns humblest thanks for his return
from wrong to right, from error to truth, from schism to unity,
from rebellion to loyalty—in a word, 'from the broad into the
narrow way which leadeth to eternal life,' [1]—how could they be
justified in anything short of separation? They could no
more continue to attend their parish church, than one who
had been a Roman Catholic could attend the mass if he had
become persuaded it was rank idolatry, or a former Protestant his old place of worship when convinced that it was a
den of mortal heresy. But between Nonjurors of the stern
uncompromising type, and those semi-Jacobites who gave
the allegiance of reason to one master, and that of sentiment
to another, there were all grades of opinion; and to all
except the most extreme among them the propriety of
attending the public prayers was completely an open question.
Tillotson ought to have known his old friend Nelson better,
than to conceive it possible that a man of such deep religious
feeling, and such sensitive honour, could be doubtful what to
do, unless it might fairly be considered doubtful. His foolish
commonplace appears indeed to have been sufficient to turn
the scale. Nelson, almost immediately after receiving this
opinion, decided on abandoning the national communion,
though he took a different and a wiser view at a later period.
In fact, Tillotson's misleading dictum seems to have contained
a double fallacy. His apparent wonder that there could be
any division of opinion among Nonjurors on the debated point
implied, in the first place, that all of them would have considered it distinctly sinful to join in the State prayers, a
premise which certainly ought not to have been assumed as
universal. In the second place, although a moderate Nonjuror, regarding the doctrine of passive obedience from his
own point of view as resting upon apostolical teaching, might
consider that he could not himself join in any prayer for the
new sovereign without evident sin, he certainly would not,
with Sancroft and Hickes, impute any such notion of sinful-
ness to those whose views differed from his own. In this

[1] *Life of Kettlewell*, App 17.

case, the question would not be whether he could join in those prayers, but only whether he could conscientiously be present while others joined in them, or, in different words, whether community of worship was consistent with disagreement in some particulars of it. Many Nonjurors and Jacobites thought not. How, said they, can we join under such circumstances in the prayer of St. Chrysostom, and thank God that ' with one accord we have made our common supplications?'[1] But many, even from the first, and eventually all but those who were bent on perpetuating the nonjuring separation, accepted the only view which is compatible with the theory of a National Church, or indeed of any common worship among a number of persons who exercise a reasonable right of private judgment. One of the ablest and saintliest of the Nonjurors, William Law, has very aptly remarked that dislike of this or that particular prayer ought not to act as a hindrance to public worship any more than the use of the imprecatory psalms.[2] If a form of worship is competent to create among fellow-worshippers a feeling of spiritual communion in the essentials of religion, there may be great diversities of opinion on minor particulars without any detriment to the sense of unity. Modern writers have very frequently dwelt on the value of multiplicity as well as of unity in the manifestations of religious life ; of the value even of the exaggerations of generous and unselfish men ; of 'dissension' within reasonable limits being not only inevitable, but a sign of healthful vitality; of the manifold loss and general waste of power when it is driven into 'dissent,'[3] and good men separate instead of agreeing to differ. At the period, however, here under consideration, these truths were far less frequently realised. Differences of opinion within the English Church were, it is true, as marked as they are now. There were greater Nonconformists, said a Mr. Truman to Dr. Bull,[4] even within her ministerial communion than ever he was. But to consider this anything short of a misfortune

[1] Lathbury, 93.

[2] Law's Letters, in *Tighe's Life*, &c. of W. Law, 68. Wall's *Dissuasive from Schism*, in Wordsworth's *Christian Institutes*, iii. 486.

[3] See, especially, G. H. Curteis' *Dissent in relation to the Church of England*, Pref. xviii. and pp. 8, 24.

[4] Nelson's *Life of Bull*, 146.

and an evil would generally have incurred a charge of dangerous Latitudinarianism. A tradition inherited equally from
Romanists and Puritans maintained very generally its ground,
and Churchmen hankered after an uniformity as wholly un-
attainable as, in the existing condition of human nature, it
would be wholly undesirable.

The circumstances of the time threw into exaggerated
prominence the particular views entertained by Nelson's Juror
and Nonjuror friends on the disputed questions connected
with transferred allegiance. But, great as were the sacrifices
which many of them incurred on account of these opinions,
—great as was the tenacity with which they clung to them,
and the vehemence with which they asserted them against all
impugners—great, above all, as was the religious and spiritual
importance with which their zeal for the cause invested these
semi-political doctrines, yet it is not on such grounds that
their interest as a Church party chiefly rests. No weight
of circumstances could confer a more than secondary value
on tenets which have no permanent bearing on the Christian
life, and engage attention only under external and temporary
conditions. The early Nonjurors, and their doctrinal sympathisers within the National Church, were a body of men from
whom many in modern times have taken pleasure in deriving
their ecclesiastical pedigree, not as upholders of nearly obsolete
opinions about divine right and passive obedience, but as the
main link between the High Churchmen of a previous age
and their successors at a much later period. To the revivers
in this century of the Anglo-Catholic theology, it seemed as
though the direct succession of sound English divines ended
with Bull and Beveridge, was partially continued, as by a side
line, in some of the Nonjurors, and then dwindled and almost
died out, until after the lapse of a hundred years its vitality
was again renewed.

On points of doctrine and discipline the early Nonjurors differed in nothing from the High Churchmen whose communion
they had deserted. Some of them called themselves, it is true,
'the old Church of England,' 'the Catholic and faithful
remnant' which alone adhered to 'the orthodox and rightful
bishops,' and bitter charges, mounting up to that of apostacy,
were directed against the 'compliant' majority. But, wide as

was the gulf, and heinous as was the sin by which, according to such Nonjurors, the Established Church had separated itself from primitive faith, the asserted defection consisted solely in this, that it had committed the sin of rebellion in forsaking its divinely appointed King, and the sin of schism in rejecting the authority of its canonical bishops. No one contended that there were further points of difference between the two communions. Dr. Bowes asked Blackburn, one of their bishops, whether 'he was so happy as to belong to his diocese?' 'Dear friend,' was the answer, 'we leave the sees open that the gentlemen who now unjustly possess them, upon the restoration, may, if they please, return to their duty and be continued. We content ourselves with full episcopal power as suffragans.' The introduction, however, in 1718, of the distinctive 'usages' in the communion service contributed greatly to the farther estrangement of a large section of the Nonjurors; and those who adopted the new Prayer-book drawn up in 1734 by Bishop Deacon, were alienated still more. The only communion with which they claimed near relationship was one which in their opinion had long ceased to exist. 'I am not of your communion,' said Bishop Welton on his death-bed, in 1726, to the English Chaplain at Lisbon, whose services he declined. 'I belong to the Church of England as it was reformed by Archbishop Cranmer.'[1] Thus too, when Bishop Deacon's son, a youth of little more than twenty, suffered execution for his share in the Jacobite rising of 1745, his last words upon the scaffold were that he died 'a member, not of the Church of Rome, nor yet of that of England, but of a pure Episcopal Church, which has reformed all the errors, corruptions, and defects that have been introduced into the modern Churches of Christendom.'[2] Yet the divergence of these Nonjurors from the National Church was, after all, far more apparent than real. It was only a very small minority, beginning with Deacon and Campbell, who outstepped in any of their ideas the tone of feeling which had long been familiar to many of the High Church party, Ever since the reign of Edward VI. the Church of England had included among its clerical and lay members some who had not ceased to regret the changes which had been made in the second

---

[1] Hearne's *Reliquiæ*, ii. 257.   [2] Lathbury, 388.

Liturgy issued in his reign, and who hoped for a restoration of the rubrics and passages which had been then expurged. This had been very conspicuous when the Scottish Liturgy had been drawn up in 1636. The bishops of Ross and Dunblane had been, it is true, the chief agents in the compilation of this book, and in the first instance, Archbishop Laud had strongly recommended that it should be identical with that used in the sister kingdom.[1] But at a later period he entirely gave up his opposition to the proposed changes. In conjunction with Juxon, Bishop of London, and Wren of Norwich, he revised the whole book when completed, and it was then published in Scotland with the understanding that it differed only in letter and nothing in substance from that which was in use in the English Church. Its speedy and unceremonious rejection is familiar to every reader. This however only showed how excessively ill-judged was the attempt to force not only the English Church, but English High Church, on a reluctant people. It serves none the worse to illustrate the fact that the usages adopted in the communion service by many of the English and Scotch Nonjurors, as still maintained in some of the Scotch episcopal congregations, and even the new Liturgy framed for their most advanced section, could be closely paralleled in an episode of English Church History a hundred years previously. There were many points of close resemblance between the Nonjuring Liturgies and the Scotch Service Book as revised by High Church English divines in 1736. Some in fact of the practices and expressions which, after the first ten or twenty years of the eighteenth century, were looked upon as all but confined to a party of Nonjurors, had been held almost as fully before yet the schism was thought of.

This was certainly the case in regard of those 'usages' which related to the sacrificial character of the Eucharist and to prayers for the dead. Dr. Hickes complained in one of his letters that the doctrine of the Eucharistic sacrifice had disappeared from the writings even of divines who had treated on the subject.[2] How far this was correct became, four years later, a disputed question. Bishop Trimnell declared it was a

---

[1] G. Grub's *Ecclesiastical History of Scotland*, ii. 377.
[2] Secretan, 37, 65.

doctrine that had never been taught in the English Church since the Reformation.[1] John Johnson, on the other hand, vicar of Cranbrook, who had originated the controversy by a book in which he ardently supported the opinion in question, affirmed that no Christian bishop before Trimnell ever denied it.[2] Evidently it was a point which had not come very prominently forward for distinct assertion or contradiction, and one in which there was great room for ambiguity. To some it seemed a palpably new doctrine, closely trenching on a most dangerous portion of the Romish system, and likely to lead to gross superstition. To others it seemed a harmless and very edifying part of belief, wholly void of any Romish tendencies, and plainly implied, if not definitely expressed, in the English Liturgy. Most of the excellent and pious High Churchmen who have been spoken of in this paper treasured it as a valued article of their faith. Kettlewell used to dilate on the great sacrificial feast of charity.[3] Bull used constantly to speak of the Eucharist as no less a sacrifice commemorative of Christ's oblation of Himself, than the Jewish sacrifices had been typical of it.[4] Dodwell, ever fruitful in learned instances, not only brought forward arguments from Scripture and the Fathers, but adduced illustrations from the bloodless sacrifices of Essenes and Pythagoreans.[5] Robert Nelson, after the example of Jeremy Taylor in his 'Holy Living and Dying,' introduced the subject in a more popular and devotional form in his book upon the Christian Sacrifice.[6] Archbishop Sharp regretted that a doctrine which he considered so instructive had not been more definitely contained in the English Liturgy, and preferred the Communion office of King Edward VI.'s Service Book.[7] Beveridge argued that if the Jews were to be punctual and constant in attending their sacrifices, how much more should Christians honour by frequent observance the great commemorative offering which had been instituted in their place, and contained within itself the benefits of them all.[8]

---

[1] Hunt, 3, 257, and Cassan's *Lives of the Bishops of Winchester*, 379. Cassan, quoting from Noble, says Trimnell was a very good man, 'whom even the Tories valued, though he preached terrible Whig sermons.' [2] Id.

[3] *Life of Kettlewell*, 56. [4] Nelson's *Life of Bull*, 178.

[5] Brokesby's *Life of Dodwell*, 363. [6] Secretan, 178-9. Teale, 297.

[7] *Sharp's Life*, by his Son, i. 355, and Secretan, 178.

[8] Beveridge's *Necessity and Advantage of Frequent Communion*, 1708.

Some observations of a somewhat similar kind may be made in regard of prayers for the departed, another subject which the English Church has wisely left to private opinion. The nonjuring 'usages,' on the other hand, restored to the Liturgy the clauses which the better judgment of their ancestors had omitted. Some went farther, and insisted that 'prayer for their deceased brethren was not only lawful and useful, but their bounden duty.'[1] All of them, however, without exception, contested with perfect sincerity that their doctrine on these points was not that of Rome, and that they entirely repudiated, as baseless and unscriptural, the superstructure which that Church has raised upon it. The nonjuring separation drew away from the National Church many who as a matter of private opinion had held the tenet without rebuke; and although, in the middle of the eighteenth century, John Wesley stoutly defended it,[2] and Dr. Johnson always argued for its propriety and personally maintained the practice,[3] an idea gained ground that it was wholly unauthorised by the English Church, and contrary to its spirit. But at the opening of the century it appears to have been a tenet not unfrequently maintained, especially among High Churchmen, whether Jurors or Nonjurors. Dr. I. Barrow, says Hearne, 'was mighty for it.'[4] In the form of prayer for Jan. 30th, 1661, there was a perfectly undisguised prayer of this kind, drawn up apparently by Archbishop Juxon.[5] It had however only the authority of the Crown, and was expunged in the authorised form of prayer for 1662. Archbishop Wake said he did not condemn the practice,[6] and Bishop Smalridge, already spoken of in the list of Robert Nelson's friends, is said to have been in favour of it.[7] So was Robert Nelson himself. After describing the death of his old and honoured friend Bishop Bull, he adds in reference to him and to his wife who had died previously:

---

[1] Lathbury, 302.

[2] In answer to Lavington, who charged him with prayers to that effect in his *Devotions for every day in the Week* (*Enthusiasm of Methodists and Papists*, 157), Wesley answered, 'In this kind of general prayer for the faithful departed, I conceive myself to be clearly justified both by the earliest antiquity and by the Church of England.' 'Answer to Lavington,' *Works*, ix. 55, also 'Letter to Dr. Middleton,' *Works*, x. 9.   [3] *Boswell's Life*, i. 187, 191, ii. 166.

[4] Hearne's *Reliquiæ*, ii. 188.   [5] Lathbury, 302.

[6] Wake's *Three Tracts against Popery*, § 3. Quoted with much censure by Blackburne, *Historical View*, &c., 115.   [7] Lathbury, 300.

'The Lord grant unto them that they may find mercy of the Lord in that day.'[1] Bishop Ken may be quoted to the same effect. Writing to Dr. Nicholas in October 1677, of the death of their friend Mr. Coles, 'cujus anima,' he continues, 'requiescat in pace.'[2] Dr. Ernest Grabe and Dean Hickes, two more of R. Nelson's intimate associates, were also accustomed to pray for those in either state.[3]

Some remarks will be made in another chapter upon the strong Protestant feeling which, at the beginning of the eighteenth century, predominated in every class of English society. The Nonjurors and High Churchmen in general, no less than the rest of their countrymen, were stout Protestants, and gloried in the name. High Churchmen had stood in the van of that great contest with Rome which had so occupied the thoughts of theological writers and the whole English people during the later years of the preceding century, and the remembrance of which was still fresh. The acrimony of argument had been somewhat abated by the very general respect entertained in England for the great Gallican divines, Pascal, Fenelon, and Bossuet. Among the Nonjurors it was further softened by political and social considerations. English Roman Catholics were almost all Jacobites, and were therefore in close sympathy with them on a matter of very absorbing interest. But although these influences tended to remove prejudices, the gap that separates Anglican and Roman divinity remained wide as ever. When the Nonjurors, or a large section of them, cut themselves away from the National Church, they did not in their isolation look towards Rome. Even the most advanced among their leaders proved, by the energy with which they continued the Protestant controversy, how groundless was the charge sometimes brought against them, that they had adopted Popish doctrines.[4]

It cannot be wondered at, that members of the nonjuring communion felt very keenly the isolated, and, so to say, the sectarian condition in which they were placed. There were

---

[1] Nelson's *Life of Bull*, 405.   [2] Bowles' *Life of Ken*, 38.

[3] Lathbury, 297, 302. The custom is spoken of as frequent among the High Churchmen of 1710-20.—*Life of Kennet*, 125.

[4] Some further remarks on their staunch Protestantism will be found in another chapter.

few words dearer to them than that word 'Catholic,' which breathes of loving brotherhood in one great Christian body. And yet outside their own scanty fold they were repelled on every side. They had been ardently attached to the English Church, and had thought that whatever its imperfections might be in practice, its theory, at all events, approached to perfection. But now, to the minds of many of them, the ideal had passed away, or had become a shadow. Not only were those whom they considered the most faithful sons of the Church a mere dismembered party, enfeebled by the late separation—not only had principles which they detested gained ground far and wide—but as a whole Church it was no longer the one they had known and loved. They might, and some of them did, boast that among themselves the pure and or- thodox Church of their fathers still survived. If it were so, there was no great satisfaction or hopefulness in the thought. Since, then, the Church in which they had been brought up had failed them, where should they find intercommunion and sympathy? Not among English Nonconformists. It is true that one of the very last acts of Archbishop Sancroft and Bishop Ken, previous to their retirement, had been to move the House of Lords for a Bill of Toleration and Comprehen- sion [1] such as might strengthen the English Church and enlarge its borders. But although they might have been willing at one time to concede much to Nonconformist scruples, yet even as fellow-members in one national Church they would have represented opposite poles of ecclesiastical sentiment; and without such a mutual bond of union, the interval which separated Dissenters and Nonjurors was wider than ever it had been. To come to any terms with Rome was quite out of the question. Such an alliance would indeed be, as Kettlewell expressed it, 'concordia discors.' [2] Could they then combine with Lutherans or other foreign Protes- tants? This at one time seemed possible. English High Churchmen, Juror and Nonjuror, were inclined to be lenient to deficiencies abroad, in order and ritual, of which they would have been wholly intolerant at home. Even Dodwell, a man of singularly straitened and rigid views, thought the prospect

---

[1] Birch, cix. Burnet's *Own Times*, 528. Hunt, ii. 70.
[2] *Life of Kettlewell*, 130.

not unhopeful. One condition, however, they laid down as absolutely indispensable—the restoration of a legitimate episcopate. To this end Dr. Ernest Grabe indefatigably laboured: Archbishop Sharp and others heartily seconded his efforts ; Frederick I. of Prussia and some of his leading clergy were by no means unfavourable to the design ; and between 1706 and 1713 there was a probability that in the dominions of that king it might be successfully carried out. But the chief promoters of the scheme died nearly coincidently ; political questions of immediate concern interfered with its farther consideration, and thus the project was dropped. The Scotch Episcopal Church remained as a communion with which English Nonjurors could fraternise. Ken and Beveridge and Kettlewell, and English High Churchmen in general, had long regarded that Church with compassion, sympathy, and interest. Dr. Hickes, the acknowledged leader of the thorough Nonjurors, had become, as chaplain to the Earl of Lauderdale, well acquainted with its bishops ; a large proportion of its clergy were Jacobites and Nonjurors ; and, like themselves, they were a depressed and often persecuted remnant. The intimacy, therefore, between the Scotch Episcopalians and many of the English Nonjurors became, as is well known, very close.

There was, however, one other great body of Christians towards whom, after a time, the nonjuring separatists turned with proposals of amity and intercommunion. This was the Eastern Church. Various causes had contributed to remove something of the obscurity which had once shrouded this vast communion from the knowledge of Englishmen. As far back as the earlier part of Charles I.'s reign, the attention of either party in the English Church had been fixed for a time on the overtures made by Cyrillus Lukaris,[1] patriarch, first of Alexandria, and then of Constantinople, to whom we owe the precious gift of the 'Alexandrian manuscript' of the Scriptures. Archbishop Abbot, a Calvinist, and one of the first representatives of the so-called Latitudinarian party, had been attracted by the inclinations evinced by this remarkable man towards the theology of Holland and Geneva. His successor and complete opposite, Archbishop Laud, had been no less

---

[1] A. P. Stanley's *Eastern Church*, 410.

fascinated by the idea of closer intercourse with a Church of such ancient splendour and such pretensions to primitive orthodoxy. At the close of the seventeenth century this interest had been renewed by the visit of Peter the Great to this island. With a mind greedy after all manner of information, he had not omitted to inquire closely into ecclesiastical matters. People heard of his conversations on these subjects with Tenison and Burnet,[1] and wondered how far a monarch who was a kind of Pope in his own empire would be leavened with Western and Protestant ideas. In learned and literary circles too, the Eastern Church had been discussed. The Oxford and Cambridge Platonists, than whom England has never produced more thoughtful and scholarlike divines, had profoundly studied the Alexandrian fathers. Patristic reading, which no one could yet neglect who advanced the smallest pretensions to theological acquirements, might naturally lead men to think with longing of an ideal of united faith 'professed' (to use Bishop Ken's familiar words) 'by the whole Church before the disunion of East and West.'[2] Missionary feeling, too, which at the beginning of the eighteenth century was showing so many signs of nascent activity, had not failed to take notice of the gross ignorance into which many parts of Greek Christendom had fallen.[3] Henry Ludolph, a German by birth, and late secretary to Prince George of Denmark, on his return to London in 1694 from some lengthened travels in Russia, and after further wanderings a few years later in Egypt, Asia Minor, and the Holy Land, persuaded some English Churchmen to publish an impression of the New Testament in modern Greek, which was dispersed in those countries through the Greeks with whom Ludolph kept up a correspondence.[4] In 1701 University men at Cambridge, when Bentley was Vice-Chancellor, were much interested by the visit of Neophytos, Archbishop of Philippopolis, and Exarch of Thrace. He was presented with a Doctor of Divinity's degree, and afterwards made a speech in Hellen-

---

[1] A. P. Stanley's *Eastern Church,* 453, 462.

[2] *Life of Ken,* by a Layman, 808.

[3] Burnet, writing in 1694, remarking on 'the present depressed and ignorant state of the Greek Churches,' speaks also with warm sympathy of their poverty and persecution—'a peculiar character of bearing the Cross.'—*Four Sermons, &c.,* 198.

[4] *Biographical Dictionary,* 'Ludolph.'

istic Greek.[1] About the same time the minutes of the Christian Knowledge Society make report of a Catechism drawn up for Greek Churchmen by Bishop Williams of Chichester, and translated from the English by some Greeks then studying at Oxford.[2] This little colony of Greek students had been established in 1689, through the cordial relations then subsisting between Archbishop Sancroft and Georgirenes, Metropolitan of Samos, who had recently been a refugee in London. It was hoped that by their residence at Oxford they would be able to promote in their own country a better understanding of ' the true doctrine of the Church of England.' They were to be twenty in number, were to dwell together at Gloucester Hall (afterwards Worcester College), be habited all alike in the gravest sort of habit worn in their own country, and stay at the University for five years.[3] Robert Nelson, ever zealous and energetic in all the business of the society, would naturally feel particularly interested in the condition of Eastern Christians on account of the business connection with Smyrna in which his family had been prosperously engaged. We are told of his showing warm sympathy in the wish of the Archbishop of Gotchau in Armenia to get works of piety printed in that language.[4] Similar interest would be felt by another leader of the early Nonjurors, Frampton, Bishop of Gloucester, who in his earlier years had served as chaplain at Aleppo, and had formed a familiar acquaintance with some of the most learned patriarchs and bishops of the Eastern Church.[5] The man, however, who at the beginning of the eighteenth century must have done most to turn attention towards the Eastern Church, was Dr. Grabe, who has been already more than once spoken of as held in great esteem by the Nonjuring and High Church party. He had found the Anglican Church more congenial to him on the whole than any other, but it shared his sympathies with the Lutheran and the Greek. He was a constant daily attendant at the English, and more especially the nonjuring services, but for many years he communicated exclusively at the Greek

---

[1] Christopher Wordsworth, *University Life in the Eighteenth Century*, 331.
[2] Secretan, 103. [3] Wordsworth, *University Life*, &c. 324-5.
[4] Teale, 302.—This was in 1707. Archbishop Sharp gave his help in furthering this work.—*Life*, i. 402. [5] Evans' *Life of Frampton*, 44.

Church. He also published a 'Defensio Græcæ Ecclesiæ.' Thus, in many different ways, the Oriental Church had come to be regarded, especially by the more studious of the High Church clergy, in quite another light from that of Rome.

In 1716 Arsenius, Metropolitan of Thebais, came to London on a charitable mission in behalf of the suffering Christians of Egypt. It will be readily understood with what alacrity a number of the Scotch and English Nonjurors seized the opportunity of making 'a proposal for a concordat betwixt the orthodox and Catholic remnant of the British Churches and the Catholic and Apostolic Oriental Church.' The correspondence, of which a full account is given in Lathbury's History of the Nonjurors,[2] although in many respects an interesting one, was wholly abortive. There appears indeed to have been a real wish on the part of Peter the Great and of some of the patriarchs to forward the project; but the ecclesiastical synod of Russia was evidently not quite clear from whom the overtures proceeded. Their answers were directed ' To the Most Reverend the Bishops of the Catholic Church in Great Britain, our dearest brothers,' and, somewhat to the dismay of the Nonjurors, copies of the letters were even sent by the Patriarch of Jerusalem to Archbishop Wake. Above all, the proposals were essentially one-sided. The nonjuring bishops, while remaining perfectly faithful to their principles, were willing to make large concessions in points which involved no departure from what they considered to be essential truths. The Patriarchs would have been glad of intercommunion on their own terms, but, in the true spirit of the Eastern Church, would concede nothing. It was ' not lawful either to add any thing or take away any thing' from ' what has been defined and determined by ancient Fathers and the Holy Œcumenical Synods from the time of the apostles and their holy successors, the Fathers of our Church, to this time. We say that those who are disposed to agree with us must submit to them, with sincerity and obedience, and without any scruple or dispute. And this is a sufficient answer to what you have written.' Perhaps the result might not have been very different, even if the overtures in question had been backed by the authority of the whole Anglican

---

[1] Secretan, ii. 220-2. Hearne's *Reliquiæ*, ii. 280.   [2] Pp. 309-59.

Church—a communion which at this period was universally acknowledged as the leader of Protestant Christendom. And even if there were less immutability in Eastern counsels, Bishop Campbell and his coadjutors could scarcely have been sanguine in hoping for any other issue. Truth and right, as they remarked in a letter to the Czar, do not depend on numbers; but if the Oriental synod were thoroughly aware how exceedingly scanty was 'the remnant' with which they were treating, and how thoroughly apart from the main current of English national life, it was highly improbable that they would purchase so minute an advance towards a wider unity by authorising what would certainly seem to them innovations dangerously opposed to all ancient precedent. It must be some far greater and deeper movement that will first tempt the unchanging Eastern Church to approve of any deviation from the trodden path of immemorial tradition.

The closing part of this chapter seems a fit place for some remarks upon the attitude of the English Church in the eighteenth century toward the early Christian fathers. Professor Blunt, in his 'Lectures' upon their 'Right Use,'[1] after showing how systematically the English Reformers, Philpot and Grindal, no less than Ridley and Jewell, appealed to their authority, goes on to specify the causes which led to their later disparagement and neglect. He speaks first of the new spirit which arose among the Puritans during the semi-religious wars of the Commonwealth, and then adds: 'But after awhile came the Revolution; an event which shed a much more disastrous influence on the taste for patristical learning, because a more enduring and insidious one, than the Rebellion.'[2] As to the nature of this influence he says but little, referring rather to such external agencies as the Establishment of Presbyterianism in the sister country, sympathy with the reformed Churches abroad, and the writings of Daillé and Barbeyrac, than to the far deeper and more potent action of ideas and forms of thought, of which (as they cannot here be discussed) it may be simply said that Locke was the most able and religious expositor. The Nonjurors, continues Dr. Blunt, in great measure 'carried away with them that regard

[1] Lecture i.   [2] Id. p. 18.

for primitive times which with them was destined by degrees almost to expire.'

It is very true that the Nonjurors and the generation of High Churchmen from among whom they came were, as a body, the last representatives in the eighteenth century of that unfeigned reverence for primitive usage and opinion which had once been general in Churchmen of every kind. The transition was a gradual one. In most controversies, opinions were still backed by arguments from the writings of the early fathers. Presbyterians as well as Episcopalians had appealed to them in support of their respective forms of Church government. Arians and Unitarians of every shade, Zuicker and Episcopius no less than Bishop Bull, Emlyn no less than Leslie, had quoted largely from the same primitive sources. Dr. Clarke, in reply to the wealth of patristic learning adduced by Waterland, maintained that, although he repudiated submission to their authority, the fathers were on his side. As for Whiston, no Nonjuror could have been more enthusiastic than he was in recurring to primitive usage in defence of the eccentric medley of opinions to which he was devoted. It seemed to him that the restoration of the Church of the first three centuries was the one panacea for all the evils which afflicted Christendom. It may be noted that among the twelve or fourteen men of various persuasions who used to meet at 'the primitive library' in his house for the promotion of this laudable object, one of the most indefatigable was Dr. John Gale, the eminent Baptist leader. Nor did the Low Church or 'Latitudinarian' divines in direct terms disparage patristic reading. Tillotson spoke with great deference of 'the Holy Fathers' and Councils;[1] Stillingfleet was very tenacious of their authority;[2] Lord Chancellor King published in 1691 a learned and profound treatise entitled 'An Enquiry into the Constitution and Discipline of the Primitive Church.' Publications of this kind did not fail to find readers. Lord King's work 'made a great sensation, and passed through many editions.'[3] The 'Bibliotheca Biblica,' a learned patristic commentary on the Old and New Testament, published in monthly parts between 1717 and 1720,

[1] S. xix. ii. 219. S. xxvii. ii. 466. [2] Hallam, *Literature of Europe*, iv. 147.
[3] Campbell's *Lives of the Chancellors*, iv. 568.

had a considerable sale. Some years later, when in 1749 Middleton published his 'Free Enquiry,' a host of answers showed how general was the disturbance and alarm excited by his assertions that the fathers were often credulous and unworthy of credit, and that their piety was more exemplary than their wisdom. John Wesley was among the first to express his indignation at Middleton's unexpected attack. Nor would it be difficult to multiply examples, in evidence that throughout the eighteenth century the Church of England by no means abandoned the old position of being to a large extent ruled in doctrine and discipline by what was 'agreeable to the mind and purpose of the old fathers.'[1]

But there was no longer any general disposition to insist strongly upon this. It was kept far more in the background than had formerly been the custom ; to be asserted in case of challenge, and to be defended against impugners, but not to be put forward in the front rank of forcible and trustworthy arguments. The early fathers would often be referred to in terms of cold respect, very barren of all sympathy, and not without a qualifying caution. 'I do not mean anything,' says Fleetwood, 'to the diminution of their credit and authority in general ; but I would have nobody so much losers by their reverence of antiquity as not to reason for themselves.'[2] They were very 'admirable,' says Swift, 'for confirming the truth of ancient doctrines and discipline, but not to be recommended for imitation in their manner of arguing and exhorting.'[3] Archbishop Potter spoke highly of their value, but was very careful in laying down the limitation under which their authority must be accepted.[4] Archbishop Secker was particular to warn his clergy against 'over-great reverence for antiquity.'[5] There was much, no doubt, that was very prudent and very true in such cautions. But the whole tone of religious thought and feeling prevalent in the eighteenth century was out of harmony with that which pervades the early patristic writers. The respect for them was mainly traditional ; the suspicion and distaste, wherever it showed itself, was thoroughly genuine. Bishop Berkeley, who in many respects stood singularly apart

---

[1] Prayer-book Preface on 'The Service of the Church.'   [2] *Works,* 700.
[3] Swift, 'Letter to a Young Clergyman,' *Works,* viii. 218.
[4] Hunt, iii. 72.   [5] Secker's Charges, 19.

from his age, strongly urged on persons of liberal education the reading of the Fathers of the Church. He thought they would find in them a spiritual depth strongly contrasting with anything they would be likely to find in the writings of their own contemporaries.[1] It would have been a useful corrective to the tendencies of a period which through conflicts with Deism, and through new revelations from the physical universe, was working out great religious problems in relation to the powers and limitations of reason, and which had manifold points of advantage over the authors of a primitive age, but greatly lacked that spiritual fervour and discernment which certainly distinguished the early fathers, whatever might be their characteristic errors. But men suit their reading to their tastes rather than to their deficiencies, and there is abundant evidence that patristic studies fell year by year into increased neglect. Whiston is perpetually lamenting this. 'Give me leave,' he says, ' to add, that I find most of our present bishops, priests, and deacons so little acquainted with the primitive writers, that not only our own dissenting brethren, who used to be far inferior to the Church of England in such learning, but the ordinary Popish priests themselves will soon be able to run them aground.'[2] Archbishop Secker, in his Latin speech before Convocation in 1761, made exactly the same complaint.[3] A good deal must be set down to the inertness which, as the century advanced, began to paralyse the intellectual no less than the spiritual energies of the Church. After the Deistical controversy had exhausted itself, the study of theology in almost all its branches rapidly declined. But even if it had not been so, patristic learning would certainly have languished. The ultimate results of the tedious but important Bangorian controversy were very great in abated respect for all kinds of Church authority. The rights of conscience and of private judgment had been vindicated in popular language and with great power. And while there was a marked inclination to resent anything like submission to the dicta of any previous age, there was as yet very little to effect a counterbalancing influence. Historical criticism was not as yet sufficiently advanced to promise a really trust-

---

[1] Berkeley's *Works* (Fraser), 272.   [2] Whiston's *Memoirs*, 310.
[3] Charges, 366.

worthy appreciation of the relative value of writings handed
down from the post-Apostolic centuries; and the turn of
religious feeling, wherever it began to revive under the Wesleyan and Evangelical movements, happened to show a marked
want of affinity in all the finer shades of sentiment with the
no less earnest religion of good men of the age of Tertullian,
Athanasius and Chrysostom. It was not only that their authority was persistently attacked by Daillé and Barbeyrac, by
Le Clerc and Bayle, by Toland and Shaftesbury and the
Deists in general, by Dr. Jortin, by Gibbon, by Priestley, and
by a host of lesser writers,—above all by Middleton, who inflicted a wound far more incurable for the time than any that
were struck by opponents more directly hostile,—but the most
orthodox and learned Churchmen often referred to them in a
thoroughly unsympathetic and even depreciatory tone. Warburton, for example, writing to his friend Hurd upon the
authors from whom he would derive assistance in a thorough
study of the Bible, tells him that ' of all the ancient commentators he need be little solicitous, except it be of St. Jerome, who
has many excellent things, and is the only father that can
be called a critic of the sacred writings, or who has followed
a just and reasonable method of criticising.'[1] The stir created
by the publication of Middleton's ' Free Enquiry' in 1749 may
be said in fact to have been almost the last symptom within the
century of anything like real interest in ecclesiastical antiquity. Even then, nothing of permanent value was elicited
in reply to Middleton's destructive criticism. After that time
patristic literature appears to have been utterly neglected.

It was far otherwise at the beginning of the century, with
that circle of learned and devout High Churchmen of whom,
in this chapter, Robert Nelson and his friends have been
fitting representatives. Some of them were deeply read in
these subjects. Bishop Bull possessed an European celebrity
for his masterly command of all that the early fathers had
written. Dodwell's knowledge of them, though it did not
show the same intellectual grasp, evinced an erudition no
less extensive. The ' Spicilegium Patrum' remains a
memorial of the industry with which Dr. Ernest Grabe
pursued his favourite study. Beveridge has left his ' Codex

---

[1] War burton and Hurd's Correspondence, 60.

Canonum.' Robert Nelson, in his elaborate defence of Bull's orthodoxy, has displayed a far more considerable acquaintance with patristic theology than could have been expected from a man whose time was so much occupied in other ways. Of Dean Hickes it was said that he was not only 'a great master of ecclesiastical antiquity,' but that he did a great deal towards creating a lively interest in it among his younger contemporaries. Three more at least of Robert Nelson's associates may be added to the list: Francis Brokesby, who wrote a 'Church History of the First Three Centuries,' Francis Lee, author of a 'History of Montanism,' and Nathanael Marshall, editor of St. Cyprian's works. Collier's Church History, Brett's Collection of Primitive Liturgies, Lawrence Howell's 'Synopsis Canonum,' and Sclater's 'Constitutions of the Primitive Church'—a treatise which was said to have caused a marked change in Lord Chancellor King's opinions— are evidences of the labour in the same field of the Nonjurors of a somewhat later date. Archbishop Wake, Wall, Bingham, Cave, Whitby, Waterland, Bentley, Atterbury, and Potter, were other English divines who in the first quarter of the last century engaged more or less deeply in patristic researches.

Robert Nelson's friends followed out their investigations of early Church history in no spirit of mere historical or antiquarian inquiry, nor yet merely to find in them a treasure-house of weapons of argument wherewith to conduct their controversies, but mainly because their whole spirit was in sympathy with what they found there. Some were profoundly learned, others had no pretensions to extensive theological acquirements, but all his most congenial associates were imbued with the same feeling of deep respect for primitive antiquity. Bishop Bull may be accepted as spokesman for them all, when he urged that 'the preferring modern authority before Catholic tradition was unreasonable and against the principle of the Church of England.' He appealed to the canon of Queen Elizabeth, which ordained that all preachers 'shall chiefly take heed that they teach nothing but what is agreeable to the doctrine of the Old and New Testament, and what the Catholic fathers and primitive bishops have thence collected.' He cited the constitution of King James I., which required all candidates in divinity 'to apply themselves seriously to the study of such books as are agreeable to the doctrine and discipline of the Church of England, and particularly to the reading of the Fathers and Councils.'[1] He quoted the testimony of many eminent writers to the same purpose. He held that the works of the fathers and ancient doctors were the best guides for interpreting those scriptures which are not plain in themselves. 'They are writ,' he said, 'with such a lively spirit of piety as is not to be met with in the writings of later centuries,' and in their interpretations there often seemed to him to be a suggestiveness and depth— *aliquid latet quod non patet*—which astonished and delighted him.[2] Of Henry Dodwell a little trait is recorded, characteristic alike of the man and of the set of religious and learned Churchmen among whom he lived. He had four miniature volumes, one or other of which was his invariable pocket companion. One was a Hebrew Bible, the second a Greek Testament, the other two were Thomas a Kempis and St. Augustine's Meditations.[3]

There was great variety of individual character in the group of Churchmen who have formed the subject of this chapter, as they did not all come into contact with one another, and some were widely separated by the circumstances of their lives. The one fact of some being Jurors and some Nonjurors was quite enough in itself to make a vast difference of thoughts and sympathies among those who had taken different sides. But they were closely united in what they held to be the divinely appointed constitution of the Church. All looked back to primitive times as the unalterable model of doctrine, order, and government; all were firmly persuaded that the English Reformation was wholly based on a restoration of the ancient pattern, and had fallen short of its object only so far forth as that ideal had as yet been unattained ; all looked with suspicion and alarm at such tendencies of their age as seemed to them to contradict and thwart the development of these principles. They were good men in a very high sense of the word, earnestly religious, bent upon a conscientious fulfilment of their duties, and centres, in their several spheres, of active Christian labours. Ken, Nelson, and Kettlewell, among Nonjurors—Bull, Beveridge,

---

[1] Nelson's *Life of Bull*, 201-2. [2] Id. 365-6. [3] Brokesby's *Life*, 303.

and Sharp, among those who accepted the change of dynasty —are names deservedly held in special honour by English Churchmen. Their piety was of a type more frequent perhaps in the Church of England than in some other communions, very serious and devout, but wholly free from all gloom and moroseness; tinged in some instances, as in Dodwell, Ken, and Hooper, with asceticism, but serene and bright, and guarded against extravagance and fanaticism by culture, social converse, and sound reading. Such men could not fail to adorn the faith they professed, and do honour to the Church in which they had been nurtured. At the same time, some of the tenets which they ardently maintained were calculated to foster a stiffness and narrowness, and an exaggerated insistence upon certain forms of Church government, which contained many elements of real danger. Within the National Church there was a great deal to counterbalance these injurious tendencies and check their growth. The Latitudinarian party, whose faults and temptations lay in a very opposite direction, was very strong. Ecclesiastical as well as political parties were no doubt strongly defined, and for a time strongly antagonistic. But wherever in a large body of men different views are equally tolerated, opinions will inevitably shade one into another to a great extent, and extreme or unpractical theories will be tempered and toned down, or be regarded at most as merely the views of a minority. Among the Nonjurors Henry Dodwell, for example, was a real power, as a man of holy life and profound learning, whose views, although carried to an extreme in which few could altogether concur, were still in general principle, and when stated in more moderate terms, those of the great majority of the whole body. As a member, on the other hand, of the National Church, his goodness and erudition were widely respected, but his theoretical extravagances were only the crotchets of a retired student, who advanced in their most extreme form the opinions of a party.

But, Jurors or Nonjurors, the very best men of the old High Church party certainly exhibited a strong bearing towards the faults of exclusiveness and ecclesiasticism. It was a serious loss to the English Church to be deprived of the services of such men as Ken and Kettlewell, but it would have been a great misfortune to it to have been represented only by men of their sentiments. Their Christianity was as true and earnest as ever breathed in the soul : nevertheless, there was much in it that could not fail to degenerate in spirits less pure and elevated than their own. They were apt to fall into the common error of making orthodoxy a far more strait and narrow path than was ever warranted by any terms of the Church apostolic or of the Church of their own country. Its strict limits, on all points which Scripture has left uncertain, had been, as it appeared to them, providentially maintained throughout the first three centuries. Then began a long period of still increasing error ; until the time of reformation came, and the Church of England fulfilled its appointed task of retracing the old landmarks, and restoring primitive truth to its ancient purity. Allowing for such trifling modifications as the difference of time and change of circumstances absolutely necessitated, the Anglican was in their estimation the Ante-Nicene Church revived. If, in the doctrine, order, and government of the English Church there was anything which would not have approved itself to the early fathers and to the first Councils, it was so far forth a falling short of its fundamental principles. They were persuaded that at all events there was nowhere outside its borders such near approach to this perfection. As for other religious bodies, the degree of their separation from the spirit and constitution of the English Church might be fairly taken as the approximate measure of their departure from the practice of primitive antiquity. Romanism, Latitudinarianism, Mysticism, Calvinism, Puritanism, whatever form Dissent might take from what they believed to be the true principles of the English Church, it was, as such, a departure from Catholic and orthodox tradition, it was but one or another phase of the odious sin of schism.

The High Anglican custom of appealing to early ecclesiastical records as an acknowledged standard of authority on all matters which Scripture has left uncertain, necessarily led this section of the English Church to repeat many of the failings as well as many of the virtues which had characterised the Church of the third and fourth centuries. It copied, for instance, far too faithfully, the disposition which primitive ages had early manifested, to magnify unduly the spiritual power and prerogatives of the priesthood. No doubt the outcry against sacerdotalism was often perverted into disingenuous uses. Many a hard blow was dealt against vital Christian doctrine under the guise of righteous war against the exorbitant pretensions of the clergy. But Sacerdotalism certainly attained a formidable height among some of the High Churchmen of the period, both Jurors and Nonjurors. Dodwell, who declined orders that he might defend all priestly rights from a better vantage ground, did more harm to the cause he had espoused than any one of its opponents, by fearlessly pressing the theory into consequences from which a less thorough or a more cautious advocate would have recoiled with dismay. Robert Nelson's sobriety of judgment and sound practical sense made him a far more effective champion. He too, like Dodwell, rejoiced that from his position as a layman he could without prejudice resist what he termed a sacrilegious invasion of the rights of the priests of the Lord.[1] The beginning of the eighteenth century was felt to be a time of crisis in the contest which, for the last three or four hundred years, has been incessantly waged between those whose tendency is ever to reduce religion into its very simplest elements, and those, on the other hand, in whose eyes the whole order of Church government and discipline is a divinely constituted system of mysterious powers and superhuman influences. It is a contest in which opinions may vary in all degrees, from pure Deism to utter Ultramontanism. The High Churchmen in question insisted that their position, and theirs only, was precisely that of the Church in early post-Apostolic times, when doctrine had become fully defined, but was as yet uncorrupted by later superstitions. It was not very tenable ground, but it was held by them with a pertinacity and sincerity of conviction which deepened the fervour of their faith, even while it narrowed its sympathies and cramped it with restrictions. A Church in which they found what they demanded ; which was primitive and reformed ; which was free from the errors of Rome and Geneva ; which was not only Catholic and ortho-

---

[1] Secretan, 195.

dox on all doctrines of faith, but possessed an apostolical succession, with the sacred privileges attached to it ; which was governed by a lawful and canonical episcopate ; which was blessed with a sound and ancient liturgy ; which was faithful (many Nonjurors would add) to its divinely appointed king ; such a Church was indeed one for which they could live and die. So far it was well. Their love for their own Church, and their perfect confidence in it, added both beauty and character to their piety. The misfortune was, that it left them unable to understand the merits of any form of faith which rejected, or treated as a thing indifferent, what they regarded as all but essential.

Fervid as their Christianity was, it was altogether unprogressive in its form. It was inelastic, incompetent to adapt itself to changing circumstances. Some of their leaders were inclined at one time to favour a scheme of comprehension. It is, however, impossible to believe they would have agreed to any concession which was not evidently superficial. They longed indeed for unity ; and there is no reason to believe that they would have hesitated to sacrifice, though it would not be without a pang, many points of ritual and ceremony if it would further so good an end. But in their scheme of theology the essentials of an orthodox Church were numerous, and they would have been inflexible against any compromise of these. To abandon any part of the inheritance of primitive times would be gross heresy, a fatal dereliction of Christian duty. No one can read the letters of Bishop Ken without noticing how the calm and gentle spirit of that good prelate kindles into indignation at the thought of any departure from the ancient ' Depositum ' of the Church. He did not fail to appreciate and love true Christian piety when brought into near contact with it, even in those whose principles, in what he considered essential matters, differed greatly from his own. He was on cordial, and even intimate terms of friendship, for example, with Mr. Singer, a Nonconformist gentleman of high standing, who lived in the neighbourhood of Longleat. But this only serves to illustrate that there is an unity of faith far deeper than very deeply marked outward distinctions, a bond of Christian communion which, when once its strength is felt, is stronger than the strongest theories. Where the stiffness of his ' Catholic and orthodox' opinions was not counteracted or mitigated by feelings of warm personal respect, Ken could only view with unmixed aversion the working of principles which paid little regard to Church authority and attached small importance to any part of a Church system that did not clearly rest on plain words of Scripture. No one, reading without farther information the frequent laments made in Ken's letters and poems, that his flock had been left without a shepherd, that it was no longer folded in Catholic and hallowed grounds, and that it was fed with empoisoned instead of wholesome food, would think how good a man his successor in the see of Bath and Wells really was. Bishop Kidder was ' an exemplary and learned man of the simplest and most charitable character.' [1]   Robert Nelson had strongly recommended him to Archbishop Tillotson. But he held a Low Church view of the Sacraments ; he was inclined to admit, on what some considered too lenient terms, Dissenters of high character into the ministry of the English Church ; his reverence for primitive tradition was slight ; he had no respect for doctrines of passive obedience and divine right. In Ken's eyes he was therefore a ' Latitudinarian Traditour.' The deprived bishop had no wish to resume his see. It was more than once offered to him in Queen Anne's reign, when the oath of allegiance would no longer have been an insuperable obstacle. But throughout the life of his first successor his anxiety about his former diocese was very great, and his satisfaction was extreme when Kidder was succeeded by Hooper, a bishop of kindred principles to his own. And Ken was in these respects a fair representative of many who thought with him. To them the Christian faith, not in its fundamentals only, but in all the principal accessories of its constitution and government, was stereotyped in forms which could not be departed from without heresy or schism. There was scarcely any margin left for self-adaptation to changed requirements and varied modes of thought, no ready scope for elasticity and development. As Christianity had been left in the age of the first three councils, so it was to remain until the end of time. The first reformers had reformed it

---

[1] Bowles' *Life of Ken,* 247.

from its corruptions once and for all. The guardians of its
purity had only to walk loyally in their steps, carry out their
principles, and not be misled by any so-called reformer of
a later day, whose meddling hands would only have
marred the finished beauty of an accomplished work of
restoration.

Such opinions, when rich in vitality and warmth of conviction, have a very important function to fulfil. Admirably
adapted to supply the spiritual wants of a certain class of
minds, they represent one very important side of Christian
truth. Good men such as those who have been the subject
of this chapter are, in the Church, much what disinterested
and patriotic Conservatives are in the State. It is their special
function to resist needless changes and a too compliant sub-
servience to new or popular ideas, to maintain unbroken the
continuity of Christian thought, to guard from disparagement
and neglect whatever was most valuable in the religious characteristics of an earlier age. Theirs is a school of thought
which has neither a greater nor a less claim to genuine spirituality than that which is usually contrasted with it. Only
its spirituality is wont to take, in many respects, a different
tone. Instead of shrinking from forms which by their abuse
may tend to formalism, and simplifying to the utmost all the
accessories of worship, in jealous fear lest at any time the
senses should be impressed at the expense of the spirit, it
prefers rather to recognise as far as possible a lofty sacramental character in the institutions of religion, to see a
meaning, and an inward as well as an outward beauty, in
ceremonies and ritual, and to uphold a scrupulous and reve
rential observance of all sacred services, as conducing in a
very high degree to spiritual edification. Churchmen of this
type may often be blind to other sides of truth ; they may
rush into extremes ; they may fall into grave errors of exclusiveness and prejudice. But if they certainly cannot become
absolutely predominant in a Church without serious danger,
they cannot become a weak minority without much detriment
to its best interests. And since it is hopeless to find on any
wide scale minds so happily tempered as to combine within
themselves the best characteristics of different religious parties, a Church may well be congratulated which can count

among its loyal and attached members many men on either
side conspicuous for their high qualities.

The beginning of Queen Anne's reign was in this respect
a period of great promise. Not only was the Church of
England popular and its opponents weak, but both High and
Low Churchmen had leaders of distinguished eminence.
Tillotson and Stillingfleet had passed away, but the Low
Church bishops, such as Patrick and Fleetwood, Burnet,
Tenison, and Compton, held a very honourable place in
general esteem. The High Churchmen no longer had Lake
and Kettlewell, but Bull and Beveridge, Sharp, and Ken, and
Nelson were still living, and held in high honour. This latter
party had been rent asunder by the nonjuring schism. The
breach, however, was not yet irreparable ; and if it could be
healed, and the cordial feeling could be restored which, under
the influence of common Protestant sympathies, had begun
to draw the two sections of the Church together, the National
Church might seem likely to root itself more deeply in the
attachment of the people than at any previous time since the
Reformation. These fair promises were frustrated, and the
opportunity lost. Before many years had passed there was a
perceptible loss of tone and power in the Low Church party,
when King William's bishops had gradually died off. Among
High Churchmen, weakened by the secession, the growth of
degeneracy was still more evident. The contrast is immense
between the lofty-minded and single-hearted men who worked
with Ken and Nelson and the factious partisans who won
the applause of ' High Church ' mobs in the time of Sacheverell. Perhaps the Church activity which, at all events in
many notable instances, distinguished the first few years of
the eighteenth century, is thrown into stronger relief by the
comparative inertness which set in soon afterwards. For a
few years there was certainly every appearance of a growing
religious movement. Church brotherhoods were formed both
in London and in many country towns and villages, missions
were started, religious education was promoted, plans for the
reformation of manners were ardently engaged in, churches
were built, the weekly and daily services were in many places
frequented by increasing congregations, and communicants

rapidly increased. It might seem as if the Wesleyan movement was about to be forestalled, in general character though
not in detail, under the full sanction and direction of some of
the principal heads of the English Church; or as if the
movement were begun, and only wanted such another leader
as Wesley was. There was not enough fire in Robert Nelson's character for such a part. Yet, had he lived a little
longer, the example of his deep devotion and untiring zeal
might have kindled the flame in some younger men of congenial but more impetuous temperament, whose zeal would
have stirred the masses, and left a deep mark upon the history
of the age.

As it was, things took a different course. The chief promoters of these noble efforts died, and much of their work
died with them. Or it may be that the times were not yet
ripe for such a revival. It may even have been better in
the end for English Christianity, that no special period of
religious excitement should interfere with the serious intellectual conflict, in which all who could give any attention to
theology were becoming deeply interested. Great problems
involved in the principles of the Reformation, but obscured
up to that time by other and more superficial controversies,
were being everywhere discussed. An interval of religious
tranquillity amounting almost to stagnation may have been
not altogether unfavourable to a crisis when the fundamental
axioms of Christianity were being reviewed and tested. And,
after all, dulness is not death. The responsibilities of each
individual soul are happily not dependent upon unusual helps
and extraordinary opportunities. Yet great efforts of what
may be called missionary zeal are most precious, and fall like
rain upon the thirsty earth. It is impossible not to feel disappointment that the practical energies which at the beginning of the eighteenth century seemed ready to expand into
full life should have proved comparatively barren of permanent results. But though the effort was not seconded as it
should have been, none the less honour is due to the exemplary men who made it. It was an effort by no means confined to any one section of the Church. There were few more
earnest in it than many of the London clergy who had worked

heart and soul with Tillotson. But wherever any great religious undertaking, any scheme of Christian benevolence, was under consideration, wherever any plan was in hand for carrying out more thoroughly and successfully the work of the Church, there at all events was Robert Nelson, and the pious, earnest-hearted Churchmen who enjoyed his friendship.

C. J. A.

CHAPTER IV.

THE DEISTS.

OF the many controversies which were rife during the first half of the eighteenth century, none raised a question of greater importance than that which lay at the root of the Deistical controversy. That question was, in a word, this— How has God revealed Himself—how is He still revealing Himself to man? Is the so-called written Word the only means—is it the chief means—is it even a means at all, by which the Creator makes His will known to His creatures? Admitting the existence of a God—and with a few insignificant exceptions this admission would have been made by all— What are the evidences of His existence and of His dealings with us?

During the whole period of pre-reformation Christianity in England, and during the century which succeeded the rupture between the Church of England and that of Rome, all answers to this question, widely though they might have differed in subordinate points, would at least have agreed in this—that *some* external authority, whether it were the Scripture as interpreted by the Church, or the Scripture and Church traditions combined, or the Scripture interpreted by the light which itself affords or by the inner light which lighteth every man that cometh into the world, was necessary to manifest God to man. The Deists first ventured to hint that such authority was unnecessary; some even went so far as to hint that it was impossible. This at least was the tendency of their speculations; though it was not the avowed object of them. There was hardly a writer among the Deists who did not affirm that he had no wish to depreciate revealed truth. They all protested vigorously against the assumption that Deism was in any way opposed to Christianity rightly understood. "Deism," they

said, " is opposed to Atheism on the one side and to superstition
on the other ; but to Christianity—true, original Christianity—
as it came forth from the hands of its founder, the Deists are
so far from being opposed, that they are its truest defenders.'
Whether their position was logically tenable is quite another
question, but that they assumed it in all sincerity there is no
reason to doubt.

It is, however, extremely difficult to assert or deny anything respecting the Deists as a body, for as a matter of fact—
they had no corporate existence. The writers who are generally grouped under the name wrote apparently upon no
preconcerted plan. They formed no sect, properly so-called,
and were bound by no creed. In this sense at least they were
genuine ' freethinkers,' in that they freely expressed their
thoughts without the slightest regard to what had been said
or might be said by their friends or foes. It was the fashion
among their contemporaries to speak of the Deists as if they
were as distinct a sect as the Quakers, the Socinians, the
Presbyterians, or any other religious denomination. But we
look in vain for any common doctrine—any common form of
worship which belonged to the Deists as Deists.[1] As a rule,
they showed no desire to separate themselves from communion
with the National Church, although they were quite out of
harmony both with the articles of its belief and the spirit of its
prayers. A few negative tenets were perhaps more or less
common to all. That no traditional revelation can have the
same force of conviction as the direct revelation which God
has given to all mankind—in other words, that what is called
revealed religion must be inferior and subordinate to natural—
that the Scriptures must be criticised like any other book, and
no part of them be accepted as a revelation from God which
does not harmonize with the eternal and immutable reason of
things ; that, in point of fact, the Old Testament is a tissue of
fables and folly, and the New Testament has much alloy

---

[1] Shedd (*History of Christian Doctrine*, vol. i. ch. iv.) defines or describes
Deism as ' a general belief in God, coupled with disbelief in a written revelation,
and of all those particular views of God and man which are taught in Scripture.'
This describes fairly enough the tendency of Deism, but there is hardly a single
Deist out of whose writings it would not be easy to quote passages which are
directly at variance with this definition, or indeed with *any* definition that could
be framed.

mingled with the gold which it contains; that Jesus Christ is
not co-equal with the one God, and that his death can in no
sense be regarded as an atonement for sin, are tenets which
may be found in most of the Deistical writings; but beyond
these negative points there is little or nothing in common
between the heterogeneous body of writers who passed under
the vague name of Deists. To complicate matters still
further, the name 'Deist' was loosely applied as a name of
reproach to men who, in the widest sense of the term, do not
come within its meaning. Thus Cudworth, Tillotson, Locke,
and Samuel Clarke were stigmatised as Deists by their
enemies. On the other hand, men were grouped under the
category whose faith did not rise to the level of Deism. Thus
Hume is classified among the Deists.[1] Yet if the term 'Deism'
is allowed to have any definite meaning at all, it implies the
certainty and obligation of natural religion. It is of its very
essence that God has revealed himself so plainly to mankind
that there is no necessity, as there is no sufficient evidence, for
a better revelation. But Hume's scepticism embraced
natural as well as revealed religion. Hobbes, again, occupies
a prominent place among the Deists of the seventeenth century,
although the whole nature of his argument in 'The Leviathan'
is alien to the central thought of Deism. Add to all this, that
the Deists proper were constantly accused of holding views
which they never held, and that conclusions were drawn from
their premises which those premises did not warrant, and
the difficulty of treating the subject as a whole will be readily
perceived. And yet treated it must be; the most superficial
sketch of English Church history during the eighteenth century
would be most imperfect if it did not give a prominent place
to this topic, for it was the all-absorbing topic of a considerable portion of the period.

---

[1] Mrs. Mallet once said to Hume, 'Allow me, Mr. Hume, to introduce myself
to you. It is right that we Deists should know each other.' 'Madam,' replied
Hume, 'I am not a Deist, and do not wish to be known under that name.' See
Hunt's *Religious Thought in England*, vol. iii. ch. xiii. p. 197. We need not
wonder at Hume's disclaiming the title; not only was his system essentially different from theirs, but he was a far more profound and consistent thinker than any
of the Deists. His friends, however, as well as his enemies, spoke of him as a
Deist. See an account of the *Life and Writings of David Hume, Esq.*, by T. E.
Richie, p. 330.

The Deistical writers attracted attention out of all proportion to their literary merit. The pulpit rang with denunciations of their doctrines. The press teemed with answers to their arguments. It may seem strange that a mere handful of not very voluminous writers, not one of whom can be said to have attained to the eminence of an English classic,[1] should have created such a vast amount of excitement. But the excitement was really caused by the subject itself, not by the method in which it was handled. The Deists only gave expression—often a very coarse and inadequate expression—to thoughts which the circumstances of the times could scarcely fail to suggest.[2]

The Scriptures had for many years been used to sanction the most diametrically opposite views. They had been the

---

[1] That is, not in virtue of anything he wrote which can be properly called Deism. Shaftesbury in his ethical and Bolingbroke in his political writings may perhaps be termed classical writers, but neither of them quâ Deists.

[2] Besides the causes enumerated in the text, the tendency of much of the philosophy of the seventeenth century was in the direction of Deism. Mr. Leslie Stephen makes a rather sweeping assertion when he says that the whole essence of the Deist's position may be found in Spinoza's *Tractatus Theologico-Politicus*, (*English Thought*, &c., i. 33), but he is substantially correct. The connexion between Spinozism and Deism is illustrated by the course which Toland ultimately took. The Cartesian philosophy, again, might be easily represented as unfavourable to a historical religion like Christianity. Descartes distinctly avowed himself to be a Christian, but the tendency of his system was, if not against Christianity, against many of the arguments by which it had been wont to be supported. There is perhaps a little unconscious irony in the closing paragraph of his *Principia* :—' Nihil affirmo ; sed hæc omnia Ecclesiæ Catholicæ auctoritati. . . . submitto !' The sentence reminds one of Shaftesbury's professions of devoted attachment to the Church ; only, Shaftesbury was probably actuated by contemptuous indifference (see *infra*, p. 187), Descartes by real timidity, and a desire to stand well with the ecclesiastical authorities.

Since the above was written, I have read Professor Fowler's admirable introduction to Bacon's *Novum Organum*. The reader may be referred to § 7, *Bacon's Religious Opinions*, for some valuable remarks on the effects of the philosophy of the seventeenth century upon the religion of the eighteenth century. Referring to the famous passage in Bacon's *Essays of Superstition*, which gives a preference to Atheism over Superstition, the writer, after having noted 'the recoil from the superstitions of the Church of Rome, and especially from the dangers with which the machinations of that Church seemed to threaten the civil power,' observes, ' This view, as stated by Bacon, bore fruit and multiplied. The undiscriminating denunciation of superstition in the seventeenth century, coupled with the free mode of enquiry into the fundamentals of religion which marked the close of the period, terminated in results, which, however much he may have contributed to them, he would probably have been among the last to welcome.'—Professor Fowler's edition of Bacon's *Novum Organum*, Introduction, p. 51.

watchword of each party in turn whose extravagances had been the cause of all the disasters and errors of several generations. Romanists had quoted them when they condemned Protestants to the stake, Protestants when they condemned Jesuits to the block. The Roundhead had founded his wild reign of fanaticism on their authority. The Cavalier had texts ready at hand to sanction the most unconstitutional measures. 'The right divine of kings to govern wrong' had been grounded on Scriptural authority. All the strange vagaries in which the seventeenth century had been so fruitful claimed the voice of Scripture in their favour.

Such reckless use of Scripture tended to throw discredit upon it as a revelation from God ; while, on the other hand, the grand discoveries in natural science which were a distinguishing feature of the seventeenth century equally tended to exalt men's notions of that other revelation of Himself which God has made in the Book of Nature. The calm attitude of the men of science who had been steadily advancing in the knowledge of the natural world, and by each fresh discovery had given fresh proofs of the power, and wisdom, and goodness of God, stood forth in painful contrast with the profitless wranglings and bitter animosities of Divines. Men might well begin to ask themselves whether they could not find rest from theological strife in natural religion? and the real object of the Deists was to demonstrate that they could.

Thus the period of Deism was the period of a great religious crisis in England. It is our present purpose briefly to trace the progress and termination of this crisis.

It is hardly necessary to remark that Deism was not a product of the eighteenth century. The spirit which in Deism appeared in its most pronounced form had been growing for many generations previous to that date. Reginald Peacock has been called the first Deist ;[1] but it is difficult to see on what grounds. If by Deism be merely meant the spirit of free inquiry rebelling against a blind submission to authority, there were Deists in England long before Peacock ; if Deism be understood in its stricter sense as indicating the frame of mind which leads to the exaltation of natural at the expense of revealed religion, the definition will not include Peacock. This

[1] Warner in Lechler's *Geschichte des englischen Deismus.*

latter spirit is not found, at least in its full development, until the seventeenth century ; and if we use the term ' Deism ' in its restricted sense we shall not be able to find a true English Deist before Lord Herbert of Cherbury.   In tone and spirit, indeed, Lord Herbert stands out in marked and favourable contrast with later writers of the same school.   Widely as he differed in many respects from his brother George, he was not wholly without the qualities which endear the name of the latter to all who love true Christianity and true poetry. It was Lord Herbert's loving spirit which could not bear to contemplate the exclusion from God's mercy of those on whom the light of revelation had never been shed, that led him into that train of thought which contains at least the germs of the Deism of the eighteenth century.   There is in his writings the same implied superiority of natural over revealed religion because the former is universal while the latter is only partial, the same insinuations that traditional religions have all been corrupted by priestcraft, and the same depreciation of Scripture, which formed the commonplaces of the eighteenth-century Deists.   Like them, he declares Christianity to be the best religion in the world ; but, like them, he seems to mean by Christianity something wider and vaguer than the distinctive, dogmatic teaching which has from the earliest times passed under that name.   His writings, however, do not properly come within the range of our present inquiry.   For the same reason we pass over the names of Hobbes, Blount, and Gildon, and come at once to a writer who, although his most notorious work was published before the seventeenth century closed, lived and wrote during the eighteenth, and may fairly be regarded as belonging to that era.

No work which can be properly called Deistical had raised anything like the excitement which was caused by the anonymous publication in 1696 of a short and incomplete treatise entitled ' Christianity not Mysterious, or a Discourse showing that there is nothing in the Gospel contrary to Reason nor above it, and that no Christian Doctrine can properly be called a Mystery.'   In the second edition, published the same year, the author discovered himself to be a young Irishman of the name of John Toland, who had been brought up a Roman Catholic.   Leland passes over this work with a slight notice ;

but it marked a distinct epoch in Deistical literature. For the first time, the secular arm was brought to bear upon a writer of this school. The book was presented by the Grand Jury of Middlesex, and was burnt by the hands of the hangman in Dublin by order of the Irish House of Commons. It was subsequently condemned as heretical and impious by the Lower House of Convocation, which body felt itself bitterly aggrieved when the Upper House refused to confirm the sentence. These official censures were a reflex of the opinions expressed out of doors. Pulpits rang with denunciations and confutations of the new heretic, especially in his own country. A sermon against him was ' as much expected as if it had been prescribed in the rubric ; ' an Irish peer gave it as a reason why he had ceased to attend church that once he heard something there about his Saviour Jesus Christ, but now all the discourse was about one John Toland.[1]

Toland being a vain man rather enjoyed this notoriety than otherwise ; but if his own account of the object of his publication be correct (and there is no reason to doubt his sincerity), he was singularly unsuccessful in impressing his real meaning upon his contemporaries. He affirmed that ' he wrote his book to defend Christianity, and prayed that God would give him grace to vindicate religion,' and at a later period he published his creed in terms that would satisfy the most orthodox Christian.[2]

For an explanation of the extraordinary discrepancy between the avowed object of the writer and the alleged tendency of his book we naturally turn to the work itself. The author begins by telling us in his preface, ' in the following discourse, which is the first of three, and wherein I prove my subject in general, the divinity of the New Testament is taken for granted. In the second, I attempt a particular and rational explanation of the reputed mysteries of the Gospel. In the

---

[1] See Hunt's *Religious Thought in England*, vol. ii. p. 244.

[2] 'I firmly believe in God, as wise, good, &c. I believe Christ is God manifest in the flesh ; that, according to the prophets, he was born of a pure Virgin ; that he rose from the dead the third day, and forty days after ascended into Heaven ; that by the sacrifice of his death he reconciled all such as do the will of the Father. I believe we are sanctified by the Divine Spirit, who worketh in us and with us.' Toland's Memorial to a Minister of State on the accession of George I.

third, I demonstrate the verity of the Divine Revelation against Atheists and all enemies of revealed religion.' The two last discourses were never published. The substance of the first is as follows :—After stating the conflicting views of divines about the Gospel mysteries, he maintains that there is nothing in the Gospel contrary to reason nor above it, and that no Christian doctrine can be properly called a mystery. He then defines the functions of reason, and proceeds to controvert the two following positions, (1) that though reason and the Gospel are not in themselves contradictory, yet according to our conception of them they may seem directly to clash ; and (2) that we are to adore what we cannot comprehend. He declares that what Infinite Goodness has not been pleased to reveal to us, we are either sufficiently capable of discovering ourselves or need not understand at all. He affirms that ' mystery' in the New Testament is never put for anything inconceivable in itself or not to be judged by our ordinary faculties ; and concludes by showing that mysteries in the present sense of the term were imported into Christianity partly by Judaizers, but mainly by the heathen introducing their old mysteries into Christianity when they were converted.

The first of Toland's positions, that there is nothing in the Gospel *contrary* to reason, was not difficult to maintain. The real difficulty lay in proving that there was nothing in the Gospel *above* reason, and that no Christian doctrine can be properly called a mystery. In proving this, Toland appeals to our knowledge of natural things. 'No Christian doctrine,' he says, ' no more than any ordinary piece of nature, can be reputed a mystery because we have not an adequate or compleat idea of whatever belongs to it. What is revealed in religion, as it is most useful and necessary, so it must and may be as easily comprehended, and found as consistent with our common notions as what we know of wood, stone, &c. ; and when we do as familiarly explain such doctrines as what we know of natural things (which I pretend we can), we may then be as properly said to comprehend the one as the other.'[1]

'Nothing is a mystery because we know not its essence, since that is neither knowable in itself nor even thought

[1] *Christianity not Mysterious*, p. 79.

of by us.'[1] 'Faith is so far from being an implicit assent to anything above reason, that this notion contradicts the ends of religion, the nature of man and the goodness and wisdom of God. . . . The question is not, whether we could discover all the objects of our faith by ratiocination ; I have proved, on the contrary, that no matter of fact can be known without revelation. But what is once revealed we must as well understand as any other matter in the world. Is reason of more dignity than revelation ? Just as much as a Greek grammar is superior to the New Testament. The uncorrupted doctrines of Christianity are not above the reach of the vulgar, but the gibberish of your divinity schools is.[2] Their own advantage was the motion that put the primitive clergy upon reviving mystery,'—and so forth.[3]

The above passages are quoted at length from this small book, not on account of its intrinsic merits (though, as the work of a young man of twenty-five, it is a remarkable performance),[4] but on account of the stir which it created, and which marks a new phase in the history of Deism. Compared with Lord Herbert's elaborate treatises, it is an utterly insignificant work ; but the excitement caused by Lord Herbert's books was as nothing when compared with that which Toland's fragment raised. The explanation may perhaps be found in the fact that at the later date men's minds were more at leisure to consider the questions raised than they were at the earlier, and also that they perceived, or fancied they perceived, more clearly the drift of such speculations. A little tract, published towards the end of the seventeenth century, entitled ' The Growth of Deism,' brings out these points ; and as a matter of fact we find that for the next half century the minds of all classes were on the alert—some in sympathy with, many more in bitter antagonism against, Deistical speculations. In his later writings, Toland went much further in the direction of infidelity, if not of absolute Atheism, than he did in his first work.[5]

---

[1] *Christianity not Mysterious*, p. 87. See also p. 135.

[2] *Ibid.* p. 165.

[3] *Ibid.* p. 166.

[4] Herder goes so far as to say that Toland surpassed all the later freethinkers in learning and quickness.—Herder's *Adrastea*, ii. p. 130.

[5] See his *Nazarenus* and later works *passim.*—If anything, he seems to have become a Pantheist. See his *Pantheisticon*—'directed,' writes Schlosser (*His-*

The next writer who comes under our notice was a greater
man in every sense of the term than Toland. Lord Shaftesbury's 'Miscellaneous Essays,' which were ultimately grouped
in one work, under the title of 'Characteristics of Men and
Manners, &c.,' only bear incidentally upon the points at issue
between the Deists and the orthodox. But scattered here
and there are passages which show how strongly the writer
felt upon the subject. Leland was called to account, and
half apologizes for ranking Shaftesbury among the Deists at
all.[1] And there certainly is one point of view from which
Shaftesbury's speculations may be regarded not only as
Christian, but as greatly in advance of the Christianity of
many of the orthodox writers of his day. As a protest
against the selfish, utilitarian view of Christianity which was
utterly at variance with the spirit displayed and inculcated by
Him 'who pleased not Himself,' Lord Shaftesbury's work
deserves the high tribute paid to it by its latest editor, 'as a
monument to immutable morality and Christian philosophy
which has survived many changes of opinion and revolutions of
thought.'[2] But from another point of view we shall come to
a very different conclusion.

Shaftesbury was regarded by his contemporaries as a
decided and formidable adversary of Christianity. Pope told
Warburton,[3] 'that to his knowledge "The Characteristics" had
done more harm to Revealed Religion in England than all the
works of Infidelity put together.' Voltaire called him 'even a
too vehement opponent of Christianity.'[4] Warburton, while
admitting his many excellent qualities both as a man and as a
writer, speaks of 'the inveterate rancour which he indulged
against Christianity.'[5]

tory of the Eighteenth Century, vol. i. ch. i.) 'against every kind of religion which
teaches belief in a personal god, and proposes to establish a Pantheistic congregation to oppose superstition, i.e., religion of every kind.'

[1] *View of the Deistical Writers,* Letter V. p. 32, &c., and Letter VI. p. 43,
&c.

[2] The Rev. W. M. Hatch. See his dedication.

[3] See Warburton's Letters to Hurd, Letter XVIII. January 30, 1749–50.

[4] See Schlosser's *History of the Eighteenth Century,* translated by D. Davison.
Schlosser himself says that Shaftesbury attacks all positive religions, especially the
Mosaic and Christian, more vehemently than any of the other Deists.

[5] See Warburton's *Dedication of the Divine Legation of Moses to the Freethinkers.* Jeffery, another contemporary, writes to the same effect.

A careful examination of Shaftesbury's writings can hardly fail to lead us to the same conclusion. He writes, indeed, as an easy, well-bred man of the world, and was no doubt perfectly sincere in his constantly repeated disavowal of any wish to disturb the existing state of things. But his reason obviously is that 'the game would not be worth the candle.' 'Populus vult decipi, decipiatur.' Perhaps his own attitude towards Christianity is best described in the following curious story :—' Three or four merry gentlemen came to a country where they were told they should find the worst entertainment and roads imaginable. One said, " The best expedient for them in this extremity would be to keep themselves in high humour, and endeavour to commend everything the place afforded." They commended every tolerable bit of road or ordinary prospect, and found reasons for the odd taste and looks of things presented to 'em at table ; they ate and drank heartily, and took up with indifferent fare so well that 'twas apparent they had wrought upon themselves to believe they were tolerably well served. Their servants kept their senses, and said their masters had lost theirs. The malicious reader might infer from this story of my travelling friends that I intend to represent it an easy matter for people to persuade themselves into what opinion or belief they pleased. It is no small interest or concern with men to believe what is by authority established, since in the case of disbelief there can be no choice left but either to live a hypocrite or be esteemed profane. In a country where faith has for a long time gone by inheritance, and opinions are entailed by law, there is little room left for the vulgar to alter their persuasions or deliberate on the choice of religious belief. When a government thinks fit to concern itself with men's opinions, and by its absolute authority impose any particular belief, there is none perhaps ever so ridiculous or monstrous in which it needs doubt having good success.'[1] No one can fail to perceive a contemptuous irony in many passages in which Shaftesbury affirms his orthodoxy,[2] or when he touches upon the persecution of the

---

[1] *Miscellaneous Reflections*, II. c. 3.

[2] ' The only subject on which we are perfectly secure and without fear of any just censure or reproach is that of faith and orthodox belief. For (1) it will appear that through a profound respect and religious veneration we have forborne

early Christians, or upon the mysteries of Christianity,[1] or upon the sacred duty of complying with the established religion [2]

so much as to name any of the sacred and solemn mystery of revelation ; and (2) as we can with confidence declare that we have never in any writing attempted such high researches, nor in practice acquitted ourselves otherwise than as just conformists to the lawful church, so we may be said faithfully and dutifully to embrace those holy mysterys, even in their minutest particulars and without the least exception on account of their amazing depth.' 'Whatever difficulties there may be in any particular speculations or mystery belonging to the faith espoused or countenanced by the magistrate, the better sort of men will endeavour to pass them over. They will believe to the full stretch of their reason, and add spurs to their faith in order to be more sociable, and conform the better with what their interest in conjunction with their good humour inclines them to receive as credible, and observe as their religious duty and devotional task. Here it is that good humour will naturally take place, and the hospitable disposition of our travelling friends [alluding to the story quoted above] will easily transfer itself into religion, and operate in the same manner with respect to the established faith [however miraculous or incomprehensible] under a mild government.'

[1] 'The Christian theology, the birth, procedure, generation, and personal distinctions of the divinity, are mysterys only to be determined by the initiated or ordained, to whom the State has assigned the guardianship and promulgation of the divine oracles. It becomes not those who are uninspired from Heaven and uncommissioned from earth to search with curiosity into the original of those holy rites and records by *law established*. Should we make such an attempt, we should probably find the less satisfaction the further we persevered to carry our speculations. Having dared once to quit the authority and direction of the law, we should easily be subject to heterodoxy and error, when we had no better warrant left us for the authority of our sacred *symbols* than the integrity, candour, and disinterestedness of their compilers and registers.'

[2] 'I was always the first to comply ; and for matters of religion was further from profaneness and erroneous doctrine than any one. I could never have the sufficiency to shock my spiritual and learned superiors. I was the furthest from leaning to my own understanding ; nor was I one who exalted reason above faith, or insisted much upon what the dogmatical men call demonstration, and dare oppose to the sacred mysterys of religion. And to show you, continued I, how impossible it is for the men of our sort to err from the Catholic and established religion, whereas others pretend to see with their own eyes what is proper and best for them in religion, *we* pretend not to see with any other than those of our spiritual guides. Neither do we presume to judge those guides ourselves, but submit to them as they are appointed by our just superiors. You who are rationalists and walk by reason in everything pretend to know all things, whilst you believe little or nothing ; we know nothing and believe all.'

After mocking modern miracles, he adds, 'but for what is recorded of ages heretofore, he seems to resign his judgment with entire condescension to his superiors. He pretends not to frame any certain or positive opinions of his own notwithstanding his best searches into antiquity and the nature of religious record and tradition ; but on all occasions submits most with full confidence and trust to the opinions of law established. If this is not sufficient to free him from the reproach of scepticism, he must be content to undergo it.'

'Though we are sensible it would be no small hardship to deprive others of a

with unreasoning faith, or upon his presumed scepticism, or upon the nature of the Christian miracles, or upon the character of our Blessed Saviour,[1] or upon the representation of God in the Old Testament, or upon the supposed omission of the virtue of friendship in the Christian system of ethics.

It is needless to quote the passages in which Shaftesbury, like the other Deists, abuses the Jews ; neither is it necessary to dwell upon his strange argument that ridicule is the best test of truth.[2] In this, as in other parts of his writings, it is often difficult to see when he is writing seriously, when ironically. Perhaps he has himself furnished us with the means of solving the difficulty. ' If,' he writes, ' men are forbidden to speak their minds seriously on certain subjects, they will do it ironically. If they are forbidden to speak at all upon such subjects, or if they find it really dangerous to do so, they will then redouble their disguise, involve themselves in mysteriousness, and talk so as hardly to be understood or at least not plainly interpreted by those who are disposed to do them a mischief.'[3] The general tendency, however, of his writings is pretty clear, and is in harmony with the Deistical theory that God's revelation of himself in Nature is certain, clear, and sufficient for all practical purposes, while any other revelation is uncertain, obscure, and unnecessary. But he holds that it would be unmannerly and disadvantageous to the interests of the community to act upon this doctrine in practical life. 'Better take things as they are. Laugh in your sleeve,

liberty of examining and searching with due modesty and submission into the nature of those subjects, yet as for ourselves, who have not the least scruple whatsoever, we pray not any such grace or favour ; being fully assured of our steady orthodoxy, resignation, and entire submission to the true Christian and Catholic doctrines of our Holy Church as by law established.'

[1] 'Our Saviour's style is . . . sharp, humourous, and witty in his repartees . . . his miracles carry with them a certain festivity, alacrity, and good humour, so that it is impossible not to be moved in a pleasant manner at their recital.' That is, as Leland quaintly adds, not to laugh at them. ' Sacred Scripture has been so miraculously preserved in its successive copies and transcriptions under the eye (as we must needs suppose) of holy and learned critics.' ' David was a hearty espouser of the merry devotion. The high dance performed by him in the procession of the sacred coffer shows he was not ashamed of expressing any ecstacy of joy or playsome humour.'

[2] A high authority (Mr. Carlyle) can find no such text in Shaftesbury's writings. The reader can only be referred to the writings themselves.

[3] *Sensus Communis* (on the Freedom of Wit and Humour), § 4.

if you will, at the follies which priestcraft has imposed upon mankind; but do not show your bad taste and bad humour by striving to battle against the stream of popular opinion. When you are at Rome, do as Rome does. The question, " What is truth" is a highly inconvenient one. If you must ask it, ask it to yourself.'

It must be confessed that such low views of religion and morality are strangely at variance with the exalted notions of the disinterestedness of virtue which form the staple of one of Shaftesbury's most important treatises. To reconcile the discrepancy seems impossible. Only let us take care that while we emphatically repudiate the immoral compromise between truth and expediency which Shaftesbury recommends, we do not lose sight of the real service which he has rendered to religion as well as philosophy by showing the excellency of virtue in itself without regard to the rewards and punishments which are attached to its pursuit or neglect.[1]

The year before ' The Characteristics ' appeared as a single work (1713), a small treatise was published anonymously which was at first assigned to the author of ' Christianity not Mysterious,' and which almost rivalled that notorious work in the attention which it excited, out of all proportion to its intrinsic merits. It was entitled ' A Discourse of Freethinking, occasioned by the Rise and Growth of a Sect called Freethinkers,' and was presently owned as the work of Anthony Collins, an author who had previously entered into the lists of controversy in connection with the disputes of Sacheverell, Dodwell, and Clarke. 'The Discourse of Freethinking' was in itself a slight performance. Its general scope was to show that every man has a right to think freely on all religious as well as other subjects, and that the exercise of this right is the sole remedy for the evil of superstition. The necessity of freethinking is shown by the endless variety of opinions which priests hold about all religious questions. Then the various objections to Freethinking are considered, and the treatise ends with a list and description of wise and

---

[1] Mackintosh considers that Shaftesbury's writings ' contain more intimations of an original and important nature on the theory of ethics than perhaps any preceding work of modern times.'—Dissertation, p. 93. See, also, Morell's *History of Modern Philosophy*, i. p. 204.

virtuous Freethinkers—nineteen in number—from Socrates to Tillotson.

In estimating the merits of this little book, and in accounting for the excitement which it produced, we must not forget that what may now appear to us truisms were 160 years ago new truths, even if they were recognised as truths at all. At the beginning of the eighteenth century it was not an unnecessary task to vindicate the right of every man to think freely ; and if Collins had performed the work which he had taken in hand fully and fairly he might have done good service. But while professedly advocating the duty of thinking freely, he showed so obvious a bias in favour of thinking in a particular direction, and wrested facts and quoted authorities in so one-sided a manner, that he laid himself open to the just strictures of many who valued and practised equally with himself the right of freethinking. Some of the most famous men of the day at once entered into the lists against him, among whom were Hoadly,[1] Swift, Whiston, Berkeley, and above all Bentley. The latter, under the title of ' Phileleutherus Lipsiensis,' wrote in the character of a German Lutheran to his English friend, Dr. Francis Hare, ' Remarks on a Discourse on Freethinking.' Regarded as a piece of intellectual gladiatorship the Remarks are justly entitled to the fame they have achieved. The great critic exposed unmercifully and unanswerably Collins's slips in scholarship, ridiculed his style, made merry over the rising and growing sect which professed its competency to think *de quolibet ente*, protested indignantly against putting the Talapoins of Siam on a level with the whole clergy of England, ' the light and glory of Christianity,' and denied the right of the title of Freethinkers to men who brought scandal on so good a word.

Bentley hit several blots, not only in Collins, but in others of the ' rising and growing sect.' The argument, *e.g.*, drawn from the variety of readings in the New Testament, is not only demolished but adroitly used to place his adversary on the horns of a dilemma. Nothing, again, can be neater

---

[1] Hoadly in one sense may be regarded as a 'Freethinker' himself; but it was the very fact that he was so which made him resent Collins's perversion of the term. The first of his ' Queries to the Author of a Discourse of Freethinking ' is ' Whether that can be justly called Freethinking which is manifestly thinking with the utmost slavery ; and with the strongest prejudices against every branch, and the very foundation of all religion ?'—Hoadly's *Works*, vol. i.

than his answer to various objections by showing that those
objections had been brought to light by Christians themselves. ' Pray, who are the discoverers of pious frauds ? '
he asks. ' The Christian priests themselves ; so far are
they from concealing or propagating them, or thinking
their cause needs them.' ' When,' he asks, ' has he or any
of his sect shown any tolerable skill in science ? What dark
passages of Scripture have they cleared, or of any book whatever ? What have they done in the language, the shell
and surface of Scripture ? ' He lays stress on the convenient
elasticity with which Collins uses the word ' freethinking,'
' juggling with it, and putting it for the common use of reason
and lawful liberty of examining.' ' If,' he adds, ' all your
freethinking does not centre in their opinions, you shall be
none of their family : claim your right as you will on the
terms of the definition, plead that you have *thought freely,*
impartially, and carefully upon all these propositions, and that
in all of them the force of evidence has drawn you to the contrary side, protest against this foul play that they themselves
impose creeds and terms of communion ; that the author, while
he rails at all guides, obtrudes himself as a guide to others ;
all this shall avail you nothing ; you shall never be incorporated into the " rising and growing sect " till you own that
that's the only freethinking to think just as they do.' He
remarks on the inconsistency of Collins in finding fault with
divines who, for want of good conduct, dispute about the
Trinity, Predestination, and so forth, while yet the whole purport of his book is that men may think *de quolibet ente.* In
short, turn where we will, we find in these Remarks a marvellous dexterity in showing up the weak points of his adversary. And yet the general impression, when one has read
Collins and Bentley carefully, is that there is a real element of
truth in the former to which the latter has not done justice ;
that Bentley presses Collins's arguments beyond their logical
conclusion ; that Collins is not what Bentley would have him
to be—a mere Materialist—an Atheist in disguise ;[1] that

---

[1] Bentley, in common with Berkeley and many writers of his day, held that
Deism was nothing but Atheism in disguise. Thus, in the first of his Boyle
Lectures, entitled ' The Folly of Atheism, and (what is now called) Deism,' he
takes for his text, Ps. xiv. ' The fool hath said in his heart there is no God,' &c.

Bentley's insinuation, that looseness of living is the cause of his looseness of belief, is ungenerous, and requires proof which Bentley has not given ; that the bitter abuse which he heaps upon his adversary as 'a wretched gleaner of weeds,' 'a pert teacher of his betters,' 'an unsociable animal,' 'an obstinate and intractable wretch,' and much more to the same effect, is unworthy of a Christian clergyman, and calculated to damage rather than do service to the cause which he has at heart.[1]

Collins himself was not put to silence. Besides other writings of minor importance, he published in 1724 the most weighty of all his works, a 'Discourse on the Grounds and Reasons of the Christian Religion.' The object of this book is to show that Christianity is entirely founded on the fulfilment of the Old Testament prophecies, and then to prove that

'There are some infidels,' he writes, 'among us who . . . . to avoid the odious name of Atheists, would shelter and skreen themselves under a new one of Deists, which is not quite so obnoxious. But I think the text hath cut them short and precluded this subterfuge ; inasmuch as it hath declared that all such wicked Principles are coincident and all one in the issue with the rankest Atheism,' &c. This was preached in 1692 ; the subsequent development of Deism certainly did not lead Bentley to alter his views.

To the same effect Berkeley, in his *Minute Philosopher*, makes 'the Freethinker to appear in the various lights of *Atheist*, Libertine, Enthusiast, Scorner,' &c. He probably alludes to Collins when he makes the Freethinker 'to have found out a demonstration against the being of a God.' But on this work *see infra.*

[1] As if it was not enough for poor Collins to have called forth the wrath of the greatest of English critics, he also found arrayed against him the greatest of English satirists. In his *Discourse*, Collins ironically commends the project of the Society for the Propagation of the Gospel for supposing 'Freethinking in matters of religion to be the duty of all men, and therefore sending out missionaries to convince the Siamese.' 'And oh !' he adds, 'that the proper persons were but employed for the execution of so glorious a design ! That such zealous divines as our S[acheverel]ls, our At[terbur]ys, our Sm[alrid]ges, our *Sw[i]fts*, were drawn out annually as our military missionarys and sent into Foreign Parts to propagate the Gospels. We might then hope to see blessed days, the doctrines and discipline of the Church of England triumph throughout the world, and faction cease at home'—(p. 43). This hint, that the removal of Swift out of the country would be a good riddance, was resented by the great satirist in a tract entitled, *Mr. Collins' Discourse of Freethinking, put into plain English, by way of abstract for the use of the Poor.* Collins' weak points are hit off in Swift's raciest style, e.g. 'The Bible says the Jews were a nation favoured by God ; but I, who am a Freethinker, say that cannot be, because the Jews lived in a corner of the earth, and Freethinking makes it plain that those who live in corners cannot be favourites of God. The New Testament all along asserts the truth of Christianity, but Freethinking denies it, because Christianity was communicated but to few, and whatever is communicated but to a few cannot be true,' &c.

these prophecies were fulfilled not in a literal, but only in a typical or secondary sense. Novelty, he argues, is a weighty reproach against any religious institution ; the truth of Christianity must depend upon the old dispensation ; it is founded on Judaism. Jesus makes claim to obedience only so far as He is the Messias of the Old Testament ; the fundamental article of Christianity is that Jesus of Nazareth is the Jewish Messiah, and this can only be known out of the Old Testament. In fact, the Old Testament is the *only* canon of Christians ; for the New Testament is not a law book for the ruling of the Church. The Apostles rest their proof of Christianity only on the Old Testament. If this proof is valid, Christianity is strong and built upon its true grounds ; if weak, Christianity is false. For no miracles, no authority of the New Testament can prove its truth ; miracles can only be a proof so far as they are comprehended in and exactly consonant to the prophecies concerning the Messias. It is only in this sense that Jesus appeals to His miracles. Christianity, in a word, is simply the allegorical sense of the Old Testament, and therefore may be rightly called ' Mystical Judaism.'

As all this bore the appearance of explaining away Christianity altogether, or at least of making it rest upon the most shadowy and unsubstantial grounds, there is no wonder that it called forth a vehement opposition : no less than thirty-five answerers appeared within two years of its publication, among whom are found the great names of T. Sherlock, Zachary Pearce, S. Clarke, and Dr. Chandler. The latter wrote the most solid and profound, if not the most brilliant work which the Deistical controversy had yet called forth.

But the strangest outcome of Collins' famous book was the work of Woolston, an eccentric writer who is generally classed among the Deists, but who was in fact *sui generis.*[1] In the Collins' Controversy, Woolston appears as a moderator between an infidel and an apostate, the infidel being Collins, and the apostate the Church of England, which had

---

[1] Collins' work not only gave birth to an eccentric writer, but was itself called forth by one scarcely less eccentric. It was professedly an answer to Whiston's *Essay towards restoring the true Text of the Old Testament, and for vindicating the citations made thence in the New Testament.*

L. .

left the good old paths of allegory to become slaves of the letter. In this, as in previous works, he rides his hobby, which was a strange perversion of patristic notions, to the death ; and a few years later he returned to the charge in one of the wildest, craziest books that ever was written by human pen. It was entitled ' Six Discourses on the Miracles,' and in it the literal interpretation of the New Testament miracles is ridiculed with the coarsest blasphemy, while the mystical interpretations which he substitutes in its place read like the disordered fancies of a sick man's dream. He professes simply to follow the fathers, ignoring the fact that the fathers, as a rule, had grafted their allegorical interpretation upon the literal history, not substituted the one for the other. Woolston was the only Deist—if Deist he is to be called,—who as yet had suffered anything like persecution; indeed, with one exception, and that a doubtful one, he was the only one who ever did. He was brought before the King's Bench, condemned to pay 25*l.* for each of his Six Discourses, and to suffer a year's imprisonment; after which he was only to regain his liberty upon finding either two securities for 1,000*l.* or four for 500*l.*; as no one would go bail for him, he remained in prison until his death in 1731.[1] The punishment was a cruel one, considering the state of the poor man's mind, of the disordered condition of which he was himself conscious. If he deserved to lose his liberty at all, an asylum would have been a more fitting place of confinement for him than a prison. But if we regard his writings as the writings of a sane man, which, strange to say, his contemporaries appear to have done, we can hardly be surprised at the fate he met with. Supposing that *any* blasphemous publication deserved punishment—a supposition which in Woolston's days would have been granted as a matter of course—it is impossible to conceive anything more outrageously blasphemous than what is

---

[1] Herder, in his generous indignation against any kind of religious persecution, gives a more sensational description of the event than that given in the text. 'Judicial persecution heated his [Woolston's] doubtless warm head ; he died—here let mankind drop a tear—the good man died in consequence of his well-meant allegories to which he reduced the miracles of Christ—in prison ! He was tenderhearted, forgiving, &c., yet such a man died, in prison !' There is no evidence to show, what Herder here insinuates, that Woolston's punishment was the cause of his death. It is the old fallacy of *Post hoc, ergo propter hoc.*

found in Woolston's wild book. The only strange part of the matter was that it should have been treated seriously at all. 30,000 copies of his discourses on the miracles were sold quickly and at a very dear rate ; whole bales of them were sent over to America. Sixty adversaries wrote against him. The Bishop of London thought it necessary to send five pastoral letters to the people of his diocese on the subject. And perhaps the most curious circumstance of all is, that even in modern times, when the temporary panic must have long ago passed away, we find this poor man's hallucinations gravely referred to as a substantive part of the Deistical controversy.[1]

The works of Woolston were, however, in one way important, inasmuch as they called the public attention to the miracles of our Lord, and especially to the greatest miracle of all—His own Resurrection. The most notable of the answers to Woolston was Thomas Sherlock's 'Tryal of the Witnesses of the Resurrection of Jesus.' This again called forth an anonymous pamphlet entitled ' The Resurrection of Jesus considered,' by a ' moral philosopher,' who afterwards proved to be one Peter Annet. In no strict sense of the term can Annet be called a Deist, though he is often ranked in that class. His name is, however, worth noticing, from his connection with the important and somewhat curiously conducted controversy respecting the Resurrection, to which Sherlock's ' Tryal of the Witnesses ' gave both the impulse and the form. Annet, like Woolston, was prosecuted for blasphemy and profanity ; and if the secular arm should ever be appealed to in such matters, which is doubtful, he deserved it by the coarse ribaldry of his attacks upon sacred things.[2]

It has been thought better to present at one view the works which were written on the miracles. This, however, is

---

[1] Schlosser, for example, gives the following extraordinary account of Woolston—whose name he spells Wollaston—confounding him, probably, with another writer, whose name is connected with the philosophical controversies of the seventeenth century. ' Wollaston applied his solid learning and extensive reading in the Christian Fathers to modify and ameliorate the limited and unreasonable notions of his Church.' Is it possible that the writer of this sentence could have read Woolston's works, especially his *Discourses on the Miracles*? See especially iv. 34, iii. 8, iv. 11, 35, 54, 67, i. 35, 5, ii. 52, &c.

[2] Mr. Ritchie could hardly have read Annet's work when he called him the famous Deist.'—*Life of Hume,* 153.

anticipating. The year after the publication of Woolston's discourses, and some years before Annet wrote, by far the most important work which ever appeared on the part of the Deists was published. Hitherto Deism had mainly been treated on its negative or destructive side. The mysteries of Christianity, the limitations to thought which it imposes, its system of rewards and punishments, its fulfilment of prophecy, its miracles, had been in turn attacked. The question then naturally arises, ' What will you substitute in its place?' or rather, to put the question as a Deist would have put it, ' What will you substitute in the place of the popular conception of Christianity?' for this alone, not Christianity itself, Deism professed to attack. In other words, ' What is the positive or constructive side of Deism?'

This question Tindal attempts to answer in his ' Christianity as old as the Creation.' The answer is a plain one, and the arguments by which he supports it are repeated with an almost wearisome iteration. ' The religion of nature,' he writes, ' is absolutely perfect ; Revelation can neither add to nor take from its perfection.' ' The law of nature has the highest internal excellence, the greatest plainness, simplicity, unanimity, universality, antiquity, and eternity. It does not depend upon the uncertain meaning of words and phrases in dead languages, much less upon types, metaphors, allegories, parables, or on the skill or honesty of weak or designing transcribers (not to mention translators) for many ages together, but on the immutable relation of things always visible to the whole world.' Tindal is fond of stating the question in the form of a dilemma. ' The law of nature,' he writes, ' either is or is not a perfect law ; if the first, it is not capable of additions ; if the last, does it not argue want of wisdom in the Legislator in first enacting such an imperfect law, and then in letting it continue thus imperfect from age to age, and at last thinking to make it absolutely perfect by adding some merely positive and arbitrary precepts ?' And again, ' Revelation either bids or forbids men to use their reason in judging of all religious matters ; if the former, then it only declares that to be our duty which was so, independent of and antecedent to revelation ; if the latter, then it does not deal with men as rational creatures. Every one is of this opinion who says we are not to read Scripture with freedom of assenting or dissenting, just as we judge it agrees or disagrees with the light of nature and reason of things.' Coming more definitely to the way in which we are to treat the written word, he writes: 'Admit all for Scripture that tends to the honour of God, and nothing which does not.' Finally, he sums up by declaring in yet plainer words the absolute identity of Christianity with natural religion. 'God never intended mankind should be without a religion, or could ordain an imperfect religion ; there must have been from the beginning a religion most perfect, which mankind at all times were capable of knowing ; Christianity is this perfect, original religion.'

In this book Deism reaches its climax. The sensation which it created was greater than even Toland or Collins had raised. No less than one hundred and fifteen answers appeared, one of the most remarkable of which was Conybeare's ' Defence of Revealed Religion against " Christianity as old as the Creation." ' Avoiding the scurrility and personality which characterised and marred most of the works written on both sides of the question, Conybeare discusses in calm and dignified, but at the same time luminous and impressive language, the important question which Tindal had raised. Doing full justice to the element of truth which Tindal's work contained, he unravels the complications in which it is involved, shows that the author had confused two distinct meanings of the phrase ' natural reason ' or ' natural religion,' viz. (1) that which is *founded* on the nature and reason of things, and (2) that which is *discoverable* by man's natural power of mind, and distinguishes between that which is perfect in its kind and that which is absolutely perfect. This powerful work is but little known in the present day. But it was highly appreciated by Conybeare's contemporaries, and the German historian of English Deism hardly knows how to find language strong enough to express his admiration of its excellence.[1]

[1] Conybeare, ' dessen Vertheidigung der geoffenbarten Religion die gediegenste Gegenschrift ist, die gegen Tindal erschien. Es ist eine logische Klarheit, eine Einfacheit der Darstellung, eine überzeugende Kraft der Beweisführung, ein einleuchtender Zusammenhang des Ganzen verbunden mit würdiger Haltung der Polemik, philosophischer Bildung und freier Liberalität des Standpunkts in diesen Buch, vermöge welcher es als meisterhaft anerkannt werden muss.'—Lech-

But Tindal had the honour of calling forth a still stronger adversary than Conybeare. Butler's 'Analogy' deals with the arguments of 'Christianity as old as the Creation' more than with those of any other book ;[1] but as this was not avowedly its object, and as it covered a far wider ground than Tindal did, embracing in fact the whole range of the Deistical controversy, it will be better to postpone the consideration of this masterpiece until the sequel.

By friend and foe alike Tindal seems to have been regarded as the chief exponent of Deism. Skelton in his 'Deism revealed' (published in 1748) says that 'Tindal is the great apostle of Deism who has gathered together the whole strength of the party, and his book is become the bible of all Deistical readers.' Warburton places him at the head of his party, classifying the Deists, 'from the mighty author of "Christianity as old as the Creation," to the drunken, blaspheming cobbler who wrote against Jesus and the Resurrection.'[2]

The subsequent writers on the Deistical side took their cue from Tindal, thus showing the estimation in which his book was held by his own party.

Tindal was in many respects fitted for the position which he occupied. He was an old man when he wrote his great work, and had observed and taken an interest in the whole course of the Deistical controversy for more than forty years. He had himself passed through many phases of religion, having been a pupil of Hickes the Nonjuror, at Lincoln College, Oxford, then a Roman Catholic, then a Low Churchman, and finally, to use his own designation of himself, 'a Christian Deist.' He had, no doubt, carefully studied the various writings of the Deists and their opponents, and had detected the weak points of all. His book is written in a comparatively temperate spirit, and the subject is treated with great thoroughness and ability. Still it has many drawbacks, even in a literary point of view. It is written in the

ler's *Geschichte des Englischen Deismus*, p. 362. Warburton calls Conybeare's one of the best reasoned books in the world.

[1] '*Christianity as old as the Creation* was the book to which, more than to any single work, Butler's *Analogy* was designed as a reply.'—Farrer's *Bampton Lectures*, 1862, ' History of Freethought.'

[2] See Watson's *Life of Warburton*, p. 293.

wearisome form of dialogue, and the writer falls into that
error to which all controversial writers in dialogue are peculiarly liable. When a man has to slay giants of his own
creation, he is sorely tempted to make his giants no stronger
than dwarfs. To this temptation Tindal yielded. His defender of orthodoxy is so very weak, that a victory over him
is no great achievement. Again, there is a want of order
and lucidity in his book, and not sufficient precision in his
definitions. But the worst fault of all is the unfairness of his
quotations, both from the Bible and other books.[1]

Perhaps one reason why, in spite of these defects, the book
exercised so vast an influence is, that the minds of many who
sympathised with the destructive process employed by preceding Deists may have begun to yearn for something more
constructive. They might ask themselves, ' What then *is* our
religion to be ? ' And Tindal answers the question after a
fashion. ' It is to be the religion of nature, and an expurgated
Christianity in so far as it agrees with the religion of nature.'
The answer is a somewhat vague one, but better than none,
and as such may have been welcomed. This, however, is
mere conjecture.

Deism, as we have seen, had now reached its zenith ;
henceforth its history is the history of a rapid decline.
Tindal did not live to complete his work ; but after his
death it was taken up by far feebler hands.

---

[1] ' Gar gern benützt er Schriftsteller und einzelne Ausdrücke der Schrift nur
seine Gedanken zu stützen, wenn jene auch oft nur als Einkleidungen erscheinen.
Wenn die Schrift sagt Gott will, dass alle zur Erkenntniss der Wahrheit kommen ;
so erweitert er dieses Wort und sagt : zu allen Zeiten hat Gott gewollt, dass die
Menschen zur Erkenntniss der Wahrheit kommen. Wenn Jesus vom Gesetz sagt :
es werde kein Iota desselben vergehen ; so deutet diess Tindal auf sein Gesetz der
Natur und sagt ; eher werden Himmel und Erde vergehen, ehe ein Iota dieses
Gesetzes geändert oder abgeschafft wird.'—Lechler, p. 341. The following are
curious instances of Tindal's perversion of Scripture texts. He finds in Romans
i. 19 a confirmation of his view that the law of nature is perfect and all-sufficient
without any other law. ' That which may be known of God (and none can know
that which may not be known) was manifest in the Gentiles.' ' Jesus does not
say, He was sent to all Israel, but to the lost sheep of the House of Israel. " I am
not come to call the righteous, but sinners to repentance," "ninety-nine just persons
which need no repentance." They certainly need no repentance who do of
themselves what would make them acceptable to Him. " The whole need no
physician, but they that are sick," would have been an improper answer, if He
thought that all stood in need of Him and his spiritual physick.'—*Christianity as
old as the Creation*, i. c. 5.

Dr. Morgan, in a work entitled 'The Moral Philosopher' or a Dialogue between Philalethes a Christian Deist, and Theophanes a Christian Jew,' follows closely in Tindal's footsteps. Like him, he insists upon the absolute perfection of the law or religion of nature, of which Christianity is only a republication. Like him, he professes himself a Christian Deist and vigorously protests against being supposed to be an enemy to Christianity. But his work is inferior to Tindal's in every respect. It is, as Schlosser calls it, 'an ill-written book.' It is mainly directed against the Jewish economy. 'The question to be debated,' says Philalethes, who represents Morgan's own views, 'is, whether the positive and ceremonial law of Moses was originally a Divine institution to be afterwards set aside by another revelation, or whether it was a mere piece of carnal worldly policy?'[1] Of course Philalethes maintains the latter; but Morgan takes a far wider range than this, embracing the whole of the Old Testament, which he appears to read backward, finding objects of admiration in what are there set before us as objects of reprobation and *vice versa*. The characters of whom he has a special abhorrence are Joseph, 'who absolutely enslaved the whole nation of Egypt, and ruined the richest and most flourishing kingdom in the world by making the Priesthood independent;' Moses, 'who trumped up the Abrahamic covenant,' &c.; Samuel, 'who usurped the High Priesthood against the fundamental constitution, and might have had the best reason in the world to know what had betided Saul's asses;' and above all David, whose 'whole life was one continued scene of dissimulation, falsehood, lust, and cruelty, contrary to all laws of nature and nations.'

On the other hand, his favourite characters are Solomon after he had fallen into idolatry, which was only 'granting general toleration or indulgence for all religions;' the Priests of Baal, who 'only desired liberty of conscience themselves, and were willing to grant the same to all others;' Ahab, who against the will of the prophets desired to establish a religion 'more friendly and beneficent to mankind, and that might not obstruct his alliance with other nations;' Jezebel, who 'was a woman of great policy,' and the Kings of Israel

[1] *Moral Philosopher*, p. 23.

generally who did evil in the sight of the Lord, that is, were
for granting a liberty of conscience.[1]

But though Morgan deals mainly with the Old Testament,
he throws considerable doubt in his third volume upon the
New. The account given of the life of Christ, still more, that
of His Resurrection, and above all, the miracles wrought by His
apostles, are all thrown into discredit.[2]

On the whole, this book marks a distinct epoch in the
history of English Deism. There is little indeed said by
Morgan which had not been insinuated by one or other of
his predecessors, but the point to be marked is that it *was*
now said, not merely insinuated. The whole tone of the book
indicates 'the beginning of the end' not far distant, that end
being what Lechler calls 'the dissolution of Deism into
Scepticism.'[3]

But there is yet one more author to be noticed whose
works were still written in the earlier vein of Deism. So
far Deism had not found a representative writer among the
lower classes. The aristocracy and the middle class had
both found exponents of their views; but Deism had penetrated into lower strata of society than these, and at length a
very fitting representative of this part of the community
appeared in the person of Thomas Chubb. Himself a working man, and to a great extent self-educated, Chubb had had
peculiar opportunities of observing the mind of the class to
which he belonged. His earlier writings were not intended
for publication, but were written for the benefit of a sort of
debating club of working men of which he was a member.
He was with difficulty persuaded to publish them, mainly
through the influence of the famous William Whiston, and
henceforth became a somewhat voluminous writer, leaving
behind him at his death a number of tracts and essays, which
were published together under the title of 'Chubb's Posthumous Works.' In his main arguments Chubb, like Morgan,
follows closely in the wake of Tindal. But his view of Deism
was distinctly from the standpoint of the working man. As
Morgan had directed his attention mainly to the Old

---

[1] *Moral Philosopher,* vol. i. pp. 239, 295, 305, 307, 313, 323, 334.
[2] *Ibid.* iii. 133, 190, 201, 261.
[3] *Die Auflösung des Deismus in Skepsis,* p. 8.

Testament, Chubb directed his mainly to the New. Like others of his school, he protests against being thought an enemy to Christianity. 'If,' he writes, in his preface to his 'Enquiry into the Ground and Foundation of the Christian Religion,' 'by Deism be meant the belief of a Deity and the governing our minds and lives suitably to such a belief (which is strictly and properly Deism), then I readily acknowledge that the following enquiry is designed and calculated to promote and encourage Deism. But how this can be done in prejudice to revealed religion in general, and to Christianity in particular, I am at a loss to discover' (p. viii.) And again, in his introduction to 'The True Gospel of Jesus Christ asserted,' 'I may possibly be deemed and represented as an unbeliever and enemy to the Gospel, than which nothing can be more unjust and ungenerous' (§ 1.) This latter work together with its sequel, 'The True Gospel of Jesus Christ vindicated,' gives the best exposition of Chubb's views. 'Our Lord Jesus Christ' he writes, 'undertook to be a reformer, and in consequence thereof a Saviour. The true Gospel is this : (1) Christ requires a conformity of mind and life to that eternal and unalterable rule of action which is founded in the reason of things, and makes that the only ground of divine acceptance, and the only and sure way to life eternal. (2) If by violation of the law they have displeased God, he requires repentance and reformation as the only and sure ground of forgiveness. (3) There will be a judgment according to works. This Gospel wrought a change which by a figure of speech is called 'a new birth' (§ 13.) Like Tindal, he contrasts the certainty of natural with the uncertainty of any traditional religion. He owns 'the Christian revelation was expedient because of the general corruption ; but it was no more than a publication of the original law of nature, and tortured and made to speak different things,'[1] and in a later page he further depreciates such a revelation.[2] He repeats

---

[1] *Enquiry into the Ground and Foundation of the Christian Religion*, p. 59.

[2] 'A religion founded on revelation, if propagated, introduces transcribers, translators, commentators, expounders, and the like ; and these, through the weakness of some and wickedness of others, introduce that great variety and contrariety and confusion and perplexity which we see at this day. True religion is grounded on the eternal reason and truth of things ; it would be hard if it depended on the sense and derivation of words, which like shuttlecocks are liable to be

Tindal's objection to the want of universality of revealed religion on the same grounds.[1] His chief attacks were, as has been said, made upon the New Testament. He demurs to the acceptance of the Gospels as infallibly true.[2]

Chubb expresses just those difficulties and objections which would naturally have most weight with the more intelligent portion of the working classes. Speculative questions are put comparatively in the background. His view of the gospel is just that plain practical view which an artisan could grasp without troubling himself about transcendental questions, on the nice adjustment of which divines disputed. 'Put all such abstruse matters aside,' Chubb says in effect to his fellow-workmen, 'they have nothing to do with the main point at issue, they are no parts of the true Gospel.' His rocks of offence, too, are just those against which the working man would stumble. The shortcomings of the clergy had long been part of the stock-in-trade of almost all the Deistical writers. Their supposed wealth and idleness gave, as was natural, special offence to the representative of the working classes. 'The enlarged revenues of the Church,' Chubb writes, 'introduced useless and superfluous clergy with pompous titles and vestments, while their principal business has been to possess great revenues, to live in pomp and grandeur, assuming and exercising dominion over their brethren.' 'Plurality of benefices, because the profit of one was not sufficient to gratify his avaricious desires, introduced supernumerary clergy, who served as journeymen to do the work for a small stipend, while the appointed guardian of the societies' souls lived lazily and idly upon the profits of it.'[3] He attacks individual clergymen,[4] inveighs against the

---

battled to and fro' according to the art and skill of opponents.'—*Enquiry*, &c. 99. For Chubb's views on the Atonement, see his *Enquiry concerning Redemption*, especially pp. 51, 64, 74, 91, and 92.

[1] It is 'repugnant to reason that God should call creatures into being and make them accountable for their actions, and yet not furnish them with capacity sufficient for the purpose.'

[2] 'As there were many persons (Matthew, &c. among others), who took upon them voluntarily to write and publish the history of Christ's life and ministry, they not having any special call to that work ; so they, like other historians, blended their own sentiments with history.'—*True Gospel of Jesus Christ asserted*, p. 21.

[3] See also Chubb's *True Gospel of Jesus Christ asserted*, § 13.

[4] Chubb's *Discourse on Miracles*, p. 101. 'If selling all and giving to the poor

'unnatural coalition of Church and State,'[1] and speaks of men living in palaces like kings, clothing themselves in fine linen and costly apparel, and faring sumptuously.

The lower and lower-middle classes have always been peculiarly sensitive to the dangers of priestcraft and a relapse into Popery. Accordingly Chubb constantly appealed to this anti-Popish feeling.[2]

Chubb, being an illiterate man, made here and there slips of scholarship, but he wrote in a clear, vigorous, sensible style, and his works had considerable influence over those to whom they were primarily addressed.

The cause of Deism in its earlier sense was now almost extinct. Those who were afterwards called Deists really belong to a different school of thought. A remarkable book, which was partly the outcome, partly, perhaps, the cause of this altered state of feeling, was published by Dodwell the younger, in 1742. It was entitled 'Christianity not founded on argument,' and there was at first a doubt whether the author wrote as a friend or an enemy of Christianity.[3]

be, according to Dr. Stebbing, necessary to constitute a disciple of Christ, then Dr. S.'s conduct as Christ's disciple is very preposterous, as the many church preferments he has got in his possession demonstrates.'

[1] 'The unnatural coalition of Church and State has answered very great purposes to men in this world, such as that those who push hard and get foremost in this pretended kingdom of Christ have their hundreds and thousands a year for now and then attending at the altar, as they affect to call it, live in palaces, cloath themselves in fine linen and costly apparel and fare sumptuously,' &c.—*Enquiry concerning Redemption.*

[2] 'Let me entreat my fellow-Protestants,' he writes, 'especially the laity, to contend for and hold fast their reason, and to follow its guidance in matters of religion and divine revelation, this being their best security against Popery, which some think gains ground among us. If once we let go our reason in matters of religion and Divine revelation, we are in danger of being captivated to the See of Rome, or to a body of clergy who may be equally injurious to us.'— Chubb's *Discourse concerning Reason,* p. 23. See also his *Reflections upon the comparative excellence and usefulness of Moral and Positive Duties,* p. 27, &c.

[3] It appears that some one who took this writer for a Christian 'earnestly recommended' his work to John Wesley, thinking no doubt that he would find in it a confirmation of his view that true Christianity cannot be attained by natural reason, but must be taught by the Spirit. Wesley, however, was far too clear-sighted to be mistaken as to the true tendency of the book. 'On a careful perusal of that piece,' he writes, 'notwithstanding my prejudice in its favour, I could not but perceive that the great design uniformly pursued throughout the work was, to render the whole of the Christian Institution both odious and contemptible. . . . His point throughout is to prove that Christianity is contrary to reason or that no

He was nominally opposed to both, for both the Deists and their adversaries agreed that reason and revelation were in perfect harmony. The Deist accused the Orthodox of sacrificing reason at the shrine of revelation, the Orthodox accused the Deist of sacrificing revelation at the shrine of reason ; but both sides vehemently repudiated the charge. The Orthodox was quite as anxious to prove that his Christianity was not unreasonable, as the Deist was to prove that his rationalism was not anti-Christian.

Now the author of 'Christianity not founded on argument' came forward to prove that both parties were attempting an impossibility. In opposition to everything that had been written on both sides of the controversy for the last half century, Dodwell protested against all endeavours to reconcile the irreconcilable.

His work is in the form of a letter to a young Oxford friend, who was assumed to be yearning for a rational faith, 'as it was his duty to prove all things.' 'Rational faith!' says Dodwell in effect, ' the thing is impossible ; it is a contradiction in terms. If you must prove all things, you will hold nothing. Faith is commanded men as a duty. This necessarily cuts it off from all connection with reason. There is no clause providing that we should believe if we have time and ability to examine, but the command is peremptory. It is a duty for every moment of life, for every age. Children are to be led early to believe, but this, from the nature of the case, cannot be on rational grounds. Proof necessarily presupposes a suspension of conviction. The rational Christian must have begun as a Sceptic ; he must long have doubted whether the Gospel was true or false. Can this be the faith that " overcometh the world "? Can this be the faith that makes a martyr ? No ! the true believer must open Heaven and see the Son of Man standing plainly before his eyes, not see through the thick dark glass of history and tradition. The Redeemer Himself gave no proofs ; He taught as one having authority, as a Master who has a right to dictate, who brought

man acting according to the principles of reason can possibly be a Christian. It is a wonderful proof of the power that smooth words may have even on serious minds, that so many have mistook such a writer as this for a friend of Christianity.'—*Earnest Appeal to Men of Reason and Religion,* p. 14.

the teaching which He imparted straight from Heaven.[1] In this view of the ground of faith, unbelief is a rebellious opposition against the working of grace. The union of knowledge and faith is no longer nonsense. All difficulties are chased away by the simple consideration "that with men it is impossible, but with God all things are possible." Philosophy and religion are utterly at variance. The groundwork of philosophy is all doubt and suspicion; the groundwork of religion is all submission and faith. The enlightened scholar of the Cross, if he regards the one thing needful, rightly despises all lower studies. When he turns to these he leaves his own proper sphere. Julian was all in the wrong when he closed the philosophical schools to the Christians. He should have given them all possible privileges that they might undermine the principles of Christ. "Not many wise men after the flesh are called." All attempts to establish a rational faith, from the time of Origen to that of Tillotson, Dr. Clark, and the Boyle lectures, are utterly useless. Tertullian was right when he said *Credo quia absurdum et quia impossibile est,* for there is an irreconcilable repugnancy in their natures between reason and belief; therefore, "My son, give thyself to the Lord with thy whole heart and lean not to thy own understanding."'

Such is the substance of this remarkable work. There can be little doubt that the object of the writer was to reduce faith to an absurdity.[2] But he hit, and hit very forcibly, a blot which belonged to almost all writers in common who took part in this controversy. The great deficiency of the age—a want of spiritual earnestness, an exclusive regard to

---

[1] A similar argument, equally ironical, was used by Hume in his *Essay on Miracles.* 'The Christian religion not only was at first attended with miracles, but even at this day cannot be believed by any reasonable person without one. Thus reason is insufficient to convince us of its veracity; and whoever is moved by *faith* to assent to it, is conscious of a continued miracle in his own person, which subverts all the principles of his understanding, and gives him a determination to believe what is most contrary to custom and experience.'—See Ritchie's *Life of Hume,* p. 324.

[2] Dodwell was the son of the learned, but eccentric and extravagant, Nonjuror of that name. It may be that his views are the result of a violent reaction against his father's teaching. Among other answers to Dodwell, one appeared from the pen of the amiable Dr. Doddridge, who, with the best intentions, played in point of fact into his opponent's hands.

the intellectual, to the ignoring of the emotional element of our nature—nowhere appears more glaringly than in the Deistical and anti-Deistical literature. What Dodwell urges in bitter irony, John Wesley [1] urged in sober seriousness, when he intimated that Deists and evidence writers alike were strangers to those truths which are 'spiritually discerned.'

There is yet one more writer who is popularly regarded not only as a Deist, but as the chief of the Deists—Lord Bolingbroke, to whom Leland gives more space than to all the other Deists put together.   So far as the eminence of the man is concerned, the prominence given to him is not disproportionate to his merits, but it is only in a very qualified sense that Lord Bolingbroke can be called a Deist. He lived and was before the public during the whole course of the Deistical controversy, so far as it belongs to the eighteenth century ; but he was known, not as a theologian, but first as a brilliant, fashionable man of pleasure, then as a politician. So far as he took any part in religious matters at all, it was as a violent partisan of the established faith and as a persecutor of Dissenters.   It was mainly through his instrumentality that the iniquitous Schism Act of 1713 was passed.   In the House of Commons he called it 'a bill of the last importance, since it concerned the security of the Church of England, the best and firmest support of the monarchy.'[2]   In his famous letter to Sir W. Wyndham, he justified his action in regard to this measure, and the kindred bill against occasional conformity, on purely political grounds.[3]   He publicly expressed his abhorrence of the so-called Freethinkers, whom he stigmatised as Pests of Society.   But in a letter to Mr. Pope, he gave some intimation of his real sentiments, and at the same

---

[1] But see note 3 on page 205.

[2] See Lord Mahon's *History of England*, Cooke's *Memoirs of Lord Bolingbroke, &c.*

[3] 'I verily think that the persecution of Dissenters entered into no man's head.   By the bills for preventing occasional conformity and growth of schism, it was hoped that their sting would be taken away.   These bills were thought necessary for our party interest, and besides were deemed neither unreasonable nor unjust.   The good of society may require that no person should be deprived of the protection of the Government on account of his religious opinion ; but it does not follow that men ought to be trusted in any degree with the preservation of the Establishment who must, to be consistent with their principles, endeavour the subversion of what is established,' &c.

time justified his reticence about them. ' Let us,' he writes, ' seek truth, but quietly, as well as freely. Let us not imagine, like some who are called Freethinkers, that every man who can think and judge for himself, as he has a right to do, has therefore a right of speaking any more than acting according to freedom of thought.' Then, after expressing sentiments which are written in the very spirit of Deism, he adds, ' I neither expect nor desire to see any public revision made of the present system of Christianity. I should fear such an attempt,' &c. It was accordingly not until after his death that his theological views were fully expressed and published. These are principally contained in his ' Philosophical Works,' which he bequeathed to David Mallet with instructions for their publication; and Mallet accordingly gave them to the world in 1754. Honest Dr. Johnson's opinion of this method of proceeding is well known. ' Sir, he was a scoundrel and a coward; a scoundrel for charging a blunderbuss against religion and morality, a coward because he had no resolution to fire it off himself, but left half-a-crown to a beggarly Scotchman to draw the trigger after his death.' This is strong language, but it is not wholly undeserved. There is something inexpressibly mean in a man countenancing the persecution of his fellow-creatures for heterodoxy, while he himself secretly held opinions more heterodox than any of those whom he helped to persecute. No doubt Bolingbroke regarded religion simply from a political point of view; it was a useful, nay, a necessary engine of Government. He, therefore, who wilfully unsettled men's minds on the subject was a bad citizen, and consequently deserving of punishment. But then, this line of argument would equally tell against the publication of unsettling opinions after his death, as against publishing them during his life-time. *Après moi le déluge*, is not an elevated maxim; yet the only other principle upon which his mode of proceeding admits of explanation is, that he wrote his last works in the spirit of a soured and disappointed man, who had been in turn the betrayer and betrayed of every party with which he had been connected.

What his motives, however, were, can only be a matter of conjecture; let us proceed to examine the opinions themselves. They are contained mainly[1] in a series of essays or letters addressed by him to his friend Pope, who did not live to read them ; and they give us in a somewhat rambling, discursive fashion, his views on almost all subjects connected with religion. Many passages have the genuine Deistical ring about them. Like his precursors, he declares that he means particularly to defend the Christian religion ;[2] that genuine Christianity contained in the Gospels is the Word of God. Like them, he can scarcely find language strong enough to express his abhorrence of the Jews and the Old Testament generally.[3] Like them, he abuses divines of all ages and their theological systems in the most unmeasured terms.[4] It is almost needless to add that, in common with his predecessors, he contemptuously rejects all such doctrines as the Divinity of the Word, Expiation for Sin in any sense, the Holy Trinity, and the Efficacy of the Sacraments.

In many points, however, Lord Bolingbroke goes far beyond his predecessors. His 'First Philosophy' marks a distinct advance or decadence, according to the point of view from which we regard it, in the history of Freethinking. Everything in the Bible is ruthlessly swept aside, except what is contained in the Gospels. S. Paul, who had been an object of admiration to the earlier Deists, is the object of

---

[1] His letters on the 'Study of History' contain the same principles.

[2] Essay iii. § 4.

[3] The God of the Jews was 'a local Deity carried about in a trunk.' In the Mosaic account of the creation, 'it is impossible to excuse all the puerile, romantic, and absurd circumstances, which nothing could produce but the habit of dealing in trifling traditions and a most profound ignorance. It is impossible to read what he [Moses] writ on this subject without feeling contempt for him as a philosopher, and horror as a divine.' 'The Jews thought themselves authorised by their religion to commit such barbarities as even they, perhaps, if they had had no religion, would not have committed.'

[4] 'Ecclesiastical tradition has been from the first and purest ages for the most part founded in ignorance, superstition, enthusiasm, and fraud. He who pretends to clear the reverend fathers and deny the charge must be very ignorant or very impudent. [In the fourth century] 'the whole body of the clergy, some few good and learned but not infallible men excepted, was ignorant, contentious, and profligate, and it did not grow better, if it could not grow worse, afterwards.' 'Theology has shortened the Decalogue, and lengthened the creed.' 'The traditional Christianity which we all profess is the word of men, and of men for the most part either very weak, very mad, or very knavish. It requires, therefore, no regard nor any inward conformity to it.'

Bolingbroke's special abhorrence. He is 'the father of artificial theology and writes confusedly and unintelligibly; when
he is intelligible, he is often absurd, or profane, or trifling.'
The Gospel of Paul is one thing, the Gospel of Christ another.
But the utmost doubt is thrown upon the authenticity and
value of the histories which contain this Gospel.[1] And not
only is the credibility of the Gospel writers impugned, Christ's
own teaching and character are also carped at. Christ's
conduct was 'reserved and cautious; His language mystical
and parabolical. He gives no complete system of morality.
His Sermon on the Mount gives some precepts which are
impracticable, inconsistent with natural instinct and quite
destructive of society. His miracles may be explained away.'

It may be said, indeed, that most of these tenets are contained in the germ in the writings of earlier Deists. But
there are yet others of which this cannot be said.

Bolingbroke did not confine his attacks to revealed
religion. Philosophy fares as badly as religion in his estimate.
'It is the frantic mother of a frantic offspring.' Plato is
almost as detestable in his eyes as S. Paul. He has the
most contemptuous opinion of his fellow-creatures, and declares that they are incapable of understanding the attributes
of the Deity.[2] He throws doubt upon the very existence of a
world to come.[3] He holds that 'we have not sufficient grounds

---

[1] 'Luke is no more than an earsay witness of what he relates. Infidels will
cavil, and sometimes plausibly, against many things that must be assumed to make
the harmony of the Gospels appear and to reconcile their differences. Luke and
Mark were not apostles, and neither of them were chosen to fill up the number
after Judas. I am not ignorant of what has been said that might weaken the
authority of Matthew.' 'Let it be that the Gospels received into the canon are
favourable to the orthodox belief [in the Trinity]; how do we know that the other
Gospels were conformable to these? The task would be infinitely harder if we
had those Gospels, to create an harmony between three or four dozen than between
four.'

[2] It is 'downright madness for a creature placed in the lowest form of intelligent
beings to unveil the mysteries of Divine Wisdom.' 'To measure the wisdom and
justice of God by a rule so inadequate as that of human intelligence is vanity and
presumption in the highest degree.'

[3] 'A future state is in the nature of it not capable of demonstration. No one
ever returned that irremeable way to give us assurance of the fact; it was originally an hypothesis, and may be a vulgar error.' 'We are wholly unable to say
what will happen hereafter.' 'If any other sanctions are necessary to enforce the
original and universal law of God, the law of our nature, they cannot be those of
a future state.'

to establish the doctrine of a particular providence, and to reconcile it to that of a general providence;' that 'prayer, or the abuse of prayer, carries with it ridicule;' that 'we have much better determined ideas of the divine wisdom than of the divine goodness,' and that to attempt to imitate God is in highest degree absurd.

There is no need to discuss here the system of optimism which Lord Bolingbroke held in common with Lord Shaftesbury and Pope;[1] for that system is consistent both with a belief and with a disbelief of Christianity, and we are at present concerned with Lord Bolingbroke's views only in so far as they are connected with religion. From the extracts given above, it will be seen how far in this system Deism had drifted away from its old moorings. To quote the words of his biographer, 'his first philosophy consisted of nothing more than the residuum which remained after rejecting every opinion, the holding which would embarrass a sceptic arguing with a Christian. A God omnipotent and all-perfect, but inconceivable in His omnipotence, and incomprehensible in His perfections. No particular providence, no future state, no immaterial soul,' &c.'[2]

After Bolingbroke no Deistical writing, properly so called, was published in England. The great controversy had died a natural death; but there are a few apologetic works which have survived the dispute that called them forth, and may be fairly regarded as κτήματα ἐs ἀεὶ of English theology. To attempt even to enumerate the works of all the anti-Deistical writers would fill many pages. Those who are curious in such matters must be referred to the popular work of Leland, where they will find an account of the principal writers on both sides.[3] All that can be attempted here is to notice one or two of those which are of permanent interest.

---

[1] And with one greater than both, Leibnitz, who was a Christian and an opponent of Deism. See his *Théodicée* passim, and Morell's *History of Modern Philosophy*, vol. i. p. 227, 'German Idealism.'

[2] Cooke's *Memoirs of Lord Bolingbroke*, vol. ii. p. 152.

[3] Or to Hunt's *History of Religious Thought* and Leslie Stephen's *English Thought in the Eighteenth Century*. In both these valuable works a far fuller account of the Deistical and anti-Deistical literature will be found than is consistent with the object of this sketch. It may be added that the present chapter was written before Mr. Stephen's book was published; but the writer

First among such is the immortal work of Bishop Butler. Wherever the English language is spoken, Butler's 'Analogy' holds a distinguished place among English classics. Published in the year 1736, when the excitement raised by 'Christianity as old as the Creation' was at its height, it was, as has been well remarked, 'the result of twenty years' study, the very twenty years during which the Deistical notions formed the atmosphere which educated people breathed.'[1] For those twenty years and longer still, the absolute certainty of God's revelation of Himself in nature, and the absolute perfection of the religion founded on that revelation, in contradistinction to the uncertainty and imperfection of all traditional religions, had been the incessant cry of the new school of thought, a cry which had lately found its strongest and ablest expression in Tindal's famous work. It was to those who raised this cry, and to those who were likely to be influenced by it, that Butler's famous argument was primarily addressed. 'You assert,' he says in effect, 'that the law of nature is absolutely perfect and absolutely certain ; I will show you that precisely the same kind of difficulties are found in nature as you find in revelation.' Butler uttered no abuse, descended to no personalities such as spoiled too many of the anti-Deistical writings ; but his book shows that his mind was positively steeped in Deistical literature. Hardly an argument which the Deists had used is unnoticed ; hardly an objection which they could raise is not anticipated. But the very circumstance which constitutes one of the chief excellences of the 'Analogy,' its freedom from polemical bitterness, has been the principal cause of its being misunderstood. To do any kind of justice to the book, it must be read in the light of Deism. Had this obvious caution been always observed, such objections as those of Pitt, that 'it was a dangerous book, raising more doubts than it solves,' would never have been heard ; for at the time when it was written,

desires to express his grateful acknowledgment both to Mr. Stephen and to Dr. Hunt for the information which he has derived from their pages. Traversing the same ground, he has not been able to avoid repeating much that they have written ; but he has in no case taken anything from their pages without recognising the fact in a note.

[1] Pattison's 'Tendencies of Religious Thought in England,' 1688-1750. In *Essays and Reviews*.

the doubts were everywhere current. Similar objections have been raised against the ' Analogy ' in modern days,[1] but the popular verdict will not be easily reversed.

Next in importance to Butler's ' Analogy ' is a far more voluminous and pretentious work, that of Bishop Warburton on ' The Divine Legation of Moses.' It is said to have been called forth by Morgan's ' Moral Philosopher.'[2] If so, it is somewhat curious that Warburton himself in noticing this work deprecates any answer being given to it.[3]

But, at any rate, we have Warburton's own authority for saying that his book had special reference to the Deists or Freethinkers (for the terms were then used synonymously).

He begins the dedication of the first edition of the first three books to the Freethinkers with the words, ' Gentlemen, as the following discourse was written for your use, you have the best right to this address.'

The argument of the ' Divine Legation ' is stated thus by Warburton himself in syllogistic form :—

' I. Whatsoever Religion and Society have no future state for their support, must be supported by an extraordinary Providence.

[1] Mr. Martineau regards *The Analogy* 'as containing, with a design directly contrary, the most terrible persuasives to atheism that have ever been produced.'— *MS. Studies of Christianity.* Miss Hennel, in an essay on the Sceptical Tendency of Butler's Analogy, considers Butler as ' the legitimate precursor of the Positive Philosopher of the present day.'-- Mr. Matthew Arnold (' Bishop Butler and the Zeit-Geist,' *Contemporary Review*, February 1876) seems to agree with the views expressed in the text so far as they concern the effectiveness of the Analogy as an answer to the Deists, but thinks it has lost all effect in the present day, because it assumes God to be a ' quasi-human being ' which the Deists would admit, but modern sceptics would not. If by a ' quasi-human being ' be meant a Personal Being with the attributes generally understood to be connoted by the name, as opposed to a mere impersonal abstraction (and it is difficult to understand the phrase in any other sense), it need only be said that the remarks in the text on the general efficacy of the Analogy *did* make such an assumption, and it is readily admitted that to those who would deny it another mode of argument would have to be addressed.

[2] Farrer's *Bampton Lectures.*

[3] ' There is a book called *The Moral Philosopher* lately published. Is it looked into ? I should hope not, merely for the sake of the taste, the sense, and learning of the present age . . . . I hope nobody will be so indiscreet as to take notice publicly of the book, though it be only in the fag end of an objection.—It is that indiscreet conduct in our defenders of religion that conveys so many worthless books from hand to hand.'—Letter to Mr. Birch in 1737. In Nichols' *Literary Illustrations of the Eighteenth Century,* ii. 70.

'The Jewish Religion and Society had no future state for their support.

'Therefore, the Jewish Religion and Society was supported by an extraordinary Providence.

'II. It was universally believed by the ancients on their common principles of legislation and wisdom, that whatsoever Religion and Society have no future state for their support, must be supported by an extraordinary Providence.

'Moses, skilled in all that legislation and wisdom, instituted the Jewish Religion and Society without a future state for its support.

'Therefore,—Moses, who taught, believed likewise that *this* Religion and Society was supported by an extraordinary Providence.'

The work is a colossal monument of the author's learning and industry: the range of subjects which it embraces is enormous ; and those who cannot agree with his conclusions either on the main argument, or on the many collateral points raised, must still admire the vast research and varied knowledge which the writer displays. It is however a book more talked about than read at the present day. Indeed, human life is too short to enable the general reader to do more than skim cursorily over a work of such proportions. Warburton's theory was novel and startling ; and perhaps few even of the Deistical writers themselves evoked more criticism and opposition from the orthodox than this doughty champion of orthodoxy. But Warburton was in his element when engaged in controversy. He was quite ready to meet combatants from whatever side they might come ; and, wielding his bludgeon with a vigorous hand, he dealt his blows now on the orthodox, now on the heterodox, with unsparing and impartial force.

Judged, however, from a literary point of view, 'The Divine Legation' is too elaborate and too discursive a work to be effective for the purpose for which it was written ;[1] and most

[1] See Charles Churchill's lines on Warburton in *The Duellist.* After much foul abuse, he thus describes *The Divine Legation* :—

> 'To make himself a man of note,
> He in defence of Scripture wrote.
> So long he wrote and long about it,
> That e'en believers 'gan to doubt it !

readers will be inclined to agree with **Bentley's verdict, that the** writer was ' a man of monstrous appetite but bad digestion.'

Of a very different character is the next work to be noticed, as one of enduring interest on the Deistical controversy. Bishop Berkeley's 'Alciphron, or the Minute Philosopher,' is one of the few exceptions to the general dreariness and un-readableness of controversial writings in the dialogistic form. The elegance and easiness of his style, and the freshness and beauty of his descriptions of natural scenery by which the tedium of the controversy is relieved, render this not only a readable, but a fascinating book, even to the modern reader who has no present interest in the controversial question. It is, however, by no means free from the graver errors incident to this form of writing. Like Tindal, he makes his adversaries state their case far too weakly. But, worse than this, he puts into their mouths arguments which they would never have used, and sentiments which they never held and which could not be fairly deduced from their writings. Not that Bishop Berkeley ever wrote with conscious unfairness. The truly Christian, if somewhat eccentric character of the man forbids such a supposition for one moment. His error, no doubt, arose from the vagueness with which the terms Deist, Free-thinker, Naturalist, Atheist, were used indiscriminately to stigmatise men of very different views. There was, for example, little or nothing in common between such men as Lord Shaftesbury and Mandeville. The atrocious sentiment of the ' Fable of the Bees,' that private vices are public benefits, was not the sentiment of any true Deist. Yet Shaftesbury and Mandeville are the two writers who are most constantly alluded to as representatives of one and the same system, in this dialogue. Indeed the confusion here spoken of is apparent

> A gentleman well-bred, if breeding
> Rests in the article of reading ;
> A man of this world, for the next
> Was ne'er included in his text,' &c. &c.

Gibbon calls *The Divine Legation* 'a monument, already crumbling in the dust, of the vigour and weakness of the human mind.'—See *Life of Gibbon*, ch. vii. 223, note. Bishop Lowth says of it ironically, *The Divine Legation*, it seems, contains in it all knowledge, divine and human, ancient and modern ; it treats as of its proper sub-ject, de omni scibili et de quolibet ente ; it is a perfect encyclopædia ; it includes in itself all history, chronology, criticism, divinity, law, politics,' &c. &c.—*A Letter to the Right Rev. Author of ' The Divine Legation,'* p. 13 (1765).

in Berkeley's own advertisement. 'The author's design being
to consider the Freethinker in the various lights of Atheist,
libertine, enthusiast, scorner, critic, metaphysician, fatalist and
sceptic, it must not therefore be imagined that every one of
these characters agrees with every individual Freethinker ; no
more being implied than that each part agrees with some or
other of the sect.' The fallacy here arises from the assumption of a sect with a coherent system, which, as has been
stated above, never had any existence.

The principle upon which Berkeley tells us that he constructed his dialogue is a dangerous one. 'It must not,'
he writes, 'be thought that authors are misrepresented if
every notion of Alciphron or Lysicles is not found precisely
in them. A gentleman in private conference may be supposed to speak plainer than others write, to improve on their
hints, and draw conclusions from their principles.' Yes ; but
this method of development, when carried out by a vehement
partisan, is apt to find hints where there are no hints, and
draw conclusions which are quite unwarranted by the premises ;
and that Berkeley did this, few unprejudiced readers who have
carefully studied the Deistical writings will deny. For
instance, were the antecedents of Alciphron and Lysicles really
a fair representation of the antecedents of the bulk of Freethinkers, whatever they may have been of individuals here and
there ? 'Alciphron is above forty, and no stranger to men
and books. I knew him first at the Temple, which upon an
estate's falling to him he quitted, to travel through the polite
parts of Europe. Since his return he hath lived in the amusements of the town, which, being grown stale and tasteless to
his palate, have flung him into a sort of splenetic indolence.
The young gentleman Lysicles is one of lively parts and a
general insight into letters, who, after having passed the
forms of education, and seen a little of the world, fell into an
intimacy with men of pleasure and freethinkers, I am afraid,
much to the damage of his constitution and his fortune. But
what I most regret is the corruption of his mind by a set of
pernicious principles, which, having been observed to survive
the passions of youth, forestall even the remote hopes of
amendment.'[1] Compare this account with what is known of

1 *Minute Philosopher*, p. 25.

the antecedents of Collins, the admired and trusted friend of Locke, or even with what is known of Toland or Chubb or Shaftesbury himself, and the contrast will be apparent.

Again, is the following a fair account of the process by which Deism lapsed into Atheism? 'Alciphron.—Was I not pinched in time, the regular way would be to have begun with the circumstantials of religion ; next, to have attacked the mysteries of Christianity ; after that, proceeded to the practical doctrines, and in the last place to have extirpated that which of all other religious prejudices, being the first taught and basis of the rest, hath taken the deepest root in our minds—I mean, the being of a God.'[1] Or is this a true picture of the representative Deist? 'Crito.—Probably, Euphranor, by the title of Deists, which is sometimes given to minute philosophers, you have been misled to imagine they worship a God according to the light of nature ; but, by living among them, you may soon be convinced of the contrary. They have neither time nor place nor form of Divine worship ; they offer neither prayers nor praises to God in public ; and in their private practice show a contempt or dislike even of the duties of natural religion.'[2] Is it a true description of Shaftesbury (Cratylus) that 'he was a man of crazy constitution and conceited mind, and that he was moral only because he had little capacity for sensual vices or temptation to dishonest ones.'[3] Was the Deist 'a downright sceptic?' Are the three following fair types of the party? 'Crito.—I know an eminent Freethinker who never goes to bed without a gallon of wine in his belly, and is sure to replenish before the fumes are off his brain, by which means he has not had one sober thought these seven years : another, that would not for the world lose the privilege and reputation of freethinking who games all night and lies in bed all day ; and as for the outside or appearance of thought in that meagre minute philosopher Ibycus, it is an effect, not of thinking, but of carking, cheating, and writing in an office.'[4] These passages have been quoted at length because they are fairly typical specimens of the sort of abuse that was heaped upon the Deists. If an amiable philanthropist and truly Christian prelate like Berkeley could deal in such

---

[1] *Minute Philosopher*, p. 35.   [2] *Ibid.* pp. 45, 46.
[3] *Ibid.* p. 128.   [4] *Ibid.* p. 331.

scurrilities, it may be imagined how less scrupulous adversaries would write. Indeed, throughout the whole of his dialogue, no less than in his papers on the same subject in the 'Guardian,' [1] Berkeley writes in a spirit quite unworthy of the general character of so great and good a man. No doubt, it was his genuine love of his religion that filled him with a zeal which in this case was not tempered with discretion. He shared in the panic and reflected only too faithfully the general bitterness of the polemics of his day. But the cause of truth is never really served by exaggeration and misrepresentation. The calm and dignified moderation of Butler was far more effectual against the minute philosophers than the vehemence of this excellent but hot-headed Irish prelate.

It is somewhat discouraging to an aspirant after literary immortality, to reflect that in spite of the enormous amount of learned writing which the Deistical controversy elicited, many educated people who have not made the subject a special study, probably derive their knowledge of the Deists mainly from two unpretentious volumes—Leland's 'View of the Deistical Writers.'

Leland avowedly wrote as an advocate, and therefore it would be unreasonable to expect from him the measured judgment of a philosophical historian. But *as* an advocate he wrote with great fairness,—indeed, considering the excitement which the Deists raised among their contemporaries, with wonderful fairness. It is not without reason that he boasts in his preface, 'Great care has been taken to make a fair representation of them, according to the best judgment I could form of their designs.' But, besides the fact that the representations of a man who holds a brief for one side must necessarily be taken *cum grano*, Leland lived too near the time to be able to view his subject in the 'dry light' of history. 'The best book,' said Burke in 1773, 'that has ever been written against these people is that in which the author has

---

[1] Bishop Berkeley wrote eleven papers in the *Guardian* against the Freethinkers, viz. Nos. 3, 27, 39, 55, 62, 70, 77, 83, 88, 89, and 126.

Commenting on a passage in Berkeley's *Theory of Vision*, in which the bishop vehemently condemns Lord Shaftesbury's *Characteristics*, Sir James Mackintosh writes, 'This most excellent man sinks for a moment to the level of a railing polemic.'—*History of Ethics*, p. 158. The same remark might be applied to most of Bishop Berkeley's writings on the Deists.

collected in a body the whole of the Infidel code, and has brought their writings into one body to cut them all off together.' If the subject was to be dealt with in this trenchant fashion, no one could have done it more honestly than Leland has done. But the great questions which the Deists raised cannot be dealt with thus summarily. Perhaps no book professedly written 'against these people' could possibly do justice to the whole case. Hence those who virtually adopt Leland as their chief authority will at best have but a one-sided view of the matter. Leland was a Dissenter ; and it may be remarked in passing, that while the National Church bore the chief part in the struggle, as it was right she should, yet many Dissenters honourably distinguished themselves in the cause of our common Christianity. The honoured names of Chandler,[1] Lardner, Doddridge, Foster, Hallet, and Leland himself (to which many others might be added), may be mentioned in proof of this assertion.

The attitude towards Deism of the authors hitherto named is unmistakable. But there are yet two great names which cannot well be passed over, and which both the friends and foes of Deism have claimed for their side. These are the names of Alexander Pope and John Locke. The former was, as is well known, by profession a Roman Catholic ;[2] but in his most elaborate, if not his most successful poem, he has been supposed to express the sentiments of one of the most

---

[1] There were two anti-Deistical writers of the name of Chandler, (1) the Bishop of Coventry and Lichfield, and (2) Dr. Samuel Chandler, an eminent Dissenter. Both wrote against Collins, but the latter also against Morgan and the anonymous author of the *Resurrection of Jesus considered*.

Sherlock's *Tryal of the Witnesses* ought perhaps to have been noticed as one of the works of permanent value written against the Deists. Wharton says that 'Sherlock's *Discourses on Prophecy and Trial of the Witnesses* are, perhaps, the best defences of Christianity in our language.' Sherlock's lawyer-like mind enabled him to manage the controversy with rare skill, but the tone of theological thought has so changed, that his once famous book is a little out of date at the present day. Judged by its intrinsic merits, William Law's answer to Tindal would also deserve to be ranked among the very best of the books which were written against the Deists ; but, like almost all the works of this most able and excellent man, it has fallen into undeserved oblivion. Leslie's *Short and Easy Method with a Deist* is also admirable in its way.

[2] But it is no want of charity to say that his Roman Catholicism sat very lightly upon him. He himself confesses it in a letter to Atterbury.

sceptical of the Deistical writers.[1] How far did the author of the 'Essay on Man' agree with the religious sentiments of his 'guide, philosopher, and friend,' Viscount Bolingbroke? Pope's biographer answers this question very decisively. 'Pope,' says Ruffhead, 'permitted Bolingbroke to be considered by the public as his philosopher and guide. They agreed on the principle that "whatever is, is right," as opposed to impious complaints against Providence ; but Pope meant, because we only see a part of the moral system, not the whole, therefore these irregularities serving great purposes, such as the fuller manifestation of God's goodness and justice, are right. Lord Bolingbroke's Essays are vindications of providence against the confederacy between Divines 'and Atheists who use a common principle, viz. that of the irregularities of God's moral government here, for different ends : the one to establish a future state, the others to discredit the being of a God.' 'Bolingbroke,' he adds, 'always tried to conceal his principles from Pope, and Pope would not credit anything against him.' Warburton's testimony is to the same effect. 'So little,' he writes, 'did Pope know of the principles of the "First Philosophy," that when a common acquaintance told him in his last illness that Lord Bolingbroke denied God's moral attributes as commonly understood, he asked Lord Bolingbroke whether he was mistaken, and was told he was.'[2]

On the other hand, there is the letter from Bolingbroke to

---

[1] Or rather of two, Bolingbroke and Shaftesbury. Mr. Leslie Stephen calls the *Essay on Man* a continuous comment upon Shaftesbury.—*English Thought in the Eighteenth Century*, vol. ii. p. 28. Schlosser says that the '*Essay on Man* brings Bolingbroke's theory into the sphere of practical life,—that the glory of God and happiness of man are not the end of human life, as a Christian would express himself.' See *History of the Eighteenth Century*, i. § iii. Dr. Blair said to James Boswell, 'Lord Bathurst told us that the *Essay on Man* was originally composed by Lord Bolingbroke in prose, and that Mr. Pope did no more than put it into verse ; that he had read Lord Bolingbroke's MS. in his own handwriting, and remembered well that he was at a loss whether most to admire the elegance of Lord Bolingbroke's prose, or the beauty of Mr. Pope's verse.' But Dr. Johnson replied, 'Depend upon it, sir, this is too strongly stated. Pope may have had from Bolingbroke the philosophic stamina of his essay ; but this is not true in the latitude Bathurst seems to imagine,' &c. &c.—Boswell's *Life of Johnson*, vii. 285.

[2] Warburton's *Works*, vol. vii. p. 572. See also pp. 573 and 858. Several of the Deists were pilloried in the Dunciad, e.g. :—

Pope quoted above ;[1] there is the undoubted fact that P
Shaftesbury,[2] and Bolingbroke so far agreed with one ano
that they were all ardent disciples of the optimistic school ; a
it must be added, there is the utter absence of anything
tinctively Christian in that poem in which one would natur
have expected to find it. For, to say the least of it, the ' Es
on Man ' might have been written by an unbeliever, as a
might the Universal Prayer. The fact seems to have b
that Pope was distracted by the counter influences of t
very powerful but two very opposite minds. Between W
burton and Bolingbroke, the poet might well become soi
what confused in his views. How far he would have agr
with the more pronounced anti-Christian sentiments of Boli
broke which were addressed to him, but which never met
eye, can of course be only a matter of conjecture. It
evident that Bolingbroke himself dreaded the influenc
Warburton, for he alludes constantly and almost nervousl
' the foul-mouthed critic whom I know you have at y
elbow,' and anticipates objections which he suspected '
dogmatical pedant ' would raise.

> ' Toland and Tindal, prompt at priests to jeer,
>
> .   .   .   .
>
> Morgan and Mandeville could prate no more.'—Bk. ii.

> ' And bade thee [Henley] live, to crown Britannia's praise,
> In Toland's, Tindal's, and in Woolston's days.'

But these passages bear but little, if at all, upon Pope's own views. The follov
is stronger :—

> ' But art thou one, whom new opinions sway,
> One who believes as Tindal leads the way,
> Who Virtue and a Church alike disowns,
> Thinks that but words, and this but brick and stones?
> Fly then, on all the wings of wild desire,
> Admire whate'er the maddest can admire.'

Lowth writes to Warburton, 'I thought you might have pilloried me in
'Dunciad,' of which you are legal proprietor.'

[1] P. 210.

[2] Pope was also clearly influenced by Shaftesbury's arguments that virtue
to be practised and sin avoided, not for fear of punishment or hope of reward,
for their own sakes. Witness the verse in the Universal Prayer :—

> ' What conscience dictates to be done,
> Or warns me not to do,
> This teach me *more than* hell to shun,
> That *more than* heaven pursue.'

There was yet another influence—is it to be called a Christian or an anti-Christian influence?—which must also be taken into account by those who would understand Pope's position in reference to the great subjects of philosophy and religion. In the vein of cynicism which runs through the 'Essay,' we recognise the caustic humour of the Dean of St. Patrick's.[1]

However, except in so far as it is always interesting to know the attitude of any great man towards contemporary subjects of stirring interest, it is not a very important question as to what were the poet's sentiments in reference to Christianity and Deism. Pope's real greatness lay in quite another direction; and even those who most admire the marvellous execution of his grand philosophical poem will regret that his brilliant talents were comparatively wasted on so uncongenial a subject.[2]

Far otherwise is it with the other great name which both Deists and orthodox claim as their own. What was the relationship of John Locke, who influenced the whole tone of thought of the eighteenth century more than any other single man, to the great controversy which is the subject of these pages? On the one hand, it is unquestionable that Locke

---

[1] Such lines as—

> ' Scarfs, garters, gold, amuse his riper stage,
>   And beads and prayer-books are the toys of age ;
>   Pleased with this bauble still, as that before,
>   Till tired he sleeps, and life's poor play is o'er.'—Ep. ii. *ad finem.*

> ' Go, teach Eternal Wisdom how to rule—
>   Then drop into thyself, and be a fool.'—Ep. ii. *ad initium.*

> ' To sigh for ribands if thou art so silly,
>   Mark how they grace Lord Umbra or Sir Billy.
>   Is yellow dirt the passion of thy life?
>   Look but on Gripus and on Gripus' wife,' &c. &c.

remind one at once of the misanthropy and feeling of the hollowness of life which characterise Swift.

[2] See Mr. Leslie Stephen's *English Thought in the Eighteenth Century*, vol. ii. p. 350, also i. 177, where he puts the matter very concisely : ' There are, indeed, many coincidences between the poem [*Essay on Man*] and Bolingbroke's fragmentary writings. But as the only question raised about Pope's verses by anybody, except Warburton, was whether the poetry was good enough to float the bad philosophy, it was hardly to be supposed that the philosophy without the poetry would be tolerable.' The last clause refers to the flatness of the reception of Bolingbroke's posthumous works.

had the closest personal connection with two of the principal Deistical writers, and that most of the rest show unmistakeable signs of having studied his works and followed more or less his line of thought. Nothing can exceed the warmth of esteem and love which Locke expresses for his young friend Collins, and the touching confidence which he reposes in him.[1] Nor was it only Collins' moral worth which won Locke's admiration ; he looked upon him as belonging to the same school of intellectual thought as himself, and was of opinion that Collins would appreciate his ' Essay on the Human Understanding ' better than anybody. Shaftesbury was grandson of Locke's patron and friend. Locke was tutor to his father, for whom he had been commissioned to choose a wife; and the author of ' The Characteristics ' was brought up according to Locke's principles.[2] Both Toland's and Tindal's views about reason show them to have been followers of Locke's system ;[3] while traces of Locke's influence are constantly found in Lord Bolingbroke's philosophical works. Add to all this that the progress and zenith of Deism followed in direct chronological order after the publication of Locke's two great works, and that in consequence of these works he was distinctly identified by several obscure and at least one very distinguished writer[4] with ' the gentlemen of the new way of thinking.'

[1] See Hunt's *History of Religious Thought in England*, vol. ii. p. 369, and Lechler's *Geschichte des Englischen Deismus*, p. 219.

[2] But Shaftesbury was bitterly opposed to one part of Locke's philosophy. ' He was one of the first,' writes Mr. Morell (*History of Modern Philosophy*, i. 203), ' to point out the dangerous influence which Locke's total rejection of all innate practical principles was likely to exert upon the interests of morality.' ' It was Mr. Locke,' wrote Shaftesbury, ' that struck at all fundamentals, threw all order and virtue out of the world, and made the very ideas of these (which are the same as those of God) unnatural and without foundation in our minds.' See also Bishop Fitzgerald in *Aids to Faith*.

[3] Toland (in explaining what reason is) ' zwar zeigt sein Sprachgebrauch und seine Ansicht vom Wissen unverkennbare Abhangigkeit von Locke's System.'—Lechler, p. 184. Also on Tindal, pp. 325, 330, ' Ueber das Wesen der Vernunft spricht sich Tindal vollkommen so aus, dass wir ihn als Schüler Locke's erkennen ; namentlich gibt er keine angebornen Prinzipien zu ausser einen der Begierde nach Glückseligkeit.'

[4] Stillingfleet. Mr. Morell, in his *History of Modern Philosophy*, expresses strongly his opinion that Locke's essay laid the foundation not only of Deism, but of scepticism :—' The only conclusion to which the whole theory [of sensationalism] can ultimately lead, is that of the most rigid scepticism,'—i. 131. ' His writings

But there is another side of the picture to which we must now turn. Though Locke died before the works of his two personal friends, Collins and Shaftesbury, saw the light, Deism had already caused a great sensation before his death, and Locke has not left us in the dark as to his sentiments on the subject, so far as it had been developed in his day.

Not much importance is to be attached to the fact that the only reference to a Deistical writer which Locke makes in his essay, is to express entire disagreement with his principles; for that disagreement was founded on philosophical, not on theological grounds. Lord Herbert's five articles, which are 'common notices or innate ideas in the soul,' contradicted verbally at least, if not really, Locke's pet theory that the mind is a *tabula rasa* which has no innate ideas, and Locke condemned the notion accordingly. Neither is much importance to be attached to the hypothesis that Locke wrote his treatise on the Reasonableness of Christianity with special reference to Herbert's system ; for this is a mere conjecture.[1] The appearance, however, of Toland's 'Christianity not Mysterious' brought Locke into more direct relation to the theological views of the Deists. Toland used several arguments from Locke's essay in support of his position that there was nothing in Christianity contrary to reason or above it. Bishop Stillingfleet, in his 'Defence of the Mysteries of the Trinity,' maintained that these arguments of Toland's were legitimate deductions from Locke's premises. This Locke explicitly denied, and moreover disavowed any agreement with the main position of Toland in a noble passage, in which he regretted that he could not find, and feared he never should find, that perfect

included, though unknown to himself, germs, which after a time bore the fruits of utilitarianism in morals, of materialism in metaphysics, and of scepticism in religion.'—i. 133, &c. M. Cousin (*Lectures on Locke*, xxi.) thinks that one part of Locke's philosophy leads to 'absolute scepticism.' But he adds, ' In the danger in which his philosophy involves him, he abandons his philosophy, and all philosophy, and he appeals to Christianity, to revelation, to faith.' For an able vindication of Locke from these charges, see Mr. Henry Rogers' 'Essay on John Locke,' in vol. iii. of his *Essays from the 'Edinburgh Review.'* Dr. Vaughan, ('Essay on Locke and his Critics,' vol. ii. of his *Essays*) though he defends Locke against M. Cousin and Mr. Morell, thinks Locke's 'Christianity was somewhat peculiar,' p. 119.

[1] See Hunt's *History of Religious Thought in England*, i. p. 453.

plainness and want of mystery in Christianity which the author maintained.[1] He also declared his implicit belief in the doctrines of revelation in the most express terms.[2] The controversy between Locke and Stillingfleet was an unhappy one for many reasons. It is painful to see two good Christians at variance ; painful to see a great and good man like Stilling-fleet, who had done eminent service to the Church, putting himself in an utterly false position ; painful to see a quite unnecessary antagonism between Christianity and a great and influential school of philosophy. The antagonism was but temporary. The warmest advocates of Christianity soon con-fessed that Locke was in the right and Stillingfleet was wrong,[3] though at the same time few will deny that Locke did not show himself at his best in this tedious dispute.

It was not, however, his essay, but his treatise on the 'Reasonableness of Christianity,' published in 1695 (the year before the publication of Toland's famous work), which brought Locke into the most direct collision with some of the orthodox of his day. In his preface Locke tells us the object and plan of his work. 'The little satisfaction and consistency that is to be found in most systems of divinity I have met with, made me betake myself to the sole reading of the Scriptures to which they all appeal, for the understand-ing of the Christian religion.' The result of his investigations was, that there was but one article of faith on which men were to be pronounced believers or unbelievers, viz., that 'Jesus Christ is the Messiah, the Son of God.'[4] Stated thus nakedly, the proposition certainly seems a startling one. But when we come to examine Locke's meaning more minutely, we find that he virtually included under this statement all the main articles of the Christian faith. His love of plainness and intelligibility, and his dread of all persecution for religious

---

[1] Locke's *Works*, vol. iv. p. 96.

[2] 'My lord, I read the revelation of Holy Scripture with a full assurance that all it delivers is true.'—Locke's *Works*, vol. iv. 341.

[3] For example, Warburton in his Dedication of the first three books of *The Divine Legation* to the Freethinkers :—'A prelate of great name was pleased to attack the *Essay on the Human Understanding*, who, though consummate in the learning of the schools, yet at that time applied his principles so very awkwardly,' &c.

[4] Locke's *Works*, vol. vii. p. 102.

opinions, made him loathe the very name of systems, and all the technical terms of scholasticism. But it was really the name rather than the thing which Locke hated. To prove this at length would be to go beyond the scope of the present inquiry, which is no further concerned with Locke's religious opinions than as they bear upon the Deistical controversy. On this point Locke has made himself perfectly clear to any reasonable mind. The host of obscure writers who immediately attacked him, if they effected little else, at least did this good, that they elicited from Locke a clear statement of his views. The opponent whom he singled out for special answer, one Edwards, a clergyman, actually represented Locke as no better than an Atheist,—Locke, who held that 'we may more certainly know there is a God than that there is anything else without us!'[1] 'He says,' complains Locke, 'that I am all over Socinianized, and a Socinian is one that favours the cause of Atheism.'[2] The vehement opposition which this little work of Locke's aroused seems to have caused the author unfeigned surprise.—'When it came out,' he writes, 'the buzz and flutter and noise which it made, and the reports which were raised that it subverted all morality and was designed against the Christian religion. . . . amazed me; knowing the sincerity of those thoughts which persuaded me to publish it, not without some hope of doing some service to decaying piety and mistaken and slandered Christianity.'[3] In another passage he tells us expressly that it was written against Deism. 'I was flattered to think my book might be of some use to the world ; especially to those who thought either that there was no need of revelation at all, or that the revelation of Our Saviour required belief of such articles for salvation which the settled notions and their way of reasoning in some, and want of understanding in others, made impossible to them. Upon

---

[1] *Essay on the Human Understanding*, bk. iv. ch. 10, § 6, and ch. 3, § 21. 'We have an intuitive knowledge of our own existence, a demonstrative knowledge of the existence of God ; of the existence of anything else, we have no other but a sensitive knowledge.'

[2] Locke's *Works*, vol. vii. 165–6.—'Vindication of the Reasonableness of Christianity from the Rev. Mr. Edwards' Reflections.' Peter Brown, afterwards Bishop of Cork, also charged Locke with a tendency to Atheism. See his book, entitled *Things Supernatural and Divine conceived by Analogy with Things Natural and Human*,' (published in 1733), p. 127, &c.

[3] Locke's *Works*, vol. vii. p. 166.

these two topics the objections seemed to turn, which were with most assurance made by Deists not against Christianity, but against Christianity misunderstood. It seemed to me, there needed no more to show the weakness of their exceptions, but to lay plainly before them the doctrines of our Saviour as delivered in the Scriptures.'[1]

The truth of this is amply borne out by the contents of the book itself. Can anything, for example, be more alien to the whole tendency of Deism than such passages as the following, which seem as if they had been written by anticipation in answer to the very arguments chiefly insisted upon by Tindal, Morgan, Chubb, and to a certain extent Bolingbroke, half a century later? 'It is true there is a law of nature, but who is there that ever did give, or undertook to give it us all entire as a law; no more nor no less than was contained in and had the obligation of that law?—Who ever made out all the *parts* of it, put them together, and showed the world their obligation?—When was there any such code that mankind might have recourse to, as their unerring rule, before our Saviour's time?'[2] 'A great many things which we have been bred up to in the belief of from our cradles (and are notions grown familiar, and as it were natural to us, under the Gospel,) we take for unquestionable, obvious truths, and easily demonstrable; without considering how long we might have been in doubt and ignorance of them had revelation been silent. And many are beholden to revelation, who do not acknowledge it. It is no diminishing to revelation, that reason gives its suffrage too to the truths revelation has discovered. But it is our mistake to think that because reason confirms them to us, we had the first certain knowledge of them from thence; and in that clear evidence we now possess them.'[3]

What a severe blow again is dealt to that want of modesty which is conspicuous in most of the Deistical writers, and which made them reject everything of which their poor finite understandings failed to grasp not only the idea, but the final cause, in the following passage :—'It is enough to justify the fitness of

---

[1] Locke's *Works,* vol. vii. p. 188, Preface to the Reader of 2nd Vindication.
[2] 'Reasonableness of Christianity,'—Locke's *Works,* vol. vii. 142.
Ibid. p. 145.

anything to be done, by resolving it into the "wisdom of God" who has done it; though our short views and narrow understandings may utterly incapacitate us to see that wisdom and judge rightly of it. We know little of this visible, and nothing at all of the state of that intellectual world, wherein are infinite numbers and degrees of spirits out of the reach of our ken or guess; and therefore know not what transactions there were between God and our Saviour, in reference to His Kingdom. We shall take too much upon us, if we call God's wisdom or providence to account, and pertly condemn for needless all that our weak, and perhaps biassed understanding cannot account for.'[1]

It is not, however, so much in direct statements of doctrine, as in the whole tenour and frame of his spirit, that Locke differed 'in toto' from the Deists: for Locke's was essentially a pious, reverent soul. But it may be urged that all this does not really touch the point at issue. The question really is, not what were Locke's personal opinions on religious matters, but what were the logical deductions from his philosophical system. It is in his philosophy, not in his theology, that Locke's reputation consists. Was then the Deistical line of argument derived from his philosophical system? and if so, was it fairly derived? The first question must be answered decidedly in the affirmative, the second not so decidedly in the negative. That Locke would have recoiled with horror from the

---

[1] 'Reasonableness of Christianity,'—Locke's *Works*, vol. vii. 134. His strong belief in the Christian revelation is almost as explicitly affirmed in the 'Essay.'—See bk. iv. ch. xvi. § 3. 'Miracles, well attested, do not only find credit themselves, but give it also to other truths, which need such confirmation,' in direct opposition to Hume's famous dictum. § 14 [a Revelation from God] 'carries with it an assurance beyond doubt, evidence beyond exception. Our assent to it is called Faith, which as absolutely determines our minds, and as perfectly excludes all wavering, as our knowledge itself; and we may as well doubt of our own Being, as we can, whether any revelation from God be true'—only, he adds, 'we must be sure that it be a Divine revelation, and that we understand it right.'—The 'Reasonableness of Christianity' shows whether he thought that the Christian revelation satisfied these conditions. In bk. iv. ch. xvii. § 23 and 24, where he distinguishes between matters above, contrary, and according to Reason, and shows that Reason and Faith are not opposite, he seems to be utterly opposed to Toland and other Deists.—'The existence of one God is according to Reason; the existence of more than one God contrary to Reason; the Resurrection of the Dead above reason.' The whole of the two chapters xviii. and xix. of bk. iv. deserve careful study, as illustrating Locke's views on religion.

conclusions which the Deists drew from his premisses, and
still more from the tone in which those conclusions were
expressed, can scarcely be doubted. Nevertheless, the fact
remains that they *were* so drawn. That Toland built upon
his foundation, Locke himself acknowledges.[1] Traces of his
influence are plainly discernible in Collins, Tindal—of whom
Shaftesbury calls Locke the fore-runner,—Morgan, Chubb,
Bolingbroke, and Hume.[2]

On the other hand, it must not be forgotten that the
opponents of Deism built upon Locke's foundation quite as
distinctly as any of the Deists did. After his death, it was
soon discovered that he was a Christian. The orthodox
Conybeare was not only an obvious follower of Locke, but has
left on record a noble testimony to his greatness and his
influence: 'In the last century there arose a very extraordinary genius for philosophical speculations; I mean Mr. Locke,
the glory of that age and the instructor of the present.'
Warburton was an equally enthusiastic admirer of our philosopher, and expressed his admiration in words very similar
to the above.[3] Benson the Presbyterian told Lardner that
he had made a pilgrimage to Locke's grave, and could hardly
help crying, 'Sancte Johannes, ora pro nobis;' and innumer-
able other instances of the love and admiration which Christians of all kinds felt for the great philosopher might be
quoted.

The question then arises, Which of the two parties, the
Deists or their adversaries, were the legitimate followers of
Locke? And the answer to this question is, 'Both.' The

---

[1] Locke's *Works*, vol. iv. 259, 260.

[2] See Morell's *History of Modern Philosophy*, i. 131 and 133.—'The principles
advocated in the 'Essay' with so much acuteness and so earnest a love of truth,
became almost universally diffused ; but unfortunately they fell into the hands of
men who, being entirely wanting in the simplicity of mind and the sincere piety
which had distinguished their author, appropriated them to purposes altogether
foreign to his intentions. The Deistical school of writers, which at this time arose,
armed themselves with many of Locke's conclusions in order to enforce their own
sceptical opinions.'

[3] 'Mr. Locke, the honour of this age and the instructor of the future' . . . .
'That great philosopher' . . . . 'It was Mr. Locke's love of it [Christianity]
that seems principally to have exposed him to his pupil's [Lord Shaftesbury's]
bitterest insults.'—Dedication of *The Divine Legation* (first three books) to the
Freethinkers.

sensational and empirical school of philosophy of which Locke was the great apostle, was the dominant school of the period. And even in the special application of his principles to religion, it would be wrong to say that either of the two parties wholly diverged from Locke's position. For the fact is, there were two sides to Locke's mind—a critical and rationalising side, and a reverent and devotional side.[1] He must above all things demonstrate the reasonableness of the Christian religion, thereby giving the key-note to the tone of theology of the eighteenth century; but in proving this point, he is filled with a most devout and God-fearing spirit. His dislike of all obscurity, and, in consequence, his almost morbid shrinking from all systematizing and from the use of all technical terms, form his point of contact with the Deists. His strong personal faith, and his reverence for Holy Scripture as containing a true revelation from God, bring him into harmony with the Christian advocates.[2] No abuse on the part of the clergy, no unfair treatment—though in his case it almost amounted to persecution [3]—could alienate him from Christianity. One cannot help speculating how he would have borne himself had he lived to see the later development of Deism. Perhaps his influence would have had a beneficial effect upon both sides; but, in whatever period his lot had been cast, it is difficult to conceive Locke in any other light than that of a sincere and devout Christian.[4]

---

[1] 'Die Verschiedenheit der Ansichten und Urtheile über Locke's Verhältniss zum Deismus, indem die einen ihn auf die Seite der Deisten verweisen, die andern ihn der entgegengesetzten vindiziren wollen, lassen sich blos dann begreifen, wenn wir anerkennen, dass sowohl ein Element der Kritik und der rationellen Freiheit, als eine supranaturalistische Anschauungsweise bei ihm sich findet. Die Entwicklung nach ihm ist durch diese Verbindung jener differenten Elemente in seinem Geist wesentlich bedingt, indem diese Elemente in mannigfaltigen Verhältnissen der Anziehung und Abstossung nachher sich neu gestatteten,' &c.—Lechler's *Geschichte des Englischen Deismus.*

[2] 'The Essay,' writes Mr. Morell (*History of Modern Philosophy*, Preface), ' is such, upon the whole, as to lead different minds to very opposite conclusions.'

[3] See Lord King's account of Locke's being deprived of his Studentship of Christ Church, and Fell, Bishop of Oxford's treatment of him.

[4] It is, however, not improbable that Locke contributed to some extent to foster that dry, hard, unpoetical spirit which characterised both the Deistical and anti-Deistical literature, and, indeed, the whole tone of religion in the eighteenth century. ' His philosophy,' it has been said, ' smells of the earth, earthy.' ' It is curious,' writes Mr. Rogers (*Essays*, vol. iii. p. 104, ' John Locke,' &c.) ' that there is

It remains for us to consider what were the effects of t
Deistical movement at home and abroad.

Its immediate effects at home were of a mixed characte
the evil being the more obvious, but the good not perhaps th
less real or less permanent.

To begin with the dark side.—The early period of the
eighteenth century was a period of controversy of all kinds,
and of controversy carried on in a bitter and unchristian spirit ;
and of all the controversies which arose, none was conducted
with greater bitterness than the Deistical.[1]   The Deists must
bear the blame of setting the example.   Their violent abuse
of the Church, their unfounded assertions that the clergy did
not really believe what they preached, that the Christian
religion as taught by them was a mere invention of priestcraft to serve its own ends, their overweening pretensions
contrasted with the scanty contributions which they actually
made either to theology or to philosophy or to philology,—
all this was sufficiently provoking.[2]

But the Christian advocates fell into a sad mistake when
they fought against them with their own weapons.   Without
attempting nicely to adjust the degree of blame attributable
to either party in this unseemly dispute, we may easily see
that this was one evil effect of the Deistical controversy,
that it generated on both sides a spirit of rancour and scurrility.

Again, the Deists contributed in some degree, though not

hardly a passing remark in all Locke's great work on any of the æsthetical or emotional characteristics of humanity ; so that, for anything that appears there, men
might have nothing of the kind in their composition.   To all the forms of the
Beautiful he seems to have been almost insensible.'   The same want in the
followers of Locke's system, both orthodox and unorthodox, is painfully conspicuous.   And again, as Dr. Whewell remarks (*History of Moral Philosophy*, Lecture
v. p. 74) 'the promulgation of Locke's philosophy was felt as a vast accession of
strength by the lower, and a great addition to the difficulty of their task by the
higher school of morality.'   The lower or utilitarian school of morality, which
held that morals are to be judged solely by their consequences, was largely followed
in the eighteenth century, and contributed not a little to the low moral and
spiritual tone of the period.

[1] The Calvinistic controversy was more bitter, but it belonged to the second,
not the first half of the century.

[2] 'They attacked a scientific problem without science, and an historical problem without history.'—Mr. J. C. Morrison's Review of Leslie Stephen's ' History
of English Thought ' in *Macmillan's Magazine* for February 1877.

intentionally, towards encouraging the low tone of morals which is admitted on all sides to have been prevalent during the first half of the eighteenth century. It was constantly insinuated that the Deists themselves were men of immoral lives.[1] This may have been true of individual Deists, but it requires more proof than has been given, before so grave an accusation can be admitted against them as a body.

But if the restrictions which Christianity imposes were not the real objections to it in the minds of the Deistical writers, at any rate their writings, or rather perhaps hazy notions of those writings picked up at second-hand, were seized upon by others who were glad of any excuse for throwing off the checks of religion.[2] The immorality of the age may be more fairly said to have been connected with the Deistical controversy than with the Deists themselves. It is not to be supposed that the fine gentlemen of the coffee-houses troubled themselves to read Collins or Bentley, Tindal or Conybeare. They only heard vague rumours that the truths, and consequently the obligations of Christianity were impugned, and that, by the admission of Christian advocates themselves, unbelief was making great progress. The *roués* were only Freethinkers in the sense that Squire Thornhill in the Vicar of Wakefield was.

Another ill effect was, that it took away the clergy from a very important part of their practical work. There was something much more attractive to a clergyman in immortalising his name by annihilating an enemy of the Faith, than in the ordinary routine of parochial work.

Bishops, too, had no time to see that the clergy did their duty. The claims of a remote diocese had to be postponed to the more pressing requirements of the defence of Christian mysteries. Not, however, that the clergy as a rule made

---

[1] 'Inquire closely into their lives,' writes Bentley (*Remarks on Discourse of Freethinking*, xv.), 'and then you will find the true reason why they clamour against religion.' Berkeley, both in the *Minute Philosopher* and in the *Guardian*, Steele, Addison, and Hughes, in the *Tatler* and *Spectator*, do not hesitate to impute the grossest immorality to the Deists as a body, but they give no proof whatever. Schlosser says, 'Tindal's laxity of moral principles injured him and his views with the middle classes,' but he too gives no proof.

[2] See Bishop Butler's charge to the clergy of Durham, 1751.—'A great source of infidelity plainly is, the endeavour to get rid of religious restraints.'

Deism a stepping-stone to preferment.[1] It would be difficult
to point to a single clergyman who was advanced to any high
post in the Church in virtue of his services against Deism, who
would not have equally deserved and in all probability obtained preferment, had his talents been exerted in another
direction. The talents of such men as Butler, Warburton,
Waterland, Gibson, Sherlock, Bentley and Berkeley would
have shed a lustre upon any profession. But none the less
is it true that the Deistical controversy diverted attention
from other and no less important matters ; and hence, indirectly, Deism was to a great extent the cause of that low
standard of spiritual life which might have been elevated, had
the clergy paid more attention to their flocks, and less to their
literary adversaries.

The effects, however, of the great controversy were not all
evil. If such sentiments as those to which the Deists gave
utterance were floating in men's minds, it was well that they
should find expression. A state of smouldering scepticism
is always a dangerous state. Whatever the doubts and difficulties might be, it was well that they should be brought into
the full light of day.

Moreover, if the Deists did no other good, they at least
brought out the full strength of the Christian cause, which
otherwise might have lain dormant. Although much of the
anti-Deistical literature perished with the occasion which
called it forth, there is yet a residuum which will be immortal.[2]

Again, the free discussion of such questions as the Deists
raised, led to an ampler and nobler conception of Christianity
than might otherwise have been gained. For there was a
certain element of truth in most of the Deistical writings. If
Toland failed to prove that there were no mysteries in Christianity, yet perhaps he set men a-thinking that there was a

---

[1] Herder, unlike himself, has somewhat ungenerously, and without giving any
proof, insinuated that they did, citing as instances Bentley and Swift, neither
of whom certainly gained any preferment in consequence of their writings against
Deists.—*Adrastea*, ii. p. 167.

[2] 'Not only,' writes Herder (*Adrastea*, ii.), 'did they [the Freethinkers]
awaken the spirit of proof and keep it awake, but (who can deny it?) they
brought out far better writers than themselves, better and opposite effects than
they had in view.'

real danger of darkening counsel by words without knowledge, through the indiscriminate use of scholastic jargon. If
Collins confounded freethinking with thinking in his own
particular way, he yet drew out from his opponents a more
distinct admission of the right of freethinking in the proper
sense of the term than might otherwise have been made.
If Shaftesbury made too light of the rewards which the
righteous may look for, and the punishments which the
wicked have to fear, he at least helped, though unintentionally, to vindicate Christianity from the charge of self-
seeking and to place morality upon its proper basis. If
Tindal attributed an unorthodox sense to the assertion that
' Christianity was as old as the Creation,' he brought out more
distinctly an admission that there was an aspect in which it
is undoubtedly true.

One of the most striking features of this strange controversy was its sudden collapse about the middle of the century.
The whole interest in the subject seems to have died away
as suddenly as it arose fifty years before. This change of
feeling is strikingly illustrated by the flatness of the reception
given by the public to Bolingbroke's posthumous works
in 1754. For though few persons will be inclined to agree
with Horace Walpole's opinion that Bolingbroke's 'metaphysical divinity was the best of his writings,'[1] yet the
eminence of the writer, the purity and piquancy of his style,
the real and extensive learning which he displayed,[2] would,
one might have imagined, have awakened a far greater interest in his writings than was actually shown. Very few
replies were written to this, the last, and in some respects the
most important—certainly the most elaborate attack that ever
was made upon popular Christianity from the Deistical stand-
point. The ' five pompous quartos' of the great statesman[3]
attracted infinitely less attention than the slight, fragmentary

[1] 'You say you have made my Lord Cork give up my Lord Bolingbroke; it is
comical to see how he is given up here, since the best of his writings, his metaphysical divinity, have been published.'—H. Walpole, ' Letter to Sir Horace
Mann,' December 1754.

[2] Hagenbach (*History of the Christian Church*, vol. i. p. 203) does not do
justice to Bolingbroke's writings when he characterises them as merely ' light and
witty.'

[3] See Horace Walpole's ' Letter ' quoted above.

treatise of an obscure Irishman had done fifty-eight years before.[1] And after Bolingbroke not a single writer who can properly be called a Deist appeared in England.

How are we to account for this strange revulsion of feeling, or rather this marvellous change from excitement to apathy? One modern writer imputes it to the inherent dulness of the Deists themselves;[2] another to their utter defeat by the Christian apologists.[3] No doubt there is force. in both these reasons, but there were other causes at work which contributed to the result.

One seems to have been the vagueness and unsatisfactoriness of the constructive part of the Deists' work. They set themselves with vigour to the work of destruction, but when this was completed—what next? The religion which was to take the place of popular Christianity was at best a singularly vague and intangible sort of thing. 'You are to follow nature, and that will teach you what true Christianity is. If the facts of the Bible don't agree, so much the worse for the facts.' There was an inherent untenableness in this position.[4] Having gone thus far, thoughtful men could not stand still.

---

[1] Dr. Newton tells us that Mallet, the editor of Bolingbroke's works, expected that they would prove a treasure, and refused three thousand pounds for the copy ; but so little did they answer his and the world's expectation, that the first impression was not sold off in twenty years. Newton's *Life of Himself*, p. 94. Warburton of course broke a lance against his old adversary.

Middleton, 'whose covert assault,' writes Mr. Stephen (i. 162), 'upon the orthodox dogmas was incomparably the most effective of the whole Deist controversy,' was received with equal flatness. Middleton, however, was not a Deist in the sense in which the term is used in this sketch. He wrote one of the numerous answers to Tindal, proving his scheme to be 'irrational, because impossible to be reduced to practice, and immoral, because, if possible, yet pernicious to the public.'—*Miscellaneous Works of Conyers Middleton*, iii. 70.

[2] Mr. Leslie Stephen, *Essays on Freethinking and Plain Speaking.* On Shaftesbury's 'Characteristics.'—'The Deists were not only pilloried for their heterodoxy, but branded with the fatal inscription of "dulness."' This view is amplified in his larger work, published since the above was written.

[3] *Aids to Faith,* p. 44.

[4] In a brilliant review of Mr. Leslie Stephen's work in *Macmillan's Magazine*, February 1877, Mr. James Cotter Morrison remarks on the Deists' view that natural religion must be always alike plain and perspicuous, 'against this convenient opinion the only objection was that it contradicted the total experience of the human race.'

'Mere Deism,' wrote Bishop Chandler, 'hath never yet been tryed in any country.'—*Defence of Prophecy against ' Grounds and Reasons,'* &c. Introd. ix.

They must go on further or else turn back. Some went forward in the direction of Hume, and found themselves stranded in the dreary waste of pure scepticism, which was something very different from genuine Deism. Others went backwards and determined to stand upon the old ways, since no firm footing was given them on the new. There was a want of any definite scheme or unanimity of opinion on the part of the Deists. Collins boasted of the rise and growth of a new sect. But, as Dr. Monk justly observes, 'the assumption of a growing sect implies an uniformity of opinions which did not really exist among the impugners of Christianity.' [1]

The independence of the Deists in relation to one another might render it difficult to confute any particular tenet of the sect, for the simple reason that there *was* no sect ; but this same independence prevented them from making the impression upon the public mind which a compact phalanx might have done. The Deists were a company of Free Lances rather than a regular army, and effected no more than such irregular forces usually do.

And here arises the question, What real hold had Deism upon the public mind at all? There is abundance of contemporary evidence which would lead us to believe that the majority of the nation were fast becoming unchristianised. Bishop Butler was not the man to make a statement, and especially a statement of such grave import, lightly, and his account of the state of religion is melancholy indeed. 'It is come,' he writes, 'I know not how, to be taken for granted, by many persons, that Christianity is not so much as a subject of inquiry, but that it is now at length discovered to be fictitious. And accordingly, they treat it as if, in the present age, this were an agreed point among all people of discernment, and nothing remained but to set it up as a principal subject of mirth and ridicule, for its having so long interrupted the pleasures of the world.' [2] Making all allowance for the

---

[1] Monk's *Life of Bentley*, vol. i. See also Berkeley's *Alciphron, or the Minute Philosopher*, 107.

[2] Advertisement to the first edition of *The Analogy*, p. xiv. See also Swift's description of the Duchess of Marlborough, in *Last Four Years of Queen Anne*, bk. i. The first and most prominent subject of Bishop Butler's 'Durham Charge,' is 'the general decay of religion,' 'which,' he says, 'is now observed

exaggeration natural in satirical writing, one can scarcely suppose that there were no grounds for the following statements in Swift's 'Argument against abolishing Christianity.' 'The curious may please to observe how much the genius of a nation is liable to alter in half an age. I have heard it affirmed for certain by some very old people that the contrary opinion was, even in their memories, as much in vogue as the other is now, and that a project for the abolishing of Christianity would then have appeared as singular and been thought as absurd as it would be at this time to write a discourse in its defence.' 'I hope no reader imagines me so weak as to stand up in defence of real Christianity as used in primitive times (if we may believe the authors of those ages,) to have an influence upon men's belief or actions; to offer at the restoring of that would indeed be a wild project; it would be to dig up foundations, to destroy at one blow all the wit and half the learning in the kingdom.' And again, 'I look upon the *mass* or body of our people here in England to be as freethinkers, that is to say, as staunch unbelievers as any of the higher rank.' Archbishop Wake's testimony is equally explicit,[1] so is Bishop Warburton's.[2] Or to take another class of evidence, Voltaire declared that there was only just enough religion left in England to distinguish Tories who had little from Whigs who had less.[3]

In the face of such testimony it seems a bold thing to assert that there was a vast amount of noise and bluster which caused a temporary panic, but little else, and that after all Hurd's view of the matter was nearer the truth. 'The truth of the case,' he writes, 'is no more than this. A few fashionable men make a noise in the world; and this clamour

by everyone, and has been for some time the complaint of all serious persons' (written in 1751). The Bishop then instructs his clergy at length how this sad fact is to be dealt with; in fact this, directly or indirectly, is the topic of the whole Charge.

[1] He wrote to Courayer in 1726,—'No care is wanting in our clergy to defend the Christian Faith against all assaults, and I believe no age or nation has produced more or better writings, &c. . . . This is all we can do. Iniquity in practice, God knows, abounds,' &c.

[2] See his works, *passim*.

[3] Quoted in Watson's *Life of Warburton*, p. 632. A well-informed modern writer asserts that 'Deism exercised an enormous, though often as unconscious influence both on the Church and the sects.'—Curteis's *Bampton Lectures* for 1871.

being echoed on all sides from the shallow circles of their admirers, misleads the unwary into an opinion that the irreligious spirit is universal and uncontrollable.' [1]   A strong proof of the absence of any real sympathy with the Deists is afforded by the violent outcry which was raised against them on all sides.   This outcry was not confined to any one class or party either in the political or religious world.   We may not be surprised to find Warburton mildly suggesting that ' he would hunt down that pestilent herd of libertine scribblers with which the island is overrun, as good King Edgar did his wolves,' [2] or Berkeley, that ' if ever man deserved to be denied the common benefits of bread and water, it was the author of a Discourse of Freethinking,' [3] and that ' he should omit no endeavour to render the persons (of Freethinkers) as despicable and their practice as odious in the eye of the world as they deserve.' [4]   But we find almost as truculent notions in writings where we might least expect them.   It was, for example, a favourite accusation of the Tories against the Whigs that they favoured the Deists.   'We' (Tories), writes Swift, ' accuse them [the Whigs] of the public encouragement and patronage to Tindal, Toland, and other atheistical writers.' [5]   And yet we find the gentle Addison, Whig as he was, suggesting in the most popular of periodicals, corporal punishment as a suitable one for the Freethinker ; [6] Steele, a Whig and the most merciful of men, advocating in yet stronger terms a similar mode of treatment ; [7] Fielding, a Whig and not a particularly straitlaced man, equally violent. [8]

This strong feeling against the Deists is all the more remarkable when we remember that it existed at a time of great religious apathy, and at a time when illiberality was far from being a besetting fault.   The dominant party in the Church was that which would now be called the Broad Church party, and among the Dissenters at least equal latitudinarianism was tolerated.   This, however, which might seem at first sight a reason why Deism should have been winked at, was

---

[1] Quoted in *Aids to Faith.*   Bishop Fitzgerald's *Essay on the Evidences of Christianity.*
[2] Watson's *Life of Warburton*, p. 293.   [3] *Guardian*, No. 3.
[4] *Guardian*, No. 88.
[5] *Examiner*, xxxix.   See also Leslie's *Theological Works*, vol. ii. p. 533.
[6] *Tatler*, No. 108.   [7] *Tatler*, No. 137.   [8] See *Amelia*, bk. i. ch. iii. &c.

probably in reality one of the causes why it was so unpopular. The nation had begun to be weary of controversy ; in the religious as in the political world, there was arising a disposition not to disturb the prevailing quiet. The Deist was the *enfant terrible* of the period, who would persist in raising questions which men were not inclined to meddle with. It was therefore necessary to snub him ; and accordingly snubbed he was most effectually.

The Deists themselves appear to have been fully aware of the unpopularity of their speculations. They have been accused, and not without reason, of insinuating doubts which they dared not express openly. But then, why dared they not express them ? The days of persecution for the expression of opinion were virtually ended. There were indeed laws still unrepealed against blasphemy and contempt of religion, but except in extreme cases (such as those of Woolston and Annet), they were no longer put into force. Warburton wrote no more than the truth when he addressed the Freethinkers thus : ' This liberty may you long possess and gratefull acknowledge. I say this because one cannot but observe that amidst full possession of it, you continue with the meanest affectation to fill your prefaces with repeated clamours against difficulties and discouragements attending the exercise of freethinking. There was a time, and that within our own memories, when such complaints were seasonable and useful ; but happy for you, gentlemen, you have outlived it.' [1] They had outlived it, that is to say, so far as legal restrictions were concerned. If they did meet with ' difficulties and discouragements,' they were simply those which arose from the force of public opinion being against them. But be the cause what it may, the result is unquestionable. ' The English Deists wrote and taught their creed in vain ; they were despised while living, and consigned to oblivion when dead ; and they left the Church of England unhurt by the struggle.' [2]

Far different was the result of the struggle in France. The French *esprits forts* derived their first inspiration from the English ' Freethinkers ;' or perhaps it would be

[1] Dedication of first three books of the *Divine Legation.* See also Pattison's Essay in *Essays and Reviews.*

[2] Farrer's *Bampton Lectures,* ' History of Free Thought.'

more correct to say that England gave back to France with interest what France had originally in part given to her. The religious wars of France in the sixteenth century produced a free spirit of religious inquiry. This passed over into England, and affected especially the higher classes of society during the period immediately subsequent to the Restoration.[1] But it was the Deistical literature of England from the time of the Revolution to the middle of the eighteenth century, which gave an impetus to that wild licence in the domain of religious thought which culminated in the formal abolition of Christianity and the deification of the Goddess Reason. During the reign of the ' Grand Monarque,' Frenchmen were accustomed to regard the English as a set of barbarians. This contempt arose from their profound ignorance of England, no less than from their national vanity. As soon as they began to know us better, a violent reaction set in, and enthusiastic admiration and imitation took the place of contemptuous disregard.

No single man contributed so materially to bring about this reaction as Voltaire. He had been intimate with Viscount Bolingbroke during the exile of the latter in France ; and when he visited England, at the very time when Deism was reaching its zenith, he was introduced by that nobleman into just that society where Deism was most fashionable. After a stay of more than two years, he returned to his own land, full of admiration for the country where he had found both religious and political liberty. ' How I love the English courage !' he exclaimed with rapture. ' How I love the people who say what they think !'[2] In England he had found men expressing with impunity sentiments far more audacious than those which had caused his own imprisonment in the Bastile ; and he determined to introduce English liberty into France. The immediate fruit of his visit to England was the publication of his first attack upon Christianity ;[3] and from that time forward he was the avowed enemy of revealed religion.

---

[1] See Lechler's *Geschichte des Englischen Deismus*, p. 444.

[2] 'Que j'aime la hardiesse anglaise ! que j'aime les gens qui disent ce qu'ils pensent !'—Letter from Voltaire, in *Correspond. de Dudeffand*, vol. ii. p. 263.

[3] ' Epître à Uranie.'

There was little or nothing original in Voltaire's system, but the influence of his writings was immeasurably greater than that of any English Deist : a fact partly, no doubt, owing to the greater readiness of the French to admit such views, but partly also because Voltaire's writings were free from two faults which greatly contributed to diminish the influence of the English Deists. He was not vague and he was not dull. There was no mistaking what his attitude towards revealed religion was. He made no fine-drawn distinctions, like those of his English prototypes, between genuine Christianity and the Christianity of priests and systematisers. He said out boldly that he was weary of hearing it boasted that twelve men had been able to plant Christianity throughout the world, and he would show that one was sufficient to destroy it. His prophecy has not been exactly fulfilled ; but in his own time there really seemed some probability that it might be, so far as France was concerned ; and he certainly did his best to bring about its fulfilment. His trumpet gave no uncertain sound. He may properly be called a Deist,[1] for he believed in a God who revealed himself in nature ; but in any other revelation of the Deity he utterly disbelieved, and expressed his disbelief in terms that were quite unmistakable. And this he did in a more attractive style than the English Deists. Not that Voltaire introduced into France a spirit of scepticism which had not existed before. Such a spirit was very general among the higher classes before his time ; what Voltaire did, was to popularise—'to grind down the grain into food for the people.'[2] He spread far and wide what had before been confined to a select circle ; and in this sense he is rightly termed *Coryphée du Déisme.* Indeed, his influence seemed to be boundless. 'The true king of the eighteenth century,' writes M. Cousin, 'is Voltaire, but Voltaire in his turn is a scholar of England. Before Voltaire knew England by his travels and by his friendships, he was not Voltaire, and the eighteenth century was not yet a fact.'[3]

---

[1] But Voltaire was vehemently opposed to the doctrine of optimism, which, in one shape or another, was held by most of our English Deists. His *Candide* was written expressly to ridicule the doctrine.

[2] Carlyle's *Essays,* vol. ii. 'Voltaire.'

[3] 'Le vrai roi du XVIII⁰ siècle, c'est Voltaire ; mais Voltaire à son tour est un écolier de l'Angleterre. Avant que Voltaire eût connu l'Angleterre, soit par ses

But though the most influential, Voltaire's is by no means the highest type even of French Deism. In profundity and grasp of his subject he is far inferior to Diderot, in spiritual earnestness to Rousseau. Indeed, the utter lack of this latter quality[1] rendered Voltaire incapable of treating adequately the subject on which he wrote so much. The organ of reverence was not highly developed in the English Deist, but in Voltaire it seems to have been absolutely non-existent. He had no sense of religion, and was in consequence no more fit to judge of a religious question than a man devoid of any natural sense is fit to judge of anything perceptible only by that sense. It has been seen that our English Deists were far more in their element when engaged in destructive than in constructive work. Still they seem to have retained some consciousness that destruction was not everything. No such misgiving seems to have troubled Voltaire. ' Down with it, down with it, even to the ground,' was the one burden of his cry, and he lived to see his mission in the fair way of being accomplished.

Rousseau was a Deist of a very different stamp ; he too derived much of his inspiration from England, and in many respects followed closely in the wake of our English Deists ; but in others he differed from them widely. He was the very reverse of a materialist ; indeed, it was his idealism which led him to reject a great part of historical Christianity. He could do so the more easily because his highly imaginative mind was able to construct, and apparently to be satisfied with, a sort of sentimental Christianity of his own.[2] But there was a truly Christian element in his wayward character which was wanting in that of the Deists generally, and notably in Voltaire. He had sufficient spiritual insight to enable him to appreciate the divine beauty of the Saviour's life and character, and especially His death, which our English Deists did very imperfectly, and Voltaire not at all.

It was not, however, the school of Rousseau—if, indeed,

voyages, soit par ses amitiés, il n'était pas Voltaire, et le XVIIIᵉ siècle se cherchait encore.'—Cousin, *Hist. de la Philos.* 1ʳᵉ série, vol. iii. pp. 38, 39.

[1] See Carlyle's Essay on Voltaire.

[2] See Hagenbach's *History of the Christian Church*, vol. i. pp. 209, &c. and Carlyle's. Essay on Voltaire, Schlegel's *Lectures on the History of Literature*, p. 359, &c.

Rousseau can be said to have founded or even to have belonged to any school of thought at all—but that of Voltaire which gave the tone to French Deism. Deism indeed, in any sense of the term, it soon ceased to be. The belief in a God was presently expunged from the creed of the new school.

Those who took the lead in this movement were largely influenced by English Deism, and that, not merely through the medium of Voltaire, but directly through English travel, and through the importation, either in the original or in translations, of English literature into France; Condillac, Diderot, Montesquieu, Helvetius, Holbach—in fact, almost all the writers in the 'Encyclopædia,'—almost all whose names are chiefly connected with the great political and religious revolution of France in the eighteenth century, were more or less influenced by English ideas. 'France stood upon the shoulders of England.'[1] But what was a mere flash in the pan in England was a mighty engine of destruction in France. How are we to account for this contrast between the influence of the same spirit in the two countries? Among other causes, may it not have been to some extent owing to the fact that in England the spirit was allowed to have free play, while in France it was not? The French authorities tried to stifle the spirit of free inquiry; the bow was so strained that at length it snapped, and the country which had so long been deprived of liberty at length broke loose, and degenerated into wild licence, which brought it to the verge of ruin.

The immediate effects of English Deism was more striking and more direct in France than in any other country, but perhaps in the long run they were yet more influential and more permanent in Germany.

Germany had been prepared for the reception of Deism by a somewhat similar process to that which had paved the way for it in England. Fierce contests between Romanists and

---

[1] 'Die deistische Literatur Englands, seit der Revolution von 1689 erstarkt und zur Blüthe gediehen, gab Frankreich die Zinse reichlich zurück. So gewiss nämlich das philosophische Jahrhundert Frankreichs ein echt nationales und eingeborenes Erzeugniss Frankreichs ist, so wenig lässt sich doch läugnen, dass die Franzosen des vorigen Jahrhunderts viele wesentliche Gedanken, viele Materialien, aus England entlehnt haben, dass sie "auf den Schultern der Engländer stehn."'[1]—Lechler, *Geschichte des Englischen Deismus*, p. 664.

Protestants, and, among Protestants themselves, between the Lutheran and the Reformed Communions, in which all the combatants claimed, of course, Scripture for their own side, had been going on without intermission for two centuries. Religious questions had been even more closely connected with the terrible Thirty Years' war in Germany than they had been with the civil wars in England. Indeed the prolongation of that desolating struggle in Germany may be distinctly traced to clerical influence.[1]

Meanwhile, both theology itself and practical religion had degenerated sadly since the days of Luther. The seventeenth century is a dark period in the history of Christianity in Germany. There were bright exceptions here and there, but these exceptions only went to prove the rule. Apostolic men like Arndt at the beginning of the century, Andrea towards the middle, and Spener at the close, made vigorous and not ineffectual efforts to revive decaying piety. But all of them drew a melancholy picture of the times in which they lived. Arndt's great work on 'True Christianity,' which created an immense sensation, and was translated into most European languages, was full of lamentations over the inefficacy of the existing system of dialectic disquisition.[2] Andrea complains that the divines of his day 'had rather explain the nature of the Trinity than worship it, prove the ubiquity of Christ than honour Him at all times and in all places, describe repentance for sin than feel it themselves, depreciate the merits of works than do good ones, finger through holy Scripture than employ themselves in the practice of Christian love.'[3] Spener, in his 'Pia Desideria' complains

---

[1] The following books may be referred to generally as confirming what is stated in the text respecting the influence of English Deism in Germany. Dorner's *History of Protestant Theology*, Hagenbach's *History of the Christian Church*, E. B. Pusey on *German Theology* (1828), H. J. Rose's *State of Protestantism in Germany* (1829), Herder's *Sämmtliche Werke*, passim, but especially the *Adrastea*. Lechler's *Geschichte des Englischen Deismus*, Carlyle's *Essay on Taylor's Survey of German Poetry*, *State of German Literature*, and his Essays on German subjects generally, Carlyle's *Life of Frederick the Great*, Schlegel's *Lectures on the History of Literature*, Baur's *Kirchengeschichte der neueren Zeit* (Tübingen, ed. 1863), Hurst's *History of Rationalism*, Morell's *History of Modern Philosophy*, and Dr. R. Vaughan's *Essays on History, Philosophy, and Theology*, two vols.

[2] See Pusey's *Historical Enquiry into the Rationalist Character in German Theology*, p. 54. [3] See Pusey, pt. ii. 246.

that few of the magistracy knew what Christianity was ; that many of the clergy lived in profligacy, many more were strangers to earnest piety, and looked upon one who was zealous for it as a Papist, Quaker, or fanatic.[1]

Theology fared no better than practical religion. Not that learned men were wanting; but their learning was for the most part misdirected. Thus, at the beginning of the eighteenth century the old orthodoxy both of Lutherans and Reformed had, to use a favourite German expression, become 'ossified.' It was a dead letter rather than a living principle, and had almost ceased to exercise any practical influence over the people.

A change in some direction was inevitable. But the next step marks an important difference between England and Germany. In England, what may be termed 'emotional religion' rose on the ruins of Deism ; in Germany it preceded that movement. The reaction against the dryness and impotency of the prevailing orthodoxy took the form of Pietism, of which Spener was the founder, and the University of Halle the centre. The Halle Pietists were excellent men, and did a great work in reviving the dying spirit of vital Christianity: but even in their earliest and palmiest days they were not equal to the task of permanently influencing the intellect of Germany. Their hearts were better than their heads, and they fell into the errors to which men of their type are most prone. Their discouragement of theological studies of the severer kind, their depreciation of human arts and sciences, their contempt for æsthetics, their precision about things indifferent, their indiscriminate condemnation of all harmless amusements, their tendency to resolve religion too much into a morbid analysis of each man's self-consciousness, —all this narrowed the influence for good which they unquestionably exercised. In short, Pietism was a system calculated rather 'to take men out of the world' than to 'keep them from the evil.' After the death of Spener, and still more after the death of Francke his successor, these defects of Pietism became more apparent. Its narrowness and bitterness against the outer world increased, and consequently its power to leaven that world decreased. There was indeed one master mind

[1] Pusey, p. 104.

which combined the good side of Pietism with a breadth and depth of thought which Pietism never possessed. This was Bengel, who sympathised heartily with the practical Christianity of the Pietists, while he deplored the narrowness into which they were drifting more and more. But Bengel was opposed by the orthodox, without altogether securing the sympathy of the Pietists. Had there been more Bengels, or had Bengel himself been able to secure a larger following, the struggle between orthodox Christianity and Rationalism might have taken a different course from what it did. As it was, Bengel could do no more than gather under his banner a select circle, which was too small to exercise much appreciable influence upon the general mind.[1]

Such was the state of religion in Germany when the first germs of Deism may be traced. There were two antagonistic tendencies discernible, both equally feeble,—a decrepit orthodoxy and a decrepit Pietism. This decrepitude extended to German literature generally. In the whole domain of thought, Germany seemed to be almost entirely dependent upon foreign resources. In the early part of the eighteenth century the Gallicomania was rampant. The Germans were becoming more and more the mere humble imitators of the French, who on their part regarded the Germans as a semibarbarous people.

This state of things may in some degree account not only for the difference in the extent and duration of the Deistical movement in Germany and in England, but also for the different treatment it met with in the two nations. In England, the orthodox of all shades at once took up a position of violent antagonism against Deism, and finally beat it out of the field. In spite of the vagueness of our Deists, in spite of their disclaiming any wish to oppose Christianity, no compromise whatever was made : there was from the first a sharp line of demarcation drawn between Deism and Christianity.

Not so in Germany. There, Deism gradually insinuated

---

[1] See Dorner's *History of Protestant Theology*, vol. ii. pp. 228 and 233. When Hagenbach (i. 375) calls Bengel ' the Spener of South Germany,' he hardly does justice to either. Spener had more extensive practical influence than Bengel, but Bengel had wider sympathies and a more powerful and cultivated mind than Spener.

itself into the current theology, gave a colour to the whole religious thought of the period, and, through many and varying phases, exercised an influence which is felt even to this day.

From its commencement, English Deism had been noticed in Germany, but only from a polemical, or at most from a historical point of view. German theologians had lifted up their voices against the spread of infidelity in England not only in general terms, but by direct attacks upon the several writers of the Deistical school. Thus Kortholt had written against Lord Herbert and Hobbes before the eighteenth century began ; the great names of Leibnitz and Mosheim are found among the antagonists of Toland ; Pfass had written an answer to Collins, Lenke to Woolston.[1] But in all this there is no trace of any positive influence exercised by English Deism over the mind of Germany. Even Toland's visits to the courts of Berlin and Hanover, great as was the attention paid to him personally at both, do not appear to have enlisted much sympathy with the school of religious thought to which he belonged.

It is not till the year 1741, when Tindal's 'Christianity as old as the Creation ' was translated into German, that we can detect any direct impression made by English Deism upon the religion of Germany.[2] The translator was J. L. Schmidt, a Wolffian ; and though he translated Foster's answer at the same time, and so supplied the antidote as well as the poison, he was severely condemned by orthodox theologians for making a Freethinker known. The change which is henceforth perceptible in the attitude of German thinkers towards Deism is in the first instance traceable to the spread of the Wolffian philosophy. To understand the nature of the process, we must go back a few years.

Christian Wolff was Professor of Mathematics in the University of Halle. He there seems to have found many sympathisers among the students with the philosophical and theological doctrines which he grounded, oddly enough, upon his mathematical teaching. But he incurred the suspicion of his brother professors, especially of Joachim Lange, through whose instrumentality he was expelled from his professorship

---

[1] Lechler, *ad finem.*   [2] Lechler, p. 448.

in 1723. The circumstances of his expulsion are ludicrous enough. King Frederick William was importuned in vain to rid the University of its obnoxious professor. The king was orthodox, but his heart was more set upon getting and keeping tall soldiers, than upon deciding nice questions of theology. At last, some one wiser in his generation than the rest put the matter in a light in which the king could understand it. 'Wolff,' he said, 'teaches some doctrines about a predetermined harmony. Follow out that, and any one of your Majesty's grenadiers might desert, and say he was predetermined to do so, and therefore had done no sin against God.' Then the king took the alarm at once, and gave peremptory orders that Wolff should quit not only Halle but the Prussian dominions within forty-eight hours, 'under pain of the halter.'[1] Wolff retired to Marburg amidst much sympathy. The king was subsequently persuaded to read Wolff's books, and not finding them, it is presumed, so dangerous as he expected, desired him to return in 1733. But Wolff was deaf to all entreaties, until a king of more congenial spirit ascended the throne. In 1740 he returned, amidst much rejoicing, to his old university, and continued to teach there until his death.

Turning to the doctrines which Wolff taught, it would seem at the first glance that they tended to strengthen rather than to weaken the cause of Christianity. Wolff indeed was not the creator of the system which bears his name. He was but the exponent of the views of a far greater man than himself, and that man a vehement and successful opponent of Deism. Wolff's mission was to bring down from the clouds the soaring speculations of Leibnitz for the use of ordinary mortals; but the teaching of the great philosopher was shorn of much of its grandeur in the descent. There is no reason to question the sincerity of the Wolffians' assertion, that their object was simply to combat infidelity with its own weapons. The Deists, especially in England, attempted to show on philosophical grounds that reason and revelation—or at least the popular views of revelation—were at variance. The Wolffian philosophy was in the first instance an attempt to show on the same grounds that a reconciliation was possible.

[1] See Carlyle's *Life of Frederick the Great*, bk. v. ch. vii. p. 623, &c.

The method adopted was the mathematical method. Leibnitz
had actually tried to prove the Lutheran view of the Lord's
Supper by algebraical formulæ.[1]   The application of mathematical evidence to moral and religious truth was a peculiar
one, and not likely to be satisfactory.   The Pietists may have
been wrong, as a general principle, in fearing that the emancipation of reason would cause an unwillingness to believe.
But the sequel showed that there was cause for alarm lest
the Leibnitz-Wolffian philosophy, when more fully developed,
might prove prejudicial to the Christian faith.   The system
placed God ordinarily at a distance from the world, and
represented the latter as being governed purely by law,
regarding it as inconsistent with the sublime conception of
the Deity that He should have much intercourse with mortals.
Without actually depreciating revelation, Wolff made Scripture too much a sealed book.   The distinction insisted upon
by the Wolffians between the natural and the revealed, i.e.
between the demonstrable religion and that which is comprehensible only through faith, paved the way for the Deistical
principle of natural religion.   Not that the Wolffians themselves ever became naturalists.   They held that natural
religion is in itself necessary and unalterable, and that consequently revealed religion could not contradict it; but they
did not, with the naturalists, accept only one ground of religion, viz. reason, and so reproach the other ground, viz.
revelation, as either false or unnecessary.   It was moreover
objected, perhaps unreasonably, that Wolff's adoption of
Leibnitz' theory of a predetermined harmony involved the
admission of fatalism, and that his rejection of some of the
methods of proving the existence of a Deity tended to atheism.
But it was the optimistic views of Leibnitz and Wolff which
more than anything else tended by a perverted application to
debase German Christianity, as we shall see presently.

From what has been said of this system, the points of
contact with English Deism which it presented will be obvious.   We need not, therefore, be surprised to find that from
the time when Wolffianism began to supersede both the old
orthodoxy and the new Pietism, that is, soon after Wolff's

---

[1] See Hagenbach's *History of the Christian Church*, vol. i. pp. 76-80.

return to Halle, English Deistical literature began to be widely circulated in Germany. From 1746 to 1767 translations of English Deistical and anti-Deistical works, notices and extracts from them, and lives of their authors, poured forth from the press, and were read with avidity. Thorschmid testifies from his own experience that in the Seven Years' war officers of high rank diligently read the writings of Collins and Tindal. In the autobiography of Laukhard (edited by Tholuck) the vivid impression made upon him by reading ' Christianity as old as the Creation ' is thus described. ' God ! ' he cries, ' with what enjoyment and support I read this remarkable book ; how are all my thoughts about mystery and revelation altered at once ! All doubts vanished from me and came no more into my soul. I became convinced, as by a mathematical certainty, that Jesus and the apostles taught nothing but natural religion, here and there adorned with pictures out of the old oriental figures of speech.' [1]

What may appear more strange is, that the English anti-Deistical works seem to have strengthened the rationalistic tendency in Germany as much as those of the Deists themselves. This is accounted for by one of the most thoughtful of English writers on the subject, ' partly because the apologists themselves had been in some degree tacitly acted upon by the systems which they opposed, partly as being too exclusively intellectual, and partly because, from the different stage in which German theology then stood, their very defences contributed to expose some of its untenable but unyielded points.'

In attributing this importance to the effects of English Deism upon Germany, it must not, of course, be forgotten that French influence also contributed to the same result. The relations between Voltaire and Frederick the Great are too well known to need description. Both strove their utmost to impose the French form of Deism upon the Germans. But what flourished luxuriantly on the light soil of France was not adapted to take permanent root on the more solid ground of Germany. The frivolous French Illuminism only stirred the surface of the German nature.[2] Indeed, it was at

[1] See Lechler.
[2] Hagenbach's *History of the Christian Church*, vol. i. p. 76.

the very time when German Deism became most prevalent, that the French influence, which had long lain like a baleful incubus over the far nobler mind of Germany, began to be shaken off. Moreover, it must be remembered that French infidelity itself drew its first inspiration from England. Such power, then, as it exerted in moulding the German mind, may be ultimately traced back to English Deism.

The process by which what in England was termed Deism, but in Germany Illuminism, Rationalism, or Neology, made its way into the latter country, was a very gradual and also a very diversified one, varying with the different minds which were affected by it. It has been said that Wolff himself never lost his hold upon the Christian faith. The same may be said of his immediate followers, although they showed a marked advance in the rationalistic direction upon their master. Baumgarten, as professor at Halle, exercised a great influence upon the students of that university. While retaining some leaven of the old Pietism, he prepared his pupils' minds for the reception of rationalistic doctrines chiefly in questions of moral theology and history. Ernesti's influence was exercised in the same direction through the exegesis of Scripture. Insisting upon a purely grammatical interpretation of the Bible, he fell into the error of applying too rigorously classical tests to Biblical language, which in more than one instance led him into the domain of neology. Contemporary with these was Michaelis, whose rationalising tendencies were promoted rather by his moral and spiritual than by his intellectual character. The influence of his father, who was a simple, earnest Pietist, prevented Michaelis from drifting away from Christianity, but he was too light-minded to take a deep, spiritual conception of Christianity ; and through his levity he contributed in a measure towards reducing Christianity to a commonplace level.

A far more interesting, complicated, and influential character than any of the three above mentioned is that of Semler, who has been termed the Father of Neology. Semler was a pupil of Baumgarten, and followed in many respects the lead of his master. He was personally a deeply religious man, and his domestic relations, especially, present a beautiful picture of tender, simple piety. But though the very reverse of a hypocrite himself, he introduced a principle which was highly dangerous, as tending to engender hypocrisy. This was the famous principle of 'accommodation.' Whatever each man's private conviction might be, he was to 'accommodate' himself to the common use of language, and outwardly to maintain a Church fellowship. As no two Christians think exactly alike, each must have, properly speaking, a different Bible. Scripture was to be tested by its 'edifying tendency;' the permanent in Christianity was to be limited to that which served for 'mending men.' It will be readily perceived how this theory would contribute to the degradation of Christianity into a mere serviceable system of morals.[1] But Semler himself recoiled from the subsequent development of his own principles. His pious soul was shocked by the coarse attacks made upon the doctrine and character of the Saviour in the 'Wolfenbüttel Fragments;' nor could he ever be reconciled to a merely secular system of education. He was deemed by many a Pietist at heart, and no doubt a remnant of Pietism did cling to him as it clung to his master, Baumgarten. Nevertheless, he contributed greatly to raise a spirit which, when raised, he could not lay.

The shape which German Deism was now taking was that of a nominal Christianity, but a Christianity shorn of all its mysteries, shorn of everything higher and deeper than what might tend to produce and increase worldly prosperity. Semler unwittingly contributed to this result, but it was mainly brought about by a perversion of the optimistic views of Leibnitz and Wolff. 'If,' it was argued, 'this is the best of all possible worlds, the wisest thing to do is to make things in it as pleasant and comfortable as can be conveniently done.'[2] If Christianity can be enlisted into the service, and moreover give us the chance of a better life into the bargain, so much the better. Thus Wolffianism drifted gradually into the 'popular philosophy.' The way was prepared for this debasement of Christianity by men like Spalding, Jerusalem, Sack, and Zollikoffer, men who themselves were Chris-

---

[1] See Hagenbach, i. 261, 263. Dorner, ii. 288, &c.

[2] 'The obverse side of Wolff's doctrine of the best possible world was a coarse Philisterism which is tolerably content with the present state of things.'—Dorner, ii. 235.

tians in a far higher sense than that of the popular philosophy. They were semi-rationalists, and strove, as one of them (Sack) expressed it, ' to keep in the temperate zone.' Their motive was a good one. Seeing that the old orthodoxy on the one hand had lost its hold upon the people by dwelling too exclusively upon the abstruse dogmas of Christianity, and Pietism on the other by a too exclusive subjectivity, by making religion too much a matter of the feelings, they aimed at steering a middle course. They preached Christian morality in the natural language of the day, instead of using a Biblical or scholastic terminology. They conceived a morbid dread of a mere emotional religion, and therefore shrunk from saying all they felt. Cold and unimaginative, they made it their one aim to be simple and practical, and held that preaching could only fulfil its mission by abstaining from everything speculative.

From this prudent abstinence from proclaiming what were termed unprofitable doctrines, it was but one step to opposing them. That step was soon made, and neological Illuminism became dominant.

The most prominent representatives of this form of German Deism were Garve, Eberhardt, M. Mendelssohn, Steinbart, Teller, Reimarus, Nicolai, and Basedow. The labours of the two last bring to notice a marked contrast between the methods of the German and the English Deists. The latter made no provision for the establishment and propagation of their system by the two most effectual ways which could be devised for such a purpose. They had no representative organ in the press, and they made no effort to promote education. The Germans did both.

Popular education was the subject to which Basedow paid special attention. He published in 1774 his elementary work, which created an educational revolution in Germany ; and he established a model school at Dessau, which he named a Philanthropin. His system was eminently calculated to propagate the principles of the new Illuminism. Religion was not altogether excluded, but the religion to be taught was one which would embrace all confessions and sects, and therefore, as may be supposed, was vague enough.

But the new cause of Illuminism was still more strengthened

by Nicolai, a bookseller at Berlin, who commenced in 1765 a periodical bearing the ambitious title of the 'Universal German Library.' The main object of this work was to disseminate the principles of the new philosophy, and to decry every work written in a different spirit. The success of the enterprise was extraordinary. It continued to be published periodically for nearly half a century, and for a long time its dicta were regarded as oracles.

The pulpit was, of course, a powerful engine for the spread of this new Gospel of comfort. The fashion set by Spalding and Jerusalem was followed and improved upon in a way those good men never dreamt of. A style of sermon came into vogue which was termed the 'Nothanker Sermon,' a name derived from a work of Nicolai called 'Sebaldus Nothanker,' in which he describes 'a preacher of utility who knew how to make use of a Bible text as a harmless means for impressing useful truths.' The model preacher 'was very studious to preach to his peasant congregation that they should rise early, attend to their cows, work in their fields and gardens, become comfortable, and get rich.' The Christian festivals were not entirely neglected by the new preachers ; they were utilised. Thus Christmas (so the rumour goes) was deemed a seasonable time to preach upon the feeding of cattle ; Easter was an obviously suitable occasion for dwelling upon the advantages of early rising.

The same utilitarian spirit was carried into hymnology. The hymns, too, must be adapted to the Illuminism of the day. It was obviously wrong, for instance, to sing such a line as 'Now slumbers *all* the world,' when, thanks to Basedow, every child knew that when it was night in one hemisphere it was day in the other. The line therefore must be altered into 'Now slumbers *half* the world.' [1]

Finally, the Bible itself must be modernised to suit the enlightenment of the eighteenth century. An attempt of this sort had been made in the Wertheim Bible of 1735, but the age was not then sufficiently enlightened to appreciate it.

To do justice, however, to this popular philosophy, it must

[1] Hagenbach's *History of the Christian Church*, i. 307-315.

be recorded that it vied with Pietism itself in works of philanthropy. Indeed, it prided itself in being the age not only
of Illuminism but also of Philanthropism. And justly so.
For not only did it give an impetus to the work of popular
education, but it set on foot all sorts of benevolent institutions;
the deaf and dumb were cared for, the condition of prisoners
improved; in short, there was more lack of Christian faith
than of Christian works.

One is so accustomed to associate German rationalism
with lofty metaphysical speculations, that it is somewhat difficult to realise that its first tendency was in the direction of a
shallow and commonplace utilitarianism. But it is with this
earlier phase, not with its later development, that English
Deism is most closely connected. It does not therefore fall
within the range of our subject to deal with the grand, if to
the Christian somewhat melancholy speculations of such deep
and earnest searchers after truth as Kant, Goethe, Schiller,
Fichte, Hegel, and Schelling. But there are yet two great
names which are distinctly, if indirectly, connected with the
influence of English Deism in Germany, and must not, therefore, be passed over. These are Lessing and Herder.

Lessing was a man of far too deep a spiritual insight to
be satisfied with the shallow empiricism of the popular philosophy. He was a man above his age, and found few with
whom he could sympathise, and was understood by few.
Indeed, it must be confessed that Lessing is a riddle not easy
to read. If he was dissatisfied with the coarse criticism of
the Illuminists, why did he lend the authority of his great
name to some of the coarsest, by publishing the 'Wolfenbüttel
Fragments?' According to the unknown Fragmentist,[1] the
purpose of Jesus was to reform Judaism and to establish an
earthly Messianic kingdom; and it was only after the failure
of this scheme that the disciples gave a spiritual meaning to
the doctrine of God's Kingdom. In this view the whole
Gospel scheme was simply a cold and cunning calculation.
These were not Lessing's sentiments; why did he publish
them? We can but give the reason he gave to Pastor Götze,
'that it is good to give vent to fire.' Again, what was the

---

[1] Reimarus? See Dorner, ii. 290, &c. Schlegel's *Lectures on the History of
Literature*, p. 415, and Hagenbach on Lessing.

bond of sympathy between Lessing and such men as Nicolaï and Moses Mendelssohn, in conjunction with whom he published the 'Library of Polite Literature' in 1757 and 'Letters on Literature' in 1759.

Lessing stands in important relation to our subject because he dealt with just those questions which were raised by the English Deists. It will be remembered that prominent among their objections to popular Christianity were its acceptance of the Old Testament as a true message from God, the particularism of earlier revelations and their omission of a future state. Lessing restored the key to the right understanding of the Old Testament in his 'Education of the Human Race.' He there represents a gradual training of the human mind by the Almighty. As in the individual so in the whole race there are three periods of life. The first is the period of childhood, and it is for this period that the Old Testament was written. The second is the period of youth, and it is for this period that the New Testament was written, for this period that Christianity as commonly understood is adapted. But this must be followed by a third period, the period of the maturity of mankind, when men will do good neither from hope nor fear, but simply because it is good.

Thus, in Lessing's view, neither the older revelation nor the later is false, but; on the other hand, no religion is absolutely true, but all religion must be developing with the development of reason. This exaltation of reason must not be confounded with that of our Deists. Lessing's view was, in fact, the very reverse of theirs. *They* would pare everything down to the level of reason in its present state, and would reject all that they could not understand. Not so Lessing. 'Though reason,' he writes, 'must decide whether a given system be a revelation or no, yet if it cannot explain things in revelation this should rather determine for revelation than against it.' Instead of magnifying reason as it is, after the fashion of the English Deists, Lessing looked forward to a visionary future when reason should be what now it is not. Instead of levelling down, his hope was that there would in time be a levelling up. That time was not to supersede Christianity; it was rather to bring about a development of it. 'The time of a new and eternal Gospel will come, which is promised to us in the elementary books of the New Testament.'

Lessing, again, supplies a missing link in the train of thought which led our Deists to reject more or less the records and chief evidences of Christianity while yet they professed their adherence to Christianity itself. Whether Lessing's explanation of the possibility of such a position be satisfactory or not is quite another question ; but, at any rate, he did not shirk the difficulty. He met it boldly in this way :—External revelations, he said, are necessary only for certain stages. The evidences of miracles and prophecies are but the scaffolding which leads to the internal substance of religion. Far from thinking that Christianity must fall with its customary evidences, he held that the sacred writings only load it with difficulties. Christianity itself consists in eternal and non-historical truths. History is no confirmation, but rather a contradiction, of it, for historical truths belong to a different sphere from that in which the eternal reason-truths move. Or, as he puts it in another place, the Bible is only the paper plan, Christianity is the building. If the Bible were lost, it would only be like the loss of the architect's plan, not the loss of the building itself.

Can we, then, agree with Schlegel's description of Lessing as 'a deep and philosophical believer?'[1] As an intensely earnest seeker after truth, as one filled with a deep religious craving, Lessing stands on a far higher plane than that on which any of our own Deists, still more than that on which any of the German Illuminists,[2] stood. But Lessing owns himself a sceptic, and, indeed, hardly seems to desire to be otherwise, for 'it is not,' he says, 'the finding of truth, but the honest search for it, that profits.'[3] The same conclusion may be drawn from the famous fable of the three rings in 'Nathan the Wise.' The moral is, that it cannot be abso-

---

[1] *Lectures on the History of Literature.*

[2] He was distinctly opposed both to those who, like Nicolai and Bahrdt, made religion a system of dry ethics, without imagination or sentiment, and to those who, like Eberhard, represented Christianity as mere Deism, or natural religion. See Dorner, ii. 303.

[3] See Carlyle's Essays, vol. i., on the *State of German Literature*, also his essay on *Taylor's Survey of German Poetry.*

lutely decided which of the rings is genuine ; and, dropping metaphor, he says distinctly, 'Nathan's declaration against all positive religion has always been mine.' That is, if we may interpret it by his other writings, he believed all positive religion to be equally false and equally true—false if any be regarded as final, true if they be regarded as temporary.

Herder, like Lessing, rose above the spirit of his age. He stands between the old Illuminism and the new Rationalism, not fully sympathising with either, and frequently brought into collision with both. He occupies an important position in relation to Deism, because he first turned the tide against that spirit which more than anything else gave birth to German Illuminism and its prototype English Deism. The Deistical controversy more than any other illustrates the prosaic character of the eighteenth century. It was conducted on both sides in a hard, cold, dry, unimaginative spirit, and if this was the case in England, still more was it so in Germany. Illuminism had well-nigh improved the poetry of life off the face of creation. It was essentially of the earth, earthy. There needed a great poetical mind, not altogether out of sympathy with the liberality of spirit of which all freethinkers boasted, to raise the Germans from this dead level. Just such a mind was Herder's.[1] A true Christian, but·yet a true free-thinker in the right sense of that term, he was able to appreciate the real good which lay in Illuminism, while at the same time both his writings and his oral teaching were a perpetual protest against the evil which lay at the root of it. Not even Germany ever produced a more universal mind than that of Herder. Take him in each *department* of intellectual eminence, and he was surpassed in all. As a poet he is far inferior to Goethe or Schiller, as a philosopher to Kant ; as an orator he was never so popular as Reinhard ; in grasp of intellect and profound earnestness of purpose he was not equal to Lessing. But take him for all in all—as poet, philosopher, orator, and intelligent and earnest thinker combined—and he stands unique. No single man embraced all these characters

---

[1] See Dorner on Herder. 'When the German nation was, in the age preceding Kant, threatening to fall a prey to a level intellectualism—nay, to a spirit of low utilitarianism—Herder struck chords which diffused a disposition for the ideal, and prepared the soil for a new epoch.' See also Pusey, pt. i. *ad finem*.

in his own person to the same extent that Herder did. The use which he made of his vast and varied powers was on the whole beneficial to Christianity, and especially in one direction in which right guidance was greatly needed.

In England Deism arose to a great extent from the inability of the Deists to throw themselves into the mind of the period, or rather periods, when the Bible was written. They *would* perversely read it in the light of the eighteenth century. It was the same with the earlier phase of German Rationalism, which really was little more than an exaggerated form of the same type of mind. Herder, on the other hand, could view the Bible with a true poet's eye. He could Orientalise himself, if the expression may be allowed; and he could thus learn to detect many a beauty which was lost upon the duller vision of English Deist and German Illuminist. Not that Herder can be cited as a consistent believer; there is too much truth in the saying that 'the most direct contradiction to Herder is Herder.' In his later years especially, after he had fallen under the neological influences of minds of a very different calibre from that of the popular philosophers, his Christianity became more and more vague and indefinite. A contemporary[1] said no more than the truth when he compared Herder's later writings to a distant cloud, of which one could not distinguish whether it *was* a cloud or a city with inhabitants. But, in spite of the increasing mistiness of his writings, Herder did a great work for the cause of Christianity in meeting the special want alluded to above.

Herder has been frequently quoted in the preceding pages in reference to our English Deists, upon whom he wrote in his 'Adrastea.' It will be a fitting conclusion to this long chapter to touch briefly upon the relation to our own countrymen of this great man who more than any other helped to give the death-blow to that tone of mind which, originating in England, passed over into Germany and in both turned many from the faith.

Herder evinced a great admiration for the English, and longed to draw closer the bonds which united the two great branches of the Teutonic family together. He mourned

[1] Garve.

bitterly over the baleful French influence, which acted like a blight upon the generation which was passing away when Herder came upon the scene. 'It is with the Britons,' he writes, 'that we stand in plainer relation. We honour them. We feel the English are men of our kind, bone of our bone. They are Germans planted on an island.'[1] He thoroughly enjoyed our literature, and, not the least, that part of it which related to the Deistical controversy. With the Deists themselves he seems in some degree to sympathise ; but it is a negative rather than a positive sympathy ; the sympathy of a generous mind, which is inclined to side with those who are down. The coarse and virulent abuse with which they were assailed pained and shocked him. But his view of Christianity, and especially of the sacred documents of Christianity, was essentially different from that of the English Deists. There was but one of them with whom he could hold any real, positive sympathy, and him he rated far above the estimate which his own countrymen formed of him. That one was Shaftesbury, whom Herder placed on a level with Locke and Leibnitz, regretting that his writings were so late translated and so little known in Germany.[2] The point of contact between Herder and Shaftesbury is obviously this: As Lessing's ideal was the True, Herder's was the Beautiful. He was attracted to Christianity by its loveliness rather than by its holiness. Those who are familiar with Shaftesbury's writings will remember that he too made the Beautiful rather than the True his ideal. But this resemblance between Herder and Shaftesbury was superficial rather than real. The falsetto of Shaftesbury's rhapsodies is not to be compared with the true ring of Herder's poetic utterances, and in depth of moral earnestness there is no comparison between the two men. It is doubtful, indeed, whether Herder really grasped the true character of English Deism. But at least we may learn this—and a useful concluding lesson it is to learn—from the criticism of a foreigner (and such a foreigner !) upon our treatment of the Deists : that virulent personal abuse, no less than persecution, is an unfit weapon for the

---

[1] *Adrastea,* xi. 283.

[2] Herder's *Sämmtliche Werke,* 'Zur Philosophie und Geschichte.' Zehnten Theil. *Adrastea,* ii., 'Das 18te Jahrhundert,' pp. 187-189.

Christian advocate ; and that, let his **adversary's sentiments**
be what they may, he will do well to lay to heart the wise
counsel, 'If he seek truth, is he not our brother, and to be
pitied ? If he do not seek truth, is he not still our brother,
and to be pitied still more ? ' [1]

J. H. O.

[1] Carlyle's Essay on Voltaire. It would transcend the limits of this chapter
to trace the influence of English Deism further. But France and Germany were
not the only foreign countries into which its influence penetrated. 'The intimate
relations,' writes Dr. Hurst in his *History of Rationalism*, ch. xv. p. 283, 'in
which Holland stood to England by the accession of William and Mary to the
British throne afforded an opportunity for the importation of English Deism.
Nowhere on the Continent was that system of scepticism so extensively propagated as among the Dutch. The Deists took particular pains to visit Holland,
and were never prouder than when told that their works were read by their friends
across the North Sea.' Those who desire to see these assertions proved and
illustrated in detail must be referred to Dr. Hurst's learned work from which the
above quotation is made.

CHAPTER V.

LATITUDINARIAN CHURCHMANSHIP.

(1) CHARACTER AND INFLUENCE OF ARCHBISHOP TILLOTSON'S THEOLOGY.

'LATITUDINARIAN' is not so neutral a term as could be desired. It conveys an implication of reproach and suspicion, by no means ungrounded in some instances, but very inappropriate when used of men who must count among the most distinguished ornaments of the English Church. But no better title suggests itself. The eminent prelates who were raised to the bench in King William III.'s time can no longer, without ambiguity, be called 'Low Churchmen,' because the Evangelicals who succeeded to the name belong to a wholly different school of thought from the Low Churchmen of an earlier age ; nor 'Whigs,' because that sobriquet has long been confined to politics; nor 'Broad Churchmen,' because the term would be apt to convey a set of ideas belonging to the nineteenth more than to the eighteenth century. It only remains to divest the word as far as possible of its polemical associations, and to use it as denoting what some would call breadth, others Latitudinarianism of religious and ecclesiastical opinion.

A really religious Latitudinarianism has no natural relationship with indifference to error. Or perhaps it should be rather said that an occasional semblance of such indifference may proceed from the very keenness with which it searches for and appreciates truth. The mind which is quick to recognise the genuine spirit of Christ under many outward forms may be tempted to disparage too much the importance of minor errors, but loves the truth too well to be careless of what clearly militates against it. Nor does it at all follow that the latitude which allows a broad margin in religious matters to individual, or national, or ecclesiastical tastes and requirements should be itself vague and colourless. Uniformity is imposing, and, under reasonable limitations, contains many elements of power ; but, so long as a general unity is maintained, it is variety, not uniformity, which is rich in life, colour, harmony. A 'Latitude man' (to use an eighteenth-century term), whose religious convictions are deep and earnest, while he is perfectly convinced that the essentials of Christianity are few and simple, and while he freely concedes to others the same ample liberty of thought which he claims for himself, does not on this account favour an undogmatic faith in non-essential matters, unless dogma be understood only of doctrinal notions authoritatively and magisterially enounced. His opinions, for example, as to the nature of the sacraments, or the best form of Church government, may be fully as definite as those of men who insist that one view only is admissible. They may even be more definite, because they may express more entirely the actual conclusion of his own mind. He may hold his own opinions, or the tenets of the Church to which he has attached himself, with great definiteness and tenacity and fervour, and yet willingly acknowledge that the necessary truths of the Gospel may be as much the possession of others as of himself; that to many persons his views may be less edifying than their own ; that arguments which seem valid to himself might not satisfy others ; that in all spiritual matters it is most desirable that everyone should be fully persuaded in his own mind ; that there may be many points on which he, and the Church to which he belongs, are more or less mistaken. A religious Latitudinarian, if he were a Roman Catholic (for the two terms are not wholly incompatible), would probably entertain a strong opinion that the Protestant neglected much that was highly edifying and instructive ; if he were a Protestant, he would think that the Romanist ran a serious risk of too much losing sight of the essentials of religion under the superstructure with which they were encumbered. In either case, both from an abstract love of truth and from a desire to see the prevalence of what he considered the most edifying form of Christianity, he might feel it his duty to do his best to combat what he believed to be error, and to promote the opinions to which he was himself attached. But, above all he would vividly realise the bond of unity which binds together in one true Church Christians of different persuasions ; he would long to see that invisible unity more visibly embodied ; he would welcome all steps to a closer intercommunion ; he would leave abundant room for wide diversities of opinion within a Church, for a regulated elasticity in modes of worship, for ready powers of self-adaptation to different classes and changing requirements ; he would be averse to all subscriptions and tests which were not plainly necessary ; and though he would wish that congregations should be sufficiently protected from opinions which run counter to the evident meaning of the formularies of their Church, and from practices to which they object, he would look with great suspicion on restrictions which went beyond this, and tended to create an idea that the clergy, the natural leaders of the people in matters of religion, could not be looked to for independent thought. He would respect the authority of a primitive age—not, however, as possessing any sovereign claim upon his veneration, but because of the opportunities it enjoyed as near the fountain-head, not forgetful that modern inquirers have counterbalancing advantages in their search for truth of which the old fathers knew nothing. He would feel little perplexity at the progress of speculations which might modify his opinions on what he considered lesser matters, that did not touch essential doctrines and deeper grounds of faith. He would be a friend to seasonable reforms ; and might probably be inclined to favour schemes of comprehension, so long as they involved no compromise of individual opinion and were fair to all, not (as has sometimes been the case) enlarging the boundaries on one side only to contract them on another. He has no idea of compromising any truth. On the contrary, he thinks that everyone should realise and embody to himself in thought and feeling to the very utmost as much of truth as he can make his own. He thinks that religious doctrine should be fertile in its associations and in suggestiveness ; that it should be no bare outline, but rich in beauty of form and feature. He does not deny the possibility of a Church or an individual attaining to complete truth, though he feels that where there is so much conflict of opinion among men of piety and thought over-confident assertion would in any case be presumptuous. And even if a Church or an individual could be absolutely certain of having reached a higher standard of truth than was elsewhere to be found, it appears to him that exclusiveness and self-glorification would still be as much out of place, as if a man who had attained a high degree of moral excellence were to vaunt himself over those who were struggling upwards at a lower level than his own. But he does not think it likely that any one Church is pre-eminently superior to all others in full realisation of Christian truth. He deems it consonant to the whole analogy of our human state that a man's perception in spiritual matters should be amply sufficient for all practical needs, and yet fall somewhat short of the clearness and precision which he would gladly lay claim to. He is content to assume that there may probably be an element of imperfection and one-sidedness in his own views, as in those of others. Of this he is sure : that if, by the defect of his mind or through lack of opportunity, a man is unable to take in a higher form of truth, it is far better that he thoroughly realise and assimilate what he can really apprehend of it, even in a lower and more imperfect shape, than that he should superficially acknowledge, in mere deference to authority, a belief which may be objectively truer, but which is too high for him, and which fails therefore in influence on his life. A man with these views cannot fail to be tolerant and sympathising in his religious opinions, but there is obviously nothing in them to encourage a negligent indifferentism.

Every temperament and tone of mind has its besetting temptations and difficulties. It seems impossible to avoid errors in one direction without incurring in an opposite direction a different set of dangers. Many 'Latitudinarian' Churchmen have been inferior to none in the depth and intensity of their religious convictions ; many, on the other hand, gain in breadth of sympathy at a great loss of power and concentration in their own opinions. In their praiseworthy appreciation of all that tends to unity they are inclined to disparage the meaning and spiritual significance of all differences that hinder it. Fully convinced that the goodness of a tree is known by its fruits—that the ultimate value of any doctrine consists in its practical influence upon the lives of men,—and unable to shut their eyes to the evident fact that almost all forms of Christianity have been adorned by noble Christian lives, they attribute the elevating, transforming influence only to that which is common to every variety of Christian creed. They unconsciously undervalue all that gives individuality, substance, detail ; not adequately realising that in religion diffuse and nebulous ideas—although, aided by philosophy and imagination, they may suffice for some—have very little power among the bulk of mankind.

Again, indifferentism bears so many superficial resemblances to what may be called a sound and wholesome latitude, that it is often confounded with it. Numberless men and women of holy lives, some simple and untaught, some cultured and intellectual, disprove the existence of any real relationship between the two. But the religion, such as it is, of the lax and the indifferent, if it does not incline, in an opposite direction, to formalism and superstition, affects a liberal breadth of view. The sceptic also, and the Deist, and those who make Christianity a moral philosophy rather than a religion, if they are not, as sometimes is the case, bigoted and dictatorial, are all in the general sense of the term Latitudinarian. Thus a religious and earnest Broad Churchman may often, on controverted questions, find himself ranged on the same side with men from whose principles he differs far more essentially than from those against which he is more immediately arguing.

The Latitudinarianism of a Tillotson or a Dr. Arnold is wholly removed from the Latitudinarianism of a Hobbes, for example, or a Bolingbroke. Yet, because they agree in some particulars, the cry is sure to be raised that they are fundamentally the same, and that the latter do but follow out conclusions which the former stop short of. The injustice and the fallacy of such a clamour is sufficiently obvious. Nevertheless there is a half-truth in it which serves to palliate the injustice and to make the fallacy plausible. It is like that familiar argument derived from the narrow end of the wedge by which, until the end of the world, every reform and every great movement will be more or less successfully opposed. There are few, if any, general principles which, once admitted, may not become dangerous by exaggeration or perversion.

No better illustration of this can be quoted than the Reformation itself. We cannot wonder that its advance was earnestly resisted by many good men. It invigorated Europe spiritually and intellectually with a full stream of fresh religious life, but it must have seemed to not a few like letting in the waters so that none could tell where the flood might end. Where was Church authority to maintain itself? Where was this new right of private judgment to be checked? Who was to decide where reformation ceased and heresy began? Open the sluices, and the bulwarks of the faith will presently be swept away; admit the wedge, and in time the Creeds will be shivered into fragments. It may be granted that it was a timorous faith which feared such dangers; but though the risk was well worth running the danger was not altogether imaginary. Roman Catholics are never weary of tracing out what they consider the disintegrating, disastrous influences of Reformation principles. Concede, they say, a right of private judgment, and Latitudinarianism has all it asks for; concede Latitudinarianism, and the Catholic faith is left bare and defenceless to the assaults of all kinds of heresies. The keenest of Protestants, less logically but no less tenaciously, have constantly held the same opinion. They love the Reformation, but they detest the principles which were really involved in it. They gladly acknowledge that a large exercise of private judgment did signal service in the sixteenth century; but henceforward, except within a far narrower field than was allowed even to the monastic disputants of a mediæval age, they look with distrust and suspicion at all free thought. They try to imagine that their own distinctive formularies are immutable truths, from which none can wander without imminent danger to themselves and grave offence to others. If all men could be got to adopt their views, how gladly then, if it were possible, and possible without persecution, would they prohibit all further inquiry! It must be acknowledged that, personally, most of the Reformers were on their side. There were very few of them who would have acknowledged the principles which lie at the basis of a religious Latitudinarianism—the first, that the real essential points of sound Christian faith, which have power to transform the life, are very few and simple; the second, that it is hopeless to expect on earth a full grasp of Divine truth ; that truth is indeed the highest object of human search, that it is a search blessed with much success and great encouragement, but that we may be 'very confident the Lord hath more truth and light yet to break forth out of His holy word ; ' [1] that no one individual, no one generation, no one Church, has a right to feel certain of having attained an understanding of Divine things which is not in some respects imperfect and one-sided, sufficient indeed for all spiritual edification, all practical needs, but not such as to warrant any presumption of an exclusive apprehension of truth, or any rash condemnation of those who may seem blind to much that we see, yet on whom light unseen to us may be flashed from other facets of that jewel of great price. Nor, in the third place, were they quick to acknowledge how much there is in the order, government, and discipline of the Church which is by its very nature variable, and of which not even apostolical and Scriptural precedent would prove more than that this or that detail was best for the necessity of the time. The disciples of Luther, of Calvin, of Cranmer, of Knox, were not content to love and admire the form of teaching to which they respectively adhered. Each believed that truth was his and his alone. 'Latitudinarianism' in all its forms, good or bad, religious or irreligious, would have been regarded as at best a disguised form of unbelief.

There were many faulty elements in the Latitudinarianism of the eighteenth century. Those who dreaded and lamented its advances found it no difficult task to show that sometimes it was connected with Deistical or with Socinian or Arian views, sometimes with a visionary enthusiasm, sometimes with a weak and nerveless religion of sentiment. They could point also to the obvious fact that thorough scepticism, or even mere irreligion, often found a decent veil under plausible professions of a liberal Christianity. There were some, indeed, who, in the excitement of hostility or alarm, seemed to lose all power of ordinary discrimination. Much in the same way as every 'freethinker' was set down as a libertine or an atheist, so also many men

---

[1] 'John Robinson to the New England Emigrants,' Dr. Wilson, *The Religious Fathers*, chap. iii.

of undoubted piety and earnestness who had done distinguished services in the Christian cause, and who had greatly contributed to raise the repute of the English Church, were constantly ranked as Latitudinarians in one promiscuous class with men to whose principles they were utterly opposed. But, after making all allowance for the unfortunate confusion thus attached to the term, the fact remains that the alarm was not unfounded. Undoubtedly a lower form of Latitudinarianism gained ground, very deficient in some important respects. Just in the same way as, before the middle of the century, a sort of spiritual inertness had enfeebled the vigour of High Churchmen on the one hand and of Nonconformists on the other, so also it was with the Latitude men. After the first ten or fifteen years of the century the Broad Church party in the Church of England was in no very satisfactory state. It had lost not only in spirit and energy, but also in earnestness and piety. Hoadly, Sherlock, Herring, Watson, Blackburne, all showed the characteristic defect of their age—a want of spiritual depth and fervour. They needed a higher elevation of motive and of purpose to be such leaders as could be desired of what was in reality a great religious movement.

For, whatever may have been its deficiencies, there was no religious movement of such lasting importance as that which from the latter part of the seventeenth until near the end of the eighteenth century was being carried on under the opprobrium of Latitudinarianism. The Methodist and Evangelical revival had, doubtless, greater visible and immediate consequences. Much in the same way some of the widespread monastic revivals of the Middle Ages were more visible witnesses to the power of religion, and more immediately conducive to its interests, than the silent current of theological thought which was gradually preparing the way for the Reformation. But it was these latter influences which, in the end, have taken the larger place in the general history of Christianity. The Latitudinarianism which had already set in before the Revolution of 1688, unsatisfactory as it was in many respects, probably did more than any other agency in directing and gradually developing the general course of religious thought. Its importance may be intimated in this, that of all the questions in which it was chiefly interested there is scarcely one which has not started into fresh life in our own days, and which is not likely to gain increasing significance as time advances. Church history in the seventeenth century had been most nearly connected with that of the preceding age; it was still directly occupied with the struggles and contentions which had been aroused by the Reformation. That of the eighteenth century is more nearly related to the period which succeeded it. In the sluggish calm that followed the abatement of old controversies men's minds reverted anew to the wide general principles on which the Reformation had been based, and, with the loss of power which attends uncertainty, were making tentative efforts to improve and strengthen the superstructure. 'Intensity,' as has been remarked, 'had for a time done its work, and was now giving place to breadth; when breadth should be natural, intensity might come again.'[1] The Latitude men of the last age can only be fairly judged in the light of this. Their immediate plans ended for the most part in disappointing failure. It was perhaps well that they did, as some indeed of the most active promoters of them were fain to acknowledge. Their proposed measures of comprehension, of revision, of reform, were often defective in principle, and in some respects as one-sided as the evils they were intended to cure. But if their ideas were not properly matured, or if the time was not properly matured for them, they at all events contained the germs of much which may be realised in the future. Meanwhile the comprehensive spirit which is absolutely essential in a national Church was kept alive. The Church of England would have fallen, or would have deserved to fall, if a narrow exclusiveness had gained ground in it without check or protest.

The principles on which the Latitudinarians of the last century founded their argument are not confined to any one party or any one age. When the Apostolic Conclave decreed that no unnecessary burden was to be imposed upon the minds and conscience of the Gentile converts; when Eusebius remarked that lesser differences do but confirm the general unity of the faith;[2] when Gregory Nazianzen affirmed that we may

[1] H. S. Skeats, *History of the Free Churches*, 315
[2] Euseb. Pamph. *Hist. Ec.*, v. 24.

without danger err as to the mode in which Christ has redeemed us ;[1] when Augustine wrote that if a man is a good and true Christian it matters not where he has found truth ;[2] when Anselm admonished the monks of Canterbury that howsoever much other things may vary with change of circumstances and differences of opinion, yet where faith, and charity, and purity, and humility, and obedience (things whereby the soul is saved) are maintained inviolate, there the true rule of St. Benedict is kept ;[3] when the great poet-theologian of the Middle Ages ranged far outside the accepted saintly calendar to picture in the highest mansions of Paradise all of every type who have been foremost in the great contest against evil ;[4] when Tusser penned for English cottagers and yeomen his homely verses on ' Points of Christianity ;' when Erasmus pressed upon the Church the need of reducing as far as possible the number of dogmas necessary to be believed, and to concede freedom of opinion on other points ;[5] when even Archbishop Laud pleaded for peaceable dissent in opinion, without schism on various non-fundamental articles[6] —in all such instances (and they might be almost indefinitely multiplied) all the principles which a moderate and religious Latitudinarian insists upon are more or less clearly contained. It was the special function of ' Latitude men,' as it is of their fellow-thinkers in every age, to maintain these principles, and to deduce true inferences from them. It is the duty of all, but the special function of those of an opposite turn of thought, to assert the due claims of authority and of established orthodox opinion, more particularly, to be on the watch that the value of dogma and of definite views be not disparaged ; that concession do not degenerate into compromise, nor liberty into laxity, nor breadth into shallowness ; above all, heedfully to guard the Church from any teaching which, under the mask of liberalism, would attack those great

---

[1] Qu. by F. Garden in *Tracts for Priests and People*, series i.
[2] Qu. by G. H. Curteis in *Dissent in Relation to the Church of England*, 7.
[3] R. W. Church, *Life of St. Anselm*, 46.
[4] Qu. R. W. Church, *Essays*, 82.
[5] Letter to Archbishop of Mayence, qu. in J. A. Froude, *Short Studies on Great Subjects*, i. 81.
[6] Qu. in J. A. Dorner, *History of Protestant Theology*, ii. 63.

essentials of Christian faith which are few, indeed, and intelligible to the simplest, but which contain the innermost life and power of Christian belief.

Liberal Church principles had had many illustrious advocates in the seventeenth century. Hooker died in 1600 ; and as he had stood almost alone in his lifetime, so also he had no immediate successors. But his statesmanlike comprehensiveness of thought, temperate and guarded though it was, did much to infuse a wider spirit among those who followed him than had existed for some length of time before. Towards the middle of the century, Broad Church principles were beginning to be strenuously asserted by many men of great piety and ability within the Church of England. Such were Lord Falkland, who threw all the weight of his influence in favour of ' a moderate and liberal Church,' and John Hales, of Eton, who discussed the bounds of 'dogmatic orthodoxy' and what might tend to ' the peace and concord of the Church.' Such was Chillingworth, the famous author of the much-belauded and much-disputed axiom of the Bible only being the religion of Protestants. Tillotson spoke of him with enthusiastic admiration as ' that incomparable person, the glory of the age and nation,' and indignantly rebutted the charges of Socinianism which were sometimes brought against him, ' for no other reason,' writes the Archbishop, ' that I know of, but his worthy and successful attempts to make Christian religion reasonable, and to discover those firm and solid foundations upon which our faith is built.' [1] Few writers have protested more strongly than Chillingworth against minor differences being made preventive of unity. This deifying of our own interpretations, and tyrannous enforcing them upon others ; this restraining of the word of God from that latitude and generality, and the understandings of men from that liberty, wherein Christ and the Apostles left them—is and hath been the only fountain of all the schisms of the Church, and that which makes them immortal.' [2] Such, again, was Jeremy Taylor, who to profound reverence for Christian antiquity and to exalted notions of

---

[1] Tillotson's *Works*, ix. 271.

[2] Chillingworth's *Religion of Protestants*, &c.   Qu. in Calamy's *Own Life*, i. 29.

Church authority added a most unfaltering loyalty to the principles of Christian liberty. Ecclesiastical laws, he said, ought always to be 'easy and charitable,' and when they are not so they oblige not. 'They should be relative to time and place, subject to changes, fitted for use and the advantage of Churches, ministering to edification and complying with charity.' As for ' cutting a man off from the communion of the Church for a trifling cause, it is to do as the man in the fable that, espying a fly on his neighbour's forehead, went to put it off with a hatchet and struck out his brains.' [1] Of a similar kind were the opinions of that exemplary and devout Churchman Lord Chief Justice Hales. Keenly alive to the prevailing impiety and moral laxity of his age, he deeply regretted the contentions with which religion was distracted— that Nonconformists, on the one hand, 'should break the peace of the Church about such inconsiderable matters as the points in difference were ;' that so many zealous Churchmen, on the other, 'should think it below the dignity of the Church to make concessions and alter laws.' It seemed to him, he said, that when men see such great weight laid upon minor questions, and 'as great fervour and animosity used for or against them as almost for any points of Christian religion, they are apt presently to throw off all religion and reckon all of the same make.' [2] Stillingfleet was another illustrious name on the same side. His ' Irenicum, or The Divine Right of Particular Forms of Government,' was a vigorous plea in behalf of a Church constituted on a broad and comprehensive basis, as tolerant to different parties within its communion as he maintained the primitive Church had been before Arians and Donatists had yet raised their exclusive pretensions. The Cambridge Platonists—Whichcote, John Smith, Cudworth, and Henry More—must least of all be omitted. They took no great part in the Church politics of their time, but their influence on educated religious thought was very great, and did much to elevate the tone of reasoning among the Latitude men of their day. There is great dignity of sentiment, for example, in the following words from Henry

Chillingworth's *Religion of Protestants*, &c. Qu. in Calamy's *Own Life*, i. 248.

[2] Qu. in *Account of the Growth of Deism*, &c. 1698, 15.

More :—' But having had such a notion of God from my very youth as represented Him to me as the most noble and excellent Being that can be, it could never enter into my mind that He was either irritable or propitiable by the omitting or performing of any mean and insignificant services such as are neither perfective of human nature nor the genuine result of that perfection : and therefore I had an early belief that he served God best that was least envious, worldly, or sensual ; that delighted most in the common good of the universe, and had the strongest faith in the bounty and mercy of God, of which His Son Jesus Christ is the most palpable pledge that He could exhibit to the world ; which constant frame of mind made me wholly incapable of the least tincture of superstition ; for it is the ignorance of better things that causes those perplexities and consternations of mind about matters of less moment.'[1]

Richard Baxter was a man of a very different order of mind from the Oxford and Cambridge Platonists ; but his popular and voluminous writings, read, as they teemed from the press, by multitudes who never heard of the names of More and Cudworth, tended in the direction of a Latitudinarianism less philosophical, no doubt, than theirs, but no less earnest and religious. Vicar of Kidderminster for four-and-twenty years, and offered the bishopric of Hereford, he by no means lost his interest in the Church of England after the unhappy ejection of 1662. Like many another, he was often far more generous and large-minded in his words than in his actions, and when he confined himself to generalities than when he descended to particulars ; and he was sometimes meddlesome and dictatorial. Yet on the whole his influence was as well deserved as it was great, and it is lamentable that the National Church should have lost the services of a man so well calculated to adorn it. His sympathies had never been restricted within close limits. To take an example quite apart from any religious questions of his time, a short passage from his ' Compassionate Counsel to Young Men ' may serve to show how far removed he was from the narrow exclusiveness which marked the Puritans of the preceding, and to a great extent

---

[1] Henry More's *Philosophical Works*, General Preface, § 9.

T 2

the Nonconformists of the next, generation :—' It will be profitable,' he tells them, ' to read the lives of the martyrs and of such Christian princes as Constantine, Theodosius, &c.; the Emperor Maximilian II., John Frederick of Saxony, Philip, Prince of Hessia, and Louis the Pious of France. Read also the lives of such heathens as Titus, Trajan, Adrian, but especially Aurelius, Antoninus, and Alexander Severus ; of such lawyers, philosophers, physicians, but especially such divines, as Melchior Adamus hath recorded in his four volumes ; and of such bishops as Cyprian, Nazianzen, Ambrose, Augustine, Basil, Chrysostom, our Usher, and others.' [1] As he grew older his foibles wore off, while the kindly Catholicity of his opinions gained both in warmth and firmness. ' The older I grew,' writes the worthy author of the ' Saint's Rest,' ' the smaller stress I laid on those controversies and curiosities (though still my intellect abhorreth confusion), as finding greater uncertainties in them than I at first discerned, and finding less usefulness where there is the greatest certainty. The Creed, the Lord's Prayer, and the Ten Commandments are now to me as my daily bread and drink ; and as I can speak and write over them again and again, so I had rather read and hear of them than of any of the school niceties. And this I observed also with Richard Hooker and with many other men.' [2] And so he continues to acknowledge how much more he had discovered his own ignorance ; how much more good and evil were mixed in men than once he had thought (' Even in the wicked generally there is more for grace to take advantage of, and more to testify to God and holiness, than I once believed there had been ') ; how much more he had learnt to appreciate the great worth of quiet godly lives which have no great gifts of utterance and make no professions ; how much more temperate he was learning to be in his censures of the Papists, whose most dangerous errors he no longer considered to be those of doctrine—errors very liable to be exaggerated by misexpression and misunderstanding—so much as those which tyrannise over the conscience or foster ignorance and superstition ; how much

---

[1] R. Baxter's *Works*, xv. 389.

[2] From ' The Things in which He Himself had Changed,' qu. in Dobney's *Free Churches*, 77.

less inclined he was to pass judgment upon the spiritual condition of those who have never heard of Christ, as 'having some more reason to think that God's dealings with such are much unknown to us;' finally, how much more sensible he was than he had been to the odiousness of spiritual pride, to the breadth and depth of the sin of selfishness, and to the excellency of 'a public mind.'[1]

The acknowledged piety and varied ability of its supporters in the seventeenth century could not fail to raise Latitudinarianism into high repute. Later writers were often accustomed to express themselves as if Latitude came in with the Revolution. It might be more correct to say that a certain deterioration in its tone began about that era to set gradually in. The pressing danger which beset the Church of England and Protestantism generally in the reign of James II. seems to have had in two ways a very beneficial effect upon the chief leaders both of the Broad and of the High Church party. It increased their earnestness of purpose, and it also brought them nearer together. Sancroft and the High Churchmen in general were at one time not indisposed to strengthen the Reformed cause, and to establish the National Church upon a broader basis, by uniting with the Liberals in some measure of comprehension which would bring in the moderate Dissenters. But the Revolution, which appeared to favour, did in reality put an end to all these hopes. The Latitudinarianism which came in from Holland was altogether of a less religious type, colder and more sceptical than that which had lately found favour among English divines. It began also to assume a far more political and party character. Low or Latitudinarian Churchmen were almost always Whigs. So also were the Dissenters. High Churchmen, on the other hand, were generally in favour of the previous dynasty. Moreover, their strength had been greatly weakened by the secession of many of their best men in the Nonjuring separation. Proposals, therefore, for a wider comprehension, which before had been either based upon broad principles or else regarded as measures of Church defence, were now suspected

[1] From 'The Things in which He Himself had Changed,' qu. in Dobney's *Free Churches*, 77.

by many as machinations of Whig policy, one-sided in their nature and distinctly intended to shift the ancient standing-point of a Church which was supposed to be not very favourable to the new régime. If such suspicions were exaggerated, there were at all events reasons which had not existed before for distrust. A really fair measure of Church comprehension had probably become for the time impossible. A very large proportion of the moderate Nonconformists might have been recovered for the work of the English Church. But it would have been at far too great a cost, if the Church, instead of enlarging her borders, had simply changed her ground and become more Protestant but less Catholic—if the High Churchmen, than whom none had served her cause more faithfully and self-denyingly, but who now, through the circumstances of the time, were partly silenced and partly estranged, should be entirely alienated, and the Nonjuring schism extended and rendered permanent. Thus, although Latitudinarianism had in many directions gained great ground, and Broad Church bishops, some of them men of great eminence, were enthroned, amid general applause, on a considerable proportion of the episcopal sees, there was a visible deterioration in its character. Other forms of religious thought suffered a no less marked decline of earnestness and spirituality. We are told that in the latter part of King James' reign, while there was a general apprehension of designs to introduce Romanism, a widespread revival of religion appeared to set in, and churches were crowded with attentive worshippers ; and that there was a lamentable contrast [1] when security came in with the Revolution, attended by new outbursts of scruples and party animosities. High Church and Broad Church (or Low Church, as it was then called) alike degenerated ; and terms, intended to be expressive of theological opinion, were caught up by multitudes who divested them of all spiritual significance, and used them as little better than electioneering cries. Under such influences it may be well understood how readily a sort of pseudo-liberalism of sentiment on religious matters adapted itself to the moral laxity and sceptical indifferentism of the

---

[1] *Life of Kettlewell*, 90–1.

time, and cast into discredit among many good men the language—similar to the ear, wholly dissimilar in real import —which had expressed the convictions of a Chillingworth or a Jeremy Taylor.

It is proposed to invite, in this chapter, a more particular attention to the writings of Archbishop Tillotson. He lived and died in the seventeenth century, but is an essential part of the Church history of the eighteenth. The most general sketch of its characteristics would be imperfect without some reference to the influence which his life and teaching-exercised upon it. Hallam contrasts the great popularity of his sermons for half a century with the utter neglect into which they have now fallen, as a remarkable instance of the fickleness of religious taste.[1] Something must certainly be attributed to change of taste. If Tillotson were thoroughly in accord with our own age in thought and feeling, the mere difference of his style from that which pleases the modern ear would prevent his having many readers. He is reckoned diffuse and languid, greatly deficient in vigour and vivacity. How different was the tone of criticism in the last age! Dryden considered that he was indebted for his good style to the study of Tillotson's sermons.[2] Robert Nelson spoke of them as the best standard of the English language.[3] Addison expressed the same opinion, and thought his writing would form a proper groundwork for the dictionary which he once thought of compiling.[4]

But it was not the beauty and eloquence of language with which Tillotson was at one time credited that gave him the immense repute with which his name was surrounded; neither is it a mere change of literary taste that makes a modern reader disinclined to admire, or even fairly to appreciate, his sermons. He struck the key-note which in his own day, and for two generations or more afterwards, governed the predominant tone of religious reasoning and sentiment. In the substance no less than in the form of his writings men found exactly what suited them—their own thoughts raised to a somewhat higher level, and expressed just in the manner

---

[1] H. Hallam, *Literature of Europe*, iv. 177.
[2] *Life of Tillotson*, T. Birch, ccxxxv.
[3] Letter to G. Hanger, in Nichols's *Lit. An.*, iv. 215.　　[4] Birch, ccxxxv.

which they would most aspire to imitate. His sermons, when delivered, had been exceedingly popular. We are told of the crowds of auditors and the fixed attention with which they listened, also of the number of clergymen who frequented his St. Laurence lectures, not only for the pleasure of hearing, but to form their minds and improve their style. He was, in fact, the great preacher of his time. Horace Walpole, writing in 1742, compared the throngs who flocked to hear Whitefield to the concourse which used to gather when Tillotson preached.[1] The literature of the eighteenth century abounds in expressions of respect for his character and admiration of his sermons. Samuel Wesley said that he had brought the art of preaching 'near perfection, had there been as much of life as there is of politeness and generally of cool, clear, close reasoning and convincing arguments.'[2] Even John Wesley puts him in the very foremost rank of great preachers.[3] Robert Nelson specially recommended his sermons to his Nephew 'for true notions of religion.'[4] ' I like,' remarked Sir Robert Howard, ' such sermons as Dr. Tillotson's, where all are taught a plain and certain way of salvation, and with all the charms of a calm and blessed temper and of pure reason are excited to the uncontroverted, indubitable duties of religion ; where all are plainly shown that the means to obtain the eternal place of happy rest are those, and no other, which also give peace in the present life ; and where every- one is encouraged and exhorted to learn, but withal to use his own care and reason in working out his own salvation.'[5] Bishop Fleetwood exclaims of him that ' his name will live for ever, increasing in honour with all good and wise men.'[6] Locke called him 'that ornament of our Church, that every way eminent prelate.' In the 'Spectator' his sermons are among Sir Roger de Coverley's favourites.[7] In the 'Guardian '[8] Addison tells how 'the excellent lady, the Lady Lizard, in the space of one summer furnished a gallery with chairs and couches of her own and her daughter's working, and at the same time heard

---

[1] *Letters*, ed. Berry, ii. 181.   [2] Birch, cccxxxviii.

[3] J. Wesley, *Works*, x. 299.   [4] Nichols, iv. 215.

[5] Sir R. Howard, *History of Religion*, 1694, preface.

[6] Fleetwood's *Works*, 516.

[7] No. 106.   [8] No. 155.

Dr. Tillotson's sermons twice over.' In the 'Tatler' he is spoken of as 'the most eminent and useful author of his age.'[1] His sermons were translated into Dutch, twice into French, and many of them into German. Even in the last few years of the eighteenth century we find references to his 'splendid talents.'[2]

At the same time the chorus of applause was by no means universal. Some were content to give a doubtful and measured approval. Dr. Johnson said he should not advise a preacher in his day to imitate him ; 'although,' he added, ' I do not know ; I should be cautious of objecting to what has been applauded by so many suffrages.'[3] Warburton's criticism of him is sound, and such as would generally commend itself to modern readers. 'The Archbishop,' he writes to his friend Hurd, 'was certainly a virtuous, pious, humane, and moderate man ; which last quality was a kind of rarity in those times. His notions of civil society were but confused and imperfect, as appears in the affair of Lord Russell. As to religion, he was amongst the class of Latitudinarian divines. . . . What I admire most were his beneficence and generosity and contempt of wealth. . . . As a preacher I suppose his established fame is chiefly owing to his being the first city divine who talked rationally and wrote purely. I think the sermons published in his lifetime are fine moral discourses. They bear, indeed, the character of their author—simple, elegant, candid, clear, and rational : no orator, in the Greek and Roman sense of the word, like Taylor ; nor a discourser, in their sense, like Barrow.'[4] He elsewhere speaks of 'those noble discourses which did such credit to religion, composed by those learned and pious men whom zealots abused by the nickname of Latitudinarian divines.' Justification by faith, a fundamental principle of the Reformation, had been by many exaggerated to the verge of Antinomianism. Tillotson and his contemporaries 'very wisely laboured in restoring

---

[1] No. 101. In the *Whig Examiner* (No. 2) it is observed, as an instance of the singular variety of tastes, that 'Bunyan and Quarles have passed through several editions, and please as many readers as Dryden and Tillotson.'

[2] *Reflections on the Clergy*, &c., 1798, iv. ; J. Napleton's *Advice to a Student*, 1795, 26.

[3] Boswell's *Life of Johnson*, iii. 250.

[4] Warburton and Hurd's *Corresp.*, 127.

morality, the other essential part of the Christian system, to its rights in the joint direction of the faithful.' [1]   Warburton goes on to show how some of Tillotson's admirers carried his principles to an extreme no less dangerous in an opposite direction.

But, as a rule, the writers of the eighteenth century seem unable to form anything like a calm estimate of the eminent bishop.   Many were lavish in their encomiums; a minority were extravagant in censures and expressions of dislike.   His gentle and temperate disposition had not saved him from bitter invectives in his lifetime, which did not cease after his death.   He was set down by his opponents as 'a freethinker.' In the violent polemics of Queen Anne's reign this was a charge very easily incurred, and, once incurred, carried with it very grave implications.   By what was apt to seem a very natural sequence Dean Hickes called the good primate in downright terms an atheist.[2]   Charles Leslie speaks of him as 'that unhappy man,'[3] and said he was 'owned by the atheistical wits of all England as their primate and apostle.'[4] Of course opinions thus promulgated by the leaders of a party descended with still further distortion to more ignorant partisans.   Tom Tempest in the 'Idler' believes that King William burned Whitehall that he might steal the furniture, and that Tillotson died an atheist.'[5]   John Wesley, as has been already observed, held the Archbishop in much respect.   He was too well read a man to listen to misrepresentations on such a matter, too broad and liberal in his views to be scared at the name of Latitudinarian, too deeply impressed with the supreme importance of Christian morality to judge anyone harshly for preaching 'virtue' to excess.   But Whitefield and Seward were surpassed by none in the unsparing nature of their attack on Tillotson, 'that traitor who sold his Lord.'[6] It is fair to add that later in life Whitefield regretted the use of such terms, and owned that 'his treatment of him had been far too severe.'[7]   With many of the Evangelicals Tillotson was in

---

[1] *Doctrine of Grace*, part iii. chap. iii. ; *Works*, iv. 712.

[2] Swift's *Works*, viii. 196.   [3] C. Leslie's *Works*, ii. 543.

[4] Id. ii. 596.   [5] No. 10.

[6] Lavington's *Enthusiasm of Meth. and Pap.*, &c., 11, and Polwhele's Introduction to id. ccxxxii.

[7] *Qu. Rev.*, 31 121.

great disfavour. It is not a little remarkable that a divine who had been constantly extolled as a very pattern of Christian piety and Christian wisdom should by them be systematically decried as little better than a heathen moralist.

The foregoing instances may serve to illustrate the important place which Tillotson held in the religious history of the eighteenth century. They may suffice to show that while there was an extraordinary diversity of opinion as to the character of the influence he had exercised—while some loved and admired him and others could scarcely tolerate the mention of him—all agreed that his life and writings had been a very important element in directing the religious thought of his own and the succeeding age. His opponents were very willing to acknowledge that he was greatly respected by Nonconformists. Why not? said they, when he and his party are half Presbyterians, and would 'bring the Church into the Conventicle or the Conventicle into the Church.'[1] They allowed still more readily that he was constantly praised by Rationalists and Deists. Collins put a formidable weapon into their hands when he called Tillotson 'the head of all freethinkers.'[2] But they also had to own that in authority as well as in station he had been eminently a leader in the English Church. A majority of the bishops, and many of the most distinguished among them, had followed his lead. The great bulk of the laity had honoured him in his lifetime, and continued to revere his memory. Men like Locke, and Somers, and Addison were loud in his praise. Even those who were accustomed to regard the Low Churchmen of their age as 'amphibious trimmers' or 'Latitudinarian traditors' were by no means unanimous in dispraise of Tillotson. Dodwell had spoken of him with esteem; and Robert Nelson, who was keenly alive to 'the infection of Latitudinarian teaching,' not only maintained a lifelong friendship with him, and watched by him at his death, but also, as was before mentioned, referred to his sermons for sound notions of religion.

A study of Tillotson's writings ought to throw light upon the general tendency of religious thought which prevailed in England during the half-century or more through which their

---

[1] Sacheverell, Nov. 5, Sermon 'On False Brethren.'   [2] Birch, ccxxxiii.

popularity lasted ; for there can be no doubt that his influence was not of a kind which depends on great personal qualities. He was a man who well deserved to be highly esteemed by all with whom he came in contact. But in his gentle and moderate disposition there was none of the force and fire which compels thought into new channels, and sways the minds of men even against their will. With sound practical sense, with pure, unaffected piety, and in unadorned but persuasive language, he simply gave utterance to religious ideas in a form which to a wide extent satisfied the reason and came home to the conscience of his age. Those, on the other hand, who most distrusted the direction which such ideas were taking, held in proportionate aversion the primate who had been so eminent a representative of them.

Tillotson was universally regarded both by friends and foes as 'a Latitude man.' His writings, therefore, may well serve to exemplify the moderate Latitudinarianism of a thoughtful and religious English Churchman at the beginning of the eighteenth century.

Perhaps the first thing that will strike a reader of his works is the constant appeal on all matters of religion to reason. That Christianity is 'the best and the holiest, the wisest and the most reasonable religion in the world ;'[1] that 'all the precepts of it are reasonable and wise, requiring such duties of us as are suitable to the light of nature, and do approve themselves to the best reason of mankind'[2]—such is the general purport of the arguments by which he most trusts to persuade the heart and the understanding. And how, on the other hand, could he better meet the infidelity of the age than by setting himself ' to show the unreasonableness of atheism and of scoffing at religion ?'[3] If the appeal to reason will not persuade, what will ? 'All that can be done is to set the thing before men, and to offer it to their choice ; and if men's natural desire of wisdom, and knowledge, and happiness will not persuade them to be religious, then there is no remedy. God has provided no remedy for the obstinacy of men ; but if they will choose to be fools, and to be miserable, He will leave them to inherit their own choice.'[4] 'Religion begins in the under-

[1] Serm. v., *Works*, i. 465.   [2] Id. i. 448.
[3] Preface to Sermons, i. ccxcv.   [4] S. i., *Works*, i. 389.

standing, and from thence descends upon the heart and life.
. . . It is the issue and result of the best wisdom and knowledge, and descends from above, from the Father of lights.'[1]

The primary and sovereign place assigned to reason in
Tillotson's conception of man as a being able to know and
serve God involved some consequences which must be mentioned separately, though they are closely connected with one
another.

It led him, if not to reject, at all events to regard with
profound distrust all assumptions of any gift of spiritual discernment distinguishable from ordinary powers of understanding. 'Reason,' he lays it down, 'is the faculty whereby
revelations are to be discerned.'[2] Nothing, he thinks, but
fanaticism and extravagance, utterly detrimental to sound
religion, can follow from a belief in direct intuitions of Divine
things. He does not question the inspiration of the sacred
writers, though he thinks it enough to believe that ' they were
so far assisted as was necessary to inform the world certainly
of the mind and will of God.'[3] But he will not allow that
there are any inward operations of the Spirit which in the
least degree supersede the exercise of reason. He does not
doubt the vast power and influence of the Spirit of God
upon the mind of man. He believes that, although the
evidence for the Divine authority of the Gospel is sufficient
to silence all opposers, faith does not become 'an abiding
and effectual persuasion in any person without the special
operation of the Holy Ghost.'[4] No man, he elsewhere
says, can doubt that God can work in the mind a firm persuasion of the truth of what He reveals, and satisfy it
beyond doubt that such a revelation is from Him.[5] All the
difficulty is in the manner in which the effectual persuasion is
brought about. Tillotson's view was that the Spirit of God
enlightens the human mind only through the reason, so that
the faith of Abraham, for example, 'was the result of the
wisest reasoning.'[6] He suggests that the spiritual presence
acts upon the reason by raising and strengthening the faculty,

[1] S. xxx., *Works* ii. 520.   [2] S. xxi., *Works*, ii. 257.
[3] S. ccxxi., *Works*, ix. 233.   [4] S. ccxxii., *Works*, ix. 248.
[5] S. ccxx., *Works*, ix. 216 and 248.   [6] S. lvi., *Works*, iv. 35.

by making clear the object of inquiry, by suggesting arguments, by holding minds intent upon the evidence, by removing the impediments which hinder assent, and especially by making the persuasion of a truth effectual on the life.[1] This, however, is the very utmost that Tillotson could concede to those who dwell upon the presence within the soul of an inward spiritual light. It would of course fail to satisfy the mystics, with whom he had no sympathy. And although his admissions, taken in a wide sense, may be so interpreted as to grant all that need be contended for, it will be felt that, in accordance with the prevalent spirit of his age, his ideas of a spiritual insight are more limited, and more closely connected with the purely reasoning faculty, than would generally be approved either in an earlier or a later theology than his own. Some, however, of his successors in the next one or two generations took a much more restricted view of the province of spiritual operations.

Tillotson gave great offence to some of his contemporaries by some expressions he has used in relation to the degree of assurance which is possible to man in regard of religious truths. He based all assent upon rational evidence. But he unhesitatingly admitted that mathematics only admit of clear demonstration ; in other matters proof consists in the best arguments that the quality and nature of the thing will bear. We can have, he said, an undoubted, but not an infallible, assurance of a Divine revelation ; the difference being that the latter ' excludes all possibility of error and mistake, the former doth not exclude all possibility of mistake, but only all just and reasonable cause why a prudent and considerate man should doubt.' [2] We may be well content with a well-grounded confidence on matters of religious truth corresponding to that which is abundantly sufficient for our purposes in the conduct of our most important worldly interests. A charge was thereupon brought against him of authorising doubt and opening a door to the most radical disbelief. The attack scarcely deserved Tillotson's somewhat lengthy defence. He had but re-stated what many before him had observed as to the exceptional character of demonstrative evidence, and the folly of

[1] S. ccxxii., *Works*, ix. 249.
[2] S. ccxxi., *Works*, ix. 236; S. i., *Works*, i. 378; S. xl., *Works*, iii. 217, &c.

expecting it where it is plainly inapplicable. A religious mind, itself thoroughly convinced, may chafe against possibility of doubt, but may as well complain against the conditions of human nature. But the controversy on this point between Tillotson and his opponents is instructive in forming a judgment upon the general character of religious thought in that age. Tillotson appears, on the one hand, to have been somewhat over-cautious in disclaiming the alleged consequences of his denial of absolute religious certainty. He allows the theoretical possibility of doubt, but speaks as if it were essentially unreasonable. He shows no sign of recognising the sincere faith that often underlies it; that prayerful doubt may be in itself a kind of prayer; that its possibility is involved in all inquiry; that there is such a thing as an irreligious stifling of doubt, resulting in a spiritual and moral degradation; that doubt may sometimes be the clear work of the Spirit of God to break down pride and self-sufficiency, to force us to realise what we believe, to quicken our sense of truth, and to bid us chiefly rest our faith on personal and spiritual grounds which no doubts can touch. In this Tillotson shared in what must be considered a grave error of his age. Few things so encouraged the growth of Deism and unbelief as the stiff refusal on the part of the defenders of Christianity to admit of a frequently religious element in doubt. There was a general disposition, in which even such men as Bishop Berkeley shared, to relegate all doubters to the class of Deists and 'Atheists.' Tillotson strove practically against this fatal tendency, but his reasonings on the subject were confused. He earned more perhaps than any other divine of his age, the love and confidence of many who were perplexed with religious questionings; but his arguments had not the weight which they would have gained if he had acknowledged more ungrudgingly that doubt must not always be regarded as either a folly or a sin. Yet although Tillotson was far from being over-indulgent to doubt, there is something in his mode of thought which from another point of view might give point to the objection that he weakened the grounds of faith. His too exclusive regard for such intellectual and moral evidence as can be definitely tested by the reasoning powers might easily lead to an under-estimate of the total weight of testimony of which spiritual truths are susceptible. When the old monk said to St. Theresa, ' My daughter, I know it by an infallible certainty which God alone bestows,' [1] he may have been right in one sense, though he was certainly wrong in another. The records of religious history abundantly testify that no intensity of conviction based upon feeling can be depended upon as a sure guide to others than the person affected. It is no more infallible than a similar intense conviction grounded upon reasoning other than demonstrative. Even where the reason and the spiritual perception are alike fully satisfied, infallibility is still unattained. But, subjectively, there is a kind of certainty which may be truly said to be infallible. The individual soul may be absolutely secure of its own possession. A man may be assured with a certainty which transcends all possibility of doubt that his faith, if not wholly void of error as regarded from without, conveys truth and light to himself. This, at all events, is truth, which may not be capable of being communicated or even of being expressed, but which has become its own evidence, as light is of the presence of light. No extraneous difficulties can invalidate it ; no consent and weight of outward testimony can appreciably augment it. Tillotson may have said that this was a kind of infallibility with which he was not dealing. Nevertheless the absence of all reference to it, when he discusses rational evidence, may be called an omission in his system.

As faith was with Tillotson an act of pure reason, aided indeed by the inspiring light of the Holy Spirit, but resting none the less upon tangible proof, he acted powerfully upon the age which succeeded him in the direction he gave to the study of the evidences of Christianity. With the most sanguine confidence he bade mankind prove their faith, and prove it in two ways—by considering in the first place its moral excellence, in the second instance its outward attestations. ' The intrinsic goodness and excellence of any religion goes half-way in the proof of its divinity ; to which if God be pleased to add the external confirmation of plain and unquestionable miracles (including prophecy), it amounts to a full demonstration, and hath all the evidence that it

[1] R. A. Vaughan, *Hours with the Mystics,* ii. 143.

is possible for any religion to have that it is from God.'[1]
'I do not say that they are the only means (for it does
not become men to limit the power and wisdom of God), but
I do not know of any other means of assurance upon which
men can securely rely.'[2] How thoroughly Tillotson has here
given a keynote to the strain which echoes with variations
from the crowd of eighteenth-century evidence writers.
Prove the faith! prove it from morals! prove it from miracles!
Until a later generation began to feel that although to do this
is well, yet that after all it is well to leave much to those other
means of assurance which we know not of, to the Spirit
breathing as it listeth in mysterious ways, and revealing itself
'with an overpowering light,'[3] perhaps through the reason,
perhaps through subtler and more spiritual channels, not to
patriarchs only and to prophets, but to all who sincerely
desire to know God's will. Tillotson had learnt much from
the Puritan and Calvinistic teaching which, instilled into him
throughout his earlier years, had laid deep the foundations of
the serious and fervent vein of piety conspicuous in all his
life and writings. He had learnt much from the sublime
Christian philosophy of his eminent instructors at Cambridge,
Cudworth and Henry More, John Smith and Whichcote,
under whom his heart and intellect had attained a far wider
reach than they could ever have gained in the school of Calvin.
But his influence in the eighteenth century would have been
more entirely beneficial, if he had treasured up from his
Puritan remembrances clearer perceptions of the searching
power of divine grace ; or if he had not only learnt from the
Platonists to extol 'that special prerogative of Christianity
that it dares appeal to reason,'[4] and to be imbued with a
sense of the divine immutability of moral principles, but had
also retained their convictions of unity with the Divine nature,
implied alike in the eternity of morality and in the supremacy of the rational faculties,— with a corresponding belief
that there may be intimate communion between the spirit
of man and his Maker, and that 'they who make reason

[1] S. ccxlii., *Works*, ix. 580. [2] S. ccxxi., *Works*, ix. 221.
[3] Tillotson's own expression in respect of direct revelation to inspired men,
ix. 216.
[4] H. More, Gen. Pref. § 3.

the light of heaven and the very oracle of God, must consider that the oracle of God is not to be heard but in His holy temple,' that is to say, in the heart of a good man purged by that indwelling Spirit.[1] Considering the immense influence which Tillotson's Cambridge teachers had upon the development of his mind, it is curious how widely he differs from them in inward tone. It is quite impossible to conceive of their dwelling, as he and his followers did, upon the preeminent importance of the external evidences.

Tillotson could not adopt as unreservedly as he did his pervading tenet of the reasonableness of Christianity without yielding to reason all the rights due to an unquestioned leader. Like Henry More, he would have wished to take for a motto 'that generous resolution of Marcus Cicero,—rationem, quo ea me cunque ducet, sequar.'[2] 'Doctrines,' he said, 'are vehemently to be suspected which decline trial. To deny liberty of inquiry and judgment in matters of religion, is the greatest injury and disparagement to truth that can be, and a tacit acknowledgment that she lies under some disadvantage, and that there is less to be said for her than for error.'[3] ''Tis only things false and adulterate which shun the light and fear the touchstone. We have that security of the truth of our religion, and of the agreeableness of it to the word of God, that honest confidence of the goodness of our cause, that we do not forbid the people to read the best books our adversaries can write against it.'[4] He has left a beautiful prayer which his editor believed he was in the habit of using before he composed a sermon. In it he asks to be made impartial in his inquiry after truth, ready always to receive it in love, to practise it in his life, and to continue steadfast in it to the end. He adds, 'I perfectly resign myself, O Lord, to Thy counsel and direction, in confidence that Thy goodness is such, that Thou wilt not suffer those who sincerely desire to know the truth and rely upon Thy guidance, finally to miscarry.'[5]

These last words are a key to Tillotson's opinion upon a question about which, in the earlier part of the eighteenth century, there was much animated controversy—in what light sincere error should be regarded. If free inquiry on religious

[1] H. More, Gen. Pref. § 6.   [2] Id. § 3.   [3] S. xx. , *Works,* ii. 277.
[4] S. xix., *Works.* ii. 540.   [5] *Works,* x. 199.

subjects is allowable and right, is a man to be held blameless if he arrives at false conclusions in respect of the fundamental articles of faith ? That the answer to be given might involve grave issues continually appeared in discussion alike with Roman Catholics and with Deists. The former had no stronger argument against liberty of private judgment than to ask how those who freely granted it could pass any moral censure on the heresies which might constantly result from it. The latter insisted that, whether they were right or wrong, no Protestant had any title to hold them in the slightest degree blameable before God or man for any opinions which were the result of conscientious research. Much was written on the subject by theologians of the generation which succeeded next after Tillotson, as for instance by Hoadly, Sykes, Whitby, Law, Hare and Balguy. But in truth, if the premises be granted—if free inquiry is allowable and the inquiry be conducted with all honesty of heart and mind—no candid person, whatever be his opinions, can give other than one answer. Kettlewell, High Churchman and Nonjuror, readily acknowledged that 'where our ignorance of any of Christ's laws is joined with an honest heart, and remains after our sincere industry to know the truth, we may take comfort to ourselves · that it is involuntary and innocent.'[1] In this he agreed with his Low Church contemporary, Chillingworth, who said that To ask pardon of simple and involuntary errors is tacitly to imply that God is angry with us for them, and that were to impute to Him this strange tyranny of requiring brick where He gives no straw ; of expecting to gather where He strewed not; of being offended with us for not doing what He knows we cannot do.'[2] Tillotson always speaks guardedly on the sub- · ject. He was keenly alive to the evil practical consequences which may result from intellectual error,—very confident that in all important particulars orthodox doctrine was the true and safe path, very anxious therefore not to say anything which might weaken the sense of responsibility in those who deviated from it. But he never attempted to evade the logical conclusion which follows from an acknowledged right of private judgment. In his practice as well as in his theory, he wholly admitted the blamelessness of error where there was ardent

[1] Qu. in J. Hunt's *Religious Thought in England,* iii. 45.   [2] Id.

sincerity of purpose. He wrote several times against the Unitarians, but gladly allowed that many of them were thoroughly good men, honest and candid in argument,[1] nor did he even scruple to admit to a cordial friendship one of their most distinguished leaders, Thomas Firmin, a man of great beneficence and philanthropy. In treating of the general subject, he dwelt much upon the text that 'If any man will do His will he shall know of the doctrine.' He thought that such moral faults as self-love, self-interest, and self-conceit, prejudice and pride were specially apt to delude and pervert the intellect.[2] As for children, and for those whose capacities or opportunities are small, God would not impute to them any dangerous error as a fault if 'they took the best and wisest course they could to come to the knowledge of the truth, by being willing to learn what they could of those whom they took to be wiser than themselves.'[3] As for others, 'When men are of a teachable temper, of a humble and obedient frame of mind, God loves to reveal Himself and His truth to them. "The meek will He guide in judgment, and the meek will He teach His way."' . . . 'Considering the goodness of God, nothing is more improbable, than that an honest mind that seeks impartially after truth should miss it, in things that are fundamentally necessary to salvation. And if we could suppose such a man to fall into such an error, either it would not be fundamental to him, having not been, perhaps, proposed to him with sufficient evidence, and would be forgiven him upon a general repentance for all sins and errors known or unknown, or he would not be permitted to continue in it; but the providence of God would find out some way or other to convince him of his error, and to bring him to the acknowledgment of the truth that he might be saved.'[4]

There was no reservation in Tillotson's mind as to the general right of private judgment. 'Any man that hath the spirit of a man must abhor to submit to this slavery not to be allowed to examine his religion, and to inquire freely into the grounds and reasons of it; and would break with any Church in the world upon this single point; and would tell them plainly, "If your religion be too good to be examined, I doubt

[1] S. xliv., *Works*, iii. 310.   [2] S. lxxxii., *Works*, iv. 524.
[3] S. lviii., *Works*, iv. 78.   [4] S. lxxxvii., *Works*, v. 35-7.

it is too bad to be believed.''[1] He grounded the right on three principles.[2] The first was, that essentials are so plain that every man of ordinary capacities, after receiving competent instruction, is able to judge of them. This, he added, was no new doctrine of the Reformation, but had been expressly owned by such ancient fathers as St. Chrysostom and St. Augustine. The second was, that it was a Scriptural injunction. St. Luke, in the Acts, St. Paul and St. John in their Epistles, had specially commended search, examination, inquiry, proof. The third was, that even those who most disputed the right were forced nevertheless to grant it in effect. Whenever they make a proselyte they argue with him, they appeal to his reason, they bid him use his judgment. If it were argued that it could not be accordant to the Divine purpose to give full scope to a liberty which distracted unity and gave rise to so much controversy and confusion,—we must judge, he replied, by what is, not by what we fancy ought to be. We could be relieved from the responsibilities of judging for ourselves only by the existence of an infallible authority to which we could appeal. This is not granted either in temporal or in spiritual matters. Nor is it needed. A degree of certainty sufficient for all our needs is attainable without it. Even in Apostolic times, when it might be said to have existed, error and schism were not thereby prevented. 'With charity and mutual forbearance, the Church may be peaceful and happy without absolute unity of opinion.'[3] Let it be enough that we have guides to instruct us in what is plain, and to guide us in more doubtful matters. After all, 'there is as much to secure men from mistake in matters of belief, as God hath afforded to keep men from sin in matters of practice. He hath made no effectual and infallible provision that men shall not sin ; and yet it would puzzle any man to give a good reason why God should take more care to secure men against errors in belief than against sin and wickedness in their lives.'[4]

Tillotson, however, did not omit to add four cautions as to the proper limits within which the right of private judgment should be exercised. (1) A private person must only judge for himself, not impose his judgment on others. His only claim

[1] S. lviii., *Works*, v. 84. [2] S. xxi., *Works*, ii. 267.
[3] Id. 273. [4] Id. 277.

to that liberty is that it belongs to all.—(2) The liberty thus possessed does not dispense with the necessity of guides and teachers in religion ; nor (3) with due submission to authority. 'What by public consent and authority is determined and established ought not to be gainsaid by private persons but upon very clear evidence of the falsehood or unlawfulness of it ; nor is the peace and unity of the Church to be violated upon every scruple and frivolous pretence.' (4) There are a great many who, from ignorance or insufficient capacity, are incompetent to judge of any controverted question. 'Such persons ought not to engage in disputes of religion ; but to beg God's direction and to rely upon their teachers ; and above all to live up to the plain dictates of natural light, and the clear commands of God's word, and this will be their best security.' [1]

Much that Tillotson has written upon free inquiry and liberty of judgment is of course no more peculiar to him than to all who, from the Reformation to the present time, have discussed the subject either from a general point of view or in one or other of its many practical bearings. His opinions on the matter call for attention not on any ground of originality, but because they acted powerfully upon the character of his mind and upon the influence which he exercised in England. Many orthodox theologians acknowledge a right of private judgment in the abstract, but either dwell little upon it or insist chiefly upon its limitations. In Tillotson's mind the duty of dispassionate reasoning upon the grounds and articles of our faith was an idea which maintained a constant influence. It coloured all his speculations as a theological writer, and all his practical measures as a ruler of the Church. There has probably been no period in which liberty of thought on religious subjects has been debated in this country so anxiously, so vehemently, so generally, as in the earlier part of the eighteenth century. The Reformation had hinged upon it ; but general principles were then greatly obscured in the excitement of change, and amid the multiplicity of secondary questions of more immediate practical interest. For a hundred and fifty years after the first breach with Rome, it may be said that private judgment was most frequently considered in

[1] S. xxi., *Works*, ii. 265-7.

nnection with a power of option between different Church
mmunions. A man had to choose whether he would adhere
the old, or adopt the new form of faith—whether he would
nain staunch to the reformed Anglican Church, or cast in his
with the Puritans, or with one or other of the rising sects,—
iether Episcopacy or Presbyterianism most conformed to his
:as of Church government. When at last these controversies
d abated, the full importance of the principles involved in
s new liberty of thought began to be fully felt. Their real
ipe and nature, apart from any transient applications, en-
zed great attention, first among the studious and thoughtful,
iong philosophers and theologians, but before long through-
t the country generally. Locke among philosophers,
llotson and Chillingworth among divines, addressed their
.sonings not to the few, but to the many. Their arguments
wever would not have been so widely and actively discussed,
i it not been for the Deists. Freethought in reference to
tain ecclesiastical topics had been for several generations
iiliar to every Englishman ; but just at a time when reflect-
; persons of every class were beginning to inquire what
s implied in this liberty of thought and choice, the term was
iappily appropriated by the opponents of revelation, and,
if by common consent, conceded to them. Notwithstanding
that could be urged by a number of eminent and influen-
. preachers and writers, freethinking became a term every-
ere associated with Deism and disbelief. It was a suicidal
or, which rapidly gained ground, and lingers still. The Deists
ned great advantage from it. They started as it were with
unchallenged verbal assumption that the most fundamental
nciple of correct reasoning was on their side. All inquiries
to truth, all sound research, all great reforms, demand free
ught ; and they were the acknowledged Freethinkers. A
ne could not have been chosen more admirably adapted to
ate, especially in young and candid minds, a prejudice in
ir favour. For the same reason, all who asserted the duty
earless investigation in the interests of Christianity could
y do so under penalty of incurring from many quarters
ily expressed suspicions of being Deists in disguise.
otson was by strong conviction an advocate of freethought.
: is a Freethinker,' said all who were afraid of liberty.

'Therefore no doubt he is undermining Revelation, he is fighting the battle of the Deists.' 'Yes,' echoed the Deists, glad to persuade themselves that they had the sanction of his authority. 'He is a Freethinker; if not one of us, at all events he is closely allied with us.' Yet, on the whole, his fame and influence probably gained by it. Many who were inclined to Deistical opinions were induced to read Tillotson, and to feel the force of his arguments, who would never have opened a page of such a writer as Leslie. Many, again, who dreaded the Deists, but were disturbed by their arguments, were wisely anxious to see what was advanced against them by the distinguished prelate who had been said to agree with them in some of their leading principles. Meanwhile liberty of thought, independently of 'Freethinking,' in the obnoxious sense of the word, attracted a growing amount of attention. The wide interest felt in the ponderous Bangorian controversy, as it dragged on its tedious course, is in itself ample evidence of the desire to see some satisfactory adjustment of the respective bounds of authority and reason. No doubt Tillotson did more than any one else, Locke only excepted, to create this interest. It was an immense contribution to the general progress of intelligent thought on religious subjects, to do as much as was effected by these two writers in removing abstract ideas from the domain of theological and philosophical speculation, and transferring them, not perhaps without some loss of preciseness and definition, to the popular language of ordinary life. The eighteenth century erred much in trusting too implicitly to the powers of 'common sense.' Yet this direct appeal to the average understanding was in many ways productive of benefit. It induced people to realise to themselves, more than they had done, what it was they believed, and to form intelligible conceptions of theological tenets, instead of vaguely accepting upon trust what they had learnt from their religious teachers. Even while it depressed for the time the ideal of spiritual attainment, the defect was temporary, but the work real. 'By clearing away,' says Dorner, 'much dead matter, it prepared the way for a reconstruction of theology from the very depths of the heart's belief.' [1]

In calling upon all men to test their faith by their reason, Tillotson had to explain the relations of human reason to

[1] J. A. Dorner, *History of Protestant Theology*, ii. 77.

hose articles of belief which lie beyond its grasp. There ras the more reason to do this, because of the difficulties rhich were felt, and the disputes which had arisen, about mysteries' in religion. Undoubtedly it is a word very apable of misuse. 'Times,' says the author last quoted, unfruitful in theological knowledge are ever wont to fall)ack upon mystery, and upon the much abused demand of 'taking the reason prisoner to the obedience of faith." They ail to see that an acceptance of that which is simply incomprehended involves a merely formal relation to the authority to which the mind is said to submit ; and that therefore such faith cannot be the mother of genuine, positive, and fruitful knowledge.' [1] History abounds in instances of the varied ill effects which have at different times arisen from a habit of Jwelling too much upon the truth that faith accepts much rhich the mind cannot comprehend. With some, religion as thus been made barren and ineffectual by being regarded s a thing to be passively accepted without being understood. Among others, it has been degraded into superstition by the ame cause. When an appetite for the mysterious has been herished, it becomes easy to attribute spiritual results to Material causes, to the confusion of the first principles alike f morality and of knowledge. Some, through an ambition)f understanding the unintelligible, have wasted their energies n a labyrinth of scholastic subtleties; others have surrendered themselves to a vague unpractical mysticism.

But, whatever may have been the errors common in other iges, it was certainly no characteristic of the eighteenth entury to linger unhealthily upon the contemplation of ysteries. The predominant fault was one of a directly pposite nature. There was apt to be an impatience of all ystery, a contemptuous neglect of all that was not self-vident or easy to understand. 'The Gospel,' it was said, professes plainness and uses no hard words.' [2] Whatever as obscure was only the imperfection of the old dispensation, r the corruption of the new, and might be excluded from le consideration of rational beings. Arguments from the ialogy of mysteries in the natural world 'have nothing to o with Divine prescriptions, which by their nature should be

[1] J. A. Dorner, *History of Protestant Theology*, ii. 255.
[2] Sir R. Howard's *History of Religion*, 1694.

plain and clear.'[1]   Even in the natural world there was most mystery in the things which least concern us; Divine providence had ordered that what was most necessary should be least obscure.   Much too was added about the priestcraft and superstition which had commonly attended the inculcation of mysterious doctrines.   In all such arguments there was a considerable admixture of truth.   But in its general effect it tended greatly to depress the tone of theological thought, to take away from it sublimity and depth, and to degrade religion into a thing of earth.[2]   Even where it did not controvert any of the special doctrines of revealed religion, it inclined men to pass lightly over them, or at all events to regard them only in their directly practical aspects, and so to withdraw from the soul, as if they were but idle speculations, some of the most elevating subjects of contemplation which the Christian faith affords.   Such reasoners were strangely blind to the thought that few could be so inertly commonplace in mind and feeling, as to rest satisfied with being fired to virtuous deeds by the purely practical side of transcendental truths, without delighting in further reflection on the very nature of those mysteries themselves.   Nor did they at all realise, that independently of any direct results in morality and well-being, it is no small gain to a man to be led by the thought of Divine mysteries to feel that he stands on the verge of a higher world, a higher nature, of which he may have scarcely a dim perception, but to which creatures lower than himself in the scale of being are wholly insensible.   There was little feeling that truths which baffle reason may be, and must be, nevertheless accordant with true reason.   It was left to William Law, a writer who stood much apart from the general spirit of his age, to remark : ' This is the true ground and nature of the mysteries of Christian redemption.   They are, in themselves, nothing else but what the nature of things requires them to be . . . but they are mysterious to man, because brought into the scheme of redemption by the interposition of God to work in a manner above and superior to all that is seen and done in the things of this world.'[3]

[1] Chubb's *Enquiry into the Ground of Religion*, 1740, 40.
[2] Cf. M. Pattison in *Essays and Reviews*, 293-4.
[3] W. Law, 'Spirit of Love,' *Works*, viii. 141.

Nothing very instructive or suggestive must be looked for from Tillotson on the subject of Divine mysteries. He was too much of an eighteenth-century man, if it may be so expressed, to be able to give much appreciative thought to anything that lay beyond the direct province of reason. Yet, on the other hand, he was too deeply religious, and too watchful an observer, not to perceive that the unspiritual and sceptical tendencies of his age were fostered by the disparagement of all suprasensual ideas. The consequence is, that he deals with the subject without ease, and with the air of an apologist. This remark does not so much relate to the miracles. Upon them he constantly insists as a very material part of distinctly rational evidence. But mysteries, apart from any evidential character which they may possess, he clearly regards almost entirely in the sense of difficulties, necessary to be believed, but mere impediments to faith rather than any assistance to it. 'Great reverence,' he says, is due to them where they are certain and necessary in the nature and reason of the thing, but they are not easily to be admitted without necessity and very good evidence.'[1] When once we are assured a thing is revealed, implicit faith becomes commendable, although we may not understand it.[2] For although nothing is to be received upon any amount of evidence which is really repugnant to reason, anything that is above reason may be accepted if we are satisfied there is reason to believe it.[3] What is a mystery to us may be based on many grounds of reason which we cannot conjecture,[4] and which it is not necessary for us to know.[5] The doctrines, for example, of the Trinity and of the Incarnation being acknowledged mysteries, the office of reason is limited to examining the evidence and establishing their credibility.[6] Above all, we must take care not 'to wade further than the Scripture goes before us, for fear we go out of our depth and lose ourselves in the profound inquiry into the deep things of God, which He has not thought fit in this present state of darkness and imperfection to reveal more plainly and fully to us.'[7] He is not sure whether much that seems mysterious

[1] S. xlvi., *Works*, iii. 359. [2] S. xlviii., *Works*, iii. 423.
[3] Id. 425. [4] S. xlvii., *Works*, iii. 387. [5] Id. iii. 351.
[6] Id. iii. 421. [7] S. xlv., *Works*, iii. 347.

may not be in some degree explained as compliances, for the sake of our edification, with human modes of thought.[1] On the whole, he is inclined to reduce within as narrow a compass as possible the number of tenets which transcend our faculties of reason, to receive them, when acknowledged, with reverential submission, but to pass quickly from them, as matters in which we have little concern, and which do not greatly affect the practical conduct of life. His extreme distaste for anything that appeared to him like idle speculation or unprofitable controversy, often blinded him in a very remarkable degree to the evident fact, that the very same mysterious truths which have given occasion to many futile speculations, many profitless disputes, are also, in every Christian communion, rich in their supply of Christian motives and practical bearings upon conduct.

Tillotson's opinions on points of doctrine were sometimes attacked with a bitterness of rancour only to be equalled by the degree of misrepresentation upon which the charges were founded. Leslie concludes his indictment against him and Burnet by saying that 'though the sword of justice be (at present) otherwise employed than to animadvert upon these blasphemers, and though the chief and father of them all is advanced to the throne of Canterbury, and thence infuses his deadly poison through the nation,' yet at least all 'ought to separate from the Church communion of these heretical bishops.'[2] Yet, if we examine the arguments upon which this invective is supported, and compare with their context the detached sentences which his hot-blooded antagonist adduces, we shall find that Tillotson maintained no opinion which would not be considered in a modern English Churchman to be at all events perfectly legitimate. Had his opponents been content to point out serious deficiences in the general tendency of his teaching, they would have held a thoroughly tenable position. When they attempted to attach to his name the stigma of specific heresies, they failed. He thought for himself, and sometimes very differently from them, but never wandered far from the paths of orthodoxy. Accusations of Socinianism were freely circulated both against him and Burnet, on grounds which

---

[1] S. xlvi., *Works*, iii. 359.   [2] C. Leslie, *Works*, ii. 669.

chiefly serve to show within what narrow grooves religious thought would have been confined by the objectors. There is a great similarity in the general line of argument adopted by Tillotson in his sermons on the Divinity and Sacrifice of Christ, and by Burnet in his second Discourse to the Sarum Clergy. Both firmly maintained the doctrine of the Church against Arians and Unitarians, and while they paid tribute to the high personal character which distinguished some of the leading members and controversialists of those bodies, insisted strongly upon the importance of the points at issue. 'I could never,' says Burnet, 'understand the pacificatory doctrines of those who think that these are questions in which diversity of opinions may well be endured without disturbing the peace of the Church, or breaking communion about them. They seem to be the fundamentals of Christianity.'[1] At the same time they showed themselves far more able to understand their point of view, and to appreciate the nature of their difficulties, than was at all usual. In some respects they made concessions which rendered their arguments far more likely to convince those to whom they were addressed, but raised much outcry among persons of timid orthodoxy. Then, as now, Unitarianism admitted many shades of opinion. Leslie quotes from Firmin that 'the Polonian Unitarians were so zealous for Divine worship to be paid to Christ, that they excommunicated and deposed from their ministry such of their own party as denied it ; which (he adds) I think they generally do in England, where likewise they are of most different faiths.'[2] The great centre of dispute with the moderate Unitarians was upon the meaning of personality as applied to the Godhead. 'Three in one Person is the Socinian Trinity,' writes Leslie.[3] It was on this point that both Tillotson and Burnet made admissions, approximating thereby to the line of least difference between themselves and the most orthodox among their opponents. They allowed that to their minds also the constant theological use of the word 'Persons' was open to objection—that it was a useful term, as serving to illustrate a revealed truth incapable of real explanation—that it was a term not to be declined, 'so long

---

[1] Burnet's *Four Discourses*, &c. 1694. Preface, vii.
[2] Leslie, ii. 656, and Burnet, *Four Discourses*, 122. [3] Id. 658.

as we mean by it neither more nor less than what the
Scripture says in other words,'[1] but not to be insisted upon
as if it were of scriptural authority. The doctrine itself also
they stated in words less removed than was often the case
from the language of moderate Unitarians. 'Oh,' said Leslie,
'that these Doctors would go fair over to the Socinian side!
To speak plainly. . . . . they aim to make the three Persons of
God only three manifestations of God.'[2] This lively and able,
but very intolerant Nonjuror was no doubt tolerably correct
in his inference, although very unwise in the wish that
accompanied it. It would have been a great misfortune to
the English Church if he could have restricted its orthodoxy
into limits as straitened as his own. Burnet, whose theological discourses received Tillotson's hearty commendation,
has fully stated what appears to have also been the less
clearly conceived opinion of the archbishop. There was no
tincture of Arianism in it; he showed on the contrary, with
much power, the utter untenability of that hypothesis. The
worship of Christ, he said, is so plainly set forth in the New
Testament, that not even the opposers of His divinity deny it;
yet nothing is so much condemned in Scripture as worshipping
a creature.[3] 'We may well and safely determine that Christ
was truly both God and Man.'[4] But he held that this true
Divinity of Christ consisted in 'the indwelling of the Eternal
Word in Christ,' which 'became united to His human nature,
as our souls dwell in our bodies and are united to them.'[5]
As Leslie said, he did in effect explain the doctrine of the
Trinity as three manifestations of the Divine nature. 'By the
first, God may be supposed to have made and to govern all
things; by the second, to have been actuated and been most
perfectly united to the humanity of Christ; and by the third,
to have inspired the penmen of the Scriptures and the workers
of miracles, and still to renew and fortify all good minds.
But though we cannot explain how they are Three and have
a true diversity from one another, so that they are not barely
different names and modes; yet we firmly believe that there
is but one God.'[6] A jealous and disputatious orthodoxy

---

[1] S. xlviii., *Works*, iii. 423, and S. xliv. iii. 333.
[2] C. Leslie, *Works*, ii. 619.   [3] Burnet's *Four Discourses*, 122.
[4] Id. 127.   [5] Id.   [6] Id. 134.

might be correct in affirming that this exposition of the Trinity was a form of Sabellianism, and one which might perhaps be accepted by some of the Unitarians. It is stated here rather to show on what scanty grounds the opponents of the 'Latitudinarian bishops' founded one of their chief accusations of Socinian heresy.

But this was only part of the general charge against them. It was also said that they were both 'rank Socinians' in regard of their views upon the doctrine of the satisfaction made by Christ for the sins of men. On the former point, however, Burnet had been considered the more heretical, Tillotson in this. Upon what was considered the crucial test of orthodoxy, Burnet had expressed himself in quite unqualified terms. He thought there could be no question whatever of the Scripture doctrine being that Christ suffered not only on our account, or for our sakes, but also in our stead.[1] The ground of offence lay in the great dislike which he shared with Tillotson for anything which seemed to savour less of Scripture or of solid inference, than of scholastic refinements in theology. ' In regard,' he said, ' of the death and sufferings of Christ, I must first observe that schoolmen and the writers of positive Divinity have upon this head laid down a great many subtleties in which the Scripture is absolutely silent. They begin with a position, that is the foundation of all their calculations, that God cannot freely forgive sin ; that punishing as well as remunerative justice is essential to Him ; that God being infinite, every offence against Him has an infinite guilt, and must be expiated either by acts of infinite value or of infinite character ; that a person of an infinite nature was only capable of acts of an infinite value; that such an one was necessary for expiating sin. But in all this gradation there is one main defect, that the Scripture sets none of these speculations before us.' There was no sanction given in the New Testament ' to these subtle weighings of infinities one against another.'[2]

Tillotson protested in much the same way against unwarranted assumptions in theology. He thought it great rashness to prescribe limits, as it were, to infinite wisdom, and to affirm that man's salvation could not possibly have

[1] Burnet's *Four Discourses*, 142.　　　[2] Id. 136.

been wrought in any other way than by the incarnation and satisfaction of the Son of God.[1]   A Christian reasoner may well concede that he can form no conjecture in what variety of modes redeeming love might have been manifested. He has no need to build theories upon what alone is possible, when the far nobler argument is set before him, to trace the wisdom and the fitness of the mode which God's providence actually has chosen. Tillotson raised no question whatever as to the manner in which redemption was effected, but stated it in exactly such terms as might have been used by any preacher of the day.   For example : ' From these and many other texts it seems to be very plain and evident, that Christ died for our sins, and suffered in our stead, and by the sacrifice of Himself hath made an atonement for us and reconciled us to God, and hath paid a price and ransom for us, and by the merits of His death hath purchased for us forgiveness of sins.'[2]

Nevertheless the charge was brought against him, as it was in a less degree against Burnet and other Low Churchmen of this time, of ' disputing openly against the satisfaction of Christ.'   This deserves some explanation.   For though in the mere personal question there can be little historical interest, it is instructive, as illustrating an important phase of religious thought.   The charge rested on three or four different grounds.   There was the broad general objection, as it seemed to some, that Tillotson was always searching out ways of bringing reason to bear even on Divine mysteries, where they held its application to be impertinent and almost sacrilegious.   His refusal, already mentioned, to allow that the sacrifice of Christ's death was the only conceivable way in which, consistently with the Divine attributes, sin could be forgiven, was a further cause for displeasure.   It did not at all fall in with a habit which, both in pulpit and in argumentative divinity, had become far too customary, of speaking of the Atonement with a kind of legal, or even mathematical exactness, as of a debt which nothing but full payment can cancel, or of a problem in proportion which admits only of one solution.   Then, although Tillotson defended the propriety of the term ' satisfaction,' he had observed that the

[1] S. xlvi., *Works*, iii. 359, and 383, 389.
[2] S. ccxxvii., *Works*, ix. 337.

word was nowhere found in Scripture, and would apparently have not regretted its disuse.   It was a graver proof of doctrinal laxity, if not of heresy, in the estimation of many, that although for his own part he always spoke of Christ suffering 'in our stead,' he had thought it perfectly immaterial whether it were expressed thus or 'for our benefit.'   It was all 'a perverse contention which signified just nothing. . . . For he that dies with an intention to do that benefit to another as to save him from death, doth certainly, to all intents and purposes, die in his place and stead.'[1]   Certainly, in these words Tillotson singularly underrated a very important difference.   Our whole conception of the meaning of Redemption, that most fundamental doctrine of all Christian theology, is modified by an acceptance of the one rather than of the other expression.   In our own days one interpretation is considered as legitimate in the English Church as the other. At the beginning of the eighteenth century, a cramped and mistaken orthodoxy, which did much harm, was apt to represent the translation 'for our sakes' as connected exclusively with Deistical or Unitarian opinions.   From that point of view, we can understand how Leslie declared with bitterness, that although the Archbishop wrote against the Socinians, 'it was really to do them service, and reconcile men more to their principles by lessening the differences which are conceived betwixt them and us.'[2]

Another cause which stirred great animosity against Tillotson as a theological writer consisted in his partial acceptance of that principle of 'accommodation' which was afterwards made so much use of by Semler and many other German writers.   Tillotson's argument was, 'that the manner and circumstances of God's dispensations are full of condescension to the weakness of mankind, and very much accommodated to the most common and deeply radicated prejudices of men concerning God and religion; and peculiarly fitted to remove and root them out of the minds of men, by substituting something in the place of them of as near a compliance with them as was consistent with the honour of Almighty God and the great design of the Christian religion.'[3]

[1] S. xlvii., *Works*, iii. 403.   [2] C. Leslie, *Works*, ii. 281.
[3] S. xlvi., *Works*, iii. 360.

He thought this principle would contribute much to an understanding, so far as our human faculties will permit, of the wisdom and reasonableness of the scheme of redemption as revealed in Scripture. Thus, the natural love of mystery which, in man's unenlightened state, had been fruitful in fantastical and unworthy superstitions, was gently guided to the contemplation of a mystery of godliness—God manifested in the flesh—so great, so wonderful, so infinite in mercy, as to 'obscure and swallow up all other mysteries.'[1] The inclination of mankind to the worship of a visible and sensible Deity was diverted into its true channel by the revelation of one to whom, as 'the brightness of His Father's glory, and the express image of His person,' divine worship might be paid 'without danger of idolatry, and without injury to the divine nature.'[2] The apotheosis of heroes, the tendency to raise to semi-divine honours great benefactors of the race, was sublimely superseded by the exaltation to the right hand of the Majesty on high of one who is not half but wholly infinite, and yet true man and the truest benefactor of our race ; One that 'was dead and is alive again, and lives for ever-more.'[3] The religious instinct which craved for mediation and intercession was gratified, and the worship of saints made for the future inexcusable, by the gift of one Mediator between God and men, a perpetual advocate and intercessor.[4] It was the same, Tillotson added, with sacrifice. On this point he dilated more at length. The sacrificial character, he said, of the atonement was not to be explained in any one manner. To open a way of forgiveness which would at the same time inspire a deep feeling of the guilt and consequences of sin, and create a horror of it, which would kindle fervent love to the Saviour, and pity for all in misery as He had pity on us; these are some of the effects which the sacrifice of Christ is adapted to fulfil, and there may be many other divine counsels hidden in it of which we know little or nothing. But he thought that further explanation might be found in a tender condescension to certain religious ideas which almost everywhere prevailed among mankind. Unreasonable as it was to suppose that the blood of slain animals could take

[1] S. xlvi., *Works*, iii. 362. [2] Id. 363.
[3] Id. 364. [4] Id. 365.

away sin, sacrifice had always been resorted to. Perhaps it implied a confession of belief that sin cannot be pardoned without suffering. Whatever the ground and foundation may have been, at all events, both among Jews and heathens, it was an established principle that 'without shedding of blood there is no remission.' God's providence may be deemed to have adapted itself to this general apprehension, not in order to countenance these practices, but for the future to abolish them, deepening at the same time and spiritualising the meaning involved in them ; 'very probably in compliance with this apprehension of mankind, and in condescension to it, as well as for other weighty reasons best known to the divine wisdom, God was pleased to find out such a sacrifice as should really and effectually procure for them that great blessing of the forgiveness of sins which they had so long hoped for from the multitude of their own sacrifices.' [1]

It is curious to see in what sort of light these not very formidable speculations were construed by some of Tillotson's contemporaries. 'He makes,' says Leslie, 'the foundation of the Christian religion to be some foolish and wicked fancies, which got into people's heads, he knows not, and says no matter how; and instead of reforming them, and commanding us to renounce and abhor them, which one would have expected, and which Christ did to all other wickedness, the doctor's scheme is, that God, in compliance with them, and to indulge men in these same wild and wicked fancies, did send Christ, took His life, and instituted the whole economy of the Christian religion.' [2] The construction put upon the Archbishop's words is curious, but deplorable. It is not merely that it exemplifies, though not in nearly so great degree as other passages which might be quoted, the polemical virulence which was then exceedingly common, and which warped the reasoning powers of such men of talent and repute as Leslie. The encouragement which attacks made in this spirit gave to the Deism and infidelity against which they were directed, was a far more permanent evil. Much may be conceded to the alarm not unnaturally felt at a time when independent thought was beginning to busy itself in the investigation of doctrines which had been generally exempt from it, and

[1] S. xlvii., *Works*, iii. 398.   [2] Leslie, ii. 562.

when all kinds of new difficulties were being started on all sides. But the many who felt difficulties, and honestly sought to find a solution of them, were constantly driven into open hostility by the unconciliatory treatment they met with. Their most moderate departures from the strictest path of presumed orthodox exposition were clamorously resented; their interpretations of Christian doctrine, however religiously conceived, and however worthy of being at least fairly weighed, were placed summarily under a ban ; and those Church dignitaries in whom they recognised some sort of sympathy were branded as 'Sons of Belial.' There can be no doubt that at the end of the seventeenth, and in the earlier part of the eighteenth centuries, many men, who under kindlier conditions would have been earnest and active Churchmen, were unconsciously forced, by the intolerance which surrounded them, into the ranks of the Deists or the Unitarians.

In the general charge preferred against Tillotson of dangerous and heretical opinion there was yet another item which attracted far more general attention than the rest. ' This new doctrine,' says Leslie, ' of making hell precarious doth totally overthrow the doctrine of the satisfaction of Christ.' [1] Of this particular inference, which would legitimately follow only upon a very restricted view of the meaning of atonement, there is no need of speaking. But the opinion itself, as stated in Tillotson's sermon on what was often described as ' the dispensing power,' is so important, that any estimate of his influence upon religious thought would be very imperfect without some mention of it. There are many theological questions of great religious consequence which are discussed nevertheless only in limited circles, and are familiar to others chiefly in their practical applications. The future state is a subject in which everyone has such immediate personal concern, that arguments which seem likely to throw fresh light upon it, especially if put forward by an eminent and popular divine, are certain to obtain very wide and general attention. Tillotson's sermon not only gave rise to much warm controversy among learned writers, but was eagerly debated in almost all classes of English society.

Perhaps there has never been a period in Christian history

[1] Leslie, ii. 596.

when the prospects of the bulk of mankind in the world beyond the grave have been enwrapped in such unmitigated gloom in popular religious conception, as throughout the Protestant countries of Europe during a considerable part of the seventeenth and eighteenth centuries. This is no place to compare Scripture texts, or to show in what various senses the words of Christ and His Apostles have been interpreted. It may be enough to remark in passing that perhaps no Christian writer of any note has ever doubted the severe reality of retribution on unrepented sin. Without further reference then to the Apostolic age, it is certain that among the early fathers of the Church there was much difference of opinion as to the nature, degree, and duration of future punishment. Hermas, in one of those allegories which for three centuries enjoyed an immense popularity, imagined an infinite variety of degrees of retribution.[1] Irenæus and Justin Martyr, in closely corresponding words, speak of its period of duration as simply dependent upon the will of God.[2] The Christian Sibylline books cherished hopes in the influence of intercession. Ambrose and Lactantius,[3] Jerome,[4] and in a far more notable degree, Clement of Alexandria[5] and Origen write of corrective fires of discipline in the next world, if not in this, to purify all souls, unless there are any which, being altogether bad, sink wholly in the mighty waters.[6] 'Augustine's writings show how widely those questions were discussed. He rejects the Origenian doctrine, but does not consider it heretical. . . . None of the first four general councils laid down any doctrine whatever concerning the everlasting misery of the wicked. Yet the question had been most vehemently disputed.'[7]

---

[1] Quotations from the *Shepherd* of Hermas, in a review of vol. i. of the *Ante-Nicene Library* in the *Spectator*, July 27, 1867, p. 836.

[2] Just. Mart. *Dial. cum Tryph.* i. b. i. § v. 20 (ed. W. Trollope, 1846); also Iren. *Hær.* ii. 34, 3, quoted in note to above.

[3] *Sibyll.* ver. 331. Ambrose, *De Psalm.* 36, v. 15; *Serm.* xx. § 12; Lactant. *Div. Inst.* vii. 21, all quoted in H. B. Wilson's speech, 1863, 102–10.

[4] Jerome, *Com. in Is.* tom. 3, ed. Ben. 514, quoted by Le Clerc, *Bib. Choisie,* i. 326.

[5] Clem. Alex. *Strom.* vii. § 6, p. 851, quoted in Blunt, J. J., *Early Fathers,* 80.

[6] Origen, *Hom.* 6, in *Ex. N.* 4, quoted by Wilson, and *De Princip.* iii. c. v–vi. quoted by Blunt, *Early Fathers,* 99, and Le Clerc, *Bibliothèque Choisie,* vii. 327.

[7] Wilson, 119 and 99.

Throughout the Middle Ages, religious terrorism in its barest and most material form was an universal, and sometimes no doubt a very efficient instrument of moral control; but small consideration is needed to perceive how these fears must have been at once tempered and partly neutralised by the belief in purgatory—tempered by the hope that pains preceding judgment might take the place of ultimate penalties, and almost neutralised by the superstitious idea that such purgatorial sufferings might be lightened and shortened by extraneous human agencies independent of the purification and renewal of the sinful soul. Throughout the earlier period of the Reformation, and especially in England, the protest of Protestantism was mainly against specific abuses in the Church, and against the Papal supremacy. Two or three generations had to pass away before habits of thought engrained for ages in the popular mind were gradually effaced. In spite of the rapid growth of Puritanism, and of the strong hold gained by an extreme form of Calvinism on some of the leading Churchmen of Queen Elizabeth's time, the faith of the mass of the people was still a combination, in varied proportions, of the old and the new. The public mind had utterly revolted against the system of indulgences ; but it would be very rash to assume that men's ideas of the eternal state were not largely and widely modified by an undefined tradition of purifying fires. Although this may not have been the case with the clergy and others who were familiar with controversy, there was certainly among them also a strong disinclination to pronounce any decided or dogmatical opinion about that unknown future. This is traceable in the various writings elicited by the omission of the latter part of the third article in the Revision under Archbishop Parker ; and is more palpably evident in the entire excision of the forty-second article, which for ten years had committed the Church of England to an express opinion as to the irreparable state of the condemned. But long before the seventeenth century had closed, orthodox opinion seems to have set almost entirely in the direction of the sternest and most hopeless interpretation possible. Bishop Rust of Dromore, who died in 1670, ardently embraced Origen's view.[1] So also did Sir Henry

---

[1] J. T. Rutt, note to Calamy's *Own Life*, i. 140.

Vane, the eminent Parliamentary leader, who was beheaded for high treason in 1662.[1] A few Nonconformist congregations adopted similar opinions. The Cambridge Platonists—insisting prominently, as most writers of a mystical turn have done, upon that belief in the universal fatherhood of God, which had infused a gentler tone, scarcely compatible with much that he wrote, even into Luther's spirit—inclined to a milder theology. Henry More ventured to hope that 'the benign principle will get the upper hand at last, and Hades, as Plutarch says, ἀπολείπεσθαι, be left in the lurch.'[2] But these were exceptions. For the most part, among religious writers of every school of thought there was perfect acquiescence in a doctrine of intolerable, never-ending torments, and no attempt whatever to find some mode of explanation by which to escape from the horrors of the conception. Pearson and Bull, Lake and Kettlewell, Bentley, Fleetwood, Worthington,[3] Sherlock, Steele and Addison, Bunyan and Doddridge—theologians and scholars, Broad Churchmen and Nonjurors, preachers and essayists, Churchmen and Nonconformists—expressed themselves far more unreservedly than is at all usual in our age even among those who, in theory, interpret Scripture in the same sense. The hideous imagery depicted by the graphic pencil of Giotto on the walls of the Campo Santo was reproduced no less vividly in the prose works of Bunyan, and with equal vigour, if not with equal force of imagination, by almost all who sought to kindle by impassioned pulpit appeals the conscience of their hearers. Young's poem of 'The Last Day,' in which panegyrics of Queen Anne are strangely blended with a powerful and awe-inspiring picture of the most extreme and hopeless misery, was highly approved, we are told, not only by general readers but by the Tory Ministry and their friends.[4] No doubt the practical and regulative faith which exercised a real influence

---

[1] Biog. D. *Vane.*

[2] H. More, *Works*, ed. 1712. *On the Immortality of the Soul*, b. iv. ch. xix. § 9.

[3] Worthington's unhesitating acceptance of the tenet in question (*Essay on Man's Redemption*, 1748, 308) is particularly noticeable, because he was an ardent believer in the gradual restoration of mankind in general to a state of perfection.

[4] *Life of Young.* Anderson's *British Poets*, x. 10.

upon life was of quite a different nature. A tenet which cannot be in the slightest degree realised, except perhaps in special moments of excitement or depression, is rendered almost neutral and inefficacious by the conscience refusing to dwell upon it.   Belief in certain retribution compatible with human ideas of justice and goodness cannot fail in practical force.   A doctrine which does not comply with this condition, if not questioned, is simply evaded. 'And dost thou not,' cried Adams, ' believe what thou hearest in Church ? ' ' Most part of it, Master,' returned the host. ' And dost not thou then tremble at the thought of eternal punishment ?' ' As for that, Master,' said he, ' I never once thought about it ; but what signifies talking about matters so far off ? ' [1] But if by the majority the doctrine in point was practically shelved, it was everywhere passively accepted as the only orthodox faith, and all who ventured to question it were at once set down as far advanced in ways of Deism or worse.

Nothing can be more confirmatory of what has been said than the writings of Tillotson himself.   His much-famed sermon ' On the Eternity of Hell Torments ' was preached in 1690 before Queen Mary, a circumstance which gave occasion to some of the bitterest of his ecclesiastical and political opponents to pretend that it was meant to assuage the horrors of remorse felt by the Queen for having unnaturally deserted her father.[2] His departure, however, from what was considered the orthodox belief was cautious in the extreme.   He acknowledged indeed that the words translated by eternal and ' everlasting ' do not always, in Scripture language, mean unending.   But on this he laid no stress.   He did not doubt, he said, that this at all events was their meaning wherever they occurred in the passages in question.   He mentioned, only to set aside the objection raised by Locke and others, that death could not mean eternal life in misery.[3]   He thought the solemn assertion applied typically to the Israelites, and confirmed (to show its immutability) by an oath that they should not ' enter into his rest,' entirely precluded

---

[1] Fielding's *Joseph Andrews*, b. ii. ch. 3.
[2] Birch, T., *Life of Tillotson*, cliv.
[3] Locke, J., *Reasonableness of Christianity*, Preface.

Origen's idea of a final restitution.[1] He even supposed, although somewhat dubiously, that 'whenever we break the laws of God we fall into his hands and lie at his mercy, and he may, without injustice, inflict what punishment on us he pleases,'[2] and that in any case obstinately impenitent sinners must expect his threatenings to be fully executed upon them. But in this lay the turning-point of his argument. 'After all, he that threatens hath still the power of execution in his hand.   For there is this remarkable difference between promises and threatenings—that he who promiseth passeth over a right to another, and thereby stands obliged to him in justice and faithfulness to make good his promise ; and if he do not, the party to whom the promise is made is not only disappointed, but injuriously dealt withal ; but in threatenings it is quite otherwise.   He that threatens keeps the right of punishing in his own hands, and is not obliged to execute what he hath threatened any further than the reasons and ends of government do require.'[3]   Thus Nineveh was absolutely threatened ; 'but God understood his own right, and did what he pleased, notwithstanding the threatening he had denounced.'   Such was Tillotson's theory of 'the dispensing power,' an argument in great measure adopted from the distinguished Arminian leader, Episcopius,[4] and which was maintained by Burnet, and vigorously defended by Le Clerc.[5] It was not, however, at all a satisfactory position to hold. Intellectually and spiritually, its level is a low one ; and even those who have thought little upon the subject will feel, for the most part, as by a kind of instinct, that this at all events is not the true explanation, though it may contain some germs of truth.   To do reasonable justice to it, we must take into account the conflicting considerations by which Tillotson's mind was swayed.   No one could appeal more confidently and fervently than he does to the perfect goodness of God, a goodness which wholly satisfies the human reason, and supplies inexhaustible motives for love and worship.   We can reverence, he said, nothing but true goodness.   A God wanting in it would be only ' an omnipotent evil, an irresistible

---

[1] S. xxxv., *Works*, iii. 85.
[2] Id. and i. 511 ; S. cxl.
[3] *Bibliothèque Choisie*, tom. vii. art. 7.
[2] Id. 84.
[4] Birch, clvi.

mischief.'[1]   But 'no religion that ever was in the world does so fully as the Christian represent the goodness of God and his tender love to mankind, which is the best and most powerful argument to the love of God.'[2]   'Did but man consider the true notion of God, he would appear to be so lovely a being, and so full of goodness and all desirable perfections, that the very persons who are of such irregular understandings as not to believe that there is a God, yet could not (if they understood themselves) refrain from wishing with all their heart that there were one. . . . If God be such a being as I have described, woe to the world if it were without him.'[3] No reader of Tillotson can fail to see that this feeling pervades his writings.   It is his strength, and sometimes his weakness. The keynote of all his speculative and practical theology, whether as regards God or men, is ever sounded on the one word 'righteousness.'

But side by side with this principal current of thought was another.   Dismayed at the profligacy and carelessness he saw everywhere around him, he was evidently convinced that not fear only, but some overwhelming terror was absolutely necessary for even the tolerable restraint of human sin and passion.   'Whosoever,' he said, 'considers how ineffectual the threatening even of eternal torments is to the greatest part of sinners, will soon be satisfied that a less penalty than that of eternal sufferings would to the far greatest part of mankind have been in all probability of little or no force. And therefore, if anything more terrible than eternal vengeance could have been threatened to the workers of iniquity, it had not been unreasonable, because it would all have been little enough to deter men effectually from sin.'[4]   Two things are set before us : 'an eternal life, and an eternal enjoyment of all things which can render life pleasant and happy ; and a perpetual death, which will for ever torment us, but never make an end of us.   These God propounds to our choice ; and if the consideration of them will not prevail with us to leave our sins and to reform our lives, what will ?   Weightier motives cannot be proposed to the understanding of man than everlasting punishment and life eternal ; than the

---

[1] S. ccxii., *Works*, ix. 84.   [2] S. v., *Works*, i. 446.
[3] S. i., *Works*, i. 366.   [4] S. xxxv., *Works*, iii. 83.

greatest and most durable happiness, and the most intolerable and lasting misery that human nature is capable of.'[1]

The result, therefore, of this twofold train of thought was this—that when Tillotson had once disburdened himself of a conviction which must have been wholly essential to his religious belief, and upon which he could not have held silence without a degrading feeling of insincerity, he then felt at liberty to suppress all further mention of it, and to lay before his hearers, without any qualification, in the usual language of his time, that tremendous alternative which he believed God himself had thought it necessary to proclaim. A perusal of the greater part of Tillotson's 254 published sermons does not authorise a quite unqualified assertion in relation to the whole ; but it may be said under correction that nowhere else than in the particular sermon which caused so much discussion did he give utterance to the opinion there put forward.[2] Even there, the passage succeeding upon the one last quoted is as follows : ' Now, considering in what terms the threatenings of the Gospel are expressed, we have all the reason in the world to believe that the punishment of sinners in another world will be everlasting. However, we cannot be certain of the contrary time enough to prevent it, nor till we come there and find by experience how it is ; and. if it prove so, it will be then too late either to prevent that terrible doom or to get it reversed.'[3] In his other sermons he has not only never scrupled, but has clearly felt it his duty to speak of never-ending torments as if he thought them perfectly certain ; and sometimes he has exerted the utmost power of his eloquence to sketch in the most vivid terms his imagination could conceive a picture of flames, and lashes, and raging anguish, and fearful despair, ' without intermission, without pity, without hope.'[4] Probably Tillotson's own mind was a good deal divided on the subject between two opinions. In many respects his mind showed a very remarkable combination of old and new ideas, and perceptibly fluctuated

---

[1] S. xxxv., *Works*, iii. 93.

[2] S. cxl. contains a slight allusion to the power of remitting threatened punishment.

[3] S. iii. 93.

[4] S. ccxlviii., *Works*, x. 65, and all the three Sermons ccxlviii., ccxlix., ccl.

between a timid adherence to tradition and a sympathy with other notions which had become unhappily and needlessly mixed up with imputations of Deism. In any case, what he has said upon this most important subject is a singular and exaggerated illustration of that prudential teaching which was a marked feature both in Tillotson's theology and in the prevailing religious thought of his age.

In spite of what Tillotson might perhaps have wished, the suggestions hazarded in his thirty-fifth sermon made an infinitely greater impression than the unqualified warnings contained in the hundreds which he preached at other times. It seems to have had a great circulation, and probably many and mixed results. So far as it encouraged that abominable system, which was already falling like a blight upon religious faith, of living according to motives of expedience and the wiser chance, its effects must have been utterly bad. It may also have exercised an unsettling influence upon some minds. Although Tillotson was probably entirely mistaken in the conviction, by no means peculiar to him, that the idea of endless punishment adds any great, or even any appreciable, force to the thought of divine retribution awaiting unrepented sin, yet there would be much cause for alarm if (as might well be the case) the ignorant or misinformed leaped to the conclusion that the Archbishop had maintained that future, as distinguished from endless punishments, were doubtful. We are told that 'when this sermon of hell was first published, it was handed about among the great debauchees and small atheistical wits more than any new play that ever came out. He was not a man of fashion who wanted one of them in his pocket, or could not draw it out at the coffee-house.' [1]   In certain drawing-rooms, too, where prudery was not the fault, there were many fashionable ladies who would pass from the scandal and gossip of the day to applaud Tillotson's sermon in a sense which would have made him shudder. [2]   Nothing follows from this, unless it be assumed that the profligates and worldlings of the period would have spent a single hour, not to say a life, differently, had he never preached the sermon which they discredited with their praise. It is possible, however, that through misapprehension, or through the

[1] C. Leslie, *Works*, ii. 596-7.   [2] Young's *Poems*, Sat. vi.

disturbing effects upon some minds, quite apart from rational grounds, of any seeming innovation upon accustomed teaching, there may have been here and there real ground for the alarm which some very good people felt at these views having been broached. It must be acknowledged that Tillotson's theory of a dispensing power is not only unsatisfactory on other grounds, but possesses a dangerous quality of expansibility. However much he himself might protest against such a view, there was no particular reason why the easy and careless should not urge that God might perchance dispense with all future punishment of sin, and not only with its threatened endlessness.

Yet, on the whole, the general effect of Tillotson's sermon must have been good. There were very strong reasons why the subject should be reverently discussed by Churchmen of ability and piety. Whatsoever may have been the reason, it had gradually got to be considered that one view only was orthodox. 'God's mercy,' said Swift, 'is over all his works ; but divines of all sorts lessen that mercy too much.'[1] Either the subject of future retribution was altogether avoided in the pulpit and elsewhere, to the great detriment of religion, as too dreadful for ears polite, or it was put forward in a manner which was beginning to do much more harm by producing secret or declared infidelity, than it did good in exciting guilty or drowsy consciences. It is not, however, to be supposed that the so-called orthodox view was acquiesced in as generally as might appear at the surface. Under no conditions would this have been the case ; still less so under the then existing tendencies of religious thought. On this point some remarks may be quoted of a man well known at the beginning of the eighteenth century, whose speculations were often extremely crotchety and extravagant, but who was personally very much respected, and was honest and truthful as the day. William Whiston, in his earlier religious meditations (1686), had dwelt upon 'the endless, ceaseless, remedyless '[2] torments of eternity in much the same language as might have been used by any other divine of that age, but afterwards altered his opinions, and published his reasons for

---

[1] Swift's 'Thoughts on Religion,' *Works,* viii. 53.
[2] Med. ix. Whiston's *Memoirs,* i. 50.

doing so, dwelling especially on the use in Septuagint and New Testament language of the word 'eternal.' 'And I think,' he says, 'I may venture to add, upon the credit of what I have discovered of the opinions of Sir Isaac Newton and Dr. Clarke, that few or no thinking men were really of different sentiments in that matter. And as to myself, to speak my mind freely, I have many years thought that the common opinion in this matter, if it were for certain a real part of Christianity, would be a more insuperable objection against it than any or all of the present objections of unbelievers put together.'[1] In another place he casually makes mention of conversation with 'a gentleman who had made the doctrine of their eternity an almost insuperable objection to the Christian religion.'[2] But at the time when Tillotson wrote his sermon, a man had need to be more than usually bold and outspoken if he gave vent to any such notions. He must expect to be regarded as a dangerous man, a heretic, a freethinker, a Deist, and very likely an atheist as well. There can be no doubt that such constrained silence did much to encourage 'freethinking' in a sense hostile to Christianity. Tillotson, with a timid and anxious cautiousness very illustrative of popular feeling on the subject, opened men's lips. Many years had yet to pass before there was any perceptible change in this point in the religious opinions of the mass. The prominence of a crude terrorism was as conspicuous in the methodistic preaching as its absence in the far more limited but somewhat analogous movement of 1875. Wesley himself, throughout all his later years, maintained a doctrine of degrees of rewards and punishments which modified to a very material extent his conception of eternal retribution.[3] But this was not the case with Whitefield, nor with the general body of subordinate preachers.[4] Perhaps, as Isaac Taylor has remarked, we may trace the hand of Providence in the fact that this great movement 'took place at the very verge of the period when the ancient belief as to future punishment was still entire.'[5] Appeals to

---

[1] Whiston's *Historical Memoirs of the Life of S. Clarke*, ed. 1748, 75.
[2] *Memoirs*, 145.
[3] J. Hunt, *Religious Life in England*, iii. 291.
[4] *Review of the Policy, &c., of the Methodists*, 1791, 23, 21.
[5] I. Taylor's *Wesley and Methodism*, 154.

the alarm which sin ought to cause is a very necessary element in a great missionary movement; and in preaching to those who were in many cases semi-heathens, brutalised by ignorance and neglect, it was more essential that the doctrine (so long as it was preached in perfect sincerity) should be strong and startling, than that it should be more correct, but at the same time more undecided. Consistently with the mode in which it has very generally operated, the Gospel,

> First by fear uncharmed the drowsed soul,
> Till of its nobler nature it 'gan feel
> Dim recollections.[1]

A period of transition, when the solemn feeling of religious fear was not yet grounded on an altered but sounder basis, and the older belief was preached in faltering or controversial tones, would have been very unfavourable to the great work which the Wesleyan leaders were called upon to perform. Among the more educated and reflective classes this period of transition had set in before Wesley began his ministrations. There was still a very great reserve on the subject, and a general disinclination to depart in any pronounced manner from the opinion which had been of late almost undisputed. This was illustrated by a very disingenuous incident in Paley's earlier life. When about to take his degree in 1762, he chose for the thesis of his disputation, ' Æternitas pœnarum contradicit divinis attributis.' Finding, however, that this would give great offence, he inserted a 'non' before the verb, and maintained the opposite position.[2] Yet the question was now felt to be more or less an open one, and was no longer avoided as if the very thought were heresy. The controversial writings of the day, the sermons, and frequent allusions in the poetry and other popular writings, often bear witness to the interest which had begun to be awakened. Even those who for their own part adhered firmly to what they believed to be the literal sense of Scripture, were sometimes ready to acknowledge that people might hold a different view and yet be good Christians. Thus Dr. Johnson, although constantly fevered and distressed by terrible apprehensions of the future

[1] S. T. Coleridge, *Religious Musings.*
[2] Paley's *Life,* prefixed to *Works,* xiii.

state, said that 'if he could not be quiet, yet he did not despair;'[1] and that the texts which so grievously disquieted him 'might admit of a mitigated interpretation.'[2]   Tillotson's mode of treating the subject cannot be considered a satisfactory one, but he did much to open the way for an unprejudiced consideration of sounder arguments and more suggestive and spiritual thoughts put forward by other inquirers. Whiston's treatise had many readers, including such men as Bishop Berkeley,[3] and would have had more if its writer had been less notable for eccentricity in his speculations. It was a question also upon which some of the Deists wrote with considerable force.   Chubb, for example, dwelt much on the great importance and concernment of the doctrine of God's future judgment of the world through our Lord Christ.[4] We cannot, he thought, insist too forcibly on 'the certain misery which will follow a vicious course of life, if the sinner's repentance and reformation does not prevent it.'[5]   But punishment, if it is to be righteous, as we are sure it will be, is proportionate, restrictive, and corrective.   The punishment might remain as long as the vile disposition remained;[6] but that vileness unsusceptible of reformation should last on through eternity, he thought inconceivable.   An idea of the perpetual duration of punishment only undermined or weakened its certainty,[7] for it was the equity and reasonableness of retribution on which its certainty depended.   If disproportionate and perpetual punishment had been the teaching of the Bible, it would only prove that all and every doctrine there contained was not a divine revelation.[8]   But it was not so.   There was much that was highly figurative in the language of Scripture, and the word translated by eternal or everlasting was sometimes used in reference to such plainly temporal things as the possession of Canaan, and the fires that consumed Sodom.[9]   There can be no doubt that the

---

[1] Boswell's *Life of Johnson*, iv. 268.   [2] Id. iii. 204.
[3] *Life and Works*, ed. Fraser, iv. 301.
[4] Chubb, T., Equity and Reasonableness of a Future Judgment,' 1734, iii. 146.
[5] Id. 'On the Parable of the Prodigal, i. 12.
[6] ' Supplement to the Equity,' &c. *Works*, i. 113.
[7] 'On the Parable,' &c. i. 14.
[8] 'Equity,' &c., iii. 132; also 'On God's Foreknowledge,' iv. 157.
[9] Id. iii. 131.

force of these and similar words was felt by many who had no sympathy with Chubb's Deistical opinions, from which indeed they are wholly separable. Much the same course of reasoning was adopted by David Hartley in his 'Observations upon Man,'[1] and by some of the so-called mystical writers, such as Dr. Francis Lee, John Byrom,[2] above all in the fervid but occasionally obscure writings of one of the saintliest characters of the eighteenth century, the Nonjuror William Law.[3]

Tillotson's theological faults were of a negative, far rather than of a positive character. The constant charges of heresy which were brought against him were ungrounded, and often serve to call attention to passages where he has shown himself specially anxious to meet Deistical objections. But there were deficiencies and omissions in his teaching which might very properly be regarded with distrust and alarm. In the generality of his sermons he dwells very insufficiently upon distinctive Christian doctrine. His early parishioners of Keddington, in Suffolk,[4] were more alive to this serious fault than the vast London congregations before whom he afterwards preached. He has himself, in one of his later sermons, alluded to the objection. ' I foresee,' he observed, 'what will be said, because I have heard it so often said in the like case, that there is not one word of Jesus Christ in all this. No more is there in the text, and yet I hope that Jesus Christ is truly preached, whenever His will, and the laws, and the duties enjoined by the Christian religion are inculcated upon us.'[5] Tillotson never adequately realised that the noblest treatise on Christian ethics will be found wanting in the spiritual force possessed by sermons far inferior to it in thought and eloquence, in which faith in the Saviour and love of Him

---

[1] D. Hartley, *Observations upon Man*, sixth edition, 1801, chap. iv. pp. 387–437.

[2] 'Penitential Soliloquy,' in J. Byrom's *Poetical Works*, Chalmers' *English Poets*, xv. 261.

[3] See chapter on ' Enthusiasm.'

[4] They complained that Jesus Christ had not been preached among them since Mr. Tillotson had been settled in the parish.—(Birch, xviii.) This was in 1663. The contrast between Tillotson's style and that of the Commonwealth preachers would in any case have been very marked, the more so as Puritanism gained a strong footing in the eastern counties.

[5] S. xlii. *Works*, iii. 275.

are directly appealed to for motives to all virtuous effort. This very grave deficiency in the preaching of Tillotson and others of his type was in great measure the effect of reaction. Brought up in the midst of Calvinistic and Puritan associations, he had gained abundant experience of the great evil arising from mistaken ideas on free grace and justification by faith only. He had seen doctrines 'greedily entertained to the vast prejudice of Christianity, as if in this new covenant of the Gospel, God took all upon himself and required nothing, or as good as nothing, of us; that it would be a disparagement to the freedom of God's grace to think that he expects anything from us; that the Gospel is all promises, and our part is only to believe and embrace them, that is, to believe confidently that God will perform them if we can but think so;'[1] 'that, in fact, religion [as he elsewhere puts it] consists only in believing what Christ hath done for us, and relying confidently upon it.'[2] He knew well—his father had been a bright example of it—that such doctrines are constantly found in close union with great integrity and holiness of life. But he knew also the deplorable effects which have often attended even an apparent dissociation of faith and morality; he had seen, and still saw, how deep and permanent, both by its inherent evil and by the recoil that follows, is the wound inflicted upon true religion by overstrained professions, unreal phraseology, and the form without the substance of godliness. He saw clearly, what many have failed to see, that righteousness is the principal end of all religion; that faith, that revelation, that all spiritual aids, that the incarnation of the Son of God and the redemption He has brought, have no other purpose or meaning than to raise men from sin and from a lower nature, to build them up in goodness, and to renew them in the image of God. He unswervingly maintained that immorality is the worst infidelity,[3] as being not only inconsistent with real faith, but the contradiction of that highest end which faith has in view. Tillotson was a true preacher of righteousness. The fault of his preaching was that by too exclusive a regard to the object of all religion, he dwelt insufficiently on the way by which it is accomplished. If some

---

[1] S. vii., *Works*, i. 495.   [3] S. xxxiv., *Works*, iii. 65.
[2] S. vii., *Works*, i. 499.

had almost forgotten the end in thinking of the means, he was apt to overlook the means in thinking of the end. His eyes were so steadfastly fixed on the surpassing beauty of Christian morality, that it might often seem as if he thought the very contemplation of so much excellence were a sufficient incentive to it. His constantly implied argument is, that if men, gifted with common reason, can be persuaded to think what goodness is, its blessedness alike in this world and the next, and on the other hand the present and future consequences of sin, surely reason itself will teach them to be wise. He is never the mere moralist. His Christian faith is ever present to his mind, raising and purifying his standard of what is good, and placing in an infinitely clearer light than could otherwise be possible the sanctions of a life to come. Nor does he speak with an uncertain tone when he touches on any of its most distinctive doctrines. Never either in word or thought does he consciously disparage or undervalue them. Notwithstanding all that Leslie and others could urge against him, he was a sincere, and, in all essential points, an orthodox believer in the tenets of revealed religion. But he dwelt upon them insufficiently. He regarded them too much as mysteries of faith, established on good evidence, to be firmly held and reverently honoured ; above all, not to be lightly argued about in tones of controversy. He never fully realised what a treasury they supply of motives to Christian conduct, and of material for sublime and ennobling thought ; above all, that religion never has a missionary and converting power when they are not prominently brought forward.

The great bitterness with which religious controversy was infected had done much to create in Tillotson's mild and kindly spirit a distaste for dealing with disputed subjects more than he could help. It was an age when the deepest and most fundamental doctrines of Christianity—the Trinity, the Incarnation, the Atonement—were being constantly discussed, sometimes in a tone of flippant scepticism, sometimes with an intolerant narrowness which would allow of no difference of views, no variety of interpretation. In either case the solemnity of the questions at issue was no bar to party innuendoes and personal abuse. When such polemics prevailed, it was certain that a great impediment would be placed to devotional and practical meditation upon those doctrines. The temper of controversy would be unfavourable to it ; and those, on the other hand, who disliked and shrank from controversy would be tempted to dwell chiefly on points of faith, less fruitful, if they had been fully aware of it, in religious power, but also less suggestive of angry debate. Some feeling of this kind is very evident in the strong sense of relief with which Tillotson, after devoting six careful sermons to the theology of Christianity, turns, as if from a subject oppressed with 'irksome and unpleasant controversy,' to discourse upon undisputed Christian duties— 'thoughts,' he adds, 'more agreeable to my temper, and of a more direct and immediate tendency to the promoting of true religion, to the happiness of human society, and the reformation of the world.'[1] Unfortunately for the permanent value of Tillotson's writings, these words did not so much imply that he was passing from a controversial to a directly practical consideration of Christian truths, as that he should base the motives of religious life less upon exclusively Christian doctrine, than upon truths on which the general conscience of mankind, when duly quickened and instructed, was agreed.

Tillotson's sermons are everywhere impressed with a deep conviction of the holiness, the beauty, the wholly inimitable excellence of the Christian faith. He did not on this account pay any the less honour to what Leslie called his 'dearly beloved'[2] natural religion. He would have held with Bishop Sherlock[3] that, with some limitations and additions, there was nothing essentially objectionable in the common dictum of the Deists, that the Gospel was a republication and restoration of the teaching of nature.[4] The notions, he said, of right and wrong implanted in our nature are truly divine and immutable; and so far as natural religion can guide men to live accordingly, it also is divine, and deserves the name of true faith.[5] A virtuous heathen might properly be said to have lived in faith. But although natural

[1] 'Preface to the Reader,' before the forty-ninth S., *Works*, iii. 440.
[2] C. Leslie, *Works*, ii. 599.
[3] T. Sherlock's sixth 'Discourse in the Temple Church,' *Works*, iii. 315.
[4] S. cii., *Works*, v. 305-6.   [5] S. ccxix., *Works*, ix. 191-8.

religion has in some cases shown itself very powerful for good, it is for the most part weak and quite insufficient, and the great purpose of Christianity has been to reinforce it with stronger motives and clearer knowledge. Still, natural religion so far, he said, retains its sovereign character, that any doctrine which does not strengthen, but contradicts it, is to be *ipso facto* rejected[1] as a mistaken reading of revelation. Natural duties he ranked higher than positive ones. The former were direct parts of right action ; the latter derived all their value from being instrumental to it. He did not hesitate to assert that the duty, for example, of a mother to nurse her own children[2] belonged to a more primary order of obligation, and was, therefore, more indispensable than obedience to an injunction which was binding, not from its own nature, but because it was divinely enjoined.

Tillotson, like many of the best among his contemporaries, believed that the greatest service he could render to religion was to insist very emphatically upon its moral teaching. This, above all things besides, seemed to be the special need of his age. He little thought that his writings would largely contribute to the growth of one of the worst religious characteristics of the century which succeeded. A period had begun to set in both in England and in the Protestant countries of Europe generally, in which Christianity severely suffered by being regarded too exclusively as a system of morality. 'Of late years,' said Dr. Bisse in a visitation sermon of 1716, 'a caution has been dinned into the ears of the clergy that they would do well to let alone the doctrinal and mysterious points of religion, as nice, useless, and often-times contentious speculations, and instead thereof to preach to the people only good, plain, practical morality, upon good moral principles levelled to their capacities ; such as the practice of sobriety, temperance, and justice, and the other moral virtues, enforcing each from the reasonableness and nature of things and their natural consequences. These things, say they, should we preach, as good and profitable

---

[1] S. cxiv., *Works*, v. 530.

[2] S. li., *Works*, iii. 488. This illustration gave great offence to Leslie (*Works*, ii. 600). But Tillotson spoke of it as by no means a minor neglect of duty, but 'one of the trying sins of the age and nation.'

unto men; but the high and abstruser points of our creeds and articles we should avoid, as knowing they do gender strife rather than godly edifying.'[1]   Pope's well-known lines,

> For modes of faith let graceless zealots fight,
> His can't be wrong whose life is in the right;
> In faith and hope the world will disagree,
> But all mankind's concern is charity,[2]

were greeted with a chorus of applause by multitudes who seemed to forget how intimately faith and hope bear upon charity and inward rectitude.   Bishop Gibson, writing to Berkeley, complained of the 'semi-infidels' who were 'making Christianity little more than a system of morality.'[3]   This was true, but it was by no means confined to them.   Kindred sentiments were constantly in the mouths of men who were in no kind of way sceptics.   In most quarters religious thought and language had shaped itself into a peculiar ethical form, so that a sort of didactic tone was quite as common in the pulpits of parish churches and Nonconformist Chapels as in the pages of those who discarded or disparaged distinctive Christian doctrine.   Thus in 1724 we find Gibson thinking it needful to remind his clergy of 'our being Christian preachers, not mere preachers of morality,'[4] and Hearne in 1735 complaining that 'the misfortune now-a-days is that the sermons are more like essays than really sermons, as having little of Scripture and divinity in them.'[5]   The life of Archbishop Secker illustrates alike the prevailing taste and the beginnings of that re-awakening from it, for which the Church was first indebted to the Wesleyan movement.   Horace Walpole, writing of him in 1751, said that he had been immensely popular[6] in his parish, but that in accordance to a

---

[1] *Pride and Ignorance the Ground of Errors of Religion*, by T. Bisse, D.D., 26–7.

[2] Pope's *Essay on Man*, iii. 303.   Perhaps, says Jortin, from Lord Herbert of Cherbury :—

> 'Digladient alii circa res religionis ;
> Quod credas nihil est, sit modo vita proba.'

Jortin's 'Critical Remarks on Various Authors,' *Tracts*, 1731, ii. 524.

[3] Gibson to Berkeley.—Berkeley's *Life and Works*, iv. 244.

[4] Gibson's *Charges*, 1744, 22.   [5] Hearne's *Reliquiæ*, iii. 183.

[6] 'When Secker preaches, the Church is crowded.'—J. Hervey's *Works*, ii. 24.

lion which he had done much to promote, his sermons e 'a kind of moral essay,' not without a certain fervour, with very little of the Gospel.[1] Seven years later, in 8, we find Secker, in his first charge as Archbishop of terbury, warning his clergy against this very fault, and ising them to counteract 'the irregularities and extravacies' of 'the new sect' by imitating and emulating what good in their teaching. 'You must be assiduous,' he tinues, ' in teaching the principles not only of virtue and iral religion, but of the Gospel. . . . You must preach to n faith in the ever-blessed Trinity. . . . You must set h the original corruption of our nature ; our redemption, irding to God's eternal purpose, by the sacrifice of the s ; our sanctification by the influence of the Divine Spirit; insufficiency of our own good works, and the efficacy of 1 to salvation ; yet handling these points in a doctrinal, controversial manner. . . . The truth, I fear, is that many, it most of us, have dwelt too little on these doctrines in sermons, by no means, in general, from disbelieving or iting them, but partly from knowing that formerly they been inculcated beyond their proportion, and even to the aragement of Christian obedience ; partly from fancying n so generally received and remembered, that little needs e said but on social obligations ; partly again from not ing studied theology deeply enough to treat of them ably beneficially ; God grant it may never have been for want iwardly experiencing their importance. But whatever be cause, the effect hath been lamentable. . . . The only plete vindication of ourselves will be to preach fully and uently the doctrines which we are unjustly accused of ing off and underrating ; yet so as to reserve always a share of our discourses, which it is generally reported e of our censurers do not, for the common duties of daily as did our Saviour Christ. But then we must enforce n by motives peculiarly Christian. I will not say only juch.'[2] Bishop Horsley in 1790 spoke to the same effect, ough by that time the evil had somewhat abated. A id, he said, of erroneous views of the mode of justification

[1] II. Walpole, *Memoirs of the Reign of George the Second*, 1846, 66.
[2] Secker's *Eight Charges*, 236-7.

by faith, and an identification of practical religion with morality, had had a pernicious influence. 'The two, taken together, had much contributed to divest our sermons of the genuine spirit and savour of Christianity, and to reduce them to mere moral essays. . . . I flatter myself that we are at present in a state of recovery from this delusion. The compositions which are at this day delivered from our pulpits, are, I think, in general of a more Christian cast than were often heard some thirty years since, when I first entered on the ministry. Still the dry strain of moral teaching is too much in use, and the erroneous maxims on which the practice stands are not sufficiently exploded.'[1]

In one of Addison's allegories, when faith and morality were placed separately on the scales, the latter outweighed the former, but when faith was conjoined with it, gained a thousandfold additional weight.[2] It was not the only time that the Christian moralist of the 'Spectator' warned his readers that morality itself would suffer by being too exclusively regarded, and would receive a vast accession of force by close combination with the sanctions and incentives of faith. Moral philosophy, so soon as it was forced into the rightful province of religion, lost in tone, and degenerated in a marked degree into some higher or lower form of utilitarianism. Shaftesbury exposed with a vigorous pen the selfish trading spirit by which, as it appeared to him, religious motives were constantly disfigured. But when he dwelt, not without much truth and force, on the native beautifulness of a virtuous life, as if that of itself could make men good, he not only failed to make any deep impression, but sometimes inconsistently fell back on the very grounds of action which he had indignantly repudiated. Such expressions as, 'It is the highest wisdom, no doubt, to be rightly selfish,'[3] although true enough in a cynical kind of way, do not well harmonise with those recommendations of virtue for virtue's sake which form the most attractive part of Shaftesbury's writings, and

---

[1] Horsley's *Charges*, 5–8. So also Blackstone, speaking of his reminiscences when he came, as a young man, to London.—'Recollections from Sir R. Inglis's Conversations,' quoted in J. C. Colquhoun's *W. Wilberforce, His Friends and Times*, 109.

[2] *Spectator*, No. 463.

[3] Sir J. Mackintosh's *Progress of Ethical Philosophy*, 1851, 44.

by which, after all, he did a timely service to his age that went far to counterbalance the evil influence of his clever and showy scepticism.

For throughout the eighteenth century the prudential considerations against which Shaftesbury and a few others protested weighed like an incubus both upon religion and on morals. ' Oh Happiness ! our being's end and aim,' [1] was the seldom failing refrain, echoed in sermons and essays, in theological treatises and ethical studies. And though the idea of happiness varies in endless degrees from the highest to the meanest, yet even the highest conception of it cannot be substituted for that of goodness without great detriment to the religion or philosophy which has thus unduly exalted it. When Tillotson, or Berkeley,[2] or Bishop Butler, or William Law, as well as Chubb[3] and Tindal,[4] spoke of happiness as the highest end, they meant something very different from ' the sleek and sordid epicurism, in which religion and a good conscience have their place among the means by which life is to be made more comfortable.' [5] William Law's definition of happiness as ' the satisfaction of all means, capacities, and necessities, the order and harmony of his being ; in other words, the right state of a man,' [6] has not much in common with the motives of expedience urged by Bentham and Paley, utilitarian systems, truly spoken of as ' of the earth, earthy.' [7] But, in any case, even the highest conception of the expedient rests on a lower plane of principle than the humblest aspiration after the right. The expedient and the right are not opposites ; they are different in kind.[8] They may be, and ought to be, blended as springs of action. No scheme of morals and no practical divinity can be wholly satisfactory in which virtue and holiness are not equally mated with prudence and heavenly wisdom, each serving but not subservient to the other. ' Art thou,' says Coleridge, ' under the tyranny of sin—a slave to vicious habits, at enmity with God, and a skulking fugitive from thine own conscience ? Oh, how idle the

[1] Pope's *Essay on Man*, Ep. 4.   [2] In *Guardian*, No. 55.
[3] ' Ground, &c., of Morality,' Chubb's *Works*, iii. 6.
[4] Dorner, iii. 81.   [5] M. Pattison in *Essays and Reviews*, 275.
[6] Quoted in F. S. Maurice's Preface to *Law's Answer to Mandeville*, lxx.
[7] Channing and Aikin's *Correspondence*, 46.

dispute whether the listening to the dictates of prudence from prudential and self-interested motives be virtue or merit, when the not listening is guilt, misery, madness, and despair.'[1] The self-love which Butler has analysed with so masterly a hand is wholly compatible with the pure love of goodness. Plato did not think it needful to deny the claims of utilitarianism, however much he gave the precedence to the ideal principle.[2]

But when the idea of goodness is subordinated to the pursuit of happiness, the evil effects are soon manifest. It is not merely that 'Epicureanism popularised inevitably turns to vice.'[3] Whenever in any form self-interest usurps that first place which the Gospel assigns to 'the Kingdom of God and his righteousness,' the calculating element draws action down to its own lower level. 'If you mean,' says Romola, 'to act nobly and seek the best things God has put within reach of men, you must learn to fix your mind on that end and not on what will happen to you because of it.'[4] It has been observed, too, with a truth none the less striking for being almost a commonplace, that there is something very self-destructive in the quest for happiness.[5] Happiness and true pleasure ultimately reward the right, but if they are made the chief object, they lose in quality and elude the grasp. 'So far as you try to be good, in order to be personally happy, you miss happiness—a great and beautiful law of our being.'[6]

Utilitarianism or eudæmonism has no sort of intrinsic connection with a latitudinarian theology, especially when the word 'latitudinarian' is used, as in this chapter, in a general and inoffensive sense. In this century, and to some extent in the last, many of its warmest opponents have been Broad Churchmen. But prudential religion, throughout the period which set in with the Revolution of 1688, is closely associated with the name of Tillotson. It is certainly very prominent in his writings. His keen perception of the exceeding beauty of goodness might have been supposed sufficient to guard

---

[1] S. T. Coleridge, *Aids to Reflection*, i. 37.
[2] Mackay, R. W., Introduction to *The Sophists*, 36.
[3] *Ecce Homo*, 114.
[4] G. Eliot, *Romola*, near the end.
[5] *Ecce Homo*, 115; cf. Coleridge, *The Friend*, Ess. xvi. i. 162.
[6] F. W. Robertson, *Life and Letters*, i. 352.

him from dwelling too much upon inferior motives. Tillotson, however, was very susceptible to the predominant influences of his time. If he was a leader of thought, he was also much led by the thought of others. There were three or four considerations which had great weight with him, as they had with almost every other theologian and moralist of his own and the following age. One, which has been already sufficiently discussed, was that feeling of the need of proving the reasonableness of every argument, which was the first result of the wider field, the increased leisure, the greater freedom of which the reasoning powers had become conscious. It is evident that no system of morality and practical religion gives so much scope to the exercise of this faculty as that which pre-eminently insists upon the prudence of right action and upon the wisdom of believing. Then again, the profligate habits and general laxity which undoubtedly prevailed to a more than ordinary extent among all classes of society, seem to have created even among reformers of the highest order a sort of dismayed feeling, that it was useless to set up too high a law, and that self-interest and fear were the two main arguments which could be plied with the best hopes of success. Thirdly, a very mistaken notion appears to have grown up that infidelity and ' free-thinking ' might be checked by prudent reflections on the safeness of orthodoxy and the dangers of unbelief. Thought is not deterred by arguments of safety ;[1] and a sceptic is likely to push on into pronounced disbelief, if he commonly hears religion recommended as a matter of policy.

In all these respects Tillotson did but take the line which was characteristic of his age—of the age, that is, which was beginning, not of that which was passing away. Something, too, must be attributed to personal temperament. He carried into the province of religion that same benign but dispassionate calmness of feeling, that subdued sobriety of judgment, wanting in impulse and in warmth, which, in public and in private life, made him more respected as an opponent than beloved as a friend. To weigh evidence, to balance probabilities, and to act with tranquil confidence in what reason judged to be the

---

[1] Cf. F. D. Maurice's Introduction to *Law on Mandeville*, xxiii.

wiser course, seemed to him as natural and fit in spiritual as in temporal matters.   This was all sound in its degree, but there was a deficiency in it, and in the general mode of religious thought represented by it, which cannot fail to be strongly felt.   There is something very chilling in such an appeal as the following : 'Secondly, it is infinitely most prudent.   In matters of great concernment a prudent man will incline to the safest side of the question.   We have considered which side of these questions is most reasonable : let us now think which is safest.   For it is certainly most prudent to incline to the safest side of the question.   Supposing the reasons for and against the principles of religion were equal, yet the danger and hazard is so unequal, as would sway a prudent man to the affirmative.'[1]   Or again, 'It is to be wise as to our main interest.   Our chief end and highest interest is happiness. . . . In a word, our main interest is to be as happy as we can, and as long as is possible. . . . This is the wisdom of religion, that upon consideration of the whole, and casting up all things together, it does advise and lead us to our main interest.'[2]   And once more : 'Besides that, it may prove a thing of a dangerous consequence to us, to deal thus strictly with God, and to drive so near and hard a bargain with him ; we may easily miss of happiness, and come short of heaven, if we only design just to get thither ; we may be mistaken in the degree of holiness and virtue which is necessary to recommend us to the divine favour and acceptance, and to make us capable of the glorious reward of eternal life.'[3]   It must not be inferred from these quotations that nobler and more generous reasonings in relation to life and goodness do not continually occur.   But the passages given illustrate a form of argument which is far too common, both in Tillotson's writings and throughout the graver literature of the eighteenth century.   Without doubt it did much harm.   So long as moralists[4] dwelt so fondly upon self-interest and expedience,

---

[1] S. ccxxiii., *Works*, ix. 275.   [2] S. i. *Works*, i. 328.
[3] S. ccxi., *Works*, ix. 75.
[4] Of Kant's influence on moral philosophy, Dorner observes : 'Kant's antagonism to eudæmonism, and the moral earnestness of his system, aroused a manly enthusiasm, and refreshed the barren land ; scarcely any other philosophical system of recent times has left such lasting marks upon theology.'— *History of Protestant Theology*, ii. 323.

and divines descanted upon the advantages of the safe side; so long as the ideal of goodness was half supplanted by that of happiness; so long as sin was contemplated mainly in its results of punishment, and redemption was regarded rather as deliverance from the penalties of sin than from the sin itself, Christianity and Christian ethics were inevitably degraded.

The making happiness to so great a degree a basis of religion and morality led to a discussion, in which there was much that was very characteristic of the age, as to the bearings of piety and virtue on temporal interests. Since every man, said Tillotson, is led by interest, and the happiness of this life is so present and sensible, 'there cannot be a greater prejudice raised against anything than to have it represented as inconvenient and hurtful to our temporal interests. Upon this account it is that religion hath extremely suffered in the opinion of many, as if it were opposite to our present welfare, and did rob men of the greatest advantages and conveniences of life. So that he that would do right to religion, and make a ready way for the entertainment of it among men, cannot take a more effectual course than by reconciling it with the happiness of mankind, and by giving satisfaction to our reason, that it is so far from being an enemy, that it is the greatest friend to our temporal interests, and that it doth not only tend to make every man happy, considered singly and in a private capacity, but is excellently fitted to the benefit of human society.'[1] He accordingly devotes two discourses to the subject, the one to show 'how advantageous religion and virtue are to the public prosperity of a nation,' the other to point out in how many ways they conduce to the happiness of the individual. Tillotson loved to expatiate on the theme that 'if men would but live as religion requires, the world would be a quiet habitation, a lovely and desirable place, in comparison of what it now is.'[2]

There was nothing in the treatment of the subject but what would be generally considered true in itself, and proper to be set forward. They were certainly arguments congenial to the age, and adapted to increase the estimation in which

---

[1] S. iii., *Works*, i. 409.   [2] Id. 416.

the Archbishop was held for reasonable, sensible, and genial piety. But at a time when there was so marked an inclination to invert the Gospel order of precedence, and to make happiness (in however high a sense), a prior consideration to goodness, the temporal rewards of virtue might readily assume an undue degree of importance. If they were denied or disparaged, the foundations of religion and of morality might seem shaken. If, on the other hand, they were over-estimated, the happiness of earth might seem to be set in competition with the happiness of heaven, and the inducements to believe in a future state seriously lessened. Hence two controversies, which attracted attention quite as much from the interest felt in the subject as from the ability of the writers engaged. One was between Atterbury and Hoadly; the other came to a point in Mandeville's 'Fable of the Bees' and in the replies which it elicited from Berkeley, Hutcheson, and William Law. In 1706, Atterbury preached and published a sermon upon the text, 'If in this life only we have hope in Christ, we are of all men most miserable.' Happiness occupied in his teaching fully as central a place as it did in that of Tillotson or any of his contemporaries. But he evidently believed that every argument which pointed at any rewards of virtue in this life invalidated trust in a recompense to come hereafter. In order to enhance the lustre of a Christian's hopes, he thought it requisite to throw his present case into deepest shade. ' If all the benefits we expect from the Christian institution were confined within the bounds of this present life, and we had no hopes of a better state after this, of a great and lasting reward in a life to come, we Christians should be the most abandoned and wretched of creatures; all other sorts and sects of men would evidently have the advantage of us, and a much surer title to happiness than we.'[1] ' If in this life only we had hope, men would really be more miserable than beasts; and the best of men often the most miserable.'[2] In such overstrained language Atterbury pressed his argument in proof of the sure hopes of immortality which requite the good for their special sufferings here on earth. Hoadly, who was at this time fast rising into eminence, at

---

[1] Quoted in Hoadly's 'Letter to Atterbury,' *Works*, i. 50.
[2] Id. 53.

once replied. St. Paul's words, he said, had special reference
to impending persecutions; the general truth was, that the
ways of heavenly wisdom are 'ways of pleasantness, and all
her paths are peace.' Doubtless, the cause of virtue did not
rest upon its natural tendency to present happiness. When
he saw how little men were moved by the prospects of a future
state, he did not suppose that the temporal rewards of goodness would prove a strong support in moments of strong
temptation. But, like Tillotson, whom he quotes with high
approval,[1] he thought the two arguments of happiness present
and to come should be combined, and that it was very
necessary to remove the counter-prejudice of religion being
unfavourable to temporal interests. At most, Atterbury's
arguments were only valid so far as happiness and misery
depend upon bodily sensations. 'It is wonderfully strange,'
he adds, speaking with a certain measured grandeur not un-
frequent in Hoadly's writings, 'that you should not consider
the chief happiness of any being, in whatsoever state it is, or
of whatsoever duration its life is, must result from the most
excellent part of its constitution; that the happiness of a
being made capable of imitating God, though for never so
short a time, must consist in that imitation; that virtue is
the imitation of God, and therefore must be the happiness of
man; that the chief happiness of a reasonable being must
consist in living as reason directs, whether he lives one day or
to eternity. . . . It is very strange likewise, that you should
not consider that the pleasures and good things of this life,
properly so called, and true happiness in this life, are two very
different things; that they are much oftener separated than
united; and that they who pursue the former within the
bounds of religion have always most of the latter, in the
ordinary course of this world.'[2]

The discussion between Atterbury and Hoadly was
carried on at some length, and attracted considerable interest.
But a few years later, in 1716, the same question, how far
virtue is, or is not, conducive to temporal interests, was reopened in a much more cynical and sceptical spirit by Dr.
Mandeville. This writer, in the 'Fable of the Bees' and the

[1] Quoted in Hoadly's Letter to Atterbury, *Works*, i. 76. So also does

subjoined 'Inquiry into the Origin of Moral Virtue,' argued that, so far from virtue being conducive to natural prosperity, a people who gave up fraud and vice and luxury would quickly sink into insignificance. Politics utilised the vices and selfishness of men, converting by a wonderful power 'their vilest and most hateful qualities into the most necessary accomplishments.' [1] He did not, he said, bring religion into debate at all ; or rather, he indicated the need of it, as intro- ducing new principles of which there was no trace in man's natural state. In that natural state men were simply rated by their desires, and virtue and vice were names invented by political wisdom under which convenient passions were flat- tered, and inconvenient ones discouraged. In most times a satirical essay such as this was, in which it was not even clear how much was written in earnest, might have had a passing circulation from the liveliness with which it was written, and would then have passed into oblivion. But at that period the public mind, so far as it was in earnest at all, was in earnest on maxims of morality, and was specially sensitive to any attack upon that union of virtue and self-interest which their principal teachers had so constantly instilled. Mandeville's production caused great alarm, and was thought extremely dangerous. It would, however, have done good service if it had led divines and moralists to reconsider whether they had been altogether on a right track in harping thus perpetually on the expedience rather than on the intrinsic excellence of right—on the happiness, present or future, of a God-serving life, rather than on an inward recognition of its entire good- ness independently of all reward.

Many of the subjects touched upon in this chapter have little or no connection with Latitudinarianism, so far as it is synony- mous with what are now more commonly called Broad Church principles. But in the eighteenth century 'reasonableness' in religious matters, although a characteristic watchword of the period in general, was especially the favourite term, the most congenial topic, upon which Latitudinarian Churchmen loved to dwell. The consistency of the Christian faith with man's best reason was indeed a great theme, well worthy to engage the thoughts of the most talented and pious men of

[1] Mandeville's *Fable of the Bees*, Preface.

the age. And no doubt Tillotson and many of his contemporaries and successors amply earned the gratitude, not only of the English Church, but of all Christian people in England. Their good service in the controversy with Deism was the first and direct, but still a temporary result of their labours. They did more than this. They broadened and deepened the foundations of the English Church and of English Christianity not only for their own day, but for all future time. They laboured not ineffectually in securing to reason that established position without which no religious system can maintain a lasting hold upon the intellect as well as upon the heart. On the other hand, their deficiencies were great, and appear the greater, because they were faults not so much of the person as of the age, and were displayed therefore in a wide field, and often in an exaggerated form. They loved reason not too well, but too exclusively; they acknowledged its limits, but did not sufficiently insist upon them. They accepted the Christian faith without hesitation or reserve; they believed its doctrines, they reverenced its mysteries, fully convinced that its truth, if not capable of demonstration, is firmly founded upon evidence with which every unprejudiced inquirer has ample reason to be satisfied. But where reason could not boldly tread, they were content to believe and to be silent. Hence, as they put very little trust in religious feelings, and utterly disbelieved in any power of spiritual discernment higher than, or different from reason, the greater part of their religious teaching was practically confined to those parts of the Christian creed which are palpable to every understanding. In their wish to avoid unprofitable disputations, they dwelt but cursorily upon debated subjects of the last importance; and in their dread of a correct theology doing duty for a correct life, they were apt grievously to under-estimate the influences of theology upon life. Their moral teaching was deeply religious, pervaded by a sense of the overruling Providence of a God infinite in love and holiness, and was enforced perseveringly and with great earnestness by motives derived from the rewards and punishments of a future state. If a reader of Tillotson feels a sense of wonder that the writings of so good a man— of such deep and unaffected piety, so sympathetic and kindly, so thoroughly Christian-hearted—should yet be benumbed by the presence of a cold prudential morality which might seem incompatible with the self-forgetful impulses of warm religious feeling, he may see, in what he wonders at, the ill effects of a faith too jealously debarred by reason from contemplations in which the human mind quickly finds out its limits. When religion, in fear lest it should become unpractical, relaxes its hold upon what may properly be called the mysteries of faith, it not only loses in elevation and grandeur, but it defeats the very end it aimed at. It takes a lower ethical tone, and loses in moral power. To form even what may be in some respects an erroneous conception of an imperfectly comprehended doctrine, and so to make it bear upon the life, is far better than timidly, for fear of difficulties or error, to lay the thought of it aside, and so leave it altogether unfruitful. Tillotson and many of his successors in the last century had a great tendency to do this, and no excellences of personal character could redeem the injurious influence it had upon their writings. His services in the cause of religious truth were very great: they would have been far greater, and his influence a far more unmixed good, if, as a representative leader of religious thought, he had been more superior to what was to be its most characteristic defect.

The Latitudinarian section of the Church of England won its chief fame, during the years that immediately followed the Revolution of 1689, by its activity in behalf of ecclesiastical comprehension and religious liberty. These exertions, so far as they extend to the history of the eighteenth century, and were continued through that period, will be considered in the following chapter.

C. J. A.

CHAPTER VI.

LATITUDINARIAN CHURCHMANSHIP.

(2) CHURCH COMPREHENSION AND CHURCH REFORMERS.

THE Latitudinarianism which occupies so conspicuous and important a place in English ecclesiastical history during the half century which followed upon the Revolution of 1689 has been discussed in some of its aspects in the preceding chapter. It denoted not so much a particular Church policy as a tone or mode of thought, which affected the whole attitude of the mind in relation to all that wide compass of subjects in which religious considerations are influenced by difference of view as to the province and authority of the individual reason. During the period mentioned such questions had come forward in more than usual prominence. Rome had been pressing with great activity, and some success, her claims to intellectual submission. Deists were asserting with confident audacity, that reason was altogether on their side. In both these controversies the compact body of Liberal Churchmen, who were headed for some years by Archbishop Tillotson, could not fail of exercising their full share of influence. Those who did them reasonable justice knew well that, whatever else might be urged against them, they were men who, at all events, combined an ardent love of reason with deep Christian feeling and thorough loyalty to the National Church.

But that which gave Latitudinarianism its chief notoriety, as well as its name, was a direct practical question. The term took its origin in the efforts made in William and Mary's reign to give such increased latitude to the formularies of the English Church as might bring into its communion a large proportion of the Nonconformists. From the first there was a disposition to define a Latitudinarian, much as Dr. Johnson did afterwards, in the sense of 'one who departs from

orthodoxy.'[1] But this was not the leading idea, and sometimes not even a part of the idea, of those who spoke with
praise or blame of the eminent 'Latitudinarian' bishops of
King William's time. Not many were competent to form a
tolerably intelligent opinion as to the orthodoxy of this or
that learned prelate, but all could know whether he spoke or
voted in favour of the Comprehension Bill. Although therefore in the earlier stages of that projected measure some of
the strictest and most representative High Churchmen were
in favour of it, it was from first to last the cherished scheme of
the Latitudinarian Churchmen, and in popular estimation was
the visible badge, the tangible embodiment of their opinions.

Comprehensiveness (in a sense however which implies
neither diffuseness nor compromise), is one of the most
ancient, as it is one of the best traditions of the English
Church. Its long and close connection with the State has
always tended to promote the feeling that, as a National
Church, it is specially called upon to shun the fault of narrowness, and to provide as much scope as its nature will permit
for the varied thoughts, ideals, and energies, under which the
spiritual life of a whole people manifests itself. How far this
noble purpose has been attained is a question which admits
of no simple answer, containing as it does within itself the
history of many centuries. There is no intrinsic reason why
a National Church should not in a very large degree accomplish the end consistently with perfect faithfulness to the
sacred 'depositum' of truth of which it is the inheritor.
There have been periods of English history in which the
Church has fulfilled this part of its office with much com-
pleteness. A reader of Mr. Freeman's graphic pages[2] will
realise how thoroughly it was an exponent of the whole
religious feeling of the nation in far gone days of Alfred and
Athelstan. It was scarcely less so while the mediæval Church
was still in its prime of popularity and energy, between the
eleventh and thirteenth centuries.[3] With the dawn of the
Reformation, the problem, always a difficult one, increased in

---

[1] S. Johnson, *Dictionary of the English Language.*
[2] E. A. Freeman, *History of the Norman Conquest,* i. 406, &c.
[3] R. W. Church, *Essays,* 123, &c. Froude's *History of England,* i. 173-5.
Short Studies, i. 48-56.

perplexity. Under the anti-national influence of Rome, a gap had begun to broaden between Church and people, deeper and more formidable than any which could have been caused by the rising difference of opinion. Year by year the English Church had become less national, more under the control of the papal conclave. If the development of our ecclesiastical had kept pace with that of our political constitution, if the convocation of the Church had been more representative, and its organisation somewhat more flexible—if, in a word, it had shown the power it once possessed of quick response to every deeper chord of popular thought and feeling, not only would it have escaped most of the abuses which were benumbing its activity, but it would have gradually found room for the new forms of religious thought which were fast beginning to gather consistency and shape. Comprehension, so far as it is legitimate, would have been a process of growth, and the necessity of violent spasmodic efforts of reform and reorganisation would have been for the most part obviated. When the Reformation in this country had once begun, its main strength consisted in the resolution embodied in it to restore the English Church to its national independence, and to its ancient position of the true Church of the people. 'Doctrinally, the Reformation was a correction of certain corruptions of faith and discipline ; ecclesiastically, it was the assertion of the right of the Church national to make such reforms for herself, and it was in this assertion of her rights as a Church national that lay the true and lawful Protestantism of the Church of England.'[1] But unless religious thought is strangely fettered or benumbed, it is always impossible for a Church to aim at being national without being in a great measure comprehensive. This was more than ever essential when there was such a mass of unsettled fluctuating opinion as in the reigns of Henry VIII. and of Elizabeth. The lines of the remodelled Church were laid down at a period when as yet there was no sharp line of division between the supporters of a Catholic and the supporters of a Puritan reformation, and while the nation, as a whole, was simply bent upon the two great objects of obtaining a spiritual independence, and of removing with a strong hand abuses and

[1] Bishop Magee, *Charge* ; October, 1872.

unrealities. Thus the revised formularies of the Reformed Church were notoriously constructed upon an avowed basis of comprehension. Comprehension was in fact an established principle long before any sound ideas of toleration had yet gained a footing.

The inclusiveness of the Reformed Church of England has never been altogether one-sided. It has always contained within its limits many who were bent on separating themselves by as wide an interval as possible from the Church of Rome, and many on the other hand who were no less anxious that the breach of unity should not be greater than was in any way consistent with spiritual independence and necessary reforms. The Reformation undoubtedly derived the greater part of its force and energy from the former of these two parties; to the temperate counsels of the latter it was indebted for being a movement of reform rather than of revolution. Without the one, religious thought would scarcely have released itself from the strong bonds of a traditional authority. Without the other, it would have been in danger of losing hold on Catholic belief, and of breaking its continuity with the past. Without either one or the other, the English Church would not only have lost the services of many excellent men, but would have been narrowed in range, lowered in tone, lessened in numbers, character, and influence. To use the terms of modern politics, it could neither have spared its Conservatives, though some of them may have been unprogressive or obstructionist, nor its Liberals, although the more advanced among them were apt to be rash and revolutionary.

At the end of the seventeenth, and at the beginning of the eighteenth centuries, Church comprehension was considered in almost exclusive relation to the Protestant Nonconformists. It had not always been so. There had once seemed a probability that a large number of those who clung to the Roman Catholic belief might still be retained within the unity of the English Church. The modern Ultramontane, if he were living in England in the latter years of Henry VIII.'s reign, would no doubt have maintained that ideas of any such comprehension were as utterly impracticable then as now. The Reformation had already reached its crisis, and all the most essential changes had been made. There was entire emancipation from all papal jurisdiction. There was liberty of judgment—liable indeed to sudden and violent checks, but still conceded both in principle and in practice, even more generally than it would be for many years yet to come. An English Bible lay open to be read or listened to in every church. English morning and evening services had taken the place of the Latin breviary. Monasticism, so far as the English Church was concerned, was a thing of the past. The whole current of religious and ecclesiastical thought had begun to flow in a fresh channel. There might seem to be very small scope for any close fellowship between the old and the new. Nevertheless for a long time the breach was far less wide than might appear. Owing in great measure to its close connection with the State, there had always been a considerable amount of freedom in English Churchmanship. National independence in spiritual, as in secular matters, was an idea closely inwoven with ancient and honourable traditions. Many English worthies, such as More and Colet, had combined with steadfast loyalty to the Church of their fathers a hearty longing for great reforms. Opinions closely akin to those which they now heard daily from the new preachers had been, for the last two or three generations, silently but widely fermenting among the mass of the people. And now, after all that had taken place, they continued to attend the same churches as heretofore, were ministered to for the most part by the same clergymen, listened to what were in substance, with a few additions, omissions, and alterations, the same prayers. It is not to be wondered at, that many good Protestants were very unwilling to set up any decided wall of separation between themselves and those of their fellow-subjects who had not yet made up their minds to renounce opinions which they had learnt in childhood ; nor, on the other hand, that many who still adhered to Rome should decline to relinquish religious communion with neighbours of more advanced opinions than their own. It was not until Roman tenets had hardened into a more unyielding form in the final session of the Tridentine Council, that the English Romanists began entirely to withdraw from the services and communions of their reformed brethren. At the

beginning of Elizabeth's reign the 'Bull Papists,'[1] as those
Roman Catholics were called who were considered specially
favourable to the supremacy of the Pope, were still in the
minority. As for the rest, their relation to the National
Church was a little analogous to that of the moderate Presbyterians towards the end of the seventeenth century, a relation
of occasional conformity, which gave some ground for a belief
that they could yet cast in their lot with the bulk of their
fellow-countrymen. There had been an evident desire to
meet their scruples. The first liturgy of Edward VI. had
been compiled with a careful purpose of combining the new
Protestantism with such latitude of expression as might
enable a conscientious Romanist to join in the service. In
the first year of Queen Elizabeth some concessions tending
to promote Church comprehensiveness were made in favour,
as of the Puritans on the one hand, so of the Romanists on
the other. The Queen herself was exceedingly desirous to
obtain a general conformity. In her opinion, and in that of
some of her best councillors, there was a strong hope that
this might be based upon the recognition of that royal
supremacy which expressed, more or less imperfectly, the
ecclesiastical independence of the nation. The oath of supre
macy was held to be a sufficient renunciation of any alien
faith. It was declared by royal proclamation that none
should be molested for religious opinions if they did not
gainsay the Scriptures or the Creed Apostolic and Catholic,
nor for matters of ceremony, if they would recognise by their
attendance the established services of the realm. In a word,
if a person professed a true Christian faith, and would abjure
the jurisdiction of the Pope, he was to be considered a
member of the National Church, free—whether his sympathies
lay in the direction of Rome or of Geneva—to put his own
interpretation upon its words and formularies, free also, apparently, to supplement what he might consider its deficiencies
by private observances more peculiarly adapted to his own
special views, but bound to join with it in worship, and at
least occasional communion.

There was the strongest ground for anticipating that a
great number of Roman Catholics would upon such a basis

[1] Southey's *Book of the Church*, 399.

gradually attach themselves to the National Church. In a period of transition, when minds were still in suspense, and people had constantly adopted the principles of the Reformed faith without yet losing their attachment to the practices of the old, conformity placed no one in any very anomalous position. The strong feeling of national unity and independence which existed among all classes of the people, greatly favoured an ecclesiastical unity in which Protestantism against Papal interference was as yet the most marked centre of agreement. And although the rejection of a foreign authority in Church matters might seem to be a question that lies on the precincts, rather than within the actual borders of religious opinion, there can be little doubt that an English Catholic who conformed upon this ground would soon find that, however little his opinions had at first altered on other controverted points, still, in rejecting the Papal jurisdiction, he had taken the decisive step which made him a Protestant. The rest would follow. There were some, no doubt, and at the beginning of the Reformation some men of influence, who had supposed that they might separate from Rome without separating from Roman doctrine.[1] But such a conception was untenable. When men had recovered by a great effort the power of self-reformation and liberty of reasoning, they could not remain where they were. They must proceed to further reformation ; and if there were any strong feeling in favour of a National Church, and if within such a Church a reasonable liberty of opinion were conceded them, they would be gained over to it, and might probably rank before long among its most devoted members. The Roman court would perhaps have acted wisely for its own interests, if from the first it had strictly prohibited any sort of conformity on the part of its members with a Church which had rejected its supremacy. But it was unwilling to break entirely with the English Church so long as it could cherish any lingering hopes of reunion. When these were reluctantly laid aside, the partial conformity that had hitherto existed [2] was put a stop

---

[1] Cf. Froude, J. A., *History of England*, i. chapter 2, p. 115, chapter 4, p. 336, and chapter 9, ii. 309.

[2] *Annals of England*, ii. 252, 272. Hallam's *Constitutional History*, i. 120, note. Gillmore, in his *Reply to Noel*, p. 168, quotes from J. Busire,

to by peremptory orders from Pius V. Elizabeth and her ministers had already done much to stop it by their very eagerness to promote it. A wise conception, well suitable to the times, which was adapted to enlarge and strengthen the National Church, and to unite in a common worship, without sacrifice of independent opinions, men of widely different views, was sorely marred by the intolerance with which it was carried out. Conformity of worship rather than uniformity of opinion, and the substitution of self-government in ecclesiastical matters in place of any foreign jurisdiction, were admirable principles upon which to lay a broad foundation for a reformed National Church. They assumed a very different character when the strongly worded oath of supremacy was thrust upon unwilling, or yet doubtful recipients, and conformity was enforced with pains and penalties.

At all events, after the first ten years of Elizabeth's rule, the efforts which had been long made to find room within the reformed Church of England for those who had hitherto held Romanist opinions, and were as yet scarcely reconciled to Protestant changes, came to an end. Before many years had elapsed, it had become quite impossible to realise how slight had been for a generation or two the gap which separated many who had accepted, from others who hesitated to accept, the reformed faith in England. The word 'Papist,' which for more than two centuries was almost the only word under which the highest, as well as the lowest English Churchmen spoke of Roman Catholics, remained to be the only relic of a past state of feeling when Protestantism, in the minds of multitudes, had mainly concentrated itself in the repudiation of Papal rule.

At the opening of the eighteenth century, all notions of a wider comprehension in favour of persons who dissented in the direction of Rome, rather than of Geneva or Glasgow, were utterly out of question. One of the most strongly-marked features in the Churchmanship of the time, was the uncompromising hostility which everywhere displayed itself

---

Diatrib. de ant. Eccl. Brit., 'toto post reformationem decennio sub Reg. Eliz. Catholici Romani communicabant cum Protestantibus sine scrupulo, donec Pius V. sua bulla interdictoria conturbavit omnia.'—Southey's *Book of the Church*, chapter xv.

against Rome. This was a direct result of the aggressive attitude of that Church towards the close of the previous century. Favoured by the reaction from Puritan extravagances, and zealously promoted by many persons of position and authority, it made considerable advances in England during the reigns of Charles II. and James II. Throughout the country, but especially in the large towns, wherever the activity of the National Church was most relaxed, wherever a clergyman was unpopular or absent—wherever, in fact, a favourable opportunity presented itself, the emissaries of the Church of Rome found entry, and made proselytes; so that in many places the alarm excited amounted almost to panic. On the Continent the successes of Rome had been far greater, more apparent, and more permanent. It almost seemed as if her prosperity were returning in a flood tide and bearing down everything before it. The Church of England, however, proved equal to the occasion. Her ablest divines, with scarcely any exception, put forth their best strength, and conducted the contest with great ability. The Nonconformists at home, and the Protestant churches abroad, felt that the National Church of England was the centre of the Protestant interest, the one great stronghold of the Reformed faith. In this contest none had taken a more energetic part than the High Churchmen of the day. The consequence was, that long after the danger had passed away, even those whose general tone of thought and reverence for Church authority brought them into nearer sympathy with Roman sentiment than was the case with others, showed nevertheless no sort of approach towards their old enemy, but gloried in the name of Protestant. Thus Robert Nelson, after denying to Rome any exclusive title to the name of Catholic, continues, 'Call us Protestants as often as you please; it puts us in mind of errors renounced by us under that name, which we are not ashamed of, so long as we know there was so great reason for it.'[1] 'The Protestant religion' is an expression evidently open to objection, and has very properly fallen into comparative disuse. But towards the end of the seventeenth century, when Sancroft felt scarcely less strongly than Tillotson the vital need of union among all who owned a re-

[1] Teale's *Life of R. Nelson*, 221.

formed faith, the term was everywhere heard. Bishop Ken, for example, on his return from a visit to Rome in 1675, wrote that 'he had great reason to give God thanks for his travels, since (if it were possible) he returned rather more confirmed of the purity of the Protestant religion than before.'[1] The High Churchmen were naturally the first to feel that the expression was not a well-chosen one ; and on the presentation of the address of Convocation to King William in 1689, there was a warm contention between the Upper and Lower Houses as to its use.[2] A few years later it had become almost a party badge. Almost the last public words of William had been a counsel that 'no other distinction be heard among us for the future but of those who are for the Protestant religion, and the present establishment,'[3]—words which were rapturously applauded by the Whigs, translated into French and Dutch, and sometimes[4] hung up, framed and decorated, in their houses. To people, on the other hand, of an opposite party the phrase became for the future a somewhat obnoxious one, and was seldom or never used by them. But they remained, on the whole, as stoutly Protestant as they had been. Although the later Nonjurors were constantly accused, as indeed even Ken and Nelson had been, of holding Papistical opinions, the charge was perfectly unfounded. It appears that a few individual Nonjurors joined the Romish Church, but this was not the case with any of their leaders, and as a body they were perfectly loyal to the Reformed faith. They remained, to use the strong words of the ejected archbishop Sancroft, 'irreconcilable enemies to the errors, superstitions, idolatries, and tyrannies of the Church of Rome.'[5] Dr. Hickes insisted as strongly as he had done in earlier years that Protestantism was nothing else than primitive Christianity ;[6] Leslie and Lawrence Howell pressed the Roman controversy with unabated zeal ;[7] Johnson set himself to prove, as Dodwell had done before,[8] that Rome

---

[1] Bowles' *Life of Ken*, 261. [2] J. Hunt's *Religious Thought in England*, iii. 2.
[3] Speech to Parliament, December 31, 1701.
[4] Calamy's *Life and Times*, i. 439.
[5] Lathbury's *History of the Nonjurors*, 77.
[6] J. Hunt's *Religious Thought in England*, ii. 54, 76. *Life of Ken*, by a Layman, 778.   [7] Lathbury's *History of the Nonjurors*, 366-7.
[8] Brokesby's *Life of Dodwell*, 43.

was evidently schismatical ; Lindsay wrote his ' Seasonable Antidote,' exposed the unreasonable pretentiousness with which that Church claimed the exclusive title of Catholic, and showed how dangerously the doctrine of transubstantiation bordered upon idolatry.[1]

If not the High Churchmen only, but even the most extreme party of the Nonjurors, who thought that the English Church had reformed itself too much—who, as active Jacobites, were often in close political and social intercourse with Roman Catholics—and who were ardently planning for affiliation with the Greek Church—were yet Protestants to the core whenever Rome was in question, this feeling had become intense to an extraordinary degree among other classes of the community. There was no party so much in favour of ' latitude ' as to concede an inch to mitigate the differences between themselves and a foe with whom their hostility was so inveterate. There were none so 'liberal' as not to hold that liberality was worse than thrown away in the dealings of Englishmen with Papists. Lord Chancellor Somers, who was always considered the great champion of toleration, a man 'of enlightened views, great talents, and unsullied integrity, the life, the soul, the spirit of his party,'[2] was as bitterly intolerant of Roman Catholics as those to whom toleration was as yet a scandal and a reproach. Lord Campbell remarks of him that the penal laws passed against Romanists while he was in office were far more severe and revolting than under Elizabeth or any of the four kings of the Stuart line.[3] 'The most curious consideration,' adds the same author, ' in looking back to those times, is, that from a general feeling among English Protestants with respect to Roman Catholics—resembling that which now (1846) prevails in the United States of America among the whites with respect to the negroes—the authors of such measures had no consciousness themselves of doing any wrong, and did not at all thereby injure their character for liberality with the great body of their countrymen.'[4] If the onesidedness of their toleration was pressed upon them, there was always,

[1] Lathbury, 401.   [2] Campbell's *Lives of the Lord Chancellors*, iv. 73, 89.
[3] Id. 221.   [4] Id. 227.

it is true, a ready explanation at hand in the assertion tha the disabilities, confiscations, and imprisonments inflicted upon Roman Catholics were but acts of civil coercion, necessary in defence of the State. 'Persecution,' says Hoadly—writing in favour of a bill to raise money upon the estates of Roman Catholics—'is the most inhumane and insociable of all crimes. But while you fly the Scylla of persecution, do not fall into the Charybdis of civil lethargy. Difference of religion has nothing to do with what is necessary for the security of the civil constitution.'[1] Upon some such plea, many who considered themselves very true friends of religious liberty became deluded into the idea that they were perfectly guiltless of persecution when they voted that any Popish priest returning to the kingdom should be hanged, or that no Papist should keep a school or be the guardian of any child, or act as a barrister or solicitor. But while Somers and Hoadly, and other advocates of unlimited toleration, thus steered their course between Scylla and Charybdis, the multitude were perfectly indifferent into what eddies of intolerance, short of downright bloodshed, they might be swept, so long as the good ship of Our Happy Constitution in Church and State could be kept well aloof from the dangerous rocks of Italy. Hatred of Rome long continued to be, as it had become in James II.'s reign, a 'ruling passion even of ploughmen and artisans.'[2] This, with not a few, seemed to be accounted the main point of Protestant Churchmanship. There were even some, as Kettlewell says, 'who did fall into Atheism for fear of Popery.'[3] Deism was, at all events, immensely promoted by the artful way in which, consciously or unconsciously, the opponents of revelation converted the popular abhorrence of 'Popish superstitions' into weapons of offence against Christianity itself. The Romanists themselves were not slow to observe and profit by this. A report circulated that their emissaries, who for the first forty years of the century were very active, sometimes personated Deistical or infidel agitators.[4] There may have been some foundation

---

[1] Letters signed 'Britannicus,' No. xvi., *Works*, iii. 58.

[2] Macaulay's *History of England*, chapter ix. Hallam's *Constitutional History*, iii. 55.	[3] *Life of Kettlewell*, 96.

[4] Swift's *Works*, 8, 76. De Foe's *Reasonable Warning*, 13.

in the rumour; but it was much more certain that the questioners of revealed truth did not need to be in the service of Rome in order to promote her immediate interests. Tindal the Deist, the writer 'against the Romish and all other priests,' brought the Vatican many more proselytes than Tindal the Roman Catholic could have done. If the reaction from superstition led any minds into bare scepticism, or a blank disbelief in spiritual existences, many adherents would be regained, as was actually the case, to a faith which bade the soul wholly distrust reason, and rest in secure submission to assumed infallible authority.

The strong hostility which at the beginning of the eighteenth century prevailed between all English Protestants and their fellow-Christians in the Roman Catholic Church, was relieved by a mitigating influence in one direction only. Churchmen in this country could not fail to feel interest in the struggle for national independence in religious matters which was being carried on among their neighbours and ancestral enemies across the Channel. The Gallican Church was in the height of its fame, adorned by names which added lustre to it wherever the Christian faith was known. No Protestant, however uncompromising, could altogether withhold his admiration from a Fénelon, a Pascal, or a Bossuet. And all these three great men seemed more or less separated, though in different ways, from the regular Romish system. The spiritual and semi-mystical piety of Fénelon[1] detached him from the trenchant dogmatism which, since the Council of Trent, had been stamped so much more decisively than heretofore upon Roman tenets. Pascal,[2] notwithstanding his mediævalism, and the humble submissiveness which he acknowledged to be due to the Papal see, not only fascinated cultivated readers by the brilliancy of his style, not only won their hearts by the simple truthfulness and integrity of his character, but delighted Englishmen generally by the vigour of the attack with which, as leader of the Jansenists, he led the assault upon the Jesuits. Bossuet's noble defence of the Gallican liberties appealed still more directly to the sym-

---

[1] Alison's *Life of Marlborough*, i. 199. Seward's *Anecdotes*, ii. 271. Jortin's *Tracts*, ii. 43. R. Savage's *Poems*, 'The Character,' &c.

[2] *Spectator*, No. 116.

pathies of this nation. It reminded men of the conflict that had been fought and won on English soil, and encouraged too sanguine hopes that it might issue in a reformation within the sister country, not perhaps so complete as that which had taken place among ourselves, but not less full of promise. In the midst of the war that was raging between the rival forms of belief, English theologians of all opinions were pleased with his graceful recognition, in the name of the French clergy, of the services rendered to religion by Bishop Bull's learned ' Defence of the Nicene Faith.' [1]

Some time after the death of Bossuet, the renewed resistance which was being made in France against Papal usurpations gave rise to action on the part of the primate of our Church, which in the sixteenth century might have been cordially followed up in England, but in the eighteenth was very generally misunderstood and misrepresented. Archbishop Wake had taken a very distinguished part in the Roman controversy, directing his special attention to the polemical works of Bossuet, but had always handled these topics in a broader and more generous tone than many of his contemporaries. In 1717, at a time when many of the French bishops and clergy, headed by the Sorbonne, and by the Cardinal de Noailles, were indignantly protesting against the bondage imposed upon them by the Bull Unigenitus, and were proposing to appeal from the Pope to a general council, a communication was received by Archbishop Wake,[2] that Du Pin, head of the theological faculty of the Sorbonne, had expressed himself in favour of a possible union with the English Church.[3] The idea was warmly favoured by De Gerardin, another eminent doctor of that university. A correspondence of some length ensued, carried on with much friendly and earnest feeling on either side. Separation from Rome was what the English archbishop chiefly pressed ;[4] ' a reformation in other matters would follow of course.'

---

[1] Nelson's *Life of Bull*, 329–30.

[2] Mosheim's *Church History*, Maclaine's edition, vol. v. ' Letter of Beauvoir to Wake,' December 11, 1717, Ap. 2, No. 2. p. 147.

[3] Id. Dupin to Wake, February 11, 1718. ' Unum addam, cum boná veniâ tuâ, me vehementer optare, ut unionis inter ecclesias Anglicanam et Gallicam viâ aliquâ inveniri posset,' &c.

[4] Wake to Dupin, October 1, 1718. Id. 134, 152, 156.

Writing as he did without any official authority, he was wise enough not to commit himself to any details. First of all they ought 'to agree,' he said, 'to own each other as true brethren and members of the Catholic Christian Church;' and then the great point would be to acknowledge 'the independence (as to all matters of authority) of every national Church on all others,' agree with one another, and communicate with one another as far as possible, and leave free liberty of disagreement on other matters. He did not see anything in our offices so essentially contrary to their principles, that they need scruple to join in them; and if some alterations were made, we also might join in theirs, on a clear understanding that on all such points of disagreement as the doctrine of transubstantiation, either body of Christians should hold the opinions which it approved. Upon such terms,[1] two great national Churches might be on close terms of friendly intercommunion notwithstanding great differences on matters not of the first moment, which might well afford to wait 'till God should bring us to a union in those also.'[2] Du Pin and De Gerardin replied in much the same spirit. The former of the two soon after died; and the incipient negotiation, which was never very likely to be followed by any practical results, fell through.[3] In fact, the resuscitated spirit of independence which had begun to stir in France was itself shortlived. 'It is disheartening to see not only the infamous Dubois, but the blameless Fleury, follow the instincts of absolutism in persecuting the appellants (from the Pope), conquering the broken-hearted De Noailles, degrading the venerable Bishop of Senez for favouring Jansenism, terrifying and 'purging' the Sorbonne by Lettres de Cachet, and pursuing in the interests of Ultramontanism a policy of reckless Erastianism and secular tyranny which carried a Nemesis with it.'[4]

The correspondence between the English primate and

[1] Wake to Dupin, Oct. 1, 1718, Ap. 3, No. 8, p. 158.

[2] Id.—It will of course be understood that Archbishop Wake's overtures were directed wholly to the Gallican Church, not to the Papacy. 'He well understood that a direct reconciliation with Rome itself was nationally, ecclesiastically, and theologically impossible.'—H. B. Wilson in *Oxford Essays*, 1857.

[3] Almost the whole correspondence is given in the eighteen letters, &c. 1717-20, of Maclaine's Appendix to *Mosheim*, vol. v.

[4] *Guardian*, May 21, 1873. Review of Jervise's *History of the Church of France*.

the doctors of the Sorbonne is an episode which stands by itself, quite apart from any other incidents in the Church history of the time. It bears a superficial resemblance to the overtures made by some of the English and Scotch Nonjurors to the Eastern Church. There was, however, an essential difference between them. Without any dishonour to Non-juring principles, and without passing any judgment upon the grounds of their separation, it must be acknowledged that those of them who renounced the communion of the English Church accepted a sectarian position. They had gained a comparative uniformity of opinion, at the entire ex-pense of that breadth and expansiveness which only national Churches are found capable of. Connection with the Eastern Church, if it could have been carried out (though the difficul-ties in the way of this were far greater than they were at all aware of), would simply have indicated a movement of their whole body in one direction only, and, in proportion as it was successful, would have alienated them more than ever from those whose religious and ecclesiastical sympathies were of a very different kind. Such communion, on the other hand, of independent national Churches as was contemplated by Du Pin and Wake might have been quite free from onesidedness of this description. It need not have interfered with or discouraged, it should rather have tended to promote, the near intercourse, which many English Churchmen were greatly desirous of, with the National Church of Scotland and with the reformed Churches of the Continent. A relation of this kind with her sister Churches on either hand would have been in perfect harmony both with the original stand-point of the Church of England, and with an important office it may perhaps be called to in the future. It was in refer-ence to the sympathetic reception given in this country to many of the proscribed bishops and clergy of France at the time of the great revolution, that the Count de Maistre made a remark which has often struck readers as well worthy of notice. ' If ever,'—he said, ' and everything invites to it—there should be a movement towards reunion among the Christian bodies, it seems likely that the Church of England should be the one to give it impulse. Presbyterianism, as its French nature rendered probable, went to extremes. Between us and those who practise a worship which we think wanting in form and substance, there is too wide an interval ; we cannot understand one another. But the English Church, which touches us with the one hand, touches with the other those with whom we have no point of contact.' [1]

Archbishop Wake, had he lived in more favourable times, would have been well fitted, both by position and character, for this work of mutual conciliation. His disposition toward the foreign Protestant Churches was of the most friendly kind. In a letter to Le Clerc on the subject,[2] he deprecated dissension on matters of no essential moment. He desired to be on terms of cordial friendship with the Reformed Churches, notwithstanding their points of difference from that of England. He could wish they had a moderate Episcopal government, according to the primitive model ; nor did he yet despair of it, if not in his own time, perhaps in days to come. He would welcome a closer union among all the Reformed bodies, at almost any price. The advantages he anticipated from such a result would be immense. Any approximations in Church government or Church offices which might conduce to it he should indeed rejoice in. Much to the same effect he wrote [3] to his ' very dear brothers,' the pastors and professors of Geneva. The letter related, in the first instance, to the efforts he had been making in behalf of the Piedmontese and Hungarian Churches. But he took occasion to express the longing desire he felt for union among the Reformed Churches—a work, he allowed, of difficulty, but which undoubtedly could be achieved, if all were bent on concord. He hoped he might not be thought trenching upon a province in which he had no concern, if he implored most earnestly both Lutherans and Reformed to be very tolerant and forbearing in the mutual controversies they were engaged in upon abstruse questions of grace and predestination ; above all, to be moderate in imposing terms of subscription, and to imitate in this respect the greater liberty of judgment and latitude of interpretation which the Church of England had wisely conceded to all who sign her articles. Archbishop Wake addressed other letters on these subjects to

---

[1] De Maistre : *Considérations sur la France*, chap. ii. p. 30.
[2] April, 1719. *Mosheim*, v. 169, Ap. 3, No. 19.
[3] Ap. 8, 1719. Id. 171–3, Ap. 3, No. 20.

Professor Schurer of Berne, and to Professor Turretin of Geneva.[1] He also carried on a correspondence with the Protestants of Nismes, Lithuania, and other countries. 'It may be affirmed,' remarks one of the editors of Mosheim's History, 'that no prelate since the Reformation had so extensive a correspondence with the Protestants abroad, and none could have a more friendly one.'[2] His behaviour towards Nonconformists at home was in his later years less conciliatory, and the inconsistency is a blemish in his character. The case would probably have been different if any schemes for union or comprehension had still been under consideration. In the absence of some such incentive, his mind, liberal as it was by nature and general habit, was overborne by the persistent clamour that the Dissenters were bent upon overthrowing the National Church, and that concession had become for the time impossible.

. It remains to mention a letter,[3] written by Wake to Jablouski, which throws much additional light upon his correspondence with the Gallican doctors of the Sorbonne. Jablouski had submitted to him two questions : Did he think that propositions of union could be entertained between the Lutheran and Roman Churches ? or, Did he rather hold that all such negotiations were dangerous and delusive ? The Archbishop replied, that all projects as at present conceived of coming to terms with the Papacy were, he was certain, utterly visionary, and would be fraught with disaster, alike to the Reformed Churches and to the interests of truth. Such negotiations were certainly possible, but only on terms (which no Pope was likely to concede) of perfect equality. All claims to infallibility, all assumptions of supreme authority, must be surrendered. Then, and not till then, a treaty for peace might be advantageously opened. On most, and those the most important, points of Christian faith there would be agreement. On other matters, it would have to be considered

---

[1] July, 1718. Id. Ap. 3, Nos. 21, 2. Turretin was intimate with Archbishop Wake, as he was with many eminent men of different Christian communions. He was a man of much learning, wide sympathies, and great tact. An account of his labours and opinions may be found in a paper by H. B. Wilson in the *Oxford Essays* for 1857.

[2] Maclaine's edition of *Mosheim*, v. 143.

[3] May 22, 1719. Mosheim, App. 3, No. 25.

how far a mutual understanding could be arrived at, and whether there were any upon which a friendly toleration of differences would be practicable. 'We may indeed,' he added, ' labour for concord and union among all Christ's disciples, and welcome it when it can be obtained on just conditions; but unjust conditions must be resolutely declined. We must not sacrifice the interests of the future to more present advantages, nor truth to the desire of peace. God avert so great a calamity from the Reformed Churches.'

After the suppression of the Gallican liberties, the hostility between the Anglican and Roman Catholic Churches was for a long time wholly unbroken. The theological controversy had abated. Pamphlet no longer followed upon pamphlet, and folio upon folio, as when, a few years before, every writer in divinity had felt bound to contribute his quota of argument to the voluminous stock, and when Tillotson hardly preached a sermon without some homethrust at Popery. But the general fear and hatred of it long continued unmitigated. So long, particularly, as there was any apprehension of Jacobite disturbances, it always seemed possible that Romanism might yet return with a power of which none could guess the force. 'The heats,' remarks Whiston, 'arisen upon the late rebellion had but too much exasperated the British Protestants against the Papists.'[1] Additions were still made to the long list of penalties and disabilities attached to Popish recusancy ; and when, in 1778, a proposition was brought forward to abate them, it is well known what a storm of riot arose in Scotland and burst throughout England. In 1768, popular feeling at Bristol was outraged by the intelligence that preparations were being made 'for opening a public mass-house under the protection of the Duke of Norfolk.'[2] An indignation meeting was held under the presidency of the Bishop and the Mayor. The Prime Minister was appealed to against 'so contemptuous a defiance of all law and authority.' Thus a stop was put to the design ; and the Roman Catholics fell back upon their private house, glad to be allowed to meet there without further molestation.

A writer of the present day, speaking of the generation immediately preceding our own, has remarked with much

[1] Whiston's *Memoirs*, 1, 602.   [2] *Bishop Newton's Life*, 117.

force upon the contrast between the feeling then entertained towards Roman Catholicism and that which now exists. Hostility was then almost entirely unmixed with interest. 'To the vast majority of even well educated and travelled English people the Roman Church, as a living institution, was a totally unknown mystery. . . . It was looked upon as a thing of the past, so far as the religious life of Englishmen was concerned. It had gone by, and had its day, being a combination of formalism, superstition, ceremonialism and cruelty. . . . The possibility of her existing as a living spiritual power at our very doors hardly crossed people's minds. There was not even a suspicion abroad that she was to be recognised as a fair competitor for the allegiance of Christians, in the midst of Protestant rival sects.'[1] Such an attitude is obviously very different not only from the Protestantism of this age, but from that which was dominant at the opening of the eighteenth century. Present feeling, less violent, though scarcely less decided in its antagonism, is at all events more discriminating for the most part, better informed, and based on better grounds. A hundred, or a hundred and thirty years before, hostility was still combined with genuine alarm, often amounting to panic, and always sensitive and jealous. But by the middle of the eighteenth century, the estrangement of indifference, which regarded the Roman system as something nearly as far removed from English Christianity as Mahomedanism itself, had already begun. When fear subsided, so also did interest ; and the real gap became wider than ever. A few exceptional incidents moved a languid interest. Le Courayer, librarian of St. Geneviève at Paris, surprised either Church by his defence of English ordinations. Expelled from his monastery, he found a hospitable refuge in England, and received an University degree. An Oxford Doctor of Divinity who was also a monk of the Roman Catholic Church would have been a very notable phenomenon, had not Le Courayer been an outlaw from his own communion.[2] Some attention was attracted by the liberal ideas and proposed reforms of Benedict XIII. on his accession to the Papal Chair. Hearne writes in his *Diary*, how

---

[1] J. M. Capes, *To Rome and Back*, 1873.
[2] *Quarterly Review*, 6, 393.

news had come from Rome that the Pope was recommending not only to the inferior clergy, but also to the people, the reading of the Holy Scriptures in the vulgar tongue, and that he was meditating a new and improved translation. 'It is said, that he has also declared, that as customs and ceremonies are not matters of faith, he is willing the Church should lay aside part of her drapery, that the Reformed may no longer have a pretence of quarrelling with their ancient mother (as they call her at Rome). Nay, some have gone so far as to say that he has some design of calling a general council, and that thus by meeting the Protestants as it were half way, he is not without hopes of drawing all Christendom under one form of Church discipline. So that though he is a person of singular piety, he appears to be no bigot. This unexpected news has made so much noise in the world, that in the Protestant Courts of Europe, it is the common saying now that the Pope has turned Protestant.'[1] But after all, the interest excited was of a very faint and transient nature. The admiration thus expressed by the recluse Nonjuror found little echo in larger circles.

A more extensive movement, which made a greater impression upon English statesmen, and was of some importance in its bearings upon Roman Catholicism in this country, originated with Febronius, the assumed name of Nicolas von Hontheim, Bishop of Treves. It was a further development of the principles which had been put forward by the leaders of the Gallican cause, disputing the supremacy of the Pope, and strongly asserting the rights of National Churches. The Febronian system, as it was entitled, caused much anxiety at Rome. It was condemned in 1764 by Clement XIII., together with another scheme put forward by the same author for the reunion of Christendom. But it produced a considerable effect upon many cultivated minds on the Continent, especially in France and Spain ; and was welcomed by many English Roman Catholics as quite in accord with the traditions of their history. In 1774, when relief was first proposed for the Roman Catholics of Ireland, a question was put to the Sorbonne as to the nature and extent of the Papal authority in civil matters. In 1791, when the exten-

---

[1] *Hearne's Diary,* ii 217.

sion of this Act to England was being considered, the English
Roman Catholics, at Mr. Pitt's desire, laid similar queries
before the Universities of Paris, Louvain, Douai, Salamanca,
Alcala, and Valladolid. The answer was the same in either
case, condemning as heretical, and contrary to the very word
of God, the doctrine of the right of Popes to depose excommunicated princes. In a document signed by a large number
of Roman Catholic laymen, and presented to Parliament, the
doctrines condemned by the six universities were accordingly
disclaimed ' as dangerous to society, and totally repugnant to
political and civil liberty.' But (adds a modern Roman
Catholic writer), [1] this most obnoxious protestation, and the
oath consequent upon it, was at once condemned, upon communication with the Holy See. The rescript of the Cardinal
Prefect of Propaganda corrected certain misconceptions, but
' gave no sanction to the detestable opinions set forth with
such pomp and circumstance by the six universities as
Catholic doctrine.' A warm dispute ensued, not without
interest to the country at large, headed by the ' Catholic
Committee ' on the one hand, and three vicars apostolical on
the other. The Anglican, or Gallican, or Febronian theory—
whatever be the name under which the ancient controversy
is renewed—is in its ultimate consequences fatal to the Roman
unity. Rome may submit to inevitable circumstances, but
will always be on the watch not to admit a principle so fraught
with danger to her assumptions. But to Englishmen, and
particularly to English Churchmen, it was a dispute suggestive of reminiscences. The protestation of their Roman
Catholic countrymen, coming seasonably as it did at the eve
of at least a partial emancipation, was a serviceable reminder
of what might seem to have been sometimes forgotten, that
all were of one family, one race, one temper, with their forefathers who had fought so long against Papal encroachments
and won their spiritual liberties at the Reformation.

It might be thought that in the dull ebb-tide of spiritual
energies which set in soon after the beginning of the eighteenth century, and prevailed wherever the Methodist movement did not reach, Rome, with her strong organisation and

---

[1] E. S. Purcell, in Archbishop Manning's *Essays on Religion and Literature,*
series ii. 444.

her experienced Propaganda, had as great a field before her
as Wesley had,—that she would have made rapid advance in
spite of all disabilities,—and that, in consequence, the Protestant fears, which had been subsiding into indifference,
would have arisen again in full force. But Rome shared in
the strange religious apathy which was dominant not in
England only, but the Continent. Her writers generally acknowledge the greater part of the eighteenth century to have
been a period of comparative inactivity,[1] broken at last only
by the violent stimulus of the Revolution. Many thought
that Romanism continued to gain ground in England, and some
cried out that still stricter laws were needed to suppress the
Papists. It is doubtful, however, whether advances in some
quarters were not more than balanced by losses elsewhere. As
the century advanced, Rome gradually ceased to be dreaded as
a subtle pervading power, full of mysterious activity, whose
force might be felt most severely at the very moment when
least preparation had been made to meet it. In 1761, Secker
spoke of Romanism as ' harbouring its strength and waiting,' [2]
but he no longer dwelt, as in 1738, on ' the zeal and artifice of
its proselytism.' [3] Later still, fear was sometimes replaced by
a confidence no less excessive. 'It is impossible,' said Mr.
Wyndham in the House of Commons, 1791, ' to deem them
(the Roman Catholics) formidable at the present period,
when the power of the Pope is considered as a mere spectre,
capable of frightening only in the dark, and vanishing before
the light of reason and knowledge.' [4]

Until the last decade of the century, Roman Catholics
were rarely spoken of in any other spirit than as the dreaded
enemies of Protestantism. There was very little recognition
of their being far more nearly united to us by the tie of a
common Christianity, than separated by the differences in it.
A man who was not a professed sceptic needed to be both
more unprejudiced and more courageous than his neighbours,
to speak of Roman Catholics with tolerable charity. In this,
as in many other points, Bishop Berkeley was superior to
his age. He ventured to propose that Roman Catholics

---

[1] *Quarterly Review.* 89, 475.
[2] ' Oratio coram Syn. Prov. Cant.,' *Works*, 354.
[3] Primary Charge, *Works*, 19.　　　[4] *Quarterly Review*, 89, 475.

should be admitted to the Dublin College without being
obliged to attend chapel or divinity lectures.[1]   He could
speak of such an institution as Monasticism in a discriminative
tone which was then exceedingly uncommon.   The passage
is worth quoting. 'It seems very expedient (he wrote) that
the world should have, among the many formed for action,
some also formed for contemplation, the influence whereof
might be general and extend to others. . . . To assist the
λύσις and φυγή of the soul by meditation was a noble purpose
even in the eyes of Pagan philosophy.   How much more so
in the eyes of Christians, whose philosophy is above all
others the most sublime, and the most calculated to wean
our thoughts from things carnal, and raise them above things
terrestrial!   That the contemplative and ascetic life may be
greatly promoted by living in community and by rules, I
freely admit. . . . I should like a convent without a vow, or
perpetual obligation.   Doubtless a college or a monastery
(not a resource for younger brothers, not a nursery for lazi-
ness, ignorance, and superstition), receiving only grown persons
of approved piety, learning, and a contemplative turn, would
be a great means of improving the Divine philosophy, and
brightening up the face of religion in our Church.'[2]   But
Berkeley was always too large-hearted to see good in one
system only of Christianity, or in one part of Christendom.
At the end of the same letter from which the above extract
is taken, 'I think it,' he says, 'a peculiar blessing to have
been educated in the Church of England.   My prayer, nevertheless, and trust is, not that I shall live and die in this or
that Church, but in the true Church.'   In Ireland he wisely
accepted the fact that the Roman Catholic priests had the
heart of the people, and shaped his conduct accordingly.
His 'Word to the Wise' was an appeal addressed in 1749
to the priests, exhorting them to use their influence to promote industry and self-reliance among their congregations.
This sort of Episcopal charge to the clergy of another Communion was received, it is said, with a no less cordial feeling
than that in which it was written.[3]

---

[1] *Berkeley's Life and Works*, ed. A. C. Fraser, iv. 243.
[2] Letter to Sir J. James, June, 1741. Id. 4, 276.
[3] *Life and Works*, iv. 321.

Dr. Johnson, a man of a very different order of mind, may be mentioned as another who joined a devoted attachment to the Church of England with a candid and kindly spirit towards Roman Catholics. Perhaps his respect for authority, and the tinge of superstition in his temperament, predisposed him to sympathy. In any case, his masculine intellect brushed away with scorn the prejudices, exaggerations, and misconstructions which beset popular ideas upon the subject. He took pleasure in dilating upon the substantial unity that subsisted between them and denominations which, in externals, were separated from them by a very wide interval. 'There is a prodigious difference,' he would say, 'between the external form of one of your Presbyterian Churches in Scotland, and a Church in Italy ; yet the doctrine taught is essentially the same.'[1]

Many of the speeches made in favour of relief, at the time of the Irish and English Emancipation Acts, were couched in terms which betoken a marked departure from the bitterness of tone which had long been customary. When the French Revolution broke out, the reaction became, for an interval, in many quarters far stronger still. In the presence of anti-Christian principles exultingly avowed, and triumphantly defiant, it seemed to many Christians that minor differences, which had seemed great before, dwindled almost into insignificance before the light of their common faith. Moreover, there was a widespread feeling of deep sympathy with the wrongs and sufferings of the proscribed clergy. 'Scruples about external forms,' said Bishop Horsley before the House of Lords, 'and differences of opinion upon controvertible points, cannot but take place among the best Christians, and dissolve not the fraternal tie ; none, indeed, at this season are more entitled to our offices of love than those with whom the difference is wide in points of doctrine, discipline, and external rites,—those venerable exiles, the prelates and clergy of the fallen Church of France, endeared to us by the edifying example they exhibit of patient suffering for conscience sake.'[2] Horsley's words were far from meeting with universal approval. Many who entirely agreed with

[1] Boswell's *Johnson*, ii. 154, 104.
[2] Sermon, January 30, 1793.

him, thought it doubtful whether he would have spoken with
equal cordiality, had the sufferers been Huguenots instead of
Gallican clergy.[1] There were some fanatics, Hannah More tells
us, who said it was a sin to oppose God's vengeance against
Popery, and succour the priests who it was His will should
starve.[2] And real sympathy, even while the occasion of it
lasted, was very often, as may well be imagined, mixed with
feelings of apprehension. These refugees might be only too
grateful. 'Principles so deeply rooted as theirs, and zeal so fervent, cannot be inactive.'[3] Thinking that salvation was obtain-
able only in their own Church, was it not likely they would use
their utmost art to extend this first of blessings to those who
had so hospitably protected them? Thus interest was
blended with anxiety in the nation which gave welcome to
the emigrants. But interest there certainly was, so general
and strong as to warrant De Maistre in saying that their reception formed an epoch in the general history of the Church.[4]
There was a friendliness in it which had long been wanting,
a promise, as it seemed to him, of peace, which may possibly
be realised in the future. At the least, it did something
towards removing the bitterness of prejudice. It was a new
thing, if the majority of cultivated Englishmen could henceforth express themselves towards Rome, not in the virulent
declamation that had been usual, but in the moderate language
of Edmund Burke. 'Violently condemning neither the
Greek nor the Armenian, nor, since heats are subsided, the
Roman system of religion, we prefer the Protestant.'[5]

The relations of the Church of England with other
Reformed bodies abroad and at home had been, since
James II.'s time, a question of high importance. Burnet
justly remarks of the year 1685, that it was one of the most
critical periods in the whole history of Protestantism. 'In
February a king of England declared himself a Papist. In
June, Charles the Elector Palatine dying without issue, the
Electoral dignity went to the house of Newburgh, a most

---

[1] Channing's *Correspondence*, 40.
[2] Roberts' *Life of H. More*, i. 531.
[3] 'Considerations on the State of Religion,' &c. 1801, 50.
[4] De Maistre, *Consid. sur la Fr.* 30.
[5] E. Burke, *Reflections on the Revolution.*

bigoted Popish family. In October, the King of France recalled and vacated the Edict of Nantes. And in December, the Duke of Savoy, being brought to it not only by the persuasion, but even by the threatenings of the court of France, recalled the edict that his father had granted to the Vaudois.'[1] It cannot be said that the crisis was an unexpected one. The excited controversy which was being waged among theologians was but one sign of the general uneasiness that had been prevailing. 'The world,' writes one anonymous author in 1682, 'is filled with discourses about the Protestant religion and the professors of it; and not without cause.'[2] 'Who,' says another, 'can hold his peace when the Church, our mother, hath the Popish knife just at her throat?'[3] But the reverses of the Reformed faith abroad greatly increased the ferment, and began to kindle Protestant feeling into a state of enthusiastic fervour. When at last, in the next reign, war was proclaimed with Louis XIV., it was everywhere recognised as a great religious struggle, in which England had assumed her place as the champion of the Protestant interest.

From the very beginning of the Reformation it had been a vexed question how far the cause of the Reformed Church of England could be identified with that of other communions which had cast off the yoke of Rome. In dealing with this problem, a broad distinction had generally been made between Nonconformists at home and Protestant communities abroad. The relation of the English Church to Nonconformity may accordingly be considered separately. So long as it was a question of communion, more or less intimate, with foreign Churches, the intercourse was at all events not embarrassed with any difficulties about schism. The preface to the Book of Common Prayer had expressly declared that 'In these our doings we condemn no other nations, nor prescribe anything but to our own people only. For we think it convenient that every country should use such ceremonies as they shall think best to the setting forth of God's honour and glory.' It was therefore acknowledged with very toler-

---

[1] Burnet's *Life and Works*, 420.
[2] *State and Fate of the Protestant Religion*, 1682, 3.
[3] *Endeavour for Peace*, &c. 1680, 15.

able unanimity that friendly relationship with Protestant Churches on the Continent was by no means inconsistent with very considerable differences of custom and opinion. The degree of assumed error which disqualified a religious body from being considered a lawful Christian Church, was a point upon which some formed a far stricter judgment than others, and some were in favour of a much closer intercourse than others thought desirable. But the sentiments of most moderate men on the matter may fairly be expressed in the words of William Wall, a writer who was certainly not regarded by the Churchmen of the day as a Latitudinarian. ' That must indeed be a pure Church,' he said, 'whose orders and rules have no fault or imperfection at all ; and yet that must be a woful Church with which a good Christian may not communicate, or under whose doctrine and discipline he may not by a godly diligence work out his salvation. Of the first sort there is none in the world. And, as I hope, no Protestant National Church of the latter sort : none, I mean, with which a good Christian may not communicate, provided they will admit him without requiring his declared assent to all their tenets.'[1] He argued that as in primitive times, Christians of Africa, if they came to Greece, complied with the Grecian usages and ceremonies, although they might like their own the best, or, if they liked the Grecian the best, still conformed to their own on returning to their native country, so it might well be now in the case of all Churches which ' neither overthrow the foundations of Christian faith nor mix any idolatry in their worship.' Members, for instance, of the Church of Denmark would have no right to separate from their fellow-members on the plea that they liked the ways of the Church of England better.

It may be said that there is a rather Erastian tone in the latter part of the passage here referred to. But men of all parties in the Church of England were ever inclined to allow great weight to the voice of constituted authority in matters which did not seem to them to touch the very life and sub-stance of religion. Without taking this into consideration, it is impossible to form a right view of the comparative tender-ness with which Churchmen passed over what they considered

[1] Wall, *History of Infant Baptism*, part ii. chap. ii. § 3.

to be defects in reformed systems abroad which they condemned with much severity among Nonconformists at home.

The relations, however, of England with foreign Protestant
bodies, though not exactly unfriendly, have been characterised
by a good deal of reserve. The kinship has been acknowledged, and the right of difference allowed ; but belief in the
great superiority of English uses, Nonconformist difficulties,
and a certain amount of jealousy and intolerance, had always
checked the advances which were sometimes made to a more
cordial intimacy. In Henry VIII.'s time, in 1533, and again
in 1535, overtures were made for a Fœdus Evangelicum, a
league of the great reforming nations.[1] The differences between the German and the English Protestants were at that
time very great, not only in details of discipline and government, but in the general spirit in which the Reformation in
the two countries was being conducted. But an alliance of
the kind contemplated would perhaps have been carried out
had it not been for the bigotry which insisted upon signature
of the Augsburg Confession. Queen Elizabeth was at one
time inclined to join on behalf of England the Smalcaldic
League of German Protestants, but the same obstacle intervened.[2] Cromwell is said to have cherished a great project
of establishing a permanent Protestant Council, in which all
the principal Reformed communities in Europe, and in the
East and West Indies, would be represented under the name
of provinces, and designs for the promotion of religion advanced and furthered in all parts of the world.[3] Such projects
never had any important results. Statesmen, as well as
theologians, often felt the need of strengthening the whole
Protestant body by an organised harmony among its several
members, something akin to that which gives the Roman
Catholic Church so imposing an aspect of general unity.
The idea was perhaps essentially impracticable, as requiring
for its accomplishment a closer uniformity of thought and
feeling than was either possible or desirable among Churches
whose greatest conquest had been a liberty of thinking. As
between England and Germany, one great impediment to a

[1] Froude's *History of England*, ii. 405.
[2] Hallam's *Constitutional History*, i. 172, note.
[3] Burnet's *History of His Own Times*, 51.

cordial understanding arose out of the differences between Lutheran and Reformed. So long as the English Church was under the guidance of Cranmer and Ridley, it was not clear to which of these two parties it most nearly approximated. In the reign of Edward VI. the Calvinistic element gained ground—a tendency as much resented by the one party abroad as it was welcomed by the other. The English clergymen who found a refuge in the Swiss and German cities were treated with marked neglect by the Lutherans, but received with great hospitality by the Calvinists.[1] At a later period, when Presbyterianism had for the time gained strong ground in England, the attitude had become somewhat reversed. The Reformed or Calvinist section of German Protestants sided chiefly with the Presbyterians; the Lutherans with the English Churchmen.[2] In a word, notwithstanding all professions of more liberal sentiment, the hankering after an impossible uniformity was, on either side of the Channel, too strong to permit of cordial union or substantial unity. It was often admitted in theory, but not often in practice, that the principles of the Reformation must be left to work out with differences and modifications according to the varying circumstances of the countries in which they were adopted. Bucer and Peter Martyr, Calvin and Bullinger, made it almost a personal grievance that the English retained much which they themselves had cast aside.[3] Laud exhibited the same spirit in a more oppressive form when he insisted that, in spite of the guarantees given by Elizabeth and James I., no foreign Protestants should remain in England who would not conform to the established liturgy.[4]

No doubt the differences between the Reformed Churches of England and the Continent were very considerable. Yet, with the one discreditable exception just referred to, there had been much comity and friendliness in all personal relations between their respective members; and the absence of sympathy on many points of doctrine and discipline was not

---

[1] Hallam's *Constitutional History*, i. 171.
[2] *Life of Archbishop Sharp*, vol. ii. 186, App. 2.
[3] Hallam's *Constitutional History*, i. 102.
[4] Perry, G.G., *History of the Church of England*, i. 453.

so great as to preclude the possibility of closer union and common action in any crisis of danger. Before the end of the seventeenth century such a crisis seemed, in the opinion of many, to have arrived. The Protestant interest throughout Europe was in real peril. In England there was as much anxiety on the subject as was compatible with a period which was certainly not characterised by much moral purpose or deep feeling. The people as a mass were not just then very much in earnest about anything, but still they cared very really about their Protestantism. They were not assured of its security even within their own coasts ; they knew that it was in jeopardy on the Continent. National prejudices against France added warmth to the indignation excited by the oppressions to which the Protestant subjects of the great monarch had been subjected. National pride readily combined with nobler impulses to create an enthusiasm for the idea that England was the champion of the whole Protestant cause.

There is nothing which tends to promote so kindly a feeling towards its objects as self-denying benevolence. This had been elicited in a very remarkable degree towards the refugees who found a shelter here after the revocation of the Edict of Nantes. Londoners beheld with a sort of humorous dismay the crowd of immigrants who came to settle among them.

> Hither for God's sake and their own they fled ;
> Some for religion came, and some for bread.
> Four hundred thousand wooden pair of shoes,
> Who, God be thanked, had nothing left to lose,
> To heaven's great praise, did for religion fly,
> To make us starve our poor in charity.[1]

But these poverty-stricken exiles were received with warm-hearted sympathy. No previous brief had ever brought in such large sums as those which throughout the kingdom were subscribed for their relief ; nor, if the increase of wealth be taken into account, has there been any greater display of munificence in our own times.[2] Churchmen of all views

---

[1] De Foe's *True-born Englishman* (Ed. Chalmers' series), vol. xx. 19.
[2] *Hallam Constitutional History*, iii. 55.

came generously forward. If here and there a doubt was raised whether these demonstrations of friendliness might not imply a greater approval of their opinions than really existed, compassion for sufferers who were not fellow-Christians only, but fellow-Protestants, quickly overpowered all such hesitation. Bishop Ken behaved in 1686 with all his accustomed generosity and boldness. In contravention of the King's orders, who had desired that the brief should be simply read in churches without any sermon on the subject, he ventured in the Royal Chapel to set forth in affecting language the sufferings they had gone through, and to exhort his hearers to hold, with a like unswerving constancy, to the Protestant faith. He issued a pastoral entreating his clergy to do the utmost in their power for ' Christian strangers, whose distress is in all respects worthy of our tenderest commiseration.' For his own part he set a noble example of liberality in the gift of a great part of 4000*l.* which had lately come into his possession.[1] We are told of Rainbow, Bishop of Carlisle, that in a similar spirit he gave to French Protestants large sums, and bore ' his share with other bishops in yearly pensions' to some of them.[2]

The burst of general sympathy evoked in favour of the French refugees happened just at a time when Churchmen of all views were showing a more or less hearty desire that the Church of England might be strengthened by the adhesion of many who had hitherto dissented from it. Sancroft was as yet at one with Tillotson in desiring to carry out a Comprehension Bill, and was asking Dissenters to join with him ' in prayer for an universal blessed union of all Reformed Churches at home and abroad.'[3] Undoubtedly there was a short interval, just before the Nonjuring secession, in which the minds not only of the so-called Latitudinarians, but of many eminent High Churchmen, were strongly disposed to make large concessions for the sake of unity, and from a desire of seeing England definitely at the head of the Protestant cause alike in England and on the Continent. They could not but agree with the words of Samuel Johnson—as good and brave a

---

[1] *Life of Bishop Ken*, by a Layman, 319–27.
[2] *Life of Rainbow*, 1688. Quoted in id. 326.
[3] Fleetwood's *Works*, 483.

man as the great successor to his name—that 'there could
not be a more blessed work than to reconcile Protestants
with Protestants.'[1] But the opportunity of successfully
carrying into practice these aspirations soon passed away.
It was utterly impossible that a great project of Church union
could come to any satisfactory issue amid the bitter party
feelings which were inflamed by the Revolution. Indeed, had
it been otherwise, there was not as yet (nor is there indeed
even in our own day) any clear conception, generally diffused,
of the principles upon which union without compromise is
attainable. When it became evident that there could be no
change in the relations of the English Church towards Nonconformity, interest in foreign Protestantism began to be
much less universal than it had been. The clergy especially
were afraid—and there was justification for their alarm—that
some of the oldest and most characteristic features of their
Church were in danger of being swept away. They had no
wish to see in England a form of Protestantism nearly akin
to that which existed in Holland. But there was a strong
party in favour of changes which might have some such effect.
The King, even under the new constitution, was still a power
in the Church, and it was well known that the forms of the
Church of England had no particular favour in his eyes.
And therefore the Lower House of Convocation, representing,
no doubt, the views of a majority of the clergy, while they
professed, in 1689, that 'the interest of all the Protestant
Churches was dear to them,' were anxious to make it very
clear that they owned no close union with them.[2] There was
a perplexity in the mode of expression which thoroughly
reflected a genuine difficulty. As even the Highest Churchmen, at the opening of the eighteenth century, were vehemently Protestant, afraid of Rome, and exceedingly anxious
to resist her with all their power, they could not help sharing
to some extent in the general wish to make common cause
with the Protestants abroad. On the other hand, there was
much to repel anything like close intercourse. The points of
difference were very marked. The English Church had
retained Episcopacy. There was no party in the Church
which did not highly value it ; a section of High Churchmen

[1] Birch's 'Life of Tillotson,'—*Works,* i. xciv.   [2] Id. cxxxv.

reckoned it one of the essential notes of a true Church, and unchurched all communions that rejected it.   The foreign Reformers, on the other hand, not, in some cases, without reluctance, and from force of circumstances, had discarded bishops.   English Churchmen, again, almost universally paid great deference to the authority of the primitive fathers and early councils.   The Reformed Churches abroad, under the leading of Daillé and others, no less generally depreciated them.[1]   Nor could it be forgotten that the sympathies of those Churches had been with the Puritans during the Civil Wars, and that in tone of thought and mode of worship they bore, for the most part, a closer resemblance to English Non-conformity than to the English Church.   Lastly, the Pro-testants of France and Switzerland were chiefly Calvinists, while in the Church of England Calvinism had for some length of time been rapidly declining.   The bond of union had need to be strong, and the necessity of it keenly felt, if it was to prevail over the influences which tended to keep the English and foreign Reformed Churches apart.

Thus, at the beginning of the eighteenth century, while there was a very general wish that the English Church should take its place at the head of a movement which would aim at strengthening and consolidating the Protestant cause throughout Europe, there was much doubt how far such a project could be carried out consistently with the spirit and principles of the Church.   Limborch, a professor of divinity at Amsterdam, dedicated one of his works in 1692 to Archbishop Tillotson as 'the common spiritual father of all Protestants who was placed at the head of the Church of England, the most eminent among the Reformed, and who was on that account in some measure the defender of the Reformed Churches in general.'[2]   Earl Stanhope, advocating in 1718 a bill for 'strengthening the Protestant interest,' looked forward to a time in which 'the Archbishop of Can-terbury would become the Patriarch of all the Protestant clergy.'[3]   Bishop Compton, in the spirit of Chillingworth and Stillingfleet, entered into correspondence in 1680 with

[1] J. J. Blunt's *Early Fathers*, 20.
[2] Birch's 'Life of Tillotson,'—*Works*, i. cxciii.
[3] Mahon's *History of England*, chap. ix.

he divines of Leyden and Charentun, and in 1707 with
he University of Geneva. In addition to the friendly feeling
vhich such intercourse was likely to promote, he hoped also
hat the expressions which it elicited of respect and esteem
or the English Church might both abate the prejudices of
Dissenters, and tend to general concord. George I., in his
address to the Nonconformist deputies, spoke of the English
Church, almost in the words used by William III., as ' Chief
of the Protestant Churches,' and 'unquestionably the main
support and bulwark of the Protestant interest ;'[1] and he
vas addressed by them as 'the common father of all Protestants,' the 'head of the Protestant, as the Emperor of
Germany was the head of the Popish interest.'[2] The correspondence of Archbishop Wake with the Protestants of
Holland, Poland, France, and Switzerland, has been already
referred to in connection with his communication with the
Gallican Church.

The hopes of High Churchmen in this direction were
based chiefly on the anticipation that the reformed churches
abroad might perhaps be induced to restore Episcopacy.
It was with this view that Dodwell wrote his ' Paraenesis to
Foreigners' in 1704. A year or two afterwards, events
occurred in Prussia which made it seem likely that in that
country the desired change would very speedily be made.
Some passing reference has already been made to it in another
chapter of this work. Frederick I., at his coronation in
1700, had given the title of bishop to two of his clergy—one
a Lutheran, the other Reformed. The former died soon
after ; but the latter, Dr. Ursinus, willingly co-operated with
the King in a scheme for uniting the two communions on a
basis of mutual assimilation to the Church of England.
Ernestus Jablouski, his chaplain, a superintendent of the
Protestant Church in Poland, zealously promoted the project.
He had once been strongly prejudiced against the English
Church ; but his views on this point had altered during a
visit to England, and he was now an admirer of it. By the
advice of Ursinus and Jablouski, the King now caused the
English Liturgy to be translated into German. This was
done at Frankfort on the Oder, where the English Church

[1] Calamy's *Life and Times*, ii. 299. [2] Id. ii. 317,

had many friends among the professors. Frederick then directed Ursinus to consult further with the Archbishop of Canterbury, and suggested that, if the plan was encouraged in England, the Liturgy should be introduced into the King's Chapel and the Cathedral Church on the 1st Sunday in Advent, 1706. It was to be left optional to other Churches to follow the example. After debate in the King's consistory, letters and copies of the version were sent to the Queen of England and to Archbishop Wake. The former returned her thanks, but the primate appeared not to have received the communication ; and the King, offended at the apparent slackness, allowed the matter to drop. Early, however, in 1709, communications were reopened. On January 14 of that year, the following entry occurs in Thoresby's ' Diary : ' ' At the excellent Bishop of Ely's [Moore]. Met the obliging R. Hales, Esq., to whose pious endeavour the good providence of God has given admirable success in reconciling the Reformed Churches abroad [Calvinists and Lutherans] one to another (so that they not only frequently meet together, but some of them join in the Sacrament), and both of them to the Church of England ; so that in many places they are willing to admit of Episcopacy, as I am creditably informed.'[1] In 1710 Frederick requested certain Prussian divines to put down in writing their several ideas upon some practical scheme of worship and discipline. Jablouski accordingly handed to Baron Prinz, President of the Berlin Council of Ecclesiastical Affairs, a document in which he warmly recommended the services and usages of the English Church. ' A conformity,' he said, ' of the Prussian with the English Church would be very agreeable in England. This is so much the more credible, for that the English Church has now at the helm so many wise and prudent men who are very sensible that the strength of the whole Protestant body consists in the harmony and firm union of its several members.' After speaking of the correspondence which had always been more or less kept up between the Reformed Churches of England and the Continent, ' Forasmuch,' he adds, ' as the English liturgy is for the most part taken from the best antiquity, not only *quoad formam, sed quoad materiam et ipsa verba,* and

---

[1] Ralph Thoresby, *Diary*, ii. 22.

is composed with so much simplicity as well as majesty, that on account of the former it may be understood by the meanest, and on account of the latter may edify and instruct the greatest capacity, therefore, it would no doubt be incomparably the shortest way to a conformity to go through the English liturgy, and see what part of it would be edifying and useful among us.' He next argues for a well-regulated Episcopacy, and continues : ' As thus, by means of this conformity, the Prussian and the English Churches shall be perfectly united, they both may join to heal the wounds of the rest of the Protestants. The Church of England, which is everywhere held in great veneration among the Lutherans, would be a proper instrument to unite the Protestants on this side the sea. On the other side, our most gracious sovereign might very gratefully and effectually employ his interest in England to unite the Nonconformists with the Established Church. His Majesty is in the highest veneration both with the Church and nation, by reason of the many proofs he has given of his great piety and patriot zeal for common welfare ; and the Nonconformists have likewise the highest trust and confidence in his Majesty. . . . There is no potentate upon earth who has better opportunities of going through with such a work than his Majesty, who, if he would show how justly he carries the name of *Friede-reich* and exert himself so as to make the effects of it felt, not only in Germany, by uniting the Protestants there, but even as far as Great Britain, by healing their divisions, the merit of it towards the Church of Christ would exceed comparison.' He thought it right to add that he did not believe that the projected conformity would give umbrage to Tories, though it might be acceptable to the Whigs. He imagined that only a section of the Tory party—'Jacobites and ill-affected persons'—would be indisposed to it. Jablouski's recommendations were translated into English, and attracted considerable attention both in England and Prussia. They were promoted by many persons of eminence, especially by Archbishop Sharp, Bishop Smalridge (who thought 'the honour of our own Church and the edification of others much interested in the scheme,') Bishop Robinson and Lord Raby, ambassador at Berlin. Secretary St. John, afterwards Lord

Bolingbroke, wrote to Raby in behalf of this 'laudable design,' informing him that the Queen was 'ready to give all possible encouragement to that excellent work,' and that if previous overtures had received a cold reception, yet that the clergy generally were zealous in the cause. Bonel, the Prussian king's minister in London, wrote in 1711 to Frederick that he thought the service of the Church of England was 'the most perfect, perhaps, that is among Protestants,' that conformity between the Prussian and English Churches would be received with great joy in England, but that the conformity desired related more to Church government than to any ritual or liturgy, and that Episcopacy was generally looked upon as the only apostolical and true ecclesiastical form of government. Later in the year, Jablouski placed in the hands of Baron Prinz his more matured 'Project for introducing Episcopacy into the King of Prussia's dominions.' Leibnitz engaged to interest the Electress of Hanover in the proposal. He was afraid, however, that the thirty-nine articles would be considered 'a little too much Geneva stamp' at Berlin. The negotiations continued, but the interest of the King had slackened; the proceedings of the Collegium Charitativum at Berlin, which sat under the presidency of Bishop Ursinus, were somewhat discredited by the wilder schemes started by Winkler, one of its chief members; the grave political questions debated at Utrecht diverted attention from ecclesiastical matters; Archbishop Sharp, who had taken an active part in the correspondence, became infirm; and the conferences were finally brought to a termination by the death, early in 1713, of Frederick I.[1] Frederick William's rough and contracted mind was far too much absorbed in the care of his giant regiment, and in the amassing of treasure, to feel the slightest concern in matters so entirely uncongenial to his temper as plans for the advancement of Church unity.

With the earlier years of the century all ideas of a closer relationship between English and foreign Protestantism than had existed heretofore passed away. The name of Protestant was still as cherished in popular feeling as ever it had been; but soon after the beginning of the Georgian period

---

[1] The full history of this correspondence is given in the *Life of Archbishop Sharp*, ed. Newcomb, i. 410–49.

ttle was heard, as compared with what lately had been the
ιse, of the Protestant cause or the Protestant interest. In
uth, when minds were no longer intent upon immediate
angers, the bond was severed which had begun to keep to-
ether, notwithstanding all differences, the Reformed Churches
ι England and on the Continent. The intercourse between
ιem had derived almost all its importance as embodying the
lea of a defensive league. A few leading spirits on either
de had been animated by those larger aspirations after
hristian unity which Grotius, Episcopius, Limborch, and
ther principal leaders of the Arminian theology had done so
ιuch to promote. But self-defence against aggressive
:omanism had been the main support of all projects of
ɔmbination. In the eighteenth century there was plenty
f the monotonous indifferentism which bears a dreary super-
cial resemblance to unity, but there was very little in the
revalent tone of thought which was adapted to encourage
·s genuine growth. And even if it had been otherwise—if
ιe National Church had ever so much widened and deepened
·s hold in England, and a sound, substantial unity had gained
round, such as gains strength out of the very differences
·hich it contains—insular feeling would still, in all proba-
ility, have been too exclusive or uninformed to care much,
·hen outward pressure was removed, for ties of sympathy
·hich should extend beyond the Channel and include French-
ιen or Germans within their hold. Quite early in the century
·e find Fleetwood [1] and Calamy [2] complaining of a growing
ιdifference towards Protestants abroad. A generation later
ιis indifference had become more general. Parliamentary
rants to 'poor French Protestant refugee clergy' and 'poor
·rench Protestant laity' were made in the annual votes of
ιpply almost up to the present reign,[3] but these were only
:ems in the public charity; they no longer bore any signi-
cance.

In 1751 an Act was brought forward for the general
aturalisation of foreign Protestants resident in England.
Iuch interest had been felt in a similar Bill which had come
efore the House in 1709. But the promoters of the earlier

---

[1] *Works*, 368.   [2] *Life and Times*, ii. 368, 482.
[3] *Life of Ken*, by a Layman, 330.

measure had been chiefly animated by the sense of close religious affinity in those to whom the privilege was offered; and those who resisted it did so from a fear that it might tend to changes in the English Church of which they disapproved. At the later period these sympathies and these fears, so far as they existed at all, were wholly subordinate to other influences. The Bill was supported on the ground of the drain upon the population which had resulted from the late war; it was vehemently resisted from a fear that it would unduly encourage emigration, and have an unfavourable effect upon English labour.[1] Considerations less secular than these had little weight. Religious life was circulating but feebly in the Church and country generally; it had no surplus energy to spare for sisterly interest in other communions outside the national borders.

The remarks that have been made in this chapter upon the relations of the English Church in the eighteenth century, especially in its earlier years, towards Rome on the one hand and the foreign Reformed Churches on the other, began with a reference to those principles of Church comprehensiveness which, however imperfectly understood, lay very near the heart of many distinguished Churchmen. But all who longed to see the Church of England acting in the free and generous spirit of a great national Church were well aware that there was a wider and more important field at home for the exercise of those principles. It was one, however, in which their course seemed far less plain. Many who were very willing to acknowledge that wide differences of opinion or practice constituted no insuperable bar to a close friendly intercourse between Churches of different countries, regarded those same variations in quite another light when considered as occasions of schism among separatists at home. Archbishop Sharp, for example, willingly communicated with congregations of foreign Protestants, wherever he might be travelling on the Continent, but could discuss no terms of conciliation with English Dissenters which were not based upon a relinquishment of Nonconformity. Liberty of opinion was not to be confused with needless infractions of Church unity.

A German writer has observed that in the British Islands

---

[1] Mahon's *History of England*, chap. xxxi.

heterodoxy has commonly assumed the form of schism, the collision in the world of practice being greater than in the world of thought; and that in the seventeenth century especially far more importance was attached in the Anglican Church to submission to Church order than to doctrinal orthodoxy. 'Even Laud,' he adds, 'declared peaceable dissent in certain non-fundamental articles allowable, while Potter required only the substance of the Christian religion for the existence of the Church—nay, called the apostolic symbol a sufficient catalogue of fundamental articles.'[1] Examples to the same effect might be multiplied almost indefinitely. Of course there has always been, in every section of the Church, a numerous body who have held almost as strict and limited ideas upon the opinions properly consistent with membership in it as the most exclusive denominationalists. There have always been even within the English Church 'sectaries, who judge and talk and live as if the world were no bigger than their synagogues and sects;'[2] Donatists, who would circumscribe the Church within their own narrow pale; Ephraims,[3] who 'dwell in a wilderness alone' by themselves. And there have always been Churchmen of another stamp from these, men of a higher culture and a wiser modesty, who are disturbed nevertheless at the wide comprehensiveness of the National Church,—who fear lest the interests of truth should suffer by the implied acknowledgment that their Church allows impartially many interpretations of it,—who would think it better that Church formularies should be defined more precisely, and that those who could not accord with their restricted sense should serve God in peace outside its borders. But such opinions, however moderately expressed, are wholly alien to the true spirit and history of the Reformed Church of England. Its general teaching has ever been that common worship is the truest bond of union. The blessedness of united worship is far more prominent in the Prayer Book than any close uniformity of belief on points in which Christians differ. No doubt there are a few detached expressions in the liturgy which sound to many too much like the

---

[1] Dorner's *History of Protestant Theology,* ii. 63.

[2] Baxter,—*Works,* vol. xv. 176.

[3] Matthew Arnold, *Culture and Anarchy,* liv.

Shibboleths of hot controversies. Yet, however much it might be desired that these could be exchanged for other words less apt to give offence, but equally or more devotional, it must always be remembered that the established usage of many generations has bestowed even upon such occasional phrases a breadth of meaning which they may not have had originally. Words which for three or four hundred years have been used in solemn acts of devotion by men of almost every shade of Christian opinion, and to which High, Low, and Broad Churchmen, in all their many varieties, have been avowedly or tacitly authorised to attach the constructions most agreeable to their views, may well be weighed less critically and scrupulously than newly minted terms not yet established in general usage. To use the words of William Wall, 'suppose that there be some particular collects or prayers, or clauses of prayers, which a man thinks to contain a mistake in them. May he not join with his brethren in the main and omit the adding of Amen to those particular clauses, especially since no man requires of him to declare his approbation of the whole and every part ? Is not this more Christianlike than to fly to that dreadful extremity of separation and total disowning for a disputable point, which may possibly be his own mistake ? ' [1] A person does not forsake the psalms because he dislikes the imprecatory ones.[2]

Sherlock, writing in 1681, was still able to say with perfect truth, 'It was never till of late days thought lawful to separate from a lawful communion, though, as the state of the Church is in this world, it were subject to some defects.'[3] Nonconformity had not even then become an established fact, to be accepted and made the best of. No one denied that secession was not justifiable only, but a duty, where communion could not be maintained without sin ; but there were very few who maintained the right and propriety of separation for any but the gravest causes. The moderate Dissenters were uncomfortable in their position, and, if their scruples had been respected, would gladly have returned into

---

[1] W. Wall, *History of Infant Baptism*, part ii. chap. xi. § 4. *Principles of the Reformation concerning Church Communion*, 1704, 202.

[2] W. Law, ' Collection of Letters,'—Tighe's *Extracts*, 68.

[3] Sherlock *On Public Worship*, chap. iii. § 1.

the National Church. An Act of Comprehension drawn up in James II.'s reign, in a statesmanlike spirit and with that feeling of respect which a Christian Church ought to feel for all reasonable scruples, would almost certainly have brought over two-thirds of the Dissenters of the time. The more violent Dissenters, on the other hand, who would entertain no ideas of reconciliation, defended themselves against the charge of schism on the ground that they considered the worship and government of the Church of England unlawful, idolatrous, and anti-Christian—that they could not, in fact, communicate with it without sin.

In Tudor times Nonconformity had been generally regarded as a transient malady.[1] It was at one time confidently expected that, when the first ferment of change had passed away, the National Church, in its reformed condition, would eventually more than fill the room it had occupied before the yoke of Rome had yet been cast off. The Lollards and Wycliffites who had disturbed its unity would be incorporated within it now. Men were not so dull as to anticipate unanimity of opinion on matters which so deeply interest the mind as questions of religion. There were multitudes of points on which the voice of the National Church was itself wavering and uncertain ; it therefore seemed perfectly reasonable that a wide margin should be left for individual differences of opinion. If English citizens could consent to join in the newly constituted forms of worship, time would gradually bring about a more cordial understanding between those who still cast regretful glances backwards, and others who were barely satisfied without new advances and further changes. Thus amid many incongruities of Church policy, and many inconsistent outbursts of harsh intolerance, space was found within the borders of the National Church alike for those who were all but Romanists except that they abjured the Pope, and for thorough Puritans who just tolerated Episcopacy. There was union, and, under wise management, prospect of greater union. If the conflict of opinion was greater, and the edge of parties in some respects sharper, than now, the forces and feelings which tended to unity were also stronger and more decided.

[1] Goldwin Smith, *On Tests*, 26.

Some remarks have already been made upon the desire that was shown to retain within the Established Church that large portion of the population who were quite alive to the necessity of sweeping away corruptions and evident abuses, but who had no wish for innovations that did not seem really necessary, and whose general sentiment was with the mode of worship to which their fathers had been accustomed.

But there was at least an equal liberty in the opposite direction. 'Is it not,' asks Coleridge, 'an historical error to call the Puritans Dissenters? Before St. Bartholomew's day they were essentially a part of the Church, and had as determined opinions in favour of a Church establishment as the bishops themselves.'[1] For several years of Elizabeth's reign it seemed, in fact, not unlikely that they would become the predominant party in the English Church, and bring the direction of it under their own control. The combined authority of the Queen, of Cecil, and of Parker was scarcely sufficient to prevent the established order in ecclesiastical matters from being not only infringed, but supplanted by ideas more consonant to those which the exiles of Mary's reign had seen flourishing at Geneva. Puritan opinions were maintained and vigorously insisted upon, not by a small turbulent minority, but by a number of the most eminent Churchmen—such as Jewel, Grindal, Sandys, and Nowell—by a considerable proportion of Parliamentary representatives, by a majority of the citizens of large towns, and by many men of great influence among the aristocracy and gentry. 'I conceive,' says Hallam, 'the Church of England party—that is, the party adverse to any species of ecclesiastical change—to have been the least numerous of the three during this reign, still excepting the neutrals, who commonly make a numerical majority, and are counted along with the dominant religion.'[2] It was not till 1570, or a year or two earlier, that even the most advanced Puritans attempted to form separate assemblies. Up to that time there were many deviations from uniformity within the English Church, but as yet no schism. There was dissension, but not yet dissent.

Presbyterianism may almost be said to have been tolerated

---

[1] Coleridge's *Table Talk*, 97.
[2] Hallam's *Constitutional History*, i. 189.

side by side with Episcopacy in the Church of England till nearly the end of the sixteenth century, or rather till the Act of Uniformity after the Restoration. In 1585 Walter Travers, who had received Presbyterian orders at Antwerp, was afternoon preacher at the Temple, and recommended to the mastership of it against Hooker by Alvie, the former master, a man loved and venerated of all, by a large part of the society of the Temple, and by Lord Treasurer Burleigh.[1] Archbishop Grindal in some cases permitted Scotch Presbyterian clergymen to preach and administer the sacraments in any part of his province.[2] In a word, Episcopacy was generally defended as an ancient and excellent form of Church government, but not by any means as a necessary and Divinely appointed institution. This comparatively neutral position was distinctly maintained by Cranmer.[3] Precisely the same view was taken by Whitgift when, in reply to Cartwright, who advocated the exclusive authority of the Presbyterian system, he argued that Christ had left the external polity[4] of His Church entirely an open question. Clarendon has remarked of the provision in the Act of Uniformity which required that no persons should hold preferment in the Church of England except such as were episcopally ordained, 'This was new, for there had been many, and at present there were some, who possessed benefices with cure of souls and other ecclesiastical promotions, who had never received orders but in France or Holland ; and these men must now receive new ordination, which had always been held unlawful in the Church, or by this Act of Parliament must be deprived of their livelihood, which they enjoyed in the most flourishing and peaceable time of the Church.' When the King was restored, the prospect of an understanding between Episcopalians and Presbyterians had seemed most hopeful. Charles owed much to the support of the Presbyterian ministers, and gladly acknowledged it. He appointed some of them to be his own chaplains, and said

---

[1] Walton's *Life of Hooker*, prefixed to *Works*, 20.

[2] Strype's *Life of Grindal*, appendix to book ii. No. xvii. Quoted by Macaulay, *History*, chap. i.

[3] J. Hunt, *Religious Life in England*, i. 14. Hallam, *Constitutional History*, chap. xi. vol. ii. 317, 337.

[4] Quoted in Skeats' *History of the Free Churches*, 18.

that he had found them not only well affected to himself,
no enemies either to Episcopacy or to a liturgy. They,
their part, declared that on doctrine all parties were agre
and that they would willingly come to a friendly settlem
on points of Church government and Church services. Tho
they had renounced 'hierarchy' and 'prelacy,' they w
willing to receive 'the true, ancient, primitive Episcopacy
the Church, in which bishops should always act in conjunct
with a presbytery. Nor did they object to a liturgy, if sc
changes were made in the existing one and it were not
rigorously imposed. The result, as is well known, was
Savoy Conference, which unhappily took the form not (
conference or consultation, as was first proposed, in
interests of peace, but of a series of argumentative excepti
and replies. 'And thus,' remarks a recent writer, 'was
the best opportunity that was ever offered of uniting into
Church the two great parties that represented between th
the religion of the nation.' [1]

The Act of Uniformity, passed in 1662, gave a standing
Dissent which it had never possessed before. Some meas
of the kind was no doubt inevitable. The confusion of
Church order which had existed during the Commonwe
could not be corrected, nor could the necessary disciplin
the Church of England be restored, without a firmnes:
action which could scarcely fail to wear some appearanc
harshness. But there was a needless rigour in the word
and provisions of the Act which is quite indefensible.
hard-cut expressions betokened the triumph of a party,
an intolerant determination to thrust out of the Church
Puritan section which had existed in it without blame,
greatly to its advantage, from the very beginning of
Reformation. 'I am past doubt,' said Baxter, speaking
the difficulties which it put in the way of conformity, '
Richard Hooker, Bishop Bilson, Archbishop Usher, and s
others, were they now alive, would be Nonconformists.'[2]
is, at all events, quite certain that many of the great Pur
divines whose piety and talents have adorned the Nati
Church would have been among the number of the ejec
A very slight accession of strength on the Liberal side wc

---

[1] Hunt, i. 295.   [2] Id. ii. 18.

have reversed the very small majority by which the bill was carried, and added modifications which might have made the measure worthy of the great opportunity which the Restoration had afforded. The immediate result of the bill was not only an immense increase of Nonconformity, but the wide spread of a feeling among many, to whom such an opinion was entirely new, that Nonconformity on account of slight differences was justifiable. There was much general sympathy with the two thousand clergy who threw up their preferments rather than submit to the requirements imposed upon them. About a score of them may have been Anabaptists, or men of wild and distempered views,[1] whom it would have been utterly impossible to retain in the ministerial service of the English Church. Some may have been unfit and ignorant men who would hardly have found their benefices except in confused times. But in almost every age, both before and after the Reformation, there had been a mixture of rude, illiterate men in the ranks of the clergy ; and at all events their self-devotion was none the less meritorious on that account. A great number, however, of those who gave up their homes and their parish churches on St. Bartholomew's day were among the very best Low Churchmen, as they would now be called, of their age. Such men carried with them, when they left their parsonages, the love of their parishioners and the deep respect of the country at large. Some of them remained in the lay communion of the English Church, but many seceded to the Nonconformists, and did not secede alone. In worldly circumstances many gained materially by what was at first a great self-sacrifice. That in no ways affected the sympathy that was felt, and the regret, frequently mixed with indignation, that deserving clergymen should suffer such treatment on account of opinions which for more than two centuries had been more or less tolerated in the Church.

The ejected clergy became in some cases bitter opponents of a Church which had been so unkind a mother to them. Yet perhaps the Church suffered more loss of popularity and influence in the justification given to Dissent by the Nonconformity of moderate men who had been made Nonconformists against their will. It was also noticed that

---

[1] *Annals of England,* App. xiv. 3, 363.

these new adherents brought into the Dissenting bodies, and especially into the Presbyterian community, a learning and a culture which had hitherto been wanting. When men of high social and intellectual eminence, such as Howe, Bates, Calamy, and Annesley, were constrained to leave the English Church, the whole level of the communion into which they transferred their allegiance was distinctly raised. In the reign of Charles II., James II., and William, the Presbyterian and a few of the Independent leaders obtained through them a position in London circles scarcely inferior to that which they would have held as dignitaries of the Established Church.

The gap, nevertheless, in feeling and opinion between moderate Nonconformists and a powerful party within the National Church was so slight, that the ejection of 1662 had been almost immediately followed by renewed efforts for comprehension. It is unnecessary to enter into a narration of the various schemes which were more or less hopefully entered into during the period which elapsed between the passing of the Act of Uniformity and the end of the century. The books and pamphlets written upon the subject from its different points of view might by themselves constitute a small library : and the whole question, although very materially connected with the history of the eighteenth century, belongs properly to that of the seventeenth. Some general remarks, therefore, must suffice.

Arguments in favour of comprehension readily suggested themselves, and were, beyond question, exceedingly strong. The differences between the Low or Latitudinarian Churchmen of the period and moderate Nonconformists were wholly insignificant. In many cases the one stumbling-block which had stood in the way of Conformity consisted in the interpretation given to the 'assent and consent' to the Book of Common Prayer, as prescribed in the Act of 1662. The expressions had undoubtedly been dictated in an overbearing spirit, very unfriendly to well-known scruples. It had received, however, an official explanation ; a declaration having been issued the year after that it should be understood only as to practice and obedience, and not otherwise. In fact, as Hoadly pointed out to Calamy, the terms of the Act itself refer assent and consent to the *use* of the book ; so that 'whoever,' adds the bishop, 'declares his assent to the truth of every proposition in it, and his consent to the use of every-thing prescribed in it, though he may not do more than he himself thinks lawful, yet he certainly does more than the Act requires.'[1] 'It means,' said another writer, 'an allowance in our circumstances of those things that must be used.'[2] But this limitation in meaning was not obvious on the surface. To many the required declaration appeared a tyrannical demand upon their intellect and consciences, to which they could not truthfully or in self-respect submit. Thus it often happened that Conformists and Nonconformists were sepa-rated by a barrier which implied no difference whatever, except only in the manner in which they construed the terms of subscription. In these cases, a slight alteration in the lan-guage of the Act would suffice for reunion between men who were divided by what might fairly be called a verbal mis-understanding.

Apart from this disputed question, and others connected with it, as to the meaning of subscription, the friends of com-prehension on either side of the line could demand with much force of reason that men whose views were so nearly identical should not be separated from one another except on very strong grounds of right or expedience. The Latitudinarian party in the English Church had, almost without exception, a bias toward Puritan opinions. To them, the differences by which they were separated from moderate Nonconformists appeared utterly immaterial, and not worthy to be balanced for an instant against the blessings of unity. Hence while, on the one hand, they did their utmost to persuade the Dis-senters to give up what seemed to them needless, and almost frivolous scruples, they were also very anxious that all ground for these scruples should be as far as possible removed. 'Sure,' they argued, ''tis not ill-becoming an elder (and so a wiser) brother in such a case as this to stoop a little to the weakness of the younger, in keeping company still; and when hereby he shall not go one step the further out of the ready road unto their Father's house.'[3] On points of Church

---

[1] Hoadly, 'Reasonableness of Conformists,'—*Works,* i. 197.
[2] *Endeavour for Peace &c.,* 1680, 26.
[3] Id. 20.

order and discipline, mitigate the terms of uniformity, do not
rigidly preclude all alternatives, admit some considered system
which will allow room for option.   Frankly acknowledge, that
in regard of the doctrine of the sacraments, divers opinions
may still, as has ever been the case, be legitimately held
within the Church, and modify here and there an expression
in the Liturgy, which may be thought inconsistent with their
liberty, and gives needless offence.   Let it not be in anywise
our fault if our brethren in the same faith will not join us in
our common worship.   They appealed to the apostolic rule
of Charity, that they who use this rite despise not them who
use it not ; and those who use it not, condemn not them that
use it.   They appealed to the example of the primitive
Church, and bade both Churchmen and Dissenters remember
how both Polycarp and Irenæus had urged, that they who
agree in doctrine must not fall out for rites.   The early
Church, said Stillingfleet,[1] showed great toleration towards
different parties within its communion, and allowed among
its members and ministers diverse rites and various opinions.
They appealed again to the practice and constitution of the
English Church since the Reformation.   They did not so
much ask to widen its limits, as that the limits which had
previously been recognised should not now be restricted.
There had always been parties in it which differed widely
from one another, Anglican and Puritan, Calvinist and
Arminian.   There never had been a time when it had not
included among its clergy men who differed in no perceptible
degree from those who were now excluded.   They appealed
to the friendly feeling that prevailed between moderate men
on either side ; and most frequently and most urgently they
appealed to the need of combination among Protestants.   It
was a time for mutual conciliation among Protestants in
England and abroad, not for increasing divisions, and for
imposing new tests and passwords which their fathers had
not known.   The National Church ought to make a great
effort to win over a class of men who, as citizens, were
prominent, for the most part, for sobriety, frugality, and
industry, and, as Christians, for a piety which might perhaps
be restricted in its ideas, and cramped by needless scruples,

---

[1] *Irenicum.*   Hunt, ii. 136.   *Endeavour &c.*, 22–7.

but which at all events was genuine and zealous. A very large number of them were as yet not disaffected toward the English Church, and would meet with cordiality all advances made in a brotherly spirit. It would be a sin to let the opportunity slip by unimproved.

The force of such arguments was vividly felt by the whole of that Latitudinarian party in the Church, which numbered at the end of the seventeenth century so many distinguished names. There was a time when some of the High Church leaders were so far alarmed by Roman aggressiveness, as to think that union among Protestants should be purchased even at what they deemed a sacrifice, and when Sancroft, Ken, and Lake moved for a bill of comprehension,[1] and Beveridge spoke warmly in favour of it.[2] The moderate Dissenters were quite as anxious on the subject as any of their conformist friends. 'Baxter protested in his latest works, that the body to which he belonged was in favour of a National State Church. He disavowed the term Presbyterian, and stated that most whom he knew did the same. They would be glad, he said, to live under godly bishops, and to unite on healing terms. He deplored that the Church doors had not been opened to him and his brethren, and pleaded urgently for a "healing Act of Uniformity." Calamy explicitly states that he was disposed to enter the establishment, if Tillotson's scheme had succeeded. Howe also lamented the failure of the scheme.'[3] The trusts of their meeting-houses were in many cases so framed, and their licences so taken out, that the buildings could easily be transferred to Church uses.[4] The Independents, who came next to the Presbyterians, both in influence and numerical strength, were more divided in opinion. Many remained staunch to the principles of their early founders, and were wholly irreconcilable.[5] Others, perhaps a majority, of the 'Congregational Brethren,' as they preferred to call themselves, were very willing to 'own the king for head over their churches,' to give a general approval

---

[1] *Burnet's Own Times*, 528. Birch's *Life of Tillotson*, cix. *Life of Ken*, by a Layman, 501. Hunt, *Religious Thought*, ii. 70.
[2] Macaulay's *History of England*, chap. xiv.
[3] Skeats, 147. [4] Id. 166.
[5] Hallam's *Constitutional History of England*, ii. 317. Hunt, *Religious Thought in England*, i. 213.

to the Prayer Book, and to be comprehended, on terms which would allow them what they considered a reasonable liberty, within the National Church.[1] They formed part of the deputation of ministers to King William, in which an ardent hope was expressed that differences might be composed, and such a firm union established on broad Christian principles 'as would make the Church a type of heaven.'[2] How far they would have accepted any practical scheme of comprehension is more doubtful. But, as Mr. Skeats remarks of the measure proposed in 1689, 'Calamy's assertion, that if it had been adopted, it would in all probability have brought into the Church two-thirds of the Dissenters, indicates the almost entire agreement of the Independents with the Presbyterians, concerning the expedience of adopting it.'[3]

The Baptists showed little or no disposition to come to an agreement with the Church. They were at this time a declining sect, who held little intercourse with other Dissenters, and were much engaged in petty but very acrimonious controversies among themselves. They had been divided ever since 1633 into two sections, the Particular and General Baptists. The former of the two were Calvinists of the most rigorous and exclusive type, often conspicuous by a fervent but excessively narrow form of piety, and illiterate almost on principle on account of their disparagement of what was called 'human learning.'[4] The general Baptists, many of whom merged, early in the eighteenth century, into Unitarians, were less exclusive in their views. But the Baptists generally viewed the English Church with suspicion and dislike. In many cases their members were forbidden to enter, on any pretext whatever, the national churches, or to form intermarriages or hold social intercourse with Churchmen.[5] Yet some may not have forgotten the example and teaching of the ablest defender, in the seventeenth century, of Baptist opinions. 'Mr. Tombs,' says Wall, quoting from Baxter, 'continued an Antipædobaptist to his dying day, yet wrote against separation for it, and for communion with the parish

---

[1] Hunt, *Religious Thought in England*, ii. 22.
[2] Skeats' *History of the Free Churches*, 147.
[3] Calamy's *Baxter*, 655 (quoted by Skeats), 149. Thoresby's *Diary*, 399.
[4] Skeats, 158–65.   [5] Id. 186.

churches.'[1] When Marshall, in the course of controversy, reproached the Baptists with separation, Tombs answered that he must blame the persons, not the general body. For his own part he thought such separation a ' practice justly to be abhorred. The making of sects upon difference of opinions, reviling, separating from their teachers and brethren otherwise faithful, because there is not the same opinion in disputable points, or in clear truths not fundamental, is a thing too frequent in all sorts of dogmatists, &c., and I look upon it as one of the greatest plagues of Christianity. You shall have me join with you in detestation of it.'[2] He himself continued in communion with the National Church until his death.

Unitarians have always differed from one another so very widely, that they can hardly be classed or spoken of under one name. Their opinions have always varied in every possible degree, from such minute departure from generally received modes of expression in speaking of the mystery of the Godhead, as need a very microscopic orthodoxy to detect, down to the barest and most explicit Socinianism. There were some who charged with Unitarianism Bishop Bull,[3] whose learned defence of the Nicene faith was famous throughout all Europe. There were many who made it an accusation against Tillotson,[4] and the whole[5] of the Low or Latitudinarian party in the Church of England. The Roman Controversialists of the seventeenth century used to go further still, and boldly assert[6] that to leave Rome was to go to Socinianism ; and the Calvinists, on their side, would sometimes argue that ' Arminianism was a shoeing horn to draw on Socinianism.'[7] A great number of the Unitarians of the seventeenth and eighteenth centuries were themselves scarcely distinguishable from the orthodox. ' For peace sake they submit to the phrase of the Church, and expressly own Three Persons, though they think the word person not

---

[1] Wall's *Dissuasive from Schism,* 477.
[2] *Tombs against Marshall,* p. 31, quoted by Wall.
[3] Nelson's *Life of Bull,* 240, 260.
[4] Birch's *Tillotson,* ccvii. Leslie's *Works,* ii. 533-600, &c.
[5] Leslie, ii. 659.
[6] Chillingworth's *Works,* vol. i. Preface, § 9.
[7] *The Principles of the Reformation concerning Church Communion,* 1704.

so proper as another word might be. If the Three Persons
should be defined by three distinct minds and spirits, or substances, the Unitarian will be lost ; but if person be defined
by mode, manifestation, or outward relation, he will be
acquitted . . . . They believe all the articles of the Apostles'
Creed . . . . They believe the law of Christ contained in the
four gospels to be the only and everlasting rule, by which they
shall be judged hereafter. . . . . They thankfully lay hold
on the message of Redemption through Christ.'[1]   Some of
the Unitarians, we are told, even excommunicated and
deposed from the ministry such of their party as denied
that divine worship was due to Christ.[2]   Of Unitarians such
as these, if they can be called by that name, and not rather
Arians or Semi-Arians, the words of Dr. Arnold may properly
be quoted : ' The addressing Christ in the language of prayer
and praise is an essential part of Christian worship.   Every
Christian would feel his devotions incomplete, if this formed
no part of them.   This therefore cannot be sacrificed ; but
we are by no means bound to inquire whether all who pray
to Christ entertain exactly the same ideas of His nature.   I
believe that Arianism involves in it some very erroneous
notions as to the object of religious worship ; but if an Arian
will join in our worship of Christ, and will call Him Lord
and God, there is neither wisdom nor charity in insisting that
he shall explain what he means by these terms ; nor in
questioning the strength and sincerity of his faith in his
Saviour, because he makes too great a distinction between
the Divinity of the Father and that which he allows to be the
attribute of the Son.'[3]   This was certainly the feeling of
Tillotson[4] and many other eminent men of the same school.
If an Unitarian chose to conform, as very many were accustomed to do, they gladly received him as a fellow worshipper.
Thomas Firmin the philanthropist, leader of the Unitarians
of his day, was a constant attendant at Tillotson's church of
St. Lawrence Jewry, and at Dr. Outram's in Lombard Street.
Yet both these divines were Catholic in regard of their

---

[1] *An Apology for the Parliament &c.*, 1697, part i.
[2] Leslie's *Works*, ii. 656.
[3] Dr. Arnold, *Principles of Church Reform*, 285.
[4] Birch's *Life of Tillotson*, ccxxvii.

doctrine of the Trinity, and wrote in defence of it. In fact, the moderate Unitarians conformed without asking or expecting any concessions. Latitudinarian Churchmen, as a party, entertained no idea of including Unitarians in the proposed act of comprehension. For his own part, said Burnet, he could never understand pacificatory doctrines on matters which seemed to him the fundamentals of Christianity.[1] So far from comprehension, Socinians were excluded even from the benefits of the act of toleration ; and more than thirty years later, in 1697, a severe Act of outlawry was passed against all who wrote or spoke against the divinity of Christ.[2] Until about 1720, Unitarians scarcely took the form of a separate sect. Either they were scarcely distinguishable from those who professed one or another form of Deism, and who assumed the title of a Christian philosophy rather than of a denomination ; or they were proscribed heretics ; or they conformed to the Church of England and did not consider their opinions inconsistent with loyalty to it.

Little need be said, in this connexion, of the Quakers. Towards the end of the seventeenth century they increased in wealth and numbers, and had begun to hold far more mitigated tenets than those of a previous age. For this they were much indebted to Robert Barclay, who wrote his 'Apology' in Latin in 1676, and translated it with a dedication to Charles II. in 1678. A few Churchmen of pronounced mystical opinions were to some extent in sympathy with them ; but, as a rule, both among Conformists and Nonconformists they were everywhere misunderstood, ridiculed, and denounced. If it had not been so, their vehement repudiation of all intervention of the State in religious matters would have compelled them to hold aloof from all overtures of comprehension, even if any had been proffered to them.

The Nonconformists, therefore, who in the latter part of the seventeenth century might have been attached by a successful measure of comprehension to the National Church, were the Presbyterians—at that time a large and influential body—a considerable proportion, probably, of the Independents, and individual members of other denominations.

---

[1] Burnet's *Four Discourses to the Clergy of Sarum,* 1694, Pref. v.
[2] Skeats, 185.

The most promising, though not the best known scheme, appears to have been that put forward by the Presbyterians, and earnestly promoted by Sir Matthew Hale, Bishop Wilkins, and others, in 1667. Assent only was to be required to the Prayer Book; certain ceremonies were to be left optional; clergymen who had received only Presbyterian ordination were to receive, with imposition of the bishop's hands, legal authority to exercise the offices of their ministry, the word 'legal' being considered a sufficient salvo for the intrinsic validity of their previous orders; 'sacramentally' might be added after 'regenerated' in the Baptismal service and a few other things were to be made discretional. Here was a very tolerable basis for an agreement which might not improbably have been carried out, if the House of Commons had not resolved to pass no bill of comprehension in that year.

Even this scheme, however, had one essential fault common to it with the projects which were brought forward at a somewhat later period. No measure for Church comprehension on anything like a large scale is ever like to fulfil its objects, unless the whole of the question with all its difficulties is boldly grasped and dealt with in a statesmanlike manner. Nonconformist bodies, which have grown up by long and perhaps hereditary usage into fixed habits and settled frames of thought, or whose strength is chiefly based upon principles and motives of action which are not quite in accordance with the spirit of the larger society, can never be satisfactorily incorporated into a National Church, unless the scheme provides to a great extent for the affiliation and maintenance in their integrity of the existing organisations. The Roman Church has never hesitated to utilise in this sort of manner new spiritual forces, and, without many alterations of the old, to make new additions to her ecclesiastical machinery at the risk of increasing its complexity. The Church of England might in this respect have followed the example of her old opponent to very great advantage. But neither in the plan of 1689, nor in any of those which preceded or followed it during the period which elapsed between the Act of Uniformity and the close of the century, was anything of the kind attempted.

Much, no doubt, could be done and was proposed to be
ne, in the way of removing from public services, where
her words, not less to the purpose and equally devotional,
uld be substituted for them, some expressions which gave
fence and raised scruples. Where this can be done without
ss, it must needs be a gain. A concession to scruples
hich in no way impairs our perception of Christian truth,
a worthy sacrifice to Christian charity. Such a work,
wever, of revision demands much caution and an excep-
nal amount of sound discretion. Least of all can it be done
any spirit of party. In proposing a change of expression
ich would be in itself wholly unobjectionable, the revisers
ve not only to consider the scruples of those whom they wish
conciliate; they must respect even more heedfully, feelings
d sentiments which they may not themselves share in, but
hich are valued by one or another party already existing in
e Church. A revision conducted by the moderates of a
urch would plainly have no right to meet scruples and
jections on the part of Puritans, outside their Communion,
ly by creating new scruples and objections among High
hurchmen within it; just as, reversely, it would be equally
justifiable to conciliate High Sacramentalists, or the lovers
a grander or more touching ceremonial, who hovered on
e borders of a Church, by changes which would be painful
its Puritan members already domiciled within it. When
en of all the leading parties in a Church are sincerely
sirous (as they ought, and, under some contingencies, are
ecially bound to be,) of removing unnecessary obstacles to
urch Communion, the work of revision will be compara-
ely easy; and changes, which to unwilling minds would
: magnified into alarming sacrifices, will become peace offer-
gs uncostly in themselves, and willingly and freely yielded.
uch then can be done in this way, but only where the
anges, however excellent and opportune in themselves, are
omoted not merely by a party, but by the Church in
neral.

Alterations, however, of this kind, although they may
nstitute a very important part of a measure of Church
mprehension, will rarely, if ever, prove sufficient to fulfil in
y satisfactory manner the desired purpose. It would be

simply ruinous to the vitality of any Church to be neutral and colourless in its formularies. Irritating and polemical terms may most properly be excluded from devotional use; but no Church or party in a Church which has life and promise in it will consent, in order to please others, to give up old words and accustomed usages which give distinctiveness to worship and add a charm to the expression of familiar doctrines.

One, therefore, of two things must be done as a duty both to the old and to the incoming members. Either much must be left optional to the clergy, or to the clergy acting in concert with their congregations, or else, as was before said, the National Church must find scope and room for its new members, not as a mere throng of individuals, but as corporate bodies, whose organisations may have to be modified to suit the new circumstances, but not broken up. When it is considered how highly strict uniformity was valued by the ruling powers at the end of the seventeenth century, the ample discretionary powers that were proposed to be left are a strong proof how genuine in many quarters must have been the wish to effect a comprehension. The difficulties, however, which beset such liberty of option were obvious, and the opponents of the bill did not fail to make the most of them. It was a subject which specially suited the satirical pen and declamatory powers of Dr. South. He was a great stickler for uniformity; unity, he urged, was strength; and therefore he insisted upon 'a resolution to keep all the constitutions of the Church, the parts of the service, and the conditions of its communion entire, without lopping off any part of them.' 'If any be indulged in the omission of the least thing there enjoined, they cannot be said to "speak all the same thing."' And then, in more forcible language, he descanted upon what he called 'the deformity and undecency' of difference of practice. He drew a vivid picture how some in the same diocese would use the surplice, and some not, and how there would be parties accordingly. 'Some will kneel at the Sacrament, some stand, some perhaps sit; some will read this part of the Common Prayer, some that—some, perhaps, none at all.' Some in the pulpits of our churches and cathedrals 'shall conceive a long crude extemporary prayer, in reproach of all the prayers which the Church with such admirable prudence and devotion hath been making before. Nay, in the same cathedral you shall see one prebendary in a surplice, another in a long coat, another in a short coat or jacket ; and in the performance of the public services some standing up at the Creed, the Gloria Patri, and the reading of the Gospel ; and others sitting, and perhaps laughing and winking upon their fellow schismatics, in scoff of those who practise the decent order of the Church.' Irreconcilable parties, he adds, and factions will be created. 'I will not hear this formalist, says one; and I will not hear that schismatic (with better reason), says another. . . . So that I dare avouch, that to bring in a comprehension is nothing else but, in plain terms, to establish a schism in the Church by law, and so bring a plague into the very bowels of it, which is more than sufficiently endangered already by having one in its neighbourhood ; a plague which shall eat out the very heart and soul, and consume the vitals and spirit of it, and this to such a degree, that in the compass of a few years it shall scarce have any being or subsistence, or so much as the face of a National Church to be known by.'[1] South's sermon was on the appropriate text, 'not give place, no, not for an hour.' His picture was doubtless a highly exaggerated one. The discretionary powers which some of the schemes of comprehension proposed to give would not have left the Church of England a mere scene of confusion, an unseemly Babel of anarchy and licence. A sketch might be artfully drawn, in which nothing should be introduced but what was truthfully selected from the practices of different London Churches of the present day, which might easily make a foreigner imagine that in the National Church uniformity and order were things unknown. Yet practically, its unity remains unbroken ; and the inconveniences arising from such divergences are very slight as compared with the advantages which result from them, and with the general life and elasticity of which they are at once both causes and symptoms. Good feeling, sound sense, and the natural instinct of order would have done much to abate the disorders of even a large relaxation of the Act of Uniformity. In 1689, before yet the

[1] R. South's *Sermons*, vol. iv. 174-95.

course taken by the Revolution had kindled the strong spirit
of party, there was nothing like the heat of feeling in regard
of such usages as the wearing of the surplice, kneeling at the
Communion, and the sign of the cross at Baptism, as there
had been in the earlier part of Elizabeth's reign. When
prejudices began to pass away, prevailing practice would
probably have been guided, after an interval, by the rule
of the 'survival of the fittest,'—of those customs, that is, which ·
best suited the temper of the people and the spirit of the
Church. The surplice, for instance, would very likely have
become gradually universal, much in the same manner as in
our own day it has gradually superseded the gown in the
pulpit. A concession to Nonconformist scruples of some
discretionary power in regard of a few ceremonies and observances would certainly not have brought upon the National
Church the ruin foreboded by Dr. South. Possibly a licensed
variety of usage might have had indirectly a somewhat wholesome influence. The mild excitement of controversies about
matters in themselves almost indifferent might have tended,
like a gentle blister, to ward off the lethargy which, in the
eighteenth century, paralysed to so great an extent the
spiritual energies of the Church. No one can doubt that
Dr. South's remarks expressed in vigorous language genuine
difficulties. But it was equally obvious that if the National
Church were to be placed on a wider basis, as the opportunities of the time seemed to demand, a relaxation of
uniformity of some kind or another was indispensable. It did
not seem to occur to the reformers and revisionists of the
time that a concession of optionary powers was a somewhat
crude, nor by any means the only solution of the difficulty;
and that it might be quite possible to meet all reasonable
scruples of Nonconformists without in any way infringing
upon customs which all old members of the Church of
England were well satisfied to retain.

But even if the schemes for comprehension had been
thoroughly sound in principle, and less open to objection,
the favourable opportunity soon passed by. While there yet
lingered in men's minds a feeling of uneasiness and regret
that the Restoration of 1660 should have been followed by
the ejection of so many deserving clergy; while the more

eminent and cultured of the sufferers by it were leavening the whole Nonconformist body with principles and sentiments which belong rather to a National Church than to a detached sect ; while Nonconformity among large bodies of Dissenters was not yet an established fact; while men of all parties were still rejoicing in the termination of civil war, in the conspicuous abatement of religious and political animosities, and in the sense of national unity; while Protestants of all shades of opinion were knit together by the strong band of a common danger, by the urgent need of combination against a foe whose advances threatened the liberties of all; while High Churchmen like Ken and Sancroft were advocating not toleration only, but comprehension ; while the voices of Nonconformists joined heartily in the acclamations which greeted the liberation of the seven bishops ; while the Upper House of Convocation was not yet separated from the Lower, nor the great majority of the bishops from the bulk of the clergy, by a seemingly hopeless antagonism of Church principles ; while High Churchmen were still headed by bishops distinguished by their services to religion and liberty; and while Broad Churchmen were represented not only by eminent men of the type of Stillingfleet and Tillotson, Burnet, Tenison and Compton, but by the thoughtful and philosophic band of scholars who went by the name of the Oxford and Cambridge Platonists—under circumstances such as these, there was very much that was highly favourable to the efforts which were being made in favour of Church comprehension. These efforts met at all times with strong opposition, especially in the House of Commons and among the country clergy. But a well-considered scheme, once carried, would have been welcomed with very general approval, and might have been attended with most beneficial results.

The turn taken by the Revolution of 1689 destroyed the prospect of bringing these labours to a really successful issue. They were pushed on, as is well known, with greater energy than ever. They could not, however, fail of being infected henceforth with a partisan and political spirit which made it very doubtful whether the ill consequences of an Act of Comprehension would not have more than counterbalanced its advantages. The High Church party, deprived of many of their best men by the secession of the Nonjurors, and suspected by a triumphant majority of Jacobitism and general disaffection, were weakened, narrowed, and embittered. Broad Churchmen, on the other hand, were looked upon by those who differed from them as altogether Latitudinarians in religion, and Whigs in politics—terms constantly used as practically convertible. Danger from Rome, although by no means insignificant, was no longer so visible, or so pressing, as it had been in James II.'s reign. Meanwhile, it had become apparent that the Church of England was menaced by a peril of an opposite kind. Not High Churchmen only, but all who desired to see the existing character of the Church of England maintained, had cause to fear lest under a monarch to whom all forms of Protestantism were alike, and who regarded all from a political and somewhat sceptical point of view, ideas very alien to those which had given the National Church its shape and colour might now become predominant. If the Royal Supremacy was no longer the engine of power it had been under some previous rulers, and up to the very era of the Revolution, the personal opinions of the sovereign still had considerable weight, especially when backed, as they now were, by a strong mass of opinion, both within the English Church, and among Nonconformists. There were many persons who drew back with apprehension from measures which a year or two before they had looked forward to with hope. They knew not what they might lead to. Salutary changes might be the prelude to others which they would witness with dismay. Moreover, changes which might have been salutary under other circumstances, would entirely lose their character when they were regarded as the triumph of a party and caused distrust and alienation. They might create a wider schism than any they could heal. The Non-juring separation was at present a comparatively inconsiderable body in numbers and general influence ; and there was a hope, proved in the issue to be well founded, that many of the most respected members of it would eventually return to the communion which they had unwillingly quitted. The case would be quite reversed, if multitudes of steady, old-fashioned Churchmen, disgusted by concessions and innovations which they abhorred and regarded as mere badges of a party triumph, came to look upon the communion of Ken and Kettlewell and Nelson as alone representing that Church of their forefathers to which they had given their attachment. It would be a disastrous consequence of efforts pressed inopportunely in the interests of peace if the ancient Church of England were rent in twain.

Thus, before the eighteenth century had yet begun, the hopes which had been cherished by so many excellent men on either side of the line which marked off the Nonconformists from their conforming friends, had at length almost entirely vanished. The scheme of 1689, well-meaning as it was, lacked in a marked degree many of the qualities which most deserve and command success. But when once William and Mary had been crowned, and the spirit of party had become strong, the best of schemes would have failed. Ralph Thoresby expressed the sentiments of not a few among his contemporaries when he wrote in his Diary for September 25, 1702,—'What a deplorable case are we reduced to, that so many attempts for reformation [comprehension] have been unsuccessful, particularly that most famous one in the beginning of the late reign, 1689, when so many incomparable persons of primitive candour were concerned therein, of which my Lord Archbishop of York [Sharp] has spoke to me with deep concern, for which disappointment all good Christians have cause for sorrow.'[1] Many, on the other hand, who once had been ardently in favour of the proposed Act, thought afterwards that there was good reason for not regretting its failure. Burnet saw therein 'a very happy direction of the providence of God. . . . For by all the judgments we could afterwards make, if we had carried a majority in the Convocation for alterations, they would have done us more harm than good.'[2]

Church comprehension never afterwards became, in any direct form, a question for much practical discussion. The interest which the late efforts had excited lingered for some time in the minds, both of those who had promoted the measure and of those who had resisted it. There was much warm debate upon the subject in the Convocation of 1702. Sacheverell and the bigots of his party in 1709 lashed themselves into fury at the very thought that comprehension could

[1] *Diary*, i. 399.　　　　[2] *Own Times*, 544.

be advocated.   It was treachery, rank and inexcusable; it was bringing the Trojan horse into the Holy City; it was converting the house of God into a den of thieves.[1]   Such forms of speech were too common just about that period to mean much, or to attract any particular notice.   As Swift said, if the zealots of either party were to be believed, their adversaries were always wretches worthy to be exterminated.[2] The Dean himself thought that 'as to rites and ceremonies and forms of prayer, there might be some useful alterations, and more which, in the prospect of uniting Christians, might be very supportable, as things declared in their own nature indifferent; to which therefore he would readily comply, if the clergy or (though this be not so fair a method) the legislature should direct.'   He thought that Government would then be able to interpose more authoritatively to pre-vent the rising and spreading of new sects.   Nevertheless, he could not altogether blame those who were unwilling to con-sent to any alterations.   Swift thus maintained a sort of inter-mediate position, which he afterwards abandoned as anomalous and untenable, between the Whigs and the Tories, between the High Churchmen and the Low Churchmen of his day. Party spirit, at this period, ran so high, both in political and ecclesiastical matters, and minds were so excited and sus-picious, that most men ranged themselves very definitely on one or another side of a clearly-marked line, and genuinely temperate counsels were much out of favour.   To the one party 'moderation,' that 'harmless, gilded name,'[3] had become wholly odious, as ever 'importing somewhat that was unkind to the Church, and that favoured the Dissenters.'[4]   There was a story, that 'a clergyman preaching upon the text, "Let your moderation be known unto all men," took notice that the Latin word "moderor" signified rule and govern-ment, and by virtue of the criticism he made his text to signify, let the severity of your government be known unto all men.'[5]   Yet it was not to be wondered at that they had got to hate the word.   The opposite party, adopting modera-

---

[1] Sermon of November 5, 709. Hunt, 3, 12.   [2] *Works*, vol. 8, 264.
[3] South's *Sermons*, iv. 227.
[4] Burnet's *Own Times*, 751. Hoadly's *Works*, i. 24.
[5] *A Brief Defence of the Church*, 1706.

n jointly with union as their password, and glorifying it
'the cement of the world,' 'the ornament of human kind,'
he chiefest Christian grace,' 'the peculiar characteristic of
is Church,'[1] would pass on almost in the same breath to
le upon their opponents indiscriminate charges of persecu-
n, priestcraft, superstition, and to inveigh against them
'a narrow Laudean faction,' 'a jealous-headed, unneigh-
urly, selfish sect of Ishmaelites.'[2] Evidently, so long as the
irit of party was thus rampant, any measure of Church
mprehension was entirely out of question. Many Low
urchmen were as anxious for it as ever. But they were no
ger in power ; and had they been a majority, they could
ly have effected it by sheer weight of numbers, and under
minent peril of disrupture in the Church. Therefore, they
i not even attempt it, and were content to labour toward
e same ends by more indirect means.

In the middle of the century thoughts of comprehension
rived both in the English Church and among the Noncon-
mists. The state of things out of which the movement
se was not a satisfactory one. Religion was undoubtedly
a very low ebb. In this all writers agree. While they
nented its condition, they could of course make the some-
at faint and melancholy allowance that it 'still restrains
ich evil, and produces much good, and serves to many
cellent purposes.'[3] They would have been no less able
add that there were thousands and tens of thousands of
useholds where a pure and unostentatious Christian faith
s as warm and bright as in any previous generation.
reover, the Wesleyan movement was everywhere gaining
und. But, apart from Methodism, zeal was out of fashion ;
d irreligion and immorality flourished, not unrebuked, but
restrained by any vigorous efforts of religious energy. It
ght be hard to light upon the golden mean between 'a
tch phlegm and a Spanish fire.'[4] But if the latter dis-
yed itself to excess in the ill-regulated ardours of some of
followers of Wesley and Whitefield, there was far too
ich of the former both among the more orthodox members of
English Church and in the Nonconformist communions.

[1] *A Brief Defence of the Church,* 1706. [2] Id. [3] Jortin's *Tracts,* i. 353.
[4] W. Clarke, in Nichol's *Lit. Anecdotes,* 4, 450.

D D 2

It was a period when 'religious animosities were out of date, and the public had no turn for controversy.'[1] The 'Church in Danger' cry had wholly passed away. 'Moderation' was no longer inveighed against. The bishops generally, and the two archbishops particularly, were eminently moderate men. The Metropolitan See was occupied by Herring. H. Walpole spoke of him as 'a harmless, good man, inclined to much moderation, and of little zeal for the tinsel of religion.'[2] Jortin spoke in more distinctly laudatory terms : 'He had piety without superstition, and moderation without meanness; an open and liberal way of thinking, and a constant attachment to the cause of sober and rational liberty, both civil and religious. Few men ever passed through this malevolent world better beloved or less censured than he.'[3] He was a Latitudinarian in theology, and was sometimes charged, on no sufficient grounds, with holding Arian opinions. Hutton, Archbishop of York, and his successor for a year in the See of Canterbury, was also a pronounced Liberal and Low Churchman, who did not hesitate to express his liking for Blackburne's 'Apology,' and to promote the author to the Archdeaconry of Cleveland. 'He was a well-bred man,' said Walpole of him, 'and devoted to the ministry.'[4]

'Those,' wrote Mosheim in 1740, 'who are best aquainted with the state of the English nation, tell us that the Dissenting interest declines from day to day, and that the cause of Nonconformity owes this gradual decay in a great measure to the lenity and moderation that are practised by the rulers of the Established Church.'[5] No doubt the friendly understanding which widely existed about this time between Churchmen and Dissenters contributed to such a result. Herring, for instance, of Canterbury, Sherlock of London, Secker of Oxford, Maddox of Worcester, as well as Warburton, who was then preacher at Lincoln's Inn, Hildersly afterwards Bishop of Sodor and Man, and many other eminent Churchmen,[6] were all friends or correspondents with Doddridge, the genial and liberal-minded leader of the Congrega-

---

[1] Walpole's *Memoirs in* 1751, iv. 148.   [2] Id.
[3] Jortin's *Tracts*, ii. 518.   [4] *Memoirs*, iv. 148.
[5] Mosheim's *Ecclesiastical History* (Maclaine's Trans.), 5, 95.
[6] Hunt, 3, 247.

tionalists, the devout author of 'The Rise and Progress of Religion in the Soul.' Much the same might be said of Samuel Chandler, the eminent Presbyterian minister. An old schoolfellow of Secker and Butler, when they were pupils together at a dissenting academy in Yorkshire, he kept up his friendship with them, when the one was Primate of the English Church, and the other its ablest theologian. Personal relations of this kind insured the recognition of approaches based on more substantial grounds. There was real friendly feeling on the part of many principal Nonconformists not only towards this or that bishop, this or that Churchman, but towards the English Church in general. They coveted its wider culture, its freer air. With the decline of prejudices and animosities, they could not but feel the insignificance of the differences by which they were separated from it. Many of them were by no means unfavourable to the principle of a National Church. This was especially the case with Doddridge. While he spoke with the utmost abhorrence of all forms of persecution, he argued that regard alike to the honour of God and to the good of society, should engage rulers to desire and labour that the people should be instructed in matters of religion, and that they could not be thus instructed without some public provision. He held, however, that such an establishment should be as large as possible, so that no worthy or good man, whose services could be of use, should be excluded. If the majority agreed in such an establishment, the minority, he thought, might well be thankful to be left in possession of their liberties. He did not see that it was more unfair that they should be called upon to assist in supporting such a Church, than that they should have to contribute to the expenses of a war or any other national object of which they might disapprove.[1] It must be added that the Nonconformists of that time were drawn towards the National Church not only by its real merits. They were in very many instances attracted, rather than repelled, by what was then its greatest defect, for it was a defect which prevailed no less generally among themselves than in it. A stiff and cold insistence upon morals and reasonable considerations, to the comparative

[1] Doddridge's *Works*, iv. 503-4.

exclusion of appeals to higher Christian motive, was the common vice of Nonconformist as well as of national pulpits. At a time, therefore, when the great cardinal doctrines of Christianity were insufficiently preached, it followed as a matter of course that differences of opinion upon religious questions of less moment dwindled in seeming importance.

Such was the frequent relation between the English Church and Dissent when a charge happened to be delivered by Gooch, Bishop of Norwich, which gave rise to some remonstrance on the part of Dr. Chandler, who had been one of his auditors. Correspondence resulted in an interview, in which Gooch, though generally considered a High Churchman, showed himself not unfavourable to comprehension. Another time Bishop Sherlock joined in the discussion. There were three points, he said, to be considered—Doctrine, Discipline, and Ceremonies. Discipline was already in too neglected and enfeebled a state, too much in need of being recast, to be suggestive of much difficulty. Ceremonies could be left indifferent. As for doctrine, both bishops were quite willing to agree with Dr. Chandler that the Articles might properly be expressed in Scripture words, and that the Athanasian Creed should be discarded. Chandler, for his part, thought that dissenting clergy would consent to a form of Episcopal ordination if it did not suggest any invalidity in previous orders. Archbishop Herring was then consulted. The Primate had already had a long conversation with Doddridge on the subject, and had fallen in with Doddridge's suggestion, that, as a previous step, an occasional interchange of pulpits between Churchmen and Dissenters might be desirable. He thought comprehension 'a very good thing;' he wished it with all his heart, and considered that there was some hopes of its success. He believed most of the bishops agreed with him in these opinions.

No practical results ensued upon these conversations. They are interesting, and to some extent they were characteristic of the time. It is not known whether Herring and his brethren on the Episcopal bench suggested any practical measure of the kind to the Ministry then in power. If they had done so, the suggestion would have met with no response. 'I can tell you,' said Warburton, 'of certain science, that not the least alteration will be made in the Ecclesiastical system. The present ministers were bred up under, and act entirely on, the maxims of the last. And one of the principal of his was, Not to stir what is at rest.'[1] Pelham was a true disciple of Sir Robert Walpole, without his talent and without his courage—a man whose main political object was to glide quietly with the stream, and who trembled at the smallest eddies.[2] He was the last man to give a moment's countenance to any such scheme, if it were not loudly called for by a large or powerful section of the community. This was far from being the case. Indifference was too much the prevailing spirit of the age to allow more than a very negative kind of public feeling in such a matter. A carefully planned measure, not too suggestive of any considerable change, would have been acquiesced in by many, but enthusiastically welcomed by very few, while beyond doubt there would have been much vehement opposition to it.

Or, if circumstances had been somewhat different, and Herring and Sherlock, Doddridge and Chandler, had seen their plans extensively advocated, and carried triumphantly through Parliament, the result would in all probability have been a somewhat disappointing one. It would infallibly have been a slipshod comprehension. Carelessness and indifference would have had a large share in promoting it ; relaxation, greater than even then existed, of the order of the Church, would have been a likely consequence. The National Church was not in a sufficiently healthy and vigorous condition to conduct with much prospect of success an enlarged organisation, or to undertake, in any hopeful spirit, new and wider responsibilities. Nor would accessions from the Dissenting communities have infused much fresh life into it. They were suffering themselves under the same defect; all the more visibly, because a certain vigour of self-assertion seemed necessary to justify their very existence as separatist bodies. The Presbyterians were rapidly losing their old standing, and were lapsing into the ranks of Unitarianism. A large majo-

---

[1] Doddridge's *Correspondence*, v. 167. Perry's *Church History*, 3, 377.
[2] Lord Mahon's *History*, chap. 31.

rity of the general Baptists were adopting similar views. The ablest men among the Congregationalists were devoting themselves to teaching rather than to pastoral work. Unitarianism was the only form of dissent that was gaining in number and influence. The more orthodox denominations were daily losing in numbers and influence, and were secluding themselves more and more from the general thought and culture of the age.

Yet it is by no means equally certain that an Act of Comprehension carried in 1750 would have proved an ultimate failure. Relaxation in the terms of subscription, and other moderate concessions which would have sufficed to satisfy such men as Doddridge and Chandler, might very possibly, under the circumstances of the age, have been detrimental rather than advantageous to the interests of religion in their immediate effect. But so far as they were just and reasonable in themselves, their beneficial action would have been experienced as the period of stagnation gradually passed away, and when the revival, which was so soon to make itself felt, had gained force. Much would have depended upon the important question whether such a measure would have modified the attitude of the Church in its relation to the Wesleyan movement. Everybody knows that for a long time Methodism had nothing to do with Nonconformity. 'The Wesleys were bitter opponents of Dissent, especially Charles, who was always harping on the Established Church, and who remarked that he would sooner see his children Roman Catholics than Protestant Dissenters.'[1] Dissenters, on their side, very frequently shared in the distrust which so many Churchmen felt towards what they were apt to call sentiment or fanaticism. If the strength of the English Church had been reinforced from the ranks of Dissent, it might perhaps have gained no increased aptitude in discerning, and availing itself of, the new power for good which Wesley would have put into its hands. Or, on the other hand, the accession of a new element might have contributed to form within the National Church a higher and wiser policy in its dealings with the Methodist revival. The terms of peace proposed by Dissenters, however moderate in themselves, would have

[1] Skeats, 382.

necessitated some modifications in the Established order. Thus the Church would have been compelled to admit the idea of changes, and to abate something of the inflexibility which routine engenders. No effort of the kind could be made without a certain heat and ferment, which at all events would have served to awaken both the Church and Dissent from the torpor which had lately prevailed. The Church, profiting by its fresh experience in gaining new helpers and assimilating new ideas, might have shaken off the alarmed perplexity with which it generally regarded the Wesleyan preachers, and, rising to the occasion, might have retained as staunch friends and ardent co-operators the army of workers, who, by an opposite treatment, were being alienated against their own wills. The renewed life which presently sprang up in Dissent would have been its own also. It can thus be imagined that a comprehension effected in a time of apathy, on a small scale, and scanty in promise, might, under favourable circumstances, have proved after a time the fruitful germ of new organisations within the National Church rich in manifold activity.

After all, the greatest question which arose in the eighteenth century in connection with Church Comprehension was that which related to the Methodist movement. Not that the word 'Comprehension' was ever used in the discussion of it. In its beginnings, it was essentially an agitation which originated within the National Church, and one in which the very thought of secession was vehemently deprecated. As it advanced, though one episcopal charge after another was levelled against it; though pulpit after pulpit was indignantly refused to its leaders; though it was on all sides preached against, satirised, denounced; though the voices of its preachers were not unfrequently drowned in the clanging of church bells; though its best features were persistently misunderstood and misrepresented, and all its defects and weaknesses exposed with a merciless hand, Wesley, with the majority of his principal supporters, never ceased to declare his love for the Church of England, and his hearty loyalty to its principles. 'We do not,' he said, 'we dare not, separate from the service of the Church. We are not seceders, nor do we bear any resemblance to them.' And when one of his bitterest opponents charged him with ' stabbing the Church to her very vitals,' ' Do I, or you,' he retorted, ' do this ! Let anyone who has read her Liturgy, Articles, and Homilies, judge. . . . You desire that I should disown the Church. But I choose to stay in the Church, were it only to reprove those who betray her with a kiss.'[1] He stayed within it to the last, and on his deathbed, in 1791, he implored his followers even yet to refrain from secession.

Comprehension had always related to Dissenters. The term, therefore, could hardly be used in reference to men who claimed to be thorough Churchmen, who attended the services of the Church, loved its Liturgy, and willingly subscribed to all its formularies. The Methodist Societies bore a striking resemblance to the Collegia Pietatis established in Germany by Spener about 1670, which, at all events in their earlier years, simply aimed at the promotion of Christian holiness, while they preserved allegiance to the ecclesiastical order of the day ;[2] or we may be reminded of that Moravian community, by which the mind of Wesley was at one time so deeply fascinated, whose ideal, as Matter has observed, was to be ' Calviniste ici, Luthérienne là, Catholique partout par ses institutions épiscopales et ses doctrines ascétiques, et pourtant avant tout Chrétienne, et vraiment apostolique par ses missions.'[3] ' At a very early period of the renewed Moravian Church,' writes the translator of Schleiermacher's Letters, ' invitations were sent from various quarters of Europe for godly men to labour in the National Churches. These men did not dispense the Sacraments, but visited, prayed, read the Bible, and kept meetings for those who, without leaving the National Churches, sought to be " built up in communion" with right-minded pious persons.'[4] These words are exactly parallel to what Wesley wrote in one of his earlier works, and requoted in 1766. ' We look upon ourselves not as the authors or ringleaders of a particular sect or

---

[1] 'Answer to Bailey,' 1750,—*Works*, vol. ix. 83.

[2] Dorner's *History of Protestant Theology*, ii. 204–6. Rose's *Protestantism in Germany*, 46–9. F. W. Farrer's *History of Religious Thought*, note 17, p. 600. M. J. Matter's *Histoire de Christianisme*, 4, 346.

[3] Matter's *Histoire de Christianisme*, 4, 368.

T. Rowan's *Life and Letters of Schleiermacher*, i. 30.

party, but as messengers of God to those who are Christians in name, but heathens in heart and life, to lead them back to that from which they are fallen, to real genuine Christianity.'[1] His followers, he added, in South Britain, belong to the Church of England, in North Britain to the Church of Scotland. They were to be careful not to make divisions, not to baptize, nor administer the Lord's Supper.[2]

The difficulties in the way of comprehending within the National Church men such as these, and societies formed upon such principles, ought not to have been insurmountable. No doubt they would have been surmounted if the Church of England had been, at that date, in a really healthy and vigorous condition. Yet it must be allowed that in practice the difficuties would in no case have been found trivial. As with Zinzendorf and his united brethren, so with Wesley and his co-workers and disciples. Their aims were exalted, their labours ` noble, the results which they achieved were immense. But intermingled with it all there was so much weakness and credulity, so much weight given to the workings of a heated and over-wrought imagination, so many openings to a blind fanaticism, such morbid extravagances, so much from which sober reason and cultivated intellect shrank with instinctive repulsion, that even an exaggerated distrust of the good effected was natural and pardonable. Wesley's mind, though not by any means of the highest order of capacity, was refined, well trained, and practical; Whitefield was gifted with extraordinary powers of stirring the emotions by his fervid eloquence. But they often worked with very rude instruments; and defects, which were prominent enough even in the leaders, were sometimes in the followers magnified into glaring faults. Wesley himself was a true preacher of righteousness, and had the utmost horror of all Antinomianism, all teaching that insisted slightly on moral duties, or which disparaged any outward means of grace. But there was a section of the Methodists, especially in the earlier years of the movement, who seemed much disposed to raise the cry so well known among some of the fanatics of the Commonwealth of 'No works, no law, no Commandments.' There were many more

---

[1] 'Remarks on the Defence to Aspasio,' &c., 1766,—*Works*, 10, 351.
[2] Id.

who, in direct opposition to Wesley's sounder judgment, but not uncountenanced by what he said or wrote in his more excited moments, trusted in impressions, impulse, and feelings as principal guides of conduct. Wesley himself was never wont to speak of the Church of England or of its clergy in violent or abusive terms.[1] Whitefield, however, and, still more so, many of the lesser preachers, not unfrequently indulged in an undiscriminating bitterness of invective which could not fail to alienate Churchmen, and to place the utmost obstacles in the way of united action. Seward was a special offender in this respect. How was it possible for them to hold out a right hand of fellowship to one who would say, for example, that 'the scarlet whore of Babylon is not more corrupt either in principle or practice than the Church of England;'[2] and that Archbishop Tillotson, of whom, though they might differ from him, they were all justly proud, was 'a traitor who had sold his Lord for a better price than Judas had done.'[3] Such language inevitably widened the ever increasing gap. It might have been provoked, although not justified, by tirades no less furious and unreasoning on the part of some of the assailants of the Methodist cause. In any case, it could not fail to estrange many who might otherwise have gladly taken a friendly interest in the movement; it could not fail to dull their perception of its merits and of its spiritual exploits, and to incline them to point out with the quick discernment of hostile critics the evident blots and errors which frequently defaced it. The attitude of Whitefield's mind at the time when he wrote in his Diary, 'went to St. Paul's and received the blessed Sacrament,' and in the evening of the same day, 'never opened my mouth so freely against the letter-learned clergy of the Church of England,' is intelligible enough. Only it cannot be wondered at that many of these 'letter-learned clergy,' to whom the whole Church owed much for the zeal with which they had devoted their learning and talents to the defence of Christian doctrine, were more repelled from Methodism by such ignorant depre-

---

[1] Wesley's 'Answer to Lavington,'—*Works*, vol. 9, 3.

[2] Seward's 'Journal,' 45, quoted by Lavington. *Enthusiasm of Methodists and Papists Compared*, 11.

[3] Seward's 'Journal,' 62. Lavington, *Id.*

ciation of their labours, than drawn towards it by a communion which was still sincere and unreserved.

Yet, as was before intimated, the difficulties in the way of union and co-operation ought not to have been insuperable. The defects of Methodism, however apparent, were precisely those to which in all ages every enthusiastic movement of the kind has been liable. What had been utilised before to the service of the dominant Church might have been utilised with the greatest advantage again. George II. always maintained that ministers should have taken his advice and made Whitefield a bishop.[1] The rulers of the National Church would have done better still if they had taken Wesley into their confidence, and without cramping her freedom of action by the limitations which necessarily attend the Episcopate, had candidly consulted with him. Except that he was sometimes inclined to be overbearing and despotic, Wesley was singularly adapted to the work, if he had been invited to undertake it, of so organising the new societies as to make them a substantive part of the fabric of the Church of England. It is not often that a great reformer, whose whole soul is possessed with one fervid idea, is also gifted with large powers of system and with a great love of order. John Wesley, however, had in a very eminent degree this important qualification. No man of his day would probably have shown greater skill in suggesting modes by which an extended Church organisation could be safely and practically introduced, without unduly disturbing the parochial machinery of the Church. Nor when it had been established, could anyone have taken a more successful part than he in supervising the newly-constituted societies, and removing or lightening the difficulties which might at first attend their working. It might have seemed to be his special and appropriate calling to be the founder of what might correspond to a great monastic order adapted to the condition of a free and reformed National Church.

Wesley had another still more essential qualification—had proper advantage been taken of it—for promoting a good understanding between Methodists and Churchmen, who, however religiously disposed, looked upon the movement with distrust. He was not only a Churchman and a clergy-

---

[1] Pattison, in *Essays and Reviews*, 323.

man of the Church, but both by disposition and education was well able to enter into its spirit, and to sympathise with the tone of feeling which generally prevailed among its devouter members. The son of an earnest-minded High Church clergyman who loved the forms and institutions of the Church of England with an attachment which bordered on the verge of bigotry,[1] and who enjoyed the friendship of Robert Nelson,[2] and other excellent men of that stamp, he retained to the last the spirit with which he had become imbued while he was yet a child under his father's roof. 'To how many,' asks a reviewer of Tyerman's work, 'does the name of Methodist suggest the Oxford Ritualist of the eighteenth century? Yet it was men like Clayton and Ingham and Hervey who, despite their ritualism, really scattered broadcast up and down the land the principles, the vitality of which Wesley had, as it were, rediscovered. . . . Ritualists, Wesley, and most of the members of the " Holy Club," were till the end of life ; but ritualism was servant, not master, except in Clayton's case, and he never "forgave Wesley for assigning a subordinate place to sacraments, fasts, penances, &c. ; " though Clayton, spite of his extreme ritualism, his Jacobite tendencies, and even priestly superciliousness, had, as these [Tyerman's] pages sufficiently show, come under the same vital influence as the most determined " Methodist " of them all.'[3] It would never have been Wesley's fault if the thought and feeling which gives ecclesiasticism its spiritual life, and which animates the ritual of the English Liturgy, had been neglected.

Nor was he less capable of appreciating the Broad Churchmen of his day. There were many points in which he might not improperly be classed among the religious Latitudinarians of the eighteenth century. Jeremy Taylor had been at one time his favourite author. He had read his writings with

---

[1] ' I resolved, as soon as I came into the country, to use what little interest I had in our election to serve those who were not likely to be partial to the Dissenters.'—S. Wesley to Hearne, sch. 28, 1708, *Relig. Hearn.* 40. 'There is a gathering making in the university for the relief of Mr. Wesley, to the great mortification of the fanatics,' Hearne in *Id.* 41.

[2] S. Wesley's poem in memory of his friend was prefixed to some of the editions of Nelson's devotional works.

[3] *Spectator*, September 6, 1873, Review of L. Tyerman's *Oxford Methodists.*

profound interest; and the breadth and liberality of view conspicuous in that great divine left an impression upon his mind never afterwards to be effaced.[1] His studies of Henry More, and of the mystical theology of William Law, had a similar effect. At a later period he vehemently denounced the mystic writers as dangerous, obscure, and unscriptural. But he never ceased to be at one with them in his sense of the comparative unimportance of the doctrinal differences which separate Church from Church, or man from man, so long as the soul is awake to the illuminating influences of the Holy Spirit, and quickened by a deep sense of the love of God. No doubt a multitude of passages might be quoted from Wesley's works, especially during the first half of his public life, which would represent him as intolerant of differences, and very narrow in his ideas of justification and saving faith. His mind, however, was always penetrated by a very different vein of large-minded liberality, which sometimes declared itself unexpectedly and even inconsistently, but which, as he grew older, became gradually more predominant. ' It is true,' he said in his 'Answer to Lavington,' ' that for thirty years past I have gradually put on a more Catholic spirit, finding more and more tenderness for those who differed from me either in opinion or modes of thought.'[2] The well-known words, ' It is a point we chiefly insist upon, that orthodoxy or right opinion is, at best, but a very slender part of religion, if any part of it at all,'[3] a saying which at different times created much indignation against him, have been somewhat misunderstood. ' I assert' (as he afterwards explained) 'first, that in a truly righteous man, right opinions are a very slender part of religion ; secondly, that in an irreligious or profane man they are not any part of religion at all, such a man not being one jot more religious because he is orthodox. It does not follow from either of these propositions that wrong opinions are not a hindrance to religion.'[4] He was very far from being indifferent to error, because he thought error interfered with the love of God and of our neighbour. On this ground he strenuously attacked Roman

---

[1] Isaac Taylor, *Wesley and Methodism*, 28.
[2] Answer to Lavington,—*Works*, 9, 55.   [3] *Plain Account*, &c.
[4] Answer to Lavington,—*Works*, 9, 56.

Catholicism ;[1] while he wrote, not inconsistently, to a Roman Catholic acquaintance : ' My dear friend, consider I am not persuading you to leave or change your religion, but to follow after that fear and love of God without which all religion is vain. I say not a word to you about your opinions or outward manner of worship. But I say, all manner of worship is abomination to the Lord unless you worship Him in spirit and in truth. . . . The love of God and man, and the doing all as unto the Lord ; this and this alone is the old religion. This is primitive Christianity. . . . Are we not thus far agreed ? . . . . We ought without this endless jangling about opinions to provoke one another to love and good works.'[2] Wherever[3] he saw piety and goodness, he never failed to recognise the true spirit of Christ. In one place, as Dr. Hunt remarks,[4] he has quoted with approbation the words of an author who said 'What the heathens call reason, Solomon wisdom, St. Paul grace, St. John love, Luther faith, Fénelon virtue, is all one and the same thing, the light of Christ shining in different degrees under different dispensations.'

If, then, Wesley had much sympathy with High Churchmen, it is no less certain that he held very much in common with the religious Latitudinarians of his day. And now that Calvinism had ceased to be the doctrine of more than a comparatively small section of the Church of England, his strongly marked Arminianism would have increased, or certainly not have lessened, confidence in him, if he had once been accepted as the leader of a new movement within it. Many rational Churchmen would have applauded him, when he vehemently exclaimed, ' I would sooner be a Turk, a Deist, yea an

[1] ' Popery calmly considered,'—*Works*, 10, 157.

[2] ' Letter to a Roman Catholic,'—*Works*, x. 84.

[3] Rowland Hill wrote against Wesley, exactly as he would have written against Morgan or Chubb. ' All the divinity we find in this wretched harangue which he (Wesley) calls a sermon, are a few bungling scraps of the religion of nature, namely, love to God and man, which a heathen might have preached as well as Mr. John, and probably in a much better manner. Erase half a dozen lines, and I defy anyone to discover whether the apostle of the Foundry be a Jew, a Papist, a Pagan, or a Turk,' &c.—Rowland Hill, *Imposture Detected*, p. 4, quoted by Wesley in his ' Answer,' &c. 1777,—*Works*, x. 453. ' You may rank,' said Hervey, once his pupil and friend, 'with the Arian and Socinian,'—*Theron and Aspasio*, quoted by Wesley in ' A Treatise on Justification,'—*Works*, x. 391.

[4] Hunt's *Religious Thought in England*, 3, 290.

Atheist, than I could believe this [doctrine of reprobation]. It is less absurd to deny the very being of God than to make Him an almighty tyrant.'[1] 'O God!' he cries in another place, 'how long shall this doctrine stand?'[2]

That there was a close relation between Wesley's preaching and the newly rising Evangelical party in the Church, is also sufficiently obvious. The two movements were far from being identical. They were sometimes warmly opposed. Hervey, Rowland Hill, and Toplady were among Wesley's keenest antagonists. Had the Calvinistic question been the only source of difference, if Wesley was strongly on one side, Whitefield was no less strongly on the other. But many Evangelicals distrusted the whole system which Wesley had established, as 'enthusiastical' and irregular. Evangelicalism, or something nearly akin to it, would certainly have arisen about the same period, even if Methodism had never existed. The relation, however, between the two was very intimate. They arose out of the same causes, were fostered by similar influences, came into close contact, and were often confused one with the other. Secker, a favourable representative of the ordinary Churchmanship of his time, was evidently much disturbed by the irregularities of Methodism. But his later charges, as compared with his earlier ones, show how deeply he was impressed by it, and how great was the stimulus which it gave to pious and thoughtful minds. In his third charge as Archbishop of Canterbury in 1766, it had clearly contributed a good deal towards awakening him to the sense that 'we have in fact lost many of our people by not preaching in a manner sufficiently evangelical.'[3] Some of the evangelical leaders owed to the instrumentality of Methodism the deep religious impressions they had received— Hervey from Wesley at Oxford, Toplady from a Wesleyan preacher,[4] John Newton from Whitefield.[5] Long before the end of the century, 'methodistical' had become a term scoffingly applied to the seriousness of a Wilberforce or a Hannah More, almost

---

[1] 'A Treatise on Justification,' 1764.—*Works*, x. 334.
[2] 'Thoughts upon Necessity,' 1774.—*Works*, x. 480.
[3] Secker, *Works*, 299.
[4] Hunt's *Religious Thought in England*, 3, 347.
[5] Newton's *Letters*, 2, 29.

as much as if they had been Methodists. It is 'a bugbear word,' Mrs. Kennicott writes, 'very ingeniously introduced to frighten people from expressing those sentiments which they ought both to cherish and avow.'[1] Those who did not care to look closely into distinctions saw little difference in manner, language, and practices between Wesley's acknowledged adherents, and others who so generally thought with them, and who were so often associated with them in the practical management of Sunday schools and religious societies,[2] but who did not attend their meetings nor approve of their separate organisations. It will be remembered too that it was not until very nearly the end of the century that the Methodists, as a body, were no longer regarded by the Evangelical party in the Church as belonging to the same communion with them.

One very important qualification which Wesley would have possessed in any negotiations with the rulers of the Church, was his respect for mental cultivation and the reasoning powers. Although one of the greatest weaknesses of Methodism has been its intellectual poverty, its leader was fully competent to discuss all the bearings of the subject with thoughtful and cultured men. He never disparaged the great gift of human reason, nor joined in the silly outcry, raised by too many of his fellow-workers, against 'human learning.' 'I believe and reason too,' he said, 'for I find no inconsistency between them. And I would just as soon put out my eyes to secure my faith, as lay aside my reason.'[3] 'I am ready to give up any opinion which I cannot by calm, clear reason defend.'[4] 'Many men make an ill use of learning. But so they do of their bibles. Therefore this is no reason for despising or crying out against it.'[5] His own intellect was not a comprehensive one, but it was acute and diligently trained. He used to speak with gratitude of the opportunities afforded during the fifteen years he had laboriously spent at Oxford, as Greek lecturer, tutor, and moderator of the classes. Logic, in which he had been an adept, he especially valued. He was well read in general

---

[1] H. More's *Memoirs*, i. 205.
[2] Polwhele's 'Introduction' to Lavington, ccxxix–xxxii.
[3] 'Dialogue between an Antinomian and his Friend,' &c. 1745.—*Works*, 10, 267.
[4] 'Answer to Downes.—*Works*, 9, 105.   [5] Id.

theology, had studied the primitive fathers, and in his discussion with Roman Catholics has shown a considerable acquaintance with many of their principal authors. In his address to the clergy, he said he wished to see them soundly learned, educated in language, in profane history, &c., in logic and metaphysics, in geometry, and in natural philosophy ('for the accurate understanding of several passages in Scripture, and for showing the wondrous works of God'). He would have them also well acquainted with the primitive fathers, especially with those who lived before the Council of Nice, as being 'the most authentic commentators on Scripture, being both nearest the foundation, and eminently endued with that Spirit by whom all Scripture was given.'[1] 'Nor did he,' he adds, 'at all undervalue such gifts as knowledge of the world, discernment of spirits, good breeding, elocution,' &c.

With such a man as this to deal with, a man too who ardently desired to advance the best interests of the Church of England, and whose personal influence over his great army of disciples was great to an almost unprecedented extent, the difficulties, considerable though they were, which stood in the way of comprehension and hearty co-operation certainly ought not to have been invincible. If the English Church had awakened a little sooner than it did to a fuller sense of its responsibilities ; even if a few men of the type of Samuel Coleridge or of Dr. Arnold had lived a little earlier, and had exercised in the cause their talents and their influence, the various bodies of Methodists might still have been English Churchmen. It is the more to be lamented that this was not the case, because a successful association of the two communions might have been most beneficial to both, each supplying the other's lack. An able writer, who has studied Methodism carefully, and has not failed to do justice to the energy and spiritual power with which it accomplished a great mission, has pointed also with much force to some of its defects. 'A ministry,' he says, 'itinerating always, and therefore never competent to discharge pastoral functions,—a crude theology, adapted indeed to the field preacher's purpose, and to nothing else,—and a style of address to the people that tended always more to produce excitement than movement

[1] 'Address to the Clergy,' 1756.—*Works*, 10, 482–4.

or than progress: such surely were the causes of this characteristic of Wesleyan Methodism—its shallowness.'[1] Itinerancy, he justly remarks, is a most valuable instrument of spiritual aggression on the irreligious masses.[2] With some modifications and improvements[3]—for the Church of England could scarcely have borne with the gross ignorance of some of Wesley's preachers—Methodism might have been incorporated into the National Church as a most efficient missionary agency. The calmest minds might have tolerated, even if they could not welcome, bursts of extravagancy which were natural and unavoidable, if considered as attendant upon the sudden awakening in rude or guilty natures of a new spiritual sense, and of overpowering religious emotions not experienced before. But when the reason and imagination had been startled, when the convert, aroused from his inertness and self-security, had grasped with trembling gratitude a salvation, capable indeed of being forfeited, but immediate and complete—when he had passed through the shock of what might often be properly described as a new spiritual birth—then the weakness of Methodism began to reveal itself. It had accomplished a specific object of inestimable importance. It had conquered; and for a time it could follow up the victory. It received the captive of the Gospel into a Christian organisation well adapted to the crisis of his need. His liberty was forfeited, he was under perpetual surveillance, he was placed under the drill of class meetings, he was called upon to give a frequent account of his doings, of his feelings, of his spiritual state. The regimen, however, which is excellently fitted to bring into subjection and to tranquillise a newly conquered domain is not good for a perpetuity, and is not meant to be perpetual. It requires to be superseded, so far as the case permits, by a freer, quieter, more constitutional government. 'Though I give the Methodists,' wrote Alexander Knox, 'all credit for making first impressions, I cannot regard

---

[1] Isaac Taylor, *Wesley and Methodism*, 345.   [2] Id. 244.
[3] The writer just quoted has remarked, no doubt with great truth, that a Church would be likely to do much good by sending out some of its best men as itinerant preachers (p. 230). At the same time it would not be well to dispense entirely with the services of the poor and illiterate, who sometimes have a power which none others possess, of bringing home to the hearts of their fellows the leading truths of the Gospel.

them as equally fitted for leading the true Christian on-
ward.' There was always in it 'too much of a kind of bellows-
blowing method.' Two sets of workmen were wanted in the
Church, 'foundation men and superstructure men—the former
teaching how to become Christians ; the latter teaching what
Christians should become.' In his own case, 'in a time of
painful hardness,' he had gained a great benefit from a
Methodist preacher ; not afterwards. 'The methods of
Methodist piety were so much pointed to present effects, to
the producing something *now.* . . . It seemed clear to me,
that a quieter, more equable, more gradual course was the one
indicated for me to walk in.' [1] Wesley himself was often
bitterly mortified by the transiency of effects in which he had
exulted, and was frequently wont to complain of 'religion
being a very superficial thing among us.' This, however, is
a lament which all powerful preachers have too often had
cause to make. It may be more to the purpose to remark
that Wesley was himself quite aware that his system was
essentially an incomplete one, not intended to stand by itself.
'In his tract "Against separation from the Church of England,"
the eighth reason against any such separation is this, that the
Methodistic society must be founded upon a different model,
which would involve a very different task, a task to which
Wesley modestly thinks neither himself nor his friends competent.' [2] In a word, the Church would have gained immensely by the comprehension of Methodism. It would have
gained in it just what it most needed. But Methodism (supposing its action to be not cramped thereby) would have
been no less a gainer. Even its more immediate followers
would have profited greatly by its special machinery being
supplemented and supported by the regular ordinances of the
Church, by its tranquil piety, by the services of a resident and
well-educated ministry, by the liberty of thought and breadth
of view which is distinctive of a national Church. Methodism
can never make any deep impression upon the cultivated
classes. It can, at best, be only the Church of the poor, and
of the lower middle classes ;—a great evil in itself, seeing that
it is not the least considerable function of a Christian Church

---

[1] Alexander Knox, *Remains*, vol. i. 72–8.
[2] Isaac Taylor, *Wesley and Methodism*, 358.

to cement together in one union and fellowship all classes of society. But, with very few exceptions, men of high education and social standing will necessarily stand aloof from a society in which religion is presented to them in what they think a crude and unattractive form, and in which learning and culture are generally, and perhaps unavoidably, neglected. Combine the organisations of Methodism and those of the National Church, and these evils are avoided. It can only be hoped that the opportunity, once passed by, is not even yet irretrievable.

At the beginning of the eighteenth century, when projects of Church Comprehension had come to an end, a great deal of angry controversy in Parliament, in Convocation, and throughout the country at large, was excited by the practice of occasional conformity. Never was a question more debased by considerations with which it ought not to have had anything to do. In itself it seemed a very simple one. The failure of the schemes for Comprehension had left in the ranks of Nonconformity a great number of moderate Dissenters—Presbyterians and others—who were separated from the Low Churchmen of the day by an exceedingly narrow interval. Many of them were thoroughly well affected to the National Church, and were only restrained by a few scruples from being regular members of it. But since the barrier remained —a slight one, perhaps, but one which they felt they could not pass—might they not at all events render a partial allegiance to the national worship, by occasional attendance at its services, and by communicating with it now and then? The question, especially under the circumstances of the time, was none the less important for its simplicity. Unhappily, it was one which could not be answered on its merits. The operation of the Test Act interfered—a statute framed for the defence of the civil and ecclesiastical constitution of the country, but which long survived[1] to be a stain and disgrace

---

[1] George III.'s determined insistence upon it led to Pitt's resignation in 1801, when some concessions were proposed in favour of Roman Catholics. He held it, he said, to be 'a fundamental maxim on which our constitution is placed, that those who hold employments in the State must be members of the Established Church, and consequently obliged not only to take oaths against Popery, but to receive the Holy Communion according to the rites of the Church of England.' 'George III. to Pitt,' in Lord Russell's *Life of C. J. Fox,* iii. 251.

to it.   A measure so miserably false in principle as to render
civil and military qualifications dependent upon a sacramental
test must in any case be worse than indefensible.   As all feel
now, and as many felt even then, to make

> The symbols of atoning grace
> An office key, a pick-lock to a place,

must remain

> A blot that will be still a blot, in spite
> Of all that grave apologists may write ;
> And though a bishop toil to cleanse the stain,
> He wipes and scours the silver cup in vain.[1]

Or, in the measured words of Bishop Hoadly : 'To make the
celebration of this institution, which was ordained and confined by our Lord Himself to the serious remembrance of His
death in the assemblies and churches of Christians, to be the
instrument of some particular sort of Christians (as well as of
infidels and Atheists) getting into civil offices, and to be the
bar against other sorts of Christians, is debasing the most
sacred thing in the world into a political tool and engine of
State.'[2]   Still, in its original design, the Test Act, though not
less objectionable in principle, had in practice a very different
character from that which it afterwards wore.   Scarcely
challenged even by the strictest Puritans, it was forced upon
Charles II. as a measure of defence against Roman Catholics.
Just as the Commons insisted that the King should cancel
the Declaration of Indulgence on penalty of being refused
supplies for the Dutch war, so, at the same time, and in the
same spirit, they passed the Test Act as an effectual means
of excluding the Duke of York and other Romanists from
places of office and command.   To receive the Communion
according to the usage of the Church of England was 'a
proof,' as the author last quoted remarked in his answer to
Sherlock, 'that the man was not a Papist, because such
a liberty was never known to be indulged to them as this of
communicating with us.   Never known (he adds) since the

---

[1] Cowper's *Poems*, 'The Expostulation.'
[2] 'Answer to the Representation of the Lower House of Convocation.'—
Works, vol. ii. 522.

beginning of the Reformation; for then, several of the Papists communicated with the Protestant Church of England, till the bad consequences of it to their own cause, and not to that of our Church, made it to be absolutely forbidden by their conductors.'[1] This Act, thus originated, which lingered in the Statute Book till the reign of George IV., which even thoroughly religious men could be so blinded by their prejudices as to defend, and which even such friends of toleration as Lord Mansfield could declare to be a ' bulwark of the Constitution,'[2] put occasional conformity into a very different position from that which it would naturally take. Henceforth no Dissenter could communicate in the parish churches of his country without incurring some risk of an imputation which is especially revolting to all feelings alike of honour and religion. He might have it cast in his teeth that he was either committing or countenancing the sacrilegious hypocrisy, the base and shuffling trick, of communicating only to qualify for office. In the bitter language of party strife, the Act which was intended to suppress the custom of occasional conformity was sometimes called a bill ' for the prevention of hypocrisy.'[3] Such a name, if it was to be used at all, should rather have been reserved for a measure which those who used it would vehemently have opposed—the long-deferred measure which, in a future generation, at last removed the scandal of the test.

It is needless here to enter into the details of the excited and discreditable agitation by which the custom of occasional conformity was at length, for a time, defeated. The contest may be said to have begun in 1697, when Sir Humphrey Edwin, upon his election as Lord Mayor, after duly receiving the Sacrament according to the use of the Church of England, proceeded in state to the Congregational Chapel at Pinner's Hall.[4] Exactly the same thing recurred in 1701, in the case of Sir T. Abney.[5] The practice thus publicly illustrated was passionately opposed both by strict Dissenters and by strict

---

[1] Hoadly, 'Common Rights,' &c.—*Works,* ii. 702.
[2] Seward's *Anecdotes,* vol. ii. (ed. 1798), 437.
[3] Rogers' *Letter to the Lords,* &c. 1704.
[4] Calamy's *Life and Times,* i. 404. Perry's *History of the Church of England,* 3, 145.
[5] Calamy, i. 465. Skeats' *History of the Free Churches,* 187.

hurchmen. De Foe, as a representative of the former, veighed against it with great bitterness, as perfectly scanlous, and altogether unjustifiable.[1] The High Church irty, on their side, reprobated it with no less severity. A ll to prevent the practice was at once prepared. In spite of ie strength of the Tory and High Church reaction, the Whig irty in the House of Lords, vigorously supported by the iberal Bishops, just succeeded in throwing it out. A conrence was held between the two houses, 'the most crowded rat ever had been known—so much weight was laid on this iatter on both sides,'[2] with a similar result. The Commons iade other endeavours to carry the Act in a modified form, id with milder penalties ; a somewhat unscrupulous minority iade an attempt to tack it to a money bill, and so effect their irpose by a manœuvre. The Sacheverell episode fanned ie strange excitement that prevailed. A large body of the untry gentry and country clergy imagined that the destinies f the Church hung in the balance. The populace caught ie infection, without any clear understanding what they ere clamouring for. The Court, until it began to be larmed, used all its influence in support of the proposed bill. verywhere, but especially in coffee-houses and taverns,[3] a ud cry was raised against the Whigs, and most of all against ie Whig Bishops, for their steady opposition to it. At last, hen all chance of carrying the measure seemed to be lost, was suddenly made law through what appears to have been most discreditable compromise between a section of the Vhigs and the Earl of Nottingham. Great was the dismay. f some, great the triumph of others. It was 'a disgraceful argain,' said Calamy.[4] To many, Nottingham was eminently i patriot and a lover of the Church.'[5] Addison makes Sir oger 'launch out into the praise of the late Act of Parliaient for securing the Church of England. He told me with reat satisfaction, that he believed it already began to take ffect, for that a rigid Dissenter, who chanced to dine at his ouse on Christmas-day, had been observed to eat very

---

[1] Calamy, i. 465.
[2] Burnet's *History of his Own Times*, 721.
[3] Hoadly, 'Letter to a Clergyman,' &c.—*Works*, i. 19.
[4] Calamy, ii. 243.   [5] *Guardian*, No. 41.

plentifully of his plum-porridge.'[1]   The Act which received the worthy knight's characteristic panegyric was repeated seven years afterwards.

Nothing could well be more alien—it may be rather said, more repugnant—to the general tenor of present thought and feeling than this controversy of a past generation. Its importance, as a question of the day, mainly hinged upon the Test Act ; and there is no fear of history so repeating itself as to witness ever again the operation of a law consigned, however tardily, to such well-merited opprobrium. Unquestionably, when Dissenters received the Sacrament in the parish churches, the motive was in most cases a secular one. ' It is manifest,' says Hoadly, 'that there is hardly any occasional communicant who ever comes near the Church but precisely at that time when the whole parish knows he must come to qualify himself for some office.'[2]   This was a great scandal to religion ; but it was one the guilt of which, in many, if not in most cases, entirely devolved upon the authors and promoters of the test. As the writer just quoted has elsewhere remarked, a man might with perfect integrity do for the sake of an office what he had always held to be lawful, and what some men whom he much respected considered to be even a duty. It was a very scandalous thing for a person who lived in constant neglect of his religious duties to come merely to qualify. But plainly this was a sin which a Conformist was quite as likely to commit as a Nonconformist.[3]

The imposition of a test on all accounts so ill-advised and odious in principle was the more unfortunate, because, apart from it, occasional conformity, though it would never have attracted any considerable attention, might have been really important in its consequences. Considered in itself, without any reference to external and artificial motives, it had begun to take a strong hold upon the minds of many of the most exemplary and eminent Nonconformists. When the projects of comprehension failed, on which the moderates in Church and Dissent had set their heart, the Presbyterian leaders, and some of the Congregationalists, turned their

---

[1] *Spectator*, No. 269.
[2] Hoadly, ' Reasonableness of Conformity.'— *Works*, i. 284.
[3] ' Letter to a Clergyman,' &c. — *Works*, i. 30.

thoughts to occasional conformity as to a kind of substitute for that closer union with the National Church which they had reluctantly given up. It was 'a healing custom,' as Baxter had once called it. There were many quiet, religious people, members of Nonconformist bodies, who, as an expression of charity and Christian fellowship, and because they did not like to feel themselves entirely severed from the unity of the National Church, made a point of sometimes receiving the Communion from their parish clergyman, and who 'utterly disliked the design of the Conformity Bill, that it put a brand upon those who least interest themselves in our unhappy disputes.'[1] This was particularly the custom with many of the Presbyterian clergy, headed by Calamy, and, before him, by three men of the highest distinction for their piety, learning, and social influence, of whose services the National Church had been unhappily deprived by the ejection of 1662—Baxter, Bates, and Howe. 'Our moderate Nonconformist Presbyterians,' writes one of their number, 'are for their stated Communions with the congregations whereof they are pastors or members; but they will join in their parish churches for occasional Communion, or else they think themselves to be guilty of schism. Thus Dr. Bates does, sometime in the year, receive the Sacrament in his parish, and Mr. Baxter did often in the parish where I am. But as for myself, I declare my stated Communion to be with the Church (where we have a very worthy, ingenious, diligent, and exemplary doctor for our minister), and my occasional communion with the Nonconformist meetings, where I go sometimes, and sometimes am called to preach. In short, I am a Nonconformist minister, but a Conforming parishioner, and I know nobody (knowing my constant principles) that is offended at it. . . . Ask your minister, when you were baptized, into what Church was it? Whether it was not into the Church Universal? Ask him then, whether that which gives a man right to be a member of the Universal Church does not give him right of occasional Communion with all true Churches that are but parts of it.'[2] Calamy, though his admonitions on this point were very inadequately attended to, used always to maintain

---

[1] Matthew Henry, in Thoresby's *Correspondence*, i. 438.
[2] J. Humphrey, in Thoresby's *Correspondence*, i. 324.

that occasionally to communicate with the Church of England was not lawful only, nor yet expedient only, but a duty which ought to be considered indispensable.[1] Many Churchmen entirely agreed with this. 'I think,' said Archbishop Tenison, 'the practice of occasional Conformity, as used by the Dissenters, is so far from deserving the title of a vile hypocrisy, that it is the duty of all moderate Dissenters, upon their own principles, to do it.'[2] However wrong they might be in their separation, he thought that everything that tended to promote unity ought to be not discountenanced, but encouraged. And Burnet, among others, argued in the same spirit, that just as it had commonly been considered right to communicate with the Protestant churches abroad, as he himself had been accustomed to do in Geneva and Holland, so the Dissenters here were wholly right in communicating with the National Church, even though they wrongly considered it less perfect than their own.[3] He has elsewhere remarked upon the unseemly inconsistency of Prince George of Denmark who voted in the House of Lords against occasional Conformity, but was himself in every sense of the word an occasional Conformist, keeping up a Lutheran service, but sometimes receiving the Sacrament according to the English rites.[4]

There were of course many men of extreme views on either side to whom, if there had been no such thing as a Test Act, the practice of occasional conformity was a sign of laxity, wholly to be condemned. It was indifference, they said, lukewarmness, neutrality; it was involving the orthodox in the guilt of heresy; it was a self-proclaimed confession of the sin of needless schism. Sacheverell, in his famous sermon, raved against it as an admission of a Trojan horse, big with arms and ruin, into the holy city. It was the persistent effort of false brethren to carry the conventicle into the Church,[5] or the Church into the conventicle. 'What could

---

[1] Calamy's Abridgment of Baxter's *History*; Hoadly, Answer to Id. — *Works*, i. 284; Calamy's *Life*, i. 473; Thoresby's *Diary*, i. 399.

[2] Speech in the House of Lords, 1704.

[3] Burnet's *Life and Times*, 741.   [4] Id. 721.

[5] At this date, as White Kennet's biographer remarks, 'the name of Presbyterian was liberally bestowed on one of the archbishops, on several of the most exemplary bishops, as well as on great numbers among the inferior clergy.'—*Life of Kennet*, 102.

not be gained by comprehension and toleration must be brought about by moderation and occasional conformity; that is, what they could not do by open violence, they will not fail by secret treachery to accomplish.'[1] Much in the same way, there were Dissenters who would as soon hear the mass as the Liturgy, who would as willingly bow themselves in the house of Rimmon as conform for an hour to the usages of the English Church; and who, 'if you ask them their exceptions at the Book, thank God they never looked at it.'[2] By a decree of the Baptist conference in 1689,[3] repeated in 1742,[4] persons who on any pretext received the Sacrament in a parish church were to be at once excommunicated. Among men, in fact, of violent opinions on either side, an argument which appeared to them unanswerable was strongly based on the preposterous assumption that the Churchman and the Dissenter held wholly different creeds, or, as De Foe broadly put it, 'two religions.'[5]

But, had it not been for the provisions of the Test Act, extreme views on the subject would have received little attention, and the counsels of men like Baxter, Bates, and Calamy, would have gained a far deeper, if not a wider, hold on the minds of all moderate Nonconformists. The effect of those counsels was already very considerable, and of much importance in its bearing upon Church and Dissent. Opponents of Church comprehension were quite right in saying that their fears had been lulled in one direction, only to be revived in another. Those, on the other hand, who had been zealous in behalf of such projects, and had been disappointed to see their failure, were thoroughly consistent in defending the growing practice of occasional conformity, and in hoping for great results from it. At the beginning of the eighteenth century, Dissent was at a very low ebb. It was not only unpopular, but it was losing ground in different directions.[6] After the Restoration, and still more after the Act of Toleration, the numbers of the Noncon-

---

[1] *Sermon before the Lord Mayor,* &c. November 5, 1709.
[2] *The Church of England free from the Imputation of Popery,* 1683.
[3] Skeats' *History of the Free Churches,* 160.   [4] Id. 346.
[5] 'Enquiry into the Occasional Conformity of Dissenters;' and *Spectator,* 1868, 324.
[6] Skeats, 245-8.

formists had begun rapidly to decrease. 'In the last year of the prince's [Charles II.] reign, their cause did seem in a manner desperate, and had he lived but a few years longer, and the same methods had been pursued, it was thought by many the Schism would have been healed, and not one open Dissenter left in England.' [1] The meeting-houses were almost deserted, and the churches thronged.[2] Burnet had remembered the London churches very poorly attended; at the end of the century he did not know of many that had not overflowing congregations.[3] Many Nonconformist ministers, especially among the Presbyterians, took Episcopal orders, and in some cases rose to great eminence in the National Church.[4] Among their number was Bishop Butler, and Archbishop Secker, Maddox, Bishop of Worcester, and Hort, Archbishop of Tuam. Leighton, Tillotson, and Samuel Wesley,[5] had been similar instances in the preceding generation. Calamy not only gives a long list of those who thus seceded from the ranks of Nonconformity, but adds, that 'they were generally persons of sobriety and unblemished character.'[6] Thus for many years there was undoubtedly a remarkable drawing towards the National Church on the part of Nonconformists; for which (though other causes contributed to it) the Church was primarily indebted to the Act of Toleration, and to the sympathetic and friendly feeling which so many leading Churchmen showed towards them. 'Toleration,' said Burnet in the House of Lords, 'hath not only set the Dissenters at ease, but has made the Church both stronger and safer. . . . The Dissenters lose as much strength as we gain by it. Their numbers are abated, by a moderate computation, at least a fourth part, if not a

---

[1] *Life of Kettlewell*, 28.

[2] Thoresby's *Correspondence*, May, 18, 1684, i. 54.

[3] Burnet, quoted in Hunt's *Religious Thought in England*, 3, 223.

[4] 'Some of the choicest examples of the firm, consistent, English Christian character have been the product of the Nonconforming and Puritanical Christian soul, blended with the better ordered and more broadly based Christian temperament of the Episcopal Church. Need we name Leighton, Tillotson, Butler, Secker, as instances? While, on the other hand, the brightest adornments of Nonconformity have been those who, having been bred in that Church, were thrust out of it.'—I. Taylor's *Wesley and Methodism*, 18.

[5] Oliphant's *Historical Sketches*, ii. 8.

[6] Calamy's *Life*, &c. ii. 503-5.

third.' Similar remarks were constantly made in the House
of Lords, in the course of the occasional conformity debates.
'Dissent,' it was once remarked, 'was so visibly abating all
over the nation, that nothing but severity could prevent its
final absorption into the Church.' There is no question that
occasional conformity greatly tended to sap the foundation
of Dissent. High and Low Churchmen, moderate and
thorough Nonconformists, were all unanimous on this one
point, that occasional, very commonly led to constant conformity. Dissent for Dissent's sake was still an almost
unheard-of dogma. But to those who acknowledged that
Dissent was indefensible in the case of any persons who could
conscientiously conform, the argument suggested by occasional conformity seemed almost irresistible. If it was lawful to communicate with the English Church sometimes, why
not always? And if it was always lawful, how could they
justify their separation? The argument was unsound. Intercommunion may be not lawful only, but most right, and
in many ways desirable, even where separation is justified on
the highest grounds of edification. But the flaw in the
reasoning was not of a kind which was likely to be obvious
to the men of that time. In any case occasional conformity
must have led them to reflect on the truth, that separation is
either a duty or a sin, 'not, therefore, to be done without
conscientious deliberation, and a deep sense of responsibility.'[1]
The moderate Dissenters were separated from the moderate
Churchmen of Tillotson's and Hoadly's time by so slight an
interval, that it was easy to foresee what issue such thoughts
as these would tend to. Occasional conformity was rapidly
bringing into the National Church a large number of people,
who retained many of the feelings of Nonconformists, and
most of their old objections, but who had begun to think that
their scruples did not warrant, or, at all events, did not require, a separation which in itself was unpopular and unattractive. It might be supposed that this would be a
movement which all Churchmen would welcome. But,
apart from the alarm excited among the Tories at what they
thought an evasion of the test, this half-hearted Churchmanship which occasional conformity tended to create, this

---

[1] Whately's *Kingdom of Christ*, 195.

conformity of men who retained the scruples of Nonconformity, was to many of them thoroughly distasteful. It seemed to them that their fears had been lulled in one direction, only to be revived in another. They had opposed and defeated all plans for Church comprehension ; and now, under a changed form, there was to be a like dangerous influx of Dissenters into the Church. Those, on the other hand, who had been zealous in behalf of projects of comprehension and had been disappointed to see their failure, were thoroughly consistent in defending the growing practice of occasional conformity, and in hoping for great results from it. The practice in question did, in fact, point towards a comprehension of which the Liberal Churchmen of the time had as yet no idea, but one which might have been based on far sounder principles than any of the schemes which had hitherto been conceived. Under kindlier auspices it might have matured into a system of auxiliary societies affiliated into the National Church, through which persons, who approved in a general way of the doctrine and order ·of the Prayer Book and Articles, but to whom a different form of worship was more edifying or attractive, might be retained by a looser tie within the established communion. A comprehension of this kind suggests difficulties, but certainly they are not insurmountable. It is the only apparent mode by which High Anglicans, and those who would otherwise be Dissenters, can work together harmoniously, but without suggestion of compromise, as brother Churchmen. And in a great Church there should be abundant room for societies thus incorporated into it, and functions for them to fulfil, not less important than those which they have accomplished at the heavy cost of so much disunion, bitterness, and waste of power. If, at the opening of the eighteenth century, the test had been abolished, and occasional conformity, as practised by such men as Baxter and Bates, instead of being opposed, had been cordially welcomed, and its principles developed, the English Church might have turned to a noble purpose the popularity it enjoyed.

A chapter dealing in any way with Latitudinarianism in the last century would be incomplete, if some mention were not made of discussions which, without reference to the removal of Nonconformist scruples, related nevertheless to the general question of the revision of Church formularies.

Improvements civil or ecclesiastical, for improvement's sake, were not much to the taste of the age of Queen Anne and the Georges. A couplet of Matthew Green's might be taken for the general motto of most leading men of the time:

> Reforming schemes are none of mine ;
> To mend the world 's a vast design.[1]

Even if the Liturgy had been far less perfect than it is, and if abuses in the English Church and causes for complaint had been far more flagrant than they were, there would have been little inclination, under the rule of Walpole and his successors, to meddle with prescribed customs. Waterland, in one of his treatises against Clarke, compared perpetual reforming to living on physic. The comparison is apt. But it was rather the fault of his age to trust overmuch to the healing power of nature, and not to apply medicine even where it was really needed. There was very little ecclesiastical legislation in the eighteenth century, except such as was directed at first to the imposition, and afterwards to the tardy removal or abatement, of disabilities upon Roman Catholics and Dissenters. Statesmen dreaded nothing much more than 'a Church clamour.'[2] Their dread was in a great measure justified by the passions which had been excited in the times of the Sacheverell and Church in Danger cries, and by the unreasoning intolerance which broke furiously out afresh when the Bill for naturalising Jews was brought forward in 1753, and when relief to Roman Catholics was proposed in 1778. At the end of the century the panic excited by the French Revolution was an effectual bar against anything that partook in any degree of the nature of innovation. Throughout the whole of the period very little was done, except in improvement of the marriage laws, even to check practices which brought scandal upon the Church or did it evident injury ; next to nothing was done with a serious and anxious purpose of promoting its efficiency and extending its popularity. The best considered plans of revision and reform would have found but small favour. It was not without

[1] M. Green's *Poems*, 'The Spleen,' Anderson's *B. Poets*, x. 754.
[2] Horace Walpole's *Memoirs*, &c. 366.

much regret that the Low or Latitudinarian party gave up all hope of procuring any of those alterations in the Prayer Book for which they had laboured so earnestly in the reign of William III. Or rather, they did not entirely give up the hope, but gradually ceased to consider the subject as any longer a practical one. After them the advocacy of such schemes was left almost entirely to men who suffered more or less under the imputation of heterodoxy. This, of course, still further discredited the idea of revision, and gave a strong handle to those who were opposed to it. It became easy to set down as Deists or Arians all who suggested alterations in the established order. And the argument followed, ' we shall never be such fools as to call in an enemy to the substance of any system, to remove its corruptions, to supply its defects, or to perfect its construction.' The 'Free and Candid Disquisitions,[1] published in 1749 by John Jones, Vicar of Alconbury, did something towards reviving interest in the question. It was mainly a compilation of opinions advanced by eminent divines, past and living, in favour of revising the Liturgy, and making certain omissions and emendations in it. Introductory essays were prefixed. The book was addressed to ' the Governing Bodies of Church and State,' more immediately to the two Houses of Convocation, and commended itself by the modest and generally judicious spirit in which it was written. Warburton wrote to Doddridge that he thought the 'Disquisitions' very edifying and exemplary. ' I wish,' he added, ' success to them as much as you can do.'[2] Some of the bishops would gladly have taken up some such design, and have done their best to further its success. But there was no prospect whatever of anything being done.[3] It was evident that the prevailing disposition

---

[1] They are carefully summarised in a series of papers in the *Gentleman's Magazine* for 1750, vols. xix. and xx. It is clear from the correspondence on the subject how much interest they aroused. See also Nichols' *Lit. An.*, vol. 3.

[2] Hunt's *Religious Thought in England*, iii. 300.

[3] ' Even in an affair of the highest consequence, how negligent is the Community ! I mean in the long-expected reformation of our Liturgy ; in which, excellent as it is on the whole, there are some passages so justly exceptionable, that every bishop in the kingdom will tell you he wishes to have them expunged ; and yet I know not for what political or timid reason it continues just as it did.' J. Hervey, Letter 155, 1756.— *Works*, 1805, vol. vi. Bishop Sherlock, in re-

was to allow that there were improvements which might and ought to be made, but that all attempts to carry them out should be deferred to some more opportune season, when minds were more tranquil, and the Church more united.[1] The effect of the ' Disquisitions' was also seriously injured by the warm advocacy they received from Blackburne and others, who were anxious for far greater changes than any which were then proposed. Blackburne, in the violence of his Protestantism, insisted that in the Reformed Church of England there ought not to be ' one circumstance in her constitution borrowed from the Creeds, Ritual, and Ordinaries of the Popish system.'[2] A little of the same tendency may be discovered in the proposals put forward in the Disquisitions. In truth, in the eighteenth, as in the seventeenth century, there was always some just cause for fear that a work of revision, however desirable in itself, might be marred by some unworthy concessions to a timid and ignorant Protestantism.[3]

Revision of the Liturgy, although occasionally discussed, cannot be said to have been an eighteenth-century question. Subscription, on the other hand, as required by law to the Thirty-nine Articles, received a great deal of anxious attention. This was quite inevitable. Much had been said and written on the subject in the two previous centuries ; but until law, or usage so well established and so well understood as to take the place of law, had interpreted with sufficient plainness the force and meaning of subscription, the subject was necessarily encompassed with much uneasiness and perplexity. Through a material alteration in the law of the English Church, the consciences of the clergy have at last been relieved of what could scarcely fail to be a stumbling-block. By an Act

ference to the *Disquisitions,* said ' it seemed to him a very proper time for applying to the Government in behalf of a Review, provided a competent number of the clergy and others should be found to favour so able and useful a design.'—Cassan's *Lives of the Bishops of Salisbury,* 262.

[1] ' Et potest ea fieri et debet : sed modestá tractatione, sed tranquillis hominum animis ; non temerariis, qualia vidimus et videmus, ausis, non inter media dissidia mutuasque suspiciones.'—Secker, ' Concio ad Convoc.,' 1761.—*Works,* 363.

[2] Blackburne's *Historical View,* &c., Introduction, xx.

[3] Schemes of revision were associated, as will be noticed a few pages later, with the movement relating to Subscription to the Articles.

passed by Parliament in 1865, and confirmed by both Houses of Convocation, an important change was made in the wording of the declaration required. Before that time the subscriber had to 'acknowledge all and every the Articles. . . . . to be agreeable to the word of God.'[1] He now has to assent to the Articles, the Book of Common Prayer, and of the ordering of priests and deacons, and to believe the doctrine therein set forth to be agreeable to the Word of God. The omission of the ' all and every,' and the insertion of the word ' doctrine ' in the singular, constituted a substantial improvement, as distinctly recognising that general adhesion and that liberty of criticism, which had long been practically admitted, and in fact authorised, by competent legal decisions, but which scarcely seemed warranted by the wording of the subscription.

Dr. Jortin, in a treatise which he published about the middle of the last century, summed up under four heads the different opinions which, in his time were entertained upon the subject. ' Subscription,' he said, ' to the Articles, Liturgy, &c., in a rigid sense, is a consent to them all in general, and to every proposition contained in them ; according to the intention of the compiler, when that can be known, and according to the obvious usual signification of the words. Subscription, in a second sense, is a consent to them in a meaning which is not always consistent with the intention of the compiler, nor with the more usual signification of the words ; but is consistent with those passages of Scripture which the compiler had in view. Subscription, in a third sense, is an assent to them as to articles of peace and conformity, by which we so far submit to them as not to raise disturbances about them and set the people against them. Subscription, in a fourth sense, is an assent to them as far as they are consistent with the Scriptures and themselves, but no further.'[1] Jortin's classification might perhaps be improved and simplified ; but it serves to indicate in how lax a sense subscription was accepted by some—the more so, as it was sometimes, in the case, for instance, of younger undergraduates, evidently intended for a mere declaration of churchmanship—and how

---

[1] Canon 36, § 3.
[2] ' Strictures on the Articles, Subscriptions, &c.,' Jortin's *Tracts*, ii. 417.

oppressive it must have been to the minds and consciences of others. From the very first this ambiguity had existed. There can, indeed, be no doubt that the original composers of the Articles cherished the vain hope of 'avoiding of diversities of opinion,' and intended them all to be understood in one plain literal sense. Yet, in the prefatory declaration, His Majesty 'takes comfort that even in those curious points in which the present differences lie, men of all sorts take the Articles of the Church of England to be for them,' even while he adds the strangely illogical inference that 'therefore' no man is to put his own sense or meaning upon any of them.

Those who insisted upon a stringent and literal interpretation of the Articles were able to use language which, whatever might be the error involved in it, could not fail to impress a grave sense of responsibility upon every truthful and honourable man who might be called upon to give his assent to them. 'The prevarication,' said Waterland, ' of subscribing to forms which men believe not according to the true and proper sense of words, and the known intent of imposers and compilers, and the subtleties invented to defend or palliate such gross insincerity, will be little else than disguised atheism.'[1] Whiston,[2] and other writers, such as Dr. Conybeare,[3] Dean Tucker,[4] and others, spoke scarcely less strongly. It is evident, too, that where subscription was necessary for admission to temporal endowments and Church preferment, the candidate was more than ever bound to examine closely into the sincerity of his act.

But the answer of those who claimed a greater latitude of interpretation was obvious. 'They,' said Paley, 'who contend that nothing less can justify subscription to the Thirty-nine Articles than the actual belief of each and every separate proposition contained in them must suppose the Legislature expected the consent of ten thousand men, and that in perpetual succession, not to one controverted position, but to many hundreds. It is difficult to conceive how this could be expected by any who observed the incurable diversity of

---

[1] Quoted in *The Church of England Vindicated*, &c., 1801, p. 2.
[2] Whiston's *Life of Clarke*, &c., 11, 40; *Memoirs*, 157, &c.
[3] Hunt's *Religious Thought in England*, 3, 305.
[4] Id. 312.

human opinions upon all subjects short of demonstration.'[1]
Subscription on such terms would not only produce total
extinction of anything like independent thought,[2] it would
become difficult to understand how any rational being could
subscribe at all.   Practically, those who took the more stringent view acted for the most part on much the same principles as those whom they accused of laxity.   They each interpreted the Articles according to their own construction of
them.   Only the one insisted that the compilers of them were
of their mind ; the others simply argued that theirs was a
lawful and allowable interpretation.   Bishop Tomline expressed himself in much the same terms as Waterland had
done ; but was indignantly asked how, in his well-known
treatise, he could possibly impose an altogether anti-Calvi-
nistic sense upon the Articles without violation of their grammatical meaning, and without encouraging what the Calvinists
of the day called 'the general present prevarication.'[3]   A
moderate Latitudinarianism in regard of subscription was
after all more candid, as it certainly was more rational.   Nor
was there any lack of distinguished authority to support it.
'For the Church of England,' said Chillingworth, 'I am persuaded that the constant doctrine of it is so pure and orthodox, that whosoever believes it, and lives according to it,
undoubtedly he shall be saved, and that there is no error in
it which may necessitate or warrant any man to disturb the
peace or renounce the communion of it.   This, in my opinion,
is all intended by subscription.'[4]   Bramhall,[5] Stillingfleet,
Sanderson,[6] Patrick,[7] Fowler, Laud,[8] Tillotson, Chief Justice
King, Baxter, and other eminent men of different schools of
thought, were on this point more or less agreed with Chillingworth.   Moreover, the very freedom of criticism which such

---

[1]   Paley's *Moral and Political Philosophy*, chap. xxii.
[2]   Mr. Buxton, Parl. Speech, June 21, 1865.
[3]   *Church of England Vindicated*, &c., 52, 161.
[4]   *Works*, vol. i. 35.
[5]   Quoted in Jortin's *Tracts*, ii. 423, and Hunt's *Religious Thought in England*, ii. 25.
[6]   Quoted in Malone's note to Boswell's *Johnson*, ii. 104.
[7]   Review of Maizeaux' 'Life of Chillingworth,' *Guardian*, November 30, 1864.
[8]   'Sense of the Articles,' &c. *Works*, vol. xv., 528-33.   'Moral Prognostication,' &c. id. xv., 440.

great divines as Jeremy Taylor had exercised without thought of censure, and the earnest vindication, frequent among all Protestants, of the rights of the individual judgment, were standing proofs that subscription had not been generally considered the oppressive bondage which some were fain to make it.

Nevertheless, the position maintained by Waterland, by Whiston, by Blackburne, and by some of the more ardent Calvinists, was strong, and felt to be so. In appearance, if not in reality, there was clearly something equivocal, some appearance of casuistry and reserve, if not of insincerity, in subscribing to formularies, part of which were no longer accepted in the spirit in which they had been drawn up, and with the meaning they had been originally intended to bear. The Deistical and Arian controversies of the eighteenth century threw these considerations into more than usual prominence. Since the time of Laud, Arminian had been so generally substituted for Calvinistical tenets in the Church of England, that few persons would have challenged the right of subscribing the Articles with a very different construction from that which they wore when the influence of Bucer and Peter Martyr was predominant, or even when Hale and Ward, and their fellow Calvinists, attended in behalf of England at the Synod of Dort. On this point, at all events, it was quite unmistakeable that the Articles (as Hoadly said)[1] were by public authority allowed a latitude of interpretation. But it was not quite easy to see where the bounds of this latitude **were** to be drawn, unless they were to be left to the individual conscience. And it was a latitude which had become open to abuse in a new and formidable way. Open or suspected Deists and Arians were known to have signed the Articles on the ground of general conformity to the English Church. No one knew how far revealed religion might be undermined, or attacked under a masked battery, by concealed and unsuspected enemies. The danger that Deists, in any proper sense of the word, might take English orders appears to have been quite overrated. No disbeliever in Revelation, unless guilty of an insincerity which precautions were powerless to guard against, could give his allegiance to the English liturgy.

[1] Answer to Rep. of Con. chap. i. § 20.—*Works,* ii. 534.

But Arian subscription had become a familiar name ; and a strong feeling arose that a clearer understanding should be come to as to what acceptance of Church formularies implied. In another chapter of this work the subject has come under notice in its relation to those who held, or were supposed to hold, heretical opinions upon the doctrine of the Trinity. The remarks, therefore, here made need only be concerned with the uneasiness that was awakened in reference to subscription generally. The society which was instituted at the Feathers Tavern, to agitate for the abolition of subscription, in favour of a simple acknowledgment of belief in Scripture, and which petitioned Parliament to this effect in 1772, was a very mixed company. Undoubtedly there were many Deists, Socinians, and Arians in it. But it also numbered in its list many thoroughly orthodox clergymen,[1] and would have numbered many more, had it not been for the natural objection which they felt at being associated, in such a connection, with men whose views they greatly disapproved of. Archdeacon Blackburne himself, the great promoter of it, held no heretical opinions on the subject of the Trinity. There was a great deal in the doctrine, discipline, and ritual of the Church of England which he thought exceptionable, but his objections seem to have been entirely those which were commonly brought forward by ultra-Protestants. His vehement opposition to subscription rested on wholly general grounds. He could not, he said, accept the view that the Articles could be signed with a latitude of interpretation or as articles of peace. They were evidently meant to be received in one strictly literal sense. This, no Church had a right to impose upon any of its members ; it was wholly

---

[1] According to Walpole (*Mems. of George III.'s Reign*, i. 8.), Bishop Lowth was inclined to subscribe to it. The most distinguished of its supporters was Edmund Law, Bishop of Carlisle, a Broad Churchman. of well-deserved repute. There are passages in his *Theory of Religion* which show great earnestness and vigour of thought. He was, however, bitterly assailed for his support of Archdeacon Blackburne and of the petition of 1772. One writer speaks of him as

'With Blackburne leagued in many a motley page,
Immortal war with Mother Church to wage.'

—'Cambridge Triumphant,' *Asylum for Fugitive Pieces*, 1785, iii. 138.

The cause, good or bad, did not gain much by the advocacy of Archdeacon, afterwards Bishop Watson.

wrong to attempt to settle religion once for all in an uncontrollable form.[1] He, and the more orthodox of his fellow-petitioners, would have taken exactly the same ground as Baxter had done. 'If any heretics (as Arians, Socinians, &c.) would creep into the ministry, there shall not be new forms of subscription made to keep them out (which it is likely, with their vicious consequences, would be ineffectual, and would open a gap to the old Church tyrannies and divisions); nor an uncertain evil be ineffectually visited by a certain greater mischief. But while he keepeth his error to himself he is no heretic as to the Church (*non apparere* being equal to *non esse*) ; and when he venteth his heresy he is responsible in the ways aforesaid, and may . . . . by the Churches be branded as none of their communion.'[2] The petition, however, had not the smallest chance of success. The Evangelicals—a body fast rising in numbers and activity—and the Methodists[3] were strongly opposed. So were all the High Churchmen ; so also were a great number of the Latitudinarians. Dr. Balguy, for instance, after the example of Hoadly, while he strongly insisted that the laws of the Church and realm most fully warranted a broad construction of the meaning of the Articles, was entirely opposed to the abolition of subscription. It would, he feared, seriously affect the constitution of the National Church.[4] The Bill was thrown out in three successive years by immense majorities. After the third defeat Dr. Jebb, Theophilus Lindsey, and some other clergymen, seceded to the Unitarians. The language of the earlier Articles admits of no interpretation by which Unitarians, in any proper sense of the word, could with any honesty hold their place in the English Communion.

---

[1] Blackburne's *Historical View*, Introd. xxxix.

[2] 'A Moral Prognostication.'—*Works*, xv. 442.

[3] H. Walpole, *Memoirs of the Reign of George III.* (Doran), i. 7, 8.

[4] Dean Tucker also distrusted the purpose of many of the petitioners. In a letter to one of them, he says, 'Produce your own plan or model. Give us a specimen of a new Confession . . . if you have any to produce ; and after that, as you have freely and severely exercised your private judgment upon ours, we ought to be allowed great liberty to scrutinise the contents of yours.'—'Apology for the present Church of England,' 1772. — *Works*, i. 55. Subscription, however, by undergraduates he desired entirely to abolish, and was not indisposed to see a revision of the Articles.

Thus the attempt to abolish subscription failed, and under circumstances which showed that the Church had escaped a serious danger. But the difficulty which had led many orthodox clergymen to join, not without risk of obloquy, in the petition remained untouched. It was, in fact, aggravated rather than not; for 'Arian subscription' had naturally induced a disposition, strongly expressed in some Parliamentary speeches, to reflect injuriously upon that reasonable and allowed latitude of construction, without which the Reformed Church of England would in every generation have lost some of its best and ablest men. Some, therefore, were anxious that the Articles and Liturgy should be revised; and a petition to this effect was presented in 1772 to the Archbishop of Canterbury.[1] Among the other names attached to it appears that of Beilby Porteus, afterwards Bishop of London and a principal supporter of the Evangelical party. Some proposed that the 'orthodox Articles' only— by which they meant those that relate to the primary doctrines of the Christian creed—should be subscribed to;[2] some thought that it would be sufficient to require of the clergy only an unequivocal assent to the Book of Common Prayer. It seems strange that while abolition of subscription was proposed by some, revision of the Articles by others, no one, so far as it appears, proposed the more obvious alternative of modifying the wording of the terms in which subscription was made. But nothing of any kind was done. The bishops, upon consultation, thought it advisable to leave matters alone. They may have been right. But, throughout the greater part of the century, leaving alone was too much the wisdom of the leaders and rulers of the English Church.

In all the course of its long history, before and after the

---

[1] *Life and Works of Bishop Porteus*, by R. Hodson, i. 38-40. Archbishop Cornwallis appears to have been in favour of it. 'What think you concerning the archiepiscopal scheme of reforming the Liturgy and Articles? Such a plan is certainly on the carpet; and it has certainly originated at Lambeth. The ostensible pretext is to expunge some exceptionable passages which are offensive to thinking men and hurtful to tender consciences. The new Lambeth Articles (if Providence do not render the design abortive) will be of a very different cast from the old ones of 1595.'—Toplady to Dr. B. February 4, 1773.—*Works*, vi. 161.
[2] *Consideration of the Present State of Religion*, &c. 1801, 11.

Reformation, the National Church of England has never, perhaps, occupied so peculiarly isolated a place in Christendom as at the extreme end of the last century and through the earlier years of the present one. At one or another period it may have been more jealous of foreign influence, more violently antagonistic to Roman Catholics, more intolerant of Dissent, more wedded to uniformity in doctrine and discipline. But at no one time had it stood, as a Church, so distinctly apart from all other Communions. If the events of the French Revolution had slightly mitigated the antipathy to Roman Catholicism, there was still not the very slightest approximation to it on the part of the highest Anglicans, if any such continued to exist. The Eastern Church, after attracting a faint curiosity through the overtures of the later Nonjurors, was as wholly unknown and unthought of as though it had been an insignificant sect in the furthest wilds of Muscovy. All communications with the foreign Protestant Churches had ceased. It had beheld, after the death of Wesley, almost the last links severed between itself and Methodism. It had become separated from Dissenters generally by a wider interval. Its attitude towards them was becoming less intolerant, but more chilled and exclusive. The Evangelicals combined to some extent with Nonconformists, and often met on the same platforms. But there was no longer anything like the friendly intercourse which had existed in the beginning and in the middle of last century between the bishops and clergy of the 'moderate' party in the Church on the one hand, and the principal Nonconformist ministers on the other. Comprehension—until the time of Dr. Arnold—was no longer discussed. Occasional conformity had in long past time received the blow which deprived it of importance. Again, the Church of England was still almost confined, except by its missions, within the limits of the four seas. Pananglicanism was a term yet to be invented. The Colonial empire was still in its infancy, and its Church in tutelage. There was a sister Church in the United States. But the wounds inflicted in the late war were scarcely staunched; and the time had not arrived to speak of cordiality, or of community of Church interests. It [illegible] English [illegible] America [illegible]

[illegible] Providence [illegible] as of [illegible] the century [illegible] stream of life which [illegible] any new [illegible] might be reserved to [illegible] century there would [illegible] striving to embrace [illegible] a part of what it already [illegible] might not be easy to recover. [illegible] would have been [illegible] and this not so much in [illegible] for the sake of tranquil days. [illegible] which a later age would regret [illegible] the Churchmen of that period had a [illegible] and of examination [illegible] They did not do that part of their [illegible] they might have done it not so well [illegible] concentrated on the special [illegible]—if they had been called [illegible] important changes in the [illegible] schemes of Church extension. [illegible] are not to be excused by un[illegible] in them: yet it is, at all events, an allowable and pleasant thing to consider whether good may not have resulted in the end. Throughout the eighteenth century the principles of the Church of England were retained, if sometimes inactive, yet at least intact, ready for development and expansion, if ever the time should come. Already, at the end of the century, our National Church was teeming with the promise of a new or reinvigorated life. The time for greater union, in which this Church may have a great part to do, and for increased comprehensiveness, may, in our day, be ripening towards maturity. Even now there is little fear that in any changes and improvements which might be made, the English Church would relax its hold either on primitive and Catholic uses, or on that precious

eritance of liberty which was secured at the Reformation.
ere may be difficulties, too great to be overcome, in the
y either of Church revision or Church comprehension;
t if they should be achieved, their true principles would
better understood than ever they were in the days of
llotson and Calamy, or of Secker and Doddridge.

C. J. A.

CHAPTER VII.

THE ESSAYISTS.

The first twenty years of the eighteenth century are distinguished both from the period which preceded and that which followed them by the important influence which periodical literature exercised over the affairs both of Church and State. Before the century began, and after its second decade closed, there was nothing of this kind which deserves to be called a power in the country.[1] But during those first twenty years, or at least a part of them, it would be scarcely too much to say that the Essayists and Pamphleteers were a more influential section of society than any other class. The present work is no further concerned with these writers than as they affected the interests of religion. But they did affect those interests in a most important particular. It is no disparagement to the excellent divines who adorned the English Church at the beginning of the eighteenth century to say that the most effectual weapon against irreligion and immorality was wielded by no hand of theirs. The circumstances of the time loudly called for the intervention of some non-official aid, to stem the torrent of vice and impiety which, by the confession of all good men, was then flooding the land. Probably no professional advocates could have brought about such a revulsion of feeling against vicious literature as was wrought by two laymen, whose sincerity was commended by the mere fact that they *were* laymen, and

[1] At least not in the same sense that the *Tatler*, *Spectator*, &c., were. The *Craftsman*, it is true, was conducted with great ability and had great influence, but though its form was precisely like that of the *Spectator*, being composed of short papers, each with a motto, and with letters and comments upon them, &c., and though it avowedly took the *Spectator* as its model ('Like my illustrial predecessor, the *Spectator*,' see No. 26), it was too purely political a paper to be ranked in the same class.

whose commerce with the outer world enabled them to adapt themselves to the lay mind better than the divines of the day could do. For at this period the distinctions between the lay and clerical order were so marked, that the latter, even with the best of intentions, could not have exerted the influence they otherwise might have done over the former. One who himself perhaps erred in the other extreme complains that 'the clergy prevent themselves from doing service to religion by affecting so much to converse with each other, and caring so little to mingle with the laity.'[1] Political causes served to widen the breach. The majority of the clergy were out of sympathy with the great mass of the nation on the question of government. Many of them were actually opposed to, and still more were but lukewarm supporters of, the Revolution Settlement. Nor can it be denied that the personal characters of too many of the clergy tended to diminish the influence of the order. The haughtiness and inordinate desire of preferment too often conspicuous in the higher clergy, and the sycophancy and illiterateness among the lower, brought about the curious result, that at a time when the Church system was most popular, its ministers were as a body most unpopular.

From these and other causes, the appearance of the 'diurnal papers' which will form the main subject of this chapter mark a distinct epoch in the history of religion and morality.

Before proceeding to notice those writers with whom this sketch is chiefly concerned, it will be well to refer to some others in the same field of literature, whose writings, if of less permanent interest, created at the time almost as much excitement as the 'Tatler' and 'Spectator' themselves. Indeed, upon the external history of the Church as a political institution, they throw more light than did the latter, who owed no small part of the beneficial effects which they produced to their prudent abstinence from Church politics.

'The Observator' of L'Estrange and 'The Rehearsals' of Charles Leslie, though in one sense they may be termed periodicals, and though both dealt with matters connected with the English Church, scarcely come within the scope of

---

[1] Swift's *Project for the Advancement of Religion.*

the present paper. The latter, indeed, like all the writings of that able controversialist, is full of talent ; but it is a periodical only in the sense that it came out in separate papers ; as it now stands, it is simply a consecutive dialogue that might equally well have been published all at once. The former never possessed any great interest, and what it once had it has now lost.

The first *bond fide* periodical which claims attention in order of date is the 'Review' of Daniel Defoe. Projected in prison and continued two or three times a week for nine years, until it swelled into nine quarto volumes all written by one single pen, the 'Review' remains [1] a standing witness to the marvellous fertility and industry of its writer. Defoe's protests against religious persecution, his warnings against the imminent danger which England ran from a combination of France and Rome, his exposure of the immoral character of occasional conformity,[2] his strictures upon clerical laxity and preferment-hunting were only too much needed. Besides his 'Review' and his larger works in prose and verse, this prolific writer published many pamphlets on subjects relating to Church and Dissent, all of which are full of shrewd common sense. Without any pretensions to the classical culture and delicate humour of Addison, or to the caustic wit of Swift, Defoe's essays and pamphlets are still an important and interesting contribution to the periodical literature of the time. His style is clear and vigorous, and though he was not without a tincture of strait-laced Puritanism,[3] he generally writes in a sensible and liberal spirit. His most famous pamphlet, 'The Shortest Way with Dissenters,' for a time deceived both friend and foe. It was professedly written by an extreme High Churchman, and was in fact a *reductio ad absurdum* of what were called in Queen Anne's days High Church principles. It was at first hailed by the extreme

---

[1] A complete edition of the *Review* is, it is believed, not extant.

[2] The subject of 'occasional conformity' gave rise to a dispute between Defoe and Howe. Defoe characterised occasional conformity as 'playing bo-peep with the Almighty.'

[3] Such a sentence as the following is of the very essence of Puritanism : 'I appeal to common knowledge, if in the first half-year of her present Majesty, almost all Maypoles in England were not repaired and re-edified, new painted, new hung with garlands, and beautified,' &c.—*Review*, ii. 330.

Church party as a vigorous exposition of their own senti-ments ; but when the trick was discovered the wrath of the 'High Flyers' knew no bounds.[1] The pamphlet was burnt by the hangman as a seditious libel and the writer fined, pilloried, and imprisoned.

Among his other pamphlets, the most striking were two, whose titles tell their own tale,—'What if the Queen should die ?' and 'What if the Pretender should come ?' For these he was again imprisoned.

But it is not on his essays and pamphlets that Defoe's fame as a writer chiefly rests. Valuable as these are as ex-pressing the sentiments of a keen and by no means illiberal Nonconformist on matters of vital interest in connection with politics and religion at a critical juncture, they naturally breathe the soured spirit of a depressed party smarting under injustice ; and this detracts from their literary merit.

From a diametrically opposite point of view, the same subjects of political Churchmanship and Dissent were handled by a far more powerful pen than that of Defoe. The position which Jonathan Swift occupied in England towards the close of Queen Anne's reign, is unique. Without any advantages except those which the sheer force of intellect confers, Swift for more than three years ruled the rulers of England ; but he never gained the object of his own ambition, and retired into comparative obscurity, a soured and disappointed man. The causes of his success and failure were identical. The same bitter and caustic humour which commended him to the Tory Ministry tempted him also to write the 'Tale of a Tub,' at once the most powerful of all his works and the most effectual bar to his preferment.

Upon the personal character of Swift and his political principles, except so far as they concerned the Church, it is not necessary here to enter ; but a few words seem requisite as to his religious sentiments. By many of his own con-temporaries,[2] and by some in our own time, he has been

---

[1] See G. Chalmers' *Life of Defoe*, 1841 ed. (first published in 1786), p. 32.

[2] In the Debate on the Schism Act (1714) the Earl of Nottingham said, ' I tremble when I think a certain divine [Swift] who is hardly suspected of being a Christian is in a fair way of being a bishop, and may one day give licenses to those entrusted with the education of youth.'—See Lord Mahon's *History of Eng-*

represented as little better than an infidel ; but the justice of the charge is at least questionable.

The only work on which such a charge can, with any show of reason, be founded, is the ' Tale of a Tub.' This extraordinary allegory, which no Christian man, still less a Christian minister, ought to have written, abounds in the grossest obscenity and blasphemy, and deservedly proved a hindrance to its author's preferment. But, to infer that it is an *anti*christian as well as *un*christian work, is to confound the accidental with the essential. Let it be remembered that Christianity itself is quite separable, in thought at least, from any outward form in which it may be clothed. It was the outer form, not the thing itself, which Swift attacked. To make what is meant quite clear, it is necessary to remind the reader of the plot of the Tale. A father leaves by will a coat having two miraculous virtues[1] to each of his three sons, Peter, Jack, and Martin. All three—notably the two former, but the latter also to a certain extent—tamper with the father's will and maltreat the coats. Now the father, the will, and the coats alone represent Christianity itself, apart from its outer forms. Swift never depreciates in any way the father's

land (1713-1783), vol. i. pp. 80, 82. Swift's *Tale of a Tub* was recommended by Voltaire to his proselytes. Sir W. Scott says Swift was ' branded as an infidel.' Cunningham (ii. 578) alludes to ' Dr. Swift, a contemner of all religions.' Swift bitterly alludes to this opinion in the lines upon himself (1713) :—

> ' By an old —— pursued,
> A crazy prelate and a royal prude ;
> By dull divines, who look with envious eyes
> On every genius that attempts to rise ;
> And pausing o'er a pipe, with doubtful nod,
> Give hints that poets ne'er believe in God. '

The 'crazy prelate' was the excellent Archbishop Sharp, whose influence with Queen Anne was exercised against Swift's preferment. It is Mr. Thackeray's belief that Swift ' suffered frightfully from the consciousness of his own scepticism,' that ' having put that cassock on, it poisoned him ; he was strangled in his bands.' Hunt (*Religious Thought in England*, iii. 93) thinks Swift's theology might be described as ' High Churchism without Religion,' and that ' his highest idea of religion was policy.' Schlosser (*History of the Eighteenth Century*) says, ' Not one of all the Encyclopædists has sneered with so much rudeness as Swift at theologians and the sanctity of religious conviction, which, at least, a man ought always to honour, if he cannot share.'

[1] *Viz.* that of lasting all the life with good wearing, and that of lengthening and widening itself so as always to fit the changes of the body.

conduct, his will, or the coats. What he does attack is the outer forms, Romanism, Dissent, and Anglicanism, represented respectively by Peter, Jack, and Martin. As Swift suggests no other form besides these three, the work has an unsettling, nay, an unchristian tendency, quite independently of the abominable filth and blasphemy with which it is interspersed. A spiritually minded man would never have written it; but on the other hand, an unbeliever, having gone so far, would have gone further: he would have ridiculed the will and the coats, which Swift never does.[1]

In none of his other writings, whether pamphlet, poem, tale, or history—though many of them are utterly unworthy of a Christian gentleman, not to say, clergyman—does Swift express or imply any unbelief in the great truths of the Christian religion. To say that he was more of a politician than a divine, is only to say that he shared the failings of too many of the clergy of his day. He defended the Church rather as a political institution than as a spiritual society; but there is no appearance of insincerity in his defence. Indeed, he was more consistent in his theology—such as it was—than in his politics. He came directly over from the Whigs to the Tories, naïvely enough confessing that he did so because he felt himself neglected by Godolphin, Halifax, and Somers, and was courted by Harley and St. John; but in ecclesiastical matters, he was from first to last a High Churchman: a High Churchman, that is, in the low sense of that term, as it was understood by the generation that was springing up, not in the far nobler sense in which it was applied by a generation that was passing away. Swift's High Churchmanship was as different from that of Ken and Nelson, Bull, Beveridge and Sharp, as light is from darkness.[2]

---

[1] Bishop Monk (*Life of Bentley*, i. c. 7) goes further, and thinks 'there was no doubt of the author's design, to uphold the Church of England.' Since the above was written, Mr. Lecky has appeared on the same side : ' From first to last an exclusive Church feeling was Swift's genuine passion. It appeared fully, though in a very strange form, in the *Tale of a Tub*.'—*History of England in the Eighteenth Century*, vol. i. ch. i. p. 157. And again (ii. ch. ix. p. 530), 'several facts in his life show that Swift had very sincere personal religious convictions.'

[2] Sir W. Scott tells us that the *Tale of a Tub* 'rendered High Church important services' (*Life of Dean Swift*, 2nd ed. 1824, p. 85). Conceive the horror of such High Churchmen of the old type as those mentioned above, if they heard a

Not only was he painfully lacking in that spiritualmindedness which indicated a depth in, and also lent a grace and beauty to, their religion; but the central idea of the Church as it existed in their minds was not his. What were to High Churchmen of the old type mere accidents, were to High Churchmen of the type of Swift all in all, while those matters which were to them all in all, hardly came within Swift's purview at all. His High Churchmanship never extended beyond the limits of a mere National Establishment, which was, as a matter of course, to teach and uphold the main truths of Christianity, but which was above all things to keep all places of power in its own hands, and if it could not harry Romanists and Dissenters (including Nonjurors) altogether off the face of the land, was at least to keep them down as low as possible.[1]

Like Defoe, Swift's popularity rests on other grounds than those of his essays and pamphlets. These latter are little known in the present day; but the effect which they produced at the time when they were written was extraordinary. His ' Conduct of the Allies,' which ran through four editions in a week, did more to reconcile the nation to the peace policy of the Tories, than all the eloquence of Bolingbroke, the tact of Harley, and the personal wishes of the Queen combined. ' The Examiner,' written, after the first twelve numbers, almost exclusively by Swift, was more than a match for all the Whig writers united. The object of this periodical, so far as Church matters went, was to show that a man might be a High Churchman and a Tory without being a Nonjuror or in any way unfavourable to the Revolution settlement and the

---

book like the *Tale of a Tub* spoken of as rendering important services to their cause !

[1] Swift's latest biographer writes of his Christianity in general and his High Churchmanship in particular,—' He would have increased her political power without enlarging her domination over conscience. His churchmanship was neither intolerant nor tantivy; and he had as little real sympathy with Atterbury as with Sacheverell, much as he admired the one and despised the other. How far he had thus early settled his own beliefs, no one can assume to say ; and most certainly there is no later evidence on which to found charges of disbelief. His respect for the ordinances of the Reformed Church, his careful observance of her usages and ritual, and his sense of what the world had gained by Christianity, there is no reason to doubt or bring in question at any time of his life.'—Forster's *Life of Swift*, bk. ii. § 1.

Hanoverian succession. But Swift wrote other tracts which were more directly theological. His 'Sentiments of a Church of England man,' his ' Letter on the Sacramental Test,' and his ' Project for the advancement of Religion,' are chiefly remarkable as illustrating the sort of political religion which in Swift's days constituted ' good Churchmanship.' The Church of England man 'thinks it highly just that all rewards of trust, profit, or dignity which the State leaves in the disposal of the Administration, should be given only to those whose principles direct them to preserve the constitution in all its parts,' i.e., only to strict Churchmen. He thinks that ' sects in a State seem only tolerated with any reason because they are already spread,' and that ' the greatest advocates for general liberty of conscience will allow that they ought to be checked in their beginnings.' But this tract might have been written by a far feebler pen than Swift's ; and the same may be said of the ' Project,' and the ' Letter.' The ' Project' simply consists of a proposal to make a religious profession a necessary step to favour and preferment — a plan better adapted to make hypocrites than Christians; while the ' Letter ' merely repeats the old arguments, or rather fallacies, which may be found in a hundred pamphlets of the day. But the ' Argument against abolishing Christianity ' is of a different calibre. The admirable gravity of such passages as the following reminds one of some of the best hits in ' Gulliver's Travels :' ' The curious may please to observe how much the genius of a nation is liable to alter in half an age. I have heard it affirmed for certain by some very old people, that the contrary opinion was, even in their memories, as much in vogue as the other is now, and that a project for the abolishing of Christianity would then have appeared as singular, and been thought as absurd, as it would be at this time to write a discourse in its defence.'[1]

The infirmities of Swift's own disposition helped to lend

---

[1] See also the passage quoted in the chapter on the Deists in this work, where Swift gravely argues that the abolishing of Christianity might possibly put the Church in danger, and the passage in which he contends that the churches cannot be said to be misapplied, for ' Where are more appointments and rendezvous of gallantry ? Where more meetings for business ? Where more bargains driven of all sorts ? and where so many conveniences or incitements to sleep?'

credit to the charge that he was in heart an infidel. There was a natural coarseness about him which disfigures almost everything he wrote, and is most of all repulsive when it appears in his religious writings. His savage misanthropy and moroseness, heightened by his own disappointments as well as his bad health, tinged all his writings with a very different spirit from that of true Christianity. But it is possible to have a thorough disbelief in man without having also a disbelief in God. Again, a brilliant wit and great powers of sarcasm, unless they are tempered and chastened by great spiritual earnestness, are dangerous possessions for a writer on controversial divinity. Swift possessed these in an extraordinary degree, and they frequently led him into veins of thought and modes of expression which were utterly unworthy of a Christian clergyman. Once more, the absence of the true spirit of poetry is a great hindrance to a high appreciation of Christianity. Swift's was an essentially prosaic mind. He wrote many clever verses but not a single line of poetry. His prose style was in its way perfect,—terse, perspicuous, plain and simple even to bareness; but not only without any ornament of diction, but without a single spark of poetical sentiment. Add to all this a far greater hankering after worldly advantages than a Christian ought to have, and there will be no difficulty in seeing how Swift could write as he did, without having recourse to the assumption that he was a hypocrite.

It was not, however, Swift or Defoe who gave the essayists and pamphleteers of the early part of the eighteenth century their high place in English literature;—the 'Review' and the 'Examiner' are now known only to the curious; but the 'Tatler' and the 'Spectator' are still household words in the mouth of every educated Englishman.

The little knot of writers to whom we are indebted for these inimitable papers, group themselves naturally round one great central figure bearing the honoured name of Addison. Without detracting from the merits of the others who were engaged with him, it is undeniable that Addison was the life and soul of the work, which but for him would never have emerged from the obscurity in which many similar adventures struggled through their little life, and soon died out of remembrance. Steele, and Tickell, and Budgell, and Hughes, and Swift, and Berkeley, and Pope, and others contributed their quota ; but it was Addison who, not only by his own contributions—though they are incomparably the gems of the series—but also by the spirit which he infused through the whole, was the real cause of their pre-eminent success.

It is difficult to conceive a greater contrast than that which existed between the two great literary monarchs of the period, Swift and Addison. They were at one time friends, and paid magnificent compliments to one another ; [1] but though they never actually quarrelled, it was impossible that an intimacy between two such opposite characters should long continue. ' Mr. Addison and I,' writes Swift,[2] 'are different as black and white ; ' and they were. Both began their careers under the same colours ; both held the then somewhat anomalous position of High Church Whigs ; but though they started from the same point, there was soon a marked divergence. In fact, the clergyman and the layman should have changed places. Swift was a politician in cassock and bands ; Addison, ' a parson in a tye wig.' [3] Swift was most brilliant in the midst of a large and brilliant society ; in such society Addison was dumb. And yet Swift's was essentially a lonely spirit ; Addison's essentially a sociable one. Swift's defects arose to a great extent from the heat of his passions ; Addison's from the coldness of his. A grossness both of sentiment and expression pervades almost all Swift's writings ; an almost feminine delicacy marks those of Addison. Swift was a savage misanthrope ; Addison the kindliest of human beings. Swift's religion was tinged with

---

[1] Addison inscribed a presentation copy of his *Travels* ' To Dr. Jonathan Swift, the most agreeable companion, the truest friend, and the greatest genius of his age.' Swift speaks of Addison as ' a most excellent person and his most intimate friend,' and writes to him ' of the great love and esteem I have always had for you.'—See Thackeray's ' Essay on Addison.' Mr. Forster (*Life of Swift*, bk. iv. § 2) quotes a letter of Swift's to Ambrose Philips, in which he says of Addison, ' That man has worth enough to give reputation to an age.'

[2] Swift's *Journal to Stella.*

[3] Mandeville's description of Addison. Sir James Mackintosh said that Addison as the Dean, and Swift as the Secretary of State, would have been a stroke of fortune, putting each into the place most fit for him.

gloominess and melancholy; Addison's was always bright and cheerful.

Having considered the essays of the former, so far as they are connected with Church matters, let us now turn to those of the latter.

It is scarcely necessary to remark that the merit of originating the papers which met with such unprecedented success is not due to Addison. Steele was from first to last the editor of the 'Tatler,' 'Guardian,' and 'Spectator.'[1] But no one recognised more fully and generously than Steele himself, the fact that to Addison was their triumph due.[2] Indeed it may be doubted whether Steele has done justice to himself, or whether posterity has done justice to him, in this matter of their joint labours.[3] For, infinitely superior as Addison was to Steele on the whole, there are still some points in which the palm belongs to the latter. There is a deeper pathos and a greater warmth about some of Steele's papers than Addison ever displayed; he had, too, a higher and nobler conception of the female character, and the position of women in society, and a better appreciation of domestic life, than his friend had; and though Addison's humour was more subtle and refined, and flowed in a more constant stream, yet flashes of wit came forth now and then from Steele's pen, which rivalled if they did not surpass the best strokes of Addison. This, however, is not the place to

---

[1] It has been thought more convenient to group the *Tatler, Spectator,* and *Guardian* together, not because they are by any means all of equal merit, but because they really formed one series. Lord Macaulay's description of the *Guardian* as a paper 'which began in dulness and ended in faction' is surely over-drawn, and his citing it as an instance of how little Steele could do without Addison is very misleading; for, in point of fact, Addison wrote almost as much of the *Guardian* as he did of the *Spectator,* and more than he did of the *Tatler.* It is true that he contributed nothing to the first volume, but when he did begin to write, he thoroughly entered into the scheme. He wrote no less than fifty-one papers.

[2] 'I claim to myself the merit of having extorted excellent productions from a person of the greatest abilities who would not have let them appear by any other means.'—*Spectator,* No. 532. He compares his situation to that of a distressed prince who calls in a more powerful neighbour to his aid, and is undone by his auxiliary.

[3] Dr. Johnson said it was wonderful how many bad papers there were in the *Spectator* in the half that was not Addison's. Lord Macaulay attributes all the success of the paper to Addison; but those who wish to see Steele's merits duly recognised may be referred to Mr. Forster's essay on the subject.

settle their respective claims, and we may turn without further preface to the papers themselves.

It is difficult at the present day to realise the influence which these papers exercised upon the general tone of society. The subjects of which they treat are those of ordinary life.; and even into these they never go very deeply. Many of the truths which they uttered now sound like truisms ; and though their exquisite grace of style and delicacy of humour will never be out of date, their literary merit at the present day is based rather upon their manner than their matter. But, in order to appreciate their real excellence, we must strive to realise the state.of society in the early part of the last century. The reaction which had set in at the time of the Restoration against religion and morality, from disgust at the straitlaced austerity of the Puritans, was subsiding. The wild licence of the second Stuart period had run its course, and society was beginning to revolt against the reckless immorality of such writers as Wycherley and Etheredge, Rochester, Congreve, and even Dryden. England had had a surfeit of licentious literature and was yearning for a more wholesome mental food. But it must not be made of the old Puritan materials. The abhorrence of the 'Reign of Saints' and all that savoured of it was still almost as strong as ever it had been. Never was there a time when a way was more open for writers who could combine wit and decency, who could write as gentlemen for gentlemen, and at the same time not forget that they were Christians.

By accident rather than by deliberate choice, Steele and his coadjutors hit exactly upon the work that was wanted. It was probably no higher motive than the 'res angusta domi' that suggested to Steele the idea of appearing before the world as a 'Tatler.'[1] His office as Gazetteer gave him access to earlier and more trustworthy news than could be derived from other sources, and the same office happily rendered it necessary for him to abstain from taking any violent part in political strife. From this humble beginning the 'Tatler' took its rise. How Addison detected his friend's

---

[1] Mr. Forster, however, thinks that 'the design of the *Tatler* was always the same,' and quotes the motto of the first paper, 'Quicquid agunt homines,' &c. in proof. —*Historical and Biographical Essays,* 'Sir R. Steele.'

hand, on observing in an early number an exquisite little criticism on Virgil borrowed from himself: how he lent his powerful aid to the enterprise: how the form of the paper was changed from a somewhat dreary medley of social gossip, literary criticism, and foreign news, into the charming series of separate papers with which we are all familiar: how the 'Tatler' died, and how his mantle and more than a double portion of his spirit fell upon his successor, the 'Spectator,' need not here be told.

Our concern with these essays only extends so far as they affected the interests of Christianity generally, and the Church of England in particular. This they did to a very material extent, both indirectly and directly. Indirectly, by acting as a kind of pioneer to the message of the Gospel, clearing away the obstacles which prevented that message from obtaining a favourable hearing, or even a hearing at all ; directly, by the advocacy of Christain doctrine and Christain practice.

The indirect influence was the most important, and claims our first attention.

It has frequently been said, that to Steele and Addison belongs the credit of enlisting wit and culture in the service of religion and morality, after they had been long employed in the service of irreligion and immorality. But this is only true with considerable modifications. The age in which South's wit was still flashing from the pulpit, in which Ken was pouring forth his melodious lyrics, in which Charles Leslie was writing with great ability on almost all the controversies of the day, in which Richard Bentley was giving to the world his inimitable criticisms, cannot, strictly speaking, be called an age in which wit and culture were divorced from Christianity. Neither can it be said that a cultivated religion belonged only to the clergy. The names of Robert Nelson, Henry Dodwell, Robert Boyle, and other laymen need only be mentioned to contradict such an idea. Nevertheless, there was real ground for the boast of the 'Spectator,' ' If I have not found a new weapon against vice and irreligion, I have at least shown how that weapon may be put to a right use, which has so often fought the battles of impiety and profaneness.' The beneficial effects of these writings are still more strongly stated by contemporaries. 'It would have been a jest,' writes an unknown hand, probably Gay's, in 1711,[1] 'some time since, for a man to have asserted that anything witty could be said in praise of a married state, or that devotion and virtue were any way necessary to the character of a fine gentleman. Bickerstaff ventured to tell the town that they were a parcel of fools, &c.,—but in such a way as pleased them. . . . It is incredible to conceive the effects his writings have had on the town ; how many thousand follies they have banished or given a check to ; how much countenance they have added to virtue and religion. His writings have set our wits and men of letters on a new way of thinking. . . . Every one writes and thinks more justly.'

The fact seems to be, that there was no lack of cultured and even witty scholars in the age in which the 'Tatler' and 'Spectator' appeared, who devoted their talents to the service of religion ; but their speculations were so mixed up with party strifes, theological and political, and were, if the expression may be used, of so professional a character, that they made little impression upon the general mass of society, and perhaps least of all upon that which calls itself 'society' *par excellence.*

At such a time there was indeed an opening for any one who could 'enliven morality with wit, and temper wit with morality.' If such an one did his work well, he might hope, without being over-sanguine, 'to recover virtue and discretion out of that desperate state of vice and folly into which the age is fallen.'[2] And Steele and Addison did their work admirably well ; they knew both what to do and what to leave undone. If they had come forward simply as mentors ; if they had shown no sympathy with the natural love of innocent pleasure, against which the Puritans had waged indiscriminate war ; if they had thrown themselves into the party strifes which were distracting the nation, they might have written with even greater talent than they did, and written in vain.

[1] *Present State of Wit.* In a letter to a friend in the country ; first printed in May 1711. See also an *Essay on the Character of Sir Richard Steele,* published in 1729.
[2] *Spectator,* No. 10 (Addison).

Partly by accident and partly by design, they avoided all these errors. They wrote like scholars, but not like bookworms; like Christians, but not like Puritans; like gentlemen, but not 'fine gentlemen;' like wits, but not buffoons. And they had a firm ground to stand upon. The nation to which they addressed themselves was still professedly Christian; and they had the good sense to appeal only to those common principles which all Christians accept, without launching upon the stormy sea of controversy.

To mention a few out of the many points in which these essays indirectly affected religion, and consequently the Church of England, its official guardian.

It has been said that the stage was one of the few literary influences which at that time affected the mass of the nation, and that in spite of some little change for the better, its influence was by no means a wholesome one. It is not surprising, therefore, that the Societies for the Reformation of Manners which originated in King William's days and continued their well-meaning if somewhat irregular efforts during the reign of Queen Anne, should have set themselves against all theatrical performances. But our Essayists took a wiser and more practicable course. They saw that it was the abuse, not the use of the theatre, which was the cause of evil. To stamp out such a popular entertainment was impossible, nor, if it were possible, would it be desirable. For the theatre, rightly conducted, might become a powerful engine for good; a help, and not a hindrance to the work of the pulpit. Therefore, in one of the early numbers of the 'Tatler,' Steele declared that 'he could not be of the same opinion with his friends and fellow-labourers, the Reformers of Manners, in their severity towards plays, but must allow that a good play acted before a well-bred audience must raise very proper incitements to good behaviour.'[1] At the same time he attacks unsparingly plays of an immoral tendency. He goes to see 'The Country Wife' acted at Drury Lane, and regrets that 'a gentleman of Mr. Wycherley's character and sense should condescend to represent the insults done to the honour of the marriage bed, without just reproof.'[2] He sees

[1] *Tatler*, No 3   [2] *Spectator*, 141.

the 'Scornful Lady' and 'is moved with the utmost indignation at the trivial, senseless, and unnatural representation of
the chaplain.'[1] He declares that 'so noble an entertainment
as the stage should be ambitious of pleasing people of the
best understanding, and leave others, who show nothing of the
human species but risibility, to bear-gardens,' &c.[2] In this
discriminating attack upon bad plays, mingled with a sensible
appreciation of good ones, Steele was well supported by Addison. 'Were our English stage,' writes the latter, 'but half so
virtuous as that of the Greeks or Romans, we should quickly see
the influence of it in the behaviour of all the politer part of
mankind. It would not be fashionable to ridicule religion or
its professors; the man of pleasure would not be the complete
gentleman; vanity would be out of countenance; and every
quality which is ornamental to human nature would meet
with that esteem which is due to it. If the English stage
were under the same regulations the Athenian was formerly,
it would have the same effect that had in recommending the
religion, the government, and public worship of its country.'[3]
But some contemporary writers of comedy 'comply with the
corrupt taste of the more vicious parts of the audience,' 'know
no difference between being merry and being lewd,'—and
much more to the same effect in several papers.

Closely connected with this subject of the stage was that
of the ties of domestic life, which in the bad plays of the
post-Restoration period were constantly held up to ridicule.
The 'Tatler' contains a pretty picture of the domestic happiness of Mrs. Jenny Bickerstaff, who found in 'Tranquillus,' her
husband, 'the fondness of a lover, the tenderness of a parent,
and the intimacy of a friend.'[4] Addison is stirred into an
unusual warmth of expression when he writes of the mischief
which seducers, 'this generation of vermin, these sons of
darkness,' produce in families. With admirable irony, he
writes in the person of a correspondent, 'For my own part I
was born in wedlock, and do not care who knows it. . . .
Nay, sir, I will go one step further, and declare to you before
the whole world that I am a married man, and at the same
time I have so much assurance as not to be ashamed of what I

[1] *Spectator*, 270.   [2] Id. 141.
[3] Id. 446.—See also 58, 65, &c. &c.   [4] *Tatler*, 104.

have done;' and then follows a pleasing description of the married state.[1]   Soon after this, the 'Spectator' is 'glad to find that his discourses on marriage are well received.' 'I am informed,' says the writer,[2] 'of several pretty fellows who have resolved to commence heads of families by the first favourable opportunity.   One of them writes me word that he is ready to enter into the bonds of matrimony provided I will give it him under my hand (as I now do) that a man may show his face in good company after he is married, and that he need not be ashamed to treat a woman with kindness who puts herself in his power for life ;'[3] but 'others say he is attempting to make a revolution in the world of gallantry, and that the consequence of it will be that a great deal of the sprightliest wit of the last age will be lost,' &c.

A very important branch of this effort to purify domestic life, was the social elevation and intellectual improvement of womankind.   Not that our essayists would have felt any sympathy with the modern advocates of woman's rights and the equality of the sexes.   Steele, whose appreciation of the female character was higher than Addison's, is of opinion that 'we have carried women's characters too much into public life,' and that 'the utmost of woman's character is contained in domestic life ; all she has to do in this world is contained within the duties of a daughter, sister, wife, and mother.' But it does not follow, because the home is the true sphere of woman's work, that therefore her mind is to be left uncultivated, that she is to be treated as a mere plaything, that dress and fashion are to be the only subject of her thoughts, and that honour and chastity are to be laughed out of polite society.   Such notions were only too prevalent among the 'fine gentlemen' of Queen Anne's reign, and too much encouraged, implicitly, at least, by the ladies themselves.

Against this vicious propensity, the 'Tatler' and 'Spectator' took up their parable.   There is no one subject which was handled in these essays more frequently and more earnestly than that of womankind.   The 'Spectator' gives notice at the outset of his work, that he shall 'dedicate a considerable share of his speculations to their service, and

---

[1] *Spectator*, 513.   [2] Id. 526 (by Hughes).

[3] Id. 342.

shall lead the young through all the becoming duties of virginity, marriage, and widowhood.' 'When,' adds the writer (Steele), 'it is a woman's day in my works, I shall endeavour at a style and air suitable to their understanding. When I say this, I must not be understood to mean that I shall lower, but exalt the subjects I treat upon. Discourse for their entertainment is not to be debased, but refined. . . . I shall take it for the greatest glory of my work, if among reasonable women, this paper may furnish tea-table talk.'[1] A few numbers later on, Addison declares the same intentions. He would 'have this paper to be served up and looked upon in families as part of the tea equipage,' and declares that 'there are none to whom this paper would be more useful than the female world.'[2] The champion of the 'fair ones,' as he calls them, is as good as his word. Now we find him warning them against 'party-rage, because it is bad for the face;' now making a sly hit at a devotee 'who professes she is what nobody ought to doubt she is, and betrays the labour she is put to, to be what she ought to be with cheerfulness and alacrity; who lives in the world and denies herself none of the diversions of it, with a constant declaration how insipid all things are to her; who is never herself but at church,' &c. Now he runs a tilt against patches, now against hooped petticoats, now he makes it his business to find suitable books for the ladies' reading. But through Addison's papers at least, on this subject, there runs a vein of half-concealed contempt for the sex whose interests he has so much at heart; his tone is not quite the tone of that religion which, more than anything else, has tended to give woman her due place in the world. Still it is a far better, a far more Christian tone, not only than that which pervaded the light literature of that and the preceding age, but also than that of the artificial and overstrained system of chivalry, which, while professing homage, really insulted rational creatures. It was chiefly in the interests of the same sex that the 'Spectator' waged war against the fine gentleman of the period. Vocifer, whose 'character is the pleasanter because he is the professed deluder of women,'[3] the 'coxcomb who, loaded with the favours of many others, is received like a victor that disdains his

[1] *Spectator*, 4.   [2] Id. 10.   [3] Id. 85.

triumphs,'[1] the beau, who 'having established his reputation
of being an agreeable rake, died of old age at twenty-five,'[2]
would all find their prototypes in real life. In contradistinction to these pretenders, the true fine gentleman is described as one who is ' honest in his actions and refined in his
language ;' he is 'modest without bashfulness, frank and
affable without impertinence, obliging and complaisant without servility, cheerful and in good humour without noise. A
true fine gentleman is what one seldom sees. He is properly
a compound of the various good qualities that embellish
mankind.'

One of the essential requisites of the fine gentleman of
the period was a nice regard for his honour : he must be
ready to kill his friend or be killed by him on the slightest
provocation. It has been said that ' Steele's admirable papers
on duelling were the first successful attempts on that remnant
of barbarism.'[3] The success was not very marked, for the
old mode of settling affairs of honour prevailed without perceptible abatement to the end of the century. But at any
rate the effort was a laudable one, and Steele threw himself
into it with all his heart and soul. The different methods in
which Addison and his friend treated this practice, are
thoroughly characteristic of the two men. Addison is content with a half-serious, half-bantering suggestion, that since
' death is not sufficient to deter men who make it their glory
to despise it ; if everyone who fought a duel were to stand in
the pillory, it would quickly lessen the number of these
imaginary men of honour, and put an end to so absurd a practice, the bane and plague of society.'[4] But Steele's righteous
indignation carries him into a higher strain. There is no
question about the earnestness of his really eloquent appeal,
which might have been made without any impropriety from
the pulpit itself. ' A Christian and a gentleman,' he says,
' are made inconsistent appellations of the same person. You
are not to expect eternal life if you do not forgive injuries,
and your mortal life is uncomfortable if you are not ready to
commit a murder in resentment of an affront. He that dies

[1] *Spectator*, 158.   [2] Id. 576.
[3] *British Essayists, Historical and Biographical*. Preface by Ferguson, p. xxxi.
[4] *Spectator*, 99.

in a duel knowingly offends God, and in that very action rushes into His offended presence. Is it possible for the heart of man to conceive a more terrible image than that of a departed spirit in this condition?'[1] And then follows a striking picture of one who 'to avoid the laughter of fools, and being the bye-word of idiots,' throws body and soul away.

Among the crying evils of the time when these essays were written, none was more conspicuous than the prevalence and virulence of party spirit. And on no subject did it arouse the angry passions more lamentably than on that of a religion whose object was to bring 'peace on earth and goodwill towards men.' Feeling strongly that 'there cannot be a greater judgment befal a country than such a dreadful spirit of division as rends a government into two distinct people,' that it is 'fatal to men's morals and understandings, sinks the virtue of a nation and destroys even common sense,'[2] Addison and his friends strove to pour oil upon the troubled waters. They felt rightly that the worst development of this evil tendency was that which affected Christianity. 'Of all the monstrous passions and opinions which have crept into the world, there is none so wonderful as that those who profess the common name of Christians should pursue each other with rancour and hatred for differences in their way of following the example of their Saviour.'[3] Sometimes, as in the passage above, they attack this spirit seriously, sometimes they try to laugh men out of it ; as, for example, when Addison proposes that 'honest men of all parties should enter into an association for the defence of one another,' and prepares the following form, which may express their intentions in the most plain and simple manner : 'We, whose names are hereunto subscribed, do solemnly declare that we do in our consciences believe that two and two make four ; and that we shall adjudge any man whatsoever to be our enemy who endeavours to persuade us to the contrary. We are likewise ready to maintain, with the hazard of all that is near and dear to us, that six is less than seven in all times and all places,' and so forth.[4]

---

[1] *Guardian*, No. 20.
[2] *Spectator*, 516.
[3] *Spectator*, 125 (Addison).
[4] Id. 126.

But this abhorrence of party spirit did not prevent them from holding and expressing very decided opinions on the best mode of worshipping God. They made no secret of their attachment to the National Church, and devoted no small space to the vindication of its system and the improvement of its services. ' I look upon it,' writes Addison, 'as a peculiar happiness that were I to choose of what religion I would be,—I should most certainly give the preference to that form of religion which is established in my own country.' [1]

But just in proportion as they admired the Church system, they lamented, and set themselves to correct its abuses. They strove to arouse in the clergy—not a greater sense of their moral and spiritual responsibilities, for, contrary to the run of writers of the period, this they assumed as generally existing—but a greater attention to the mode of performing the beautiful services. In several papers the bad reading of the liturgy is commented on ; in others improvements in Church psalmody are suggested ; in another, the extempore prayers before the sermon, which were more common then than now, are criticised ; above all things, they protested against the cold and apathetic style of preaching then prevalent. [2]

The severest strictures, however, are reserved for the congregation. [3] One of the best papers on this subject is that in which Addison represents the Indian kings describing the impression made upon them by a visit to St. Paul's. The admirable gravity of the humour reminds one of Swift's happiest vein :—' It is most probable,' so their comment runs, ' that when this work was begun many hundred years ago, there must have been some religion among this people ; for they give it the name of a temple and have a tradition that it was designed for men to pay their devotions in. And, indeed, there are several reasons which lead us to think that the natives of this country had formerly among them some sort of worship ; for they set apart a seventh day as sacred ; but upon my going into one of these holy houses, I could not observe any circumstance of devotion in their

---

[1] *Spectator*, 287. See also *Spectator*, 392.
[2] *Tatler*, 66, and *Spectator*, 407, &c.　　　　[3] *Spectator*, 239, &c.

behaviour. There was, indeed, a man in black, mounted
above the rest, who seemed to be uttering something with
a great deal of vehemence; but as for those underneath
him, instead of paying their worship to the Deity of the
place, they were most of them bowing and curtseying to
one another, and many were fast asleep.' [1]

A marked respect for the clergy is conspicuous in these
essays. The clergyman who belongs to the Spectator's Club
is a gentleman to whom the whole club pay a particular
deference. The chaplain at Coverley Hall is 'a very venerable man,' 'a person of good sense and some learning, of a
very regular life and obliging conversation.' 'There has not
been a law-suit in the parish since he has lived among them;
if any dispute arises, they apply themselves to him for the
decision.' [2] The ignominious treatment of domestic chaplains
generally is strongly reprobated. The 'Tatler' is shocked at
'the indecency of discharging the holiest man from the
table as soon as the most delicious parts of the entertainment are served,' and 'blushes to see gentlemen of more
wit and learning than himself, of the same university, treated
so ignominiously.' [3]

Thus, in a very unpretentious but very real way, these
good men helped on the great work which every true Churchman must have had at heart. They looked upon their efforts
not as superseding, but as supplementing those of the pulpit.
'There are many little enormities in the world,' writes Addison, 'which our preachers would be very glad to see removed,
but at the same time dare not meddle with, for fear of be-
traying the dignity of the pulpit. For this reason I look
upon myself to be of great use to these good men. While
they are employed in extirpating mortal sins and crimes of a
higher nature, I should be glad to rally the world out of
indecencies and venial trangressions.' [4] Sometimes, however,
they soar above this humble office of handmaid to religion,
and treat of subjects which would not only not be out of

---

[1] *Spectator*, 50.   [2] Id. 106; see also 110.
[3] *Tatler*, 255. See also 258. The work of Christian education and the charity
schools, the duty of kindness to animals, and other matters indirectly connected
with religion, were also treated of.
[4] *Guardian*, 116.

place in the pulpit, but which a Christian preacher must necessarily deal with constantly.

Faithful to his purpose, to pave the way for the preacher, Addison devoted his Saturday papers to these higher topics. The papers form not the least bright of the many bright gems which sparkle in these essays. In elegance and purity of style, in refinement of sentiment and in the genuine spirit of piety which pervades them, the religious meditations of Addison have rarely, if ever, been surpassed. But if they be regarded as an exhaustive account of Christian doctrine and Christian practice, they must be pronounced defective. In fact, though Addison had the profoundest reverence for holy Scripture, the majority of these meditations might really have been written by a mere Theist, who had never heard of Christianity. An essay, of course, is not to be tried by the same standard as a sermon, especially an essay whose writer expressly disclaims any attempt to usurp the office of the preacher. Still, it is somewhat strange that Addison, with his strong sense of the boundless love of the great Creator, should dwell so little upon the highest proof and the crowning instance of that love, the Gospel. The only essay which recognises fully and worthily the work of the Redeemer was written, not by Addison, but by Steele.[1] So far as they go, however, Addison's religious meditations are, in their way, perfect. There is nothing affected, nothing artificial, nothing far-fetched about them ; they are for the most part suggested by the common incidents of every-day life. He walks, for instance, out into the country on a fine spring morning, and turning the exhilarating influences of the season into a pious channel, 'would have his readers endeavour to moralise this natural pleasure of soul and improve this vernal delight into a Christian virtue.' 'The cheerfulness of heart,' he adds, ' which springs in us from the survey of nature's works, is an admirable preparation for gratitude. The mind has gone a great way towards praise and thanksgiving that is filled with such a secret gladness : a grateful reflection on the Supreme Cause who produces it, sanctifies it in the soul, and gives it its proper value.'[2] The difficulty which many feel in employing properly their leisure hours, suggests to

[1] *Spectator,* 356 (on Good Friday).   [2] Id. 393.

him among other expedients the pleasure to be derived from
' that intercourse and communication which every reasonable
creature ought to maintain with the great Author of his being.
The man who lives under an habitual sense of the Divine
presence keeps up a perpetual cheerfulness of temper, and
enjoys every moment the satisfaction of thinking himself in
company with his dearest and best of friends. The time
never lies heavy upon him ; it is impossible for him to be
alone. His thoughts and passions are the most busied at
such hours when those of other men are the most unactive.' [1]
He thinks of the helplessness and wretchedness of man, subject every moment to the greatest calamities and misfortunes,
and finds comfort in the thought that 'we are under the care
of one who directs contingencies, and has in his hands the
management of everything that is capable of annoying or
offending us.' [2]

Nor is it in his Saturday papers alone that the overflow-
ings of Addison's pious soul find a vent. Religious thoughts
suggest themselves in the midst of his more secular speculations. He glances with playful humour at the folly of
popular superstitions, and turns quite naturally from their
ludicrous aspect into the following serious reflections : ' I know
but one way of fortifying my soul against these gloomy
presages and terrors of my mind, and that is, by securing to
myself the friendship of that Being who disposes of events
and governs futurity. He sees at one view the whole thread
of my existence, not only that part of it which I have already
passed through, but that which runs forward into all the
depths of eternity. When I lay me down to sleep, I recommend myself to His care ; when I awake, I give myself up to
His direction.' [3] He walks by himself in Westminster Abbey,
and the sight of the tombs around him awakens a train
of reflections, half humorous, half solemn, but so happily
blended, that the transition from one to the other never
shocks us. When he sees the epitaphs of persons who have
nothing else recorded of them but that they were born on
one day and died on another, the whole history of their lives
being comprehended in those two circumstances that are

---

[1] *Spectator*, 387.   [2] Id. 441.   [3] Id. 7.

common to all mankind, he is reminded of his favourite classical writers, 'where persons are mentioned in the battles who have sounding names given them, for no other reason but that they may be killed, and are celebrated for nothing but being knocked on the head,' while others 'are covered with such extravagant epitaphs, that if it were possible for a dead person to be acquainted with them, he would blush at the praises which his friends have bestowed on him.' But amidst all this playful humour there is nothing jarring to the feelings in the serious reflections with which he concludes his paper, ending with this sentence of exquisite beauty: 'When I read the several dates of the tombs, of some that died yesterday, and some six hundred years ago, I consider that great day when we shall all of us be contemporaries and make our appearance together.'[1] And again, in one of his most humorous papers, on the subject of ghostly apparitions, he passes quite naturally into the following serious admonition :—' If we believe, as many wise and good men have done, that there are such phantoms and apparitions as those I have been speaking of, let us endeavour to establish to ourselves our interest in Him who holds the reins of the whole creation in His hands, and moderates them after such a manner, that it is impossible for one being to break loose upon another, without His knowledge and permission.' Indeed, it is this happy art of turning 'from grave to gay, from lively to severe' that constitutes the peculiar charm of Addison. He describes himself with perfect accuracy when he says 'for my own part, though I am always serious, I do not know what it is to be melancholy ; and can therefore take a view of nature in her deep and solemn scenes, with the same pleasure as in her most gay and delightful ones.' ' It is not religion,' he argues, ' that sours a man's temper, but his temper that sours his religion.' ' Human nature is not so miserable, that we should be always melancholy ; nor so happy, that we should be always merry. In a word, a man should not live as if there were no God in the world, nor at the same time as if there were no men in it.' This is the key-note of Addison's religious philosophy. An habitual sense of the Divine Presence, combined with a full conviction that He doeth all things well,

[1] *Spectator,* 26.

should produce a cheerful, bright, and equal frame of spirit ; and Christians should recommend their religion by 'the joy, the cheerfulness, the good humour, that naturally spring up in this happy state, like the spies bringing along with them the clusters of grapes and delicious fruits, that might invite their companions into the pleasant country which produced them.'

No doubt this aspect of religion is the more insisted upon by Addison, because he felt very keenly the mischievous results produced by the sour austerity of the Puritans. The exquisite humour with which he describes the Puritan head of a College examining a candidate for a fellowship or a scholarship after the fashion of the times, and 'the boy, *who had been bred up by honest parents,* frighted out of his wits at the solemnity of the proceeding,' and Sombrius, who 'looks on a sudden fit of laughter as a breach of his baptismal vow,' represents one side, but only one side, of the truth. The awful nature of sin and the ravages it had made and was making in this fair work of the Creator on which Addison so loved to dwell, were hardly realised by him to their full extent. To borrow a simile from his friend Steele, 'he sounded a flute when there was need of a trumpet.' The irreligion and immorality of the times could hardly be dealt with by his pious optimism. It requires among other things, a greater .amount of culture and reflection than most men possess—not indeed to understand, for extreme simplicity is not the least of the beauties of these essays—but really to appreciate and to be practically affected by the inducements to a pious life which Addison loved to dwell upon. Compare him with the two great religious reformers of the century—John Wesley and Dr. Johnson. The genuine spirit of piety is quite as conspicuous in his writings as in any of theirs. The 'Saturday Papers' are in one sense infinitely superior to the finest passages in Wesley's sermons or the 'Rambler ;' but he never did and never could have done the work which both these great and good men in very different ways did for religion. Without going so far as to say of his essays what was said of Blair's sermons, 'they are polished as marble—and as cold,' it must be owned that there was not enough of fire and vigour in his temperament, not enough of distinctive Christianity as opposed to mere Theism in his teaching, to enable him to do the work of a missionary, when such a work was sorely needed.

Indeed, it was not those papers in the 'Tatler' and 'Spectator,' which bore exclusively upon religious subjects—exquisitely beautiful as they are, that helped most the cause of religion. It was those papers which cleared away the obstacles to the reception of religious truth. The essayists were more successful as guides to the portals within which others might teach, than as teachers themselves. Concealing a serious purpose under a playful humour, they fairly laughed men out of that false modesty which made them ashamed of owning themselves on the Christian side. Lotius, whom the 'Tatler' 'had long suspected of being a little pious, though no man ever hid his vice with greater caution than he did his virtue;'[1] the well-bred man who is 'obliged to conceal any serious sentiment, and appear a greater libertine than he is, that he may keep himself in countenance among the men of mode;' the master of the house, who is 'so very modest a man, that he has not the confidence to say grace at his own table;'[2] the 'young missionaries from the universities,' who, for fear of being thought straitlaced, 'dress and move and look like young officers'—are all admirable and truthful representations of a too prevailing tendency of the times. In these and similar passages, the satire is so kindly, the purpose of the writers so evidently honest and single, the tone so thoroughly gentlemanly and good-natured, that they gave very little offence.

There was one, and only one, exception to the general kindliness and fairness of the Essayists' attacks. There was one subject which roused even Addison out of his usually placid demeanour. Genially tolerant of almost every other class of offenders, he was absolutely intolerant of 'the Freethinkers and Atheists'—terms which in those days were used almost synonymously. These men are 'apostates from reason;' 'miscreants,' who 'endeavour by trash and sophistry to weaken the principles for the vindication of which freedom of thought became at first laudable;' 'wretches who, without any show of wit, learning, or reason, publish their crude conceptions with an ambition of appearing more wise than the rest

[1] *Tatler*, 211.   [2] *Spectator*, 458.

ot mankind ; ' [1] 'vermin,' to punish whom by legal penalties would be to disgrace persecution ; ' [2] for whom 'a solemn judicial death would be too great an honour.' [3] Now if we regard all this as criticism upon the so-called Freethinkers, it cannot be said to possess much value.   Indeed, with the exception of Bishop Berkeley, whom Steele gladly welcomed as an ally in this crusade in the 'Guardian,' the writers do not show any traces of having even read the authors whom they so vehemently condemned.   Still, from Steele's and Addison's point of view, the condemnation is not unnatural, nor, perhaps, altogether unreasonable.   For when they wrote, they had in their eye not Toland and Collins and Shaftesbury, but Vocifer and Lotius and Will Honeycomb.   In the words of a modern writer, [4] ' the loose Deism of fashionable circles had a tendency to minimise religion and morality, to reduce and impair their authority on the part of free-living people who said, *We are Deists*, as the least they could say ; as another mode of saying, " We think little of religion in general, and of Christianity in particular." '

Now, it was just for the benefit of these fashionable circles that the Essayists wrote ; as staunch supporters of ' religion in general, and Christianity in particular,' they felt it to be their mission to nip in the bud such mischievous teaching, and they did so without any particular regard to the justice or injustice of their attacks upon those writers who, whether consciously or unconsciously, were in the first instance responsible for the mischief done.   The Deistical controversy, now at its height, did no doubt affect many who had never read a word of what was written on either side.   The beaux and witlings of the coffee-houses seized hold of the fact that the doctrines of Christianity were impugned as a pretext for disregarding the obligations of religion and morality.   Steele himself lets us into the secret of his savage indignation against these ' minute philosophers.' ' It is a melancholy reflection,' he writes, ' to consider that the British nation, which is now at a greater height of glory for its councils and conquests than it ever was before, should distinguish itself by a certain looseness of principles and falling off from those

[1] *Tatler*, 135.   [2] Id. 111.   [3] *Spectator*, 389.
[4] Mr. Pattison in *Essays and Reviews*.

schemes of thinking, which conduce to the happiness and perfection of human nature;'[1] and then he proceeds to lay the whole fault at the door of the Deists.

But this fierce and excited mode of writing was, as has been said, limited to this one class of opponents; in other cases the Essayists, and especially Addison, err, if anything, on the other side. Moderation was of the very essence of their religion; enthusiasm and zeal were the objects of their special abhorrence. We can well understand how a calm, retiring temperament, like that of Addison, would shrink with horror from anything approaching to religious excitement. The religion which led to endless strife was utterly out of accord with his gentle, peaceful spirit. He loved the Church of England and her services chiefly on account of their 'soothing influence.'[2] He was even nervously anxious lest the Church should diverge one step to the right hand or to the left from that moderation which it was her glory to maintain.[3] She alone hit the happy mean between enthusiasm and superstition. In the ecclesiastical thermometer 'the Church should be exactly midway between the two extremes; that is the situation in which she always flourishes, and in which every good Englishman wishes her.'

One can hardly help reading these essays on the beauty of moderation and the danger of zeal in the light of after-events. In the days of hot strife when Addison wrote, it was no doubt necessary to dwell upon the virtue of moderation. To recur to his own simile, the ecclesiastical thermometer showed a dangerous tendency to rise; but in the early Hanoverian period its tendency was to fall—moderation sank to the dead level of indifference; and one cannot but feel that those cautions against zeal became not only superfluous, but liable to be misinterpreted as encouraging apathy. Such a result would have been inexpressibly painful to the devout soul of Addison; for among the many excellencies of his beautiful speculations on religion, none is more conspicuous than their thorough reality and earnestness of purpose. But Addison is not the first writer who, with the very best intentions, has, owing to a change of popular

---

[1] *Tatler*, 111. [2] See Preface to Keble's *Christian Year*. [3] *Tatler*, 220.

pinion, produced a very contrary effect to that which he
med at.

This subject naturally leads us to consider what was the
ltimate result of these essays, so far as religion and morality
ere concerned.

That their effect was marvellous in turning the current
' wit, which had for some time flowed in an irreligious
nd immoral direction, is unquestionable. 'Addison,' writes
Iacaulay, 'retorted on vice the mockery which had been
irected against virtue ; since his time, the open violation of
ecency has been held the sure mark of a fool.'[1] Contem-
orary testimony to the beneficial effects produced has been
ready quoted. The writers themselves were astonished
: their own success. 'When I broke loose,' says the 'Spec-
tor' (Addison), 'from that great body of writers who have
nployed their wit and parts in propagating vice and irre-
zion, I did not question but I should be treated as an odd
nd of fellow that had a mind to appear singular in my way
' writing ; but the general reception I have found con-
nces me that the world is not so corrupt as we are apt to
agine.'[2]

As a matter of fact, however, was there any appreciable
ange for the better in morals and religion after the publica-
n of these essays ? Truth compels us to own that there
as not.[3] The chroniclers of the period complain year after
ar with melancholy iteration of the increasing laxity of
orals and the wide spread of irreligion.[4] Indeed, contem-
orary evidence of all kinds proves with overwhelming force
at the picture of an able writer of our own day is not over-
awn. 'The historian of moral and religious progress [during
e thirty years which succeeded the Peace of Utrecht] is
der the necessity of depicting it as one of decay of religion,
entiousness of morals, public corruption and profaneness

---

[1] Macaulay's *Essay on Addison.*   [2] *Spectator*, 262.
[3] 'This contrast [of Taste—Essayists, Pope, Hogarth, &c.—enlisted on the side
virtue, while fashion remained on that of vice] is needful to understand if one
uld be just to the Evangelical movement. They did, what the literary spirit of
e time tried and failed to do. Taste and culture attempted to regenerate society,
d failed.'—*John Wesley and the Evangelical Reaction of the Eighteenth Century,*
Julia Wedgwood, p. 118.
[4] See Rapin, Smollett, &c. *passim.*

of language ; an age destitute of depth and earnestness, of light without love, whose very merits were of the earth, earthy.'[1] Indeed, the early part of the Hanoverian period contrasts unfavourably in respect of practical religion and morality with that which preceded it.

At the same time, bad as the state of morals and religion was in the era of the first two Georges, it would probably have been still worse, had the general tone of light literature continued to be as reckless and impure as it was before Addison and his friends turned the tide of popular feeling. Reasons in abundance might be given to account for the lamentable state of things referred to above. Men's minds had become thoroughly unsettled on matters of vital importance. There had been a removal of the old landmarks. The Deistical controversy, the Arian and Socinian controversy, the Divine Right and Passive Obedience controversy, and many others, though in the end productive of good, were, in the first instance, in many respects demoralising. Many men lost confidence in their old guides without finding trustworthy new ones. Before the great revival of Wesley, there was hardly any party left, either inside or outside the National Church, which could exercise any appreciable influence for good over the nation at large. The inveterate prejudices against anything in the least degree savouring of Puritanism were still as strong as ever. The Dissenting interest was numerically, intellectually, and spiritually weak. The old High Church party was almost defunct ; what remained of it was, with a few exceptions, confined within the narrow limits of the Nonjuring communion, which was too much depressed—not to say persecuted—to effect any extensive good. The dominant party in the Church was, with some bright exceptions, narrow, unspiritual, and self-seeking. The example of the Court was as bad as that of Charles II., without its superficial polish. The personal character of the sovereign was as immoral as that of Charles, and more gross. The prevalence of Sir R. Walpole's venal principles in politics was debasing to the last extent.

Against these and similar evil influences, a far stronger

[1] Pattison's Essay on the *Tendencies of Religious Thought in England.* 1688-1750.

force than that which the essays we are considering could pretend to exercise would have been unavailing. For, in point of fact, their influence for good was of a negative rather than a positive character. They set the example of writing in a gentlemanly and scholarlike style, without being irreligious and immoral. This was good as far as it went, but it did not go very far. There is some truth in the unfavourable criticism of a foreigner upon these writings. He complains that they were 'artificial works, destitute of strength and sap ;' that 'there is no kindling fire, no kernel in them ;' that 'Addison's morality was stiff, and his truth so represented as to be suitable to everybody, but neither calculated to terrify nor to dazzle ;' that 'to make himself agreeable, he always put forward the claims of duty in the mildest form.'[1] Although in the passage from which the above extracts are taken the writer shows a provoking want of appreciation of the true merits of the Essayists, he certainly hits a real blot in their system. Reformers of manners are made of sterner stuff than Steele and Addison were. Such a reformation as they proposed and effected was not more than skin-deep. But we must take men as we find them, and be thankful to the Essayists for what they did, without complaining unreasonably of what they failed to do—what men of their temperament were incapable of doing. Instead of swelling the number of the few dissentient voices, educated churchmen will join in the almost universal chorus of applause with which they were greeted by their contemporaries, and which, in the case of Addison, found its noblest expression in the touching elegy of his most faithful friend and satellite,[2] an extract from which will form a fitting conclusion to these remarks on this great and good man :—

> Or dost thou warn poor mortals left behind,
> A task well suited to thy gentle mind ?

[1] Schlosser's *History of the Eighteenth Century*, translated by D. Davison, on 'Addison and Steele.' 'Dull prosaists in whom there was not a spark of poetry.'

[2] Tickell. Addressed to the Earl of Warwick, on the death of Mr. Addison. The poem is more valuable as a testimony of the estimation in which Addison was held than as an appreciative critique on his work. In it occur the well-known lines—

> He taught us how to live, and (oh ! too high
> The price for knowledge) taught us how to die,

Oh ! if sometimes thy spotless form descend,
To me thine aid, thou guardian genius, lend.
When rage misguides me, or when fear alarms,
When pain distresses, or when pleasure charms,
In silent whisperings, purer thoughts impart,
And turn from ill a frail and feeble heart ;
Lead through the paths thy virtue trod before,
Till bliss shall join, nor death can part us more.

If imitation be the sincerest form of flattery, never were writers more flattered than those of the ' Tatler ' and ' Spectator.' Almost to the end of the century, essays from time to time continued to be published, written exactly on the model of these master-pieces. The 'Mirror,' the 'World,' the ' Connoisseur,' the ' Adventurer,' the ' Rambler,' the 'Idler,' the ' Lounger,' are, with one exception, names little known to the reader of the present day. Of course the great name of Dr. Johnson prevents the ' Rambler ' from sinking into oblivion, though few will reckon it the most successful of his works. There are, too, some great names among the contributors to the others. The poet Cowper, for instance, was a contributor to the ' Connoisseur ; ' Lord Chesterfield and Horace Walpole to the ' World,' which was, perhaps, the best of these abortive efforts. For abortive they were. The attempt to write like Addison was an attempt to imitate the inimitable. No weaker hand could string Ulysses' bow.

The decline of periodical literature after 1720 is probably attributable to the shameful venality which under the Walpole administration extended through all departments of politics. The famous maxim, inaccurately attributed to Walpole, that every man has his price, was applied to and justified by the conduct of the writers of periodical literature. It is said that upwards of 50,000*l.* of Government money was paid to the writers and printers of newspapers during the fourth decade of the century.[1] Scurrility and scandal formed the staple of

---

[1] John, Lord Hervey takes a very different view. ' Never was writing in England at a higher pitch either for learning, strength of diction, or elegance of style than in this reign [George II.]. All the good writing too was confined to political topics, either of civil, military, or ecclesiastical government, and all the tracts on these subjects printed in pamphlets. It might very properly be called the Augustan age of England for this kind of writing.'—Hervey's *Memoirs of the Reign of George II.* vol. i. p. 305.

these periodicals, and they are now, for the most part, deservedly forgotten; but probably the immense reputation of the ' Tatler ' and 'Spectator ' was in no slight degree enhanced by the contrast which they in every way presented to their degenerate successors in the same field of literature.

J. H. O.

CHAPTER VIII.

THE TRINITARIAN CONTROVERSY.

IN an age which above all things prided itself upon its reasonableness, it would have been strange indeed if that doctrine of Chistianity which is objected to by unbelievers as most repugnant to reason, had not taken a prominent place among the controversies which then abounded in every sphere of theological thought. To the thoughtful Christian, the question of questions must ever be that which forms the subject of this chapter. It is, if possible, even a more vital question than that which was involved in the Deistical controversy. The very name 'Christian' implies as much. A Christian is a follower of Christ. Who, then, is this Christ? What relation does He bear to the Great Being whom Christians Jews, Turks, Infidels, and Heretics alike adore? What do we mean when we say that He is the Son of God Incarnate? That He is still present with his Church through his Holy Spirit? These are only other forms of putting the question, What is the Trinity? The various answers given to this question in the eighteenth century form an important part of the ecclesiastical history of the period.

The subject carries us back in thought to the earliest days of Christianity. During the first four centuries, the nature of the Godhead, and the relation of the Three Persons of the Trinity to each other, were directly or indirectly the causes of almost all the divisions which rent the Church. They had been matters of discussion before the death of the last surviving Apostle, and the three centuries which followed his decease were fruitful in theories upon the subject. These theories reappear with but little alteration in the period which comes more immediately under our present consideration. If history ever repeats itself, it might be expected to do so on the revival of this discussion after an abeyance of many centuries. For it is one of those questions on which modern research can throw but little light. The same materials which enabled the inquirer of the eighteenth century to form his conclusion, existed in the fourth century. Moreover, there was a tendency in the discussions of the later period to run in an historical direction ; in treating of them, therefore, our attention will constantly be drawn to the views of the earlier thinkers. With regard to these, it will be sufficient to say that their speculations on the mysterious subject of the Trinity group themselves under one or other of these four heads.

1. The view of those who contend for the mere humanity of Christ—a view which, as will be seen presently, is often claimed by Unitarians as the earliest belief of Christendom.

2. The view of those who deny the distinct personality of the Second and Third Persons of the Blessed Trinity. This was held with various modifications by a great variety of thinkers, but it passes under the general name of *Sabellianism.*

3. The view of those who hold that Christ was something more than man, but less than God ; less than God, that is, in the highest, and indeed the only proper, sense of the word God. This, like the preceding view, was held by a great variety of thinkers, and with great divergences, but it passes under the general name of *Arianism.*

4. The view of those who hold that 'there is but one living and true God,' but that 'in the Unity of this Godhead there are three Persons, of one substance, power, and eternity —the Father, the Son, and the Holy Ghost.' This view is called by its advocates *Catholicism,* for they hold that it is, and ever has been, the doctrine of the Universal Church of Christ ; but, inasmuch as the admission of such a name would be tantamount to giving up the whole point in question, it is refused by its opponents, who give it the name of *Athanasianism.*

In the early Church, the real struggle lay between the advocates of the third and fourth of these views. In the latter part of the fourth century, the Arian view seemed likely to predominate. But this prevalency of Arianism, when examined more closely, loses much of the significance which at the first glance it seems to possess. Its importance has perhaps been exaggerated by a misapprehension of the famous remark of S. Jerome, 'The whole world groaned and wondered to find itself Arian.' This remark was made after the Council of Rimini (A.D. 360), when the Emperor Constantius, in his desire to bring about a Concordat between the contending parties, persuaded the Arians to confess that 'the Word was God, begotten of God before all time, and not a creature, *as other creatures are.*' The Catholics, upon this, consented to suppress the term consubstantial, and the Arians boasted that the expression 'not a creature as other creatures are' was in itself an acknowledgment that the Word *was* a creature in effect, though much more excellent than others. *Then* the world, as S. Jerome says, was surprised to find themselves, whether they would or no, become Arian, though they were not so, but were led into a trap by the use of equivocal words.[1]

After the suppression of Arianism by Theodosius in the East, by Clovis in Gaul, and by Justinian in Africa and Italy, the Trinitarian question lay at rest for nearly nine centuries. Indeed, throughout the sixteenth century, it can scarcely be said to have taken any prominent place among the many theological questions then discussed. The great name of Erasmus indeed is claimed by the anti-Trinitarians as a favourer of their views ; and the question assumed a factitious importance from its connection with the famous case of Servetus, who was burnt by the advice of Calvin for his heterodoxy on the subject of the Trinity. But these were only isolated cases.

With the commencement, however, of the seventeenth century there arose a revival of the old disputes under a new form. Poland was the scene of the revival, and its originator was one Faustus Socinus, who gave his name to a new sect, which to this day retains the title of Socinians. Socinianism differed from Arianism, so far as it related to the subject of the Trinity, mainly in asserting that Jesus Christ had no pre-existence before He was born of the Virgin Mary. Not that

---

[1] See Maimbourg's *History of Arianism*, vol. i. p. 226 ; Waddington's *History of the Christian Church*, p. 88, &c. Arianism was adopted by the half-barbarians in the fourth century on political rather than theological grounds.

this opinion was first held by Socinus. It dates from the very earliest days of Christianity.[1] All that Socinus did was to give a more simple and definite form to a variety of opinions which had been floating about in the country of his adoption for several years before his appearance on the scene.

In England, the Trinitarian question does not appear to have been generally agitated until later on in the same century. Possibly the interest in the subject may have been stimulated by the migration into England of many anti-Trinitarians from Poland, who had been banished from the country by an Order of Council in 1660. At any rate, the date synchronises with the re-opening of the question in this country. It is probable, however, that under any circumstances the discussion would have arisen.

Before the publication of Bishop Bull's first great work in 1685, no controversial treatise on either side of the question —none, at least, of any importance—was published in this country. There had of course been individual anti-Trinitarians in England long before that time. M. L'Amy is of opinion that 'what introduced modern Arianism into England was an excessive compliance shown in 1535 to some Dutch Anabaptists, who took refuge here after the ruin of the Anabaptist party in Amsterdam.'[2] But they seem to have made no great way. In 1551 a German was burnt in London for professing Arianism, and in 1555 an Englishman was burnt at Uxbridge for the same reason. Both Elizabeth and James I. treated with the greatest severity any who were thought to be unsound on the subject of the Trinity. During the Commonwealth, one John Biddell, a schoolmaster in Gloucester, made sufficient impression to be able to form a sect called from his name Biddellians; but the society was short-lived, and the very name passed away after the death of its founder. Anonymous

---

[1] The Ebionites and Cerinthians seem to have held it in the times of the Apostles themselves. Theodotus of Byzantium in the second century, Paul of Samosata, and perhaps Sabellius himself, in the third, and Photinus of Sirmium, a little later, all agreed with Socinus on this point, and all drew after them a certain number of disciples. The Phantastic theory found also great acceptance in the early days of Christianity. 'The body of our Lord,' writes S. Jerome, 'was declared to be a phantom while the Apostles were still in the world, and the blood of Christ was still fresh in Judæa.'—*Advers. Lucif.* xxiii. vol. ii. p. 197.

[2] *History of Socinianism,* by M. L'Amy.

tracts were from time to time published, and the Unitarian doctrines were secretly gaining ground; but so far, the English anti-Trinitarians, the chief of whom were Biddell, Firmin (a worthy man, the friend of Tillotson), and Gilbert Clarke, were little more than importers of foreign novelties.[1] A proof of the little impression which they made may be found in the fact that in Bishop Bull's 'Defensio Fidei Nicænæ' no allusion occurs to any English contemporary writer, the whole work being directed against three foreigners.

A few words on this first great defence of the Catholic Doctrine of the Trinity will be a fitting introduction to the controversy which belongs properly to the eighteenth century. Bishop Bull's defence was written in Latin and was therefore not intended for the unlearned. It was exclusively confined to this one question: What were the views of the ante-Nicene fathers on the subject of the Trinity, and especially on the relation of the Second to the First Person? But though the work was addressed only to a very limited number of readers, and dealt only with one, and that a very limited, view of the question, the importance of thoroughly discussing this particular view can scarcely be exaggerated for the following reason. When the attention of any one familiar with the precise definitions of the Catholic Church which were necessitated by the speculations of Arians and other heretics, is called for the first time to the writings of the ante-Nicene Fathers, he may be staggered by the absence of equal definiteness and precision in them. Bishop Bull boldly met the difficulties which might thus occur. He minutely examined the various expressions which could be wrested into an anti-Trinitarian sense, showing how they were compatible with the Catholic Faith, and citing and dwelling upon other expressions which were totally incompatible with any other belief. He showed that the crucial test of orthodoxy, the one single term at which Arians and semi-Arians scrupled—that is, the Homoousion or Consubstantiality of the

---

[1] In 1702, Thomas Emlyn, a Presbyterian minister in Dublin, avowed Unitarian opinions and was driven from his pulpit.—See Curteis' *Bampton Lectures* for 1871, p. 296. The famous *Letter to a Convocation Man*, written in 1697, says that the land had been deluged with Socinian pamphlets.

Son with the Father—was actually in use before the Nicene Council, and that it was thoroughly in accordance with the teaching of the ante-Nicene Fathers. This is proved, among other ways, by the constant use of a simile which illustrates, as happily as earthly things can illustrate heavenly, the true relation of the Son to the Father. Over and over again this is compared by the early fathers to the ray of light which proceeding from the sun is a part of it, and yet without any division or diminution from it, but actually consubstantial with it. He fully admits that the early fathers acknowledged a certain pre-eminence in the First Person, but only such a pre-eminence as the term Father suggests, a pre-eminence implying no inequality of nature, but simply a priority of order, inasmuch as the Father is, as it were, the fountain of the Deity, God in Himself,[1] while the Son is God *of* God, and, to recur to the old simile incorporated in the Nicene Creed, Light *of* Light.[2] Summing up all that he had written, he says, ' I have shown by many and plain proofs that primitive antiquity agreed with the Nicene fathers on these four heads : 1. That Christ the Lord existed in His own higher nature before the most blessed Virgin Mary, aye, and before the creation of the world, and that He was Himself the Creator of the universe. 2. That in His own true nature He was consubstantial with the Father, that is, not of any created and changeable essence, but of entirely the same nature with the Father, and therefore true God ; consequently that He was also co-eternal with the Father, that is, a Divine Person co-existent with the Father from eternity, but nevertheless that He was subordinate to the Father as the author and principle of himself.' (He dwells more especially upon this second point, because it was the hinge upon which the controversy turned.) ' 3. That the greater and better part of the primitive fathers professed their belief in the Son's eternity; and that if a few of them attributed a certain generation to the Son beginning with some commencement, however they might disagree with the former in words, yet in fact they fully agreed with them. 4. That the ante-Nicenes attributed no other subordination of the Son to the Father than that which

---

[1] αὐτόθεος.

[2] φῶς ἐκ φωτός.

the Catholics acknowledged who wrote after and against the heresy of Arius.'[1]

It may seem strange that one of the antagonists (Petavius) against whom Bishop Bull wrote should have been a Jesuit, who of course would hold on the subject of the Trinity the same views as Bull himself. But the Jesuits' line of argument would, no doubt, be this. The early Church leaned towards Arianism or Unitarianism ; therefore it is obvious that neither Scripture nor primitive antiquity gives a sufficient rule of faith, but that regard must be had to the living voice of the Church speaking authoritatively on the doctrines of Christianity. Petavius is by no means the only instance of a Romanist turning the unsettlement of men's minds on the subject of the Trinity to the advantage of his own system.[2]

Bishop Bull's two subsequent works on the subject of the Trinity (' Judicium Ecclesiæ Catholicæ ' and ' Primitiva et Apostolica Traditio ') may be regarded as supplements to the ' Defence.' The object of the ' Judicium ' was to show, in opposition to Episcopius, that the Nicene fathers held a belief of Our Lord's true and proper divinity to be an indispensable term of Catholic communion ; his latest work was directed against the opinion of Zuicker that Christ's divinity, pre-existence, and incarnation were inventions of early heretics.[3]

It is somewhat remarkable that although in the interval which elapsed between the publication of these and of his first work the Trinitarian controversy in England had been assuming larger proportions and awakening a wider interest, Bull never entered into the arena with his countrymen. But the fact is, his point of view was different from theirs. He confined himself exclusively to the historical aspect of the question, while other defenders of the Trinity were ' induced to overstep the boundaries of Scripture proof and historical

---

[1] Bishop Bull's *Defensio Fidei Nicænæ*, vol. ii. pp. 291–2. 'Multis iisque perspicuis testimoniis ostendi consentiri cum Nicænis Patribus antiquitatem primæ-vam de his quatuor capitibus : (1) Christum Dominum in potiori suâ naturâ ante beatissimam Virginem Mariam adeoque ante mundi creationem extitisse perque ipsum condita fuisse universa,' &c. &c.

[2] See Maimbourg's *History of Arianism*, vol. ii. *ad finem* ; L'Amy's *History of Socinianism*, p. 10 ; *Encyclopédie*, Article, ' Unitarian,' quoted in Toulmin's *Memoirs of Faustus Socinus*.

[3] See Van Mildert's *Life of Waterland*, § 3, p. 29.

testimony, and push their inquiries into the dark recesses of metaphysical speculation.'[1] Chief among these was Dr. W. Sherlock, Dean of St. Paul's, who in 1690 published his 'Vindication of the Trinity,' which he describes as 'a new mode of explaining that great mystery by a hypothesis which gives an easy and intelligible notion of a Trinity in Unity and removes the charge of contradiction.'[2] In this work Sherlock hazarded assertions which were unquestionably 'new,' but not so unquestionably sound. He affirmed among other things that the Persons of the Godhead were distinct in the same way as the persons of Peter, James, and John, or any other men. Such assertions were not unnaturally suspected of verging perilously near upon Tritheism, and his book was publicly censured by the Convocation of the University of Oxford. On the other hand, Dr. Wallis, Professor of Geometry, and the famous Dr. South, published treatises against Dr. Sherlock, which, while avoiding the Scylla of Tritheism, ran dangerously near to the Charybdis of Sabellianism. Like all his writings South's treatise was racy, but violently abusive,[3] and such irritation and acrimony were engendered, that the Royal authority was at last exercised in restraining each party from introducing novel opinions, and requiring them to adhere to such explications only as had already received the sanction of the Church.

Chillingworth, in his Intellectual System, propounded a theory on the Trinity which savoured of Arianism; Burnet and Tillotson called down the fiercest invectives from that able but fiery controversialist Charles Leslie, for 'making the Three Persons of God only three manifestations, or the same Person of God considered under three different qualifications and respects as our Creator, Redeemer, and Sanctifier,' while Burnet argued that the inhabitation of God in Christ made Christ to be God.

---

[1] Van Mildert's *Life of Waterland.*

[2] Sherlock's *Vindication of the Holy and ever Blessed Trinity and the Incarnation of the Son of God* was written in answer to the many tracts which were published and dispersed through the country, chiefly by the exertions of Thomas Firmin.

[3] South says: 'The Socinians are impious blasphemers, whose infamous pedigree runs back from wretch to wretch in a direct line to the Devil himself, and who are fitter to be crushed by the civil magistrate as destructive to government and

Thus at the close of the seventeenth century the subject of the Trinity was agitating the minds of some of the chief divines of the age. It must be observed, however, that so far the controversy between theologians of the first rank had been conducted within the limits of the Catholic Faith.[1] They disputed, not about the doctrine of the Trinity itself, but simply about the mode of explaining it.

Still these disputes between English Churchmen strengthened the hands of the anti-Trinitarians. These latter represented the orthodox as divided into Tritheists and Nominalists, and the press teemed with pamphlets setting forth with more or less ability the usual arguments against the Trinity. These were for the most part published anonymously; for their publication would have brought their writers within the range of the law, the Act of 1689 having expressly excluded those who were unsound on the subject of the Trinity from the tolerated sects. One of the most famous tracts, however, 'The Naked Gospel,' was discovered to have been written by Dr. Bury, Rector of Exeter College, Oxford, and was burnt by order of the Convocation of that University. 'A Historical Vindication of the Naked Gospel,' was also a work of considerable power, and was attributed to the famous Le Clerc. But with these exceptions, the anti-Trinitarians, though they were energetic and prolific in a certain kind of literature, had not yet produced any writer who had succeeded in making his mark permanently upon the age.

Thus the question stood at the commencement of the eighteenth century. In one sense the controversy was at its height; that is to say, some of the ablest writers in the

---

society, than confuted as merely heretics in religion.'—See Toulmin's *Memoirs of Faustus Socinus,* p. 300.   Dr. Jane also entered the lists.

[1] The great name of Sir Isaac Newton has been cited as on the Arian side, but the evidence of his Arianism is, at least, doubtful. Moreover, Newton can hardly take a place among '*theologians* of the first rank;' his true greatness lay in another direction. Dr. Vaughan asserts that Locke 'was not a believer in the Trinity; he did not hold the proper Deity of the Son or of the Holy Spirit' (*Essays* by R. Vaughan, vol. ii. p. 119, 'Locke and his Critics'). It is perilous to assert a negative, but after a very careful study of all Locke's writings, I cannot find anything which directly proves this, though I admit that Locke is not so clear upon the point as could be wished. However, Locke, like Newton, won his reputation on other grounds than theology. He, too, can scarcely be placed among *theologians* of the first rank.

Church had written or were writing upon the subject; but the real struggle between the Unitarians (so called) and the Trinitarians had hardly yet begun, for under the latter term almost all the disputants of high mark would fairly have come.

The new century found the pen of that doughty champion of the Faith, Charles Leslie, busy at work on the Socinian controversy. His letters on this subject had been begun some years before this date ; but they were not finally completed until the eighteenth century was some years old. Leslie was ever ready to defend what he held to be the Christian faith against all attacks from whatever quarter they might come. Deists, Jews, Quakers, Romanists, Erastians, and Socinians, all fell under his lash ; his treatise on the last of these, being the first in order of date, and by no means the last in order of merit among the eighteenth-century literature on the subject of the Trinity, now comes under our notice.

Although his dialogue is nominally directed only against the Socinians, it is full of valuable remarks on the anti-Trinitarians generally ; and he brings out some points more clearly and forcibly than subsequent and more voluminous writers on the subject have done. For example, he meets the old objection that the doctrine of the Trinity is incredible as involving a contradiction, by pointing out that it rests upon the fallacy of arguing from a nature which we know to quite a different nature of which we know little or nothing.[1] The objection that the Christian Trinity was borrowed from the Platonists he turns against the objectors by asking, ' What is become of the master argument of the Socinians that the Trinity is contradictory to common sense and reason ?— Yet now they would make it the invention of the principal and most celebrated philosophers, men of the most refined reason.'[2]

On the whole this is a very valuable contribution to the apologetic literature on the subject of the Trinity, for though

---

[1] 'We cannot charge anything to be a contradiction in one nature because it is so in another, unless we understand both natures. Because a nature we understand not, cannot be explained to us but by allusion to some nature we do understand.'—Leslie's *Theological Works*, vol. ii. p. 402, ' The Socinian Controversy.'

[2] Leslie's *Theological Works*, ii. 405.

Leslie, like his predecessors, sometimes has recourse to ab-struse arguments to explain the 'modes' of the divine presence, yet he is far too acute a controversialist to lay himself open, as Sherlock and South had done, to imputations of heresy on any side ; and his general method of treating the question is lucid enough, and full of just such arguments as would be most telling to men of common sense, for whom rather than for profound theologians the treatise was written.[1]

About the same time that this treatise was published, there arose what was intended to be a new sect, or, according to the claims of its founders, the revival of a very old one—a return, in fact, to original Christianity. The founder or reviver of this party was William Whiston, a man of great learning and of a thoroughly straightforward and candid dis-position, but withal so eccentric, that it is difficult sometimes to treat his speculations seriously. His character was a strange compound of credulity and scepticism. 'Whiston,' writes Macaulay, ' believed everything but the Trinity.' He was 'inclined to believe true' the legend of Abgarus' epistle to Christ, and Christ's reply.[2] He published a vindication of the Sibylline oracles ' with the genuine oracles themselves.'[3] He had a strong faith in the physical efficacy of anointing the sick with oil.[4] But his great discovery was the genuine-ness and inestimable value of the Apostolical Constitutions and Canons. He was ' satisfied that they were of equal value

---

[1] On March 22, 1701, a book called *The Balance of Power*, by Dr. C. Da-venant, which had been affixed on the door of Westminster Abbey, was discussed in the Upper House of Convocation. It contained these words, ' Are not a great many of us able to point out several persons whom nothing has recommended to places of the highest trust, and often to rich benefices and dignities, but open enmity, almost from their cradles, to the Divinity of Christ ? ' It was determined that the writer should be called upon ' to point out whom he knows to be guilty of the charge, that they may be proceeded against in a judicial way, which will be esteemed a great service to the Church. Otherwise the passage will be looked on as a public scandal.'—See Cardwell's *Synodalia*, vol. ii. § xxxiii. Socinianism was a favourite charge against the Latitudinarian bishops. Tillotson, Burnet, Hoadly, &c. were constantly charged with it.

[2] Whiston's *Essays*, published 1713.

[3] *Memoirs of Whiston*, by himself, p. 236.

[4] ' I, William Whiston, have enquired of Mr. Stanger, whose elder brother was a Baptist bishop or messenger who anointed a sick woman and she recovered.' —Whiston's *Memoirs*, p. 448. Many other instances of the efficacy of unction are given.

with the four Gospels ;' nay, 'that they were the most sacred of the canonical books of the New Testament ; that polemical controversies would never cease until they were admitted as the standing rule of Christianity.'[1] The learned world generally had pronounced them to be a forgery, but that was easily accounted for. The Constitutions favoured the Eusebian doctrines, and were therefore repudiated of course by those who were interested in maintaining the Athanasian heresy.[2]

Whiston had many missions to fulfil. He had to warn a degenerate age against the wickedness of second marriages ; he had to impress upon professing Christians the duty of trine immersion[3] and of anointing the sick ; he had to prepare them for the Millennium, which, according to his calculations when he wrote his Memoirs, was to take place in twenty years from that time. But his great mission of all was to propagate Eusebianism and to explode the erroneous notions about the Trinity which were then unhappily current in the Church.[4] His favourite theory on this subject may be found in almost all his works ; but he propounded it *in extenso* in a work which he entitled 'Primitive Christianity revived.' Whiston vehemently repudiated the imputation of Arianism.[5] He called himself an Eusebian, 'not,' he is careful to tell us, 'that he approved of all the conduct of Eusebius of Nicomedia, from which that appellation was derived ; but because that most uncorrupt body of the Christian Church which he so much approved of had this name originally bestowed upon them, and because 'tis a name much more proper to them than Arians.'[6] He sums up his creed

---

[1] See *Memoirs of William Whiston*, by himself, pp. 179, 195, 389, &c.

[2] 'When Rundle, who was once an Eusebian, gained preferment at Salisbury, I was informed, that though he had appeared before so zealous for the genuine antiquity of the Apostolical Constitutions, he said they were not written till the fourth century. I replied, "Make but Dr. Rundle Dean of Durham and they will not be written till the fifth." '—*Memoirs*, 273.

[3] 'In 1714,' he writes with great complacency, 'I baptized Mr. J. and Mr. E. Shelwall with trine immersion according to the Form published by myself.' The close of his *Memoirs* is full of instances of the recovery of sick who had been anointed.

[4] Whiston found all his favourite notions in the Apostolical Constitutions and Canons.

[5] See the first of Whiston's *Three Essays, ad finem* (published 1713).

[6] Whiston's *Essay on the Council of Nice vindicated from the Athanasian Heresy.*

on the subject of the Godhead and the Trinity in words to this effect.—'That there is one supreme God, the Father of Jesus Christ. That God the Father alone is to be primarily worshipped, or, in the most proper sense, he alone being the object of the supreme de⌣ ιee of such divine worship through Jesus Christ. That Jesus Christ is truly God and Lord; that is, really by the appointment of the Father our God, Lord, King, and Judge,' ('this article,' he adds, 'was agreed to by Eusebians, Athanasians, and Arians; as also that he is God by nature and was such before his incarnation; nay, before the creation of the world, and not only by office and appointment afterwards, as the old Ebionites and modern Socinians affirm'), 'but that he is not equal to the supreme God. That Jesus Christ is the first-begotten of all creatures, that is, a Divine Being or Person created or begotten by the Father before all ages, or before all subordinate creatures visible or invisible, but that the Arian interpretation that he was made out of nothing is heretical. That the hypothesis of a human rational soul besides the Logos in his composition as assumed at the incarnation is a later notion. That Jesus Christ will at the consummation of all things resign the kingdom, which the supreme God installed him in after his resurrection, into the Father's hands, and will thenceforward with all other dependent beings be entirely subject to the Father. That super-eminent and divine honour and worship is due to the Son of God, not only by obeying Him as our Lord, by baptizing into his name, by wishing grace and peace from Him and by doxologies, but by proper adoration; by direct and distinct invocation and thanksgiving. That the Holy Spirit of God is a Divine Person made under the supreme God by the Saviour superior to all subordinate creatures, but inferior and subordinate to the Father and the Son. That the Holy Spirit is never in Scripture or most primitive antiquity called directly God or Lord; nor is he properly invocated by any Christian.'

Such was in the main the system of Whiston. It has been set forth at length under his name, because it is in fact the system of what were called 'modern Arians,' only it was propounded in a more fearless and outspoken manner by him than by others, who had more fear of breaking entirely with the Established Church.[1] Whiston formed a sort of society which at first numbered among those who attended its meetings men who afterwards attained to great eminence in the Church ; among others, B. Hoadly, successively Bishop of Bangor, Hereford, Salisbury and Winchester, Rundle, afterwards Bishop of Derry, and then of Gloucester, and Dr. Samuel Clarke. But Whiston was a somewhat inconvenient friend for men who desired to stand well with the powers that be. They all fell off lamentably from the principles of primitive Christianity,—Hoadly sealing his defection by the crowning enormity of marrying a second wife.

Poor Whiston grievously lamented the triumph of interest over truth, which these defections implied. Neither the censures of Convocation nor the falling off of his friends had any power to move *him*. He still continued for some time a member of the Church of England. But his character was far too honest and clear-sighted to enable him to shut his eyes to the fact that the Liturgy of the Church was in many points sadly unsound on the principles of primitive Christianity. To remedy this defect he put forth a Liturgy which he termed ' The Liturgy of the Church of England reduced nearer to the Primitive Standard.' It was in most respects precisely identical with that in use, only it was purged from all vestiges of the Athanasian heresy. The principal changes were in the Doxology, which was altered into what he declares was its original form,[2] in the Prayer of St. Chrysostom,[3] in the first four petitions of the Litany,[4] and one or two

---

[1] A somewhat different view is taken of Whiston by Dr. Hunt. He contends that Whiston cannot be considered as a representative man, which is true enough, but only in the sense that he was not so cautious as his contemporaries. It is difficult to see any substantial difference between his views on the Trinity (with which alone we are concerned) and those of the modern Arians generally. When Dr. Hunt hints that Dr. Clarke differed from him among other things in disavowing Arianism, surely he forgets that Whiston made precisely the same disavowal (see *supra*). They *did* differ to a certain extent in the fact that Whiston attributes more weight to the early fathers, but in little else.

[2] ' Glory be to the Father, *through* the Son, *in* the Holy Ghost.'

[3] The Prayer of St. Chrysostom was altered into ' Almighty God, . . . who *by Thy beloved Son* dost promise that when two or three are gathered together in *His* name thou will grant their requests.'

[4] The first three petitions are altered so as to make them agree with Eusebian views, and the fourth is omitted altogether.

others,[1] and in the collect for Trinity Sunday. The Established Church was, however, so blind to the truth, that she declined to adopt the proposed alterations, and Whiston was obliged to leave her communion. He found a home, in which, however, he was not altogether comfortable, among the general Baptists.

The career of this singular man is a curious episode in the Trinitarian controversy. In an age which was only too conspicuous for subterfuges and evasions, in which preferment rather than the pursuit of truth was too often the object of able men, it is refreshing to find a man of marked ability and learning who was honest enough to say what he thought, and act up to what he said, regardless of consequences. But the speculations of Whiston are mixed up with so much eccentricity that they can scarcely be said to possess much permanent value.

The real reviver of modern Arianism in England was Whiston's friend, Dr. Samuel Clarke. It has been seen that hitherto all theologians of the highest calibre who had taken part in the Trinitarian controversy would come under the denomination of Trinitarians, if we give that term a fairly wide latitude. In 1712 Dr. Clarke, who had already won a high reputation in the field of theological literature,[2] startled the world by the publication of his 'Scripture Doctrine of the Trinity.' This book was long regarded as a sort of text-book of modern Arianism. The plan of the work was to make an exhaustive collection of all the texts in the New Testament which bear upon the nature of the Godhead—in itself a most useful work, and one which was calculated to supply a distinct want in theology. No less than 1,251 texts, all more or less pertinent to the matter in hand, were collected by this industrious writer, and to many of them were appended explanations and criticisms which bear evident marks of being the product of a scholar and a divine. But the advocates of the Catholic doctrine of the Trinity had no need to go further than the mere headings of the chapters of this famous work to have their suspicions justly awakened respecting its tendency. Chapter i. treated 'of God the

---

[1] 'By the mystery of *Thy Son's* holy incarnation, by *his* nativity,' &c.

[2] By his famous 'à priori' arguments for the Being and Attributes of God, and by his answers to the Deists generally.

Father;' chapter ii. 'of the Son of God;.' chapter iii. 'of the Holy Spirit of God.' The natural correlatives to 'God the Father' would be 'God the Son' and 'God the Holy Ghost;' there was something suspicious in the change of these expressions into 'the Son of God' and 'the Holy Spirit of God.' A closer examination of the work will soon show us that the change was not without its significance. 'The Scripture Doctrine' leads substantially to a very similar conclusion to that at which Whiston had arrived. The Father alone is the one supreme God; the Son is a Divine being as far as divinity is communicable by this supreme God; the Holy Ghost is inferior both to the Father and the Son, not in order only, but in dominion and authority. Only Dr. Clarke expresses himself more guardedly than his friend. He had already made a great name among theologians, and he had no desire to lose it.

We may take the appearance of Dr. Clarke's book as the commencement of a new era in this controversy, which after this time began to reach its zenith. Various opponents at once arose attacking various parts of Dr. Clarke's scheme. Dr. Wells complained that he had taken no notice of the Old Testament, that he had failed to show how the true sense of Scripture was to be ascertained, and that he had disparaged creeds, confessions of faith, and the testimony of the fathers; Mr. Nelson complained, not without reason, of his unfair treatment of Bishop Bull; Dr. Gastrell pointed out that there was only one out of Dr. Clarke's fifty-five propositions to which an Arian would refuse to subscribe.[1]

These and others did good service on particular points; but it remained for Dr. Waterland to take a comprehensive view of the whole question, and to leave to posterity not only an effective answer to Dr. Clarke, but a masterly and luminous exposition, the equal to which it would be difficult to find in any other author, ancient or modern. It would be wearisome even to enumerate the titles of the various 'Queries,' 'Vindications,' 'Replies,' 'Defences,' 'Answers to Replies,' which poured forth from the press in luxuriant abundance on either side of the great controversy. It will be sufficient to indicate generally the main points at issue between the combatants.

[1] Potter also, subsequently Archbishop of Canterbury, entered into the lists against Clarke.

Dr. Clarke then, and his friends [1] (who all wrote more or less under his inspiration,) maintained that the worship of God is in Scripture appointed to one Being, that is, to the Father *personally*. That such worship as is due to Christ is the worship of a mediator and cannot possibly be that paid to the one supreme God. That all the titles given to the Son in the New Testament, and all powers ascribed to him, are perfectly well consistent with reserving the supremacy of absolute and independent dominion to the Father alone. That the highest titles of God are never applied to the Son or Spirit. That the subordination of the Son to the Father is not merely nominal, consisting in the mere position or order of words, which in truth of things is a *co*-ordination; but that it is a *real* subordination in point of authority and dominion over the universe. That three persons, that is, three intelligent agents in the same individual, identical substance, is a self-evident contradiction, and that the Nicene fathers, by the term Homoousion, did not mean one individual, identical substance. That the real difficulty in the conception of the Trinity is *not* how three persons can be one God, for Scripture nowhere expresses the doctrine in those words, and the difficulty of understanding a Scripture doctrine ought not merely to lie wholly upon words not found in Scripture, but *how* and in what sense, consistently with everything that is affirmed in Scripture about Father, Son, and Holy Ghost, it is still certainly and infallibly true that to us there is but 'one God the Father' (1 Cor. viii. 6). 'If the one God and Father of all be above all' (Eph. iv. 6), 'tis manifest that all

---

[1] Dr. Whitby (already favourably known in the theological world by his commentary on the Bible), Mr. Sykes, and Mr. Jackson, Vicar of Rossington and afterwards of Doncaster, &c. 'As to Dr. Whitby,' wrote Randolph in 1775, 'he was in the vigour of his age a zealous assertor of the doctrine of the Trinity; and in his Annotations has vindicated several texts of Scripture from the misconstructions of Socinus. . . . He lived to a great age : and in his latter days, when Dr. Clarke wrote his *Scripture Doctrine of the Trinity*, he sided with him, and wrote a treatise entitled *Disquisitiones modestæ in Bulli defensionem Fidei Nicænæ*, wherein he passes censure on a book which he had before, in a treatise on Christ's Divinity, cried up as a most excellent performance. Dr. Whitby was a man of learning, and had done good service to the Church, and to the learned world. But we must appeal from Dr. Whitby in his dotage to Dr. Whitby in his sober senses.'—Randolph's *Vindication of the Worship of the Son and Holy Ghost, against Theophilus Lindsey*, p. 100.

worship, all prayer and thanksgiving, must terminate in him, and must either immediately or mediately be directed to him : and if this be so, then it is evident likewise that all honour or worship paid to a mediator in any capacity must be mediatorial only. The worship paid to Christ and to God through him, as through the alone mediator, is not a separate, independent worship of the person of Christ, but a part of the worship of the Father by his command and to his glory. And this does not open the door to idolatrous worship generally, for God has *commanded* that to *one* only mediator of his *own* appointment every knee shall bow, and has *forbidden* paying worship to angels or any other mediators whom men, contrary to the command of God, select for themselves. If there cannot be anything between the Supreme Father of all things and that system of beings which we call creatures, it follows that the Son of God must be either the Supreme Father himself or a mere creature. The latter was the opinion of the Arians, who held that the Son of God was made out of nothing, and that there was a time when he was not. This was never asserted by Dr. Clarke, nor has he ever affirmed anything from which either notion can be justly inferred. If it be asked how is Christ called God, it replied, 'the word God in Scripture is always a relative word of office, signifying personal dominion, dignity, or government.' The divinity of the Son is shown by those passages of Scripture which declare that before his incarnation he was the Word, that he was in the beginning with God, and was himself God or a divine Person, that he had glory with God before the world was, that he was in the form of God and was the brightness of His glory and the express image of His person, the image of the invisible God, the beginning (or head) [1] of the creation, He by whom God created all things, and that after his incarnation and resurrection all power was given unto him in heaven and earth, and a name above every name ; but all this is perfectly consistent with reserving the supremacy of absolute and independent dominion to the Father alone. As to the claims of the Holy Ghost to be worshipped on an equality with the Father, there is really no

[1] ἀρχή.

one instance in Scripture of any direct act of adoration or invocation being paid to Him at all.

Such is the outline of the system of which Dr. Clarke was the chief exponent. The various arguments by which it was supported will be best considered in connection with that great writer who now comes under our notice—Dr. Waterland. Among the many merits of Waterland's treatment of the subject, this is by no means the least—that he pins down his adversary and all who hold the same views in any age to the real question at issue. Dr. Clarke, for example, admitted that Christ was, in a certain sense, Creator. ' Either, then,' argues Waterland, ' there are two authors and governors of the universe, *i.e.* two Gods, or not. If there are, why do you deny it of either; if not, why do you affirm it of both ? ' Dr. Clarke thought that the divinity of Christ was analogous to the royalty of some petty prince, who held his power under a supreme monarch. ' I do not,' retorts Waterland, ' dispute against the notion of one king under another; what I insist upon is that a great king and a little king make two kings ; (consequently a supreme God and an inferior God make two Gods).' Dr. Clarke did not altogether deny omniscience to be an attribute of Christ, but he affirmed it to be a relative omniscience, communicated to him from the Father. ' That is, in plain language,' retorted Waterland, ' the Son knows all things, except that he is ignorant of many things.' Dr. Clarke did not altogether deny the eternity of the Son. The Son is eternal, because we cannot conceive a time when he was not. ' A negative eternity,' replies Waterland, ' is no eternity ; angels might equally be termed eternal.'

One point on which Waterland insists constantly and strongly is that the scheme of those who would pay divine honours to Christ, and yet deny that he is very God, cannot escape from the charge of polytheism. ' You are tritheists,' he urges, ' in the same sense as Pagans are called polytheists. One supreme and two inferior Gods is your avowed doctrine ; that is, three Gods. If those texts which exclude all but one God, exclude only supreme deities, and do not exclude any that are not supreme, by such an interpretation you have voided and frustrated every law of the Old Testament against idolatry.' Dr. Clarke and his friends distinguished between that supreme sovereign worship which was due to the Father only, and the mediate, relative, inferior worship which was due to others. 'What authority,' asks Waterland, 'is there in Scripture for this distinction? What rules are there to regulate the intention of the worshipper, so as to make worship high, higher, or highest as occasion requires? All religious worship is determined by Scripture and antiquity to be what you call absolute and sovereign.' 'Scripture and antiquity generally say nothing of a supreme God, because they acknowledge no inferior God. Such language was borrowed from the Pagans, and then used by Christian writers. So, too, was the notion of "mediatorial worship" borrowed from the Pagans, handed on by Arians, and brought down to our own times by Papists.'

But Dr. Clarke and his friends maintained that they were not Arians, for they did not make Christ a creature. 'Impossible,' replies Dr. Waterland; 'you assert, though not directly, yet consequentially, that the Maker and Redeemer of the whole world is no more than a creature, that he is mutable and corruptible; that he depends entirely upon the favour and good pleasure of God; that he has a precarious existence and dependent powers; and is neither so perfect in his nature nor exalted in privileges but that it is in the Father's power to create another equal or superior. There is no middle between being essentially God and being a creature.' Dr. Clarke cannot find a medium between orthodoxy and Arianism. He has declared against the consubstantiality and proper divinity of Christ as well as his co-eternity. He cannot be neutral. In condemning Arians he has condemned himself. Nay, he has gone further than the Arians. 'Sober Arians will rise up in judgment and condemn you for founding Christ's worship so meanly upon I know not what powers given after his resurrection. They founded it upon reasons antecedent to his incarnation, upon his being God before the world, and Creator of the world of His own power.'

Waterland showed his strength in defence as well as in attack. He boldly grappled with the difficulties which the Catholic doctrine of the Trinity unquestionably involves, and his method of dealing with these difficulties forms not the least valuable part of his writings on the subject.

Into the labyrinths, indeed, of metaphysical speculation he distinctly declined to follow his opponents. They, as well as he, acknowledged or professed to acknowledge the force of the testimony from Scripture and the fathers. He is ready to join issue on this point, 'Is the Catholic doctrine true?' but for resolving this question he holds that we must have recourse to Scripture and antiquity. 'Whoever debates this question should forbear every topic derived from the *nature* of things, because such arguments belong only to the other question, whether the doctrine be *possible*, and in all reason possibility should be presupposed in all our disputes from Scripture and the fathers.' He consistently maintains that our knowledge of the nature of God is far too limited to allow us to dogmatise from our own reason on such a subject. 'You can never fix any certain principles of individuation, therefore you can never assure me that three real persons are not one numerical or individual essence. You know not precisely what it is that makes one being, one essence, one substance.' There are other difficulties in the nature of the Godhead quite as great as any which the doctrine of the Trinity involves. 'The Omnipresence, the Incarnation, Self-existence are all mysteries, and eternity itself is the greatest mystery of all. There is nothing peculiar to the Trinity that is near so perplexing as eternity.' And then he finely adds: 'I know no remedy for these things but a humble mind. If we demur to a doctrine because we cannot fully and ade-quately comprehend it, is not this too familiar from a creature towards his Creator, and articling more strictly with Almighty God than becomes us?'

Is the Trinity a mysterious doctrine? 'The tremendous Deity is all over mysterious, in His nature and in His attri-butes, in His works and in His ways. If not, He would not be divine. If we reject the most certain truths about the Deity, only because they are incomprehensible, when every-thing about Him must be so of course, the result will be Atheism; for there are mysteries in the works of nature as well as in the Word of God.'

If it be retorted, Why then introduce terms and ideas

which by your own admission can only be imperfectly understood? Why not leave such mysteries in the obscurity in
which they are shrouded, and not condemn those who are
unable to accept without understanding them? The reply
is, 'It is you and not we who are responsible for the discussion and definition of these mysteries. The faith of the
Church was at first, and might be still, a plain, simple, easy
thing, did not its adversaries endeavour to perplex and
puzzle it with philosophical niceties. Early Christians did
not trouble their heads with nice speculations about the
modus of the Three in One.' 'All this discourse about *being*
and *person* is foreign and not pertinent, because if both these
terms were thrown out, our doctrine would stand just as
before, independent of them, and very intelligible without
them. So it stood for about 150 years before *person* was
heard of in it, and it was later before *being* was mentioned.
Therefore, if all the objection be against these, however innocent, expressions, let the objectors drop the name and accept
the thing.' It was no wish of Waterland's to argue upon
such mysteries at all. ' Perhaps,' he says, 'after all, it would
be best for both of us to be silent when we have really nothing
to say, but as you have begun, I must go on with the argument. . . . It is really not reasoning but running riot with
fancy and imagination about matters infinitely surpassing
human comprehension. You may go on till you reason, in a
manner, God out of his attributes and yourself out of your
faith, and not know at last when to stop.' These are weighty
and wise words, and it would be well if they were borne in
mind by disputants on this profound mystery in every age.
But while deprecating all presumptuous prying into the secret
nature of God, Waterland is perfectly ready to meet his
adversaries on that ground on which alone he thinks the
question can be discussed.

Summing up and setting in one compendious view all
that the modern Arians taught in depreciation of Christ,
Waterland showed that in spite of their indignation at being
represented as teaching that Christ was a mere creature, they
yet clearly taught that he was ' brought into existence as well
as any other creature, that he was precarious in existence,
ignorant of much more than he knows, capable of change

from strength to weakness, and from weakness to strength; capable of being made wiser, happier, and better in every respect; having nothing of his own, nothing but what he owes to the favour of his lord and governor.' By the arguments which they used to prove all this, they put a most dangerous weapon into the hands of Atheists, or at least into the hands of those who denied the existence of such a God as is revealed to us in Holy Scripture. 'Through your zeal against the divinity of the Son, you have betrayed the cause to the first bold Marcionite that shall deny the eternal Godhead of the Father and the Son, and assert some unknown God above both. The question was, whether a particular Person called the Father be the Eternal God. His being called God would amount to nothing, that being no more than a word of office. His being Creator, nothing; that you could elude. His being Jehovah, of no weight, meaning no more than a person true and faithful to his promises. Almighty is capable of a subordinate sense. The texts which speak of eternity are capable of a subordinate sense. The term "first cause" is not a Scriptural expression.'

Waterland boldly faces the objection against the Catholic doctrine of the Trinity which was derived from certain texts of Scripture which taken by themselves might seem to favour the Arian view. How, for example, it was asked, could it be said that all power was *given* unto Christ (Matt. xxviii. 18), and that all things were put under his feet after his resurrection (Eph. i. 22), if He was Lord long before? 'The Logos,' replies Waterland, 'was from the beginning Lord over all, but the God man ($\Theta\epsilon\acute{a}\nu\theta\rho\omega\pi\sigma$) was not so till after the Resurrection. Then he received in that capacity what he had ever enjoyed in another; he received full power in both natures which he had heretofore only in *one*.'[1] The passage on which the Arians insisted most of all, and which they constantly asserted to be by itself decisive of the whole question, is 1 Corinthians viii. 6. There, they asserted, the Son is excluded in most express words from being one with the Supreme God. Dr. Clarke told Waterland in downright

[1] He proceeds to explain S. Matthew xxiv. 36, S. Luke ii. 52, and S. John v. 19, in a sense consistent with the Catholic doctrine.

terms that 'he should be ashamed when he considered that he falsified St. Paul, who said, " To us there is but one God, the Father."' ' But,' replies Dr. Waterland, ' do we who make the Son essentially the same God with that one, and suppose but one God in all, or you who make two Gods, and in the same *relative* sense, God *to us,* falsify St. Paul? *We* can give a reason why the Son is tacitly included, being so intimately united to the Father as partaker of the same divine nature, but that any creature should not be excluded from being God is strange.'

To turn now from Scripture to antiquity. The question as to what was the opinion of the ante-Nicene fathers had been so thoroughly handled by Bishop Bull, that Waterland (his legitimate successor) had no need to enter upon it at large over again. But Bishop Bull had done his work too well to suit the theory of Dr. Clarke and his friends. Although the latter professed to find in the early fathers a confirmation of their views, yet from a consciousness, perhaps, of the unsatisfactoriness of this confirmation they constantly depreciate the value of patristic evidence. In connection, therefore, with the subject of the Trinity, Waterland clearly points out what is and what is not the true character of the appeal to antiquity. The fathers are certain proofs in many cases of the Church's doctrine in that age, and probable proofs of what that doctrine was from the beginning. In respect of the latter they are inferior additional proofs when compared with plain Scripture proof ; of no moment if Scripture is plainly contrary, but of great moment when Scripture looks the same way, because they help to fix the true interpretation in disputed texts. Waterland, however, would build no article of faith on the fathers, but on Scripture alone. If the sense of Scripture be disputed, the concurring sentiments of the fathers in any doctrine will be generally the best and safest comments on Scripture, just as the practice of courts and the decisions of eminent lawyers are the best comments on an Act of Parliament made in or near their own times, though the obedience of subjects rests solely on the laws of the land as its rule and measure. To the objection that interpreting Scripture by the ancients is debasing its majesty and throwing Christ out of his throne, Waterland replies in somewhat stately terms, 'We think that Christ never sits more secure or easy on his throne than when he has his most faithful guards about Him, and that none are so likely to strike at his authority or aim at dethroning him as they that would displace his old servants only to make way for new ones.' But this respect for the opinion of antiquity in no way involved any compromise of the leading idea of all eighteenth century theology, that it should follow the guidance of reason. Reason was by no means to be sacrificed to the authority of the fathers. Indeed, 'as to authority,' he says, ' in a strict and proper sense I do not know that the fathers have any over us ; they are all dead men ; therefore we urge not their *authority*, but their testimony, their suffrage, their judgment, as carrying great force of reason. Taking them in here as lights or helps *is* doing what is *reasonable* and using our own understandings in the best way.' ' I follow the fathers,' he adds, ' as far as reason requires and no further ; therefore, this *is* following our own reason.' In an-age when patristic literature was little read and lightly esteemed this forcible, and at the same time highly reasonable, vindication of its importance had a value beyond its bearing upon the doctrine of the Trinity, in connection with which the subject was introduced by our author.[1]

Here our notice of the points at issue between Dr. Water-land and the modern Arians, so far as they concerned the truth of the Catholic doctrine of the Trinity, may fitly close. But there was yet another question closely connected with the above which it concerned the interests of morality, no less than of religion, thoroughly to sift. It was no easy task which Dr. Clarke and his friends undertook when they essayed to prove from Scripture and antiquity that the Son and Holy Ghost were not one with the supreme God. But they attempted a yet harder task than this. They contended that their views were not irreconcilable with the formularies and Liturgy of the Church of England. The more candid and ingenuous mind of Whiston saw the utter hopelessness of this endeavour. It was, he says, an endeavour 'to wash the blackmore white,' and so, like an honest man as he was, he retired from her communion. Dr. Clarke could not, of course,

---

[1] See vols. i. ii. and iii. *passim* of Waterland's *Works*, edited by Van Mildert.

deny that there was at least an apparent inconsistency between his views and those of the Church to which he belonged. One of the chapters in his 'Scripture Doctrine of the Trinity' is devoted to a collection of 'passages in the Liturgy which may seem in some respects to differ from the foregoing doctrine.' But he and his friends were 'ready to subscribe any test containing nothing more than is contained in the Thirty-nine Articles; their avowed principle being that 'they may do it in their own sense agreeably to what they call Scripture.' In his 'Case of Arian Subscription' Dr. Waterland had no difficulty in showing the utter untenableness of this position. He maintained that 'as the Church required subscription to *her own* interpretation of Scripture, so the subscriber is bound to that and that only.' 'The rules,' he says, 'for understanding what her sense is are the same as for understanding oaths, laws, &c.—that is, the usual acceptation of words, the custom of speech at the time being, the scope of the writer from the controversies then on foot,' &c. It is but a shallow artifice for fraudulent subscribers to call their interpretation of Scripture, Scripture. The Church has as good a right to call her interpretation Scripture. Let the Arian sense be Scripture to Arians; but then let them subscribe only to Arian subscriptions.

The Arians justified their conduct by maintaining that, at the worst, they only followed the example of those who, like Waterland himself, repudiated Calvinism and yet subscribed to Calvinistic Articles. Had Dr. Waterland possessed the light which has been thrown upon the history of our Articles in the present day, his answer to this *tu quoque* argument (for at the best it amounted to nothing more) would have been even more effective. But, as it was, his distinction between the two cases is quite conclusive. 'The article on predestination,' he argues, 'is left in *general* terms. Both sides may subscribe *in the same sense*, which sense reaches not to the particulars in dispute. One believes predestination to be absolute, the other conditional. But the propositions concerning the Trinity are not general but special and determinate in the very points of difference between the Catholics and the Arians (*e.g.* on the consubstantiality, coeternity, and coequality of the Son) in as clear and strong words as can be devised.' Dr. Waterland sets in strong contrast Dr. Clarke's faith as gathered from his works, and the faith which he was obliged to profess as a clergyman of the Church of England. ' My faith is, that the Father only, in opposition to all other persons whatever, is very and eternal God, and that therefore the Son is not. Yet I profess that the Son *is* the " very and eternal God." My faith is, that there are *not* three eternal persons, yet I confess that " it may be proved by certain warrants of Scripture that there are." I do not believe that the Father, Son, and Holy Ghost are one God, because that would be contradictory to St. Paul, yet I am content to say, " O holy, blessed, and glorious Trinity, three persons in one God " '—and much more to the same effect.[1] In answer to the accusation of narrowness and bigotry, Waterland brings out clearly a distinction which his adversaries had confused. ' The writer,' he says, ' cannot distinguish between ejecting and not admitting, nor between Church communion and Church trusts. I said not a word about ejecting any man out of communion ; I pleaded only against admitting any to Church trusts that must come in by iniquity or not at all.'

But strongly as Dr. Waterland felt and expressed his sense of the disingenuousness of those who were ready to subscribe to forms which were evidently contrary to their own opinions, Dr. Clarke's friend Whiston expressed himself still more strongly : ' It is not justifiable,' he thinks, ' but contradictory to the direct meaning and design of those forms, and of most pernicious consequence in all parallel cases.'

The case of Arian subscriptions was really part of a larger question. There were some who, without actually denying the *truth* of the doctrine of the Trinity, doubted whether it was of sufficient *importance* or clearly enough revealed to make it a necessary article of the Christian faith. These were sometimes called Episcopians, a name derived from one Episcopius, an amiable and not unorthodox writer of the seventeenth century, who was actuated by a charitable desire to include as many as possible within the pale of the Christian Church, and to minimize the differences between all who

---

[1] Waterland's ' Case of Arian Subscription Considered.'—*Works*, vol. ii. p. 330, &c.

would, in any sense, own the name of Christians. The prevalence of such views in Dr. Waterland's days led him to write one of his most valuable treatises in connection with the Trinitarian controversy. It was entitled, ' The Importance of the Doctrine of the Trinity Asserted,' and was addressed to those only who believed the *truth* of the doctrine but demurred to its importance. Waterland, on the contrary, shows that 'it is of prime consideration for directing and determining our worship. It is no mere barren speculation, but intimately and directly practical. How much greater is the love of Christ to man on Trinitarian than on anti-Trinitarian principles. If he were very God, it was an act of infinite love and condescension to become man and die for us. But if he were a mere creature, it was no surprising act of condescension to embark in so glorious a work as being Saviour of mankind, and such as would advance him to be lord and judge of the world. Where is the condescension in a creature submitting to be highly honoured? What creature could modestly aspire to it and not think it above his pretensions and highest ambition?' Waterland concludes this work, which is rather a practical than a controversial treatise, with some wise words of caution to those persons of ' more warmth than wisdom,' who from a mistaken liberality would make light of heresy.[1]

It is now time to close this sketch of the method in which this great writer—one of the few really great divines who belong to the eighteenth century—handled the mysterious subject of the Trinity. Not only from his profound learning and acuteness, but from the general cast of his mind, Waterland was singularly adapted for the work which he undertook. To treat this subject of all subjects, the faculties both of thinking clearly and of expressing thoughts clearly are absolutely essential. These two qualifications Dr. Waterland possessed in a remarkable degree. He always knew exactly what he meant, and he also knew how to convey his meaning to his readers. His style is nervous and lucid, and he never sacrifices clearness to the graces of diction. His very deficiencies were all in his favour. Had he been a man of a

[1] Waterland's 'Importance of the Doctrine of the Holy Trinity Considered.'— *Works*, vol. iii. pp. 475, 479, 485, &c.

London, half recanting and half explaining his explanations.[1] These documents appear to have satisfied nobody except perhaps the bishops. The Lower House resolved 'that the paper subscribed by Dr. Clarke and communicated by the bishops to the Lower House doth not contain in it any recantation of the heretical assertions, &c., nor doth give such satisfaction for the great scandal occasioned by the said books as ought to put a stop to further examination thereof;' while his outspoken friend, Whiston, wrote to him, 'Your paper has occasioned real grief to myself and others, not because it is a real retractation, but because it is so very like one, yet is not, and seems to be penned with a plain intention only to ward off persecution,' and told him face to face that '*he* would not have given the like occasion of offence for all the world.' However, the bishops were satisfied and the matter proceeded no further.

Subsequently Dr. Clarke was taken to task by his diocesan, the Bishop of London, for altering the doxology into an accordance with Arianism. He was neither convinced nor silenced by Waterland; and though his influence may (as Van Mildert tells us) have perceptibly declined after the great controversy was closed, he was not left without followers, and maintained a high reputation which survived him. He was for many years known among a certain class of admirers as 'the great Dr. Clarke.'[2] Among those who were at least interested in, if not influenced by the doctor was Queen Caroline, the clever wife of George II.

Nor was the excitement caused by the speculations of Dr. Clarke on the doctrine of the Trinity confined to the Church of England alone. It was the occasion of one of the fiercest disputes that ever arose among Nonconformists.

---

[1] See Cardwell's *Synodalia*, xxxviii. &c., and Tindal's *Continuation of Rapin*, xviii. 344.

[2] Hoadly declared to the world that he wished to be distinguished after death by no other title than the friend of Dr. Clarke.—Nichol's *Literary Anecdotes of the Eighteenth Century*, quoted in Mrs. Thomson's *Memoirs of Lady Sundon*, &c. Dr. Clarke's reputation, however, was founded not so much upon his contributions to the Trinitarian controversy as upon his famous *à priori* demonstration of a Deity and upon his ethical speculations. He was the chief opponent of those who found all moral obligation on the will of God, and the assertor of the independent and necessary character of moral distinctions.

Exeter was the first scene of the spread of Arianism among the Dissenters. Two ministers gave great offence to their congregations by preaching Arianism. The alarm of heresy spread rapidly, and there was so great an apprehension of its tainting the whole county that—strange as it may sound to modern ears—the judge at the county assize made the prevalence of Arianism the chief subject of his charge to the grand jury. Among Churchmen, some were alarmed lest the heresy should spread among their own body, while others rather gloried in it as a natural result of schism. A statement of the case was sent to the dissenting ministers in the metropolis. The Presbyterian ministers at Exeter, in order to allay the panic, agreed to make a confession of faith, every one in his own words *vivâ voce.* This caused a revival of the old discussion as to whether confessions of faith should be made in any but Scripture language. The matter was referred to the ministers in London, and a meeting was held at Salters' Hall, at which the majority agreed to the general truth that ' there is but one living and true God, and that the Father, Son, and Holy Ghost are that one God.' Numbers, however, of the Presbyterians, and some of the Baptists, adhered to Arianism and thence drifted into Socinianism or rather simple Unitarianism.

This, indeed, was the general course inside as well as outside the Church. The very name of Arian almost died out, and the name of Socinian took its place. The term Socinian is, however, misleading. It by no means implies that those to whom it was given agreed with the doctrine of Faustus Socinus. It was often loosely and improperly applied on the one hand to many who really believed more than he did, and on the other to many who believed less. In fact, the stigma of Socinianism was tossed about as a vague, general term of reproach in the eighteenth century, much in the same way as ' Puseyite,' ' Ritualist,' and ' Rationalist' have been in our own day. Many were called Socinians who certainly were thorough believers in the divinity of Jesus Christ in its highest sense. Thus Warburton was suspected of being tainted with Socinianism. So was Herring, Archbishop of York. This very inaccurate use of the word Socinian may in part be accounted for by remembering that one important feature in the system of Socinus was his utter denial of the doctrine of the atonement or satisfaction made by Christ in any sense. ' Christ,' he said, 'is called a mediator not because he made peace between God and man, but because he was sent from God to man to explain the will of God and to make a covenant with them in the name of God. A mediator (a medio) is a middle person between God and man.'[1]   Now there is abundance of evidence that before and at the time of the Evangelical revival in the Church of England, this doctrine of the atonement had been, if not denied, at least practically ignored. Archbishop Secker, in his Charge in 1758, complains bitterly of the teaching of mere virtue and natural religion, and urges his clergy to dwell more on the doctrine of the Trinity, on Christ's sacrifice, and on sanctification by the Spirit.[2]   Bishop Horsley, in his Charge in 1790, says that matters in this respect were better than they were thirty years before, when he first entered the ministry, but still he felt it necessary to prove the fallacy of supposing that the peculiar doctrines of the Trinity, Incarnation, Expiation, Intercession, and Communion with the Holy Spirit are above the reach of the common people.[3]   These two writers have been quoted because, as they did not belong to that party to whom the Church is mainly indebted for again bringing the distinctive doctrines of Christianity into prominence, they will not be suspected of over-stating the case.   In the writings of the early Evangelical party we find, of course, constant complaints of the general ignoring of these doctrines.   Now it is probable that the term Socinian was often applied to those who kept these doctrines in the background, and not, indeed, applied altogether improperly ; only, if we assume that all those who were termed Socinians disbelieved in the true divinity or personality of the Son and the Holy Ghost, we shall be assuming more than was really the case.

On the other hand, many were called Socinians who really believed far less than Socinus and the foreign Socinians did.   It is true that Socinus 'regarded it as a mere

---

[1] Toulmin's *Memoirs of Faustus Socinus*, p. 191.
[2] Archbishop of Canterbury's First *Charge*, 1758.
[3] Bishop of St. David's *Charge*, 1790.

human invention, not agreeable to Scripture and repugnant to reason, that Christ is the only begotten Son · of God, because he and no one besides him was begotten of the divine substance ; '[1] but he also held that ' Scripture so plainly attributes a divine and sovereign power to Christ as to leave no room for a figurative sense.'[2] And the early Socinians thought that Christ must not only be obeyed but his assistance implored, and that he ought to be worshipped, that ' invocation of Christ or addressing prayers to him was a duty necessarily arising from the character he sustained as head of the church ; ' and that ' those who denied the invocation of Christ did not deserve to be called Christians.'[3]

Let us now return to the history of our own Socinians, or, as they preferred to be called, Unitarians ; we shall soon see how far short they fell in point of belief of their foreign predecessors.

The heresy naturally spread more widely among Nonconformists than it could in the Church of England. As the biographer of Socinus remarks, ' The Trinitarian forms of worship which are preserved in the Church of England, and which are so closely incorporated with its services, must furnish an insuperable objection against conformity with all sincere and conscientious Unitarians.'[4] If the common sense and common honesty of Englishmen revolted against the specious attempts of Dr. Clarke and his friends to justify *Arian* subscription, a much more hopeless task would it have been to reconcile the further development of anti-Trinitarian doctrines with the formularies of the Church.

At the same time it must be admitted that the cessation or abatement of anti-Trinitarian efforts in the Church after the death of Dr. Clarke is not to be attributed solely to the firmness and earnestness of Churchmen's convictions on this subject. It arose, in part at least, from the general indisposition to stir up mooted questions. Men were disposed to rest satisfied with ' our happy establishment in Church and State ;' and it was quite as much owing to the spiritual torpor

---

[1] Toulmin's *Memoirs of Faustus Socinus*, p. 180. [2] Id. 211.
[3] Id. p. 467.
[4] Toulmin, p. 281. See also on this point Thomas Scott's interesting account of his own religious opinion in the *Force of Truth*, and in his biography by his son.

which overtook the Church and nation after the third decade of the eighteenth century, as to strength of conviction, that the Trinitarian question was not further agitated.

Among the Nonconformists, and especially among the Presbyterians, the case was different. The Arianism which led to the Salters' Hall conference drifted by degrees into Unitarianism pure and simple. Dr. Lardner was one of the earliest and most distinguished of those who belonged to this latter school. He passed through the stage of Arianism, but the mind of the author of 'The Credibility of Gospel History' was far too clear and logical to allow him to rest there, and he finally came to the conclusion that 'Jesus Christ was a mere man, but a man with whom God was, in a peculiar and extraordinary manner.' This is not the place to refer to the various Nonconformists, such as Caleb Fleming, Hugh Farmer, James Foster, Robert Robinson, John Taylor, and many others who diverged more or less from the Catholic doctrine of the Trinity. But the views of one Nonconformist whose name is a household word in the mouth of Churchmen and Dissenters alike, and some of whose hymns will live as long as the English language lives, claim at least a passing notice.

Isaac Watts belonged to the Independents, a sect which in the first half of the eighteenth century was less tainted with Socinianism than any of 'the three denominations.' His 'Treatise on the Christian Doctrine of the Trinity,' and that entitled, 'The Arian invited to the Orthodox Faith,' were professedly written in defence of the Catholic doctrine. The former, like most of Dr. Watts's compositions, was essentially a popular work. 'I do not,' he writes, 'pretend to instruct the learned world. My design here was to write for private and unlearned Christians, and to lead them by the fairest and most obvious sense of Scripture into some acquaintance with the great doctrine of the Trinity.'[1] In some respects his work is very effective. One point especially he brings out more forcibly than almost any other writer of his day. It is what he calls 'the moral argument' for the Trinity. There is real eloquence in his appeal to the 'great number of Christians

---

[1] 'The Christian Doctrine of the Trinity,' by Isaac Watts, vol. vi. of *Works*, p. 155.

who, since the Apostles, under the influence of a belief in the Divinity of the Son and the Spirit, have paid divine honours to both, after they have sought the knowledge of the truth with the utmost diligence and prayer ; when they have been in the holiest and most heavenly frames of spirit, and in their devoutest hours ; when they have been under the most sensible impressions of the love of the Father and the Son, and under the most quickening influences of the Blessed Spirit himself ; in the devotions of a death-bed, and in the songs and doxologies of martyrdom.' 'Now can we,' he asks, ' suppose that in such devout and glorious seasons as these, God the Father should ever thus manifest his own love to souls that are degrading Him by worshipping another God ? That Christ Jesus should reveal himself in his dying love to souls that are practising idolatry and worshipping himself instead of the true God ? '

But there are other passages of a very different tendency, in which Dr. Watts virtually gives up the whole point at issue, and apparently without being conscious that he is doing so. On the worship of the Holy Ghost, for example, he writes: 'There is great silence in Scripture of precepts or patterns of prayer and praise to the Holy Spirit.' 'Therefore,' he thinks, 'we should not bind it on our own consciences or on others as a piece of necessary worship, but rather practise it occasionally as prudence and expediency may require.'[1] On the famous question of the Homoousion, he thinks ' it is hard to suppose that the eternal generation of the Son of God as a distinct person, yet co-equal and consubstantial or of the same essence with the Father, should be made a fundamental article of faith in the dawn of the Gospel.' He is persuaded therefore 'that faith in Him as a divine Messiah or all-sufficient and appointed Saviour is the thing required in those very texts where he is called the Son of God and proposed as such for the object of our belief; and that a belief of the natural and eternal and consubstantial sonship of Christ to God as Father was not made the necessary term or requisite of salvation ; ' neither can he ' find it asserted or revealed with so much evidence in any part of the Word of God as is

---

[1] 'The Christian Doctrine of the Trinity,' by Isaac Watts, vol. vii. of *Works*, p. 196.

necessary to make it a fundamental article of faith.'[1] And once more, on the Personality of the Holy Ghost, he writes: 'The general and constant language of Scripture speaks of the Holy Ghost as a power or medium of divine operation.' Some places may speak of him as personal, but 'it was the frequent custom of Jews and Oriental nations to speak of powers and qualities under personal characters.' He can find 'no plain and express instance in Holy Scripture of a doxology directly and distinctly addressed to the Holy Spirit,' and he thinks the reason of this may be 'perhaps because he is only personalised by idioms of speech.'[2]

Now anyone who has studied the course of the Trinitarian controversy will see at once that an anti-Trinitarian would require no further concessions than these to prove his point quite unanswerably. The amiable design of Dr. Watts's second treatise was 'to lead an Arian by soft and easy steps into a belief of the divinity of Christ,'[3] but if he granted what he did, the Arian would have led him, if the controversy had been pushed to its logical results.'

To return to the Church of England. About the middle of the eighteenth century there was a revival of one phase of the Trinitarian controversy. A movement arose to procure the abolition of subscription to the Articles and Liturgy. The spread of Unitarian opinions among the clergy is said to have originated this movement, though probably this was not the sole cause. One of the most active promoters of this attempt was Archdeacon Blackburne; he was supported by Clayton, Bishop of Clogher, who boldly avowed that his object was to open the door for different views upon the Trinity in the Church.[4] His own views on this subject expressed in a

---

[1] Watts, p. 200.

[2] 'The Arian Invited to an Orthodox Faith.'—*Works*, vol. vi. p. 348.

[3] Id. 225.

[4] One of the ablest opponents of Bishop Clayton was Dr. Randolph, President of C.C.C. Oxford. See his *Vindication of the Doctrine of the Trinity from the Exceptions of a late Pamphlet entituled an Essay on Spirit*, published 1754. Dr. Randolph published a supplement to this treatise in 1775, entitled 'A Vindication of the Worship of the Son and the Holy Ghost against the Exceptions of Mr. Theophilus Lindsey from Scripture and Antiquity.' Edmund Law, Bishop of Carlisle, Rundle, Bishop of Derry, and Hare, Bishop of Chichester, were all thought to be more or less unsound on the doctrine of the Trinity. The latter certainly vindicated the opinions of Whiston and Clarke.

treatise entitled 'An Essay on Spirit' were certainly original and startling. He held that the Logos was the Archangel Michael, and the Holy Spirit the angel Gabriel!

This treatise and that of Blackburne, entitled 'The Confessional,' called forth the talents of an eminent Churchman in defence of the received doctrine of the Trinity—Jones of Nayland. His chief work on the subject was entitled 'The Catholic Doctrine of the Trinity,' and was drawn up after the model of Dr. Clarke's famous book, to which, indeed, it was partly intended to be an antidote. It was written on the principle that Scripture is its own best interpreter, and consisted of a series of well-chosen texts marshalled in order with a brief explanation of each, showing its application to the doctrine of the Trinity. On one point Jones insists with great force, viz., that every article of the Christian faith depends upon the Catholic doctrine of the Trinity; and he illustrates this by applying it to 'our creation, redemption, sanctification, resurrection, and glorification by the power of Christ and the Holy Spirit.'[1] Jones did, perhaps, still more useful if less pretentious work in publishing two little pamphlets, the one entitled 'A Letter to the Common People in Answer to some Popular Arguments against the Trinity,' the other 'A Preservative against the Publications dispersed by Modern Socinians.' Both of these set forth the truth, as he held it, in a very clear and sensible manner, and at a time when the Unitarian doctrines were spreading widely among the multitudes who could not be supposed to have either the time or the talents requisite to grapple with long, profound, and elaborate arguments, they were very seasonable publications.

But the most curious contribution which Jones made to the Trinitarian controversy was a pamphlet entitled 'A Short Way to Truth, or the Christian Doctrine of a Trinity in Unity, Illustrated and Confirmed from an Analogy in the Natural Creation.' He shows that the powers of nature by which all natural life and motion are preserved are three—air, fire, and light. That these three thus subsisting together in unity are applied in Scripture to the Three Persons of the Divine

---

[1] Address to the Reader, p. viii. prefixed to *The Catholic Doctrine of the Trinity,*

Nature, and that the manifestations of God are always made under one or other of these signs. These three agents support the life of man. There is a Trinity in the body (1), the heart and blood vessels; (2) the organs of respiration; (3) the nerves, the instruments of sensation; these three departments are the three moving principles of nature continually acting for the support of life. 'Therefore,' he concludes, 'as the life of man is a Trinity in Unity, and the powers which act upon it are a Trinity in Unity, the Socinians being, in their natural capacity, formed and animated as Christians, carry about with them daily a confutation of their own unbelief.'[1]

In the year 1782, the Trinitarian controversy received a fresh impulse from the appearance in it of a writer whose eminence in other branches of knowledge lent an adventitious importance to what he wrote upon this subject. In that year, Dr. Priestley published his 'History of the Corruptions of Christianity,' which, as Horsley says, was 'nothing less than an attack upon the creeds and established discipline of every church in Christendom.' Foremost among these corruptions were both the Catholic doctrine of our Lord's divinity and the Arian notion of his pre-existence in a state far above the human. The general scope of the book, so far as it concerned the Trinity, is not unfairly summed up by Bishop Horsley in these words :—' The doctrine of the Trinity, in the form in which it is now maintained, is no older than the Nicene Council, and is the result of a gradual corruption of the doctrine of the Gospel which took its rise in an opinion first advanced in the second century by certain converts from the Platonic school, who, by expounding the beginning of St. John's Gospel by the Platonic doctrine of the Logos, ascribed a sort of secondary divinity to our Saviour, affirming that he was no other than the second principle of the Platonic Triad, who had assumed a human body to converse with man. Before this innovation, of which Justin Martyr is made the author, the faith of the whole Christian Church, but particularly the Church of Jerusalem, was simply and strictly Unitarian. The immediate disciples of the apostles conceived our Saviour to be a man whose existence com-

---

[1] Jones of Nayland's *Theological Works*, vol. i. p. 214, &c.

menced in the womb of the Virgin, and they thought him in no respect the object of worship. The next succeeding race worshipped him indeed, but had no higher notions of his divinity than those which were maintained by the followers of Arius in the fourth century.[1] The same opinions are expressed by Dr. Priestley in his 'History of the Early Opinions about Jesus Christ.' He came to these conclusions in spite of a strong prepossession to the contrary derived from his early training. He was educated, he tells us, in the strictest principles of Calvinism, and having from his early years had a serious turn he was very zealous in his belief of the Trinity. About the age of twenty he saw reason to change and became an Arian, and continued so for fifteen years. From reading Lardner's letters on the Logos he became a Socinian, and was greatly confirmed in this doctrine after he was fully satisfied that man is of an uniform composition and wholly mortal, and that the doctrine of a separate, immaterial soul capable of sensation and action when the body is in the grave is a notion borrowed from heathen philosophy and unknown to Scripture.[2] He thinks that to be convinced of the proper humanity of Christ men must begin as he did with the study of Scripture.[3]

The train of reasoning by which Priestley supported his conclusion was as follows. 'Since all Jewish Christians were called Nazarenes or Ebionites, and all writers that mention them speak of the doctrine of those sects *in general* as being that Christ was a mere man, the inference is that those sects of Jewish Christians did, in all times after they became so distinguished (just before or just after the destruction of Jerusalem) hold that doctrine. Then, is it not almost certain that the apostles themselves must have taught it? Could the whole Jewish Church have abandoned the doctrine of the divinity of Jesus Christ so soon after the apostles, if they had received it from them?'[4] With regard to the apostles themselves, 'they evidently conversed with Christ at first on the supposition of his being a man as themselves. What

[1] *A Charge to the Clergy of the Archdeaconry of St. Albans*, pp. 87, 88.
[2] Priestley's *Tracts*, in controversy with Bishop Horsley, Preface vi.
[3] Id. viii.
[4] Id. p. 32.

must have been their surprise on being informed that he was not a man but God ! No one, he is confident, would ever call that being a man, after he was convinced he was God.'[1] Again, 'the great objection of the Jews to Christianity was that it enjoined the worship of more gods than one. There is no such objection raised in the Acts of the Apostles. Therefore the divinity of Christ could not have been preached to them.'[2] How then did the notion of the Trinity arise ? 'It was derived from no other source than the Platonic philosophy. The real truth of the matter may be gained from an expression of Tertullian, who says that the "idiotæ" of his time were Unitarians, and were shocked at the notion of a Trinity. This exactly tallies with the explanation given of the origin of the Trinity. It would, of course, be the learned Christians alone who would become enamoured of the philosophy of Plato ; therefore, the great body of the unlearned (idiotæ) continued to be Unitarians long after the learned had adopted the notion of the Trinity.' The latter were misled by the principles of Platonism of which they were great admirers, and from the three Platonic principles got the idea of the Three Persons of the Trinity. But they modified the Platonic notions to suit their own theories. 'The Logos of the Platonists had in their opinion always had a personal existence, because Plato supposed the creation to have been eternal ; but this was not the opinion of the platonising Christians, who held that the world was not eternal ; and therefore, retaining as much of Platonism as was consistent with that doctrine, they held that there was a time when the Father was alone and without a Son ; his Logos or reason being the same in him that reason now is in man.'[3]

Priestley held that there was no censure of Unitarianism in the New Testament, although Unitarians certainly existed in the time of St. John. The term heresy was long used as synonymous with Gnosticism, and was not applied to Cerinthians, Ebionites, and Nazarenes, of whose existence St. John at any rate knew without condemning them. The one

---

[1] Priestley's *Tracts*, in controversy with Bishop Horsley, p. 92.
[2] Id. p. 132.
[3] Id. p. 74. See also p. 478.

expression, ' Christ came in the flesh,' which, taken by itself, might seem to imply his pre-existence, was really directed against the Gnostics, who held that Christ had no real body, and therefore though he was *come* according to the prophecies concerning him, he was not *come in the flesh.* This also is the meaning of Polycarp and others when they use this phrase. The Jews expected their Messiah to come as a mere man, and never changed in this opinion.

The great antagonist of Dr. Priestley was Dr. Horsley, who, first in a Charge to the clergy of the Archdeaconry of St. Albans, and then in a series of letters addressed to Priestley himself, maintained with conspicuous ability the Catholic doctrine of the Trinity.

An able modern writer [1] says that the Unitarian met at the hands of the bishop much the same treatment as Collins had received from Bentley. But the comparison scarcely does justice either to Horsley or Priestley. From a purely intellectual point of view it would be a compliment to any man to compare him with ' Phileleutherus Lipsiensis,' but the brilliant wit and profound scholarship displayed in Bentley's remarks on Collins were tarnished by a scurrility and personality which, even artistically speaking, injured the merits of the work, and were quite unworthy of being addressed by one gentleman (not to say clergyman) to another. Horsley's strictures are as keen and caustic as Bentley's ; but there is a dignity and composure about him which, while adding to rather than detracting from the pungency of his writings, prevent him from forgetting his position and condescending to offensive invectives. Priestley, too, was a more formidable opponent than Collins. He was not only a man who by his scientific researches had made his mark upon his age, but he had set forth Unitarianism far more fully and powerfully than Collins had set forth Deism. Still he unquestionably laid himself open to attack, and his opponent did not fail to take advantage of this opening.

Horsley distinctly declines to enter into the general controversy as to the truth or possibility of the Christian Trinity. Everything, he thinks, that can be said on either side, has been said long ago. But he is ready to join issue

[1] Hunt's *History of Religious Thought*, iii. 349.

with Priestley on the historical question. This he feels it practically necessary to do, for 'the whole energy and learning of the Unitarian party is exerted to wrest from us the argument from tradition.'[1]

He shows, then, that so far from all the Church being originally Unitarian, there was no Unitarian before the end of the second century, when Theodotus, 'the learned tanner of Byzantium,' who had been a renegade from the faith, taught for the first time that his humanity was the whole of Christ's condition, and that he was only exalted to Heaven like other good men. He owns that the Cerinthians and Ebionites long before that had affirmed that Jesus had no existence previous to Mary's conception, and was literally and physically the carpenter's son, and so asserted the mere humanity of the Redeemer, 'but,' he adds, 'they admitted I know not what unintelligible exaltation of his nature upon his Ascension by which he became no less the object of worship than if his nature had been originally divine.'[2] He acknowledges that the Cerinthian Gnostics denied the proper divinity of Christ, but, he adds very pertinently, 'if you agree with me in these opinions, it is little to your purpose to insist that Justin Martyr's reflections are levelled only at the Gnostics.'[3]

Like Waterland, and indeed all defenders of the Catholic doctrine, Horsley fully admits the difficulties and mysteriousness of his subject, 'but,' he asks, 'is Christianity clear of difficulties in any of the Unitarian schemes? Hath the Arian hypothesis no difficulty when it ascribes both the first formation and perpetual government of the Universe not to the Deity, but an inferior being? In the Socinian scheme is it no difficulty that the capacity of a mere man should contain that wisdom by which God made the universe?'[4]

Horsley rebukes his opponent in severe and dignified language for presuming to write on a subject on which, by his own confession, he was ignorant of what had been written. In reply to a passage in Horsley's 'Charge,' in which it was asserted that Priestley's opinions in general were the same as those propagated by Daniel Zuicker, and that his arguments were in essential points the same as Episcopius had used, Priestley had

---

[1] *Charge*, p. 67.
[2] Id. 43, &c.
[3] *Letter X. to Dr. Priestley*, p. 183.
[4] *Letters to Dr. Priestley*, p. 249.

said that he had never heard of Zuicker, and knew little of Episcopius ; he also let slip that he had only 'looked through' the ancient fathers and the writings of Bishop Bull, an unfortunate phrase, which Horsley is constantly casting in his teeth.[1] On the positive proofs of his own position, Horsley cites numerous passages from the ante-Nicene fathers. He contends that in the famous passage of Tertullian on which Priestley had laid so much stress, Tertullian meant by 'idiotæ,' not the general body of unlearned Christians, but some stupid people who could not accept the great mystery which was generally accepted by the Church. He shows that the Jews in Christ's time *did* believe in a Trinity, and expected the Second Person to come as their Messiah. He maintains that when Athanasius spoke of Jews who held the simple humanity of Christ, he meant what he said, viz., Jews simply, not Christian Jews, as Priestley asserted.

There is a fine irony in some of his remarks on Priestley's interpretations of Scripture. 'To others,' he says in his 'Charge,' 'who have not the sagacity to discern that the true meaning of an inspired writer must be the reverse of the natural and obvious sense of the expressions which he employs, the force of the conclusion that the Primitive Christians could not believe our Lord to be a mere man because the Apostles had told them he was Creator of the Universe (Colossians i. 15, 17) will be little understood.'[2] In the famous text which speaks of Christ as 'come in the flesh,' for 'come *in* the flesh' Priestley substitutes 'come *of* the flesh.' 'The one,' says Horsley, 'affirms an Incarnation, the other a mortal extraction. The first is St. John's assertion, the second Dr. Priestley's. Perhaps Dr. Priestley hath discovered of St. John, as of St. Paul, that his reasoning is sometimes inconclusive and his language inaccurate, and he might think it no unwarrantable liberty to correct an expression, which, as not perfectly corresponding with his own system, he could not entirely approve. It would have been fair to advertise his reader of so capital an emendation, an emendation for which no support is to be found in the Greek Testament or any variety of manuscripts.'[3] In a similar tone, he trusts 'that

---

[1] *Letters*, &c. p. 91, &c.   [2] *Charge*, p. 14.   [3] Id. p. 17.

the conviction of the theological student that his philosophy is Plato's, and his creed St. John's, will alleviate the mortification he might otherwise feel in differing from Dr. Priestley.'[1]

One of the most important and interesting parts of Horsley's letters was that in which he discussed the old objection raised by Priestley that the Christian doctrine of the Trinity was borrowed from Plato. There is, and Horsley does not deny it, a certain resemblance between the Platonic and the Christian theories. The Platonists asserted three Divine hypostases, the Good Being ($\tau\dot{a}\gamma\alpha\theta\acute{o}\nu$), the word or reason ($\lambda\acute{o}\gamma\sigma\varsigma$ or $\nu\hat{o}\hat{v}\varsigma$), and the Spirit ($\psi\upsilon\chi\acute{\eta}$) that actuates or influences the whole system of the Universe (*anima mundi*), which had all one common Deity ($\tau\grave{o}$ $\theta\epsilon\acute{\iota}o\nu$), and were eternal and necessarily existent.[2] Horsley can see no derogation to Christianity in the resemblance of this theory to that of the Christian Trinity. He thinks that the advocates of the Catholic Faith in modern times have been too apt to take alarm at the charge of Platonism. ' I rejoice,' he says, ' and glory in the opprobrium. I not only confess, but I maintain, not a perfect agreement, but such a similitude as speaks a common origin, and affords an argument in confirmation of the Catholic doctrine for its conformity to the most ancient and universal traditions.'[3] For was this idea of a Triad peculiar to Plato? or did it originate with him? 'The Platonists,' says Horsley, ' pretended to be no more than expositors of a more ancient doctrine which is traced from Plato to Parmenides ; from Parmenides to his master of the Pythagorean sect ; from the Pythagoreans to Orpheus, the earliest of Grecian mystagogues ; from Orpheus to the secret lore of Egyptian priests in which the foundations of the Orphic theology were laid. Similar notions are found in the Persian and Chaldean theology ; even in Roman superstition from their Trojan ancestors. In Phrygia it was introduced by Dardanus, who carried it from Samothrace.' In short, ' the Trinity was a leading principle in all ancient schools of philosophy and religion.'[4]

---

[1] *Charge*, p. 73.
[2] See Maimbourg's *History of Arianism*, i. 6, note 3.
[3] *Letters*, p. 215.
[4] *Charge*, p. 43. Horsley rather lays himself open in this passage to the charge

Not, of course, that Horsley approved of the attempts made at the close of the second century to meet the Platonists half-way by professing that the leading doctrines of the Gospel were contained in Plato's writings. He strongly condemned, *e.g.*, the conceit of the Platonic Christians that the external display of the powers of the Son in the business of Creation is the thing intended in Scripture language under the figure of his generation. 'There is no foundation,' he thinks, 'in Holy Writ, and no authority in the opinions and doctrines of preceding ages. It betrayed some who were most wedded to it into the use of very improper language, as if a new relation between the First and Second Persons took place when the creative powers were first exerted.' He condemns 'the indiscretion of presuming to affix a determinate meaning upon a figurative expression of which no particular exposition can be drawn safely from Holy Writ.' 'But,' he adds, 'the conversion of an attribute into a person, whatever Dr. Priestley may imagine, is a notion to which they were entire strangers.'[1] On the main question of the Trinity he asserts, in opposition to Dr. Priestley, that they were quite sound. 'The Platonic fathers, though they held the eternity of the Second Person no less than the First, imagined that his generation signified a particular transaction which took place at a certain time. And it is probable that though they held the eternity of the Holy Spirit, yet they conceived that the procession expressed some projection of his energies which took place at the same time with that which they understood to be the generation of the Son. But they conceived that the Second Person had ever been the word, the Third ever the wisdom.' The three names, therefore—God, the Word, and the Wisdom—in the language of Theophilus' age, were equivalent to Father, Son, and Holy Ghost.'[2]

Adopting the same line of argument which Leslie had used before him, Horsley dexterously turns the supposed resemblance between Platonism and Christianity, which, as has been seen, he admits, into a plain proof that the doctrine

---

of confounding history with mythology ; but probably all he meant was to show the extreme antiquity of Trinitarian notions.

[1] *Charge*, p. 59.

[2] Id. 70. See also *Letters to Priestley*, 235, 460, &c.

of the Trinity cannot be such a contradiction as the Unitarians represented it to be. ' In the opinions of the Pagan Platonists,' he says, ' we have in some degree an experimental proof that this abstruse doctrine cannot be the absurdity which it seems to those who misunderstand it. Would Plato, Porphyry, or even Plotinus, have believed the miracles of Mahomet or the doctrine of Transubstantiation ? But they all believed a doctrine which so far at least resembles the Nicene as to be loaded with the same or greater objections.' [1]

The controversy between Priestley and Horsley brings us nearly to the close of the eighteenth century. There had been a considerable secession of English clergymen to the Unitarians,[2] and Horsley's masterly tracts were a very opportune defence of the Catholic doctrine. On one point he and his adversary thoroughly concurred—viz., that there could be no medium between making Christ a mere man and owning Him to be in the highest sense God. Arianism in its various forms had become by this time well-nigh obsolete in England. It was a happy thing for the Church that this point had been virtually settled. The alternative was now clearly set before English Churchmen—' Choose ye whom ye will serve ; if Christ be God, follow him ; if not, be prepared to give up all notions of a creature worship.' The Unitarians at the close of the eighteenth century all took their stand on this issue. Such rhapsodies as those which were indulged in by early Socinians as well as Arians were now unheard. The line of demarcation was strictly drawn between those who did and those who did not believe in the true Godhead and distinct personality of the Second and Third Persons of the Blessed Trinity, so that from henceforth men might know on what ground they were standing.

———————

Here the sketch of this famous controversy, which was certainly a marked feature of the eighteenth century, may fitly close. But a few general remarks in conclusion seem requisite.

And first as to the nomenclature. The name claimed

---

[1] *Charge*, p. 70.
[2] Evanson, Disney, Jebb, Gilbert Wakefield, &c.

by the anti-Trinitarians has, for want of a better, been perforce adopted in the foregoing pages. But in calling them Unitarians, we must do so under protest. The advocates of the Catholic doctrine might with equal correctness be termed, from one point of view, Unitarians, as they are from another point of view termed Trinitarians. For they believe in the Unity of God as firmly as they believe in the Trinity. And they hold that there is no real contradiction in combining those two subjects of belief; for that the difficulty of reconciling the Trinity with the Unity of the Godhead in reality proceeds simply from our human and necessary incapacity to comprehend the nature of the union. Therefore they cannot for a moment allow to disbelievers in the Trinity the title of Unitarians, so as to imply that the latter monopolise the grand truth that 'the Lord our God is our Lord.' They consent reluctantly to adopt the term Unitarian because no other name has been invented to describe the stage at which anti-Trinitarians had arrived before th e close of th e eighteent century. These latter, of course, differed essentially from the Arians of the earlier part of the century. Neither can they be properly termed Socinians, for Socinus, as Horsley justly remarks, 'though he denied the original divinity of Our Lord, was nevertheless a worshipper of Christ, and a strenuous asserter of his right to worship. It was left to others,' he adds, 'to build upon the foundation which Socinus laid, and to bring the Unitarian doctrine to the goodly form in which the present age beholds it.' [1] Indeed, the early Socinians would have denied to Dr. Priestley and his friends the title of Christians, and would have excommunicated them from their Society. 'Humanitarians' would be a more correct designation; but as that term is already appropriated to a very different signification, it is not available. For convenience' sake, therefore, the name of Unitarians must be allowed to pass, but with the proviso that so far from its holders being the sole possessors of the grand truth of the unity of the Godhead, they really, from the fact of their denying the divinity of two out of the three Persons in the Godhead, form only a very maimed and inadequate conception of the one God.

[1] *Letters,* &c. 243.

The outcry against all mystery, or, to use a modern phrase, the spirit of rationalism, which in a good or bad sense pervaded the whole domain of religious thought, orthodox and unorthodox alike, during the eighteenth century, found its expression in one class of minds in Deism, in another in anti-Trinitarianism. And here rises the question, What was the connection between these two heresies? Were they simply different phases of one and the same habit of thought, or were they totally distinct? The former was the view taken by many contemporary writers. It was but one step, they said, from Socinianism to Deism—nay, the Socinians were for the most part only Deists under a thin disguise.[1]

In many respects unquestionably the Deists and Socinians were in perfect accord. In the essential points in which the Socinians differed from the orthodox the Deists were, to a man, Socinians. They agreed in denying the original divinity of Christ; they agreed in denying the personality of the Holy Ghost; they agreed in rejecting all notions of a satisfaction or atonement for sin brought about by the death of Christ; they agreed in finding a stumbling-block in the mysteries of Christianity; they agreed in their exorbitant exaltation of reason. But then, did they arrive at these conclusions from the same line of argument, and were they agreed on other points equally important? Professedly, at least, quite the reverse. The Deists thought any revelation from God beyond that which He has given us in Nature unnecessary, and in particular they rejected all that God is supposed to have revealed in the Old Testament and almost all in the New. The anti-Trinitarians, on the contrary, whether Arians, Socinians, or Unitarians, professed quite as much reverence for the authority of the Bible as the Trinitarians themselves did. It was to the Bible that they appealed. They could not believe in the Trinity because they could find no traces of the doctrine in the Old Testament, nor any in the New, except what could be easily explained in accordance with their own theories. They rejected the notion of three persons not only or chiefly because it was offensive to their reason, but because it was contrary to the grand old Bible truth of the Unity of the

---

[1] Jones of Nayland called even Dr. Clarke, who by no means went all the lengths even of Socinianism, a Deist.

Godhead. Such was their profession, and we must not gratuitously assume that they were insincere in it. The sufficiency of natural religion, which was the keynote of Deism, found no place in anti-Trinitarianism. But if the systems were not identical or even kindred systems, yet, as a matter of fact, did the one lead to the other? There is not sufficient evidence to show that it did. It is easy to trace the natural and logical descent from Arianism to Socinianism, from Socinianism to Unitarianism, pure and simple ; and it is equally easy to perceive the stages by which Deism lapsed into Pyrrhonism, and Pyrrhonism into Atheism. But the link between Unitarianism and Deism is missing. There may have been exceptions, but it was certainly not the usual course for Unitarians to become Deists. Indeed, the historical sequence of events, if nothing else, proves the contrary. Unitarianism, in its latest and fullest development, hardly arose— at least, hardly made itself felt as a force—till Deism proper was well-nigh extinct. One of the earliest of English Unitarians, Dr. Lardner, was himself a distinguished writer against the Deists. The course of the history of Deism differs widely from that of Unitarianism. Deism in England made a vast sensation for about half a century and then was hardly ever heard of more. Unitarianism never created the excitement that Deism did ; but its influence was far more lasting ; it constantly changed its form, but it was always essentially the same thing. At the present day, when the Deist, in the proper sense of that term, is almost extinct, Unitarians abound, and though they may vary in some respects, are still the legitimate descendants of the Unitarians of the eighteenth century. Deism and Unitarianism, therefore, can hardly be regarded as kindred systems ; neither can one be regarded as the natural development of the other. But though both disavowed any opposition to real Christianity, yet both in reality allow no scope for what have been from the very earliest times to the present day considered essential doctrines of the Gospel. If the Deist strikes at the very root of Christianity by questioning the evidence on which it rests, no less does the Unitarian divest it of everything distinctive—of the divine condescension shown in God taking our nature upon him, of the divine love shown in God's unseen presence even now in His Church by His Holy Spirit. Take away these doctrines, and there will be left indeed a residuum of ethical teaching, which some may please to call Christianity if they will ; but it differs as widely from what countless thousands have understood and still understand by the term, as a corpse differs from a living man.

J. H. O.

CHAPTER IX.

ENTHUSIASM.

FEW things are more prominent in the religious history of England in the eighteenth century, than the general suspicion entertained against anything that passed under the name of enthusiasm. It is not merely that the age was, upon the whole, formal and prosaic, and that in general society serenity and moderation stood disproportionately high in the list of virtues. No doubt zeal was unpopular; but, whatever was the case in the more careless language of conversation, zeal is not what the graver writers of the day usually meant when they inveighed against enthusiasts. They are often very careful to guard themselves against being thought to disparage religious fervour. Good and earnest men, no less than others, often spoke of enthusiasm as a thing to be greatly avoided. Nor was it only fanaticism, though this was especially odious to them. Some to whom they imputed the charge in question were utterly removed from anything like fanatical extravagance. The term was expressive of certain modes of thought and feeling rather than of practice. Under this theological aspect it forms a very important element in the Church history, and is well worthy of attentive consideration.

Enthusiasm no longer bears quite the same meaning that it used to do. A change, strongly marked by the impress of reaction from the prevailing tone of eighteenth-century feeling, has gradually taken place in the usual signification of the word. In modern language we commonly speak of enthusiasm in contrast, if not with lukewarmness and indifference, at all events with a dull prosaic level of commonplace thought or action. A slight notion of extravagance may sometimes remain attached to it, but on the whole we

use the words in a decidedly favourable sense, and imply in
it that generous warmth of impetuous, earnest feeling without
which few great things are done. This meaning of the word
was not absolutely unknown in the eighteenth century, and
here and there a writer may be found to vindicate its use as
a term of praise rather than of reproach. It might be applied
to poetic [1] rapture with as little offence as though a bard
were extolled as fired by the muses or inspired by Phœbus.
But applied to graver topics, it was almost universally a term
of censure. The original derivation of the word was generally
kept in view. It is only within the last one or two generations that it has altogether ceased to convey any distinct
notion of a supernatural presence—an afflatus from the Deity.
But whereas the early Alexandrian fathers who first borrowed
the word from Plato and the ancient mysteries had Chris-
tianised it and cordially adopted it in a favourable signification, it was now employed in a hostile sense as ' a misconceit
of inspiration.' [2] It thus became a sort of byeword, applied in
opprobrium and derision to all who laid claim to a spiritual
power or divine guidance, such as appeared to the person by
whom the term of reproach was used, fanatical extravagance, or,
at the least, an unauthorised outstepping of all rightful bounds
of reason. Its preciser meaning differed exceedingly with the
mind of the speaker and with the opinions to which it was
applied. It sometimes denoted the wildest and most credulous fanaticism or the most visionary mysticism ; on the
other hand, the irreligious, the lukewarm, and the formalist
often levelled the reproach of enthusiasm, equally with that
of bigotry, at what ought to have been regarded as sound
spirituality, or true Christian zeal, or the anxious efforts of
thoughtful and religious men to find a surer standing ground
against the reasonings of infidels and Deists.

A word which has not only been strained by constant
and reckless use in religious contests, but is also vague in
application and changeable in meaning, might seem marked
out for special avoidance. Yet it might be difficult to find a

---

[1] Or to a painter's imagination. The *Idler*, not however without some fear of
'its wild extravagances' even in this sphere, allows that 'one may very safely
recommend a little more enthusiasm to the modern painters; too much is certainly
not the vice of the present age.'—No. 79.

[2] Henry More, *Enthus. Triumphatus*, § 4.

more convenient expression under which to group various forms of subjective, mystic, and emotional religion, which were in some cases strongly antagonistic to one another, but were closely allied in principle and agreed also in this, that they inevitably brought upon their supporters the unpopular charge of enthusiasm. All were more or less at variance with the general spirit of the century. But, in one shape or another, they entered into almost every religious question that was agitated; and, in many cases, it is to the men who in their own generation were called mystics and enthusiasts that we must chiefly turn, if we would find in the eighteenth century a suggestive treatment of some of the theological problems which are most deeply interesting to men of our own time.

At the opening of the period before us a great many causes had combined to create a strong prejudice against outbreaks of religious excitability. The preceding century had completed, in great measure, the long history of the Reformation and its more immediate consequences. Up to the time of the Revolution the struggle had been incessant, and the country had never felt safe from relapse into Romanism on the one hand, or wild sectarian confusion on the other. The 'Church in danger' cry survived for some years yet to come; but this favourite alarm, degenerating as it soon did into little more than a party watchword, was but a very faint echo of the real and imminent perils from which not the English Church only, but English Protestantism, had at last emerged. As for dangers yet in store, those which were most dreaded became yearly less formidable, and no one thought as yet of the greater danger which beset a time of somnolent tranquillity. The old troubles were past. Sober-minded Englishmen had been worried to the utmost with the fanaticism and furious religious fervours of the Commonwealth, and the very notion of enthusiasm under any form had become abhorrent to them. The last great struggle with Rome in the time of James the Second had not very powerfully agitated spirits unnerved by the general reaction which had set in with the Restoration. But it had caused much excitement and temporary panic. These fears also had been set comparatively at rest. And now, amid all the differences of Whig and Tory, the religion of the country

eemed, on the whole, thankful to repose for a time at peace
nder the shelter of 'our present happy establishment in
Church and State.' Schemes of Church comprehension had
ailed ; but the efforts made on either side had had a con-
iliatory effect upon Nonconformists, and the Toleration Bill
ad removed for the time their most urgent grievances.
Dissent was, in fact, very greatly weakened, and English
'rotestants in general, with the exception of a very insignifi-
ant minority, were well content to see the Reformed National
Church placed at last upon a sound and permanent footing.
Everywhere there was an inclination to rest, and to enjoy
vithout disturbance the vaunted blessings of sobriety and
noderation. All the leading political conditions tended to
onfirm these feelings. The country acquiesced in the new
dynasty apathetically, and without any cordiality. There
vas nothing to stir the emotions and kindle the imagination.
Loyalty of the old kind was dead, or survived only under the
aint of disaffection and possible rebellion. Under different
ircumstances the great war with France, full as it was of
eligious and political interest, might have stirred the English
nation to its depths, almost as when the hearts of the people
vent forth with their queen in the days of Elizabeth and the
Armada. There could be no such exaltation of patriotic
entiment amid the conflicting interests, the intrigues, and
party animosities, which threw their shade over the most
plendid victories of Marlborough. Thus in the political, as
n the religious atmosphere, there was a sort of dulness
broad, a lack of elasticity and energetic life, which was
itterly unfavourable to all forms of enthusiasm.

Meanwhile, with the passing away of old controversies,
new subjects for investigation came prominently forward.
Now that a period of greater ecclesiastical tranquillity had
arrived, when Church writers no longer felt bound to exert
all their powers of argument against Rome or rival modes of
Protestantism, and when disputes about forms of government,
rites and ceremonies, and other externals of religion ceased
o excite any strong interest, attention began to be turned in
good earnest to the deeper and more fundamental issues
nvolved in the Reformation. There arose a great variety of
nquiries as to the principles and grounds of faith. Into

all of these entered more or less directly the important question, How far man has been endowed with a faculty of spiritual discernment independent of what is properly called reason.   It was a subject which could not be deferred, although at this time encompassed by special difficulties and beset by prejudices.   The doctrine of 'the inner light' has been in all ages the favourite stronghold of enthusiasts and mystics of every kind, and this was more than enough to discredit it.   All the tendencies of the age were against allowing more than could be helped in favour of a tenet which had been employed in support of the wildest extravagances, and had held the place of highest honour among the opinions of the early Quakers, the Anabaptists, the Muggletonians, the Fifth Monarchy men, and other fanatics of recent memory.   Did not the very meaning of the word 'enthusiasm,' as well as its history, point plainly out that it is grounded on the belief in such inward illumination?   And who, with the examples of the preceding age before him, could foretell to what dangerous extremes enthusiasm might lead its excited followers?   Whenever, therefore, any writers of the eighteenth century had occasion to speak of man's spiritual faculties, one anxiety was constantly present to their minds.   Enthusiasm seemed to be regarded with continual uneasiness, as a sort of unseen enemy, whom an incautious expression might let in unawares, unless they watchfully guarded and circumscribed the province which it had claimed as so especially its own.

It is certainly remarkable that a subject which excited so much apprehension should have entered, nevertheless, into almost every theological discussion.   Yet it could not be otherwise.   Controversy upon the grounds of faith and all secondary arguments and inferences connected with it gather necessarily round four leading principles—Reason, Scripture, Church Authority, Spiritual Illumination.   Throughout the century, the relation more particularly of the last of these principles to the other three, became the real, though often unconfessed centre alike of speculation and of practical theology.   What is this mystic power which had been so extravagantly asserted—in comparison with which Scripture, Reason, and Authority had been almost set aside as only lesser lights? Is there indeed such a thing as a Divine illumination, an inner light, a heavenly inspiration, a directing principle within the soul? If so—and that there is in man a spiritual presence of some kind no Christian doubts—what are its powers? how far is it a rule of faith? What is its rightful province? What are its relations to faith and conscience? to Reason, Scripture, Church authority? Can it be implicitly trusted? By what criterion may its utterances be distinguished and tested? Such, variously stated, were the questions asked, sometimes jealously and with suspicion, often from a sincere, unprejudiced desire to ascertain the truth, and often from an apprehension of their direct practical and devotional value. The inquiry, therefore, was one which formed an important element both in the divinity and philosophy of the period, and also in its popular religious movements. It was discussed by Locke and by every succeeding writer who, throughout the century, endeavoured to mark the powers and limits of the human understanding. It entered into most disputes between Deists and evidence writers as to the properties of evidence and the nature of Reasonable Religion. It had to do with debates upon inspiration, upon apostolic gifts, upon the Canon of Scripture, with controversies as to the basis of the English Church and of the Reformation generally, the essentials and nonessentials of Christianity, the rights of the individual conscience, toleration, comprehension, the authority of the Church, the authority of the early fathers. It had immediate relation to the speculations of the Cambridge Platonists, and their influence on eighteenth-century thought, upon such subjects as those of immutable morality and the higher faculties of the soul. It was conspicuous in the attention excited in England, both among admirers and opponents, by the reveries of Fénelon, Guyon, Bourignon, and other foreign Quietists. It was a central feature of the animated controversy maintained by Leslie and others with the Quakers, a community who, at the beginning of the century, had attained the zenith of their numerical power. It was further illustrated in writings upon the character of enthusiasm elicited by the extravagances of the so-called French Prophets. In its aspect of a discussion upon the supra-sensual faculties of the soul, it received some additional light from the transcendental conceptions of Bishop Berkeley's philosophy. In its relation with mediæval mysticism on the one hand and with some distinctive aspects of modern thought on the other, it found an eminent exponent in the suggestive pages of William Law ; with whom must be mentioned his admirer and imitator, the poet John Byrom. The influence of the Moravians upon the early Methodists, the controversy of Wesley with Law, the progress of Methodism and Evangelicalism, the opposition which they met, the ever repeated charge of 'enthusiasm,' and the anxiety felt on the other side to rebut the charge, exhibit the subject under some of its leading practical aspects. From yet another point of view, a similar reawakening to the keen perception of other faculties than those of reason and outward sense, is borne witness to in the rise of a new school of imaginative art and poetry, in livelier sympathy with the more spiritual side of nature, in eager and often exaggerated ideals of what might be possible to humanity. Lastly, there remains to notice the very important influence exercised upon English thought by Coleridge, not only by the force of his own somewhat mystic temperament, but by his familiarity with such writers as Kant, Lessing, Schleiermacher, and Schelling, who had studied far more profoundly than any English philosophers or theologians, the relation of man's higher understanding to matters not cognisable by the ordinary powers of human reason.

But it is time to enter somewhat further into detail on some of the points briefly suggested. Reference was made to the Cambridge Platonists, for although they belong to the history of the seventeenth century, some of their opinions bear too directly on the subject to be entirely passed over. Moreover, Cudworth's 'Immutable Morality' was not published till 1731, at which time it had direct reference to the controversies excited by Mandeville's 'Fable of the Bees.' The popularity also of Henry More's writings continued into the century after his death, and a new edition of his ' Discourse of Enthusiasm' appeared almost simultaneously with writings of Lord Shaftesbury, Dr. Hickes, and others upon the same subject. It might have been well if the works of such men as H. More and Cudworth, J. Smith and Norris, had made a deeper impression on eighteenth-century thought.

Their exalted but[1] restrained mysticism and their lofty
system of morality was the very corrective which the tone of
the age most needed. And it might have been remembered
to great advantage, that the doctrine of an inner light, far
from being only the characteristic tenet of the fanatical
disciples of Fox and Münzer, had been held in a modified
sense by men who, in the preceding generation, had been the
glory of the English Church—a band of men conspicuous for
the highest culture, the most profound learning, the most
earnest piety, the most kindly tolerance. Cudworth, at all
events, held this view. Engaged as he was, during a lengthened period of intellectual activity, in combating a philosophical system which, alike in theology, morals, and politics,
appeared to him to sap the foundations of every higher
principle in human nature, he was led by the whole tenour of
his mind to dwell upon the existence in the soul of perceptions
not derivable from the senses, and to expatiate on the immutable distinctions of right and wrong. Goodness, freed from
all debasing associations of interest and expedience, such as
Hobbes sought to attach to it, was the same, he was well
assured, as it had existed from all eternity in the mind of God.
To a mind much occupied in such reflections, and nurtured
in the sublime thoughts of Plato, the doctrine of an inner
light naturally commended itself. All goodness of which
man is capable is a participation of the Divine essence—an
effluence, as it were, from God ; and if knowledge is communicable through other channels than those of the outward senses,
what is there which should forbid belief in the most immediate intercourse between the soul and its Creator, and in a
direct intuition of spiritual truth ? We may attain a certain
comprehension of the Deity, ' proportionate to our measure ;
as we may approach near to a mountain, and touch it with
our hands, though we cannot encompass it all round, and
enclasp it within our arms.'[1] In fact, Cudworth's general

---

[1] Cudworth's *Intellectual System*, book v. *Works*, iii. 222. The whole passage
is remarkable, especially for the succession of vivid metaphors by which he illustrates apprehension, as distinguished from comprehension of the Deity. See also
Sir J. Mackintosh, *Progress of Ethical Philosohy*, § 5 ; Hunt's *Religious Thought
in England*, iii. 185 ; Pattison in *Essays and Reviews*, 290. The applicability of
Cudworth's writings to present controversies is spoken of in *Edinburgh Review*,
January 1875, 8.

train of reasoning and of feeling brought him into great sympathy with the mystics, though he was under little temptation of falling into the extravagances which had lately thrown their special tenets into disrepute. He did not fail, indeed, to meet with some of the customary imputations of enthusiasm, pantheism, and the like. But an ordinary reader will find in him few of the characteristic faults of the mystic writers and many of their merits. In him, as in his fellow Platonists, there is little that is visionary, there is no disparagement of reason, no exaggerated strain of self-forgetfulness. On the other hand, he resembles the best mystics in the combination of high imaginative with intellectual power, in warmth of piety, in fearlessness and purity of motive. He resembles them too in the vehemence with which he denies the liberty of interpreting Scripture in any sense which may appear to attribute to God purposes inconsistent with our moral perceptions of goodness and justice—in his horror of the more pronounced doctrines of election—in his deep conviction that love to God and man is the core of Christianity—in his disregard for controversy on minor points of orthodoxy,[1] and in the comprehensive tolerance and love of truth and liberty which should be the natural outgrowth of such opinions.

The other Cambridge Platonist whose writings may be said to have a distinct bearing on the subject and period before us, is Henry More. Even if there were no trace of the interest with which his works continued to be read in the earlier part of the eighteenth century, it would still seem like an omission if his treatise upon the question under notice were passed over. For perhaps there never was an author more qualified than he was to speak of 'enthusiasm' in a sympathetic but impartial spirit. He felt himself that the subject was well suited to him. 'I must,' he said, 'ingenuously confess that I have a natural touch of enthusiasm in my complexion, but such, I thank God, as was ever governable enough, and have found at length perfectly subduable. In

---

[1] His object, he said, 'was not to contend for this or that opinion, but only to persuade men to the life of Christ, as the pith and kernel of all religion.' 'Sermon before the House of Commons,' quoted in J. J. Tayler's *Retrospect of the Religious Life in England*, 211.

virtue of which victory, I know better what is in enthusiasts than they themselves, and therefore was able to write what I have wrote with life and judgment, and shall, I hope, contribute not a little to the peace and quiet of the kingdom thereby.'[1] He was in truth, both by natural temperament and by the course which his studies had taken, thoroughly competent to enter into the mind of the mystics and enthusiasts against whom he wrote. It was perhaps only his sound intellectual training, combined with the English attribute of solid practical sense, that had saved him from running utterly wild in fanciful and visionary speculations. As it is, he has been occasionally[2] classed among the so-called Theosophists, such as Paracelsus and Jacob Behmen. His exuberant imagination delighted in subjects which, since his time, have been acknowledged to be closed to all efforts of human reason, and have been generally abandoned to the dreams of credulity and superstition. He revelled in ingenious conjectures upon the condition of the soul in the intermediate state after death, upon the different stages and orders of disembodied spirits, and upon mysterious sympathies between mind and matter. We have continually to remember that he wrote before the dawn of the Newtonian philosophy, if we would appreciate his reasonings and guesses about strange attractions and affinities, which pointed as he thought to an incorporeal soul of the world, or spirit of nature, acting as 'a great quartermaster-general of Providence' in directing relations between the spiritual and material elements of the universe.[3]

Such was Henry More in one side of his character. The counterbalancing principle was his unwavering allegiance to reason, his zealous acknowledgment of its excellence as a gift of God, to be freely used and safely followed on every subject of human interest. He held it to be the glory and adornment of all true religion, and the special prerogative of Christianity. He nowhere rises to greater fervour of expression than where he extols the free and devotional exercise of reason in a pure

---

[1] *Philosophical Writings of H. More,* fourth edition, 1712. General preface, §3.

[2] *Quarterly Review,* xxviii. 37.

[3] H. More, *On the Immortality of the Soul,* b. iii. ch. 12 ; and the whole treatise, especially the third and fourth books.

and undefiled heart; and he is convinced of the high and
special spiritual powers which under such conditions are
granted to it. ' I should commend to them that will successfully philosophise the belief and endeavour after a certain
principle more noble and inward than reason itself, and
without which reason will falter, or at least reach but to mean
and frivolous things. I have a sense of something in me
while I thus speak, which I must confess is of so retruse a
nature that I want a name for it, unless I should adventure to
term it Divine sagacity, which is the first rise of successful
reason. . . . All pretenders to philosophy will indeed be
ready to magnify reason to the skies, to make it the light of
heaven, and the very oracle of God : but they do not consider
that the oracle of God is not to be heard but in his Holy
Temple, that is to say, in a good and holy man, thoroughly
sanctified in spirit, soul, and body.' [1]

Believing thus with all his heart both in the excellence
of reason and in a true inspiration of the spirit granted to
the pure in heart, but never dissociating the latter from the
former; well convinced that ' Christian religion is rational
throughout,' and that the suggestions of the Holy Spirit are
in all cases agreeable to reason—More wrote with much force
and beauty of argument his ' Exorcism of Enthusiasm.' He
showed that to abandon reason for fancy is to lay aside the
solid supports of religion, to trust faith to the mere ebb and
flow of ' melancholy,' and so to confirm the sceptic in his
doubts and the atheist in his unbelief. He dwelt upon the
unruly power of imagination, its deceptive character, its intimate connection with varying states of physical temperament—upon the variety of emotional causes which can produce
quakings and tremblings and other convulsive forms of
excitement—upon the delusiveness of visions, and revelations,
and ecstacies, and their near resemblance to waking dreams—
upon the sore temptations which are apt to lead into sin
those who so closely link spirituality with bodily feelings,
making religion sensual. He warned his readers against that
sort of intoxication of the understanding, when the imagination is suffered to run wild in allegorical interpretations of

---

[1] H. More, *Phil. Works*, General Preface, § 6 ; and *Enthusiasmus Triumphatus*, § 52.

Scripture, in fanciful allusions, in theories of mystic influences and properties which carry away the mind into wild superstitions and Pagan pantheism. He spoke of the self-conceit of many fanatics, their turbulence, their heat and narrow scrupulosity, and asked how these things could be the fruits of heavenly illumination. He suggested as the proper remedies against enthusiasm, temperance (by which he meant temperate diet, moderate exercise, fresh air, a due and discreet use of devotion), humility, and the sound tests of reason—practical piety, and service to the Church of God. Such is the general scope of his treatise; but the most interesting and characteristic portion is towards the close and in the Scholia appended to it, in which he speaks of 'that true and warrantable enthusiasm of devout and holy souls,' that 'delicious sense of the Divine life'[1] which the spirit of man is capable of receiving. If space allowed, one or two fine passages might be quoted in which he describes these genuine emotions. He has also some good remarks upon the value, within guarded limits, of disturbed and excited religious feelings in rousing the soul from lethargy, and acting as external aids to dispose the mind for true spiritual influences.

Henry More died the year before King William's accession. But his opinions were, no doubt, shared by some of the best and most cultivated men in the English Church during the opening years of the eighteenth century. After a time his writings lost their earlier popularity. Wesley, to his credit, recommended them in 1756 to the use of his brother clergymen.[2] As a rule, they appear at that time to have been but little read; their spiritual tone is pitched in too high a key for the prevalent religious taste of the period which had then set in. Some years had to pass before the rise of a generation more prepared to draw refreshment from the imaginative and somewhat mystical beauties of his style and sentiment.[3]

[1] § 62. [2] 'Address to the Clergy.'—Wesley's *Works*, 492.

[3] Coleridge seems to have read H. More with much enjoyment.—*Aids to Reflection*, i. 106–10. 'Occasional draughts,' Channing writes, of More and other Platonists, 'have been refreshing to me.' . . . Their mysticism was noble in its kind, 'and perhaps a necessary reaction against the general earthliness of men's minds. I pardon the man who loses himself in the clouds, if he will help me upwards.'—W. E. Channing's *Correspondence*, 338.

Dr. John Scott was another writer of the seventeenth century, who claims nevertheless some notice in reference to the subject before us. His book upon the Christian Life was written in 1686, and reached its tenth edition in 1739. He deplores the unhappiness of the age 'wherein the best Church and religion in the world are in such apparent danger of being crucified, like their blessed Master, between those two thieves (and both, alas! impenitent), superstition and enthusiasm.'[1] His object, he says, is to do what he can to divert men from such contentions to that Christian practice which is the only proper sphere of true zeal. But it is noticeable that while he fully shared the general aversion for 'enthusiasm,' he resembled Henry More in his cordial sympathies with a sort of quietistic contemplativeness on the one hand, and with a vigorous exercise of the powers of reasoning on the other. It is a salutary combination of qualities, but one in which the eighteenth century was generally very deficient. The most ardent votaries of reason could scarcely in warmer terms express their reverence for the object of their admiration. But with Scott, as with More, the highest efforts of devotional reason are transfigured with a heavenly light, and rise into a loftier region than any in this world of sense. To the mind of this professed enemy of all enthusiasm the utmost ecstasies of spiritual rapture are by no means inconsistent with sober, steadfast loyalty to reason, first of all human properties, 'the root and groundwork of all other virtues.'[2] There are passages in his writings where he speaks of absorption from earthly things, and of the bliss of 'the still and quiet regions of the blessed' enjoyed by foretaste in contemplation,[3] which might rather be supposed to come from the meditations of those mystics and quietists who were most apt to disparage the ordinary gifts of reason. Scott was too well persuaded of the Divine origin of all intellectual powers, to be jealous of them; too confident of the truth of religion, to be afraid of 'heat, and light, and motion'[4] in it; too large-minded, to think it could be involved in petty issues of sect and party; too full of compassion for the 'poor, longing mind which gropes about for truth in a

[1] J. Scott, *Christian Life*, &c., vol. i. Epistle Dedicatory.
[2] Id. chap. iii. i. 48 o.   [3] Id. 90-1.   [4] Id. 285.

ark dungeon of error and ignorance,'[1] to distrust the use of
any faculties of mind or spirit, ordinary or transcendental,[2]
by which it can gain fresh glimpses of the heavenly light;
and too convinced that 'the Christian life, next only to the
angelical, approaches nearest to the life of God,'[3] to doubt
hat our Maker does indeed 'reveal to it special tokens of
His presence and of His favour.

The philosophy of Locke, and the deep, general, and
lasting impression which it left, can here be only touched
upon, so far as it is closely connected with the present subject.
It has been truly remarked that it 'constitutes the diverging
point at which the religious thought of the eighteenth century
separates itself from that of the preceding ages.'[4] His influence is by no means to be measured only by the sway,
powerful though it was, which it exercised over the minds of
learned writers, and of those who were able to study and
appreciate his reasonings. Directly or indirectly, it penetrated
society, and gave a marked bias to the direction of popular
as well as philosophical opinion. His system had no primary
and direct reference to religious questions. These, in the
first instance, he had rather avoided ; his object being to mark
out more distinctly than had yet been done, the powers and
limitations of man's reasoning faculties. But the publication
of his works fell in opportunely with the beginning of a great
controversy which was already, by a combination of causes,
inevitable, and gave it definiteness and impetus. To use a
forcible expression of Mr. Pattison, 'the title of Locke's
treatise, "The Reasonableness of Christianity," may be said
to have been the solitary thesis of Christian theology in
England for great part of a century.'[5] When once he had
overcome the first weight of resistance, he reigned almost
supreme.[6] His writings were an inexhaustible treasure-house

---

[1] J. Scott, *Christian Life*, &c., 90.

[2] Alexander Knox quotes a passage from Scott in which he speaks of the impossibility of accurately distinguishing direct spiritual influence from reason and
conscience co-operating with it.—*Remains*, i. 21.

[3] Scott's *Christian Life*, Preface.   [4] *Quarterly Review*, July 1864, 79.

[5] *Essays and Reviews*, 258.

[6] 'At first,' said Warburton, 'Locke had neither followers nor admirers :
but being everywhere clear, and everywhere solid, he at length worked his way ;
and afterwards was subject to no reverses.'—*Letters to Hurd*, No. 127. At the
end of the century his authority was waning. 'De 1792 à 1800, j'ai rarement

of argument for the combatants on either side ; and his authority was appealed to with equal reverence by men singularly opposite to one another in the whole bent and character of their minds. Bolingbroke and Isaac Watts,[1] for example, were on common ground in their mutual admiration of a philosopher, to whom meanwhile the worldly scepticism of the one disciple, and the gloomy supralapsarianism of the other, would have been almost alike intolerable.

When once the genius of Locke was in the ascendant, more spiritual forms of philosophy fell into disrepute. Descartes, Malebranche, Leibnitz were considered almost obsolete ; More and Cudworth were out of favour ; and there was but scanty tolerance for any writer who could possibly incur the charge of transcendentalism or mysticism. It is not that Cartesian or Platonic, or even mystic opinions, are irreconcileable with Locke's philosophy. When he spoke of sensation and reflection as the original sources of all knowledge, there was ample room for innate ideas,[2] and for intuitive perceptions, under the shelter of terms so indefinite. Moreover, the ambiguities of expression and apparent inconsistencies of thought, which stand out in marked contrast to the force and lucidity of his style, are by no means owing only to his use of popular language, and his studied avoidance of all that might seem to savour of the schools. His devout spirit rebelled against the carefully defined limits which his logical intellect would have imposed upon it. He could not altogether avoid applying his system to the absorbing subjects of theology, but he did so with some unwillingness and with much reserve. Revelation, once acknowledged as such, was always sacred ground to him ; and though he often appears to reduce all evidence to the external witness of the senses, there is something essentially opposed to materialistic notions, in his feeling that there is that which we do not know simply

---

entendu citer Locke en Angleterre : son système, disait-on, était vieilli, et il passait pour faible en idéologie.'—Chateaubriand, *Essai sur la Litt. Angl.* 1836, ii. 273.

[1] ' Locke hath a soul wide as the sea,
Calm as the night, bright as the day.'
Watts's *Lyric Poems.*

[2] Sir J. Mackintosh, ' Philosophical Genius of Bacon and Locke.'—*Works,* 156.

by reason of our want of a new and different sense, by which, if we had it, we might know our souls as we know a triangle.[1] Locke would have heartily disowned the conclusions of many who professed themselves his true disciples, and of many others whose whole minds had been trained and formed under the influences of his teaching, and who insisted that they were but following up his arguments to their legitimate consequences.[2] The general system was the same ; but there was nothing in common between the theology of Locke and Toland's repudiation of whatever in religion transcended human reason, or Bolingbroke's doubts as to the immortality of the soul, or the pronounced materialism of Hartley and Condillac, or the blank negative results at which Hume arrived.

But though Locke and multitudes of his admirers were profoundly Christian in their belief, the whole drift of his thought tended to bring prominently forward the purely practical side of religion and the purely intellectual side of theology, and to throw into the background, and reduce to its narrowest compass, the more entirely spiritual region which marks the contact of the human with the Divine. Its uncertain lights and shadows, its mysteries, obscurities, and difficulties, were thoroughly distrusted by him. He did not— a religious mind like his could not—deny the existence of those feelings and intuitions which, from their excessive prominence in that school, may be classed under the name of mystic. But he doubted their importance and dreaded their exaggerations. Not only could they find no convenient place, scarcely even a footing, in his philosophical system, but they were out of accord with his own temperament and with the opinions, which he was so greatly contributing to form, of the age in which he lived. They offended against his love of clearness, his strong dislike of all obscurity, his wish to see the chart of the human faculties mapped out and defined, his desire to translate abstract ideas into the language of sound, practical, ordinary sense, divested as far as could be of all that was open to dispute, and of all that could in any

---

[1] Quoted by Bishop Berkeley, *Theory of Vision*, pt. i. § 116.
[2] Schlosser, *History of the Eighteenth Century*, chap. 1, i. Horsley's *Charges*, 86. *Quarterly Review*, July 1864, 70-9.

way be accounted visionary. His perpetual appeal lay to
the common understanding, and he regarded, therefore, with
much suspicion, emotions which none could at all times
realise, and which to some minds were almost, or perhaps
entirely unknown. Lastly, his fervent love of liberty indisposed him to admissions which might seem to countenance
authority over the consciences of men on the part of any who
should assert special claims to spiritual illumination.

It was with good reason, therefore, that Lord Lyttelton,
in one of his ' Dialogues of the Dead,' makes Locke express
himself as ' the declared enemy of enthusiasm.' [1] Into the
fourth book of his work on the ' Human Understanding '
Locke introduced a chapter not contained in the first edition,
in which enthusiasm is discussed. He explains it as ' a third
ground of assent, as confidently relied upon by some as
faith or reason,' but ' really substituting ungrounded fancies
for both, and making them a foundation both for opinion and
conduct.' ' Reason,' he says, ' is natural revelation. Revelation is natural reason enlarged by a new set of discoveries
communicated by God immediately, which reason vouches
the truth of, by the testimonies and proofs it gives that they
come from God.' But some—those especially ' in whom
melancholy has mixed with devotion '—want an easier guide
by direct revelation, and ' flatter themselves with a persuasion
of an immediate intercourse with the Deity. Their minds
being thus prepared, whatever groundless opinion comes to
settle itself strongly upon their fancies is an illumination
from the Spirit of God, and presently of Divine authority.'
Such enthusiasm, he continues, when once it has taken root
in them, becomes almost incradicable. ' Reason is lost upon
them, they are above it : they see the light infused into their
understandings, and cannot be mistaken : it is clear and
visible there like the light of bright sunshine ; shows itself,
and needs no proof but its own evidence : they feel the hand
of God moving them from within, and the impulses of the
Spirit, and cannot be mistaken in what they feel. . . . They
are sure because they are sure, and their persuasions are right
because they are strong in them.' Unless it is *known* that a
particular impression is made by the Holy Spirit, ' how great

---

[1] Lord Lyttelton's *Works*, 365. Dialogue xxiv.

ʃ

soever the assurance is that I am possessed with, it is groundless ; whatever light I pretend to, it is but enthusiasm.'
Reason, 'our last judge and guide in everything,' is the only
means of obtaining this knowledge ; to set up belief or fancy
in its place is to run into extravagant errors, and to make
God the Father not only of lights, but of opposite and contradictory lights.   The holy men of old were not left to their
own persuasions alone ; outward signs were given to attest
the author of those revelations.   He by no means denied that
the immediate influence of the Holy Spirit is sometimes
given to enlighten men's minds and to excite them to good
actions.   The point to be insisted upon was that ' no strength
of private persuasion could warrant it to be a light and motion
from heaven.   Nothing could do that but the written word
of God without us, or that standard of reason which is common
to us with all men.' [1]

These remarks of Locke are very characteristic of his age,
and might with great ease be paralleled with passages—not
always so moderately and cautiously expressed—from numberless other writers throughout the whole of the eighteenth
century.   He struck a keynote which was harped upon by a
host of theologians and moralists after him, whenever, as was
constantly the case, they had occasion to raise their voice
against that dreaded enemy, enthusiasm.   There were many
who inveighed against ' the new modish system of reducing
all to sense,' when used to controvert the doctrines of revelation.   But while with vigour and success they defended the
mysteries of faith against those who would allow nothing but
what reason could fairly grasp, and while they dwelt upon
the paramount authority of the Spirit which inspired Holy
Scripture, they would allow no sort of spiritual influence to
compete with reason as a judge of truth.   Reason, it was
perpetually argued, is sufficient for all our present needs.
Revelation is adequately attested by evidence addressed to
the reason.   We need no other proof or ground of assent ; at
all events, none other is granted to us.   It was not so indeed
in the first age of the Church.   Special gifts of spiritual
knowledge and illumination were then given to meet special
requirements.   The Holy Spirit was then in very truth im-

[1] Locke *On the Human Understanding*, b. iv. chap. 19.

mediately present in power, the greatest witness to the truth, and its direct revealer to the hearts of men. Many of the principal preachers and theological writers of the eighteenth century dwell at length upon the fulness of that spiritual outpouring. But it is not a little remarkable to notice with what singular care they often limit and circumscribe its duration. A little earlier or a little later, but, at all events, at the end of a generation or two after the first Christian Pentecost, a line of demarcation was to be drawn and jealously guarded. The question is not so much one of miracles. Even in regard to spiritual powers of wisdom, knowledge, teaching, inspiration, illumination, it was generally thought necessary to lay down with almost anxious care an impassable distinction between the transient, extraordinary gifts of the Spirit and those which remained behind as the ordinary and constant endowment of the Church of Christ. Warburton's ' Doctrine of Grace ' is, no doubt, a somewhat exaggerated instance of this disposition. Nor should we omit to add that in a later note he complains of his opinions on the subject having been misrepresented. But there is no doubt that from the dread which he shared with the bulk of his contemporaries for anything approaching to ' enthusiastical ' pretensions, he gave much countenance to what William Law and John Byrom said of him, that he represented Scripture, rather than the hearts of good men, to be the temple of the Holy Ghost. ' The Scriptures,' he writes, 'of the New Testament were given by inspiration of God. And thus the prophetic promise of our blessed Master, that the Comforter should abide with us for ever, was eminently fulfilled. For though, according to the promise, His ordinary influence occasionally assists the faithful in all ages, yet His constant abode and supreme illumination is in the sacred Scriptures of the New Testament.' [1] The aid of the Holy Spirit might be given to enlighten the understanding or to rectify the will; but Scripture once established as a sufficient Rule of Faith wanted no other interpreter than ordinary human reason. It was only fanatics who spoke as if further Divine communications could be needed to explain obscurities or supply deficiencies. J. Byrom, in the prosaic but often impressive

[1] ' Doctrine of Grace,' chap. v.—Warburton's *Works*, iv. 564.

rhymes in which he chose to write theology, says not amiss of Warburton and his fellow anti-enthusiasts :—

> They think that now religion's sole defence
> Is learning, history, and critic sense ;
> That with Apostles, as a needful guide,
> The Holy Spirit did indeed abide :
> But having dictated to them a rule
> Of faith and manners, for the Christian school,
> Immediate revelation ceased, and men
> Must now be taught by Apostolic pen.
>
> .   .   .   .   .   .
>
> To look for inspiration is absurd ; .
> The Spirit's aid is in the written Word :
> They who pretend to His immediate call,
> From Pope to Quaker are fanatics all.[1]

He justly adds of his own Church of England—

> If to expect the gifts, however great,
> Be popish and fanatical deceit,
> She in her offices of every kind
> Has also been fanatically blind.

In the second book of Warburton's 'Doctrine of Grace' there is a singular instance of apparent incapacity on the part of a most able reasoner to acknowledge the possible existence in his own day of other spiritual influences than those which, in the most limited sense of the word, may be called ordinary. He is speaking of the splendour of the gifts which shed their glory upon the primitive Church and afterwards passed away. He dwells with admiration upon the sudden and entire changes which were made in the dispositions and manner of those whom the Holy Spirit had enlightened. Sacred antiquity, he says, is unmistakeable in its evidence on this point, and even the assailers of Christianity confessed it. Conversions were effected among early Christians such as could not be the result of mere rational conviction. It is utterly impossible for the magisterial faculty of reason to enforce her conclusions with such immediate power, and to win over the will with such irresistible force, as

---

[1] 'On Warburton's Sermon on the Operation of the Holy Spirit.'—Chalmers' *British Poets*, xv. 305.

to root out at once inveterate habits of vice. 'To what must we ascribe so total a reform, but to the all-powerful operation of grace?'[1] These remarks are true enough; but it seems incredible that, writing in the very midst of an extraordinary religious outburst, he should calmly assume the impossibility in all but primitive times of such sudden changes from irreligion to piety, and should even place the miraculous conversions of apostolic times at the head of an argument against Methodist enthusiasts. Well might Wesley remark with some surprise, 'Never were reflections more just than these,'[2] and go on to show that the very same changes were constantly occurring still.

One more example may be taken from the writings of an author of repute in the eighteenth century, Lord Barrington, Bishop successively of Llandaff, Salisbury, and Durham. He has left a treatise on 'The Teaching and Witness of the Holy Spirit.'[3] In his opening sentence he says that feeling the Holy Spirit to be the greatest of all witnesses to the truth of the Christian religion, he desires to consider that evidence with all the care in his power. The essay he thus introduces shows study and ability, but it is strange to read on to the end of it, and to find that he has treated this great subject as if the witness of the Spirit had been granted only for the first settlement of Christianity in apostolic times. He of course does not deny that the same Divine power continues, in some sense, to operate in the Church of every age, but he evidently considers this so subordinate a branch of the subject as not even to bring it into mention. From all that appears in his treatise, the teaching of the Holy Spirit might be simply an important feature in the ancient history of Christianity, and an early evidence to its truth. Without attributing too much weight to an omission which is certainly a remarkable one, it may fairly be said that there have been few ages of the Church in which a lengthened theological essay published under such a title could have been so strikingly limited in its scope.

It would not be reasonable to expect in any one age an even apprehension of different sides of truth. We must be

---

[1] Warburton's *Works*, iv. 568.
[2] 'Letter to the Bishop of Gloucester.'—Wesley's *Works*, ix. 151.
[3] Republished in Bishop Watson's *Theological Tracts*, 1791, vol. v.

content for the most part to find predominant convictions sincerely expressed.[1] If they be too ardently and blindly followed, some kind of reaction will presently follow, and the needful balance will be in great measure restored. Rationalism, in the unprejudiced uses of the word, was the special glory of the eighteenth century. The Reformation had at last achieved its natural result, and a great crisis had gradually and quietly arrived. Reason had become politically, if not socially, emancipated. It was as desirable as it was inevitable, in the interests of religion and of the human mind in general, that, being thus free, it should not hesitate to put forth its utmost power. A reformed theology could not, if it would, evade a thorough scrutiny, and would incur fatal suspicion if it were protected, or sought to be protected, from it. Religion must rather welcome reason, as light sent from the Father of lights, both to disseminate its glories and to lay bare deficiencies. Even if there be danger lest reason, freely exercised, should transgress its rightful limits, it is only by such free exercise that it can learn where its powers end, and where it must give place to revelation or to some faculty in man more purely spiritual than itself. At the opening of the period under review, there was a far keener sense of the powers of reason than its limitations. But in any case, its authority had begun to command universal reverence. Christianity was called upon to submit its evidence to the proof, and its defenders for the most part fearlessly accepted the challenge. A flood of sober reasoning poured from the pulpit ; and while Deists and Sceptics demanded that all mysteries should, under penalty of rejection, be made clear to human understanding, preachers and evidence writers were well content to insist in all their arguments upon the marvellous reasonableness of the Christian belief, and to retort upon their opponents the unreasonableness and fatuity of unbelief.

Under such circumstances, there was little room for what the age banned under the name of enthusiasm, little patience for any mode of religion which relied upon the existence of a faculty different from, and in some respects superior to reason. There has never been a period when there were not in every class of society, earnest and devout men who ardently believed

[1] Cf. F. D. Maurice, *Theological Essays,* 3–4.

in an immediate spiritual apprehension of truths not cognisable by the understanding. The eighteenth century was no
exception. It may be added, that not indirectly only by reaction, but as the direct result of careful inquiries into the
province of reason, the rationalists, orthodox and unorthodox,
of the time were preparing the way for a wide acceptance of
what may be called a sound and moderate mysticism. But
in the meanwhile the most representative writers of the day,
both those who addressed themselves to the learned, and
those who appealed to a more popular audience, scouted
all such ideas. It will be understood that enthusiasm in
the more general sense of zeal is not here in question.
There is no doubt a very close connection between the two
meanings of the word. An age in which cool reason is
reverenced as sole and sovereign arbiter in all religious debate,
is sure to be affected with a certain deficiency of practical
religious zeal. But this branch of the subject is at all events
entirely separate from the point now under discussion. The
prevalent aversion to enthusiasm was by no means confined
to those who either from indifference, or from any other
motive, might be expected to discourage all fervid outbursts
of religious feeling. Lax and thoughtless writers would be
sure to heap together in very undiscriminating contempt such
terms as superstition, enthusiasm, bigotry, and rant. Those
who shrank, not without frequent cause, but with some excess
of fastidiousness, from 'unmannered zeal' and 'indiscreet
fervours of devotion' might naturally dismiss with a smile as
'intimates of heaven' whosoever asserted a direct communication of the soul with God. Bolingbroke was consistent with
himself in calling it not enthusiasm only, but blasphemy, to
suppose that man partakes in the Divine nature, and that God
breathes upon our spirits. So too was Shaftesbury, when he
ridiculed all such ideas as a mere disorder of the imagination ;
and his opinion would be shared by Swift, in whose morose
and cynical mind all 'violent zeal even for truth has a
hundred to one odds to be either petulancy, ambition, or
pride.'[1] Neither could we expect much sympathy with
enthusiasm of any kind from that distinguished list of
'moderate' prelates, whose calm reasoning, serene piety, and

---

[1] Dr. Swift, 'Thoughts on Religion.'—*Works*, viii. 53.

tolerant opinions have won them high and enduring esteem. Tillotson, in the methodically ordered argument usual to him, points out six chief ways in which the Divine Spirit aids the reason and makes it effectual upon the life ; but, fully satisfied that the evidence of reason is sufficient by itself to convince the mind, and to confute opposition, can only view with mild compassion the claims to illumination, and the 'wild freaks of enthusiasm,' which he finds outside the favoured borders of his Church. Butler was startled into words very unlike the self-restrained language of reasoning habitual to him, when, in his conversation with Wesley, he exclaimed, 'Sir, the pretending to extraordinary revelation and gifts of the Holy Ghost is a horrid thing, a very horrid thing.'[1] Hoadly couples together 'zeal and fury,'[2] and could not brook any approach to language which seemed to him hostile to the composure of a reasonable Christian service. Secker-and men like him, although not indisposed, as the century advanced, to bestow a measured approbation upon a manner somewhat more impassioned than had of late been at all customary in the Church of England, were yet strongly prejudiced by all the traditions of their theological training against any evidence which was not plainly grounded on solid foundations of sober reasoning. But it is needless to add names.[3] It may be said without any disparagement of a host of eminent English divines of the eighteenth century, that their entire sympathies were with the reasonable rather than with the spiritual side of religion. Their ideal of Christian perfection was in many respects an elevated one, but absolutely divested of that mystic element which in every age of the Church has seemed to be inseparable from the higher types of saintliness. If we may

---

[1] Quoted by Hunt, 3, 289.

[2] Hoadly's *Answer to Report of Convocation*, chap. ii. §9.

[3] Besides the authors quoted in this chapter, the following names may be mentioned of writers against 'Enthusiasm,' in the eighteenth century :—J. Drake, in his *Memorial*, &c. 1705 ; Hunter *On Enthusiasm*, 1709 ; Bishop Gibson's *Charge* of 1724 ; Bishop P. Browne, *On the Human Understanding*, c. 1725 ; Dr. J. Trapp's *Four Sermons*, 1739 ; Bishop E. Law, *Theory of Religion*, 1745 ; Dr. S. Chandler, *Sermons*, vol. i. 1725 ; G. Campbell, *Discourse on Enthusiasm*, c. 1750 ; Archbishop Synge (Tuam) on *Religion Tried by the Test of Reason*, 1761 ; J. Langhorne on *Melancholy and Enthusiasm*, 1762 ; Bishop Douglas's *Apology*, 1755, and his *Criterion*. Bishop Watson, in 1799, entered into the controversy more doubtfully.—*Life*, i. 378–380.

judge from the treatises of Lord Lyttelton and Dean Graves, the character even of the apostles had to be carefully vindicated from all suspicion of any taint of enthusiasm if they were to maintain their full place of reverence as leaders and princes of the Christian army. Only it must not be supposed that this religious characteristic of the age was by any means confined to the sceptical and indifferent on the one hand, or to persons of a sober and reflective spirit on the other. It was almost universal. John Wesley, for example, repeatedly and anxiously rebuts the charges of enthusiasm which were levelled upon him from all sides. He would have it understood that he had for ever done with enthusiasm when once he had separated from the Moravians. The same shrinking from the name, as one of opprobrium, is shown by Dr. Watts;[1] and one of the greatest troubles in Hannah More's life seems to have been her annoyance, that she and other faithful members of the English Church should be defamed as encouragers of enthusiasm.[2]

The eighteenth century was indeed an age when sober reason would hear of no competitor, and whose greatest outburst of religious zeal characteristically took its name from the well-ordered method with which it was organised. It will not, however, be inferred that enthusiasm, as the word was then commonly understood, scarcely existed. On the contrary, the vigour and constancy of the attack points with sufficient clearness to the evident presence of the enemy. In fact, although the more exaggerated forms of mysticism and fanaticism have never permanently thriven on English soil, there has never been an age when what may be called mystical religion has not had many ardent votaries. For even the most extravagant of its multiform phases embody an important element of truth, which cannot be neglected without the greatest detriment to sound religion. Whatever be its particular type, it represents the protest of the human soul against all that obscures the spirituality of belief. But of all the accidents and externals of religion, there is not one, however important in itself, which may not be made unduly

---

[1] Dedication to his *Three Sermons*, quoted by H. S. Skeats, *History of the Free Churches*, 333.

[2] W. Roberts, *Memoirs of Hannah More*, i. 500, ii. 61, 70, 110.

prominent, and under such circumstances interfere between the soul and the object of its worship. It will be readily understood, therefore, upon how great a variety of grounds that protest may be based, how right and reasonable it may sometimes be, but also how easily it may itself run into excess, and how quickly the understanding may lose its bearings when once, for fear of the abuse, it begins to dispense with what was not intended to check, but to guide and regulate the aspirations of the Spirit. Mystical and enthusiastical religion, whether in its sounder or in its exaggerated and unhealthy forms, may be a reaction against an over-assertion of the powers of reason in spiritual matters and questions of evidence, or against the undue extension, in subjects too high for it, of the domain of 'common sense ;' or it may be a vindication of the spiritual rights of the uneducated against the pretensions of learning ; or an assertion of the judgment and conscience of the individual against all tyranny of authority. It may be a protest against excessive reverence for the letter of Holy Scripture as against the Spirit which breathes in it, against all appearance of limiting inspiration to a book, and denying it to the souls of living men. It may express insurrection against all manner of formalism, usages which have lost their significance, rites which have ceased to edify, doctrines which have degenerated into formulas, orthodoxy which has become comparatively barren and profitless. It may represent a passionate longing to escape from party differences and sectarian strife into a higher, purer atmosphere, where the free Spirit of God bloweth where it listeth. It often owes its origin to strong revulsion against popular philosophies which limit all consciousness to mere perceptions of the senses, or against the materialistic tendencies which find an explanation for all mysteries in physical phenomena. It may result from endeavours to find larger scope for reverie and contemplation, or fuller development for the imaginative elements of religious thought. It may be a refuge for spirits disgusted at an unworthy and utilitarian system of ethics, and at a religion too much degraded into a code of moral precepts. All these tendencies, varying in every possible degree from the healthiest efforts after greater spirituality of life to the wildest excesses of fanatical extravagance, may be copiously illustrated from the history of enthusiasm. The writers of the eighteenth century were fully alive to its dangers. It was easy to show how mystical religion had often led its too eager, or too untaught followers into the most mischievous antinomianism of doctrine and life, into allegorising away the most fundamental grounds of Christianity, and into the vaguest Pantheism. They could produce examples in abundance of bewildered intellects, of ' illuminations' obscurer than any darkness, of religious rapture, in its ambitious distrust of reason, lapsing into physical agencies and coarse materialism. They could hold up, in ridicule or warning, profuse illustrations of exorbitant spiritual pride, blind credulity, infatuated self-deceit, barefaced imposture. It was much more congenial to the prevalent temper of the age to draw a moral from such perversions of a tone of feeling with which there was little sympathy, than to learn a useful lesson from the many truths contained in it. Doubtless, it is not easy to deal with principles which have been maintained in an almost identical form, but with consequences so widely divergent, by some of the noblest, and by some of the most foolish of mankind, by true saints and by gross fanatics. The contemporaries of Locke, Addison, and Tillotson, trained in a wholly different school of thought, were ill-fitted to enter with patience into such a subject, to see its importance, to discriminate its differences, and to solve its perplexities.

At the opening of the eighteenth century, the elements of enthusiasm were too feeble to show themselves in any acknowledged form either in the Church of England or in the leading Nonconformist bodies. In England, no doubt, as in every other European country, there were, as Mr. Vaughan observes, ' Scattered little groups of friends, who nourished a hidden devotion by the study of pietist and mystical writings.... Whenever we can penetrate behind the public events which figure in history at the close of the seventeenth, and the opening of the eighteenth century, indications are discernible, which make it certain that a religious vitality of this description was far more widely diffused than is commonly supposed.' [1] But these recluse societies made no visible impression

---

[1] R. A. Vaughan's *Hours with the Mystics*, ii. 391.

upon the general state of religion. If it were not for the evident anxiety felt by many writers of the period to expose and counteract the dangers of a mystical and enthusiastical bias, it might have been supposed that there never was a time when the Church was so entirely free from any possible peril in that direction. Their fear, however, was not without some foundation. When an important phase of spiritual truth is comparatively neglected by established authorities and in orthodox opinion, it is sure to find full vent in another less regular channel. We are told that in the first years of the century, the Quakers had immensely increased. 'They swarm,' said Leslie, 'over these three nations, and they stock our plantations abroad.'[1] It is 'a frightful and stupendous prospect,' he adds in dismay, a 'wide-spread infection, all the more dangerous because it seizes so many well-meaning and devout persons.'[2] Quakerism had met with little tolerance in the previous century. Churchmen and Dissenters had unanimously denounced it, and Baxter, large-minded as he often proved himself, denied its adherents all hope of salvation. But the sect throve under persecution ; and in proportion as its follies and extravagances became somewhat mitigated, the spirituality of belief, which even in its most exaggerated forms had always been its soul of strength, became more and more attractive to those who felt its deficiency elsewhere. Between the passing of the Toleration Act and the end of William III.'s reign it made great progress. After that it began gradually to decline. This was owing to various causes. Some share in it may perhaps be attributed to the continued effects of the general religious lethargy which had set in some years before, but may have now begun to spread more visibly among the classes from which Quakerism was chiefly recruited. Again, its intellectual weakness would naturally become more apparent in proportion to the daily increasing attention paid to the reasonable aspects of faith. The general satisfaction felt, except by the pronounced High Church and Jacobite party, at the newly established order in Church and State, was unfavourable to the further progress of a communion which, from its rejection of ideas common to every other ecclesiastical body,

---

[1] C. Leslie, 'Snake in the Grass.'—*Works,* iv. 21.   [2] Id. 4.

seemed to many to be rightly called 'the end and centre of all confusion.'[1] It may be added that as the century advanced, there gradually came to be within the confines of the National Church a little more room than had lately existed for the upholders of various mystical tenets. With the rise of Wesleyanism enthusiasm found full scope in a new direction. But the power of Quakerism was not only silently undermined by the various action of influences such as these. In the first years of the century it received a direct and serious blow in the able exposure of its extravagances written by Leslie. The vagaries of the French 'Prophets' also contributed to discredit the assumption of supernatural gifts in which many Quakers still indulged.

It is needless to dwell with Leslie on the wild heretical opinions into which the over-strained spirituality of the disciples of Fox and Penn had led them. Certainly, the interval between them and other Christian communities had sometimes been so wide that there was some justification for the assertions made on either side, that the name of Christian could not be so widely extended as to be fitly applied to both. Archbishop Dawes, for example, in the House of Lords, roundly refused them all claim to the title;[2] and there were thousands of Quakers who would retaliate the charge in terms of the most unsparing vigour. To these men, all the Gospel was summed up in the one verse that tells how Christ is the light that lighteth every man that cometh into the world. Leslie was able to produce quotations in plenty from acknowledged authorities among them which allegorised away all belief in a personal Saviour, and which bade each man seek within himself alone for the illuminating presence of his Christ and God.

It was well that the special dangers to which Quakerism and other forms of mysticism are liable should be brought clearly and openly into view. But after all it is not from the

---

[1] Dr. Sherlock, *On Public Worship*, chap. iii. § 1, 4.

[2] Tindal's 'Continuation of Rapin,' quoted in H. B. Wilson's *History of Merchant Taylors' School*, ii. 966 ; Atterbury spoke scarcely less strongly. Id. W. Wall said that many denied them the title, though he did not.—*Dissuasive from Schism*, § 8. Ingham, writing to J. Wesley in 1734, asked his opinion, 'whether it be convenient or lawful for a Christian to dwell with a Quaker, when under no compulsion.'—L. Tyerman's *Oxford Methodists*, 60.

extravagances and perversions of a dogma that the main lesson is to be learnt. With the Bible open before them, and with hearts alive to the teachings of holiness, the generality of religious minded Quakers were not likely to be satisfied with what Warburton rightly called not so much a religion as 'a divine philosophy, not fit for such a creature as man,'[1] nor with a religious vocabulary summed up, as the latter humorously said, in the three words, 'Light,' 'Friend,' and 'Babylon.'[2] There was no reason why the worship of the individual should not be very free from the prevalent errors of the sect, and be in a high sense pure and Christian. For the truths which at one time made Quakerism so strong are wholly separable, not only from the superficial eccentricities of the system, but from its gravest deficiencies in form and doctrine. There is nothing to forbid a close union of the most intensely human and personal elements of Christian faith with that refined and pervading sense of a present life-giving Spirit which was faithfully borne witness to by Quakers when it was feeblest and most neglected elsewhere. If Quaker principles, instead of being embodied in a strongly antagonistic form as tenets of an exclusive and often persecuted sect,[3] had been transfused into the general current of the national religious life, they would at once have escaped the extravagances into which they were led, and have contributed the very elements of which the spiritual condition of the age stood most in need. Not only in the moderate and constantly instructive pages of Barclay's 'Apology' for the Quakers, but also in the hostile expositions of their views which we find in the works of Leslie and their other opponents, there is frequent cause for regret that so much suggestive thought should have become lost to the Church

[1] Warburton's 'Alliance.'—*Works*, 1788, iv. 53.
[2] *Tatler*, No. 257.
[3] Canon Curteis remarks of the early Quakers, 'What was urgently wanted, and what Christ (I think) was really commissioning George Fox and others to do, was not a destructive, but a constructive work,—the work of breathing fresh life into old forms, recovering the true meaning of old symbols, raising from the dead old words that needed translating into modern equivalents.'—G. H. Curteis, *Dissent in Relation to the Church of England*, 268. The importance of the best principles of Quakerism was not always overlooked. Davenant had predicted that in a hundred years religion would come to a settlement in a kind of 'ingenious Quakerism.'—J. Stoughton's *Church of the Revolution*, 458.

at large.   The Quakers were accustomed to look at many
important truths in somewhat different aspects from those in
which they were commonly regarded ; and the Church would
have gained in power as well as in comprehension, if their
views on some points had been fully accepted as legitimate
modes of orthodox belief.   English Christianity would have
been better prepared for its formidable struggle with the
Deists, if it had freely allowed a wider margin for diversity of
sentiment in several questions on which Quaker opinion
almost universally differed from that of the Churchmen of the
age.   It was said of Quakers that they were mere Deists,
except that they hated reason.[1]   The imputation might not
unfrequently be true ; for a Quaker consistently with his
principles might reject some very essential features of
Christianity.   Often, on the other hand, such a charge would
be entirely erroneous, for, no less consistently, a Quaker
might be in the strictest sense of the word a thorough and
earnest Christian.   But in any case he was well armed
against that numerous class of Deistical objections which
rested upon an exclusively literal interpretation of Scripture.
This is eminently observable in regard of theories of inspiration.   To Quakers, as to mystical writers in general, biblical
infallibility has never seemed to be a doctrine worth contending for.   They have always felt that an admixture of human
error is perfectly innocuous where there is a living spirit
present to interpret the teaching of Scripture to the hearts of
men.   But elsewhere, the doctrine of unerring literal inspiration was almost everywhere held in its straitest form.   Leslie,
for example, quotes with horror a statement of Ellwood, one
of his Quaker opponents, that St. Paul expected the day of
judgment to come in his time.   'If,' answers Leslie, 'he
thought it might, then it follows that he was mistaken, and
consequently that what he wrote was not truth ; and so not
only the authority of this Epistle, but of all the Epistles, and
of all the rest of the New Testament, will fall to the ground.'[2]
Such specious, but false and dangerous reasoning is by no
means uncommon still ; but when it represented the general
language of orthodox theologians, we cannot wonder that

[1] C. Leslie, ‘Defence, &c.’—*Works*, v. 164.
[2] Id. *Works*, iv. 428.

the difficulties started by Deistical writers caused wide-spread disbelief,[1] and raised a panic as if the very foundations of Christianity were in danger of being overthrown.

There were other ways in which profound confidence in direct spiritual guidance shielded Quakers from perplexities which shook the faith of many. They had been among the first to turn with horror from those stern views of pre-destination and reprobation which, until the middle of the seventeenth century, had been accepted by the great majority of English Protestants without misgiving. It was doctrine utterly repugnant to men whose cardinal belief was in the light that lighteth every man. The same principle kept even the most bigoted among them from falling into the prevalent opinion which looked upon the heathen as altogether without hope and without God in the world. They, almost alone of all Christian missionaries of that age, pointed their hearers (not without scandal to their orthodox brethren) to a light of God within them which should guide them to the brighter radiance of a better revelation. Nor did they scruple to assert that 'there be members of this Catholic Church both among heathens, Jews, and Turks, men and women of inte-grity and simplicity of heart, who, though blinded in some things of their understanding, and burdened with superstition, yet, being upright in their hearts before the Lord, ... and loving to follow righteousness, are by the secret touches of the holy light in their souls enlivened and quickened, thereby secretly united to God, and thereby become true members of this Catholic Church.'[2] Such expressions would be generally assented to in our day, as embodying sound and valuable truths, which cannot be rejected on account of errors which may sometimes chance to attend them. At the beginning of the eighteenth century there were few, except Quakers, who were willing to accept from a wholly Christian point of view

---

[1] 'The chief advantage which the writers on the side of infidelity have had, and which they have well understood how to use for the service of their cause, has been drawn from what unguarded expressions and injudicious and unfavourable representations they could pick up out of the writings of its friends, which they turned as arguments against religion itself. This hath occasioned several points to be reconsidered of late, by which means they have been set in a clearer light.'—W. Worthington, *Essay on the Scheme of Redemption,* 2nd ed. 1748, Pref.

[2] R. Barclay's *Apology for the Quakers,* 259.

ing title to the name of 'National,' that it has been able to learn from the sects which have grown up around it. Cautiously and tardily—often far too much so for its own immediate advantage—it has seldom neglected to find at last within its ample borders some room for modes and expressions of Christian belief which, for a time neglected, had been growing up outside its bounds. It was so with Methodism ; it was so also with Quakerism. When Quakers found that its more reasonable tenets could be held, and find a certain amount of sympathy within the Church, it quickly began to lose its strength. A remark of Boswell's in 1776, that many a man was a Quaker without his knowing it,[1] could scarcely have been made in the corresponding year of the previous century. At the earlier date there was almost nothing in common between the Church and a sect which, both on its strongest and weakest side, was marked by a conspicuous antagonism to established opinions. At the latter date Quakerism had to a great extent lost both its mystic and emotional monopolies. After a few years' hesitation Southey concluded that he need not join the Quakers simply because he disliked 'attempting to define what has been left indefinite.'[2] The semi-mystical turn of thought which is most keenly alive to the futility of such endeavours was no longer a tenable ground for secession. Or if a man believed in visible manifestations of spiritual influences, he would more probably become a Methodist than a Quaker ; and the time was not yet come when to be a Methodist was to cease to be a Churchman. In one respect, however, Quakerism possessed a safeguard to emotional excitement which in Methodism was wanting.[3] It was that notion of tranquil, tarrying, and spiritual quiet which was as alien to the spirit of later Methodism as it is congenial to that of mysticism. The language of the Methodist would entirely accord with that of the Quaker in speaking of the pangs of the new birth, and of the visible tokens of the

---

[1] Boswell's *Life of Dr. Johnson,* ii. 456.

[2] Southey's ' Letters,' quoted in *Quarterly Review,* 98, 494.

[3] ' I fancy that most of the Churches need to learn and receive of one another ; and I have often wished that the zealous Methodist, for instance, who lives so much in action and in the atmosphere of religious excitement, could sometimes enter thoroughly into the spirit of the more religious Friends.'—H. H. Dobney, *Free Churches,* 106.

Spirit's presence; but the absence of reserve and the mutual 'experiences' of the Methodist stand out in a strong, and to many minds unfavourable, contrast with the silence and self-absorption of which Quakerism had learnt the value.

> Then comes the Spirit to our hut,
> When fast the senses' doors are shut;
> For so Divine and pure a guest
> The emptiest rooms are furnished best.[1]

Or, in the words of one of the saintliest of the mediæval mystics, 'In the chamber of the heart God works. But what He works in the souls of those with whom He holds direct converse none can say, nor can any man give account of it to another; but he only who has felt it knows what it is; and even he can tell thee nothing of it, save only that God in very truth hath possessed the ground of his heart.'[2]

It may here be observed that what has been said of Quakerism, so far as it was at one time representative of that mystic element which the eighteenth century called enthusiasm, will be a sufficient reason for passing all the more briefly over other branches of the same subject. The idea of self-surrender to the immediate action of spiritual influence is a bond of union far more potent than any external or ecclesiastical differences. Whatever be the period, or Church, or state of society in which it is found, mysticism is always very nearly the same both in its strength and in its weakness. It exhibits, indeed, the most varied phases, according to the direction and degree in which it falls into those excesses to which it is peculiarly liable, but such extravagances are very independent of the particular community in which they happen to appear. Different as are the associations connected with such names as Plato and Pythagoras, Plotinus and Dionysius, St. Bernard and T. a Kempis, Eckhart and Tauler, More and Norris, Fénelon and Guyon, Arndt and Spener, Law and Byrom, Quakers and Moravians, Schleiermacher and Schelling, yet passages might be collected from each, often striking and sometimes sublime, which show

---

[1] J. Byrom's *Poems.*

[2] Tauler's *Sermon for Epiphany*; Winkworth's *History and Life, with twenty five Sermons translated,* 223.

very close and essential points of affinity. And just in proportion as each form of mysticism has relaxed its hold upon steadying grounds of reason, the diversified dangers to which it is subject uniformly recur. Every successive type of mystic enthusiasm, if once it has passed its legitimate bounds, has produced exactly analogous instances of pantheism, antinomianism, or fanaticism.

Early in the eighteenth century, when Quakerism was just beginning to lose its influence, its wild assumptions of an earlier date were paralleled by a new form of fanatical enthusiasm. In 1706 there arose, says Calamy, 'a mighty noise as concerning new prophets.'[1] These were certain Camisards,[2] as they were called, of the Cevennes, who, after the revocation of the Edict of Nantes, had risen in the cause of their religion, and had been suppressed with great severity by Marshals Montrevel and Villars. Suffering and persecution have always been favourable to highly-wrought forms of mysticism. In their sore distress men and women have implored for and obtained consolations which transcend all ordinary experience. They have cried in agonies of faith and doubt for cheering visions of brighter things.

> Father, O Father, what do we here,
> In this land of unbelief and fear?
> The land of dreams is brighter far,
> Above the light of the morning star.[3]

Not only have they been comforted by what they feel to be direct intuitions of a Divine Presence in them and about them, but their imaginations have been kindled into fervent anticipations of triumphs near at hand and of judgments soon to fall upon their oppressors. From excited feelings such as these it is but a very little step for illiterate and undisciplined· minds to pass into the wildest phrensies of fanaticism. So it was with these 'French prophets.' The cause of foreign Protestantism was at this time very popular in England ; and when a number of them found their way hither as refugees they met at first with much sympathy, and had many admirers.

---

[1] Calamy's *Own Life*, ii. 71.
[2] W. M. Hatch's edition of Shaftesbury's *Characteristics*, Appen. 376-8.
[3] W. Blake, *Miscellaneous Poems*, 'The Land of Dreams.'

Some men even of learning and reputation, as Sir Edward Bulkeley and John Lacy, threw themselves heart and soul into the movement, on the not unreasonable ground that the dulness of religion and the degeneracy of the time needed a new dispensation of the Spirit, and that a great revival had begun. It is unnecessary to follow up the history in any detail. The impulse had been very genuine in the first instance, and had stood the test of much fierce trial. Transplanted to alien soil, it rapidly degenerated, and presently became degraded into mere imposture. For a time, however, it not only created much excitement throughout England, and even as far north as Aberdeen, but also attracted the anxious attention of several men of note. Harley, Chief Secretary of State, and Lord Godolphin made inquiries into it through Dr. Calamy, who was intimately acquainted with the subject, Lacy having been his personal friend and a leading member of his congregation.[1] Hoadly wrote his 'Vindication of the Ancient Prophets,'[2] in answer to Sir Richard Bulkeley's 'Defence.' Lord Shaftesbury entered into the field against these claimants to supernatural gifts. The first paper of his 'Characteristics,' headed 'Enthusiasm,' is mainly directed against them. It is not to be supposed that a philosopher of sceptical views, who chose for the motto of the very work in question the words πάντα ὑπόληψις ('Everything is supposition'), should feel any sympathy with religious enthusiasm, far less with a fanatical form of it. Still Shaftesbury was not altogether an irreligious man. In a letter written by him in 1702 to his brother Maurice,[3] after giving an interesting account of a strange interview he had had with a certain Quakeress prophet, he adds that the Sunday next after he went to church and received the Sacrament, 'never with truer zeal, in a better disposition, or with wholesomer affections,' blessing that good Providence which had placed him in a Church 'where zeal was not phrensy nor devotion extravagance.' And although in the 'Characteristics' he treats of enthusiasm as a mere contagious disorder of the mind, bred

---

[1] Calamy's *Own Life*, ii. 75–8, 95–7.

[2] Hoadly's *Works*, i. 108–123.

[3] Quoted by Hatch, App. ii. to his edition of Shaftesbury's *Characteristics*, 393.

of melancholy, at times when, he says, men are most unfitted to judge of themselves or of things above them, yet it is curious to note how, in spite, as it were, of himself, he feels obliged to make some concessions in its favour. 'Many of our first Reformers, it is feared, were little better than enthusiasts, and God knows whether a warmth of this kind did not materially help us in throwing off that spiritual tyranny.' [1] He allows, too, that enthusiasm is wonderfully powerful, and that there is a true inspiration, a real feeling of Divine presence, not easily to be distinguished from the false. And again, 'Something there will be of extravagance and fury when the idea or images received are too big for the narrow human vessel to contain.' [2] Persecution of fanatical excesses he entirely disapproves of, and urges, in his wonted strain, that raillery and ridicule furnish both a fiercer and a better test. The experience, he says, both of Socrates' times and of our own shows that the characters and doctrines which can stand that proof may be accepted as solid and just.

There could not be many subjects on which Hoadly and Shaftesbury, Spinckes the Nonjuror, Whiston and Calamy could all be writing contemporaneously on the same side. But it was so in this case. Whiston, in his 'Boyle Lectures' for 1707, insisted that the convulsive agitation of the French prophets must be caused not by good but by evil spirits,[3] and charged them with doctrinal errors closely corresponding to those imputed by Leslie to Bourignon. Spinckes,[4] following the example of his friend Dr. Hickes, who a few years before had published against the Quakers his 'Enthusiasm Exorcised,' took in hand Lacy's 'Warnings' and 'Cry from the Desert,' and exposed in numerous quotations the gross follies into which fanaticism had led him. Lee wrote at the same time his 'History of Montanism,' and from it pointed his warning against the insidious advances of enthusiasm or pretended inspiration. It is all the more dangerous, he says, because its germs are so universally diffused. Like other fevers, enthusiastic passion has its recurrent periods of special energy, and sometimes becomes an instrument in the hands of Providence

[1] Shaftesbury's *Characteristics*, chapter on 'Enthusiasm,' § 3.   [2] Id. § 7.
[3] Whiston's *Memoirs*, 137.
[4] N. Spinckes, *New Pretenders to Prophecy Examined*, 1709.

to work great revolutions in politics and religion. But 'there are very few in the world who can be said to be perfectly free from it. Even those that are phlegmatic are sometimes fermented by it; and all generally have some bias or other, some extraordinary warmth or confidence as to this or that, some waking dreams and some strong impulses whereof they can give little or no account. . . . Everyone, therefore, will do well to take warning, and will see good reason to pity rather than laugh at that infirmity of nature, since he himself may be as well seized by this as by any other distemper.'[1]

The commotion caused by these Camisard refugees quickly passed away, but left its impression on the public mind, and made the educated classes more than ever indisposed to bear with any outbursts of religious feelings which should in any way outstep the bounds of sobriety and order. When strange physical manifestations began to break out under the preaching of Wesley and Whitefield, the quakings and tremblings, the sighings and convulsions, which middle-aged people had seen or heard of in their younger days were by many recalled to memory, and helped to strengthen the unfortunate prejudices which the new movement had created. Wesley himself was vexed and puzzled at the obvious resemblance. He was quite ready to grant that such agitations betokened ' natural distemper '[2] in the case of the French prophets, yet the remembrance of them embarrassed him, for he was convinced that what he saw around him were veritable pangs of the new birth, the undoubted effects of spiritual and supernatural agencies.

About the same time that the Protestant enthusiasts of the Cevennes were conspicuously attracting the admiration or derision of the English public, another form of mysticism imported from Catholic France was silently working its way among a few persons of cultivated thought and deep religious sentiment. Fénelon was held in high and deserved esteem in England. Even when vituperation was most unsparingly lavished upon Roman Catholics in general, his name, conjointly with those of Pascal and Bossuet, was honourably excepted. His mild and tolerant spirit, his struggles with the

---

[1] *History of Montanism*, by a lay gentleman, 344.
[2] Wesley's *Third Journal*, p. 24, quoted by Lavington, *Enthus. of Meth. and Pa. Comp.*, 252.

Jesuits, the purity of his devotion, the simple, practical way in which he had discussed the evidences of religion, and, lastly, but perhaps not least, the great popularity of his 'Telemachus,' combined to increase his reputation in this country. The Duke of Marlborough, at the siege of Bouchain, assigned a detachment of troops to protect his estates and conduct provisions to his dwelling.[1] Steele copied into one of the Saturday papers of the ' Guardian,'[2] with a preface expressive of his high admiration of the piety and talents of its author, the devotional passage with which Fénelon concluded his ' Demonstration.' Lyttelton made Plato welcome him to heaven as ' the most pure, the most gentle, the most refined, disciple of philosophy that the world in modern times has produced.'[3] Richard Savage spoke of him as the pride of France.[4] Jortin, in reference to him and other French Churchmen of his stamp, observed that no European country had produced Romanists of so high a type.[5] But Fénelon is thoroughly representative of a pure and refined mysticism. He is, indeed, singularly free from the various errors which closely beset its more exaggerated forms. Yet no admirer of his who had become at all penetrated with the spirit that breathes in his writings could fail to sympathise with the fundamental ideas common to every form of mystic theology. An age which abhorred enthusiasm might have found, nevertheless, in the author whom all extolled, opinions closely analogous to those by which the wildest fanatics had justified their extravagancies. The doctrines of an inner light, of perfection, of reason quiescent amid the tumult of the soul, of mystical union, of disinterested love, are all strongly maintained by the Archbishop of Cambray. He wrote his 'Maximes des Saints' with the express purpose of showing how, in every age of the Church, opinions identical with those held by himself and Madame Guyon had been sanctioned by great authorities.[6] It was, in fact, a detailed defence of the Quietism

---

[1] A. Alison's *Life of Marlborough*, chap. ix. § 30.
[2] *Guardian*, No. 69.
[3] Lord Lyttelton's *Dialogues of the Dead*, No. 3.
[4] R. Savage's *Miscellaneous Poems*, ' Character of Rev. J. Foster.'
[5] Jortin's *Letters*, ii. 43.
[6] R. H. Vaughan, *Hours with the Mystics*, ii. 226.

and moderated mystical views which had excited the violent
and unguarded attack of Bossuet.

Fénelon, with instinctive ease, escaped the pitfalls with
which his subject was encompassed; but it was not so with
Madame Guyon, whose opinions he had so vigorously defended
and all but identified with his own. There could scarcely be
a better example of the insensible degrees in which, by the
infirmity of human nature, sound spiritualism may decline
into visionary fancies and a morbid state of religious emotion,
than to notice how the writings of Guyon and Bourignon form
transitionary links between Fénelon and the extreme mystics.
Their principles were the same, but the meditations of Madame
Bourignon, although sometimes ranked in devotional value
with those of A Kempis and De Sales, fell, if Leslie and
others may be trusted,[1] into most of the dangerous and
heretical notions into which an unreined enthusiasm is apt to
lead. A defence of her opinions, published in London in
1699, and a collection, which followed soon after, of her translated letters, had considerable influence with many earnest
spirits[2] who chafed at the coldness of the times, and cared little
for other faults so long as they could find a religious literature
in which they could, at all events, be safe from formalism
and scholastic or sectarian disputings.

Lyttelton, in the same paper in which he pronounces his
panegyric on Fénelon, calls Madame Guyon a 'mad woman'
and 'a distracted enthusiast.' So much depends upon the
greater or less sobriety with which views are stated; and
excellent as Madame Guyon was, her effuse and somewhat
morbid form of devotional sentiment can never be altogether
congenial to English feeling, still less to English feeling such
as it was in the first half of the eighteenth century. But her
hymns, made familiar to readers in this country by Cowper's

---

[1] C. Leslie's 'Snake in the Grass.'—*Works*, iv. 1–14. So also Lavington's
Enthusiasm, &c., 346.

[2] 'In England her works have already deceived not a few.'—Leslie, Id. 14.
'What think you too of the Methodists? You are nearer to Oxford. We have
strange accounts of their freaks. The books of Madame Bourignon, the French
visionnaire, are, I hear, much enquired after by them.'—Warburton to Doddridge, May 27, 1738. Doddridge's *Correspondence*, &c., iii. 327.

Francis Lee, the Nonjuror, an excellent man, one of Robert Nelson's friends,
was 'once a great Bourignonist.'—Hearne to Rawlinson, App. iii. 1718, quoted in
H. B. Wilson's *History of Merchant Taylors' School*, ii. 957.

translations, were received by many with the same welcome
as the works of Madame de Bourignon. If there were few
who could appreciate the high-strung mystic aspirations after
perfect self-renunciation, self-annihilation, and absorption in
the abyss of the Divine infinity, the ecstatic joy in self-denial
and suffering, whereby the soul might be so refined from
selfishness as to surrender itself wholly to the will of God, and
to see the marks of His love equally present everywhere—if
to religious men and women outside the cloister this seemed
like vainly striving

> To wind ourselves too high
> For sinful man beneath the sky,

yet in the general spirit of her verses they could gain refreshment not always to be found elsewhere. They could sympathise with the intense longing for a closer walk with God, with
the hunger and thirst after a purer righteousness, a more
unselfish love, a closer mystical union with the Divine life.

Yet, after all, it is not France, but Germany that has been
for many centuries the chosen abode of every variety of mystic
sentiment. The most exalted forms of spiritual Christianity
have prospered there, and, on the other hand, the vaguest
reveries and the grossest epidemics of fanaticism. We turn
from the influence in the England of the eighteenth century
of French revivalists and French Pietists to that exercised by
one of the most remarkable of German mystics, Jacob Behmen.
If it was an influence no longer popular and widely spreading,
as it once had been, yet it directly and profoundly impressed
one of the most eminent of our theologians, and indirectly its
effects were by no means inconsiderable.

The history of 'the Teutonic theosopher,' 'the illuminated
Behmen,' as his admirers were wont to call him, can be but
briefly touched upon. Born in 1575, he was often, while yet
an apprentice at Gorlitz, absorbed in a dreamland of visionary
meditation. Above all he pondered longingly and wonder-
ingly what might be the full meaning of those words, 'Your
Father in heaven will give the Holy Spirit to them that ask
Him.'[1] The mystery of evil everywhere mingled with the
good had oppressed him with ' melancholy and heavy sadness.'

---

[1] *Jacob Behmen's Life and Works*, by W. Law, 1764; *Life*, xv.

He could not find comfort in Scripture, and idle and evil thoughts troubled him. 'But when in this affliction and trouble I elevated my spirit, which then I understood very little or nothing at all what it was, I earnestly raised it up into God as with a great storm and onset, wrapping up my whole heart and mind, as also all my thoughts and whole will and resolution, incessantly to wrestle with the love and mercy of God, and not to give over unless He blessed me—that is, unless He enlightened me with His Holy Spirit, whereby I might understand His will and be rid of my sadness. . . . But when in my resolved zeal I gave so hard an assault, storm, and onset upon God and upon all the gates of hell, as if I had more reserves of virtue and power ready, with a resolution to hazard my life upon it, which assuredly were not in my power without the aid of the Spirit of God, suddenly, after some violent storms made, my spirit did break through the gates of hell, even into the innermost birth and geniture of the Deity, and there I was embraced with love, as a bridegroom embraces his dearly beloved. But the greatness of the triumphing that was in the spirit I cannot express either in speaking or writing, neither can it be compared to anything but with that wherein the life is generated in the midst of death, and it is like the resurrection of the dead. In this light my spirit suddenly saw through all ; and in and by all the creatures, even in herbs and grass, it knew God, who He is and how He is, and what His will is.'[1]   These are words which, like many passages from John Bunyan, have the ring of intense conviction, and mark a man well fitted to sway religious feeling. He began to publish in 1612, and died in 1624 with the often-quoted words upon his lips, ' Now I go hence into Paradise.'[2] His writings, which during those twelve years were voluminous, travelled rapidly throughout Europe, found readers in every class, and are said to have been widely instrumental in recalling unbelievers to a Christian faith. They popularised and gave an immense extension to mysticism of every kind, good and bad. In Germany they largely contributed[3] to form the opinions of Arndt and Andreas, Spener and Francke, men to whom their country was indebted for a re-

---

[1] Behmen's *Aurora*, b. xix. § 9-12.   [2] *Life*, p. xxii.
[3] M. J. Matter, *Histoire du Christianisme*, iv. 344.

markable revival of spiritual religion. Their further influence may, perhaps, be traced through Francke on Count Zinzendorf and the Moravians,[1] and through Wolff on the mystic rationalism of later Germany. The German Romanticists of the end of the last and the beginning of this century were extravagant in his praises,[2] Schlegel declaring that he was superior to Luther. Novalis was scarcely less ardent in his admiration. Kahlman protested that he had learnt more from him than he could have learnt from all the wise men of his age together.[3] In England, both in the seventeenth and eighteenth centuries, he had many devoted followers and many violent opponents. Henry More speaks of him as a good and holy man, but at the same time 'an egregious enthusiast,' and regrets that he 'has given occasion to the enthusiasts of this nation in our late troublesome times to run into many ridiculous errors and absurdities.'[4] J. Wesley admitted that he was a good man, but says 'the whole of Behmenism, both phrase and sense, is useless.'[5] With an absence of appreciation almost amounting to a want of candour, not uncommon in this eminent man towards those from whom he disagreed, he will not even allow that he had any 'patrons'[6] who have adorned the doctrine of Christ. 'His language is barbarous, unscriptural, and unintelligible.' 'It is most sublime nonsense, inimitable bombast, fustian not to be paralleled.' Bishop Warburton also refers to him in the most unqualified[7] terms of contempt. William Blake, most mystical of poets and painters, delighted, as might well be expected, in Behmen's writings.[8] A far weightier testimony to their value is to be found in the high estimate which William Law—

[1] Francis Okely, one of the most distinguished of the English Moravians of the last century, was a great student and admirer of Behmen.—Nichol's *Literary Anecdotes*, iii. 93.

[2] Schelling and others, says Dorner, 'sought out and utilised many a noble germ in the fermenting chaos of Böhme's notions.'—J. A. Dorner's *History of Protestant Theology*, 1871, ii. 184.

[3] R. A. Vaughan, *Hours with the Mystics*, ii. 349.

[4] H. More's *Works*, 'Antidote against Atheism,' note to chap. xliv.

[5] J. Wesley, 'Thoughts upon Jacob Behmen.'—*Works*, ix. 509.

[6] Id. 513.

[7] Unqualified, even for Warburton. 'Doctrine of Grace,' b. iii. ch. ii.—*Works*, iv. 706.

[8] A. Gilchrist's *Life of Blake*, i. 16.

a theologian of saintly life, and most thoughtful and suggestive in his reasonings—formed of the spiritual treasury which he found there. He can scarcely find words to express his thankfulness for 'the depth and fulness of Divine light and truth opened in them by the grace and mercy of God.' [1]

This extreme contrast of opinions may be easily accounted for. To most modern readers Jacob Behmen's works must be an intolerable trial of patience. They will find page after page of what they may very pardonably call, as Wesley did, 'sublime nonsense' or unintelligible jargon. Repetitions, obscurities, and verbal barbarisms abound in them, and the most ungrounded fancies are poured profusely forth as the most indubitable verities. But it is like diving for pearls in a deep and turbid sea. The pearls are there, if patiently sought for, and sometimes of rare beauty. To Behmen's mind the whole universe of man and nature is transfigured by the pervading presence of a spiritual life. Everywhere there is contest against evil, sin, and death; everywhere there is a longing after better things, a yearning for the recovery of the heavenly type. Everywhere there is a groaning and travailing in pain until now, awaiting the adoption—to wit, the redemption of the body. Heaven and earth are full of God; and if our eyes could be opened, as the eyes of Stephen or Elijah's servant, or St. Paul when he saw things unutterable, we might behold 'the holy angels converse and walk up and down in the innermost birth of this world by and with our King Jesus Christ, as well as in the uppermost world. . . . And where should the soul of man rather be than with its King and Redeemer Jesus Christ? For near and afar off us God is one.' [2] None felt more keenly than Behmen that heaven is truly at our doors, and God not far away from every one of us. The Holy Spirit is to him in very deed Lord and Giver of all life, and teaches all things, and leads into all truth. He is well assured that to him who thirsts after righteousness, and hath his conversation in heaven, and knoweth God within him, and whose heart is prepared by purity and truth, such light of the eternal life will be granted that, though he be simple and unlearned, heavenly wisdom

[1] W. Law's introduction to his translation of Behmen's *Works.*
[2] *Aurora,* chap. xix, §§ 56-8.

will be granted to him, and all things will become full of meaning. He puts no limit to the grand possibilities and capabilities of human nature. To him the soul of man is indeed 'larger than the sky, deeper than ocean,'[1] but only through union and conformity with that Divine Spirit which 'searcheth all things—yea, the deep things of God.' He would have welcomed as a wholly congenial idea that grand mediæval notion of an encyclopædic wisdom in which all forms of philosophy, art, and science build up, as it were, one noble edifice, rising heavenwards, domed in by Divine philosophy, the spiritual and intellectual knowledge of God ; he would have agreed with Bonaventura that all human science 'emanates, as from its source, from the Divine Light.'[2] He felt also that in the unity of 'the selfsame Spirit, dividing to every man severally as He will,' would be found something deeper than all diversities in religion, which would reconcile them, and would solve Scripture difficulties and the mysteries which have tormented men.

These and suchlike thoughts, intensely realised, and sometimes expressed with singular vividness and power, possessed great attraction to minds wearied with the religious controversies or spiritual dulness of the time, and which were not repelled by the wilderness of verbiage, the hazy cloudland, in which Behmen's conceptions were involved. William Law, the Nonjuror, was thoroughly fascinated by them, and their influence upon him forms an episode of considerable interest in the religious history of the period.

Yet if it had been only as the translator and exponent of 'the Teutonic theosophy' that William Law had become prominent, and incurred on every side the hackneyed charge of 'enthusiasm,' this excellent man might have claimed but a passing notice. His theological position in the eighteenth century is rendered chiefly remarkable by the power he showed (in his time singularly exceptional) of harmonising the ideas of mediæval mysticism with some of the most characteristic features of modern religious thought. A man of deep and somewhat ascetic piety, and gifted with much originality and with a cultured and progressive mind, he had

[1] H. Coleridge, *Sonnet on Shakspeare.*
[2] Quoted in *Christian Schools and Scholars*, ii. 85.

many readers and a few earnest and admiring adherents, yet was never greatly in sympathy with the age in which he lived. Three or four generations earlier, or three or four generations later, he would have found much more that was congenial to one or another side of his intellectual temperament. At the accession of George I. in 1716 he declined to take the oaths, and resigned his fellowship at Cambridge, although, like others among the moderate Nonjurors, he remained to the last constant to the communion of the National Church.[1] In 1726 he wrote the 'Serious Call,' one of the most remarkable devotional books that have ever been published. Dr. Johnson, upon whom it made a profound and lasting impression, describes it as 'the finest piece of hortatory theology in any language.'[2] Gibbon, in whose father's house Law lived for some time as tutor and chaplain, says of it that 'if it found a spark of piety in the reader's mind it would soon kindle it to a flame.'[3] Southey remarks of it that 'few books have made so many religious enthusiasts.' The reading of it formed one of the first epochs in Wesley's religious life. It did much towards forming the character of the elder Venn. It was mainly instrumental in effecting the conversion from profligacy to piety of the once famous Psalmanazar.[4] Effects scarcely less striking are recorded in 1771 to have resulted upon its copious distribution among the inhabitants of a whole parish.[5] And lastly it may be added that Bishop Horne made himself thoroughly familiar with a kindred work by the same author—on 'Christian Perfection'—and was wont to express the greatest admiration of it.

From his retirement at Kingscliffe,[6] where he lived a life of untiring benevolence, Law took an active part in the

---

[1] A sketch of his life is given in Bishop Ewing's *Present-Day Papers*, 13-17.
[2] Boswell's *Johnson*, ii. 125.
[3] E. Gibbon, *Memoirs of My Life*, 13.
[4] *Quarterly Review*, 103, 310.   [5] Ewing's *Present-Day Papers*, 14.
[6] In Leslie Stephen's *English Thought in the Eighteenth Century* we have a vivid picture of the retreat at Kingscliffe—the devotional exercises, the unstinted almsgiving, and Law's little study, four feet square, furnished with its chair, its writing-table, the Bible, and the works of Jacob Behmen. 'Certainly a curious picture in the middle of that prosaic eighteenth century, which is generally interpreted to us by Fielding, Smollett, and Hogarth.'—Chap. xii. 6 (70).

religious controversies of the time ; refusing, however, all payment for his publications. He entered the lists against Tindal, Chubb, and Mandeville, against Hoadly, against Warburton, against Wesley. His answer to Mandeville is called by J. Sterling 'a most remarkable philosophical essay,' full 'of pithy right reason,'[1] and has been republished by Frederick Maurice, with a highly commendatory introduction. The authority last mentioned also speaks of him as ' a singularly able controversialist in his argument with Hoadly ; ' and adds : ' Of all the writers whom he must have irritated— Freethinkers, Methodists, actors, Hanoverians,—of all the nonjuring friends whom he alienated by his quietism, none doubted his singleness of purpose.' It may be added that there were few of his opponents who might not have learnt from him a lesson of Christian courtesy. Living in an age when controversy of every kind was, almost as a rule, deformed by virulent personalities, he yet, in the face of much provocation, kept always faithful to his resolve that, ' by the grace of God, he would never have any personal contention with anyone.'[2]

Such was the man who, from about 1730 to his death in 1761, was a most earnest student of mystical theology. ' Of these mystical divines,' he says, ' I thank God I have been a diligent reader, through all ages of the Church, from the Apostolical Dionysius the Areopagite down to the great Fénelon, the illuminated Guyon, and M. Bertot.'[3] Tauler made a great impression on his mind, but Jacob Behmen most of all. Of these writers in general he speaks in grateful terms, as true spiritual teachers, purified by trials and self-discipline, and deeply learned in the mysteries of God, ' truly sons of thunder and sons of consolation, who awaken the heart, and leave it not till the kingdom of heaven is raised up in it.'

William Law was a man of far too great intellectual ability to be a mere borrower of ideas. What he read he thoroughly assimilated ; and Behmen's strange theosophy, after passing through the mind of his English exponent, reappeared in a far more logical and comprehensible form.

[1] F. S. Maurice, Introduction to Law's *Answer to Mandeville,* v.
[2] *Works,* vi. 216.   [3] *Answer to Dr. Trapp.—Works,* vi. 319.

It cannot be said that Law was altogether a gainer by his later studies. To many of his contemporaries the result appeared quite the contrary ; and he was constantly reproached with having become a mere mystic or a hopeless enthusiast. No doubt, he borrowed from his favourite authors some of their faults as well as many of their virtues. Jacob Behmen's most glaring faults in style and phraseology are sometimes transferred with little mitigation to his pages. A person who gathered his ideas of William Law from Wesley's critique would probably turn with impatience, and something like aversion, from one who could use upon the gravest subjects what might seem a strange jargon compounded out of Gnostic cosmogonies and alchemistic fancies. We take Jacob Behmen for what he was—a man in some respects of extraordinary spiritual insight, but perfectly illiterate ; living at a time when the fame of Agrippa and Paracelsus was still recent, and accustomed to refer all his conceptions to immediate revelation from heaven. But we do not expect to find in a cultivated scholar of the eighteenth century such outlandish sayings as ' Nature is in itself a hungry, wrathful fire of life,' or pages of argument grounded upon the condition and fall of angels before the creation of the world. Such phraseology and such reasonings, even if culled from Law's writings less unrelentingly and more fairly than by Wesley and Warburton, are quite sufficient to create a reasonable prejudice against his opinions. Yet these are blemishes which lie comparatively on the surface. They are always found in reference to certain views which he had adopted about creation and the fall of man. Although, therefore, they occur constantly—for the Fall is always a very essential feature in the whole of Law's theology—they do not interfere with the general lucidity of his argument, or the devotional beauty of his thought.

Independently of occasional obscurities of language and visionary notions, Law does not altogether escape those more serious objections to which mystic writers are almost always liable. When he speaks of heavenly illumination, and of the birth of Christ within the soul, or of the all of God and the nothingness of man, or when he refers over slightingly to ' human reason ' or ' human learning,' or to the outward machinery of religion in contrast to the direct communion of the soul with its Creator, it is impossible not to feel that he sometimes approaches over nearly to the dangerous verge where sound spiritualism loses self-control.

The ascetic austerity of Law's life and teaching was at once a recommendation and an impediment to the influence of his writings. From the beginning to the end of his active life he would never swerve an atom from the high and uncompromising type of holiness which he constantly set before himself as the bounden goal of all human effort. His mysticism only intensified this feeling. Assured as of a certain truth that, corrupt, fallen, and earthly as human nature is, there is nevertheless in the soul of every man 'the fire and light and love of God, though lodged in a state of hiddenness, inactivity, and death, . . . overpowered by the workings of flesh and blood,'[1] it seemed to him the one worthy object of life, by purification and by mortification of the lower nature, to remove all hindrances to the enlightening efficacy of the Holy Spirit. So only could the Divine Image, the life of the Triune God within the soul, be restored, and the heavenborn Spirit, 'that angel that died in Paradise,'[2] be born again to life within us. His words sound like a Christian paraphrase of what Plato had said in the 'Republic,' where he compares the present appearance of the soul to an image of the sea god Glaucus, so battered by waves, so disfigured by the overgrowth of shells, and seaweed, and all kinds of earthy substances, that it has almost lost the similitude of the immortal likeness.[3] No one could have felt more keenly than William Law the overpowering need of this restorative process, and the fervent longing of the awakened soul to be delivered from that bondage of corruption which presses like a burden too heavy to be borne, not upon man only, but upon all creation, groaning and travailing in sympathetic pain, to be delivered from the evil and misery and death with which it is laden.[4] He will allow of no ideal short of the highest pattern of angelic[5] goodness, nor concede that we are

---

[1] *Way to Divine Knowledge*, 2nd ed. 1762, p. 7.—*Works*, vol. vii.
[2] Id.　　　　　　　　　[3] Plato, *Republic*, b. x. § 611.
[4] *Appeal to all that Doubt*, 3rd ed. 1768, p. 131.—*Works*, vol. vi. *Spirit of Prayer*, 1st part, 73, vol. vii.　　　　[5] Id. 24.

called upon to pray, ' God's will be done on earth as it is in heaven,' without its full accomplishment being in human power. This height of aspiration gives great stimulative power to Law's writing, but, as is unfortunately apt to be the case, it is a source of weakness as well as of power. With him, as with many mystic writers, all other elements of human nature are slighted and neglected in the absorbing thirst for holiness. His ideal is indeed lofty, but it fails in expansiveness. When he speaks of absorption into the Divine will—of seeking 'deliverance from the misery and captivity of self by a total continual self-denial' [1]—of converting 'this poison of an earthly life into a state of purification' [2]—of 'turning from all that is earthly, animal, and temporal, and dying to the will of flesh and blood, because it is darkness, corruption, and separation from God;' [3] when— sound and thoughtful reasoner as he often is—he speaks with thorough distrust of ' the guidance of our own Babylonian reason,' [4] and of learning as good indeed within its own sphere, but ' as different from Divine light as heaven from earth,' [5] and wholly useless to one who would 'be well qualified to write notes upon the spirit and meaning of the words of Christ;' [6] it is impossible not to feel that he is approaching very closely to the morbid pietism of the recluse. His was indeed no mere contemplative asceticism, but fruitful in practical virtues ; and even its weaker points stand out in noble contrast with the deficiencies of an age which admired prudential religion, and took in good earnest the words of the Preacher as to being righteous overmuch. [7] But his writings would

---

[1] *Answer to Dr. Trapp*, 38-39, vol. vi.   [2] Id.

[3] *Way to Divine Knowledge*, 14.

[4] Id. 93. But he adds soon after, ' I am no more an enemy to learning than to grinding corn, but it must keep within its own sphere '—(Id. 95.) There is no reason to believe that he would have repudiated passages from his earlier works such as the following: ' The more we act according to order, truth, and reason, the more we make ourselves like unto God, who is truth and reason itself. This is the strong and immoveable foundation of moral virtue, having the same certainty as the attributes of God.'—*Answer to Mandeville*, F. Maurice's ed. p. 27.

[5] *Answer to Dr. Trapp*, 244.

[6] *Way to Divine Knowledge*, 98.

[7] The special reference is to Dr. Joseph Trapp's ' Four Sermons on the Folly, Sin, and Danger of being Righteous overmuch ; with a particular view to the Doctrines and Practices of Modern Enthusiasts,' 1739. The work had an extensive sale. S. Johnson's *Works* (R. Lynam), v. 497. It should be added that, from

probably have had greater and wider influence if his piety had been less austere, and his ideal of life more comprehensive.

Yet, on the whole, William Law's mysticism had a most elevating effect on his theology, and has done much toward raising him to the very foremost rank of eighteenth-century divines. It broadened and deepened his views, so that from being only a luminary of the estimable but somewhat narrow section of the Nonjurors, he became a writer to whom some of the most distinguished leaders of modern religious thought have thankfully acknowledged their obligations. He learnt to combine with earnest piety and strong convictions an unreserved sympathy, as far as possible removed from the sectarianism of religious parties, with all that is good and Christlike wherever it might be found, wherever the Light that lighteth every man shines from its inward temple. He would like no truth, he said, the less because Ignatius Loyola or John Bunyan or George Fox were very zealous for it;[1] and while he chose to live and die in outward communion with the Church of England,[2] he desired to 'unite and join in heart and spirit with all that is Christian, holy, good, and acceptable to God in all other Churches.'[3] He deplored the ' partial selfish orthodoxy which cannot bear to hear or own that the spirit and blessing of God are so visible in a Church from which it is divided.'[4] He grieved that 'even the most worthy and pious among the clergy of the Established Church are afraid to assert the sufficiency of the Divine Light, because the Quakers who have broken off from the Church have made this doctrine their corner-stone.'[5] Of Romanism he remarked that 'the more we believe or know of the corruptions and hindrances of true piety in the Church of Rome, the more we should rejoice to hear that in every age so many eminent spirits, great saints, have appeared in it, whom we should thankfully behold as so many great lights hung out by God to show the true way to heaven.'[6]

Nor would he by any means limit the operations of true

their own point of view, the sermons contain much sound sense and are by no means deficient in religious feeling.

[1] *Appeal*, &c. 278. [2] Id. 279. [3] Id. 280.
[4] Id. 282. [5] Id. 275. [6] Id. 282

redeeming grace to the bounds of Christendom. Ever impressed with the sense that 'there is in all men, wherever dispersed over the earth, a divine, immortal, never-ending Spirit,'[1] and that by this Spirit of God in man all are equally His children, and that as Adam is spoken of as first father of all, so the second Adam is the regenerator of all,[2] he insisted that 'the glorious extent of the Catholick Church of Christ takes in all the world. It is God's unlimited, universal mercy to all mankind.'[3] Understood rightly, Christianity might truly be spoken of as being old as the Creation ; for the Son of God was the eternal life and light of men, quite independently of the infinitely blessed revelation of Himself afforded in the Gospel. There is a Gospel Christianity, which is as the possession compared with the expectation. There is an 'original, universal Christianity, which began with Adam, was the religion of the Patriarchs, of Moses and the Prophets, and of every penitent man in every part of the world that had faith and hope towards God, to be delivered from the evil of this world.'[4] The real infidel, whether he be a professed disciple of the Gospel, of Zoroaster, or of Plato, is he who lives for the world and not for God.[5]

There was probably no one man in the eighteenth century, unless we except Samuel Coleridge, so competent as William Law to appreciate, from a thoroughly religious point of view, spiritual excellence in Christian and heathen, in Anglican, and Roman Catholic, and Methodist, and Quaker. Much in the same way, although a firm believer in revealed religion and a vigorous opponent of the Deists, engaged 'for twenty years in this dust of debate,'[6] he did not yield even to Bishop Butler in his power of recognising what was most forcible in their objections. The mystical tendencies of his religion, whatever may have been the special dangers incidental to them, at all events enabled him to meet the Deists with advantage on their own chosen ground. How he met Tindal's 'Christianity as Old as Creation' has been already mentioned. As Eusebius and St. Augustine and many others had done before him, he accepted it as to a great extent true, while he

---

[1] *Appeal*, &c., 4.   [2] Id. 70; *Spirit of Prayer*, pt. i. 56–8.
[3] *Spirit of Prayer*, pt. i. 57.
[4] *Way to Divine Knowledge*, 78, and 31. *Appeal*, &c., 5.
[5] *Way to Divine Knowledge*, 14.   [6] Id. 15.

declined to accept Tindal's inferences from it.[1] So of the Atonement, which was always considered the cardinal point in the controversy with Deists. Law willingly acknowledged the justice of many of their arguments, but maintained that the opinions they impugned were simply a mistaken view of true Christianity. The author of ' Deism fairly stated,' &c.— a work which excited much attention at its publication in 1746—had said, 'That a perfectly innocent Being, of the highest order among intelligent natures, should personate the offender and suffer in his place and stead, in order to take down the wrath and resentment of the Deity against the criminal, and dispose God to show mercy to him—the Deist conceives to be both unnatural and improper, and therefore not to be ascribed to God without blasphemy.' ' What an arrow,' answers Law, ' is here : I will not say shot beside the mark, but shot at nothing ! . . . The innocent Christ did not suffer to quiet an angry Deity, but as co-operating, assisting, and uniting with that love of God which desired our salvation. He did not suffer in our place or stead, but only on our account, which is a quite different matter.'[2] ' Our guilt is transferred upon Him in no other sense than as He took upon Him the state and condition of our fallen nature . . . to heal, remove, and overcome all the evils that were brought into our nature by the fall . . . His merit or righteousness is imputed or derived into us in no other sense than as we receive from Him a birth, a nature, a power to become the sons of God.'[3] There is nothing here said which would not now be widely assented to among members of most sections of the Christian Church. William Law's writings will not be rightly estimated unless it be remembered that in his time orthodox theology in England scarcely allowed of any other than those scholastic and forensic notions of the Atonement which he deprecates. Other views were commonly thought

---

[1] One of the passages on the title-page of Tindal's *Christianity as Old as the Creation*, was the following sentence from the *Retractations* of St. Augustine : ' The thing which is now called the Christian Religion was also among the ancients, nor was it wanting from the beginning of the human race, until Christ came in the flesh, when the true religion that then was began to be called Christian.'—Quoted in Hunt's *Religious Thought in England*, ii. 434.

[2] *Spirit of Love*, pt. ii. 124, vol. viii.

[3] *Appeal*, &c., 199–200. *Spirit of Prayer*, pt. ii. 159.

to savour of rank Deism or rank Quakerism. His theological opponents seemed somewhat to doubt under which of these denominations he should be placed, or whether he would not more properly be referred to both.[1]

Law's unwavering trust in a Spirit which guides faith and goodness into all necessary truth, led him to take a different course from the evidence writers of his time. ' I would not,' he says, ' take the method generally practised by the defenders of Christianity. I would not attempt to show from reason and antiquity the necessity and reasonableness of a Divine revelation in general, or of the Mosaic and Christian in particular. Nor do I enlarge upon the arguments for the credibility of the Gospel history, the reasonableness of its creeds, institutions, and usages ; or the duty of man to receive things above, but not contrary to his reason. I would avoid all this, because it is wandering from the true point in question, and only helping the Deist to oppose the Gospel with a show of argument, which he must necessarily want, was the Gospel left to stand upon its own bottom.'[2] To follow up the line of thought suggested by these words would be in itself a treatise. It is a first axiom among all mystics, that light is its own witness. With what limitations and precautions this is to be transferred to the spiritual region, and how far Christianity is independent of other testimony than its own intrinsic excellence—is a question of profound importance, and one which various minds will answer very differently. Law's unhesitating answer is another example of the way in which he was wont to combat Deists with their own weapons.

The vigour and success with which Law controverted the reasonings of those who grounded human society upon expedience, was also owing in large part to what was styled his mysticism or his enthusiasm. A religious philosophy which led him to dwell with special emphasis on the Divine element inherent in man's nature, and his faculties of communion with the Infinite, inspired him with the strongest force of conviction in combating theories such as that expressed in its

---

[1] Wesley's ' Letter to W. Law.'—*Works*, ix. 488—. Also Warburton on Middleton ; and ' Doctrine of Grace,' part iii.—*Works*, vol. iv.

[2] *Way to Divine Knowledge*, 10. *Appeal*, &c., 325.

barest form by Mandeville—that, in man's original state, right and wrong were but other expressions for what was found to be expedient or otherwise, that not rarely

> Vice is beneficial found,
> When it's by justice lopt and bound ;[1]

and that 'moral virtues' (unless regarded as dictates of a special revelation) ' are but the political offspring which flattery begot on pride.'[2] The answers even of Berkeley and Hutchinson had been comparatively feeble. They could not altogether escape from being hampered by those favourite reasonings of the day about the wisdom of morality and the advantages of religion, which after all were much like the very same argument from expedience, clothed in fairer garb. Law wrote in a different strain. Addressing himself to Deists who, whatever else might be their doubts, rarely departed from belief in a God, he bade them find their answer in that belief. 'Once turn your eyes to heaven, and dare but own a just and good God, and then you have owned the true origin of religion and moral virtue.' 'Suppose that God is of infinite justice, goodness, and truth . . . this is the strong and unmoveable foundation of moral virtue, having the same certainty as the attributes of God.'[3] Thence came that original excellence of man's nature which is essentially his healthy state, his sound and perfect condition, and of which all evil is the corruption and disease. Examine goodness, analyse it with unsparing strictness ; and see 'whether the investigation does not prove that evil is *not* the substantial part of any act which is acted, or thought which is thought, in this world ; but, on the contrary, the destructive element of it, that which makes it unreal and false.'[4]

Closely connected with this unfaltering conviction of the immutable character of right and wrong, that the light of our souls come direct from the source of light, and that the principles of justice, truth, and mercy cannot be otherwise than identical in God and His reasoning creatures—came William Law's speculations about the ultimate destinies of

---

[1] Mandeville's *Fable of the Bees*, 1714, l. 425.
[2] Mandeville's *Enquiry into the Origin of Moral Virtue*, p. 12.
[3] W. Law's *Answer to Mandeville*, 27.
[4] F. D. Maurice's Preface to Id.

man. It has been truly observed that 'the first step commonly taken by Protestant mysticism is an endeavour to mitigate the gloom which hangs over the future state.'[1] This is very strongly marked in all the later productions of Law's mind. He was very far from taking anything like an optimist view of the world around him. There is no writer of his age who shows himself more impressed with an abhorrence of sin, and with the sense of its widespread and deeply rooted influences. He is austere even to excess in his views of what godliness requires. His whole soul is oppressed with the wilful ruin of spiritual life which he everywhere beholds. Yet he can conceive of no hope except by the recovery of that spiritual life, no atonement except by the extinguishing of sin,[2] no salvation nor redemption except by regeneration of nature,[3] no forgiveness of sin but by being made free from sin.[4] But paramount above all such thoughts is his ever-ruling conviction of the perfect love of God. 'Ask what God is? His name is Love; He is the good, the perfection, the peace, the joy, the glory and blessing of every life. Ask what Christ is? He is the universal remedy of all evil broken forth in nature and creature. He is the destruction of misery, sin, darkness, death, and hell. He is the resurrection and life of all fallen nature. He is the unwearied compassion, the long-suffering pity, the never-ceasing mercifulness of God to every want and infirmity of human nature. He is the breathing forth of the heart, life, and Spirit of God into all the dead race of Adam. He is the seeker, the finder, the restorer of all that was lost and dead to the life of God.'[5] Law utterly rejected the possibility of Divine love contradicting the highest conceptions which man can form of it; and he turned with horror from the arbitrary sovereignty suggested in the Calvinistic scheme. Nations or individuals, he said, might be chosen instruments for special designs, but 'elect' ordinarily meant 'beloved.' In any other sense the evil nature only in every man is reprobated, and that which is divine in him elected.[6] 'The goodness and love of God,' he

---

[1] R. A. Vaughan, *Hours with the Mystics*, ii. 246.
[2] *Spirit of Love*, pt. ii. 87.
[3] *Spirit of Prayer*, pt. i. 53. Also, Id. 39, *Way to Divine Knowledge*, 96.
[4] W. Law's *Letters*, in R. Tighe's *Life of Law*, 72.
[5] *Spirit of Prayer*, pt. ii. 127. [6] *Spirit of Love*, pt. ii. 161.

asserted, 'have no limits or bounds, but such as His omnipotence hath.'[1] It was indeed conceivable that there may be spirits of men or fallen angels that have so totally lost every spark of the heavenly nature, and have become so essentially evil, that restoration is no more consistent with their inner-most nature than for a circle to have the properties of a straight line. If not, 'their restoration is possible, and they will infallibly have all their evil removed out of them by the goodness of God.'[2] Christianity, he said, is the one true religion of nature, because man's corrupt state 'absolutely requires two things as its only salvation. First, the Divine life must be revived in the soul of man. Secondly, there must be a resurrection of the body in a better state after death.'[3] ·That religion only can be sufficient to the want of his nature which can provide this salvation. God's redeeming love, said Law, will not suffer the sinner to have rest or peace until, in time or in eternity, righteousness is restored and purification completed.[4] He expressed in the strongest language his belief that 'every act of what is called Divine vengeance, recorded in Scripture, may and ought, with the greatest strictness of truth, to be called an act of the Divine love. If Sodom flames and smokes with stinking brimstone, it is the love of God that kindled it, only to extinguish a more horrible fire. It was one and the same infinite love, when it preserved Noah in the ark, when it turned Sodom into a burning lake, and overwhelmed Pharaoh in the Red Sea.'[5] If God did not chastise sin, that lenience would argue that He was not all love and goodness towards man. And so far from its being a lessening of the just 'terrors of the Lord,' to say that His punishments, however severe, are inflicted not in vengeance but in love, such wholesome terrors are placed on more certain ground. Every work of piety is turned into a work of love; but from the licentious all false and idle hopes are taken away, and they must know that there is 'nothing to trust to as a deliverance from misery but the one total abolition of sin.'

[1] *Appeal to all that Doubt,* 88.   [2] *Way to Divine Knowledge,* 65.
[3] *Spirit of Love,* pt. ii. 140.
[4] *Letters,* in Tighe, 73; and *Spirit of Love,* pt. ii. 107-8.
[5] *Spirit of Love,* pt. ii. 80.   [6] Id. 112-9.

William Law's views upon the relations of man to outward nature, and of physical to moral evil, are too much mixed up with Jacob Behmen's imaginative reveries, to be of much interest. It is time to pass on from this brief review of the writings of a man who would have been worthy of attention in any age, but in his own generation was exceptionally remarkable. A few words, however, may be added upon what was said of enthusiasm by one who was generally looked upon as the special enthusiast of his age. How much the usual meaning of the word has altered since the middle of the last century, is well illustrated by the length at which he argues that 'enthusiasm' ought not to be applied only to religion, and that it should be used in a good as well as in a bad sense.[1] It is 'a miserable mistake,' he says, 'to treat the real power and operation of an inward life of God in the birth of our souls, as fanaticism and enthusiasm.'[2] 'It is the running away from this enthusiasm that has made so many great scholars as useless to the Church as tinkling cymbals, and all Christendom a mere Babel of learned confusion.'[3] Instead of being blamable, the enthusiasm, which meant perfect dependence on the immediate inspiration and guidance of the Holy Spirit in the whole course of life, was one, he said, in which every good Christian should endeavour to live and die.[4] But he was too wise a man not to warn his readers against expecting uncommon illuminations, visions, and voices, and revelations of mysteries. Extraordinary operations of the Holy Spirit granted to men raised up as burning and shining lights are not matters of common instruction.[5] Many a fiery zealot would be fitly rebuked by his words, 'Would you know the sublime, the exalted, the angelic in the Christian life, see what the Son of God saith, "Thou shalt love the Lord thy God with all thy heart, and thy neighbour as thyself." And without these two things no good light ever can arise or enter into your soul.'[6]

John Byrom, whose life and poetical writings will be found in Chalmers' edition of the British poets, has already

[1] *Appeal*, &c., 301–13.
[2] *Spirit of Love*, pt. ii. 46. *Spirit of Prayer*, pt. i. 55.
[3] *Answer to Dr. Trapp*, 87. [4] *Appeal*, &c. 310–3.
[5] *Spirit of Prayer*, pt. ii. 202. [6] Id.

been slightly referred to. His works would demand more attention at this point, were they not to a great degree an echo in rhyme of William Law's prose works. One of his longest poems was written in 1751, on the publication of Law's 'Appeal,' &c., upon the subject of 'Enthusiasm.' It may be said of it, as of several other pieces he has left, that although written in very pedestrian verse, they are worth reading, as containing some thoughtful remarks, expressed occasionally with a good deal of epigrammatic force. A few of his hymns and short meditations rise to a higher poetical level. They are referred to with much praise by Mr. G. Macdonald,[1] who adds the just remark that 'The mystical thinker will ever be found the reviver of religious poetry.' Like Law, John Byrom was a great admirer of Behmen. He learnt High Dutch for the purpose of studying him in the original, and, nowise daunted by the many dark parables he found there, paraphrased in his halting rhymes what Socrates had said of Heraclitus :—

> All that I understand is good and true,
> And what I don't, is I believe so too.[2]

The same influences, springing from a German origin, which thus deeply and directly impressed William Law, and a few other devout men of the same type of thought, acted upon the national mind far more widely, but also far more indirectly, through a different channel. The Moravian brethren, though dating in the first instance from the time of Huss, owed their resuscitation to that wave of mystic pietism which passed through Germany in the seventeenth century,[3] showing its early power in the writings of Behmen, and reaching its full tide in the new vigour of spiritual life inspired into the Lutheran Church by the activity of Arndt and Spener. Their work was carried on by Francke, 'the S. Vincent de Paul of Germany.' Educated by him, and trained up in the teaching of Spener's School at Halle, Count Zinzendorf imbibed those

---

[1] G. Macdonald's *England's Antiphon*, 288.
[2] Chalmers' *English Poets*, xv. 269. *Thoughts on Human Reason.*
[3] M. J. Matter, *Histoire de Christianisme*, vol. iv. 347. H. J. Rose, *Protestantism in Germany*, 46-9. Dorner's *History of Protestant Theology*, ii. 217–227.

principles which he carried out with such remarkable success
in his Moravian settlement at Herrnhut. There he organised
a community to which their severest critics have never refused a high amount of admiration ; a society which set itself
with simple zeal to lead a Christian life after the primitive
model—frugal, quiet, industrious, shunning temptation and
avoiding controversy,—a band of brethren who held out the
hand of fellowship to all in every communion who, without
giving up a single distinctive tenet, would unite with them in a
union of godly living—which sent out labourers into Christian
countries to convert but not to proselytise—whose missionaries were to be found among the remotest heathen savages.
That they should fall short of their ideal was but human
weakness ; and no doubt they had their special failings.
They might be apt, in the fervency of their zeal, to speak too
disdainfully of all gifts of learning ; [1] they might risk alterna-
tions of distressing doubt by too presumptuous expectations
of visible supernatural help ; [2] they might think too lightly of
all outward aids to religion.[3]   Such errors might, and sometimes did, prove very dangerous.   But one who knew them
well, and to whom, as his mind expanded, their too parental
discipline, their timid fears of reasoning, their painful straining
for experiences, had become intolerable, could yet say of
them, ' There is not throughout Christendom, in our day,
a form of public worship which expresses more thoroughly
the spirit of true Christian piety, than does that of the Herrnhut brotherhood. . . . It is the truest Christian community, I
believe, which exists in the outward world.' [4]

The first Diaspora, or missionary colony, established by
the Moravians in England was in 1728, at the instance of a
lady in that centre of intellectual and religious activity, the
Court of Queen Caroline.   They did not, however, attract
much attention.   Whiston, ever inquisitive and unsettled,
wanted to know more about them, and began to read some of
their sermons, but ' found so much weakness and enthusiasm
mixed with a great degree of seriousness,' that he did not care

---

[1] Matter, *Histoire*, &c. 348.
[2] Lavington's *Enthusiasm of Methodists and Papists*, 1747, § 14.   [3] Id. 20.
[4] Schleiermacher, in a Letter to his Sister, 1805 ; F. Rowan's *Life of Schleiermacher*, ii. 23.

to go to their worship.[1] Their strictly organised discipline was in itself a great impediment to success among a people so naturally attached to liberty as the English. In the middle of the century, their missionary enterprise secured them special privileges in the American colonies. More than this. At the instance of Gambold, who was exceedingly anxious that the Brotherhood should gain ground in England within the bosom of the Anglican Church, a Moravian synod, held in 1749, formally elected Wilson, the venerable Bishop of Sodor and Man, 'into the order and number of the Antecessors of the General Synod of the brethren of the Anatolic Unity.' With this high sounding dignity was joined 'the administration of the Reformed Tropus' (or Diaspora) 'in our hierarchy, for life, with full liberty, in case of emergency, to employ as his substitute the Rev. T. Wilson, Royal Almoner, Doctor of Theology, and Prebendary of St. Peter's, Westminster.' It is further added that the good old man accepted the office with thankfulness and pleasure.[2] Here their success ended. Soon afterwards many of the English Moravians fell for a time into a most unsatisfactory condition, becoming largely tainted with Antinomianism, and with a sort of vulgar lusciousness of religious sentiment, which was exceedingly revolting to ordinary English feeling.[3] After the death of Zinzendorf in 1760, the Society recovered for the most part a healthier condition,[4] but did not regain any prospect of that wider influence in England which Gambold and others had once begun to hope for, and perhaps to anticipate.

Warburton said of Methodism, that 'William Law was its father, and Count Zinzendorf rocked the cradle.'[5] The remark was no doubt a somewhat galling one to Wesley, for he had afterwards conceived a great abhorrence of the opinions

---

[1] Whiston's *Life*, by Himself, 575.

[2] Hatton's *Memoirs*, p. 246, quoted in L. Tyerman's ' Life of J. Gambold,' in his *Oxford Methodists*, 188.   Archbishop Potter, in 1737, wrote a Latin letter to Zinzendorf, full of sympathy and interest.   It is given in Doddridge's *Correspondence*, v. 264.

[3] Mosheim's *Ecclesiastical History*, 1758, vol. v. 86. Doddridge's *Correspondence*, v. 271, note.. Remarks on Stinstra's ' Letters,' in J. Hughes' *Correspondence*, 1772, ii. 204-5.

[4] Tyerman, *Oxford Methodists*, 197.

[5]. Warburton's ' Doctrine of Grace,' chap. vi.—*Works*, 1788, 4, 626.

both of the father and the nurse. But it was perfectly just; and Wesley, though he might have been unwilling to own it, was greatly and permanently indebted to each. The light which, when he read Law's 'Christian Perfection and Serious Call,' had 'flowed so mightily on his soul that everything appeared in a new view,' was rekindled into a still more fervent flame by the glowing words of the Moravian teacher on the morning of the day from which he dated his special 'conversion.' Nor was his connection with men of this general turn of thought by any means a passing one. His visit to William Law at Mr. Gibbon's house at Putney in 1732—the correspondence he carried on with him for several years afterwards—his readings of the mystic divines of Germany—his loving respect for the company of Moravians who were his fellow travellers to Georgia in 1736—his meeting with Peter Böhler in 1738—the close intercourse which followed with the London Moravians—the fortnight spent by him at Herrnhut, 'exceedingly strengthened and comforted by the conversation of this lovely people,'[1]—his intimate friendship with Gambold, who afterwards completely threw in his lot with the United Brethren and became one of their bishops,[2]—all these incidents betoken a deep and cordial sympathy. It is true that all this fellow-feeling came at last to a somewhat abrupt termination. Passing, at first, almost to the bitter extreme, he even said in his 'Second Journal' that 'he believed the mystic writers to be one great Anti-Christ.'[3] Some years afterwards he retracted this expression, as being far too strong. He had, he said, 'at one time held the mystic writers in great veneration as the best explainers of the Gospel of Christ;'[4] but added, that though he admired them, he was never of their way; he distrusted their tendency to disparage outward means. 'Their divinity was never the Methodist doctrine. They could not swallow either John Tauler or Jacob Behmen.'[5] His friendly correspondence with Law ceased after a few years. He continued to 'admire and love' his personal character, but

---

[1] Wesley's *Journal*. Quoted in *Wesley's Life*, Religious Tract Society, 34.

[2] 'Life of Gambold,' in L. Tyerman's *Oxford Methodists*, 155–200.

[3] *Second Journal*, p. 26–7. (Quoted by Lavington, § 21); and *Works*, ed. x. 438.

[4] 'Remarks on Mr. Hill's Review,' &c.—*Works*, x. 438.

[5] 'Answer to Lavington.'—*Works*, ix. 49.

attacked his opinions [1] with a vehemence contrasting somewhat unfavourably with the patience and humility of Law's
reply.[2]   As for the Moravians, not Warburton, nor Lavington,
nor Stinstra, nor Duncombe, ever used stronger words against
'these most dangerous of the Antinomians—these cunning
hunters.'[3]   Count Zinzendorf, on the other hand, published a
notice that his people had no connection with the Wesleys.

Like many other men who have been distinguished in
divinity and religion,[4] John Wesley, as he grew older, became
far more charitable and large-hearted in what he said or
thought of opinions different from his own.   Methodism also
had become, by that time, well established upon a secure
basis of its own.   Wesley had no longer cause to be disturbed by its features of relationship with a school of theology
which he had learnt greatly to distrust.   The fanciful and
obscure philosophy of Dionysius, of Behmen, or of Law had
been repugnant to him from the first.   He had beheld with
the greatest alarm Law's departures from commonly received
doctrine on points connected with justification, regeneration,
the atonement, the future state.   Above all, he had become
acquainted with that most degenerate form of mysticism,
when its phraseology becomes a pretext to fanatics and
Antinomians.   Much in the same way as in the Germany of
the fourteenth century the lawless Brethren of the Free Spirit [5]
had justified their excesses in language which they borrowed
from men of such noble and holy life as Eckhart [6] and Tauler,
and Nicolas of Basle, so the flagitious conduct, at Bedford
and elsewhere, of some who called themselves Moravians
threw scandal and odium on the tenets of the pure and simple-
minded community of Herrnhut.   This was a danger to which
Wesley was, without doubt, all the more sensitive, because

---

[1] 'Letter to Mr. Law.'—*Works*, ix. 466-509.

[2] I. Taylor, *Wesley and Methodism*, 33.

[3] 'Short View,' &c.—*Works*, x. 201.   'My soul,' he wrote in one of his
journals, 'is sick of their *sublime* divinity.' Quoted in H. Curteis, *Dissent in
Relation to the Church of England*, 366.

[4] Dean Stanley instances, in addition to Wesley, Athanasius, Augustine,
Luther, and Baxter.—*Speech at Edinburgh*, January 2, 1872.

[5] S. Winkworth's *Tauler's Life and Times*, 86.

[6] Id.; also a review of F. Pfeiffer's 2nd vol. of *Deutsche Mystiker* (Meister
Eckhart) in *Saturday Review*, January 9, 1858, and *British Quarterly*, October
1874, 300-5.

he lived among hostile critics who were only too ready to
discredit his teaching by similar imputations on its tendencies.
The truth is that Methodism, in its different aspects, had so
many points of contact with the essential characteristics of
mysticism, both in its highest and most spiritualised, and in
its grosser and more fanatical forms, that Wesley was exceedingly anxious his system should not be confused with
any such 'enthusiasm,' and dwelt with jealous care upon its
more distinctive features.

It has been already observed that a French historian of
Christianity speaks of Quakerism and Methodism as the two
chief forms of English mysticism.[1] To an educated man of
ordinary observation in the eighteenth century, especially if
he regarded the new movement with distrust, the analogy
between this and different or earlier varieties of 'enthusiasm'
appeared still more complete. Lord Lyttelton, for example,
in discussing a favourite theological topic of that age—namely,
the absence of enthusiasm in St. Paul, and his constant
appeals to the evidence of reason and the senses—contrasts
with the life and writings of the Apostles the extravagant
imaginations, and the pretensions to Divine illumination, of
'mystics, ancient and modern,' mediæval saints, 'Protestant
sectaries of the last age, and some of the Methodists now.'[2]
Montanus and Dionysius, St. Francis and Ignatius Loyola,
Madame Bourignon, George Fox, and Whitefield are all
ranked together in the same general category. Methodists,
Moravians, and Hutchinsonians are classed as all nearly-
related members of one family. Just in the same way[3] Bishop
Lavington, in his 'Enthusiasm of Methodists and Papists,' has
entered into an elaborate comparison between what he finds in
Wesley's journals and in the lives and writings of saints and
mystics of the Roman Church.[4] Nor does he fail to discover
similar resemblances to Methodist experiences among the old
mystic philosophers, Montanists, Quakers, French Quietists,
French prophets, and Moravians. The argumentative value
of Lavington's book may be taken for what it was worth. To
his own contemporaries it appeared the achievement of a

---

[1] M. J. Matter's *Histoire du Christianisme*, 4, 343.
[2] *Works of George, Lord Lyttelton*, 239.   [3] Id. 271.
[4] *Enthusiasm of Romanists and Methodists Compared*, passim.

great triumph if he could prove in frequent cases an almost identical tone of thought in Wesley and in Francis of Assisi or Francis de Sales. To most minds in our own days it will rather seem as if he were constantly dealing blows which only rebounded upon himself, in comparing his opponent to men whose deep piety and self-denying virtues, however much tinged by the errors of their time and order, worked wonders in the revival of earnest faith. On the whole Lavington proved his case successfully, but he only proved by what easy transitions the purest and most exalted faith may pass into extravagancies, and, above all, the folly of his own Church in not endeavouring to find scope for her enthusiasts and mystics, as Rome had done for a Loyola and a St. Theresa. He himself was a typical example of the tone of thought out of which this infatuation grew. What other views could be looked for from a bishop who, though himself an awakening preacher and a good man, whose dying words [1] were an ascription of glory to God (δόξα τῷ Θεῷ), was yet so wholly blind to the more intense manifestations of religious fervour that he could see nothing to admire, nothing even to approve, in the burning zeal of the founders of the Franciscans and of the Jesuits? Of the first he had nothing more to say than that he was 'at first only a well-minded but weak enthusiast, afterwards a mere hypocrite and impostor;' of the other he spoke with a certain compassion as 'that errant, shatterbrained, visionary fanatic.' [2] And the Methodist, he thought, had a somewhat 'similar texture of brain.'

The Methodist leaders were wholly free from some dangerous tendencies which mysticism has been apt to develop. They never disparaged any of the external aids to religion; their meaning is never hidden under a haze of dim conceptions; above all, they never showed the slightest inclination to the vague and unpractical pantheistic opinions which are often nurtured by a too exclusive insistance on the indwelling and pervading operations of the Divine Spirit. In the two latter points they resembled the Quietist and Port-Royal mystics of the French school, who always aimed at lucidity of thought and language, rather than those of German

[1] Polwhele's *Introduction to Lavington*, clxxx.
[2] Lavington's *Enthusiasm*, &c., § 2.

Q Q 2

origin. From mystics generally they differed, most of all, in adopting the Pauline rather than the Johannine phraseology.

But, with some important differences, there can be no question that Methodism rose and prospered under the same influences which in every age of Christianity, or rather in every age of the world, have attended all the most notable outbursts of mystic revivalism. Its causes were the same ; its higher manifestations were much the same ; its degenerate and exaggerated forms were the same; its primary and most essential principle was the same. As the religious brotherhoods of the Pythagoreans rose in spiritual revolt against the lax mythology and careless living of the Sybarites in Sicily ; [1] as in the third century of the Christian era Neoplatonism concentrated within itself whatever remains of faith and piety lingered in the creeds and philosophies of paganism ; [2] as in the Middle Ages devout men, wearied with forms and controversies, and scholastic reasoners seeking refuge from the logical and metaphysical problems with which they had perplexed theology, sought more direct communion with God in the mystic devotion of Anselm and Bernard, of Hugo and Bonaventura ; [3] as Bertholdt and Nicolas, Eckhart and Tauler,[4] organised their new societies throughout Germany to meet great spiritual needs which established systems had wholly ceased to satisfy ; as Arndt and Spener and Francke in the seventeenth century breathed new life into the Lutheran Church, and set on foot their 'collegia pietatis,' their systematised prayer-meetings, to supplement the deficiencies of the time[5]—so in the England of the eighteenth century, when the force of religion was chilled by drowsiness and indifference in some quarters, by stiffness and formality and over-cautious orthodoxy in others, when the aspirations of the soul were being ever bidden rest satisfied

---

[1] G. Grote's *History of Greece*, chap. xxxvii. There is a full and interesting account of the Pythagorean revival in Dr. F. Schwartz's *Geschichte der Erziehung*, 1829, 301-21.

[2] H. H. Milman, *Early History of Christianity*, 1840, ii. 237.

[3] H. H. Milman, *Lat. Christianity*, 1857, iii. 270, vi. 263, 287 ; R. A. Vaughan, *Hours with the Mystics*, i. 49, 152.

[4] Milman's *Lat. Christianity*, vi. 371-80 ; Winkworth's *Life and Times of Tauler*, 186.

M. J. Matter's *Histoire du Christianisme*, 4, 347 ; H. T. Rose, *Protestantism in Germany*, 50.

with the calculations of sober reason, when proofs and evidences and demonstrations were offered, and still offered, to meet the cry of those who called for light, how else should religion stem the swelling tide of profligacy but by some such inward spiritual revival as those by which it had heretofore renewed its strength? If Wesley and Whitefield and their fellow-workers had not come to the rescue, no doubt other reformers of a somewhat kindred spirit would have risen in their stead. How or whence it is useless to speculate. Perhaps Quakerism, or something nearly akin to it, might have assumed the dimensions to which a half-century before it had seemed not unlikely to grow. The way was prepared for some strong reaction. Past aberrations of enthusiasm were well-nigh forgotten, and large masses of the population were unconsciously longing for its warmth and fire. It was highly probable that an active religious movement was near at hand, and its general nature might be fairly conjectured; its specific character, its force, extent, and limits, would depend, under Providence, upon the zeal and genius of its leaders.

Nothing could be more natural than that to many outside observers early Methodism should have seemed a mere repetition of what England, in the century before, had been only too familiar with. The physical phenomena which manifested themselves under the influence of Wesley's and Whitefield's preaching were in all points exactly the same as those of which the annals of imaginative and excited religious feeling have in every age been full. Swoons and strange convulsive agitations, however impressive and even awe-inspiring to an uninformed beholder, were undistinguishable from those, for example, which had given their name to English Quakers [1] and French Convulsionists,[2] which were to be read of in the Lives of Guyon and St. Theresa,[3] and which were a matter of continual occurrence when Tauler preached in Germany.[4] It is no part of this inquiry to dwell upon their cause and nature, or upon the perplexity Wesley himself felt

---

[1] C. Leslie's *Works*, 'The Snake in the Grass,' and 'Defence &c.' Id. vols. iv. and v. passim; R. A. Vaughan's *Hours with the Mystics*, ii. 255–60; Barclay's *Apology*, 339.

[2] N. Spinckes, *New Pretenders to Prophecy*, 1709, 402, &c.

[3] Vaughan, ii. 165–208.   [4] Winkworth's *Life of Tauler*, 172.

on the subject. Occasionally he was mortified by the discovery of imposture or of superstitious credulity, and something he was willing to attribute to natural causes.[1] On the whole his opinion was that they might be rejoiced in as a glorious sight,[2] visible evidences of life-giving spiritual agencies, but that the bodily pain was quite distinct and due to Satan's hindrance.[3] He sometimes added a needful warning that all such physical disturbances were of a doubtful nature, and that the only tests of spiritual change which could be relied upon were those indisputable fruits of the Spirit which the Apostle Paul enumerates.[4] His less guarded words closely correspond with what may be read in the journals of G. Fox and other early Quakers. When he writes more coolly and reflectively we are reminded not of the first fanatical originators of that sect, but of what their distinguished apologist, Barclay, has said of those 'pangs of the new birth' which have often accompanied the sudden awakening to spiritual life in persons of strong and undisciplined feelings. 'From their inward travail, while the darkness seeks to obscure the light and the light breaks through the darkness . . . . there will be such a painful travail found in the soul that will even work upon the outward man, so that oftentimes through the working thereof the body will be greatly shaken, and many groans, and sighs, and tears, will lay hold upon it.'[5]

Wesley himself was protected both by disposition and training from falling deeply into some of the dangers to which enthusiastic and mystical religion is very liable. He was credulous, and even superstitious, but he checked his followers in the credence which many of them were inclined to give to stories of ecstasies, and visions, and revelations. He spoke slightingly of orthodoxy, and held that 'right opinions were a very slender part of religion;'[6] but, far from countenancing anything like a vague undogmatic Pietism, his

[1] J. Wesley, 'Letter to the Bishop of Gloucester.'—*Works*, ix. 137, 142.
[2] Wesley's *Journal*, quoted by Lavington, *Enthusiasm*, &c., 271.
[3] *Works*, ix. 121; and *Journal*, 1738-43, quoted by Warburton, 'Doctrine of Grace,' *Works*, iv. 605-73.
[4] *Works*, ix. 143.
[5] Barclay's *Apology*, 330. Cf. Wesley's 'Letter to W. Dewsbury,' 1759. *Works*, ix. 104-5.
[6] Wesley's *Plain Account of the People called the Methodists*, 6th ed. 1761, 4.

opinions went almost to the opposite extreme of precise definition. Neither could it be said of him that he spiritualised away the plain meaning of Scripture—a charge to which the old Quakers were constantly liable, and which was sometimes alleged against the later Methodists. He himself never spoke contemptuously—as the mystics have been so apt to do—of the value of learning ; and of reason he said, in the true spirit of Henry More, 'I believe and reason too, for I find no inconsistency between them. And I would as soon put out my eyes to secure my faith, as lay aside my reason.'[1] But the Methodists, as a body, were far less inclined to act on this principle. Without disparagement to the conspicuous ability of some individual members of their communion, both in the present and in the past, it may be certainly said that they have always utterly failed to attract the intellect of the country at large. Great, therefore, as was its moral and spiritual power among large classes of the people, Methodism was never able to take rank among great national reformations.

There was one point in which neither Wesley nor the Wesleyans have ever yielded to a mischievous tendency which has beset most forms of mysticism. They have never, in comparison with the inward worship of the soul, spoken slightingly of 'temples made of stones,'[2] or of any of the chief outward ordinances of religion. Their opponents often attempted to make it a charge against them, and thought, no doubt, they would be sure to prove it. But they never did so. Wesley was always able to answer, with perfect correctness, that what was thus said might be true of Moravians, or of Tauler, or of Behmen, or of St. Theresa, or of Madame de Bourignon, or of the Quakers, or even of William Law, but that he himself had never done otherwise than insist most strongly on the essential need of making use of all the external helps which religion can offer.[3]

By far the gravest imputation that has ever been brought against the disciples of each various form of mystical or emotional religion is that, in aspiring after some loftier ideal

---

[1] 'Predestination calmly Considered,' 1745.—*Works*, x. 267.

[2] Behmen, *Three Principles*, chap. xxvi.

[3] 'Answer to Lavington.'—*Works*, ix. 50 ; 'Letter to Mr. Law,' id. 505.

of spiritual communion with the Divine, they have looked
down with a kind of scorn upon 'mere morality,' as if it were
a lower path. And it must be acknowledged that men of the
most pure and saintly lives have, nevertheless, used expressions which misguided or unprincipled men might pervert into
authority for lawlessness. Tauler, whom an admiring contemporary once called 'the holiest of God's children now
living on the earth,'[1] could yet say of the higher elevation of
the Christian life that, 'where this comes to pass, outward
works become of no moment.'[2] What wonder that the
fanatical Beghards, or Brethren of the Free Spirit, against
whom he contended with all his energies,[3] should seek to
confuse his principles with theirs, and assert that, having
attained the higher state, they were not under subjection to
moral commandments? So, again, of the early Quakers
Henry More[4] observed that, although their doctrine of special
illumination had guided many into much sanctity of life, the
more licentious sort had perverted it into a cloke for all kinds
of enormity, on the ground that they were inspired by God,
and could be guilty of no sin, as only exercising their rights of
liberty. Madame de Bourignon was an excellent woman, but
Leslie and Lavington[5] showed that some of her writings
seem dangerously to underrate good works. Moravian
principles, rightly understood, made Herrnhut a model
Christian community; misunderstood, they became pretexts
for the most dangerous Antinomianism.[6] An example may
even be quoted from the last century where the nobler
elements of mystic enthusiasm were found in one mind
combined with the pernicious tendency in question. In that
very remarkable but eccentric genius, William Blake, mysticism was rich in fruits of faith and love, and it is needless,
therefore, to add that he was a good man, of blameless morals;
yet, by a strange flaw or partial derangement in his profoundly spiritual nature, 'he was for ever, in his writings,

[1] Winkworth's *Life, &c. of Tauler*, 96.
[2] Tauler, 'Sermon for Third Sunday after Epiphany,' Id. 223.
[3] Id. 86, 137-8.
[4] H. More's note to § 44 of *Enthus. Triumphatus*.
[5] C. Leslie, *Works*, iv. 5-8; Lavington, 346.
[6] Mosheim's *Ecclesiastical History*, 1758, v. 86 (note); Tyerman, *Oxford Methodists*, 194; Wesley, continually; &c.

girding at the "mere moral law" as the letter that killeth. His conversation, his writings, his designs, were equally marked by theoretic license and virtual guilelessness.' [1]

The dangerous bias thus illustrated is owing to a sort of pantheistic confusion of right and wrong, occasionally found among enthusiasts who have so exaggerated and distorted the doctrine of inward illumination as to attribute the suggestions of their own mind to the promptings of the Divine Spirit. We have seen that the sayings of one of the greatest preachers of righteousness whom Germany in the fourteenth century produced were wrested into a meaning from which his soul abhorred. But of Tauler it has been correctly said that 'he often seems to tread to the verge of the pantheistic abyss, though he never falls into it;' [2] John Wesley, on the other hand, was wholly free from any sort of approximation to it; yet, like Tauler, Wesley also was perpetually charged with being an enthusiast whose doctrines undermined immutable distinctions of right and wrong. He deserved the accusation as little as Tauler did. The soul and heart of all his teaching,[3] from which it chiefly gained its searching power, was the faith in a deliverance from, and a victory over, sin. He could appeal with pride, such as might worthily swell in an apostle's breast, to the results which proved the moral strength with which he led the reaction against moralities. 'If,' says he, 'you do not find that the greater part of these [certain Cornish Methodists] were a year or two ago notoriously wicked men, yet the main doctrines they have heard since were, "Love God and your neighbour, and carefully keep His commandments," and that they have since exercised themselves therein and continue so to do—I say, if any reasonable man, who will be at the pains to enquire, doth not find this to be an unquestionable fact, I will openly acknowledge myself an enthusiast, or whatever else he shall

---

[1] A. Gilchrist's *Life of W. Blake*, 331.

[2] R. A. Vaughan, *Hours with the Mystics*, i. 254. Warburton charged W. Law with teaching pantheism.—*Doctrine of Grace*, chap. vii. 'A mystic philosophy,' says I. Taylor (*History of Enthusiasm*, 302), 'is essentially pantheistic.' The term, however, is far too vague to mean much without further definition.

[3] Cf. F. D. Maurice, *Theological Essays*, 28.

please to call me.'[1] It may well be that some of the arguments employed to excite the imagination and stir the conscience were such as would repel rather than attract more
educated and thoughtful audiences than those among whom
Wesley and Whitefield won their greatest spiritual harvests.
Any form of religion, once eagerly accepted by the multitude,
is sure to contract some grosser properties,[2] although they may
not impair to any great extent its vital essence. All such
imperfections will be lightly passed over in taking account of
a movement undoubtedly rich in abundant fruits of good
works. Nor is the high tone of Wesley's moral teaching to
be estimated only by its effects, or by his constant insistance
upon outward as well as inward holiness. The dangers of
Antinomianism were constantly present to his mind. He
turned with alarm from the Moravians as soon as he saw in
some of their congregations a tendency in this direction. He
promised never again to use intentionally the term 'imputed
righteousness,' when once he found the 'immense hurt which
the frequent use of this unnecessary phrase had done.'[3] Much
of his hostility to Calvinism arose from suspicion of its ethical
bearings. He saw that his own doctrine of Christian perfection might be used to countenance the same error, and carefully sought to counteract the danger by teaching the possibility of losing the gift.

These examples may serve to show with what anxious care
Wesley sought to guard against the approaches of an Antinomianism which he undoubtedly thought the worst of all
possible heresies ; but they also indicate that he felt cause
for anxiety, and point to weaknesses which many a keen-
sighted critic had been quick to observe and exaggerate. It
was not impracticable to find even in Wesley's works passages
which, like some parallel sayings of Luther, might be abused
into meaning that a man might sin boldly, for Christ would
pay the debt.[4] And when he wrote that 'true religion doth

---

[1] Wesley's 'Answer to Lavington.'—*Works*, ix. 20.
[2] Cf. Newman's 'Letter to Pusey,' 1866, quoted in Hatch's *Notes on Shaftesbury*, 16.
'Treatise on Justification,' 1764.—*Works*, x. 311 ; *Remarks on Mr. Hill's
Remarks*, &c., 1772, x. 376.
[4] *Third Journal*, 18, quoted by Lavington, 347.

not consist in any or all of these three things : the living harmless, using the means of grace, and doing much good ; ' that 'a man may do all this and yet have no true religion at all,' for this 'consists in God's dwelling and reigning within the heart,'[1] no later qualifications could remove the impression, that such words must have an ill effect on minds less penetrated than his own with the conviction that a pure and lofty morality is absolutely essential to the very idea of holiness. There seems little doubt that to some extent this was the case, not so much during the earlier stages of the movement as later in the century. After making large allowances for prejudice and aversion on the part of its opponents, it appears that the Antinomianism which Wesley so greatly dreaded did gain some footing[2] in the societies established by him. No form of emotional or mystic religion has altogether escaped its contamination. Notwithstanding, it may be said of Methodism that to many thousands of souls it was an unmixed blessing. It stirred the sluggish spiritual nature to its depths ; it awoke the sense of sin and an eager longing to be delivered from it. To the age and Church in general its quickening action was scarcely less important, as providing to a considerable extent the very stimulus and corrective which prevailing tendencies most required. In all these respects it greatly resembled other revivals of spiritual religion which had taken place in previous ages in England and on the Continent. As contrasted with these, it had some characteristic defects, but more perhaps than a corresponding advantage in its closer adherence to the words of Scripture and its clearer definition of the objects of faith. Like them, it supplied those appeals to the heart and inward consciousness in which the religion of the time was most deficient ; like them, it was apt to develop those particular errors to which 'religion of the heart.' becomes

---

[1] *Journal*, 1739-1761, quoted by Warburton, *Doctrine of Grace*, ch. xi.

[2] This is evident not only from the writings of the opponents of Methodism, such as Lavington, Warburton, Downes, Dr. Horne, &c. (also *Review of the Doctrines and Policy of the Methodists*, 1791), but from the alarm occasionally evinced by Wesley himself on observing signs of it. Dorner speaks of it as beginning to show itself in some of their societies about 1770.—*History of Protestant Theology*, ii. 93.

susceptible when once it begins to decline into sentiment and impulse.

Methodism was, in most respects, a practical and not a theological movement. Yet that which Lavington triumphantly denounced in it as 'the true spirit and very essence of enthusiasm '—the belief, as held by Wesley, in an inward illumination, a Divine guidance of the spiritual understanding —brings it indirectly into the most intimate connection with the general history of religious thought. It must be allowed that Wesley's views on this subject were uncertain, if not inconsistent. On one occasion a complaint occurs in his journal of ' a spirit of enthusiasm breaking out among some of us, many charging their own imaginations on the will of God, and that not written, but impressed on their hearts. If these impressions be received as the rule of action, instead of the written word, I know nothing so wicked or absurd but we may fall into, and that without remedy.' [1] These are decisive words, and, taken by themselves, might seem to place Wesley among the ranks of those who entirely distrusted the evidence of inward feeling. But this, it need scarcely be remarked, was very far from being the case. He held fast to two guarantees against what he considered to be enthusiasm. One was that all supposed inspirations should be proved by their consistency with Scripture, or (to use his own favourite expression) ' should be brought to the only certain test—the law and the testimony.' The other was that no special gifts of inspiration are to be laid claim to but such as are part of the common inheritance of all faithful Christians.[2] If, therefore, an asserted revelation were in accord with Wesley's interpretation of ' the law and the testimony,' it only remained to ask whether it were a gift of Divine guidance such as any true believer might fairly hope to receive. Here Wesley unconsciously left an opening to a considerable amount of credulity. For, to his mind, God's government of the world implied a very frequent interposition of Divine power, over-ruling all ordinary agencies. His journals abound in accounts of special providences which he allows to be scarcely distinguishable from miracles, and of

---

[1] *Fourth Journal,* quoted by Lavington, 121.
[2] 'Answer to Church,' 39, quoted in Lavington, 123, and 'Letter to Rev. Mr. Bailey,' 1750.—*Works,* ix. 91.

spiritual assistances and inspirations exactly analogous to those, for example, which are to be found in the early Quaker narratives, except only in this, that Wesley would not allow that they lay, in any proper sense, beyond the range of ordinary experience.

This exception is, however, one of essential importance. Wesley was quite right in assuming that enthusiasm gives cause for grave distrust only when it begins to lay claim to extraordinary gifts and revelations in which humanity in general has no share. Calmer reasoning and wider experience soon correct any credulity to which a heated imagination has given rise, when their conclusions must be grounded on no exceptional phenomena, but on a wide range of spiritual experience. From a general point of view it mattered little that, personally, Wesley was somewhat inclined to a superstitious belief in prodigies. The impression left by his preaching upon theological thought was effected by the conviction it produced of too little attention having been paid to spiritual powers which, so far from being prodigies, are the inalienable possession of all men. Although Wesley's views of un-Christianised human nature were very dark, he has quoted with approbation as ' a great truth' the saying of an ancient philosopher which ascribes to every soul of man an element of Divine inspiration,—' Nemo sine afflatu divino fuit.'[1] How much more so in those in whom the light of Christian faith has fully risen ! To men bred up in the shallow theology of the age, who made bare reason arbiter of all truth, and only smiled to remark how

> Modern Methodists derive
> Their light from no Divine alive,[2]

Wesley answered that this belief in spiritual inspiration, which they spoke of as if it were but feeble enthusiasm, was one of the fundamental doctrines of Christianity, and that they who deny it stab the Church to her very vitals.[3] The Liturgy, the Articles, the Homilies, the great expounders of her creeds, all, he said, dwell upon the necessity of the enlightening

---

[1] ' On the Doctrine of Original Sin,' 1756.— *Works,* ix. 201.

[2] J. G. Cooper's *Poems,* Epistle IV.

' Answer to Bailey.'— *Works,* x. 83.

operation of the Holy Spirit. And yet on the mentioning of these great truths, even among men of education, the cry immediately arises, 'An enthusiast! an enthusiast!'[1] and while 'in the desk the clergy prayed God to cleanse the thoughts of their hearts by the inspiration of the Holy Spirit, in the pulpit they said there was no such thing as inspiration since the time of the Apostles.'[2]

There may be some slight exaggeration in the tone of Wesley's words on this subject; but, at all events, the Methodist revival marked a decided turn, not only in popular feeling on religious topics and in the language of the pulpit, but also in theological and philosophical thought in general. It was scarcely possible for those who had witnessed the effects of Wesley's and of Whitefield's preaching to speak or write as if a firm conviction of Christian truth could proceed only from the logic of evidences. Warburton might argue in dignified language that it 'could be no wisdom from above which, instead of giving the Christian faith the manly support of moral demonstration, resolves all into internal feelings and mystic spiritualism.'[3] There lurked a fallacy in the word 'all.' Wesley never disparaged reason; but henceforth inward feeling and spiritual discernment were to reassume a place in the analysis of religious thought which for a long time had been denied to them. The arguments both of Deists and of evidence-writers rapidly became obsolete, when it was felt that both one and the other—the latter even more than the former—had almost omitted from their reasonings faculties which might prove to be among the most important of which human nature is capable, but which had been contemptuously given over to the speculations of so-called mystics and enthusiasts. Wesley himself was evidently somewhat doubtful how to define the inspired illuminating power by which man is enabled to apprehend Divine truth. It might sometimes seem as if he were disposed almost to identify it with justifying faith in a narrowed sense of the term. Elsewhere he speaks of it unhesitatingly as a light refused to none. His firm belief in this great spiritual gift certainly widened his

---

[1] ' Letter to Bishop of Gloucester.'— *Works*, ix. 170.
[2] ' Letter to Rev. Mr. Potter,' 1758.— *Works*, x. 107.
[3] ' Doctrine of Grace,' chap. vii. — *Works*, iv. 633.

charity, and enabled him to speak of good men of every creed or denomination with a liberality which greatly scandalised some of his followers, and provoked Rowland Hill into exclaiming that 'he defied anyone to discover whether the apostle of the Foundry were a Jew, a Papist, a Pagan, or a Turk.' [1]

There is an interesting passage in Wesley's letter to Middleton, in which he dwells upon the testimony, amounting to positive assurance, which spiritual realities receive from inward experience. 'This,' he says, 'I conceive to be the strongest evidence of the truth of Christianity. I do not undervalue traditional evidence. Let it have its place and due honour. It is highly serviceable in its kind and in its degree. And yet I cannot set it on a level with this. It is generally supposed that traditional evidence is weakened by length of time, as it must necessarily pass through so many hands in a continued succession of ages. But no length of time can possibly affect the strength of this internal evidence. . . . It passes at once, as it has done from the beginning, into the believing soul. Traditional evidence is of an extremely complicated nature. . . . On the contrary, how plain and simple is this, and how level to the lowest capacity! The traditional evidence of Christianity stands, as it were, a great way off . . . . whereas the inward evidence is intimately present to all persons, at all times, and in all places. It is nigh thee, in thy mouth and in thy heart, if thou believest in the Lord Jesus Christ. . . . If, then, it were possible (which I conceive it is not) to shake the traditional evidence of Christianity, still he that hath this internal evidence would stand firm and unshaken. . . . I have sometimes been almost inclined to believe that the wisdom of God has, in most later ages, permitted the external evidence of Christianity to be more or less clogged and encumbered for this very end, that men (of reflection especially) might not altogether rest there, but be constrained to look into themselves also, and attend to the light shining in their hearts. Nay, it seems (if it may be allowed to pry into the reasons of the Divine dispensations) that, particularly in this age, God suffers all kinds of objections to be raised against the traditional evidences of

---

[1] Rowland Hill's *Imposture Detected*, and Wesley's *Answer*, 1777, x. 453.

Christianity, that men of understanding may not rest the whole strength of their cause thereon, but seek a deeper and a firmer support for it. Without this I cannot but doubt whether they can long maintain their cause ; whether, if they do not obey the loud call of God, and lay far more stress than they have hitherto done on this internal evidence of Christianity, they will not, one after another, give up the external and (in heart at least) go over to those whom they are now contending with, so that in a century or two the people of England will be fairly divided into real Deists and real Christians. . . . Nay, perhaps it would be the speediest— yea, the only effectual—way of bringing all reasonable Deists to be Christians.' A few lines after, turning to the Deists, he exclaims, ' Go on, gentlemen, and prosper. Shame these nominal Christians out of that poor superstition which they call Christianity. Reason, rally, laugh them out of their dead, empty forms, void of spirit, of faith, of love. . . . Press on, push your victories, till you have conquered all that know not God. And then He, whom neither they nor you know now, shall rise and gird Himself with strength, and go forth in His almighty love and sweetly conquer you all together.'[1]

No apology is needed for this lengthened quotation, both because it is one of the finest and most thoughtful passages in Wesley's writings, and because it pointedly expresses the intimate connection of the Methodist movement, and the train of thought which it evolved, with the Deistical con- troversies of the first half of the century, and the influence exercised by S. Coleridge and others towards its close. Strange as it may at first seem, Wesley was sometimes accused by his Calvinistic opponents[2] of expressing just such opinions as might be expected from a Deist. It was, in fact, the same charge which Wesley himself had brought against

---

[1] 'Letter to Dr. Middleton,' 1749.—*Works*, x. 76-7.

[2] Thus Hervey wrote: ' You scarce distinguish yourself by this language from a heretic. You may rank with the Arian and Socinian.' (Quoted by Wesley in his ' Treatise on Justification,' a reply to Hervey's ' Theron and Aspasio.'—*Works*, x. 391.) Rowland Hill wrote, ' All the divinity we find in this wretched harangue, which he calls a sermon, are a few bungling scraps of the religion of nature . . . . which a heathen might have preached as well as Mr. John, and probably in a much better manner.' (Quoted by Wesley in his ' Answer to R. Hill.' *Works*, x. 433.)

William Law [1] and the mystics in general, and was grounded
for the most part upon the same objection of making Christianity too wide, too undefined and subjective, too dependent
upon ideas and feelings, too neglectful of orthodoxy and
traditional formulas. The so-called 'Christian Deists' themselves sometimes appealed to the Methodists in confirmation of
their position that facts and history were too slender supports
on which to rest the entire superstructure of revelation. Thus
Henry Dodwell, in his 'Christianity not Founded upon Argument,' [2] published in 1742—a work written professedly against

[1] 'Letter to W. Law,'—*Works,* ix. 480, 493.

[2] The general argument of this treatise was that faith was grounded, not
upon reason, with which it had little or nothing in common, but upon what he
termed 'inspiration,' or 'infused evidence,' or 'internal sense,' imparted to
individuals by special grace of the Holy Spirit, but capable of being improved
by diligence. (Cf. Bishop E. Law's criticism of it in *Considerations upon
the Theory of Religion,* 21.) 'In a predestinarian manner,' says Dorner
(*Hist. of Prot. Theol.* ii. 87), 'he approximates to Quakerism.' The Deistical
tendency of the book was generally recognised by all who were contending on
either side, for or against 'the reasonableness of Christianity.' Opinion, however, was very much divided about it, and some very religious people welcomed
it with delight. Doddridge said of it, 'It is a most artful attempt, in the person
of a Methodist, but made indeed by a very sagacious Deist, to subvert Christianity ;
and it wounds as a two-edged sword, tending most dangerously to spread mad
enthusiasm among some and utter irreligion among others.' 'It is in high reputation,' he adds, 'among the nobility and gentry' (Doddridge's *Diary and
Corresp.* 111, 110.) The Methodists were, generally, not at all inclined to
repudiate their unexpected supporter. 'Our good Methodists do not much
approve of your answer to *Christianity not Founded upon Argument.* Seagrave
(a Cambridge Methodist of much repute) was but this day in the coffee-house
vindicating the book you wrote against' (Jennings to Doddridge, id. 179.)
The real intention of the author has always been uncertain. 'More than once
the irony is apparent' (Hunt, *Rel. Th.,* 9, 111, 180). Nevertheless even the
irony may be unintentional, and often he appears to be quite in earnest. In
any case the treatise was suggestive of thought, and highly characteristic of a
period when many minds, unsettled and perplexed by Deistical arguments, were
turning their attention, with a half-incredulous hope, to Methodism, not so much
with any intention of joining the movement as from the idea of discovering in it
a new ground upon which to base more firmly a Christian faith. Dodwell, though
a man of very different opinions from his father, the Nonjuror, seems to have
inherited the same propensity of unintentionally confuting himself by pressing his
arguments to *ad absurdum* extremes. In the last pages of his treatise he quotes
Beveridge—'that a man may as soon read the letter of the Scripture without eyes
as understand the mysteries of the Gospel without grace' (p. 103), and soon
after continues, reasonably enough, 'Be satisfied henceforth that there is a kind
of evidence of power beyond what reason can ever pretend to furnish, such as
brings with it that cordial peace and assurance of mind to which all conviction
by human means is an utter stranger' (p. 115). His concluding words are

the Deists, but, in some respects, taking very much their point of view—calls the Methodists living witnesses of the thesis he had undertaken to prove. Thomas Chubb also quoted the Methodists in his support. No doubt they differed from him essentially ; for he acknowledged no guide in matters of religion but reason,[1] and they believed in Divine impressions, of which he, on his part, felt quite disqualified to say more than that he entirely distrusted them.[2] But they agreed with him, he said, in holding that Christian faith was not grounded upon reason.[3] His argument was good for its immediate purpose. The Methodists did undoubtedly act as unintentional allies of the Deists in so far as this, that they did much to attach a stamp of insufficiency on the most conscientious labours of the evidence-writers. But if they were allies in one respect they were among their most formidable opponents in another. About the time 'when Wesley's power Gathered new strength from hour to hour'[4] theological opinion was in much the same state in England as that described by Goethe[5] as existing in Germany when he left Leipzic in 1768 ; it was to a great extent fluctuating between an historical and traditionary Christianity on the one hand and pure Deism on the other. William Law in his own way and among a select but somewhat limited body of readers, Wesley in a more practical and far more popular manner, did very much to restore to English Christianity the element that was so greatly wanting—the appeal to a faculty with which the soul is gifted to recognise the inherent excellence, the beauty, truth, and divinity of a Divine Object once clearly set before it. Whatever may have been the respective deficiencies in the systems and

those in which the wise man bids his son ' Trust thou in the Lord with all thine heart, and lean not unto thine own understanding.' But he could not be satisfied with temperate conclusions. Almost at the beginning he lays it down as his ' full persuasion that the judging at all of religious matters is not the proper office of reason, nor indeed an affair where it has any concern ' (p. 7).

[1] Thomas Chubb, *Collection of Tracts*, 1732-4, title to ' Treatise on the Sufficiency of Reason,' vol. i. No. 1.

[2] Id., 'Ground of Morality,' &c., vol. iii. No. 7, p. 51.

[3] See two passages quoted by Hunt, *Rel. Th. in Eng.* III, 396.

[4] Chatterton's *Poems*, ' Apostate Will.'

[5] Goethe's *Life*, i. 247. qu. in H. J. Rose, *German Protestantism*, App. 8.

teaching of these men, they achieved at least this great result ; nor is it too much to say that it gave a death-blow to the then existing forms of Deism.

The intended limits of this chapter have already been considerably exceeded, and the subject has been so far illustrated that whatever remains to add may be very briefly touched upon.

Bishop Berkeley's name could not be passed over even in such a sketch as this without a sense of incompleteness. He was, it is true, strongly possessed with the prevalent feeling of aversion to anything that was called enthusiasm. When, for example, his opinion was asked about John Hutchinson—a writer whose mystic fancies as to recondite meanings contained in the words of the Hebrew Bible [1] possessed a strange fascination for William Jones of Nayland, Bishop Horne, and other men of some note [2]—he answered that he was not acquainted with his works, but ' I have observed him to be mentioned as an enthusiast, which gave me no prepossession in his favour.' [3]   But the Christianity of feeling, which lies at the root of all that is sound and true in what the age called enthusiasm, was much encouraged by the theology and philosophy of Berkeley.   It may not have been so to any great extent among his actual contemporaries.   A thoroughly prosaic generation, such as that was in which he lived, was too unable to appreciate his subtle and poetic intellect to gain much instruction from it.   He was much admired, but little understood.   ' He is indeed,' wrote Warburton to Hurd, ' a great man, and the only visionary I ever knew that was.' [4]   It was left for later reasoners, in England

---

[1] Warburton called him and his followers 'our new Cabalists.'—Letter to Doddridge, May 27, 1758.

[2] A full statement of Hutchinson's views may be found in the *Works of G. Horne,* by W. Jones (of Nayland), Pref. xix.-xxiii., 20-23, &c. His own views were visionary and extreme. Natural religion, for example, he called ' the religion of Satan and of Antichrist.' (Id. xix.) But he had many admirers, including many young men of promise at Oxford. (Id. 81.) They were attracted by the earnestness of his opposition to some theological tendencies of the age. It was to this reactionary feeling that his repute was chiefly owing. 'Of Mr. Hutchinson we hear but little ; his name was the match that gave fire to the train.' (Id. 92.)

[3] Berkeley to Johnson, July 25, 1751—*G. Berkeley's Life and Works,* ed. A. C. Fraser, iv. 326.

[4] Warburton and Hurd's *Correspondence,* Letter xx.

and on the Continent, to separate what may be rightly called
visionary in his writings from what may be profoundly true,
and to feel the due influence of his suggestive and spiritual
reflections.

The purely mystic element in Berkeley's philosophy may
be illustrated by the charm it had for William Blake, a man
of whom Mr. Swinburne says that 'his hardest facts were the
vaguest allegories of other men. To him all symbolic things
were literal, all literal things symbolic. About his path and
about his bed, around his ears and under his eyes, an infinite
play of spiritual life seethed and swarmed or shone and
sang.'[1] To this strange artist-poet, in whose powerful but
fantastic mind fact and imagination were inextricably
blended, whose most intimate friends could not tell where
talent ended and hallucination began, whom Wordsworth
delighted in,[2] and whose conversation in any country walk is
described as having a marvellous power of kindling the
imagination, and of making nature itself seem strangely more
spiritual, almost as if a new sense had awakened in the mind
of his hearer[3]—to William Blake the theories of Berkeley
supplied a philosophy which exactly suited him.[4] Blake's
ruling idea was that of an infinite spiritual life so imprisoned
under the bondage of material forces[5] that only by spiritual
perception—a power given to all to cultivate—can true
existence be discovered.[6] He longed for the full emancipation which a better life would bring.

[1] Alg. C. Swinburne, *W. Blake: a Critical Essay*, 41.
[2] A. Gilchrist's *Life of W. Blake*, i. 303.
It was not only that Wordsworth was at one with Blake in his intense feeling
of the mysterious loveliness of nature. There is also an occasional vein of
mysticism in his poetry. Thus it is observed in Ch. Wordsworth's *Memoirs of
his Life* (p. 111), that his *Expostulation and Reply* (1798) was a favourite with the
Quakers. It is the poem in which these verses occur :—

> 'Nor less I deem that there are powers
>   Which of themselves our minds impress ;
> That we can feed these minds of ours
>   In a wise passiveness.
>
> Think you, mid all this mighty sum
>   Of things for ever speaking,
> That nothing of itself will come,
>   But we must still be seeking ? '—*Poems*, iv. 180.

[3] Gilchrist, i. 311.   [4] Id. 190–1.
[5] Swinburne, 274.   [6] Gilchrist, 321.

> When will the Resurrection come, to deliver the sleepy body
> From corruptibility? Oh, when, Lord Jesus, wilt Thou come?[1]

Meanwhile it was the special task of that discerning faculty
of the soul—that enthusiasm[2] which is 'the first principle of
knowledge'—

> To open the eternal worlds : to open the immortal eye
> Of men inwards—into the world of thought—into eternity,
> Ever expanding in the bosom of God.[3]

Such were the leading principles of William Blake's inward
life ; and it may be easily understood how Bishop Berkeley
should have been one of his most favourite authors, because
no other philosophy helped him so much to the conception
of spiritual realities disengaged from material conditions.

But it must be acknowledged that there is a something
very incongruous in the notion of Berkeley's polished pages
inspiring, alternately with the 'Aurora' of Jacob Behmen, the
'fire and mist'[4] rhapsodies—as even his greatest admirers
must call them—of Blake. It is undoubtedly an association
which to the Bishop himself would have been as distasteful
as it would have seemed impossible. For although to both
matter appeared wholly unsubstantial as contrasted with
spiritual reality, and both were equally concerned in vindicating the absolute, unconditional supremacy of intelligence
over the forms in which it manifests itself, Berkeley's lucid
and practical mind would have acknowledged no sympathy
with any kind of mysticism. His whole scheme of philosophy
had a direct argumentative purpose as a contribution to the
controversy with the Deists. That portion of it which directly
relates to the spiritual discernment of Divine things had reference to the reasonings of Peter Browne, afterwards Bishop
of Cork, who had urged against Toland on the one hand,
and against all 'enthusiasts' on the other, that whatever has
been revealed to us of the nature of God must remain none
the less a mystery,—that reason and the bodily senses are our
only channels of knowledge,—that we can have no idea of
spirit and no direct knowledge of supra-sensual things, such

---

[1] Blake's *Milton*, qu. by Swinburne, 266. [2] Gilchrist, 261.
[3] Blake's *Jerusalem*, qu. by Gilchrist, i. 185. [4] Swinburne, 3.

as the Divine nature and attributes, except only by analogy from the outward world of sense.[1] In substance his argument denied all power of judging the contents of revelation, and threw the proof of Christianity entirely upon its external evidences. To this the whole tone of Bishop Berkeley's mind and the whole tenor of his philosophy were opposed. It seemed to him that we have a far more certain knowledge of spirit than of anything else besides. Of all outward objects of sense we only know that the mind is sentient of this or that combination of phenomena. We have no guarantee whatever of their having any substantial existence of their own, independent of the conscious intelligence.[2] Spirit, by which we act, and think, and perceive, he held to be the only certain existence ; and by analogy from ourselves the existence is made known to us of other spirits like to ourselves, in whom similar thoughts and ideas are manifested. 'After the same manner,' he adds, ' we see God,[3] and (since the existence of other spirits is known by their operations or the ideas by them excited in us) we may even assert that the existence of God is far more evidently perceived than the existence of men, because the effects of nature are infinitely more numerous and considerable than those ascribed to human agents.'[4] It is impossible to condense fairly into two or three sentences the ingenious reasonings and apt illustrations by which Berkeley supports his theories, but what has been said may sufficiently intimate the train of thought by which he reasons that God is known to us in 'His spirituality, omnipresence, providence, omniscience, infinite power and goodness,'[5] by manifestations no less conspicuous than those by which alone we are cognisant of human minds, and even of our own being.

In one of Berkeley's letters there are some interesting remarks on the special subject of ' enthusiasm.' Speaking of the general shallowness of contemporary theology, he observes that ' most modern writings smell of the age, and there are no books so fit to make a soul advance in spiritual per-

---

[1] J. Hunt, *Rel. Thought in Eng.* ii. 247, iii. 127-8, 380.
[2] Bishop Berkeley's *Works*, ed. A. C. Fraser, vol. i., 'Theory of Vision,' pt. i. § 37, 91.   [3] Id. § 148.
[4] Id. § 147.   [5] Id., 'Hylas and Philonous,' i. 354.

fection as the Scriptures and the ancient Fathers. He agrees with his correspondent that 'the Christian religion is spiritual and the Christian life supernatural, and that there is no judge of spiritual things but the Spirit of God.' He believes that the saying of our Lord that he that doeth God's will shall know of the doctrine extends to all saving truths. Belief is no mere product of reason or authority. 'There is a secret unction, an inward light and joy, that attends the sincere, fervent love of God and His truth. . . . There is an internal, as well as an exterior, λόγος to inform me. . . . The sincere Christians of our communion are governed, or led, by the inward light of God's grace, by the outward light of His written word, by the ancient and catholic traditions of the Christian Church, by the ordinances of our National Church, which we take to consist all and hang together. But then we see, as we all must do, with our own eyes,—not with a common light, but each by his own private eyes. . . . Some, indeed, go further, and, without regard to the Holy Spirit, or the word of God, or the writings of the primitive Fathers, or the universal, uninterrupted traditions of the Church, will pretend to compass every mystery, every step of Providence, and reduce it to the private standard of their own fancy. Such as these I give up and disown. . . . Light and heat are both found in a religious mind duly disposed. Light, in due order, goes first. It is dangerous to begin with heat—that is, with the affections. To balance earthly affections by spiritual affections is right. But our affections should grow from enquiry and deliberation ; else there is danger of our being superstitious and enthusiasts.'[1]

At the very close of the century, in the year 1798, an elaborate treatise on enthusiasm was published by Richard Graves, Dean of Ardagh, a man of considerable learning and earnest piety. It is needless to enter into the arguments of his 'Essay on the Character of the Apostles and Evangelists.' Its object was to prove that they were wholly free from the errors of enthusiasts ; that in their private conduct, and in the government of the Church, they were 'rational and sober, prudent and cautious, mild and decorous, zealous without violence, and steady without obstinacy ;' that their writings

[1] Berkeley to Sir J. James, June 1741, iv. 270-2.

are plain, calm, and unexaggerated . . . . natural and rational
. . . . without any trace of spiritual pride, any arrogant claims
to full perfection of virtue . . . . teaching heartfelt piety to
God without any affectation of rapturous ecstasy or extravagant fervour.'[1] On the other hand, he illustrates the extravagances into which enthusiasts have been led, from the
history of Indian mystics and Greek Neoplatonists, from
Manichæans and Montanists, from monastic saints, from the
Beghards of Germany, the Fratricelli of Italy, the Illuminati
of Spain, the Quietists of France, from Anabaptists, Quakers,
and French prophets. He refers to what had been written
against enthusiasm within the preceding century by Stillingfleet, Bayle, Locke, Hickes, Shaftesbury, Lord Lyttelton,
Barrington, Chandler, Archibald Campbell, Stinstra, Warburton, Lavington, and Douglas—a list the length of which is in
itself a sufficient evidence of the sensitive interest which the
subject had excited. He remarks on the attempts made by
Chubb and Morgan to attach to Christianity the opprobrium
of being an enthusiastic religion, and reprobates the assertions
of the younger Dodwell that *faith* is not founded on argument. The special occasion of his work[2] arose out of more
recent events—the publication at Geneva in 1791 of Bou-
langer's 'Christianity Unmasked,' and the many similar
efforts made during the period of the French Revolution to
represent fanaticism and Christianity as synonymous terms.

But while Dean Graves was writing in careful and moderate language his not unseasonable warnings, thoughts
representative of a new and deeper strain of theological feeling
were passing through the mind of Samuel Coleridge. His
was a genius singularly receptive of the ideas which emanated
from the leading intellect of his age in England or abroad.
He was probably better acquainted than any other of his
countrymen with the highest literature of Germany, which
found in him not only an interpreter but a most able and
reflective exponent. Few could be better fitted than he was
· no one certainly in his own country and generation—to
deal with those subtle and intricate elements of human nature
upon which enthusiasts and mystics have based their specu-

[1] R. Graves' *Works*, 'The Apostles not Enthusiasts,' i. 199-200.
[2] Id., *Memoirs*, i. lvi.

lations, and hopelessly blended together much that is sublime
and true with not a little that is groundless and visionary, and
often dangerous in its practical or speculative results.   In the
first place, he could scarcely fail in sympathy.   He was
endowed with a rich vein of that imaginative power which is
the very life of all enthusiasm.   It is the most prominent
characteristic of his poetry ; it is no less conspicuous in the
intense glow of excited expectation with which he, like so
many other young men of rising talent, cherished those
millennial visions of peace and brotherhood, and simple faith
and love, which the French Revolution in its progress so rudely
crushed.   Mysticism also must have had great charms for
one who could write verses so imbued with its spirit as are
the following :—

> He first by fear uncharmed the drowsèd soul,
> Till of its nobler nature it 'gan feel
> Dim recollections ; and thence soared to hope,
> Strong to believe whate'er of mystic good
> The Eternal dooms for His immortal sons ;
> From hope and firmer faith to perfect love
> Attracted and absorbed ; and centred there,
> God only to behold, and know, and feel,
> Till by exclusive consciousness of God,
> All self annihilated, it shall make
> God its identity—God all in all !
> We and our Father one !
>   And blest are they
> Who in this fleshly world, the elect of heaven,
> Their strong eye darting through the deeds of men,
> Adore with steadfast, unpresuming gaze
> Him, nature's essence, mind, and energy ;
> And gazing, trembling, patiently ascend,
> Treading beneath their feet all visible things
> As steps, that upward to their Father's throne
> Lead gradual.[1]

If we would further understand how far removed must
have been Coleridge's tone of thought from that which for so
long a time had regarded enthusiasm in all its forms as the

---

[1] S. T. Coleridge's *Poetical Works*, 'Religious Musings,' i. 83-4.

greatest enemy of sober reason and sound religion, we should only have to consider what a new world of thought and sentiment was that in which Coleridge was living from any of which the generation before him had experience. The band of poets and essayists represented by Coleridge and Wordsworth, Southey, Lamb, De Quincey, and we may add Blake, were in many respects separated by a wider gulf, except only in time, from the authors of twenty years before, than they were from the writers of the Elizabethan age. New hopes and aspirations as to the capabilities of human life, new and more spiritual aspects of nature, of art, of poetry, of history, made it impossible for those who felt these influences in all the freshness of their new life to look with the same eyes as their fathers on those questions above all others which related to the intellectual and spiritual faculties of the soul.

In the course of his theological and philosophical researches Coleridge was often led to reflect on the powers possessed by man of discerning religious truth. It will be readily understood that his was not a mind to rest satisfied with the logical array of proofs and demonstrations on which a long succession of divines had spent their labour. He was far from disparaging their eminent services. But it was not what he wanted. 'Evidences of Christianity!' he writes, 'I am weary of the word. Make a man feel the want of it. Rouse him, if you can, to the self-knowledge of his need of it, and you may safely trust it to its own evidence—remembering only the express declaration of Christ Himself, 'No man cometh to me unless the Father draw him.'[1] On the other hand, notwithstanding his highly imaginative and somewhat mystical turn of thought, he was far from falling into that besetting temptation of all enthusiasts to attribute an excessive importance to inward feelings and experiences. A strong feeling of the unmanliness of sentimental religion,[2] and of the indignities to which sound reason has been submitted by many of those who have discoursed most upon immediate consciousness of the spirit, sometimes led him almost to the opposite extreme. Coleridge certainly descends for the time to a lower spiritual level than his own when he writes with triumph of the pretensions which had been

---

[1] *Aids to Reflection*, i. 320. [2] Id. 21.

'pilloried by Butler, sent to Bedlam by Swift, gibbeted by Warburton, and anatomised by Bishop Lavington.'[1] His real attitude in relation to enthusiasm corresponded not to any of those whom he has here mentioned, but rather to Henry More, whom he greatly admired and often quotes. He was keenly sensible how impoverished Deism had been by the absence of a feeling of a living communion with the Spirit.[2] He was no less convinced that, so far from reason being forbidden to set foot on holy ground and gaze at sacred mysteries, man's highest rational faculties find their noblest exercise in the field of pure theology. It was quite true, he said, that deep feelings have a remarkable tendency to combine with obscure and undefined ideas,[3] and that the Holy Spirit sometimes acts upon the soul in modes that are essentially incommunicable [4]—'groanings that cannot be uttered.' There was all the more reason, therefore, why a deaf ear should be turned to the effusions of those who idly babble on matters too deep for words and on spiritual operations which by their nature can be made evident only by their results, and why the fullest light of reason should be poured on all ideas which are susceptible of clear conception. Religion was not like a stove, heat without light, nor yet light without heat, like the moon, but like the sun itself, whence light and heat stream forth conjointly.[5] He cordially agreed with Henry More that reason in close union with conscience is a truly spiritual organ, by which man can effectually reach the cognisance of eternal realities, in a degree amply sufficient for all purposes of practical guidance.[6] Inspiration itself he judged to be an elevated [7] form of it, so that the instructed spirit, which he elsewhere speaks of as coincident [8] with man's highest reason, can share in the perceptions of the inspired writers, and enter into the mind of God the giver, who is Himself the Supreme Reason.[9] The Neoplatonists themselves had not more exalted notions than Coleridge of the spiritual

---

[1] *Aids to Reflection*, 52.
[2] Id. 56.
[3] *The Friend*, i. 138 (note).
[4] *Aids to Reflection*, i. 47.
[5] *The Friend*, i. 136.
[6] Id. 209 ; A. S. Farrar on Coleridge, in *Critical History of Free Thought*, 464–9.
[7] Farrar, Id. 467.
[8] *Aids to Reflection*, i. 260.
[9] *The Friend*, i. 209.

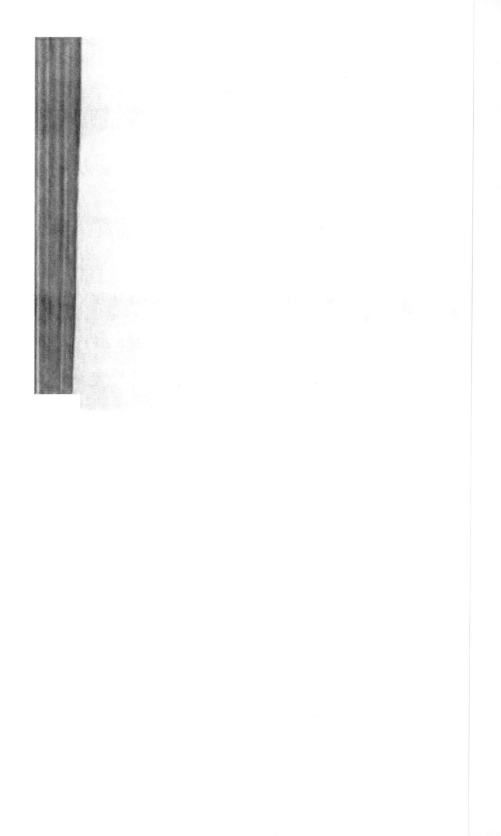

unite its sublimer powers with conscience as a divinely given 'inner light,' to combine in one the highest exercise of the intellectual and the moral faculties. Emotional religion had exhibited on a large scale alike its powers and deficiencies. Thoughtful and religious men could scarcely do better than set themselves to restore the balance where it was unequal. They had to teach that faith must be based, not only upon feeling and undefined impulse, but on solid intellectual apprehension. They had to urge with no less earnestness that religious truth has to be not only outwardly apprehended, but inwardly appropriated before it can become possessed of true spiritual efficacy. It is most true that vague ideas of some inward illumination are but a miserable substitute for a sound historical faith, but it is no less true that a so-called historical faith has not become faith at all until the soul has received it into itself, and made of it an inward light. In the eighteenth century, as in every other, mystics and enthusiasts have insisted only on inward illuminations and spiritual experiences, while of men of a very different cast of mind some have perpetually harped upon authority and some upon reason and reasonableness. It may be hoped that our own century may be more successful in the difficult but not discouraging task of investigating and harmonising their respective claims.

C. J. A.

END OF THE FIRST VOLUME.

LONDON: PRINTED BY
SPOTTISWOODE AND CO., NEW-STREET SQUARE
AND PARLIAMENT STREET

LaVergne, TN USA
10 April 2011
223600LV00008B/100/P

9 781163 310151